PATHWAYS OF CREATIVE RESEARCH
TOWARDS A FESTIVAL OF DIALOGUES

Pathways of Creative Research
Towards a Festival of Dialogues

edited by
ANANTA KUMAR GIRI

foreword by
JAMES L. PEACOCK

PRIMUS
BOOKS

PRIMUS BOOKS

An imprint of Ratna Sagar P. Ltd.

Virat Bhavan

Mukherjee Nagar Commercial Complex

Delhi 110 009

Offices at CHENNAI   LUCKNOW

AGRA AHMEDABAD BANGALORE COIMBATORE DEHRADUN GUWAHATI HYDERABAD
JAIPUR KANPUR KOCHI KOLKATA MADURAI MUMBAI PATNA RANCHI VARANASI

© *Ananta Kumar Giri for Editorial selection 2017*

© *Individual contributors for their respective essays 2017*

All rights reserved. No part of this publication may be reproduced,
stored in a retrieval system or transmitted, in any form or by any means,
without the prior permission in writing from Primus Books, or as
expressly permitted by law, by licence, or under terms agreed with
the appropriate reproduction rights organization.
Enquiries concerning reproduction outside the scope of the above
should be sent to Primus Books at the address above.

First published 2017

ISBN: 978–93–84082–05–5 (hardback)
ISBN: 978–93–86552–18–1 (POD)

Published by Primus Books

Laser typeset by Sai Graphic Design
Paharganj, New Delhi 110 055

Printed at Replika Press Pvt. Ltd.

This book is meant for educational and learning purposes. The author(s) of the book
has/have taken all reasonable care to ensure that the contents of the book do not violate any existing
copyright or other intellectual property rights of any person in any manner whatsoever. In the
event the author(s) has/have been unable to track any source and if any copyright has been
inadvertently infringed, please notify the publisher in writing for corrective action.

For

PROFESSOR T.K. OOMMEN

RACHEL CORRIE

OVE JACOBSEN

and

SURESH CHANDRA SHUKLA

Contents

Foreword

The reader is invited to a remarkably rich and suggestive conversation, rather like that which I witnessed between the editor, Ananta Kumar Giri, and students at the Daily Grind.[1] We followed Ananta there, after spilling out of his remarkable talk, and entered his intimately engaging and fast-moving ruminations about subjects which are mirrored in this volume.

I hint at several themes detected both in the introductory essay and the outline of queries guiding this 'festival' not as summation but rather as invitation. One of them is disenchantment/reenchantment. Disenchantment, as Ananta notes, is a term borrowed from Max Weber. In his still-to-be-properly-explored work on the Protestant Ethics, Weber blames the Puritans. In fact, one can trace a simple progression from Durkheim to Weber: Durkheim in his *Elementary Forms of Religious Life* offering the model of the enchanted community, enchanted because the sacred is immanent in social life, exemplified by rituals. Puritans—not just Protestants but Puritans as a category, an ideal type—destroy this enchantment by elevating God to a transcendent position which leaves society as fallen, even sinful and depraved. Ritual therefore is denigrated, as is all of life on this earth.

Further, this fallen earth, harbours monsters. In Western mythologies, these are vampires, ghosts, zombies and evil people who threaten good people. What is the antidote? Rationality. Rationality is best exemplified by science or scientific method. In early modern fiction, such heroes as Sherlock Holmes and Dracula's opponent Van Helsing illustrate this. These men (and they are usually men, while women are the vulnerable victims) are virtuosos of rationality. Holmes is utterly analytical; hence his power to discern evil and defeat it. Doing so, he, Van Helsing, and other scientists represent a counter point 'the evil ones'. Where this distinction is not maintained, the monster can enter our lives, as with Frankenstein—spawn of the impure scientist, or with Jekyll and Hyde. In these images lie sources and mirrors of what became the great modernist method—science—with all of alienating as well as salvation-giving qualities.

Reenchantment is envisioned in this volume in many dimensions. One fundamental example is stated by Gadamer in his *Truth and Method*

(Methode und Wahrheit) which posits that method *is* truth. Why and how? Because method is not merely an alienated intellectual query or procedure, it is also a mode of being. This is because in discerning an object, one discerns one's self and not merely one's individual personal self but also the 'horizon' or tradition—anthropologists would say 'culture'—and history of which one is part. And discernment implies, or even is, action and experience.

Research, then, is necessarily engagement. This is true in fieldwork, especially in ethnographic research.

What is implied by research is driven by engagement which compared to engagement driven by research? In development work, for example, is 'engaged' research necessarily the most powerful means to the end of development, whether economic, educational, clinical, or social? As noted, statistics, surveys and other tools of orthodox science or social science are often deployed in development or other 'applied' and 'engaged' efforts to create change. These tools alienate at the level of the individual researcher, they may be engaging at the policy level in a way that 'engaged' research may fail to be. This is precisely because of expectations of policymakers? This is a thought-provoking question, often explored by authors in this 'festival' of enquiry.

Does research embed itself in engagement? For example, scholars have researched religious belief and practice for more than a century. Is it the case, therefore, that research is becoming an aspect of religious belief and practice? Yes, in some ways, but is it so in the most fundamental ways? That is, does a believer include in his or her belief, research into the features and context of that belief like that ventured by anthropologists and social scientists? When so, what happens to belief under this kind of scrutiny?

Globalism or globalization are implicated in all such questions. For example, the challenge to belief when one joins a company of seemingly varied believers (Tony Blair famously proposed this as the basis for world peace). Engagement operates locally, in a certain space, among certain persons in a group, and electronic or other seemingly space-transcending modes either change or challenge localized engagements. Is 'grounded globalism' feasible? That is, now that the first blush of globalism is past, how are localized engagements manifesting themselves—is it in globalized ways? No one is more equipped to address that question than anthropologists; the question is, how?

Reminiscent of Ananta as a singular catalyst among students, I witnessed in February in Pune, India, a gathering of forty-five speakers on the topic of peace. That event in many ways resembled this volume—a 'festival'—of visions and of ideas. Readers should prepare for an energetic engagement that stretches their creative capacities, being open to the potential for a kind of intellectual, spiritual and kinetic integration.

University of North Carolina   JAMES L. PEACOCK
at Chapel Hills (USA)

Note

1. Daily Grind is a café at University of North Carolina at Chapel Hill, USA.

Preface

The promise of a movement is its future victory; whereas the promises of incidental moments are instantaneous, such moments include, life-enhancingly or tragically, experiences of freedom in action. . . . Such moments—as no historical 'outcome' can ever be—are transcendental, are what Spinoza termed eternal, and they are as the stars in an expanding universe. . . . Today the infinite is beside the poor — JOHN BERGER

Out beyond the ideas of wrongdoing and right doing, there's a field. I'll meet you there. . . . Don't worry about saving these songs! And if one of our instruments breaks, it doesn't matter. We have fallen into the place where everything is music. — RUMI

The nature of creativity is heavenly. It is one of its attributes. The next attribute of creativity is that it is very natural to humans. And the third attribute is that it is an awesome superhuman process. These three attributes of the creative act—its divine nature, its absolute naturalism, and its superhuman character are woven together thus making it so inspiring, mysterious, compelling and inevitable.

So, why must we create? Because the Cosmos does it through us. Because it is joy to do so. Because creativity is the surest vehicle of self-realization.
— HENRYK SKOLIMOWSKI (2010), *Let there be Light:*
The Mysterious Journey of Cosmic Creativity, pp. 133–4.

At the horizon line of the near future toward which we gaze, pragmatically assessing the utility of truth, there lies a more distant future that we can never really forget. Rorty alludes to this with the term solidarity, which I propose to read directly in the sense of charity, and not just as the means of achieving consensus but as an end in itself. Christian dogma teaches that *Deus Caritas est*, charity is God himself. From a Hegelian viewpoint, we may take the horizon to be that absolute spirit which never allows itself to be entirely set aside but becomes the final horizon of history that legitimates all our near-term choices.
— GIANNI VATTIMO (2011), *A Farewell to Truth*, pp. 139–40.

Creativity is an epochal calling of our times. Contemporary changes in life, culture and society invite us to embody this in our various walks of life, including in our practices of learning and research. This invitation is meant for all concerned human beings, to all students of life, and to professional social scientists. This invitation is to embody creativity in one's self and in social enquiry and to allow ourselves to be challenged to transgress boundaries. This includes boundaries between everyday life and social science research, between action and reflection, between theory and practice, between ontology and epistemology, and between activists and scholars.

The present work is an invitation to a more creative way of doing and thinking about social research. I have been interested in rethinking such theories and methods for almost the last two decades, and the present work builds upon journeys and discussions with concerned friends and fellow seekers. It began with my organization of a seminar on the theme of 'Creative Social Research: Rethinking Theories and Methods' in 1997 which was part of our Institute's annual Interdisciplinary Research Methodology Workshop and held in collaboration with Professor S. Uma Devi of Department of Economics of University of Kerala in Thiruvanthapuram. This led to publication of *Creative Social Research: Rethinking Theories and Methods* edited by me in 2004. In my introduction to the book, I had explored a new pathway of thinking, research and knowledge gathering called ontological epistemology of participation which goes beyond the dualism between the epistemic and the ontological and builds upon transformative moves in both as well as across. Once during a journey of life in Europe in 2007 when I was visiting several European universities as a fellow of Alexander von Humboldt Foundation based at University of Freiburg in Germany, it dawned upon me that it would be enriching to offer some of the proposals of pathways of creative research and ideas such as ontological epistemology of participation to fellow seekers. I invited many friends and seeking souls I met on the roads to join us in this festival of dialogue and collaborative quest. Many friends have joined in this journey which we began in 2007 and now after ten years of wear and tears this trilogy on creative research is finally dancing with the light of our world. Our present book, *Pathways of Creative Research: Towards A Festival of Dialogues*, is the first in this series which is followed by *Cultivating Pathways of Creative Research: New Horizons of Transformative Practice* and *Collaborative Imagination and Research as Realization: Science, Spirituality and Harmony*. The present volume focuses on some of the themes explored in my introductory essay such as ontological epistemology of participation and experimental creativity in research, self and society. The second volume focuses on the challenge of cultivating pathways of creative research in social sciences and humanities such as sociology, anthropology, philosophy and education. It also explores further the theme of relationship between scholarship and activism and the vocation of a scholar activist. The third volume in our trilogy deals with the theme of research as realization which includes self-realization as well as co-realization of potential of reality and research, self and the other. It also deals with the challenge of transcending boundaries between religion and science and cultivate new pathways of harmony and spirituality which can be called transformative harmony and practical spirituality (see Giri 2017a, 2017b).

My introductory essay, 'Pathways of Creative Research: Rethinking Theories and Methods and the Calling of an Ontological Epistemology of Participation', inviting us to this festival of dialogues, has been presented in many places over the last fifteen years. I am grateful to kind hosts and participants for comments and reflections, especially John Clammer, D.P. Dash, Chitta Ranjan Das, Ingrid Dash, Wendy Olsen, Lennart Svensson, Petr Skalnik and Piet Strydom. I thank my dear student Carsten Brinkmeyer from Aalborg University, Denmark, for his help with diagrams in the text.

I dedicate this work with gratitude to Professor T.K. Oommen, Rachel Corrie, Ove Jacobssen and Suresh Chandra Shukla. Professor T.K. Oommen is a social scientist of India who has inspired many of us with his generosity, continued pursuit of insight and his humour. I remember with gratitude many moments spent with Professor Oommen in many corners of the world and present this as a small token of what we collectively owe to this smiling, inspiring, insightful, kind and enthusiastic sociologist of humanity.

Rachel was a young student from the US who gave her life in defending a Palestinian home in Gaza. On 16 March 2003, she was crushed to death in front of a bulldozer. Although I never knew her personally, Rachel's life is as significant to many as the life of Antigone, Jesus or Gandhi. Her email to her family days before her death is heart-touching:

When that explosive detonated yesterday it broke all the windows in the family's house. I was in the process of being served tea and playing with two small babies. I am having a hard time right now. Just feel sick to my stomach a lot, being doted on all the time, very sweetly by people who are facing doom. . . . Honestly a lot of time the sheer kindness of the people here, coupled with the overwhelming evidence of the wilful destruction of their lives, makes it seem unreal to me. I can't really believe that something like it can happen in the world without a bigger outcry about it. It really hurts me, again, like it has hurt me in the past, to witness how awful we can allow the world to be.

Rachel's pathway of participation inspires us to strive for a different kind of world through different forms of learning, dedication and transformation.

Ove Jacobssen from Denmark was a dedicated seeker who came to India quite young and worked with Mitraniketan, a centre for community development and education, in Kerala in the 1960s. In his work he embodied selfless devotion and for four decades he was a bridge between the people of India and Denmark. In the last phase of his life, with his friend Margerethe Bonner, Ove brought many people from Denmark and Europe, to Mitraniketan and south India and created a new space for cross-cultural experience and learning. Ove was devoted to the cause of education and passionate about Mitraniketan People's College (modelled upon a Danish Folk High School). I first met Ove in 1993, in a seminar to establish this folk high school in Kerala. Ever since, Ove has been a kind of co-walker and co-dreamer though he left his physical body in 2010. Finally, Suresh Chandra Shukla was an inspiring teacher with a devotion to learning and love. I had the good fortune to spend many enriching moments with him and know he would have loved to join in the festival of dialogue of this book. When he breathed his last, he was editing a book on education and with an essay of mine on integral education to be a part of it. I hope Shuklaji joins us in his eternal spirit, as do Rachel and Ove in this journey.

This book has been a long journey and I am grateful to all our fellow contributors for their kindness, patience and trust. I am grateful to Professor James L. Peacock of University of North Carolina, Chapel Hill, USA for his foreword and to Dr Marcus Bussey of University of Sunshine Coast, Australia and Miriam Sannum of Gothenburg, Sweden for their afterword to this book.

Finally, I hope this work creates the much-needed transdisciplinary, transparadigmatic and border-crossing body and spirit of knowledge which helps us acknowledge limits of the restraints imposed by the epistemic violence of one-dimensional understanding within our inherently multidimensional fields of living, learning and research. I also hope that it helps us embody a multi-valued logic of autonomy and interrelatedness in our lives, society and the world.

Madras Institute of Development Studies   ANANTA KUMAR GIRI
Chennai

References

Skolimowski, Henry (2010), *Let there be Light: The Mysterious Journey of Cosmic Creativity.*

Vattimo, Gianni (2011), *A Farewell to Truth*, New York: Columbia University Press.

Giri, Ananta Kumar (ed.) (2004), *Creative Social Research: Rethinking Theories and Methods*, Lanham, MD: Lexington Books.

———— (2017a), *Transformative Harmony*, New Delhi: Studera Press.

———— (2017b), 'Practical Spirituality and Human Development', Mansucript.

PART ONE

NEW PERSPECTIVES AND HORIZONS OF RESEARCH

Pathways of Creative Research:
An Adventure and Invitation

ANANTA KUMAR GIRI

Understanding is like water flowing in a stream. . . . Penetration means to enter something, not just to stand outside of it. . . . To comprehend something means to pick it up and be one with it. . . . you have to enter in order to be one with what you want to observe and understand. . . . you can no longer stand and remain just an observer. Today many scientists prefer the word participant to the word observer.

> – THICH NHAT HANH (1997: 8), *The Heart of Understanding.*

The world cannot be put into words, and the ultimate questions of being cannot be answered. But insofar as we have no option but to speak, think, and act, we are bound to struggle for the kind of language, the kind of thought, and the kind of action that does greatest justice to life as it is lived.

> —MICHAEL JACKSON (2007: xi), *Excursions.*

. . . all science depends on observation, and all observation depends upon participation—that is, on a close coupling, in perception and action, between the observer and those aspects of the world that are the focus of attention. If science is to be a coherent knowledge practice, it must be built on the foundation of openness rather than closure, engagement rather than detachment. And this means regaining the sense of astonishment that is so conspicuous by its absence from contemporary scientific work. Knowing must be connected with being, epistemology with ontology, thought with life.

> – TIM INGOLD (2006), 'Rethinking the Animate, Re-animating Thoughts'.

We must develop multiple schemas of interpretation with respect not only to others but ourselves. We must learn to keep the channels of communications open between various levels of consciousness. We must realize that . . . there are multiple realities and human growth requires the ability to move easily between them and will be blocked by setting up one as a despot to tyrannize over the others. . . . The radical split between knowledge and commitment that exists in our culture and in our universities is not ultimately tenable.

> Differentiation has gone about as far as it can go. It is time for a new integration.
>
> — ROBERT N. BELLAH (1970: 254, 257), *Beyond Belief.*

An Introduction and An Invitation

Pathways of Creative Research is an invitation to all concerned with exploring new pathways of learning, being and co-living—learning with the self and the world, while holding the hands of and looking up to the face of the Other. My opening essay in Part One of the volume, 'Pathways of Creative Research: Rethinking Theories and Methods and the Calling of an Ontological Epistemology of Participation', presents some pathways of rethinking theories and methods. It presents ontological epistemology of participation embodying deep and rigorous engagement in epistemic learning as well as in ontological self-cultivation as a creative way of doing research as well as thinking about the world. It also seeks to cultivate non-dual modes of understanding, a new comparative global learning nurtured by creative transdisciplinary interpenetrations such as between philosophy and fieldwork, a new vocation of social research and learning, a new art of wholeness and integration. The opening essay is an invitation for dialogue, and some contributions in the volume engage with the themes raised in opening essay, while many others bring related reflections and meditations on the challenge of creative research, understanding and transformations in the world.

The festival of dialogues begins with the opening essay 'Pathways of Creative Research: Rethinking Theories and Methods and the Calling of an Ontological Epistemology of Participation'. Part Two, 'Pathways of Creative Research: Crossing Boundaries, Stimulating Creativity', begins the journey with the essay 'Crossing Boundaries, Stimulating Creativity: The Horizon of Integral Meta-Studies' by Markus Molz and Mark Edwards. It presents creative ways of crossing boundaries and carrying out integral mega studies. Integral understanding is an important challenge of modern times and it helps in moving towards a 'new integrative vision' in today's research practice and imagination. In the subsequent chapter, 'Body-Place-Commons: Reclaiming Professional Practice, Reclaiming Democracy', Betsy Taylor invites readers to be with the pathways of life and learning in new ways. Taylor especially enriches pathways of ontological epistemology of participation in four ways. First, Taylor looks at actual political ecology that results from what is described in the opening essay as one-dimensional epistemic violence. Second, Taylor looks at 'the narrowing of knowledge to epistemology as a problem of power and social relationships among professionals'. Third, Taylor critiques postmodern social theory that tries to overcome the one-dimensionality of epistemic violence by denying dimensionality itself. Finally, to respond to the call for ontological epistemology of participation, Taylor proposes a new folded ontology and to 'reground theoretical practices in embodied, placed care for the commons'.

Taylor urges readers to understand the violence of absolutism in politics and knowledge. Taylor's essay, in tune with the spirit of the book, urges all to find non-absolutist and non-violent ways in science, politics, culture, religion and spirituality. Her essay helps to realize that subject-object dualism is a dominating part of dominant reality today. This constitutes the 'problematic kind of subject formation'. In this context, exploration of new pathways of creative research calls for interrogation and transformation of existing logic of reductionist dualism—what Taylor calls 'logic of fungibility' and existing structures of authority, especially the authority of expert knowledge. Taylor's deep and profound critique of reduction of knowledge to expert knowledge finds a resonance in the contribution of Åse Møller-Hansen in the volume when she writes: 'You can only be an expert in your own limited field, but the problems of the world are connected'. She also urges to reflect upon the implication of domination of experts in peoples' lives: 'Just a minority are recognized as formal experts, with positions, and there is a trend that you shall not speak about serious matters if you are not an expert'.

In her contribution, Taylor enriches the explorations of this volume, especially pathways of ontological epistemology of participation, with her pathways of 'folded' rather than 'flat' ontology. Folded ontology contains 'manifolds of ontologies—multileveled, flat, but mostly curved/curving and (un) folded/ing. The folded ontology is not only a noun but also a verb (Giri 2012a).

Taylor's call for understanding one's location and habitation in body-place-commons finds a resonance in the subsequent dialogue of Scott Schaffer, 'Kairos and an Ethics of Space: Towards Reconceptualizing Conversations and Their Loci'. Schaffer urges the reader to realize how he/she 'conceptualize the present is crucial' for rethinking society, subjectivity and social theory. For Schaffer, the present is not only a temporal category but also a spatial one and it contains circles of autonomy and interpenetration of different dimensions of self and society. Schaffer's reflections contribute to contemporary rethinking of what Foucault calls 'ontology of the present' and Gianni Vattimo (2011) 'ontology of actuality'.[1]

Taylor concludes her reflections with a call for rethinking the universal with a concept of the transversal. The subsequent contribution of Boike Rehbein, 'Configurational Dialectics', also continues this quest by presenting configurational dialectics as an important part of creative research. Rehbein helps to understand different elements of eurocentrism in social theory and also come to terms with it and move beyond. In configurational dialectics, 'each configuration is regarded as particular—but neither general nor singular. It refers to something more general but not to an all-encompassing totality that would determine all other configurations in the same way'. Configurational dialectics involves work of Wittgenstein's 'family resemblances' and this resonates with the proposal for a new global comparative engagement where the objective is not wholescale comparison of societies but finding partial connections as well as partial differences between them.

These essays are then followed by an insightful contribution of Des Gasper on 'Creative and Social Research: Ideas from Discourse Analysis and Creative Thinking'. At the very beginning Gasper says that explorations of new ways of understanding reality and social research faces 'obstacles, educational, logistical and socio-political' and 'not solely obstacles set by widespread philosophical presuppositions'. For Gasper, 'centralized power breeds a demand for generalized forms of knowledge claim'. Gasper discusses new experimentations with learning and thinking pioneered by parallel and creative thinking especially that of De Bono. Gasper draws attention to De Bono's 'six hats method' in group discussion and work which 'turns discussion into a team effort, during which everybody works together in construction, and in criticism, and in the other activities, rather than having personalized duels as too easily occur otherwise'. For Gasper, 'De Bono sees a connection between a combative/defensive, ego-based, self-righteous approach in argumentation and a traditional essentialist conception that there is one, absolute, truth'. Gasper also urges one to learn from discourse analysis where 'one of the ways of getting into other people's minds, in both teaching and research, is through intensive text analysis'.

Gasper's essay is followed by Peter Herrmann's on 'Research as Searching for Nescience' in which he challenges one to go beyond science as control and practice new ways of state and policy work. This is followed by Mihir Shah who talks about the fundamental existence of uncertainty that social research has to take note of. He also shares some illuminating reflections on transformative initiatives of today, including visions of such leaders as Martin Luther King, Jr. His elaboration of King's pathway of *agape* urges to bring *agape* to the practice of research as well, which would help to go beyond all categorical boundaries and realize new solidarity:

Agape implies understanding. It intimates a creative, redeeming goodwill for all, an overflowing love which seeks nothing in return. *Agape* is not a weak, passive love. It is love in action.

— (also see Taylor 2007, 2013; Giri 2012b).

Nurturing Experimental Creativity:
Gandhi, Illich, Vygostky, Panikkar and Beyond

It is appropriate that Part Two concluding with Shah's inspiring reflections should be accompanied by Part Three entitled, 'Nurturing Experimental Creativity: Gandhi, Illich, Vygostky, Panikkar and Beyond'. This section brings many important reflections together and touches on new areas of collaboration between creative social research and transformative action. It begins with Åse Møller-Hansen who in her dialogue, 'Global Movements, Gandhi and the Progress of Humanity', presents pathways of learning and research emerging from participation in transformative movements, local as well as global where 'former students of life are becoming students of life and are still searching for solutions in solitude or through networking with people'. She says: 'This is the kind of creative research I want to reflect upon. The quest for hope, knowledge and necessary action—on the grassroots'. Møller-Hansen as an activist creatively picks up the challenge of moving beyond ethnocentric assumptions and take part in trans-civilizational dialogues. Here she brings Gandhi as a co-walker to the pathways of explorations but urges all not to forget that it is necessary to find partners of dialogue from other traditions as well, especially Islam. For Møller-Hansen, bringing Gandhi to the dialogue is not just about 'our enigmatic past but about our new humanity'. She believes that in the course of knowledge about globalization, Gandhi's legacy could hopefully give more direction about 'inter-religious dialogue and ethics, sustainable development, inclusive economies, conflict solution and non-violence, and the art of democracy'. About the concern for transcendence in this exploration of creative social research, Møller-Hansen writes: 'Though the Western science is still not very open for the existence of a transcendent, people on the grass-root though are experiencing this on their own'.

Like many participants in these dialogues, without drawing a dualism between the material and non-material, Møller-Hansen draws attention to the non-material aspects of life and in his contribution, 'Towards an Organic Process of Substantial Sociology', Karl-Julius Reubke brings his profound knowledge of philosophy, theology, science and social action to speak about 'substance without matter' building on the seminal work of Thomas Aquinas. Reubke says, 'Looking at sociology as a chemist though leaving the materialistic point of view of our science behind, I was interested in chemistry of formation and transformation of social entities'. By substance without matter Reubke draws attention to the work of ideas in creation and human life. But without being confined only to the ideational realm as a chemist of social experimentation and formation, Reubke explains how new substances and spaces are created in society, which might be called civil society. Sharing his participation with Ekta Parishad, a people's movement inspired by Gandhi, Reubke felt in the village congregation the origin of a new 'substance' of community.

Reubke resonates with the proposal of ontological epistemology of participation also in an interesting way. Instead of holding 'ontology and epistemology as opposing strategies', for him, ontological epistemology of participation focuses attention 'on a completely new and more "practical" approach of the "being" or "evolving" society which is still in need of its own understanding'.

The following two contributions present many insights from Ivan Illich. In his essay, 'Pathways of Creative Research: Ivan Illich's Regenerative Methodologies', Trent Schroyer speaks about Illich's methods where his purpose is to be regenerative in the interests of retrieval of greater capacity for practical judgments of the right proportion in common sense living in hospitable worlds. The following essay of Paul Schwartzentruber presents and appraises Illich's own proposal for a 'post-industrial' alteration of method toward 'personal learning' and 'convivial tools' assisted by 'counterfoil research'. A counterfoil research which is ethically directed towards the preservation of personal knowledge, would have, Illich proposes, 'two major tasks: to provide guidelines for detecting the incipient stages of murderous logic in a tool; and to devise tools and tool systems that optimize the balance of life, thereby maximizing liberty for all'.

Illich also links *askesis* to renunciation urging readers to realize epistemological renunciation or what he called 'epistemological *askesis*'. One can now link this to the pathway of ontological epistemological participation nurtured in this book. One can realize that the project of ontological epistemology of participation can cultivate an integral practice of renunciation vis-à-vis epistemology, ontology and participation. Illich's epistemological *askesis* purges ourselves and epistemologies 'of those corrupting concepts that give "fictitious substances" the semblance of a sensible existence' (ibid: 50). Similarly it can also be useful for cultivating ontological and participatory *askesis* in a spirit of pregnant and possibility-engendering renunciation and not just reproducing a logic of mortification. By renunciation, Illich himself specified that he did not mean mortification. This epistemological and ontological *askesis* resonates with what I have elsewhere called practical renunciation, which can now become a part of the journey of ontological epistemology of participation.[2]

It is appropriate that a journey with Illich in this volume is followed by walking together with Leo Vygotsky who was a revolutionary thinker and practitioner in the Soviet Union and continues to inspire creative experiments in research and practice across the globe. In her contribution in this volume, Lois Holzman presents Vygotsky's concept of Zones of

Proximal Development or ZPD. Presenting Vygotsky's pathways and building upon her quarter-century of work with creative social therapy, Holzman suggests how one can create zones of proximal development as a process of creative togetherness in which people help each other develop their potential. This is followed by Anthony Savari Raj's essay on cultural innovation and a new hermeneutics of reality in which he presents important insights from Raimundo Panikkar, a creative border-crosser of modern times, a mutational man, who also resonates with the spirit of Illich and Vygotsky. Panikkar states that Reality is *cosmotheandric* in which three dimensions of Reality—the divine, human and the cosmic dwell within one another. This dwelling within one another can be related to pathways of multi-valued logic and being of autonomy and interpenetration presented in my opening essay of the volume. Panikkar here presents the following interlinked challenges for creative research: 'Our task and responsibility are to accumulate wisdom of the bygone traditions and, having made it our own, to allow it to grow' (Panikkar 2010: xxvii).[3]

Cultivating Pathways of Non-Dual Realizations and New Horizons of Ontological Epistemology of Participation

With these explorations and dialogues comes Part Four, which focuses on the key theme of the volume, the challenge of non-dual realization in life and research and the vision and practice of ontological epistemology of participation. This begins with Binod Kumar Agarwala's essay on 'The Ontology of Humanities and Social Sciences', which presents a Gadamerian perspective on ontology and social research. This is then followed by Piet Strydom's 'Ontology Today: Social Science as Discursive Practice Participating in World Creation' in which he calls for an understanding of social research as part of a discursive practice of world creation. Strydom brings together his admirable and formidable knowledge of philosophy and sociology, especially the continental tradition of critical theory and American tradition of pragmatism, to rethink the available conceptions of practice and cognition. To the call for ontological participation in this volume, Strydom brings rich insights from the pragmatic tradition, especially that of C.S. Peirce.

For Strydom, according to Peirce, 'the semiotic pragmaticist', the production and employment of knowledge is a process in which signs mediate between reality and those who interpret signs and engage with reality. All three moments are at all times involved in the temporal semiotic process. Far from being simply an imaginary concatenation of figments of the mind, signs are an essential element in the process of evolution and hence to use signs correctly and appropriately, and to learn to do so is to acquire the ability to participate responsibly in the process of evolution, both natural and social.

Peirce's call for self-understanding as sign-mediating agents opens up new vistas for looking at participation and practice as simultaneously natural and social. Strydom also challenges one to rethink general conception of human in the light of new developments in cognitive science and genetic technology. Human beings simultaneously belong to Nature as well as the cultural-historical world and this realization should transform pathways of creative research, which is usually based upon a dualism between nature and culture.

Strydom raises some profound questions about ontology, which is discussed in the concluding section of this essay. Continuing the journey, the issue of ontological epistemology of participation finds a creative, critical and experiential resonance in Wendy Olsen's contribution, 'Three Ontological Contributions to Knowing About Praxis'. For Olsen, 'The knower and that which is known are not just separate-but-related; they are part of a single whole, too. ... The ontological argument is that weneed to conceive of people in non-individualistic ways.' In his generous and critical contribution, 'Critical Distance and Dualism: A Tangential Response' Andrew Smith resonates affirmatively with some of the proposals from the opening essay. He writes: 'We are, ineluctably, part of the world which we study. To deny this ... involves not just a methodological mistake, but also an ontological one'. Smith begins by sharing a learning from his own experience of teaching a course on African literature in an extra-mural setting in Glasgow where students read the texts with involvement not with detachment but nonetheless produced critical reflections.

Smith says not to put dualism under the carpet in the name of any a priori valorization of non-dualism and to this the subsequent contribution of Jens Seiffert, 'Beyond Boundaries: Dualism, Non-Dualism and Creative Research', brings further insights. For Seiffert, while one cannot put dualism under the carpet, dualism is also not the final destiny as even dualism in social reality what to speak of methods of study is encompassed by a reality of non-duality. In her following essay, 'Shifting Boundaries in the Process of Self and the Process of Coming to Know', Ingrid Dash presents the following interpretation of the practice of ontological epistemology of participation:

1. Both the researcher/teacher and the informant/pupil participate in a learning process, were ontological assumptions are contested, rather than pre-determined. A multi-valued logic underlines that in a statement there are more or less differentiated meanings;

2. An intercultural perspective not only means a continuous change in perspectives and shifts in taken-for-granted dualisms, it also underpins a creative research approach/teaching approach which includes an intercultural sensitivity to how meanings are created and identities (here: learning identities) are constituted in different contexts.

In her subsequent contribution in this section, 'Neither Theos nor Logos: Indic Divine Mother Beyond "Ontotheology"' Neela Bhattacharya Saxena brings the exploration of ontological epistemology of participation to a new depth when she writes: 'Giri's call for an "ontological epistemology of participation" can be truly realized when full divinity is accorded to the body of the woman who equally participates in the socio-political as well as spiritual realms. While spirituality is not the exclusive realm of women or any particular religious tradition, often the spiritual core of most religions reveal the intimation of a Divine Feminine who as the totality of Being or as Wisdom incarnate marks our humanity as we plunge in the dark depths of her womb and realize the not-self as our true "identity".'

A more philosophical aspect of the journey begins with Prasenjit Biswas's wide-ranging essay on 'Sociality and Subjectivity: An Ontological Return to the Other'. Biswas helps clarify some of the deep philosophical issues to think about sociality and subjectivity. This is followed by Alec Schaerer who raises some foundational questions about thinking and research in his essay 'Creating Dialogical Creativity'. For Schaerer, 'In research and knowledge creation, due to the predominant (and insofar "normal") habit of setting out from fundamental assumptions—known as axiom, definition, hypothesis, postulate, premise, etc.—today's normal research (in contrast to creative research) cannot achieve fully the required "listening" mode'. This is then followed by Ranjan Kumar Panda's essay on 'Knowing and Sharing: A Dialogical Journey' in which Panda reflects 'on an alternative methodology in which knowing and sharing are integrated and open up a new space of creative thinking and learning'.

At the Mid-Point of Our Dialogues: Painting Our Questions and Seeking Answers Together

The above presents a glimpse of what awaits in the walk together in this journey of dialogues. Participants in this dialogue have also raised some profound questions to the proposals for creative research presented in the opening essay. For example, in his dialogue, Piet Strydom has raised a number of important questions. He agrees that 'as against positivism or logical empiricism's one-dimensional ontology Giri obviously has an expanded ontology in mind'. But Strydom still looks at ontology mainly through his approach to Heidegger who, according to him, dismissed epistemology out of hand in the name of an idealist ontology. But as in my opening essay in this volume, my ontology is not solely derived from Heidegger. I also do not build solely on Roy Bhaskar, the philosopher of critical realism, and my ontology of self-expansion is a multidimensional ontology where ontology is not so much a noun but a verb, a meditative verb, and it is integrally linked to epistemic practices of learning and is part of an ontological epistemology of participation.[4] Though I agree with Strydom that 'different social scientific approaches do not have not only distinct methodologies but also their corresponding epistemologies and ontologies', the real difference lies in tending to make ontology derivative of either methodology or epistemology or vice versa. In keeping with the spirit of autonomy and interpenetration proposed in my opening essay, I would like to plead for exploring relations among them, as Strydom urges to explore, in the same spirit of autonomy and interpenetration where one is not reduced to the other. In such a non-reductive mode of engagement it can be realized that ontology is not an adjunct to either essentialist epistemology or essentialist ontology.

Resonating with Taylor's conception of folded ontology, I explore a multilayered and multidimensional conception and practice of ontology where it is a process of self-creation, world creation and creation of appropriate intersubjective relations. But unlike Strydom, this ontology is not solely discursive; this does not belittle the significance of discourse but it is, at the same time, non-discursive and trans-discursive as suggested in the reflections of Taylor in this volume. Strydom finds problem in the proliferation of the adjective 'ontological' in my text but this may be understood as not just my individual limitation but also a reflection of limits of available language to represent ontology as a verb. Ontological is not separated from ontological epistemology of participation as self-cultivation is not from world creation though one is not reducible to the other. In exploring pathways of ontology as a verb, I build upon significant moves in the field such as Vattimo's pathways of 'weak ontology', Dallmayr's 'practical ontology' and Clammer et al's 'relational and anthropological ontology' (Vattimo 1999; Dallmayr 1984; Clammer et al. 2004). Strydom quite insightfully presents the evolving perspective of 'weak naturalism' and it is fertile to look at reality at the cross-section of both weak ontology and weak naturalism as part of a new art of integration (cf. Giri 2013a, 2013b; Strydom 2013).[5] Therefore, my ontology is not solely Heideggerian. Strydom looks at Heidegger only as an idealist but there are also significant pragmatic pathways in Heidegger going beyond a facile dualism between idealism and pragmatism. In fact, there is also an alternative tradition of pragmatism where practice is not looked through the dualistic prism of either idealism or realism or theory and practice. One can embody practice in different ways with differential emphasis of the ontological or the epistemic, ideal or the practical, spiritual or material without being a prisoner of dualism. Similarly, my conception of theory is not just interpretative, especially that of Gadamer, as Strydom thinks. I do not so much explore ontology as I explore meta-ontology as a verb. Also, I explore some meta-theoretical questions where theory is not only a noun but also a verb. Additionally, I argue that this cannot be separated from the process of theorizing which is a conditional process and it has relevance for understanding the genesis and work of all kinds of theories, not only interpretative ones. However, my conception of theory is not just interpretative.

Strydom writes: 'Modernity is the only form of life which is aware of its own contingency and tries to live with it'. But how do people who do not consider modernity as their telos look at it? Such a view reflects the post-traditional telos of much of modernistic sociology, which itself needs critical self-examination. Ontology in ontological epistemology of participation is not an escape from modernity, especially its epistemology; rather, it is a creative mode of living with modernity but not solely on its own terms. The vision and practice of ontological epistemology of participation helps in realizing that one is not condemned to live with and in modernity only in a modernistic way. One can embody and inhabit plural ways of being and knowing in this contemporary world with creative crossing of boundaries between ontology and epistemology; between modern, non-modern and postmodern ways of living and with linked border-crossing between art, science, religion and spirituality.

Strydom considers that I have a narrow view of self-cultivation but my multidimensional conception of self and self-cultivation, consisting simultaneously of interconnecting and autonomous circles of unconscious, techno-practitioner and the transcendental, involves cultivation of all these circles of reality, thus making self-cultivation overflow to varieties of practices of world creation. Strydom considers that I have not been charitable in arguing that critical social science has 'lacked sufficient acknowledgment of the transcendental dimension of our co-present reality'. For Strydom, authentic critical social science

from its start in Marx throughout its elaboration up to Habermas and Axel Honneth . . . has been precisely about transcendence—i.e., non-arbitrary learning, transformation, and change on the level of the individual, institutions, culture and society aimed at a closer approximation to an authentically lived, reasonable and humane social form of life beyond what we are familiar with. . . .

I agree. But this is mainly one particular kind of transcendence, a sociological transcendence that Habermas calls 'transcendence from within'. But for many seekers of life, science and spirituality, there is also another interpenetrating reality of transcendence, which is not just social; even though Habermas might call this 'transcendence from without', this is beyond the dualism of within and without. Modernity and modern social science have been isolated from such a broader reality and realization of transcendental. It is in this context that transcendental in pathways of ontological epistemology of participation includes Nature, Divine and the human-social. Of course, Strydom's weak naturalism would be open to transcendental as simultaneously containing natural and human-social but it can now invite, as modern science, the Divine (including in non-religious ways). Social science then becomes not only a discursive practice of world-creation but also, at the same time, becomes a meditative practice of self-cultivation and world-creation with a broadened and deepened realization of both self and the world as multidimensional—simultaneously practical and transcendental; transcendental in both human-social as well as natural-divine ways.

Olsen argues that I uncritically adopt Roy Bhaskar's conception of transcendental identification. Yes, I agree that it is important to explore the work of the transcendental not only through the prism of identification but also through differentiation and disjunction. Transcendental works simultaneously through the process of identification as well as differentiation and this is also true of the field of ontological epistemology of participation. Ontological epistemology of participation contains the work of the transcendental through processes of identification, differentiation and disjunction.

In his critical reflections, Andrew Smith urges one not to sweep movements of dualism under the carpet in the name of enthusiastic valorization of non-duality. For Smith, 'oppositional thought has been centrally important to many of the most progressive political struggles of the modern world and "dualist models" have been hugely important in promoting critical consideration of the status quo'. Here Smith provides the examples of both class struggles, anti-colonial struggles for liberation as well as struggle for gender justice. But, as Smith quite insightfully argues, all these dualisms are not essentialistic. I agree that one cannot wish away dualism but it depends upon how he or she relates to reality of duality. One can relate to reality of duality as the ultimate or one can relate duality to non-duality in a permanent processual and non-absolutist ways. Oppositional thought has played an important role in progressive political struggle in the modern world but all these struggles also have been accompanied by the murder of the very goals for which the struggles had been undertaken. In this case, is it not necessary to learn from the contingent histories and practice of oppositional politics, even politics of dual confrontation with a sensitivity to non-dual grounds and horizons? This is an epochal question of human and social evolution too and there are no easy answers. Here, learning from movements for liberation in modernity one can practise a new art of liberation which can be called an art of compassion and confrontation. In this art of new political and spiritual struggle one confronts sources of exploitation but does not forget the responsibility of compassion. Though dualistic construction of the other has been the hallmark of many anti-colonial struggles there has also been other anti-colonial and post-colonial struggles where the colonizer and the colonized have not been constructed through the dualism of self and other.

Smith also makes another significant observation about the contemporary field of knowledge production, namely, the academy. For Smith, universities today are being invaded and transgressed by the logic of neoliberal market and in this context my plea for transcending the identity of scholars may be construed differently by different stakeholders some using it for colonizing the very social space of scholarship itself. But much depends upon what is the process and agent of transgression. One would have to resist the forces of neo-liberal market transgressing the bounds of academic reflections but, at the same time, one can make the field of reflection much more part of a flow of conversations and transformation between university and society, science and life. Furthermore, while defending individual identity onecannot escape the call for responsibility. Critique of neo-liberal audit cultures in the academy, sometimes forget this calling of responsibility (cf. Giri 2000). Thus, in transgressing the identity as scholars, one is simultaneously transformative and it is this act of transformation, which can be a saving grace. Smith quite rightly writes that scholars have their own habitus, the way they speak and even in the way they walk. But should not this be now broadened and should not the practice embody both intellectual and manual labour while transforming both into spiritual praxis of *shramabhakti* (devotional labour)? Exploring and taking part in pathways of creative research then becomes a *shramabhakti*—devotional labour—combining knowledge, action and devotion in a multi-valued spirit of autonomy and interpenetration.

Pathways of Creative Research: Festival of Dialogues and the Tasks Ahead

This book thus discusses these challenges of creative research, practice and transformations at present. These dialogues are now cultivated together by bringing critical and creative reflections and practice to them. Thus the journey and dialogue continues.

Notes

1. Here what Vattimo (2011: 21) writes deserves careful consideration:
   'In the age of democracy, the event (of Being) to which thought must turn its attention is something much broader, perhaps, and less well-defined, something more like politics. The only aid we have in thinking it is an expression from the late Foucualt, which I adopt and use it in an autonomous sense: "the ontology of actuality". The event (of Being) to which thought has the task of corresponding in the age of democracy is the mode in which Being is configured on an ongoing basis in the collective experience.'
   Vattimo (2011: 23) further says:
   'I will use "ontology" in a sense I take from Heidegger, for whom it denotes the thought of Being in both senses, the subjective and objective, of the genitive. [This is different from] most ontologists who reduce ontology to a theory of objects. As for actuality, I use this term to refer to the common conditions of our life at present

2. I explore vision and practice of practical renunciation in my poem: Sacrifice

   Sacrifice
   You said
   Sacrifice is the foundation of life
   But is not sacrifice
   Linked to violence?
   Sacrificial lamb and sacrificial Christ?
   Christ the yogi of Love
   Becomes a Justification for
   Sacrificing Millions
   In the name of sacrifice
   We sacrifice women, children and
   Each other
   Religion of love
   Becomes a religion of sacrifice
   Sacrifice!
   Gift of virgins
   Exchange of women
   Is this sacrifice
   Or renunciation?
   Renunciation is different
   A path of love and communication
   Let the violence of sacrifice
   Be transformed with the sadhana of
   Practical renunciation
   A new art of co-responsibility

Exchange of gifts
Exchange of selves
An economy of Gift
A politics of renunciation
A spirituality of transformation

[Montesserat, Barecelona, 17 January 2003]

3. About his own journey, Panikkar (2010: xxvi) explains: 'My originality, if any, will be that of giving to the origins—not to do archaeology or to make anachronistic interpretations, as if the beginnings were always exemplary, but to perform the task of latter-day hunter-gatherer, re-collecting life from the stupendous field of human experience on Earth. . .'.

4. Meditative verb as different from just active verb is the verb which combines action and meditation (see Giri 2012).

5. Strydom and myself have now taken part in such a dialogue in a preliminary way. I have edited a special symposium on the theme of integration in *Sociological Bulletin* in 2013 in which both of us have explored the need to bring weak ontology and weak naturalism together (see Giri 2013; Strydom 2013).

References

Bellah, Robert N. (1970), *Beyond Belief*, New York: Harper & Row.

Cayley, David (2007), *Ivan Illich in Conversation*, 1992; repr., Toronto: House of Anansi Press.

Clammer, John, Sylvie Piorier and Eric Schwimmer (2004), 'Introduction: The Relevance of Ontologies in Anthropology: Reflections on a New Anthropological Field', in *Figured Worlds: Ontological Obstacles in Intercultural Relations*, ed. John Clammer et al., Toronto: Toronto University Press, pp. 3–22.

Dallmayr, Fred (1984), *Polis and Praxis: Exercises in Contemporary Political Theory*, Cambridge, MA: The MIT Press.

Giri, Ananta Kumar (2000), 'Audited Accountability and the Imperative of Responsibility: Beyond the Primacy of the Political', in *Audit Cultures: Anthropological Studies in Accountability, Ethics and the Academy*, ed. Marilyn Strathern, London: Routledge, pp. 173–95.

————(2012), 'Beyond Adaptation and Meditative Verbs of Co-Realizations', in *Sociology and Beyond: Windows and Horizons*, ed. Ananta Kumar Giri, Jaipur: Rawat Publications.

————(2013a), 'Networks of Agape and Creativity: Learning Across Boundaries and the Calling of Planetary Realizations', *Integral Review*, vol. 9, no. 2, pp. 38–45.

————(2013b), 'Towards a New Art of Integration', *Integral Review*, vol. 9, no. 2, pp.113–22.

Hanh, Thich Nhat (1997), *The Heart of Understanding*, New Delhi: Full Circle Publishing House.

Ingold, Tim (2006), 'Rethinking the Animate, Re-animating Thoughts', *Ethnos*, vol. 71, no. 1, pp. 9–20.

Jackson, Michael (2007), *Excursions*, Durham, NC: Duke University Press.

Panikkar, Raimundo(2010), *The Rhythm of Being: The Unbroken Trinity*, The Gifford Lectures, New York: Orbis Books.

Strydom, Piet (2013), 'Cooperation, Coordination and the Social Bond: On Integration from a Critical Cognitive Social-Theoretical Perspective', *Sociological Bulletin*, vol. 62, no. 1, pp. 115–21.

Vattimo, Giani (1999), *Belief*, Cambridge: Polity Press.

———(2011), *A Farewell to Truth*, New York: Columbia University Press.

Taylor, Charles (2007), *A Secular Age*, Cambridge, MA: Harvard UniversityPress.

———(2011), *Dilemmas and Connections: Selected Essays*, Cambridge, MA: Harvard University Press.

Thoreau, David (1975), 'Walking', in *The Portable Thoreau*, ed. Carl Bode, Penguin.

2

Pathways of Creative Research: Rethinking Theories and Methods and the Calling of an Ontological Epistemology of Participation

ANANTA KUMAR GIRI

Theoria and the contemplative life, which the philosophical tradition has identified as its highest goal for centuries, will have to be dislocated onto a new plane of immanence. It is not certain that, in the process, political philosophy and epistemology will be able to maintain their present physiognomy and difference with respect to ontology.

— GEORGIO AGAMBEN (1999: 239), *Potentialities: Collected Essays in Philosophy.*

What is the contemporary field of possible experience? Here it is not a question of an analytic of truth, but of what one might call an ontology of the present, an ontology of ourselves. . . .

—MICHEL FOUCAULT (1986), *Kant on Enlightenment and Revolution.*

Faithful to the Platonic motto of 'wondering' (thaumazein), the reflective theorist in the global village must shun spectatorial allures and adopt the more modest stance of participant in the search for truth: by opening mind and heart to the puzzling diversity of human experiences and traditions—and also to the possibility of jeopardizing cherished preoccupations or beliefs.

— FRED DALLMAYR (1999), *Border Crossing: Toward a Comparative Political Theory.*

This amounts to saying that theory of knowledge and theory of life seem to us inseparable. A theory of life that is not accompanied by a criticism of knowledge is obliged to accept, as they stand, the concepts which the understanding puts at its disposal: it cannot but enclose the facts, willing or not, in pre-existing frames which it regards as ultimate. . . . On the other hand, a theory of knowledge which does not replace the intellect in the general evolution of life will teach us neither how the frames of knowledge have been constructed nor how we can enlarge or go beyond them. It is necessary that these two inquiries, theory of knowledge and theory of life, should join each other, and, by a circular process push each other unceasingly.

— HENRI BERGSON (1912), *Creative Evolution.*

The Problem

Modern social research, as it is known now, emerged as a part of the rise of modern social sciences in the context of transition to modernity. As an enterprise of modernity, social research reflected some of the foundational assumptions of modernity. For example, the project of sociology was closely tied to the project of nation state, embodying in its epistemology what Ulrich Beck (2002) calls methodological nationalism. Social research also proceeded within the bounded logic of disciplines. Another assumption of modernity that social research reflected was modernity's primacy of epistemology and the neglect of ontology which short-circuited 'ontological issues by assuming that once the right procedure for attaining truth as correspondence or coherence is reached, any remaining issues will be either resolved through that method or shown to be irrelevant' (Connolly 1995: 6). In the modernist mode, social research was considered only an epistemic engagement, a project of knowing about the world with proper procedure and scientific method. But this only embodies a questionable 'social ontology' which in its 'empiricist version . . . treats human beings as independent objects susceptible to representation, or at least, a medium in which the designative dimensions of concepts can be disconnected rigorously from the contexts[1] of rhetoric/action/evaluation in which they originate' (Connolly 1995: 6). But all these assumptions of modernity as well as their social manifestations have been subjected to fundamental criticisms and interrogations in the last decades. Both anti-systematic socio-cultural movements and critical discursive movements and new movements of ideas have challenged the modernist paradigms of pathology and normality as well as distinction between ontology and epistemology. There has been some foundational criticism of the bounded logic of both the disciplines and nation state and awareness of the need for post-national[2] transformations, planetary realizations and a creative trans-disciplinarity (Giri 2004a; Strathern 2004). In the background of critiques of modernity, social movements and processes of transformations the present essay submits some proposals for a creative and critical social research. It explores ways of moving beyond mere denunciations and critiques and embodying transformational theories and methods, which would facilitate creative and critical research. The essay also calls for a new vocation of social research by pleading for a simultaneous engagement in activism and creative understanding, fieldwork and philosophical reflections, ontological self-cultivation and epistemic labour of learning.

The present essay presents some proposals for rethinking theories and methods. It discusses ways of rethinking society and subjectivity and pleads for a frame of ontological sociality. It submits some proposals for rethinking method, especially overcoming the dualism of qualitative and quantitative, ontology and epistemology. It pleads for border crossing between philosophy and social sciences, a multi-valued logic of autonomy and interpenetration and an ontological epistemology of participation. As the limitations of any such single engagement can be appreciated, the present essay is not able to present an exhaustive critical description of all relevant thoughts and thinkers and presents only some glimpses from this vast field of rethinking and reconstruction of theories and methods of social sciences.

Creative Social Research and Rethinking Theories and Methods

THE CALLING OF SOCIAL MOVEMENTS

In the last quarter century, social movements have been a very important dimension of normative horizon and domain of social practice. Study of social movements has enabled social scientists to rethink theories of self and society as well as be engaged in new methodological formulations. As Veena Das tells us:

The emergence of social movements around issues of environment, gender inequalities, and health (to name a few) have similarly offered important critiques of the disciplines by interrogating notions of normality and pathology around which conceptual distinctions have been organized. For instance, the role of the women's movement in bringing the issue of sexual violence into public discourse has also provided an impetus for rethinking ideas about heterosexuality, reproduction and sexual geographies in the classic field of kinship and marriage (2003: 20).

In the evocative phrase of Alain Touraine (1977), social movements are agents of 'self-production of society' and embody a new dialectic of self and society (Melucci 1996). They embody the self-transcendence of culture and society and point to the 'non-identity of society with itself' (Fuchs 2004: 44). Social movements show the limitations of looking at society only through its own logic of identity, through its code of 'self-referentiality'. Reflections on social movements have been innumerable in recent years and Martin Fuchs, an insightful scholar in the field, states that social movements 'express the self-defining subjectivity—identity and distantiation, (self-) reflexivity and (self-) transformation in an exemplary way and as social act' (2004: 44). Study of social movements also calls for a new methodology of dialogue, hermeneutics and interpretation. It calls for a

change in the relationship between the social analyst and those he is analysing. The analyst would have to be more of a hermeneute, an interpreter of the ways in which collective or individual actors link up with discourse and representations and appropriate or reject (i.e., interact with) them; a listener to ideas and imaginations which crop up in the ongoing negotiation of sociality (social relationship). Instead of just a distant observer of society the analyst has to become an interlocutor of the actors . . . . (Fuchs 2004: 44).

But while study of society provides an opportunity for rethinking theories and methods, especially rethinking society and self, it has to be borne in mind that study of social movements cannot be just an act of valorization—just paraphrasing representations and articulations of movements and their words and worlds. In this context, Andre Beteille's distinction between sociological engagement and activistic engagement is important to keep in mind. For Beteille, 'The social activist is a partisan, and partisanship undermines the very conditions of sociological enquiry and analysis . . . it is fair-mindedness and not partisanship, that is the defining virtue of the sociologist' (2002: 9). But as helpful as such a critical perspective is, it still leaves some fundamental questions untouched. Are participation and partisanship the same thing? Does fair-mindedness stand for a spectatorial stance or a pure view of the observer? How can fair-mindedness arise without the sociologist also participating in the aspirations and struggles of the activists? In this regard what may be considered is that participation may not be partisanship because while participating in the dreams and struggles of the activists a sociologist or anthropologist does not have to abandon one's vocation of critical understanding.

In fact it is the virtue of fair-mindedness that also requires of the sociologist to participate in the life worlds of actors. This participation is however an engagement of simultaneous sympathetic participation and critical understanding. Instead of a confident and valorizing distinction between the activist and the sociologist there needs to be a dialogue between them and through this dialogue contribute to the making of the transgressive and transformative genre of scholar-activists. But much of this dialogue so far has remained either half-hearted or empty because the concerned actors here are too anxious to guard their identity either as an activist or a scholar rather than learn from each other in a transgressive manner and strive to embody the vision and practice of both, i.e. to be a scholar-activist. The worlds of scholarship and critical social actions have their own autonomies but they are also related to each other in a spirit of embodied interpenetration. To be a scholar–activist is to realize this logic of autonomy and interpenetration in one's own vision and practice, ontology and epistemology, embodying a labour and love of learning (cf. Giri 2004b).

RETHINKING THEORIES

Social research has been influenced by several theories in philosophy and social sciences, notable among the recent ones being structuration theory, theories of reflexivity, varieties of postmodernism and post-structuralism. A detailed rethinking of all these theories is outside the scope of this essay. Here I am engaged particularly with three issues: first, rethinking of the theory itself, rethinking of society and rethinking of self and subjectivity (cf. Turner 1996). To begin with the former, so far theory has been thought of as a body of prescriptive and predictive rules and regulations. Now theory has to be thought of in a new way as a companion rather than as a master, as a moving lighthouse which gives possible direction in the sea of complex reality, rather than as a fixed star. It involves a critique of 'theoreticist theory'—a 'theoretical logic' which is not grounded in a concrete research practice (Bourdieu and Wacquant 1992: 32). Rethinking theory also involves an acknowledgement of limits of theory or of what Dallmayr (1987: 3) calls formulating purely 'philosophical questions' in the hope of finding for them 'philosophical solutions'. Building on Oakeshott's distinction between theory and theorizing, Dallmayr presents the notion of a conditional, non-systematic mode of theorizing: 'Although propelled by an "unconditional" commitment to learning, theorizing in this view does not pretend to systematic epistemic knowledge, but only to an ongoing clarification of its own limitations or conditions of possibility'[3] (Dallmayr 1984: 6). It also calls for abandonment of theoretical arrogance, lying at the heart of modernity, of solving problems of practice solely through theoretical means.[4]

RETHINKING SOCIETY: THE CALLING OF AN ONTOLOGICAL SOCIALITY

Creative social research involves a reconceptualization of society and subjectivity and an important task here is to understand what can be called the work of ontological sociality in self, culture and society. One important challenge here is to go beyond the false dichotomy between individual and society. As Norbert Elias tells us:

We have the familiar concepts of 'individual' and 'society', the first of which refers to a single human being as if he or she were an entity existing in complete isolation . . . Society is understood either as a mere accumulation, an additive and unstructured collection of many individual people, or as an object existing beyond individuals and incapable of further explanation. . . the words available to us, the concepts which decisively influence the thought and action of people growing up within their sphere, make it appear as if the single human being, labelled the individual, and the plurality of people conceived as society, were two ontologically different entities (1991: i).

For Elias, '. . . the individual person is able to say "I" because he can at the same time say "we". Thus society consists of a simultaneously "I" and "we" but the balance between them has changed historically' (1991: 61). At the contemporary juncture it is the 'I' dimension which seems to be getting more primacy and attention in modern and late modern societies, which Zygmunt Bauman calls individualized society (Bauman 2001). In such societies there is a recognition of the limits of the social in many spheres of life such as education, love and ethics (cf. Beck 2000; Beck and Beck-Gernsheim 1995). The ideal of society is now being foundationally rethought as providing a space for self-development of individuals. For example, Andre Gorz (1999) argues that educative relation is not just a social relation.[5] Similarly ethics is not just acting in accordance with social conventions but acting in accordance with post-conventional awareness and realizations where, as Habermas says, conventional norms of society turn out to be 'instances of problematic justice' (1990: 108). Morality is not just obeying pre-given command by either society or a benevolent dictator or a wise master but acting according to one's conscience (Giri 1998a). It is probably for this reason that Touraine writes in his recently provocatively titled essay 'Sociology after Sociology:'

One of the main themes of sociology is therefore the reversal of the conception and role of institutions. These were defined by their function in the integration of a social system. They defined and imposed respect for the norms and instruments for the defense of individuals which enable them to defend themselves against norms. Our society is less and less a society of the subjected and more and more a society of volunteers. (2007: 191)

The field of society is also a work of ontological sociality, which is not confined only to contemporary late modern or individualized societies. It is a reality and possibility in all kinds of societies though degrees may vary (cf. Touraine 2000). In this context what Michael Frietag writes deserves careful consideration: 'Contrary to a misguided reading of Max Weber's well known texts, the ontological aspect—the immanent normativity of human/ social and historical being is primary, and an understanding of it involves another break with the Weberian heritage: the idea of an ontological reciprocity of individual and society should replace methodological individualism' (2001: 2). But acknowledging the ontological aspect of society does not mean only acknowledging its normative dimension but also its 'subjective existence' (Frietag 2001: 2). As has been already suggested, in recent social experience in the work of varieties of social movements this ontological dimension of society comes into play—creativity of self, return of the actor, and self-production of society. Some scholars of social movements suggest that in social movements one gets a glimpse of the pathways of an alternative sociality which can be called ontological sociality, the basic ontological relationship characterized by interpretative action. As Martin Fuchs argues:

Humans not only refer to their self and their social environment, the sociality or polity they live in but the world as a . . . latent 'surplus of meaning', as exceeding. The basic (ontological) relationship would be interpretative action. This broadens the reference of human action and interpretation or, rather, transcends the idea of a specific referent . . . Instead of seeing subjectivity as constitutive of the world [. . . we have to see it] as open to the world. (2004)

Now, there is a recognition of an ontological dimension in varieties of life and disciplines. For example, insofar as the domain of economy and the field of economics is concerned, Irene van Staveren explains: '. . . There is a methodological alternative to the utilitarian paradigm of economics to be found in ontology' (2004: 86). Like Frietag's discussion of ontological reciprocity in sociology pointing to the normative and subjective dimensions of self and society, in van Staveren, an ontological approach to economics urges one to understand the value commitments of actors. An ontological approach to economics relies on people's value commitments but these values should not be understood as only utility maximization or profit maximization but reflect values of justice and care, and these values should not be understood through 'the dualistic methodology of mainstream economics, separating values from economic behaviour' (2004: 86). In her outline of an alternative economic methodology (an ontological methodology for economics grounded on human values) and conceptualization of economics as concerned with provisioning rather than exchange, van Staveren builds on Aristotle but reformulates the essentialist traces of an Aristotelian ontology in the direction of movement and pluralism.

For van Staveren, economic actors have plural value commitments of freedom, justice and care. So far the ontology of economics has been narrowly defined in terms of freedom, market and exchange. For van Staveren however, the domains of justice and care are also integral parts of the reality of economic life. These domains of the economy are autonomous yet interdependent and what is helpful in realizing is that there is a non-instrumental relationship between them. What van Staveren writes can open new vistas of imagination in methodological engagement: '. . . in an economic ontology grounded in human values, economic value domains are interdependent but not instrumentally related. Each domain functions on its own terms but at the same time it is a precondition for the functioning of other domains, without being instrumental' (2004: 98).

There are glimpses of an ontological sociality going beyond subject-object dualism in classical formulations of society. For example, building on both Indian and Greek traditions, philosopher Binod Kumar Agarwala (2004) says that play was central to Greek and Vedic imagination of society. Central to the practice of play is that the actor or subject loses himself in the play. Furthermore, 'The mode of being of lila [play] does not permit the jiva [person] to behave towards the lila as to an object';'the self-understanding of jiva is inevitably involved in understanding of lila in such a way that the medium is not differentiated from it' (Agarwala 2004: 263). This suggests an ontology and epistemology of participation that are important components of a creative social research but Agarwala urges one to be open towards the dimension of beyond or transcendence in this ontology and epistemology of participation. Self-consciousness here cannot be completely dissolved into self-knowledge: 'There is always a remainder, an excess of what we are beyond what we know of ourselves' (2004: 263, emphasis mine).

RETHINKING SOCIETY:
SOME FURTHER CONSIDERATIONS

The perspective of ontological sociality helps to rethink society in a foundational way, which can be understood in conjunction with other recent efforts. For example, many contemporary sociologists point to the need for thinking about sociology beyond society. John Urry and Karin Knorr-Cetina point to this, which has a much wider currency than acknowledged by anxiety-stricken sociologists of today.[6] John Urry writes in his *Sociology Beyond Societies*: 'New rules of sociological method are necessitated by the apparently declining power of national societies (whether or not we do in fact live in a global society), since it was these societies that had provided the social context for sociological study until the present' (2000: 1–2). Urry looks at the emergence of 'natural-social' hybrids for contemporary citizenship and explores whether 'notions of chaos and complexity' can assist in the 'elaboration of a "sociology beyond societies"'(2000: 190).

Social theorist and sociologist of science Karin Knorr-Cetina takes this exploration of sociology beyond society to inspiring height and depth. Writes Knorr-Cetina in her provocatively titled essay 'Postsocial relations: Theorizing Society in a Postsocial Environment': 'Sociality is very likely a permanent feature of human life. But the focus of sociality is nonetheless changing—in conjunction with concrete historical developments' (Knorr-Cetina 2001: 521). And one of the most important aspect of the contemporary development is 'the loss of social imagination, the slow erosion of the belief in salvation by society' (2001: 523). The post-social environment today not only consists of subject-centred imagination but also objects and the non-human world, which challenges one to go beyond anthropocentrism. The very starting lines of Knorr-Cetina (2001: 520) deserve careful attention from the point of view of overcoming the tight-grip of anthropocentrism in one's thinking:

we take it for granted that social reality is the world of human affairs, exclusively . . . Luckman raised the issue from a phenomenological perspective arguing that the boundary we see between the human social and the non-human, non-social was not an essential structure of the life-world. One reason for this was that our sense of humanness itself is not an original or universal projection but arises from revisions and modifications of other distinctions, for example that between living and non-living beings.

For Knorr-Cetina, social reality in contemporary consumer culture and society consists not only of subjects but also objects. Living in this reality leads to the emergence of a new self: the self as a structure of wanting and the shift from 'the inner censor to the mirror image self'. Knorr-Cetina writes, building on his dialogue with George Herbert Mead and Jacques Lacan: 'The lack-wanting system describes contemporary selves better than the I-you-me system' (2001: 527). Here self is characterized by wanting and though in contemporary consumer culture individuals want fulfilment in having more objects, this object-centred consumption may not be the individual's destiny and the structure of wanting has the potential to make him/her seeker of a more authentic solidarity, an intimate relation with self, other, Nature and God. The task here is to realize the challenge of an emergent subjectivity and what Foucault had written vis-à-vis Nietzsche: 'For Nietzsche, the death of God signifies the end of metaphysics, but God is not replaced by man, and the space remains empty' (quoted in Carretto 1999: 85; see also Uberoi 2002; Bhaskar 2002a, 2002b).

In Knorr-Cetina's insightful formulation, solidarity is central to a post-social sociality but solidarity here is not entrapped in a logic of nation state and society but carries the signature of an ontological sociality. Post-social sociality also calls for a new epistemology of participation. Writes Knorr-Cetina: '. . . we can do less without positioning ourselves on the object's side when the object is non-human than when it is human . . . .The process of position-taking involves the subject's "becoming the object," a sort of cross-over through which the subject attempts to see the object world from inside, to "think" as it does, and to feel its reactions'. In the words of a biologist, 'if you want to really understand about a tumour, you've got to be a tumour' (2001: 531).

But such an ontology and epistemology of participation calls for overcoming not only anthropocentrism but also egoism. What is interesting is that such a calling seems to be articulated now by scholars with a Marxist background. In his presidential address to World Congress of Sociology, 'The Heritage of Sociology, the Promise of Social Science', Wallerstein writes: 'Human arrogance has been humanity's greatest self-imposed limitation. . . . In all these arrogances we have betrayed first of all ourselves, and closed off our potential' (1999: 250). Wallerstein transforms the whole logic of familiar sociological discourse when he talks about cosmic creativity which prepares the ground for far deeper radical proposals of thinkers such as Roy Bhaskar to follow, who talks about cosmic envelope and transcendental identification: 'We live in an uncertain cosmos, whose single greatest merit is the permanence of . . . uncertainty, because it is this uncertainty that makes possible creativity—Cosmic Creativity, and with that of course human creativity' (1999: 250).

In the same essay, Wallerstein presents sociology six challenges: the challenge of rethinking rationality; the challenge of overcoming its initial Eurocentric bias; rethinking time and temporality; reckoning with complexities and uncertainties; coming to terms with feminist challenges not only in social relations but also in epistemology; and questioning objectivity in not only social sciences but also in natural science and finally rethinking modernity by acknowledging that modernity, the centre piece of all one's work, has never really existed (1999: 241) which urges one to realize that the relations between self, other and the world can be more meaningfully imagined and lived than what has been done under the regime of European modernity (Uberoi 2002).

Out of these challenges, one can elaborate the challenge of rethinking rationality and universality as a starting point of a multidimensional foundational rethinking of the very category of society itself. The conception of society in sociology suffers from a 'myth of rationality' and 'myth of stability' (cf. Toulmin 2001). But society is not only the ground of the rational, society is also the base of much irrational and also the ground for supra-rational aspirations, as Nietzsche and Sri Aurobindo from their very different positions would urge one to understand (Connolly 2002; Giri 2004a). And, insofar as universality is concerned, there is a dimension of universality as a reality as well as possibility in particular cultures calling the US to transcend the dichotomy between universalism and particularism and understanding the work of a contingent universal. Wallerstein et al. (1996) many years ago had thrown a challenge to understand the work of 'particularistic universalism'. This is akin to a relational and perspectival universality articulated by literary theorist Radhakrishnan (2003: 34) which is always in process. In their work on cosmopolitanism, Sheldon Pollock et al. (2000) urge all to understand the similar work of what they call 'situated universality'[7] which is different from an opposition between global and local, universal and particular. Ulrich Beck (2002) in this regard also talks about cosmopolitanism with roots and wings. In rethinking universality, along with perspectives such as situated universality and perspectival universality one is also enriched by a perspective of dialectical universality recently developed by Roy Bhaskar in his project of a deepened critical realism. For Bhaskar, for rethinking universality, one must go beyond abstract universality, understand it dialectically, and relate universality to 'irreducible uniqueness' (Bhaskar 2002a: 122). For Bhaskar, dialectical universality of particular beings is sustained by 'genuine non-duality and relations of identity' (2002b: xxv). For Bhaskar, 'once you describe the world in an abstract universal way as consisting in constant conjunctions of events or actualized empirical uniformities then you put a halt to history' (2002b: 122). It reflects 'ontological monovalence' and a sense of fatalism that the present society is the best of all possible worlds. Instead,

universality had to be understood dialectically—that is universality together with differentiations and mediations, together with geo-historical trajectories, or what I call rhythmics, and together with irreducible uniqueness, all of which defines the concrete singularity of every instance, everything that ever occurs. This would mean in concrete terms that the two members of the working class or two members of human race would always have to be understood in their mediations, that is whether they are women or men, what kind of work they do, and also in terms of their geo-historical trajectories, where they are coming from, their place and past, and where they are going, what their tangential future (2002b: 122).

Rethinking Subjectivity

In his introduction to an anthology of contemporary European social thought on 'Rethinking the subject', James D. Faubion argues that while Kant's ontology is that of autonomous subject which was followed by Durkheim as he reformulated it in terms of making society 'the genuine referent of Kant's transcendental subject', contemporary European thinkers go beyond this in offering an ontology of techno-praxis of the 'techno-practitioner'. For Faubion, the works of Habermas and Bourdieu reflect this shifting subjectivity:

For Habermas, the hallmark of the techno-practitioner is his or her capacity—no longer nominal, but instead the product and profit of all in this world that mankind has learned—at once to recognize, accept, and follow the normative principles immanent in communication. For Bourdieu, the hallmark of techno-practitioner is his or her capacity to play a game, to use his or her material and symbolic resources strategically in order to win a context more or less local in its rule but everywhere the same in its covert end: domination (Faubion 1995: 15).

Rethinking the subject as a techno-practitioner, for Faubion, should remind one of Aristotle to realize its promise and limits. For Faubion, 'The Ethics [Nichomachean Ethics of Aristotle] sets the technician to one side; it features only the practitioner. But the practitioner it features is, like those of his lineage, a being neither transcendental nor natural but instead a being constructed, trained, and socialized, a being of acquired competence and acquired habit' (1995: 15). But Aristotle would also urge all to understand the limit of the contemporary techno-practitioner in terms of 'ethical formalism' of Habermas and Bourdieu's 'perverse teleology' [This is what Faubion himself writes]. Aristotle's hallmark is eudaimonia—happiness—and the techno-practitioner must not only argue and strategize but embody a striving for eudaimonia a striving which takes her beyond the contemporary models of the subject as coming from Habermas and Bourdieu. Realization of happiness is not a matter of social practice but also of appropriate subjective cultivation; realization of eudaimonia also calls for a spiritualization of practice, as can shortly be seen, and also going beyond Aristotle.

SUBJECT AS NOT ONLY A TECHNO–PRACTITIONER BUT ALSO A TRANSCENDENTALLY REAL SELF

Thus rethinking the subject urges one to realize the limits of the models of the techno-practitioner, which is closer to the earlier sociological model of homo sociologicus presented by Ralph Dahrendorf. Neither the techno-practitioner nor homo sociologicus as occupants of social roles, exhaust the reality and possibility of the subject (see Cohen 1994; Giri 1998) and here it is also helpful to acknowledge that the subject is also a transcendentally real self. Such a deepening and widening of perspective is suggested by Roy Bhaskar. Bhaskar, the pioneer in the movement of critical realism, has now deepened the quest of realism to touch spiritual quest of self-development and social emancipation. Even much before his contemporary spiritual deepening of critical realism Bhaskar had posed some foundational challenges to social sciences. For Bhaskar, in thinking about society one should not commit a collectivist or individualist fallacy as society consists of neither the collective nor the individual but relations. But what is at the core of relationship? For Bhaskar, it is the ideal and practice of identification what he calls 'transcendental identification'. Transcendental identification is the work of the transcendentally real self; so in rethinking the subject one has to think of her as also a transcendentally real self and not merely a 'techno-practitioner'. For Bhaskar, '. . . transcental identification is absolutely basic to life. This means non-duality is absolutely basic to life' (Bhaskar 2002a: 140). And this 'non-duality is not something "mystical", not something that depends on any kind of belief or faith, but the necessary condition for the most quotidian states and acts' (Bhaskar 2002a: 261). For Bhaskar, ontology has to be 'vastly expanded to allow for the possibility for the enfolding layers of being' (2002a: 16). Parallel to Knorr-Cetina's notion of self as a structure of wanting, Bhaskar refers to absence that affects ontology and epistemology:

The whole process is really structured by absence: first in the form of incompleteness which initiates it; second it is negativity in the form of contradiction which stimulates the crisis which motivates you to transcend an existing problem field. And, what happens when you are transcending it is that you have a moment of creative discovery which actually cannot be induced or deduced from the existing subject matter; so it comes from the epistemically unknown (2002a : 130).

Acknowledging that the subject is also a transcendentally real self urges one to rethink differentiation from a perspective of identification. Bhaskar takes the discourse and practice of identification to a new depth and height by talking of ground state, cosmic envelope and co-presence. Bhaskar writes: 'When your action is coming from your ground-state you will see no preference for your own development over the development and freedom of any other being in the universe' (2002a: 148). Bhaskar urges social scientists to be open to these new pathways of connectivity at work in people's lives rather than just be preoccupied with difference:

The critique of postmodernism involves accepting the emphasis on uniqueness and differentiation without throwing out concepts of universality and connection. Indeed the ground-state and cosmic envelope are just precisely the concepts we need to understand differentiation within a unity. But these aspects of being, on which all other aspects ultimately depend, are precisely those which through the generalized theory of co-presence, allows us to see that everything is implicitly enfolded or contained and may be brought to consciousness, implicit or explicit, in everything else, so that anything can be traced or manifest in anything else. The world becomes one in which a quasi-magical or generalized (dialectically universalized) synchronicity is potentially capable of being manifest anywhere. (2002a: 248)

Max Weber spoke about the disenchantment of the world in which modern scientific world view played an important role. Modern social science took part in this disenchantment of the world in the process making Man unable to live authentically. Now there is a need to go beyond the crisis of European sciences and to live a non-dual life and through ontology and epistemology contribute to the experience and making of a re-enchanted world where 'knowledge of' cannot be dissociated from 'knowing with' (cf. Sunder Rajan 1998). Bhaskar urges one to attend to this calling of re-enchantment both as subjects and scientists which involves collapse of 'subject-object duality' and 'fact-value distinction'[8] (Bhaskar 2002b: xxxvii). For Bhaskar all are enchanted beings, i.e. 'bearers of values, meaning and change'. Bhaskar writes: 'We are involved as totalities in a world which is enchanted in the sense that it is the bearer of values, of meaning and change. This level of critique also enables one to see that the world consists of emergent totalities' (2002b: 247). Bhaskar elaborates the dynamics of an expanded ontology as a reflection of and striving towards a dynamically moving re-enchanted world:

we perspectivally re-totalise the field, which we all daily experience, and which is plummeting into global crisis, under the categories of transcendence, duality and non-duality, in the context of an expanded ontology, in which we not only, as in hitherto critical realism, think being, thing being processually, and as a totality, and as incorporating transformative agency and reflexivity; but also now think being as multi-planar and n-dimensionally generalized, with mental and emotional sui generis realities, bound together within a more basic level which is not only beyond thought but beyond sight, which I have called the cosmic envelope; and within this vastly expanded conception of being, and the very extended ontology it necessitates, we now see being as re-enchanted, that is as valuable, meaningful and containing invisible (more generally unknown and even unmanifest), subtle, mysterious and even magical qualities and connections, which our contemporary sciences know nothing of. (2002b: 257–8)[9]

Rethinking Methods

OVERCOMING DUALISM: TOWARDS A MULTI-VALUED LOGIC OF AUTONOMY AND INTERPENETRATION AND AN AESTHETICS OF DISCOVERING THREADS OF CONNECTIONS

Realization of non-duality in a world of duality is an important challenge before us, both ontologically as well as epistemologically, i.e. whatever reality one tries to understand has a non-dual dimension and the method of understanding it ought to embody this non-dual sensitivity. As shall be seen, an ontology and epistemology of non-duality is neither one of total absorption nor uncritical holism nor monism[10] as it is sensitive to disjunction and antinomies between different dimensions or parts of reality. Building on the earlier discussion about subject, subject is simultaneously a techno-practitioner or homo sociologicus and transcendentally real self. Furthermore, building on Freud, Jung and Victor Frankl, the subject has also a dimension of unconscious. Thus the subject has, at least, three dimensions, in her multi-planar existence—unconscious, role player/techno-practitioner, and transcendentally real self. But how do they relate to each other? Does one totally exhaust the other or is opposed to the other? The relationship between these dimensions is one of autonomy and interpenetration, i.e. these dimensions of subject exist as concentric and interpenetrative circles having simultaneously an autonomous and relational existence. For example, whatever one does as role occupants and techno-practitioners is influenced by both the dimensions of unconscious and transcendentally real self.[11] But neither of these exist in a situation of either or nor can one be unproblematically reduced to or subsumed under the other.

The perspective taken for granted is that the world is unitary but in fact a plural world consisting of multiple domains which are simultaneously irreducible to each other and at the same time in relationship with each other is emerging in varieties of domains of reflections now.[12] For example, van Staveren (2001), argues that the field of economy consists of not only the domain of market exchange but also domains of justice and care and they are not related to each other in a dualistic or exclusionary manner. Such a plural but interconnected and relational conceptualization of a field of study is also emerging in domains such as history. For example, philosopher R. Sunder Rajan argues that history does not consist of only power and reason but also of vision. Taking cues from this in his efforts to rethink modernist historiography, I (2004) critically discussed Amartya Sen's view of history as an enterprise of knowledge (cf. Sen 2001). For me, as an enterprise of knowledge, history is 'neither unitary nor rational'. There are different domains in the enterprise of history such as history as power, history as reason and history as vision. But like van Staveren's conceptualizations of different domains of economy, I argued that these different domains of history are simultaneously autonomous and interpenetrative where they 'illumine each other revealing unsuspected dimensions of each other' (Sunder Rajan 1996: 193).

One finds a similar sensitivity to autonomy and interpenetration emerging in anthropologist Frederik Barth's approach to and conceptualization of knowledge. Barth (2002) argues that knowledge consists of three domains—substantive corpus, communicative medium, and social organization—but they are related to each other. Barth writes:

I am not inviting you to take a highly generalized and abstract unity (knowledge) and divide into three parts (substantive corpus, communicative medium, and social organization) and then progressively break each of these parts down further till we finally arrive at the level of particular human actions and events. On the contrary, my thesis is that these three faces of knowledge appear together precisely in the particulars of action in every event of the application of knowledge . . . ..Their mutual determination takes place at those specific moments when a particular item of substantive knowledge is cast in a particular communicative medium and applied in an actor by an action positioned in a particular social organization: their systematic interdependence arises by virtue of the constraints in realization that these three aspects impose on each other in the context of every particular application. (2002: 3; italics in the original)

As a final example of this proposed ontology of autonomy and interpenetration one can look at the field of development. Building on three fundamental Kantian questions—what can be done? What can be known? And what can be hoped for?—Quarles van Ufford and I (2003) argue that the discourse and practice of development consist of domains of hope, politics and administration, and critical understanding. Autonomous as well as interconnected knowledge and actions arise in these domains. But these domains though autonomous already presuppose the other in their constitution, genealogy and dynamics. The domain of development as hope has or ought to have within itself an awareness of the issues emerging from domains of politics and application, and critical understanding. The same simultaneous logic of autonomy and interpenetration is true of domains of politics and critique as well.

But in order to understand this relationship of autonomy and interpenetration a new logic is needed that philosopher J.N. Mohanty (2000), building on both the Jaina tradition of Svedavada and Husserl's phenomenology, calls multi-valued logic or which sociologist J.P.S. Uberoi (2002), building on Goethe, Gandhi and the Hermetic tradition of Europe, calls 'the four-fold logic of truth and method'. What Mohanty writes below helps to understand the proposed multi-valued logic of autonomy and interpenetration:

The ethic of non-injury applied to philosophical thinking requires that one does not reject outright the other point of view without first recognizing the element of truth in it; it is based on the belief that every point of view is partly true, partly false, and partly undecidable. A simple two-valued logic requiring that a proposition must either be true or false is thereby rejected, and what the Jaina philosopher proposes is a multi-valued logic. To this multi-valued logic, I add the Husserlian idea of overlapping contents. The different perspectives on a thing are not mutually exclusive, but share some contents with each other. The different 'worlds' have shared contents, contrary to the total relativism. If you represent them by circles, they are intersecting circles, not incommensurable, [and it is this model of] intersecting circles which can get us out of relativism on the one hand and absolutism on the other. [Emphasis mine] (2000: 24)

Thus taking inspiration form Mohanty one can represent the previous examples of fields in terms of following a series of overlapping and concentric circles:

But though these different domains or dimensions of life and science— self, knowledge, history, economy and development—embody a logic

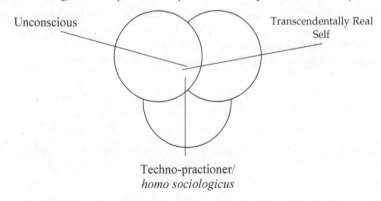

Self

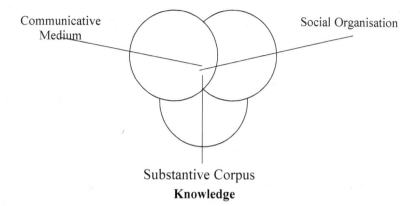

Communicative
Medium

Social Organisation

Substantive Corpus
Knowledge

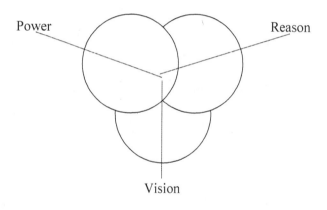

Power

Reason

Vision

History

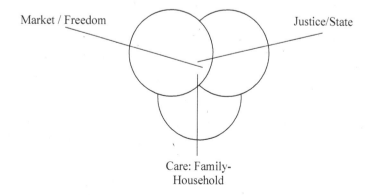

Market / Freedom

Justice/State

Care: Family-
Household

Economy

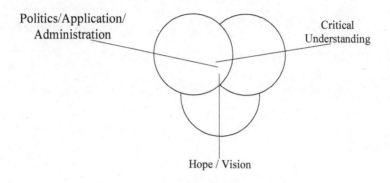

Development

autonomy and interpenetration it requires a bit of effort to discover their threads of connections. There is a dimension of autonomy among these domains and many a time they present themselves as well as are perceived as incommensurabilities. In this context, a move from autonomy trapped inside incommensurability as fate to discovering threads of connections requires work on self and science, ontology and epistemology. For philosopher and historian Ankersmit (2002), it calls for an aesthetic cultivation, which enables one to deal with immensurabilities and discover threads of connections without suppressing gaps or disjunctions.[13] It also calls for the work of a 'transversal reason' which takes one beyond the exclusionary rationality of each of the domains, for instance, cognitive or ethical (Ankersmit 2002: 233–4). Transversal reason, which is connected to both aesthetics[14] and transcendence (cf. Schrag 1997; Quarles van Ufford and Giri 2003), works across boundaries and has the unique 'capacity of dealing with incommensurability' (Ankersmit 2002: 233–4). Thus moving from the dimension of autonomy which is perceived as incommensurability to discovering threads of connections or to the locus of the intersecting circles calls for an aesthetics of transversal reason and non-violence in both thought and action, as non-violence is linked to understanding the world in a plural but interconnected way.[15]

RETHINKING THE OPPOSITION BETWEEN
QUANTITATIVE AND QUALITATIVE

The need for overcoming dualism is most urgent in the sterile and now lazy fight over the primacy of either the qualitative or the quantitative methods of research. Social research is wedded to a cult of the quantitative but here as economist Achin Chakraborty (2004) tells us, just bringing the tool of qualitative research to the methodological kit box of a field like economics, for example, which is wedded to a positivist Methodology is not enough. As 'Monotheism reigns supreme in Methodology' (Bourdieu

1992: 226) what is called for here is a plural and reflexive methodology which does not valorize reflection at the expense of fieldwork or what Pierre Bourdieu calls getting 'hands dirty in the kitchens of empirical research' (Bourdieu 1990: 19). Bourdieu's outstanding works show how new insights emerge by combining ethnological fieldwork with statistical research.[16] In this context, Mats Alversson and Kaj Skoldberg (2000) present some helpful insights. For them the issue is not quantitative versus qualitative, or standardization or non-standardization. They write:

It is not methods but ontology and epistemology which are the determinants of good social science. These aspects are often handled better in the qualitative research—which allows for ambiguity as regards interpretive possibilities, and lets the researcher's construction of what is explored become more visible—but there are also examples of the use of the quantitative methods in which figures, techniques and claims to objectivity are not allowed to gain the upper hand . . . (Alversson and Skoldberg 2000: 4).

In fact now there is an emergent new qualitative method which combines rich description and deep reflections: 'While it remains descriptively rich, it is also privileged to engage the thorny epistemological questions that arise when researchers attempt to document the contours and workings of a constructed, yet substantial, world of everyday life' (Gubrium and Holstein 1997: vii).

In fact, insofar as an emergent qualitative method is concerned, in their reformulation of development ethics as emergent ethics I and Quarles van Ufford (2004), speak about emergent empiricism, which looks at data as part of an emergent situation. Emergent empiricism looks at possible data in a given situation always open to horizon of emergence in the empirical world itself. Development ethicist Des Gasper (2003), brings a new dimension to this emergent empiricism by urging all to go beyond the division between the quantitative and qualitative as monolithic and unitary things. For Gasper, what is often labelled as case-approach includes varieties of cases or different kinds of cases, for example—'thick case studies; thin case studies; real life choice situations; real life anecdotes and other illustrations; conceivably true fictions; and impossible fictions' (Gasper 2003: 196). Gasper discusses the implications of different kinds of cases and engagement with cases for ethical argumentation and action; for example in some cases it is helpful to have thick case studies, in others like Rawls's discussion of the original situation it is helpful to have impossible fictions as cases. One implication of Gasper's pluralization of the case study approach, which is usually considered unitary, is that the practice of research and critical social action should embody a creative pluralism of cases. It has a further ethical dimension too in real life action on the part of researchers, policymakers and activists. For example, if a dam is being built then before taking such a decision it is an ethical imperative for the policymakers and decision-making politicians to engage themselves with a thick case study of communities and people at risk. This may not alter the footsteps of the monolithic giants involved but it can create a space of possibility for the marginalized and powerless and also for all concerned. This is much more so when powers that be almost always 'see like a state' and do not engage themselves in a situation, which would give them an opportunity for a thick description and thick experience of the life of people. The need for such a thicker case engagement has become all the more important now when in the name of audit culture in economy, academy and development organizations, a new myopia and organized blindness is being promoted which looks at only quick and short-term results collected at the tip of a finger by clicking the button of the mouse (cf. Strathern 2000). There is an imperial triumph of the survey method now to the exclusion of participation with the life of the people and now many academic researchers even do not do this themselves, subcontracting their survey research to other people as part of a flexible dismantling of research labour. In this context, combining varieties of methods—qualitative and quantitative—and varieties of cases from the qualitative—has important implications, ethical as well as epistemological. But the very practice and choice of doing so is not dependent on epistemology alone; it depends upon nature and quality of self-cultivation and commitment, understood broadly as touching both self and institutions.

This issue raises the challenge of overcoming expediency. For example, how does one overcome the temptation for expediency when epistemologically and ethically required to embody methodological pluralism, for example the task and responsibility of being engaged in a thick understanding of a damaged, vulnerable form of life? In this context Narendar Pani's (2004) discussion of 'Gandhian economic methods and the challenge of expediency' is helpful. For Pani, though Gandhian economic method shares with pragmatism a focus on human practice, Gandhi's concept of knowledge is more inclusive and includes practices of self-reflection and self-development, which enables one not to use one's knowledge expeditiously. Gandhi reduced the scope for 'expediency by refusing to accept moral justification for promoting self-interest' (Pani 2004).

DIALOGUE BETWEEN PHILOSOPHY AND SOCIAL SCIENCES

As the ground has been prepared a bit, for creative and critical social research border crossing between philosophy and social scientists is not just a matter of fancy, whim or benevolence but also now a matter of necessity. As Aversson and Skoldberg write:

Referring to philosophical ideas without really using them is pointless, bewildering and means a waste of time and energy for the researcher and of his or her unfortunate readers. Interplay between philosophical ideas and empirical work marks high-quality social research. While philosophical sophistication is certainly not the principal task of social science, social research without philosophically informed reflection easily grows so unreflexive that the label "research" becomes questionable (ibid.: 7).

But here the caution from Andrew Sayer needs to be borne in mind: 'But while I believe social scientists can learn from philosophy they should not be in awe of it, for they can also inform it' (Sayer 1992: 3). Thus what is called for here is a mutually transforming border crossing between philosophy and social sciences where philosophers do fieldwork[17] and field working social scientists themselves become philosophers in reflecting upon the foundations of their presuppositions and not just become servants of the awe-inspiring philosophical masters no matter whether the master is Plato, Kant, Heidegger or Derrida the new prophet of today. Johan Godfried Herder had asked long ago: 'What fruitful new developments would not arise if only our whole philosophy would become anthropology' (quoted in Zammito 2002). Anthropology similarly could ask a similar self-transcending question: 'What fruitful new developments would not arise if only our whole anthropology would become philosophy.'

Fortunately for us, from both sides now there are self-critical, transgressive and transformational moves.[18] From philosophy, just as an example, Richard Rorty (1990) and J.N. Mohanty (2002), in their many different ways reiterate the significance of description. Mohanty brings to philosophical description a sense of pathos, which is enriching. Writes Mohanty (2002):

A genuinely descriptive philosophy [and we can add here sociology, anthropology or social sciences] is bound to be characterized by a tragic sense not merely because everywhere phenomena exhibit discontinuity and gaps which he would not fill in, but also because he is haunted by the gap which continues to persist and which he only tries to make up asymptotically, between philosophical reflection and unreflective experience. His is thus a never-ending endeavour, his is an open system. The speculative metaphysician, on the other hand, closes the system . . .

Even though Mohanty is a philosopher, he brings to philosophical description a tragic sense of life but is it found in Clifford Geertz, the celebrated anthropologist of thick description? Where is a sense of tragedy in Geertz's Balinese cockfight, where are Geertz's tears in his (Geertz 1973) description of bleeding cocks? In his *Available Light: Anthropological Reflections on Philosophical Themes*, Geertz (2000) says that Wittgenstein has been a sort of Guru to him and Geertz has been a guru to many anthropologists and many others. Here one may wonder how the trajectory of cultural anthropology would have developed had Heidegger also been some sort of a guru to Geertz? Surely it would not have been that easy for anthropologists to hide behind the category of language game and neglect the question of ontology. Going beyond a formulaic denunciation of Heidegger's complicity with Nazism (cf. Bourdieu 1991b), it would have certainly urged them to come to terms with the calling of what Dallmayr (1987) calls 'practical ontology'.[19]

Wittgenstein is not only a guru to Geertz but also to many philosophically engaged anthropologists of modern times such as Pierre Bourdieu (1990, 2000) and Veena Das (1995, 1999). Veena Das develops a passionate project of anthropology of suffering taking inspiration from Wittgenstein, which poses important transformational challenges for Geertz whose Wittgensteinian anthropology does not embody the pains of a groaning humanity.[20]

The lack of sufficient attention to issues of ontological cultivation is not the only limitation with much of contemporary philosophical anthropology. Another foundational limitation of the project of philosophical anthropology or anthropological philosophy as it has emerged in the Euro-American world in the last fifty years, is that it is too parochial (its philosophical sources such as Pascal, Wittgenstein, Heidegger, Pierce or Kenneth Burke come from a very narrow part of the world) and lack a transcultural and transcivilizational dialogue as, for example, found in the works of seekers such as Fred Dallmayr (cf. Dallmayr 1996, 1998, 2001, 2002).[21]

PAYING ATTENTION TO DISJUNCTION AND GAPS:
ATTENDING TO ANTINOMIES IN SELF AND SOCIETY

Mohanty speaks about attending to gaps between systems. Theoretically and methodologically one needs to go beyond preoccupation with an unproblematic whole or sociology of the black box and attend to gaps and disjunctions in between. Here Foucault and Ankermit are helpful in providing a new theoretical imagination. In his reflection on Kant, Foucault (1984a) endorses Kant's distinction between three domains of knowledge (knowledge related to political action, knowledge related to critical reflection, and knowledge related to hope) as constitutive of Enlightenment but urges to acknowledge the lack of fit between them. Similarly, Ankersmit (1996, 2002) points to the incommensurabilities between domains and how they can be dealt with artistically but cannot be forcefully absorbed into a system. Beteille also urges us to bring attending to antinomies to the heart of sociological understanding as he defines antinomies as 'contradictions, oppositions and tensions inherent in the norms and values through which societies regulate themselves and continue their existence' (Beteille 2000: 1).

PAYING ATTENTION TO CONTINGENCY

Along with paying attention to disjunctions, as students of self, culture and society, one needs to be aware of the work of contingencies in society and history. Contingency points to one's embeddedness in many webs of relationships, which simultaneously determines and opens up spaces of possibilities. Contingent engagement is also a creative one, as Santos, building on Ilya Prigogine tells us, now instead of necessity one now has creativity and contingency (Santos 1995: 19).

An engagement with contingency points to the contextual dimension in the work of self, culture and society and frees one from confinement with abstractions and law-like generalizations. An awareness of contingency enables one to realize that a particular mode of development also could have been different thus freeing one from notions of historical inevitability which reflects an 'ontological monovalence' (Bhaskar 2002a: 123). As social theorist Nancy Weiss Hanrahan tells us: '. . . the outcome of social processes are always contingent in that things could turn out otherwise'[22] (Hanrahan 2000: 35; also see Hawthorn 1991; Walker 1998).

CONTINGENCY AND PHRONESIS:
NEW METHODOLOGICAL OUTLINES

Taking contingency seriously means paying importance to context. This is in tune with paying importance to practice as has been suggested by Bourdieu and many others. Recently some scholars have urged to draw new methodological and theoretical insights by drawing upon Aristotle, namely, his emphasis on phronesis. One of the most important dialogues with Aristotle in contemporary social science is Bent Flyvbjerg's *Making Social Sciences Matter: Why Social Inquiry Fails and How it can Succeed Again* (Flyvbjerg 2001). In building on Aristotle in reconstructing social sciences, Flyvbjerg primarily focuses on Aristotelian phronesis rather than techne and episteme. For Flyvbjerg, 'Phronesis is most important because it is that activity by which instrumental rationality is balanced by value-rationality, and because such balancing is crucial to the sustained happiness of the citizens in any society' (Flyvbjerg 2001: 4). A focus on phronesis enables one to understand context-dependence but 'context-dependence does not mean just a more complex form of determinism. It means an open-ended, contingent relation between contexts and actions and interpretations' (Flyvbjerg 2001: 43). In tune with a running concern of cultivation of a non-dual mode in ontology and epistemology, an engagement with phronesis also facilitates this. In Flyvbjerg's words: 'There are rules, and there is the particular. This much can be observed phenomenologically. . . To amputate one side in these pairs of phenomena into a dualistic "either-or" is to amputate understanding. Rather than the "either or", one should develop a non-dualism and pluralistic "both-and"' (2001: 49).

Flyvbjerg's outline of a new methodology is in tune with many of the proposals in this essay. But there still seems to be an unconscious streak of dualism in his proposal when he talks about 'looking at practice before discourse'. Though I do not believe that practice is discursively constituted it is helpful to study practice and discourse simultaneously. Flyvbjerg is also within the modernist regime of denial of ontology when he writes the following to elaborate his advice of doing narrative: 'Narratology, understood as the question of "how best to get an honest story honestly told" is more important than epistemology and ontology' (2001: 137).

For Flyvbjerg, 'The horizon of meaning is that of the individual practice' (2001: 135). But the horizon of meaning also lies beyond practice, or in a beyond, which is a dimension in the immanent domain of practice. There is insufficient recognition of this dimension of beyond in contemporary social sciences even though Wittgenstein, another key source in contemporary creative reconstruction of social sciences, had said long ago: 'The meaning of a word lies outside a word.' Here along with empowering Aristotle, as Flyvbjerg suggests, one also has to spiritualize him, a spiritualization which enables one to embody normative alternative to the will to power or realizing what Dallmayr, building on Heidegger says, a 'power-free existence' (cf. Dallmayr 2001). In critical social science there is not only a lack of sufficient acknowledgement of the transcendental dimension of the co-present reality but there is an anxiety to distantiate one's initiative of reconstruction from any engagement with transcendence. A case in point here is the work of Hardt and Negri referred to earlier. They write in their influential critical treatise on the contemporary condition Empire: 'The multitude today, however, resides on the imperial surfaces where there is no God the Father and no transcendence. Instead there is immanent labour.... The multitude has no reason to look outside its own history to lead towards its constitution as a political subject' (Hardt and Negri 2000: 396). But though there is no point in asserting transcendence there is also no point in denying it and what is called for here is an openness to transcendence as a real and possible dimension of self, culture and society.

A COMPARATIVE GLOBAL ENGAGEMENT

Social research now needs to embody a comparative global engagement by simultaneously studying the self and other. Comparative method has been a hallmark of social sciences such as sociology and social anthropology for long but this reflected a nation state centred ethnocentrism and suffers from what Radhakrishnan calls a 'dominant universalizing tendency' (Radhakrishnan 2003: 73). Now there is a need to embody a new comparative global engagement by simultaneously studying the self and other, not only discursively but also ethnographically to the extent possible. Multi-sited ethnography of a discursive theme of comparison ought to be a companion of a globally engaged social science (cf. Marcus and Fischer 1986). Here one has to move beyond systemic comparisons and attend to complexities that lie in between and beyond. As Beteille (1983) tells us, the whole scale comparison of civilizations such as India as 'Homo Hierarchicus' and West as Homo Equalis is not only unhelpful but perpetuates Western ethnocentrism. Similar also is the perspective of Touraine who argues that the distinction between modernity and tradition in terms of individualism and hierarchy—a la Louis Dumont—is not helpful to understand either of them. As he writes:

The distinction between social and non-social definitions of the individual seems to me to be even more important than that between the holistic societies of old and modern individualistic societies. Both types of society are Janus-faced, because there is no fundamental difference between an individual who is trapped in the roles imposed on him by the community and an individual whose actions are determined by his social situation and the highly effective blandishments of the market. At the same time, there is a similarity between the renouncer and the modern individual who appeals to the universal rights of man and in particular the dissident or resister who risks his life by challenging a social order which, in his view, is an affront to human dignity. (2000: 86; emphasis mine)

Thus one needs a comparative global and even planetary engagement which is interested to explore pathways of partial connections rather than wholesale comparison of civilizations and systems: 'Partial connections require images other than those taxonomies or configurations that compel one to look for overarching principles or for some core or central features . . .' (Strathern 1991: xviii). Based on her work in New Guinea, Marilyn Strathern puts forth: '. . . attempts to produce a typology of societies from the application of constant principles may also evaporate. For instance, principles of reciprocity as they affect the organization of transactions and the role of leaders as Great Men or Big Men may well appear to discriminate effectively between a handful of cases; but the discrimination cannot be necessarily sustained at that level—an expanded version reveals that principles radically distinguishing whole cluster of societies are also replicated within them' (Strathern 1994: xviii; also see Gingrich and Fox 2002).

But a global comparative anthropology not only calls for multi-sited fieldwork[23] in the global ethnoscape; it also calls for a trans-civilizational dialogue on one's foundational presuppositions about self, culture and society. Social research cannot just be a surface level engagement of doing fieldwork on practices without entering into the foundational ways in which people constitute themselves and their worlds. For example in *Bhagavad Gita*, a spiritual text from Indian civilization journey, it is written: *Sradhha Maya Ayam Purusha Jo Jat Sraddha Sa Ebasa:* (This Purusha [the human person] is characterized by sraddha—capacity for love and reverence—one is what one who loves or reveres). These lines also offer some presuppositions about self, culture and society as the presuppositions about power offered by Weber and Foucault and justification offered by Habermas. For a broadened understanding of culture and society should not there be a dialogue among such presuppositions? (cf. Giri 2003). The need for a trans-civilizational dialogue for social theory as part of a comparative global engagement becomes a little more clear when the issue of Japan, modernity and social theory is taken. John Clammer writes in his provocative work *Difference and Modernity: Social Theory and Contemporary Japanese Society:* 'While mainstream social theory has largely assumed the separateness of man from nature, the Japanese understanding has always been "ecological": that man as part of nature not only in the obvious sense of dependence on the biosphere for good, air, water and warmth, but also in the sense that processes and rhythms in nature parallel, reinforce or are identical with patterns of human interaction' (Clammer 1995: 61). Clammer further says that in the Japanese way, 'the non-duality of nature and non-duality of human selfhood are . . . intimately linked' (1995: 73). Furthermore there is a connection between ethics and aesthetics: '. . . aesthetics here does not imply just "art" but the integration of art and life based on a holistic understanding of the universe' (Clammer 1995: 66; also see Peacock 2002).

Creative and Critical Social Research: Towards a New Vocation

Creative social research at the contemporary juncture has to renew its commitment to the realization of beautiful and dignified worlds. Creative social research can help a person to recognize his/her own ontological power and the ontological power of the multitude. By recording the narratives of struggles and strivings for a better world in the face of the ideology of 'end of history' creative social research can participate in multiple breakthroughs. One finds such a commitment to creative social research in some of the contemporary interlocutors. Michael Hardt and Antonio Negri state in their Empire to 'subvert the hegemonic languages and social structures and thereby reveal an alternative ontological basis that resides in the creative and productive practices of the multitude' and participate in the 'constructive and ethico-political' striving for a better world (Hardt and Negri 2000, 1994). Similar is also Arjun Appadurai's calling in his provocative and inspiring reflection, 'Grassroots Globalization and Research Imagination' (2000). Reflecting on the contemporary predicament of globalization and the pessimist tendency of resignation on the part of the academics, Appadurai asks: 'Can we retain the methodological rigour of modern social science while restoring some of the prestige and energy of earlier visions of scholarship in which moral and political concerns were central? Can we find ways to legitimately engage scholarship by public intellectuals here and overseas whose work is not primarily conditioned by professional criteria of criticism and dissemination?' (2000: 14). For Appadurai, '. . . globalization is not simply the name for a new epoch in the history of capital or in the biography of the nation-state. It is marked by a new role for imagination in social life' (2000: 13). Creative social research has to be receptive to this work of imagination in the life of self and society (see Gatens and Lloyd 2001). Appadurai elaborates:

If globalization is characterized by disjunctive flows that generate acute problems of social well-being, one positive force that encourages an emancipatory politics of globalization is the role of imagination in social life. The imagination is no longer a matter of individual genius, escapism from ordinary life, or just a dimension of aesthetics. It is a faculty that informs the daily lives of ordinary people in myriad ways. It allows people to consider migration, resist state violence, seek social redress and design new forms of civic association and collaboration, often across national boundaries. (2000: 6)

In the midst and face of such works of imagination, Appadurai articulates the following challenge before research:

Critical voices who speak for the poor, the vulnerable and the marginalised in the international fora in which global policies are made to lack the means to produce a systematic grasp of the complexities of globalization. A new architecture for producing and sharing knowledge about globalization could provide the foundations of a pedagogy that closes this gap and helps to democratice the flow of knowledge about globalization itself. Such a pedagogy could create new forms of dialogue between academics, public intellectuals, activists, and policy makers in different societies. (2000: 18)

Creative social research has to resist the temptation and security of paraphrasing the logic of global capital and the police state and has to contribute towards democratization of the public sphere with its insights of research. Such a commitment has a particular salience in the contemporary climate of terror where the world is being so easily classified into good and evil. After the 11 September attack on the World Trade Center, New York there is now a globalization of war on terrorism, which is itself a terrorist campaign and in this context the commitment to interpretative social science as a critical democratic engagement needs to be renewed. For Veena Das, the challenge here is: 'Might we be able to mourn with the survivors of 11 September without the needing to appropriate their grief for other grander projects' (Das 2001: 111). As Michele Fine states: 'Perhaps we can exhibit our most bold and radical democratic presence by refusing the freezing of conversation and imagination' (Fine 2002: 141). Fine cautions us: 'Descriptive research, I worry, will not do. In our research we are now obliged to interrogate Why, assuring that analyses of history and justice are joined; discussion of what "is" is yoked to "what has been" and "what must be." Why raises hard questions, negotiated genesis stories, contentious histories.'

The Calling of an Ontological Epistemology of Participation

But practising such a vocation of research calls for adequate preparation in self and society. Research is not just an epistemic activity; it also calls for cultivation of appropriate virtues transgressing the conventional boundaries between epistemology and ontology. As John Greco writes: 'Just as virtue theories in ethics try to understand the normative properties of actions in terms of the normative properties of moral agents, virtue theories in epistemology try to understand the normative properties of beliefs in terms of the normative properties of cognitive agents' (Greco 2001: 136). Virtue epistemology makes activities of research 'person-based rather than belief-based' (Greco 2001: 136). While in epistemology there is a move towards 'virtue epistemology' in ontology there are moves towards 'weak ontology'[24] as pioneered by Vattimo (1999), 'practical ontology' and 'critical ontology' as striven by Dallmayr (1984, 1987, 1991), and 'ontological anthropology' as striven by Clammer et al. (2004), which interestingly embodies a 'relational epistemology' (Clammer et al. 2004: 17). Vattimo's weak ontology embodies vulnerability, self-emptying (kenosis), love and non-violence; similar is also Dallmayr's strivings of a practical ontology which touches the height and depth of a practical spirituality. One can bring 'virtue epistemology', 'weak ontology', 'practical ontology', 'ontological anthropology' and Bhaskar's expanded ontology or ontology of self-expansion and nurture the ground for an ontological epistemology of participation.

In ontological epistemology of participation, there is attentiveness to and interpenetration of both the subjective and the objective and the whole challenge is to arrive at an objective in spite of one's irreducible subjectivity. This calls for a new conception of both the subjective and the objective. As suggested, subjective also refers to the dimension of transcendental or non-dual self in the actor/subject/scientist and this would be a companion of an aspired for objectivity. As Eric Fromm tells us: 'Objectivity does not mean detachment, it means respect; that is, the ability not to distort and to falsify things, persons and oneself' (Fromm 1950: 105). Furthermore, 'To be objective is possible only if we respect the things we observe; that is, if we are capable of seeing them in their uniqueness and interconnectedness' (Fromm 1950: 104) (Compare this to Bhaskar's perspective of dialectical universality paying attention to uniqueness and singularity.)

Ontological epistemology of participation differs from participant observation, as it is conventionally understood. Bourdieu asks of participant observation: 'How can one be both subject and object, the one who acts and the one who, as it were, watching himself acting?' (Bourdieu 2003: 282). As an alternative Bourdieu proposes participant objectivation: 'By participant objectivation I mean the objectivation of the subject of objectivation, of the analyzing subject—in short the researcher herself?' (Bourdieu 2003: 282). But how can one watch oneself acting and be both subject and object? Does it not involve work on oneself or cultivation of some kind of witnessing self what is called *sakhi pursusha* in Indian spiritual traditions or impartial spectator by Adam Smith (cf. Sen 2002; Smith 1976)? Can this be only epistemic and doesn't it also involve some ontological work on oneself? Bourdiue speaks about 'epistemic reflexivity' (cf. Bourdiue and Wacquant 1992: 38). His application of statistical analysis to self-understanding is helpful but does it also not involve ontological nurturance?[25]

In this context, Ankersmit's most recent discussion of the methodology of historical representation helps to understand the work of ontological epistemology of participation in a new way. Ankersmit states that historical representation of a period may present a 'coherent whole of developments on domains that are incommensurable with each other' such as the 'cognitive, ethical, aesthetic, religious or technical preoccupations of a period' (Ankersmit 2002: 234). For Ankersmit such a connected picture and free movement 'from one domain to another' is possible because of historical representation. He goes on to write: 'If we ask ourselves how representation may enable us to do this, the answer is that the unique contribution of representation . . . is that it involves the knowing subject.... The self is activated by representation in a way that would mean the end of objective knowledge. And from the point of view recommended by representation, suddenly a common ground can be discerned for domains that seemed hitherto completely unrelated and incommensurable' (2002: 234; emphasis mine).

Here Ankersmit presents the example of epistemology and politics in seventeenth century France. For Ankersmit, 'at first sight seventeenth-century rationalist philosophy and absolutism will have nothing in common for us. But then the historian may suggest the point of view of the transcendental ego [or it may emerge from any self-initiated historical engagement, not just from historian as a professional expert], of a self that withdraws from the world but in order to get a firmer hold of it' (2002: 234). 'And this point of view makes us aware of what the Cartesian self, doubting all knowledge in order to gain access to absolute certain knowledge, has in common with Louis XIV withdrawing from the bustle of Paris to Versailles in order to confirm his absolutist mastery of France' (Ankersmit 2002: 234). Thus, the perspective of transcendental ego born of historical enquiry and representation, an engagement in which all seeking souls can participate, not only professional historians, helps to understand the connection between epistemology and politics in seventeenth-century France. For Ankersmit, one may not totally identify with such a perspective, which emerges from the work of historical representation but nonetheless it shapes one's personality and what that person is. From the perspective of the calling of an ontological epistemology of participation, what Ankersmit writes deserves careful considerations: 'Nevertheless, becoming acquainted with the possibility of many such points of view will, add each time, a new, though tiny stone to the mosaic of our personality. And in the end this cannot fail to have its effect on the kind of person that we are' (Ankersmit 2002: 235).

Conclusion

In this essay I have touched some of the themes and challenges in the vocation of a creative and critical social research which point to the need for cultivation of an appropriate ontology in the engagement of research which can help one come to terms with not only some of the theoretical problems such as the postmodern imprisonment within difference but also realize the practical task of establishing solidarity across divides. As seen, this includes the challenge of cultivating non-dual modes within oneself as subjects of investigation. Such an ontological cultivation has an epochal significance as many theories and methods have been imprisoned within the modernist privileging of epistemology over ontology. Bringing ontological cultivation back to social research enables one to go beyond the conventional slogan of renewing social research with participation. For the last quarter century participatory research has been much valorized—it has been on everybody's lips starting from anthropologists to development practitioners, and now the agents of World Bank. But the approach to and involvement with participatory research has been generally procedural and instrumental. In this context, one needs to think about and practise research in a new way, in an ontological way, where the whole self—not just the inquiring mind—is involved with research. The valorized discourse of participatory research today needs a radical supplement from Gandhi and Heidegger where research becomes a time and space of laying open oneself and realization of co-being (cf. Dallmayr 1996). The time of research becomes both a time of communication and silence[26]—a time of 'lived time'—and the space of research becomes a space of dwelling, in fact a 'poetics of dwelling' (cf. Ingold 2004), rather than building. Here what Pillai writes about Gandhi's modes of participation in social service from a Heideggerian point of view can be helpful in going beyond an instrumentalist approach to participatory research: 'Gandhi's participation in the life of his time was always (at the same time) an interior journey, an exploration of his being, and not just working out of a pre-established strategy.[27] It is this insistent questioning of himself which distinguishes his action from all self-sanctifying "social service" based on representation. Every decision for Gandhi was simultaneously the laying open of himself' (Pillai 1985: 77).

Bringing ontological cultivation to the discourse and practice of social research is an important calling of today. But while embodying ontological cultivation one can proceed in the spirit of a journey and evolution rather than with an essentialist, fixed ontology. Much talk of ontology has in the past suffered from the dangers of essentialism and fixation. But one is not destined to commit the same errors nor should one valorize ontology to the point of excluding the epistemic activity of learning. A way out of the modernist privileging of epistemology and neglect of ontology is not to valorize ontology at the expense of the epistemic practices of learning and enquiry. Here one can supplement Heidegger with Gandhi, not only in politics but also in epistemology, thus rescuing one from complicity with any politics of mastery in the name of the resoluteness of Dasein and making Dasein and self an involved and emergent participant in learning[28] (cf. Bourdieu 1991; Dallmayr 2001; Srinivasan 1998). One arresting aspect of Gandhi's life and work is his insatiable passion for learning and experiments with truth. At the ripe age of eighty when he was travelling from village to village and trying to calm the fire of communal violence in riot-torn Noakhali, he was devoting an hour everyday to learning the alphabets of the language of the locality, Bengali. It is this passion for learning and self-cultivation that can make a person humble and rescue him/her from the danger of using the acquired knowledge, including the knowledge generated out of research, as an aid to the will to power—an instrument of authority, including ethnographic authority; it can help one realize that what is needed is not so much 'self-mastery' as an 'ethics of servanthood', and a 'pathos of shakenness' (cf. Giri 2002: Shanks 2001). As commitment to creative social research as a companion to the activity of understanding self, society and the world and transforming it is renewed, one has to realize that ontology emerges as much from contestation, conversation and learning as it is an initial participant in self and science. Ontology itself should be opened to a journey of homelessness (cf. Dallmayr 2001) and an epistemic practice of learning, thus crossing the boundaries between ontology and epistemology—a border-crossing which becomes a paradigmatic activity of multiple border-crossing between philosophy and fieldwork, creative research and critical action, self and other, society and cosmos. To sing it with Rabindranath Tagore, the immortal poet of Gitanjali: 'Life is perpetually creative because it contains in itself that surplus which ever overflows the boundaries of immediate time and space, restlessly pursuing its adventure of expression in the varied forms of self-realization' (Tagore 1961: 45).

Notes

1. Connolly urges us to understand the gaps modern social sciences have left in not paying attention to ontology. In this context, Charles Taylor also urges to acknowledge this similar problem. For Taylor, 'What the ontology of mainstream social science lacks is the notion of meaning as not simply for an individual subject; of a subject who can be a "we" as well as an "I"' (Taylor 1971: 32). But many contemporary thinkers would still like to maintain a self-confident distance from any ontological consideration. Jurgen Habermas seems to be foremost among them. For Habermas, '. . . as long as philosophy remains caught in ontology, it is itself subject to an objectivism that disguises the connection of its knowledge with the human interest in autonomy and responsibility' (Habermas 1971: 311). But why this should necessarily be the case? What is to be noted that the situation is not much different even after forty years of Habermas. For example in his project of a cosmopolitan social science Ulrich Beck (2002) talks about 'methodological cosmopolitanism' but this seems to be primarily epistemological and lacks any engagement of ontological nurturance.
2. This is especially urgent as much of social research not only in India but also in many parts of the world, has been conducted 'under the sign of the nation' (Das 2003: 1). A critical genealogy is needed as to the complicity of such a nation state directed sociology with many violent projects of the nation state.
3. For Oakeshott, a non-totalizing mode of theorizing 'does not claim for philosophy any special source of knowledge hidden from other forms of

experience' or any 'immunity' from contingent events (quoted in Dallmayr 1984: 5–6). What Oakeshott writes deserves our careful consideration: 'My use of "theorizing" as a transitive verb is not an inadvertence; it is the recognition of the enterprise as one of learning to understand; that is, as a transitive engagement' (quoted in Dallmayr 1984: 6).

4. A famous example in this regard is the structure-agency problem in sociology. So much has been written about it from Parsons to Giddens but none of the protagonists seem to acknowledge that this problem is not amenable only to a theoretical resolution. While theoretical meditations can illumine a contextual and provisional resolution of this problem, this also crucially depends upon the nature and quality of practice of both structure and agency, self and society.

5. Gorz (1999) writes the following about education, which embodies a critique of society-centred sociological reasoning and signature of an ontological sociality:

> This cannot be taught; it has to be stimulated. It can arise only out of the affective attachment of children or adolescents to a reference group who makes them feel deserving of unconditional love, and confident of their capacity to learn, act, undertake projects and measure themselves against others—who gives them, in a word 'self-esteem.' The subject emerges by virtue of the love with which another subject calls it to become a subject and it develops through the desire to be loved by that other subject. This means that the educative relation is not a social relation and is not socializable.

In this context, what Touraine (2007: 191) writes below also deserves our careful attention:

> The combination of economic participation and cultural identity cannot be realized at the level of society; it is only at the level of the individual that participation in the global economy and the defense or formation of a cultural identity—legacy or new project—can combine. That is why, in both family and school, we are seeing the triumph—despite resistance—of the idea that it is the child or the pupil who must be at the centre of the institution. The protracted debates in France between advocates and opponents of the so-called college unique, the system in which all students attend the same middle school, lead us to the conclusion that the preservation of the latter is not possible without substantial individualization of the relations between the teachers and the taught.

6. This seems to be the case with Anthony Giddens whose very title, In Defense of Sociology, suggests this anxiety. It is no wonder then that Giddens laments the disappearance of the 'capacity of sociology to provide a unifying centre for the diverse branches of social research' (Giddens 1996: 2). To be fair to Giddens he is surely not alone; traces of this anxiety are to be found in Andre Beteille (2000) as well. An anxiety to defend one's discipline is not confined to sociology. Habermas (1990) seems to be worried that one day philosophy may be replaced by cultural anthropology and Sidney Mintz (2000) is worried about this being replaced by cultural studies.

7. What Pollock et al. write below vis-à-vis their elaboration of what they call as cosmo-feminism as an example of situated universalism deserves our careful attention:

> Any cosmo-feminine would have to create a critically engaged space that is not just a screen for globalization or an antidote to nationalism but is rather a focus on projects of the intimate sphere conceived as a part of the cosmopolitan. Such a critical perspective would also open up a new understanding of the domestic, which would no longer be confined spatially or socially to the private sphere. This perspective would allow us to recognize that domesticity itself is a vital interlocutor and not just an interloper in law, politics and public ethics. From this reconfigured understanding of the public life of domesticity and intimacy it follows that spheres of intimacy generate legitimate pressure on any understanding of cosmopolitan solidarities and networks. The cosmo-feminine could thus be seen as subverting those larger networks that refuse to recognize their own nature as specific systems of relations among others. That is, we would no longer have feminism as the voice of the specificity interrogating the claims of other putative universals. Instead we would have the cosmo-feminine as the sign of an argument for a situated universalism that invites broader debate based on a recognition of their own situatedness. A focus on this extensional understanding of domesticity and intimacy could generate a different picture of more public univeralisms, making the domestic sphere subversive of thin claims to universalism (Pollock et al., 2000: 584/585; emphases added).

8. Re-enchantment for Baskar also involves a 'collapse of the distinction between sacred and profane' (2002b: xxxviii). For him, 'Once this distinction goes we can read the spiritual into the structure of everyday life' (Bhaskar 2002b: xxxviii).

9. Bhaskar's subsequent elaboration deserves our careful attention:

> Our task is to re-become non-dual beings in a world of duality, opposition and strife. Freedom is the elimination of the non-dual components within my embodied personality; that is the elimination of everything inconsistent with my ground-state, the cessation of negative incompleteness. In order to do this, I had to experience duality, heteronomy and change, to grow and fulfil my intentionality. When I have fulfilled my intentionality, when I have no more non-me within me, I am one with my ground state, and one with the ground-states of all other beings in the rest of creation too. I am one with the whole of creation; and as such will reflect back to its creator his work, formation, creation, will or intentionality; and perfectly reflecting his intentionality, I am one with him too. This is self-realisation, the realisation of the divine ingredient within me . . ..
>
> But this is not the end of the odyssey in the world of duality. I am still positively incomplete, in so far as other beings are co-present, enfolded within me, are negatively incomplete, that is, unfree. When the whole of creation is self-realized, when it reflects back its own divinity, then and only then will there be peace. Even then this peace is only the end of pre-history.

I know in the meantime that I will grow and develop while I strive for this goal, a development to which I can see no conceivable end; so if there is an expanded plenitude of possibilities packed into my non-dual being, my agentive self in the world of duality, we cannot even begin to anticipate what possibilities lie within eudemonia. This eudenomia is not something removed from ordinary secular speculation..; rather, we have found it everywhere as a presupposition of even the most crude and rudimentary forms of ethics. (2002b: 261–2).

10. Here it is important to keep in mind what Isiah Berlin writes about pluralism and monism: 'The enemy of pluralism is monism—the ancient belief that there is a single harmony of truths into which everything, if it is genuine, in the end must fit. The consequence of this belief is that those who know should command those who do not' (Berlin 2001: 14).

11. Building on transformations in psychoanalysis and spiritual traditions of the world, Chitta Ranjan Das argues that the Unconscious itself is the repository of not only the libido or the irrational but also the highest possible in self, world and cosmos.

12. Bourdieu also speaks about 'plurality of worlds' with 'consideration of the plurality of logics corresponding to different worlds, that is, to different fields as places in which different kinds of common sense, different common place ideas and different systems of topics, all irreducible to each other, are constructed' (Bourdieu 1990: 21). Also note what Bourdieu suggests about a far deeper interpenetrative logic:

> Thus Sociology partakes at once of two radically discrepant logics: the logic of the political field in which the force of ideas is mainly a function of the power of groups that take them to be true; and the logic of the scientific field, which, in its most advanced states, knows and recognizes only the 'intrinsic force of true idea' of which Spinoza spoke (Boudieu 1991, in epilogue).

13. Our multi-valued logic of autonomy and interpenetration and the aesthetics of discovering threads of connections does not suppress disjunctions nor does it want to forcibly force connections as part of an a priori teleological grid about which Strathern rightly warns the following which needs to be kept in mind: 'A problem that jumps out of twenty-first-century imaginings of a connected-up ('globalized') world is the connecting work that the language of connection seems to do. Its epistemological effect (making connections) makes thinkers lazy. . ... Like "network", the very term seems intrinsically benign, desirable; also like network, it gobbles up all the spaces between—a continentalizing empire, leaving nothing that is not potentially connectable to everything else' (Strathern 2002: xv).

14. In their creative interpretation of what they call John Dewey's 'aesthetic ecology of public intelligence' Herbert Reid and Betsy Taylor also urge us to understand the significance of aesthetics in moving beyond fixed boundaries and discovering emergence and interconnections: 'aesthetic practices are necessary to the Knower's ability to grasp the emergent qualities of the thing. . .' (Reid and Taylor 2009: 12). Another important recent development

which connects aesthetics and the ability to have relational logic is the pioneering work of John Clammer et al., who talk about 'figured worlds' and 'relational logic' at the same time: 'Figured worlds are discourses built up by relational logic, linking people, cultural forms, and social positions by facts of experience in specific historical worlds' (Clammer et al. 2004: 9).

15. In fact, the multi-valued logic of Mohanty draws inspiration not only from Jaina tradition and Husserlian phenomenology but also from Gandhian experiments in non-violence. (See Mohanty 2000b).

16. In the words of Bourdieu:

> I was stupefied to discover, by the use of statistics—something that was very rarely done in ethnology—that the type of marriage considered to be typical in Arabo-Berber societies, namely marriage with the parallel girl cousin, accounted for about 3–4 per cent of cases, and 5–6 per cent in Marabout families, that are stricter and more orthodox. This forced me to think about the notion of kinship, rule, and rules of kinship, which led me to the antipodes of structuralist tradition. And then it was, I think, necessary for me to leave ethnology as a social world, by becoming a sociologist, so that the raising of certain unthinkable questions could become possible (Bourdieu 1990: 9).

17. Bourdieu (1990) speaks about 'fieldwork in philosophy' but many philosophers may not be that enthusiastic about themselves carrying out fieldwork. During a discussion Karl Otto-Apel, a doyen of contemporary continental philosophy, told me that while he is open to using ethnographic data, he himself does not feel the need for doing fieldwork himself as, among other things, this would cut into his time for philosophical reflections and disturb the division of labour between philosophers and anthropologists.

18. From anthropology one finds glimpses of it in the following lines of Michel Fisher (1999: 456):

> Emergent forms of life 'acknowledge an ethnographic datum, a social theoretic heuristic, and a philosophical stance regarding ethics. The ethnographic datum is the pervasive claim . . . by practitioners in many contemporary arenas of life . . . that traditional concepts and ways of doing no longer work, that life is outnumbering the pedagogies in which we have been trained. The social theoretic heuristic is that complex societies, including the globalized regimes under which late and post-modernities operate, are always compromise formations among . . . emergent, dominant and fading historical horizons. The philosophical stance towards ethics is that 'giving grounds' for belief comes to an end somewhere and that 'the end is not an ungrounded presupposition; it is an ungrounded way of acting'—a sociality of action, that always contains within it ethical dilemmas or, in the idiom of Emmanuel Levinas, the face of the other.

19. Dallmayr elaborates his pathway of practical ontology thus:

> By 'ontology' I mean substantive (but non-positivist) mode of thinking and acting, a mode of exceeding the confines of a purely formal analysis; the adjective 'practical' is added to accentuate the aspect of lived engagement. Basically the phrase stands opposed to a traditional or strictly theoretical

ontology founded on the contemplation of ultimate substances, primal causes, or foundational structures' (Dallmayr 1987: 3).

20. To be fair to Geertz, Geertz is reported to have intervened for the release of some human rights activists and political prisoners during the authoritarian rule in Indonesia (see Inglis 2000). But such a practice now needs to foundationally reconfigure Geertzian symbolic anthropology.

21. From the perspective of trans-civilizational dialogues, it seems Veena Das's project of an anthropology of suffering can be enriched by a trans-civilizational dialogue with Buddhism. See, Clammer (forthcoming).

22. From a contingent perspective it would be interesting to ask, as Uberoi suggests, how science and social sciences would have looked like had Goethe, with his more non-dualistic perspective and not Newton, been our main source of inspiration (cf. Uberoi 1978; 1984; 2002). This is not just a hypothetical question but has important implications for the way people look at their present and future. As Veena Das argues, 'A tunnel view of history shapes our understanding of the emergence of social science and modernity in which relatively little attention is paid to those ideas which were defeated or simply failed to be realized' (Das 2003: 3). This question of contingency then would make the confident formulation of sociology as a modern, as opposed to postmodern or traditional, discipline problematic. For Beteille (2002), sociology is a modern and not postmodern discipline. Beteille also says that sociology is not an ideology but if modernity, as Veena Das (2003: 3) suggests, 'functions as the ideology of social sciences' then in making sociology a part of a teleological part of modernity is not Beteille making sociology an ideological project? How far such an ideological project then can sympathetically, what to speak of even objectively, understand and take part in both postmodernity as well as tradition?

23. Unfortunately many of our advocates of comparative method do not do fieldwork in multiple sites integrally relevant to the themes of their own discursive formation. For example, Beteille takes Dumont to task for not having based his comparison of India and the West on fieldwork in the West but Beteille himself has not pursued his comparative engagement on this simultaneous theme of equality and hierarchy by carrying out fieldwork in the West as well (cf. Giri 1993).

24. In the words of Vattimo: '. . .We derive an ethics of non-violence from weak ontology, yet we are led to weak thought, from its origin in Heidegger's concern with the metaphysics of objectivity, by the Christian legacy of the rejection of violence at work within us' (Vattimo 1999 : 44).

25. This may still be a helpful step despite Bourdieu's own disdain for 'the political ontology of Martin Heidegger' (Bourdieu 1991b). A way out is not to be trapped inside the abominable walls of Heideggerian political ontology and to explore the pathways of spiritual ontologies taking inspiration, for example, from Dallmayr's (1993) exploration of another Heidegger.

26. Consider here what Niklas Luhman, the sociologist of communication writes: '[People need] to make a digression at this point and consider whether the

participation of consciousness is not perhaps best conceived as a silence' (Luhman 2001: 16).

27. It is also enriching here to read what Dallmayr writes about his own vocation of journey, which takes inspiration from both Gandhi and Heidegger:

> The notion of experience as a journey or of man as homo viator, is no longer much in vogue today—having been replaced by the sturdier conceptions of man as fabricator or else as a creative assembler and dissembler of symbolic designs. In invoking or reclaiming the eclipsed notion of a 'journey' I wish to dissociate myself, however, from a number of accretions clouding the term. First of all, I do not identify the term with a deliberate venture or project (in a Sartrean or broadly existentialist sense)—irrespective of the deliberative or reflective posture of participants. Shunning the planned delights of organized tourism, I prefer to associate the term with unanticipated incidents or adventures, which one does not so much charter as undergo. Moreover, journeying in my sense does not basically travelling along a well-demarcated route in the direction of a carefully chosen or clearly specified goal. Rather, being properly underway or 'abroad' denotes to me also frequenting byways, detours, and uncharted trails—sometimes exploring dead-ends, cul-de-sacs . . . (Dallmayr 1987: 1)

28. It must be noted however that in his later seeking Heidegger himself made a shift from his earlier preoccupation with resoluteness. As Dallmayr helps us understand in an original reinterpretation of the Heideggerian pathway: '. . .Heidegger's middle and later writings came to see the pitfalls and streamlining effects of linear power-seeking and to adumbrate a realm beyond power and impotence, domination and submission under the rubric of a "power-free" (machtlos) dispensation that allows being(s) "to be"' (Dallmayr 2001b: 190).

References

Agarwala, Binod (2004), 'Humanities and Social Sciences in the New Millennium: Theorizing in/for Society as Play', in *Creative Social Research: Rethinking Theories and Methods*, ed. Ananta Kumar Giri, Lexington Books, pp. 253–72.

Alversson, Mats and Kaj Skoldberg (2000), *Reflexive Methodology: New Vistas for Qualitative Research*, London: Sage.

Ankersmith, F.R. (1996), *Aesthetic Politics*, Stanford: Stanford University Press.

———(2001), The Sublime Dissociation of the Past: Or How to Be(come) What One is No Longer', *History and Theory*, vol. 40, no. 3, pp. 295–323.

———(2002), *Political Representation*, Stanford: Stanford University Press.

Appadurai, Arjun (2000), 'Grassroots Globalization and Research Imagination', *Public Culture*, vol. 12, no. 1, pp. 1–19.

Barth, Frederik (2002), 'Anthropology of Knowledge', *Current Anthropology*, vol. 43, no. 1, pp. 1–18.

Bauman, Zygmunt (2001), *The Individualized Society*, Cambridge: Polity Press.

Beck, Urlich (2000), *The Brave New World of Work*, Cambridge: Polity Press.

————(2002),'The Cosmopolitan Society and its Enemies', *Theory, Culture and Society*, vol. 19, nos. 1–2, pp. 17–44.

Beck, Ulrich and Elizabeth Beck-Gernsheim (1995), *The Normal Chaos of Love*, Cambridge: Polity Press.

Berlin, Isaih (2001), *The Power of Ideas*, New York: Pimlico.

Bergson, Henri (1912), *Creative Evolution*, London: Macmillan.

Beteille, Andre (1983),'Homo Hierarchicus, Home Equalis', in *The Idea of Natural Inequality and Other Essays*, ed. Andre Beteille, Delhi: OUP.

————(2000), *Antinomies of Society*, Delhi: OUP.

————(2002), *Sociology: Essays on Approach and Method*, Delhi: OUP.

Bhaskar, Roy (2002a), *Reflections on Meta-Reality: Transcendence, Everyday Life and Emancipations*, New Delhi: Sage.

———— (2002b), *Meta-Reality: The Philosophy of meta-Reality*, vol. 1, *A Philosophy for the Present. Creativity, Love and Freedom*, The Bhaskar Series, New Delhi, Thousand Oaks and London: Sage.

Bochi, G. and M. Ceruti (2002), *The Narrative Universe*, Cresskill, New Jersey: Hampton Press Inc.

Bourdieu, Pierre (1990), *In Other Words: Towards a Reflexive Sociology*, Cambridge: Polity Press.

————(1991a), 'Epilogue: On the Possibility of a Field of World Sociology', in *Social Theory for a Changing Society*, ed. Pierre Bourdieu and James S. Coleman, Boulder: Westview, pp. 373–87.

————(1991b), *The Political Ontology of Martin Heidegger*, tr. Peter Collier, Cambridge: Polity Press.

————(1992),'The Practice of Reflexive Sociology (Paris Workshop)', in *An Invitation to Reflexive Sociology*, ed. Bourdieu and Wacquant, Cambridge: Polity Press.

————*The Weight of the World: Social Suffering in Contemporary Society*, Cambridge: Polity Press.

————(1999, 2000), *Pascalian Meditations*, Cambridge: Polity Press.

————(2003),'Participant Objectivation', *Journal of Royal Anthropological Institute*, n.s., vol. 9, pp. 281–94.

Bourdieu, Pierre and Loic J.D. Wacquant (1992), *An Invitation to Reflexive Sociology*, Cambridge: Polity Press.

Burawoy, Michael et al., eds. (1991), *Ethnography Unbound: Power and Resistance in the Modern Metropolis*, Berkeley and Los Angeles: University of California Press.

Carretto, Jeremy ed. (1999), *Religion and Culture by Michel Foucault*, Manchester: Manchester University Press.

Clammer, John (1995), *Difference and Modernity: Japan and Social Theory*, London: Kegan Paul.

————'Beyond Power: Alternative Conceptions of Being and Reconstitution of Social Theory', in *Modern Prince and Modern Sage: Transforming Power and Freedom*, ed. Ananta Kumar Giri (Forthcoming).

Clammer, John, Sylvie Piorier and Eric Schwimmer (2004), 'Introduction: The Relevance of Ontologies in Anthropology: Reflections on a New Anthropological

Field', in *Figured Worlds: Ontological Obstacles in Intercultural Relations*, ed. John Clammer et al., Toronto: Toronto University Press, pp. 3–22.

Chakraborty, Achin (2004), 'The Irrelevance of Methodology and the art of the Possible: Reading Sen and Hirschman', in *Creative Social Research: Rethinking Theories and Methods*, ed. Ananta Kumar Giri, Lanham, MD: Lexington Books, pp. 169–84.

Cohen, Anthony (1994), *Self-Consciousness: An Alternative Anthropology of Identity*, London: Routledge.

Connolly, William (1995), *The Ethos of Pluralization*, Minneapolis: University of Minnesota Press.

———(2002), *Neuropolitics*, Minnesota: University of Minnesota Press.

Dallmayr, Fred (1984), *Polis and Praxis: Exercises in Contemporary Political Theory*, Cambridge, MA: The MIT Press.

———(1987), *Critical Encounters: Between Philosophy and Politics*, Notre Dame: University of Notre Dame Press.

———(1991), *Between Freiburg and Frankfurt: Toward a Critical Ontology*, Amherst: University of Massachusetts Press.

———(1993), *The Other Heidegger*, Ithaca: Cornell University Press.

———(1996), *Beyond Orientalism: Essays on Cross-Cultural Encounter*, Albany: SUNY Press.

———(1998), *Alternative Visions: Pathways in the Global Village,* Lanham, MD: Rowman & Littlefield.

——— ed. (1999), *Border Crossings: Toward a Comparative Political Theory*, Lanham, MD: Lexington Books.

———(2001a), *Homelessness and Homecoming: Heidegger on the Road*, University of Notre Dame: Manuscript,.

———(2001b), 'Resisting Totalizing Uniformity: Marin Heidegger on the *Macht* and Machenschaft', in *Achieving Our World: Toward a Global and Plural Democracy*, ed. Fred Dallmayr Lanham, MD: Rowman & Littlefield.

———(2002), *Dialogue Among Civilizations: Some Exemplary Voices*, New York: Palgrave.

———(2004), *Peace Talks—Any Body Listening?*, Notre Dame: University of Notre Dame Press.

Dallmayr, Fred R. and Thomas A. McCarthy (1977), 'Introduction: The Crisis of Understanding', in *Understanding and Social Inquiry*, ed. Fred R. Dallmayr and Thomas A. McCarthy, Notre Dame: University of Notre Dame Press, pp. 1–15.

Das, Veena (1995), *Critical Events: Anthropological Perspectives on Contemporary India*, Delhi: OUP.

———(1999), 'Wittgenstein and Anthropology', *Annual Review of Anthropology.*

———(2001), 'Violence and Translation', *Anthropological Quarterly*, vol. 75, no. 1, pp. 105–12.

———(2003), 'Social Sciences and the Publics', in *Introduction to The Oxford Indian Companion to Sociology and Social Anthropology*, ed. Veena Das, Delhi: OUP, pp. 1–29.

Dogan, Mattei and Robert Pahre, eds. (1990), *Creative Marginality: Innovations at the Intersections of Social Sciences*, Boulder: Westview Press.

Eisenstadt, S.N. (1992), 'Intersubjectivity, Dialogue, Discourse and Cultural Creativity in the work of Martin Buber', in *Martin Buber on Intersubjectivity and Cultural Creativity,* ed. S.N. Eisenstadt, Chicago: University of Chicago Press.

————(2002), 'Martin Buber in the Postmodern Age: Utopia, Community and Education in the Contemporary Era', in *Martin Buber: A Contemporary Perspective,* ed. Paul Mendes-Flohr, Syracuse: Syracuse University Press.

Elias, Norbert (1991), *The Society of Individuals,* Cambridge, MA: Basil Blackwell.

Faubion, James D., ed. (1995), *Rethinking the Subject: An Anthology of Contemporary European Social Theory,* Boulder, Co: Westview Press.

Fine, Michelle (2002), 'The Mourning After', *Qualitative Inquiry,* vol. 8, no. 2, pp. 137–45.

Foucault (1984), 'What is Enlightenment?', in *The Foucault Reader,* ed. P. Rabinow, NY: Pantheon Books.

Flyvbjerg, Bent (2001), *Making Social Science Matter: Why Social Inquiry Fails and How It can Succeed Again,* tr. Steven Sampson, Cambridge: CUP.

Frietag, Michel (2001), 'The Contemporary Social Sciences and the Problem of Normativity', *Theses Eleven,* no. 65, pp. 1–25.

Fromm, Eric (1950), *Man for Himself,* London: Routledge and Kegan Paul.

Fuchs, Martin (2004), 'Articulating the World: Social Movements, the Self-Transcendence of Society and the Question of Culture', in *Creative Social Research: Rethinking Theories and Methods,* ed. Ananta Kumar Giri, Lanham, MD: Lexington Books.

Gasper, Des (2003), 'Anecdotes, Situations, Histories: Varieties and Uses of Cases in Thinking About Ethics and Development Practice', in *A Moral Critique of Development: In Search of Global Responsibilities,* ed. Philip Quarles van Ufford and Ananta Kumar Giri, London: Routledge, pp. 194–220.

Giddens, Anthony (1996), *In Defense of Sociology: Essays, Interpretations and Rejoinders,* Cambridge: Polity Press.

Gatens, Moira and Genevieve Lloyd (1999), *Collective Imaginings: Spinoza, Past and Present,* London: Routledge.

Geertz, Clifford (1973), *Interpretation of Cultures,* New York: Basic Books.

————(2000), *Available Light: Philosophical Reflections on Anthropological Topics,* Princeton: Princeton University Press.

Gingrich, Andrew and Richard Fox, eds., (2002), *Anthropology, By Comparison,* London: Routledge.

Giri, Ananta Kumar (1998), 'Self, Other and the Challenge of Culture', in *Global Transformations: Postmodernity and Beyond,* ed. Ananta Kumar Giri, Jaipur: Rawat.

————(2002), *Conversations and Transformations: Toward a New Ethics of Self and Society,* Lanham, MD: Lexington Books and Rowman and Littlefield.

————(August 2003), 'Social Science Research: Call of Home and the World', *Economic and Political Weekly.*

————(2004, 2004a), 'Knowledge and Human Liberation: Jurgen Habermas, Sri Aurobindo and Beyond', *European Journal of Social Theory.*

————(2004b), *Reflections and Mobilizations: Dialogues with Movements and Voluntary Organizations,* New Delhi: Sage.

————(2004c), 'Self-Development, Inclusion of the Other and Planetary Realizations', in *The Religion of Development, Development of Religion,* ed. Ananta

Kumar Giri, Anton von Harshkamp and Oscar Salemnink, Lanham, MD: Lexington Books.

———(2004d), 'Rethinking Modernist Historiography', in *Creative Social Research: Rethinking Theories and Methods*, ed. Ananta Kumar Giri, Lanham, MD: Lexington Books.

Giri, Ananta Kumar and Philip Quarles van Ufford (2004), 'A Moral Critique of Development: Ethics, Aesthetics and Responsibility', *Review of Development and Change*.

Gorz, Andre (1999), *Reclaiming Work: Beyond the Wage-Based Society*, Cambridge: Polity Press.

Greco, John (2001), 'Virtues and Rules in Epistemology', in *Virtue Epistemology: Essays on Epistemic Virtue and Responsibility*, ed. Abrol Fairweather and Linda Zagzebski, Oxford: OUP, pp. 117–41.

Greer, Scott (1989[1969]), *The Logic of Social Inquiry*, New Brunswick: Transaction Publishers.

Gubrium, Jaber F. and James A. Holstein, eds. (1997), *The New Language of Qualitative Method*, New York: OUP.

Habermas, Jurgen (1971), *Knowledge and Human Interest*, Boston: Beacon Press.

———(1990), *Moral Consciousness and Communicative Action*, Cambridge: Polity Press.

Hanrahan, Nancy (2000), *Difference in Time: A Critical Theory of Culture,* Westport, CT: Praeger.

Harding, Sandra, ed. (1987), *Feminism and Methodology: Social Science Issues*, Indiana University Press and Open University Press.

Hardt, Michael and Antonio Negri (2000), *Empire*, Cambridge, MA: Harvard University Press.

———(1994), *Labor of Dionysus: A Critique of the State-Form*, Minneapolis: University of Minnesota Press.

Harvey, David (2000), *Spaces of Hope*, Edinburgh: University of Edinburgh Press.

Hawthorne, Geoffrey (1991), *Plausible Worlds*, Cambridge: CUP.

Kovacs, George (2001), 'Heidegger in Dialogue with Herder: Crossing the Language of Metaphysics toward Be-ing-historical Language', *Heidegger Studies,* vol. 17, pp. 45–63.

Knorr-Cetina, Karen (2001), 'Postsocial Relations: Theorizing Society in a Postsocial Environment', in *Handbook of Social Theory*, ed. George Ritzer and Barry Smart, London: Sage.

Luhman, Niklas (2001), 'Notes on the Project 'Poetry and Social Theory', *Theory, Culture & Society,* vol. 18, no. 1, pp. 15–27.

Inglis, Fred (2000), *Clifford Geertz: Culture, Custom and Ethics*, Cambridge: Polity Press.

Ingold, Tim (2004), 'A Circumpolar Night's Dream', in *Figured Worlds: Ontological Obstacles in Intercultural Relations*, ed. Clammer et al., Toronto: Toronto University Press, pp. 25–57.

Marcus, George and Michel Fischer (1986), *Anthropology as Cultural Critique: An Experimental Moment in the Human Sciences,* Chicago: University of Chicago Press,.

Mintz, Sidney W. (2000), 'Sow's Ears and Silver Linings: A Backward Look at Ethnography', *Current Anthropology*, vol. 41, no. 2, pp. 169–89.

Melucci, Alberto (1996), *The Playing Self: Person and Meaning in the Planetary Society*, Cambridge: CUP.

Mohanty, J.N. (2000a), *Self and Other: Philosophical Essays*, Delhi: OUP.

———(2000b), 'Gandhi's Truth', in *Fusion of Horizons: Socio-Spiritual Heritage of India*, ed. Krishna Roy, Delhi: Allied Publishers.

———(2002), *Explorations in Philosophy: Western Philosophy*, Delhi: OUP.

Monk, Ray (1990), *Ludwig Wittgenstein: The Duty of Genius*, London: Vintage Books.

Pani, Narendar (2004), 'Gandhian Economic Method and the Challenge of Expediency', in *Creative Social Research: Rethinking Theories and Methods*, ed. Ananta Kumar Giri, Lanham, MD: Lexington Books.

Peacock, James (2002), 'Action Comparison: Efforts Towards a Global and Comparative yet Local and Active Anthropology', in *Anthropology, By Comparison*, ed. Gingrich and Fox, London: Routledge, pp. 44–69.

Pillai, P.V. (1985), 'Hind Swaraj in the Light of Heidegger's Critique of Modernity', in *Hind Swaraj: A Fresh Look*, Delhi: Gandhi Peace Foundation.

Pollock, Sheldon et al. (2000), 'Cosmopolitanisms', *Public Culture*, vol. 12, no. 3, pp. 577–89.

Quarles van Ufford, Philip and Ananta Kumar Giri, eds. (2003), *A Moral Critique of Development: In Search of Global Responsibilities*, London: Routledge.

Ried, Herbert G. and Betsy Taylor (2009), 'Globalization, Democracy and the 'Aesthetic Ecology of Emergent Publics' for a Sustainable World: Working From John Dewey', in *Modern Prince and the Modern Sage: Transforming Power and Freedom,* ed. Ananta Kumar Giri.

Rorty, Richard (1990), *Contingency, Irony and Solidarity*, Cambridge: CUP.

Radhakrishnan, R. (2003), *Theory in an Uneven World*, Cambridge, MA: Basil Blackwell.

Santos, Baaventura de Sousa (1995), *Toward a New Common Sense: Law, Science and Politics in the Paradigmatic Transition*, London: Routledge.

Sayer, Andrew (1992 [1984]), *Method in Social Science: A Realist Approach*, 2nd edn., London: Routledge.

Schrag, Calvin (1997), *The Self After Postmodernity*, Yale University Press.

Shanks, Andrew (2001), 'What is Truth?', in *Towards a Theological Poetics*, London: Routledge.

Sen, Amartya (2001), 'History as an Enterprise of Knowledge', *Frontline,* 2 February, pp. 86–91.

Smith, Adam, (1976), *A Theory of Moral Sentiments*, Oxford: OUP.

Srinivasan, Amrit (1998), 'The Subject of Fieldwork: Malinowski and Gandh', in Meenakshi Thapan, ed. *Anthropological Journeys: Reflections on Fieldwork*, Hyderabad: Orient Longman.

Strathern, Marilyn (1994), *Partial Connections*, Savage, MD: Rowman & Littlefield.

———(2002), 'Foreword', in *Anthropology, By Comparison*, ed. Gingrich and Fox, London: Routledge, pp. xi–xvii.

———(2004), *Commons and Borderlands: Working Papers on Interdisciplinarity,*

Accountability, and the Flow of Knowledge, Oxon, UK: Sean Kingston Publishing House.

———— ed. (2000), *Audit Cultures: Anthropological Studies in Accountability, Ethics, and the Academy*, London: Routledge.

Sunder Rajan, R. (1998), *Beyond the Crises of European Science: vol. 1, New Beginnings*, Shimla: Institute of Advanced Studies.

————(1996), 'Notes towards a Phenomenology of Historiographies', *Journal of Indian Council of Philosophical Research*, January–April, pp. 187–207.

Strydom, Piet (2000), *Discourse and Knowledge: The Making of Enlightenment Sociology*, Liverpool: Liverpool University Press.

————(2001), 'The Problem of Triple Contingency in Habermas', *Sociological Theory*, vol. 19, pp. 165–86.

Tagore, Rabindranath (1961), *On Art and Aesthetics*, Calcutta: Orient Longman.

Tuner, Bryan S., ed. (1996), *The Blackwell Companion to Social Theory*, Oxford: Blackwell.

Toulmin, Stephen (2001), *Return to Reason,* Cambridge, MA: Harvard University Press.

Touraine, Alain (1977), *Self-Production of Society*, Chicago: University of Chicago Press.

————(2000), *Can We Live Together? Equality and Difference*, Cambridge: Polity Press.

————(2007), 'Sociology After Sociology', *European Journal of Social Theory*, vol. 10, no. 2, pp. 184–93.

Uberoi, J.P.S. (1978), *Science and Culture*, Delhi: OUP.

————(1984), *The Other Mind of Europe: Goethe as a Scientist,* Delhi: OUP.

————(2002), *The European Modernity: Truth, Science and Method*, New Delhi: OUP.

Urry, John (2000), *Sociology Beyond Societies: Mobilities for the Twenty-First Century*, London: Routledge.

Vattimo, Gianni (1999), *Belief*, Cambridge: Polity Press.

Van Staveren, Irene (2001), *The Values of Economics: An Aristotelian Perspective*, London: Routledge.

————(2004), 'Caring for Economics', in *Creative Social Research: Rethinking Theories and Methods*, ed. Ananta Kumar Giri, Lanham, MD: Lexington Books.

Walker, Ralph C. (1998), 'Contingency', in *Routledge Encyclopeadia of Philosophy*, ed. Edward Craig, vol. 2, London: Routledge.

Wallerstein, Immanuel et al. (1996), *Open the Social Sciences*, Stanford: Stanford University Press.

————(1999), *The End of the World as We Know It: Social Science for the Twenty-First Century*, Minneapolis: University of Minnesota Press.

Zammito, John H. (2002), *Kant, Herder, and the Birth of Anthropology*, Chicago: University of Chicago Press.

PART TWO

PATHWAYS OF CREATIVE RESEARCH: CROSSING BOUNDARIES, STIMULATING CREATIVITY

3

Crossing Boundaries, Stimulating Creativity
The Horizon of Integral Meta-Studies

MARKUS MOLZ and

MARK EDWARDS

I think we may safely say that the studies preliminary to the construction of great theory should be at least as deliberate and thorough as those that are preliminary to the building of a dwelling-house. That systems ought to be constructed architectonically has been preached since Kant, but I do not think the full import of the maxim has by any means been apprehended. What I would recommend is that every person who wishes to form an opinion concerning fundamental problems, should first of all make a complete survey of human knowledge, should take note of all the valuable ideas in each branch of science, should observe in just what respect each has been successful and where it has failed . . . I . . . give emphasis to one special recommendation, namely, to make a systematic study of the conceptions out of which a philosophical theory may be built, in order to ascertain what place each conception may fitly occupy in such a theory, and to what uses it is adapted. — CHARLES S. PEIRCE (1891: 162).

The most important task today is, perhaps, to learn to think in a new way.

— GREGORY BATESON (1972: 327).

No knowledge without knowledge of knowledge.

— EDGAR MORIN (1986: 25).

In this chapter we put forward the case for a broad-range, multilayered and integrative view of the social sciences. While integrative and boundary-crossing forms of research have a long tradition, its methods, aims and advantages have not been well articulated. This multilayered view is closely connected to the idea that an integral pluralism regarding theories and research paradigms is a desirable and even essential quality for the ongoing development of the social sciences. However, in the era of almost exponential growth of specialized knowledge, this pluralism has not only resulted in a productive differentiation but also in a confusing fragmentation. Today, countless theories and models co-exist in a rather disconnected fashion in great many separate subdisciplines, research streams and institutional contexts. This fragmentation conceals the crucial difference between actual and apparent creativity, i.e. between true innovation and re-invention, and it fundamentally inhibits boundary crossing research which is vital for addressing the deep transformational challenges currently impacting society, nature and self.

While we concentrate in this contribution on situating meta-layer approaches in the overall landscape of social studies, we think that they are equally relevant for the humanities and the sciences. We address both modern and postmodern critiques raised against meta-narratives and discuss how contemporary meta-studies can respond to them. We propose that the framework of an integral meta-studies can incorporate important ideas from different disciplinary and interdisciplinary streams to develop and connect integrative, embodied and contextualized forms of boundary-crossing research. Based on insights drawn from several overarching research approaches, we attempt to identify the main branches of an integral meta-studies consisting of an interconnected cycle of metatheory, meta-method, meta-data-analysis and meta-hermeneutics. Integral meta-studies is a collaborative form of research that enables researchers to critically select, connect, combine and analyse sense-making tools such as conceptual dimensions and lenses, metaphors, theories and methods, through an appreciative stance towards contemporary pluralism. The essay concludes with reflections on how this view contributes to creativity and dialogue within and between social science disciplines and beyond while honouring and connecting the unique roles and trajectories of existing approaches.

Creating and Crossing Boundaries

> If the Kosmos is ... a fragmented and jumbled affair, with no common contexts or linkings or joinings or communions—then fine, the world is the jumbled mess the various specialities take it to be. But if the world is holistic and holonic, then why do not more people see this? And why do many academic specialities actively deny it? If the world is whole, why do so many people see it as broken? And why, in a sense, is the world broken, fragmented, alienated, divided?   − KEN WILBER (2000: XIII).

> Reflection constitutes the ecology of knowledge. It is the self-consciousness of intellectual practices. It gets at what is behind them, at what they actually do and how they work. Thinking is not automatically reflexive. Thinking that occurs in terms of disciplines, does not usually reflect on itself or the wider world.   − MARTIN DAVIES (2003:10).

There are recurrent boundaries of many different kinds in scientific research: geographical, linguistic, socio-cultural, disciplinary, paradigmatic, theoretical, methodological, and terminological. These boundaries lie between the domains of humanity's knowledge and between the methods used to build knowledge. Boundaries define what and how one studies. In a fundamental way, they set the parameters of one's imagination. These boundaries are not merely passive demarcations for administrative convenience but possess real social, psychological, and material significance (Morin 1986). One uses them on a daily basis in powerful and very concrete ways, not only to do research on social life but also to live the life of social researchers. They first appear as anchoring signals, belief systems, and identity markers and some of them coalesce into research schools, disciplinary traditions, employment opportunities and distinct fields of study (Abbott 2001; Gasper 2004; Giri 2002). The process of institutionalization and materialization continues with the creation of specialized journals and publishers, focused programmes of teaching and funding and separate buildings located on distinct regions within university campuses (Russell 2005). As a result, 'academics frequently have little or nothing to do with their colleagues on the same campus from supposedly sister disciplines' (Gasper 2004: 318). Further on, these demarcations diffuse into, and largely shape, almost all domains of contemporary societies (Turner 2000). It is possible to observe how these disciplinary divides are etched into forms of technological innovation, industry, social policy and in educational streams and funding criteria. The heavily compartmentalized and enduring structure of the contemporary research enterprise has become the guiding blueprint for thinking and acting, not only for scholars and teachers, but also for practitioners and professionals, employers and employees, citizens and politicians.

The benefits that flow from the concentration of scientific activities into schools, disciplines and research paradigms are obvious. Boundaries provide orientation and indicate what to consider as relevant and even more so what to legitimately neglect as irrelevant. They constitute manageable frames for building scientific and cultural knowledge. They enable people to make seemingly well-founded choices and allow them to label, define and communicate their understandings within circumscribed communities of peers. Funders can resource target areas of specific need, students can identify their domains of interest and scholars can develop world-class sophistication in specialized topics. More importantly, these boundaries provide clear-cut faculty career paths, which can be projected in advance, allowing for the reproduction of research lineages across generations (Abbott 2001). Overall, 'academic disciplines provide wealth, prestige, power and acclaim to the practising professionals' (Giri 2002: 111).

Eventually, however, 'we look at the world through the eyes of the discipline to which we belong and tend to think that the whole world is characterized by a disciplinary significance' (Giri 2002: 104). Indeed, 'each specialist, when he is broadminded, tends to see the whole world from his specialized point of view. The principles essential to his area of competence are seen as essential structures in his world view. But to the extent that he has neglected principles essential to the viewpoints of other scientists who also project them as world view structures, his view may be judged deficient' (Bahm 1980: 35). This can bear dramatic effects because in addition there is a tendency that 'disciplines fossilize' (Turner 2000: 64), cause 'mental sclerosis' (Gusdorf 1977: 588) and produce 'a new ignorance, a new obscurantism, a new pathology of knowledge' (Morin 1986: 14). At least, specializations narrow down into extremely precise fields shared only by often very small communities of scholars. After a century of almost exponential growth of research disciplines, the world is now probably approaching 10,000 recognized research fields (Clark 1995). By its very nature, this process results in highly technical enclaves of specialized knowledge, methods, languages and instrumental technologies. Even though there is an ongoing dynamics of borrowing between fields, splitting and merging of subdisciplines, the early movers who managed to get institutionalized out of the fuzzy pre-disciplinary research landscape are to this day extremely stable and dominant (Abbott 2001; Turner 2000) because 'the boundaries of academic departments and institutes tend to determine boundaries of study and to perpetuate themselves' (Valen 1972: 418).

Such disadvantages of this self-perpetuating process of differentiation, if not epistemological disintegration (Bendle 1996) of the overall research and knowledge-building endeavour are much less acknowledged. The very core assumptions of the largest part of institutionalized research currently conducted are uncritically, if not unconsciously, shaped by a heavy specialization bias constricting research paradigms into vying conceptual systems rather than complementary and coordinated perspectives. At the same time, the numerous attempts at multidisciplinary and interdisciplinary projects have contributed little to a lasting connection and integration of knowledge (Nicolsecu 2002; Rescher 1999; Turner 2000; Weingart 2000). 'The very attempt to counteract fragmentation produces new fragments' (Rescher 1999: 53). We seem to be together prisoners of

an unending cycle leading to ever more specialized but ever more cross-fertilized areas. Scientific fields show continually growing specialization, narrowing focus, and subdivisions: the creation of subdisciplines. This produces deeper work, but also leaves gaps and progressively encounters diminishing returns. Innovators then identify higher returns from cross-border hybridization with another specialized fraction, often from another discipline. A new, more specialized, sub-field emerges; and the cycle then repeats, again and again. (Gasper 2004: 315)

Even though there are principled boundaries to the knowledge quest (Barrow 1999; Cilliers 2005; Dupré 2003; Morin 1986; Nicolsecu 2002; Rescher 1999; Stenmark 2008), and even though 'rethinking theory also involves an acknowledgement of limits of theory' (Giri 2006a: 232), most of the above-mentioned reified boundaries are not principled, but socially constructed in a way that, over time, limits our individual and collective capacity to find connection, to perceive cross-cutting patterns, and to develop boundary-crossing and integrative approaches to world-scale future enabling. Indeed, 'this inwardly referential character of modern discipline forms a major barrier to updating our approach to contemporary problems' (Rodgers et al. 2003: 2).

Even before the information technology revolution became pervasive this requirement for crossing boundaries, creating new relationships and integrating disconnected areas, was anticipated by some exceptional scholars who took a broad view on research and society. For example, Ernest Boyer, who was United States Commissioner of Education and President of the Carnegie Foundation for the Advancement of Teaching, stated in a presentation of a commissioned report on the future priorities of the professoriate (Boyer 1994: 118):

In the coming century, there will be an urgent need for scholars who go beyond the isolated facts; who make connections across the disciplines; and who begin to discover a more coherent view of knowledge and a more integrated, more authentic view of life.

And in the report itself, he said that 'by integration, we mean making connections across the disciplines, placing the specialities in larger context, illuminating data in a revealing way, often educating non-specialists too' (Boyer 1990: 18). On the basis of an attitude of 'respected complementarity' (Eckensberger 2002), building connection across what were previously assumed to be unconnected or incommensurable ideas and research streams is not only useful, it is also illuminating. It allows to discover new types of knowledge and more authentic world views through the balancing of specialized with overarching perspectives. A European research group involved in originating trans-disciplinary research approaches makes an interesting point in this regard.

The pluralization of culture, the depths of the sciences and the arts achieved by specialists and specialization are worthy accomplishments of our culture. We believe, however, that the fragmentation of our culture should be a starting point for a new effort at integration, one that explicitly takes into account these achievements. It is for this reason that . . . a new communication among these diverse specializations must be created (Aerts et al. 2007 [1994]: 8).

Aerts and his colleagues are making the point that the task of integration across boundaries also needs to recognize the plurality of views and the contributions of specialized fields and the reductionist sciences. What is required here is a pluralistic integration that retains the diversity of specialities, not a dominant and monistic integration that reduces everything to one overarching grand theory.

Meta-Perspectives and Meta-Critiques

> We understand our universe to a much greater extent than we often recognize, but we fail to realize this fact because we have not pulled together existing theories.   — JONATHAN TURNER (1991: 252).

When social studies were institutionalized in the Western world into various academic disciplines, big picture world views such as neo-Thomism, Hegelianism, Darwinism and the early versions of Marxism and Freudian Psychoanalysis were widely studied and were very influential. They provided philosophical and scientific frameworks, which were totalizing in their approach to psychosocial reality. Although in many respects opposed to each other, each of them contained a potent mix of inspiring concepts and hypotheses on the one hand, and philosophical suppositions on the other. They stimulated rich veins of empirical and conceptual research. However, particularly since the 1950s, big pictures and totalizing streams of theory-building and research have fallen on hard times. There are at least two major reasons for this. First, social research did not escape the overall pressure to specialize and to empirically test research questions in specific contexts on the basis of small- and middle-range models and theories.

> The attempt to formulate general social or political philosophies thus came to be treated as little better than a confused and old-fashioned failure to keep up with the scientific times. Connected with this was the positive injunction to abandon the study of the grand philosophical systems of the past, with their unsatisfactory mixture of descriptive and evaluative elements, in order to get on with the truly scientific and purportedly value-neutral task of constructing what came to be called 'empirical theories' of social behaviour and development. The effect of this was to make appear that two millenia of philosophizing about the social world had suddenly come to an end. (Skinner 1985: 4)

This 'middle range strategy produced a vast array of theories' (Turner and Boyns 2006: 355) and a proliferating number of research paradigms and quickly reached the point where theoretical overviews of many fields of social research were beyond the means of even the most encompassing reviews. Integrative meta-approaches can contribute to balance this lopsided focus on theory testing of the middle range. Indeed, as Turner and Boyns (2006: 376) observe:

there are now so many different theories that it seems impossible to gain a vision of the social universe as a whole; rather, our theories have chopped up reality in so many arbitrary ways that it is difficult to see the forest through the trees.

The proliferation of theories and research paradigms has led to the specialization and creation of research silos that have no place for endeavours that aim to connect ideas at the meta-level. The second reason for the more recent neglect of meta-layer research is that a positivist-empiricist critique of big picture narratives arose, which dismissed such work on the basis of methodological grounds. Paul Colomy refers to this positivist devaluing of metatheory saying that: 'A now-classic critique castigates grand theory as being nothing more than association and dissociation of concepts typically presented in confused verbiage and amounting to little more than elaborate and arid formalism' (Colomy 1991: 272).

Of course there are armchair attempts to meta-layer studies to which this critique can be rightly raised. There is no doubt that there were actually 'fatal flaws in earlier explicitly meta-theoretical works', which were, in addition, often 'at odds with one another' (Ritzer 1992: 12). This critique, however, became overgeneralized in time and space while failing to consider that concepts, models and theories can serve themselves as 'data' as thoroughly processed as empirical data (see section 4). Amongst other factors, this recurrent empiricist critique has created a long-standing disregard for meta-studies within a mainstream science made up by the dominant schools of middle-range theory testing in each discipline. Accordingly, 'piecemeal empirical research in the human sciences was alone commended, while Marxism, psychoanalysis, and all forms of Utopian social philosophy were together consigned to the dustbin of history' (Skinner 1985: 5). This neglect has had unfortunate outcomes for both broad-range and middle-range theory building. As a state of affairs revealed by looking into today's specialized journals, much empirical research is done without any substantial philosophical or meta-theoretical reflection. On the other hand, a good deal of academic philosophizing seems to freely float above the messy realities that are the focus of empirical labour and the uncountable small and middle-scale theoretical frameworks that deal with every widening range of applied fields (Morin 1986; Weinstein and Weinstein, 1992). For these and other reasons, meta-level research, if it has any profile among contemporary researchers, has little credibility among the sciences in general and the social sciences in particular.

Apart from these critiques issuing from the modernist concern for theory-testing, operationalization and empirical support, a second wave of fierce criticism swept over meta-level approaches when postmodern philosophies gained influence in the social sciences from the 1970s to the 1990s. The 'incredulity towards meta-narratives' (Lyotard 1984: xxiv) has been offered as one of the core defining elements of a postmodern approach, i.e. a 'contesting of the unified and coherent self [and a] general questioning of any totalizing or homogenizing system' (Hutcheon 1993: 252). West (1993: 577) has pointed out that:

Distinctive features of the new cultural politics of difference are to trash the monolithic and homogeneous in the name of diversity, multiplicity and heterogeneity; to reject the abstract, general and universal in light of the concrete, specific and particular, to historicize, contextualize and pluralize by highlighting the contingent, provisional, variable, tentative, shifting and changing.

Ritzer and Goodman (2006: 154) summarize the attitudes of postmodern and interpretivist writers and researchers as follows:

For the postmodernist, deconstruction is to be followed by further deconstruction without end. . . . For postmodernists totalizations are only useful in order to make 'war on totality' (Lyotard 1993: 16) and the only useful grand narrative is 'a grand narrative of the decline of the grand narrative' (Lyotard 1993: 29). . . . Thus, totalizations and grand narratives, where they exist in the social world or in the social sciences, are seen as terroristic and to be avoided at all costs. Wherever they are found they are to be deconstructed.

In addressing modernist and postmodernist critiques of the big picture research, it is important to distinguish between the pluralism of integrative meta-layer approaches and the totalizing world views of theoretical monism. Integral pluralistic approaches take the above-mentioned empiricist and postmodern criticisms very seriously and are actually deeply engaged with both, empirical research and pluralism. Using an appreciative rather than combative metaphoric, integral approaches serve to detect and balance the excesses and inconsistencies of:

1. Unwarranted and overgeneralizing meta-narratives lending themselves to ideological misuses by specific interest groups, i.e. a monistic and totalizing grand theorizing;
2. An empiricism based on a narrow and one-dimensional understanding of evidence, i.e. a monistic and totalizing empiricism; and
3. An exaggerated, self-contradictory relativism and disassembling contextualism, i.e. a monistic and totalizing relativism.

Today, those defending the value of integrative approaches are not satisfied with leaving in its wake a deconstructed set of relativized and localized viewpoints, whether they are empirically supported or critically deconstructed. The task is only half finished at this point on a difficult journey of reconnection and discovery of intersecting languages, interests and approaches (Dussel 2008; Giri 2006b; Wilber 2000a)—a journey that needs to be undertaken on the basis of different parameters than in the past, in an appreciative and dialogic mode rather than an imperialistic or extremely relativistic one. An appropriate meta-perspective today should not only point out boundaries but actually show ways to cross them. It does this by creating an expanded r(el)ationality that uncovers underlying connections and establishing new ones and, in so doing, advances the creative and emancipatory capacities of the diversity of views and practices.

As long as one is unconscious of the influence of the meta-layer assumptions that necessarily frame all theories and ways of thinking about and acting upon the world, one will always be subject to their partialities and reductionisms and reproduce those distortions in all aspects of research and practice. Bahm (1980: 35) contended a generation ago in his programmatic 'interdisciplinology' that:

Most people, including most scientists, have a world view, clear or vague. Most world views have been projected from viewpoints with comparatively limited perspectives. . . . The task of achieving a most adequate world view involves both accepting and incorporating demonstrated principles from each science and rejecting and excluding any conclusions inferred by scientists from their own principles implying that true conclusions in other sciences are false.

Such a 'calling for transdisciplinarity requires a practice of interperspectivity' (Giri 2002: 106). In order to accomplish the huge task of developing conscious and targeted interperspectivity, we need to come together to methodically conduct meta-layer studies so that we can become more conscious of the interdependencies between the core assumptions of respective world views and the ways they make us interpret and shape reality. With the emergence of varieties of meta-studies during the last two decades or so, which are pluralistic and integrative at the same time there can indeed be a substantiated and legitimated 'return of grand theory' (Skinner 1985; Turner and Boyns 2006). But rather than the a priori, monistic or relativistic grand theorizing of former times, a new type of boundary-crossing research is arising now that should and could not be confounded with its modernist and postmodernist predecessors. This integrative approach does not supplant theoretical alternatives but accommodates them and can even develop specialized theory under its purview. Many researchers are calling for such a new kind of integrative vision:

In contrast to current trends towards specialization, both inside and outside of theorizing proper, we argue that specialized theories are best developed within a more encompassing vision of how the social universe unfolds. Only grand theory can provide this vision. (Turner and Boyns 2006: 376)

There are actually many substantial examples of research streams that can be characterized by such a non-exclusionary meta-perspective, even though they are often marginalized in various ways as 'arguments, promising or otherwise, identified with discredited traditions or segments' that 'will often be discounted and dismissed for reasons having little to do with their social scientific merits' (Colomy 1991: 278). The impact of criticism and neglect from both the modernist and postmodernist branches has indeed left the potential of these meta-layer approaches underutilized and often ignored by the mainstream of research activity, thus cutting itself off from a major source of creative stimulation. Rather than dismissing grand theorizing as too grand in our eyes most of the justly criticized historical grand theorizing was never grand enough to encompass, accommodate and elucidate the actual diversity of research approaches, including the criticizing ones. But instead of refraining as a consequence from grand, i.e. boundary-crossing meta-layer research altogether, instead of limiting in the research enterprise to disconnected small and middle-scale research, we might rather attempt to make grand theory grand enough, through sustained trans-paradigmatic, trans-disciplinary and trans-civilizational dialogues (Dussel 2009; Giri 2002, 2006b).

Lev Vygotsky can serve here as a historical example. While Vygotskian ideas have finally made inroads internationally in applied fields like education and communication studies, the larger implications of his socio-historical approach and his meta-psychology have gone largely unnoticed. The conceptually integrative capacities possessed by the Vygotskian meta-constructs of mediation and the proximal zone of development and the general dialectical approach that Vygotsky developed have been relatively ignored. As Robbins (2003: 305) points out, Vygotsky used these and other methods to survey and systematically integrate much of the theoretical landscape of his time:

An integral part of the understanding of Vygotskian dialectical synthesis relates to the construction of a system of thought that does not jettison all older . . . theories of the past, nor does it try to replicate a bricolage model of additive and summative constructions within a microlevel of analysis.

This active pursuance of cross-boundary conceptual integration of partial models and a non-separating take on psychosocial reality has continued in the Vygotskian tradition until today in the work of scholars such as Yrjö Engeström (2009) and Jaan Valsiner (2000). There are many contemporary examples reflecting a basically similar attitude of a conceptual and 'methodological cosmopolitanism' which rejects 'the either-or principle and assembles a this-as-well-as-that principle . . . thinking and living in terms of inclusive oppositions' (Beck 2002: 19). Among the many examples of these integrative principles are those brought to our attention by Giri (2006a):

There are rules, and there is the particular. This much can be observed phenomenologically. . . . To amputate one side in these pairs of phenomena into a dualistic 'either-or' is to amputate our understanding. Rather than the 'either-or', we should develop a non-dualism and pluralistic 'both-and' (Flyvbjerg 2001: 49).

The ethic of non-injury applied to philosophical thinking requires that one does not reject outright the other point of view without first recognising the element of truth in it; it is based on the belief that every point of view is partly true, partly false, and partly undecidable. (Mohanty 2000: 24)

There are many more important streams of this boundary-crossing, appreciative and integrative research attitude. These streams are characterized by a self-reflexive capacity for 'complex thinking' (Morin 1986), 'relational and contextual reasoning' (Reich 2002) or 'vision logic' (Wilber 2000: 192) related to a planetary world view. Our view is that such meta-research streams have the potential to cross-fertilize with each other even though they are not necessarily yet interacting much with each other, as the following three more philosophically tuned examples might show:

1. Roy Bhaskar, in his critical realism (1998), now expanded into the philosophy of meta-reality (Bhaskar 2002), has systematically 'argued against the dualisms and splits that dominated the . . . contemporary human sciences . . . between positivism and hermeneutics; between collectivism and individualism; structure and agency; reason and cause; mind and body; fact and value'. In each case he comes up with 'a third sublating position which could reconcile these stark polarities and oppositions, and which could situate the two extremes as special cases of the more general sublating position' (Bhaskar 1999), thus exemplifying how an integrative attitude can be adopted towards arguments and paradigms opposing each other.
2. Enrique Dussel is sensing through his philosophy of liberation (1985) that 'a global project of a trans-modern pluriverse (other than universal, and not post-modern), appears on the horizon'

(2008: 10). 'Subsuming the best of globalized European and North American modernity, "trans"-modernity affirms "from without" the essential components of modernity's own excluded cultures in order to develop a new civilization for the twenty-first century' (Dussel 2002: 223–4). Dussel here is emphasizing a simultaneously appreciative, critical and connective attitude towards cultural perspectives stemming from concrete, localized historical experiences of interacting human collectivities.

3. Ken Wilber's (2000a, 2000b) so-called AQAL 'Integral model is post-disciplinary in that it can be used successfully in the context of approaches considered as disciplinary, multidisciplinary, interdisciplinary, and transdisciplinary' (Esbjörn-Hargens and Wilber 2006: 524–5), exemplifying the very possibility of crossing and transcending the disciplinary boundaries through a widely applicable, domain-unspecific framework.

Even though these thinkers have initially developed and subsequently expanded their approaches quite independently from each other, their respective works reflect important resonances and commonalities regarding their basic intention. If we have taken each of them to highlight a specific quality each oeuvre actually covers all these qualities in one way or the other. So, let us summarize the commonalities: those meta-layer forms of research aim specifically at accommodating and connecting paradigms, disciplines, theories, and cultural world views and traditions of knowledge. Boundary-crossing in this new sense does not mean, however, to espouse a single encompassing truth, to fix the one and best (meta)methodology, or to justify the dominance of a certain culture, world view or framework. It is not seeking domination at all. Rather, meta-layer research recognizes and values pluralism and diversity while at the same time finding shared patterns, shared fundamental values and shared platforms for communication that contribute to the development of constructive, useful and emancipatory knowledge. Wilber (2000b: 24) expresses this goal of an integral pluralism circumventing the problems of relativist pluralism and universal monism as follows:

Many of the waves and streams of the spectrum of consciousness are indeed local, culturally specific, and not universal. But research has consistently confirmed that many of these patterns of richly interwoven textures are common to humanity as a whole; others are common to large areas of humanity or to various epochs; and some are merely local and idiosyncratic, varying from culture to culture and individual to individual. Acknowledging and honouring the common and cross-cultural patterns in consciousness is not necessarily a marginalizing, oppressive endeavour; in its non-marginalizing form, it is in fact the basis of universal integralism.

Meta-layer approaches can substantially contribute to create such pluralistic connections because they provide a basis for analysing, critiquing and integrating the landscape of contemporary research and thought. More specifically they: contribute to enhancing true creativity in social research by differentiating between necessary and unnecessary limits built in the assumptions that underpin modern and postmodern research endeavours (see prior sections); can identify omissions, weaknesses and blind spots in specific research streams (Edwards 2010); prevent the pervasive unnoticed repetition and wasteful reinvention of models and theories within separated fields of study (Abbott 2001); determine adequate boundaries of research perspectives that have come to colonize and dominate knowledge and social life beyond their domain of helpful and valid application (Wilber 2000a); and invite scientific researchers to intentionally consider reflexivity in the development of their conceptual frameworks in order to substantiate their approach (Ashmore 1989; Fuchs 1992; and Maton 2003).

Introducing Integral Meta-studies

> Metatheorising cannot progress until its practitioners have a clear sense of what they are doing and then communicate to others the procedures involved.   – GEORGE RITZER (1991: 316).

So far we have touched upon some of the major criticisms raised against big picture theorizing and we have mentioned a selection of contemporary authors pursuing this kind of meta-layer research. We will now consider a variant of meta-layer research that we call integral meta-studies (Edwards 2008, 2010). Integral meta-studies are fundamentally compatible with all of the above-mentioned meta-layer approaches while explicating more precisely their overall character and contours. In the following section we will outline an extended agenda as well as the field of application for meta-layer research as a whole, across various meta-streams and fields of research. In order to perform this task two ideas will be introduced here, which help support the integral meta-studies framework that is presented here. These ideas concern: the relationship between the meta-, middle-range and empirical layers of scientific research and how together they form, what might be called, a holarchy of (scientific) sense-making, and a general model of knowledge development, and particularly of scientific knowledge, that might be called an integral cycle of learning.

THE COMPLEXITY OF SENSE-MAKING

There are many categorizing systems used in the academic world to order its constituents into meaningful and hopefully useful categories, from pervasive but simplistic ones, e.g. the 'two cultures' (Snow 1958) or the commonly used three worlds of the natural sciences, the humanities and the social sciences (Kagan 2009), to more sophisticated attempts at ordering forms of scientific knowledge creation (e.g. Szostak 2004). The application of these concepts labels boundaries between the various forms of knowledge creation for the purpose of, among other things, demarcating and identifying one area of activity and validity from another (e.g. Wilber 2000a), or for devising alternative forms of organization (e.g. Jantsch 1972; Wallerstein 1995). There is the ordering of scientific traditions in terms of disciplines, sub-disciplines and sub–sub-disciplines, but as well in terms of disciplinary, multidisciplinary, interdisciplinary and transdisciplinary endeavours (Nicolescu 2002). There are delineations between pure research, applied research and participatory action enquiry or cooperative enquiry (Chandler and Torbert 2003; Heron 1996), between empirical and theoretical research (Törnebohm 1971), and between qualitative and quantitative methodologies (Creswell 2009). Creating these distinctions has its advantages and disadvantages. While such boundaries provide the means for performing research within recognized communities of researchers, as already mentioned, they also create ideational and institutional divisions that block the communication of ideas and the cross-fertilization of insights.

One dimension of delineation that we have been using repeatedly here is that between middle-layer and meta-layer research. Often little clarity reigns regarding this crucial distinction. Where middle-layer research, or 'primary research' as it is also called, focuses on the construction of conceptual models based on empirical events, meta-layer frameworks, or 'secondary research' (Zhao 1991), is based on the analysis of middle-layer models or theories themselves. This distinction is crucial to the model proposed here and the following quote stresses what the 'meta' in meta-studies actually means:

The prefix 'meta' connotes 'after', 'about', and 'beyond', and is often used in describing 'second-order' studies. ... The second-order study, or meta-study, is thus the study of the study, which transcends as well as succeeds the first-order study. Meta-study may involve the continuous monitoring of first-order studies by those doing the studies through self-examination and self-direction. Meta-study also can be undertaken by others interested in examining a study or set of studies. (Ritzer et al. 2006: 113–14)

Although the authors here were referring to the meta-study of sociology theories, these distinctions hold true beyond the sociological domain. Meta-studies address a crucial and often neglected or not sufficiently differentiated dimension of sense-making and scientific research. As Shweder (1984: 40) posited a long time ago:

a frame, paradigm, or absolute presupposition is a statement about the world whose validity can be neither confirmed nor disconfirmed. A frame violates no empirical evidence, nor is it dictated by any evidence. A frame violates no principle of logic nor does it follow from logic.

Accordingly, meta-studies are taking those frames of thinking, or entire frameworks, as their specific object of study, those frames or frameworks that otherwise constitute the inevitable and unattended background assumptions from which primary research operates.

As this layering lies at the heart of the current proposition we wish to substantiate it by showing that diverse sources converge in this respect and provide strong support for the necessity and usefulness of a fully differentiated meta-perspective of and for (scientific) enquiry. We contend that three distinct processes are the required minimum for describing the relationship between meta-, middle and empirical layers of research. In just the same way that, for example, 'for any intelligent process to happen ... performance components operate on data, meta-components operate on other components' (Sternberg 1984: 312) we suggest that the scientific process can be usefully viewed as consisting of at least three layers of sense-making. It is worth quoting Salthe (1985: 75) at some length here:

... in the face of a potentially overwhelming complexity of transactions between entities at different levels we must seek to discover what might be the basic minimal set of relationships that would satisfactorily frame most (or the most important) relationships. A reading of some of the literature on systems reveals for us what that structure is. The smallest cluster of levels required to represent fundamental interactive relationships is a triad of contiguous levels, so that we can simultaneously examine some process (or the events the process produces), the context of these events, and their causes.

Precisely, many theorists from various different domains proposed three layers or realms as core to their (meta) research approach, among them:

- Pitirim Sorokin's (1958) complementary channels of cognition: empirical-sensory, rational, and superrational.
- Margaret Masterman's (1970) resetting of Kuhn's paradigm concept into a data-based construct level, a 'sociological' level of accepted habits for research achievements, and finally a metaphysical level.
- Gregory Bateson's (1972) famous levels of learning: learning I (choice of response alternatives), learning II (change of the set of response alternatives) and learning III (change of the system of sets of response alternatives).
- The three levels of John van Gigch's (1991) meta-system approach: the real world enquiring system, the science enquiring system, and the meta-level or epistemology enquiring system.

- George Lakoff's and Mark Johnson's (1999) model of embodied cognition as based on universally shared kinaesthetic image schemata informing creative abstract reasoning which in turn shapes entire philosophical systems in specific ways.
- Haridimos Tsoukas's and Christian Knudsen's (2003) Object, Theory and Metatheory levels of organizational research.
- Lutz Eckensberger's (2003) action levels: first-order world-oriented actions, second-order action-regulating actions, and third-order actor-oriented actions reflecting on values, priorities and self.
- John Christopher's and Mark Bickhard's (2007) 'Three Knowing Levels' of interaction with the physical world, reflective abstraction and meta-values.

We are not claiming exact correspondences between these independently developed frameworks. Nevertheless, across time, cultures and research domains we can state an amazing level of confluence of core distinctions in this respect. So, in accord with these and many more frameworks, integral meta-studies are based on the distinction between the experiential and empirical layer, the conceptual, model building layer and the reflective meta-layer of sense-making (Figure 4.1). This multilayered format should not be regarded as a traditional hierarchy of levels of abstraction but as co-creating and mutually constitutive layers of meaning making and developmental dynamics. In other words, the layering of empirical, theoretical and meta-theoretical form a holarchy of sense-making, a holarchy being a way of representing a layered system that includes both hierarchy and heterarchy, i.e. the vertical and the horizontal, the whole and the part, the synthetic and the analytical.

However, we want to emphasize that the holarchy lens is but one way to represent those minimum three crucial ingredients for any sense-making endeavour, scientific or mundane. Another metaphorical representation is a three-dimensional space as introduced by Holton (1973) to locate different types of scientific statements appropriately. Holton's space is made up of an X-axis (phenomenic dimension), a Y-axis (analytic dimension) and a Z-axis (thematic preconceptions). Gülerce (1997) is also using a three-dimensional representation for what she calls the 'transformational unit'. The two complementary metaphorical representations, holarchy and three-dimensional space, are shown in Figure 3.1.

Whichever of these or other metaphors is preferred, their commonality resides in the mutualizing relationship between layers/axial dimensions that co-create and shape the overall sense-making endeavour. Although those layers/dimensions are simultaneously efficacious one has the tendency to focus attention on one of them at a time. Then, any one may be taken as

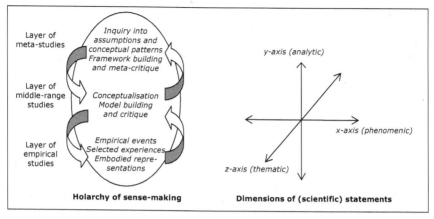

FIGURE 3.1: Two Metaphorical Models of (Scientific) Sense-Making

the point of departure. As one of the possibilities we will describe this as a process starting from the empirical. Observations, impressions and feelings rooted in immediate sensory experience provide a field in which experiences selected through the focus of attention and awareness are channelled, interpreted and transformed in terms of kinaesthetic schemata, and then further into basic symbols and concepts (which themselves act on and may be expressed as part of the empirical field). In symbolizing the experiences in more complex ways, conceptual systems are created in the form of models and theories (which themselves substantiate and are reworked back into the empirical and factual realms as designs, programmes, systems, practices and interventions). From the analysed patterns represented by middle-range theory overarching frameworks are built, or meta-models up to entire world views. These in turn generate and shape models and theories in specific ways which then influence the empirical field through the 'double hermeneutic' (see Ghoshal 2005; Giddens 1987). There is no dominant direction of causation apart from the interweaving and co-creation of each layer or dimension with the others. This means that each of these layers or dimensions of sense-making is involved in the process of (re)creating the empirical, symbolic, social and scientific worlds that all of us inhabit in one way or the other, from the most mundane to the most sophisticated.

THE CYCLE OF LEARNING

Mapping the branches of a comprehensive vision of metatheorizing requires some foundation in a general model of learning and scientific knowledge development. At a basic level, learning for both individuals and communities can be usefully considered as a cycle of at least four phases. Learning is an integration of at least four interconnected engagements: (1) the review, uptake and co-production of extant or condensed social knowledge, and behavioural instructions, which lead to (2) observing and experiencing specific phenomena within a specified domain; which is connected to (3) immediate ('felt sense') or intermediate (interpretive) sense-making attempts which allows for the (4) justification, validation, appreciation or critique of those interpretations within a social context. (Figure 4.2). Within the particular learning context of middle-range scientific research these engagements typically emerge as theories, methods, aggregated data sets and interpretations which are typically reflected in the traditional structure of research papers (Szostak 2004).

Actually, there are numerous models of epistemology, learning, development and intervention corroborating this fourfold distinction (see, for example, Engeström 1987; Kolb 1984; Scharmer 2007; Torbert 1991). Once again we do not claim exact correspondences between these models. Nevertheless, given the different contexts in which they have been developed and used there are striking resonances and sufficient similarities to suspect a cross-cutting pattern. At least, within each of these models it appears impossible to reduce any of the components to one of the others. As a consequence, an entire learning cycle cannot be conceived with less than four components. Simpler models fall short of accounting for learning processes.

In practice there is no privileged entry or exit point to the cycle we have proposed in Figure 3.2 even though there are standard forms of presenting research within certain paradigms or fields of research which might give the impression of a linear process. Rather, multiple individual and collective micro- and macro-cycles with different entry points, directions of flow and emphasis on parts of the integral cycle of learning supersede and cross each other. But overall, these engagements form iterative learning loops that potentially spiral up and result in knowledge

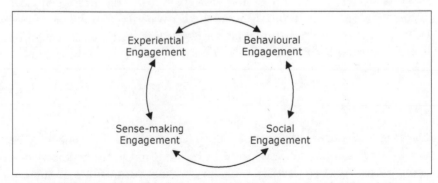

FIGURE 3.2: Basic Phases/Aspects in Developing (Scientific) Knowledge

development at many levels of complexity. Increasing complex contexts for these learning and knowledge cycles take the form of various 'learning loops' such as the double, triple if not quadruple loops described by Bateson (1972), Torbert (1991) and others. Knowledge development dynamics are not only fuelled by striving for internal coherence between theory, method, data and interpretation in any given study or research project but also by competing and conflicting views within a given field regarding valid theories, appropriate methods, relevant data, and convincing interpretations.

A FRAMEWORK FOR INTEGRAL META-STUDIES

Crossing the integral cycle of learning (Figure 3.2) with the various layers, realms or dimensions of sense-making described earlier (Figure 3.1) provides a framework for arranging the central activities of the scientific process (see the simplified compilation in Table 3.1). Table 3.1 shows the layers of empirical, middle-range and meta-studies, where empirical refers to the narrow forms of purely descriptive research, the middle-range refers to more general theory-based explanations of phenomena and meta-studies refer to reflective approaches crossing over multiple middle-level boundaries. The table is an extremely static and, therefore, rather inadequate way of depicting the dynamic relations that exist between the layers and engagements of scientific research but it does give a sense of the general domains that a more integrative and pluralistic approach to science needs to include if it is to account for all the core activities in scientific research. The boundaries that exist between these domains cut across the conventional boundaries mentioned in the first section in novel and challenging ways. This can contribute to reorientate one's perception of the relationships between existing and emerging meta-layer sciences.

TABLE 3.1: The Meta-studies Framework

Layers of scientific research	*The behavioural engagement*	*The experiential engagement*	*The sense-making engagement*	*The social engagement*
The layer of meta-studies	meta-method	meta-data-analysis and synthesis	meta-hermeneutics	meta-theory
The layer of middle-range studies	method	data	interpretation	theory
The layer of empirical studies	behavioural procedures	observations and experiences	primary meaning	descriptions/ explanations

As already mentioned, meta-theory is built on the analysis of middle-range theory (Fuchs 1992; Overton 2007; Ritzer 1991, 1992; Ritzer et al., 2006): 'A meta-theory M may represent the specific point of view on a certain class or set of theories T and this viewpoint generates meta-properties of T. Meta-properties are the consequence of the relation between M and T, but they are not the properties of any T application domain' (Gadomski 2001). So, too, the other meta-layer engagements of meta-method, meta-data analysis and meta-hermeneutics are built up from the middle-range studies of method, data analysis and interpretive studies respectively.

Taking the area of method for example, in recent decades a move could be observed towards employing multiple forms of methods and techniques to gather data. The methods of, for example, triangulation (Hassard 2005), multi-methodology (Mingers 2006), mixed methods (Creswell 2009) and integral methodological pluralism (Esbjörn-Hargens 2005), result from the meta-methodological concern for more comprehensive and interconnected approaches to data collection (Szostak 2004). An integral meta-method would contribute a systematic and boundary crossing approach to the study of methods and the various meta-layer lenses that generate them. All too often research methods are adopted purely for reasons of familiarity or through the habits and advantages of following some research tradition. There needs to be a more conscious comparison of the limitations or benefits of particular methods and a more concerted effort to combine multiple methods, techniques and instruments in performing research.

An integral meta-method introduces a systematic appraisal of the landscape of methods and, among other contributions, could identify the complementarities that exist between different methods and the possibilities of disclosing and evincing rich seams of data. Such complementarities and comparisons cannot be identified when researchers operate solely from within one methodological school, however developed in techniques that school might be. In such instances there is a lack of awareness about the conditions of creation of artefacts by adopting the same kinds of methods. Indeed, as Fox (1996: 110) notes: 'Methodology is done, even methodically, but usually not with explicitly articulated or self-conscious method. There is no orthodox meta-methodology; the question is simply rarely considered.'

Similarly, an integral meta-hermeneutics has much to offer in studying different interpretive frameworks from a meta-perspective. Traditionally, this has been the territory of all those, especially postmodern approaches that took an 'interpretive turn' towards treating the task of explanation and understanding as a function of epistemology rather than ontology, including the psychological, sociological, socio-historical, economic and geopolitical conditions, contexts, positions and interests of the researcher and respective communities. However, rather than simply focusing on the deconstructive analysis of epistemologies, an integral meta-hermeneutics would also move on towards the constructive task of finding connections and developing integrative frameworks for the plurality of interpretive positions. An integral meta-hermeneutics would not reject or replace the contributions of postmodernist interpretivism (in all its different varieties) but rather build on these analyses by including contemporary approaches to a balanced, embodied and relational realism such as the approaches offered by Edgar Morin (1986), Roy Bhaskar (2002), Ted Slingerland (2008) and others.

Finally, an integral approach to meta-data analysis and synthesis would take further the contemporary developments in the meta-analysis of research data, to establish a more holistic meta-layer research perspective. Ritzer has defined the basic elements of meta-data analysis as follows: 'meta-data-analysis takes as its subject a range of studies of a given phenomena and seeks to gain an overall sense of them and to aggregate the data in order to come to a more general conclusion about a given issue' (Ritzer 2006: para 6). Such an approach has been sketched out within the field of health research by Margaret Sandelowski and her colleagues (Sandelowski, Barroso and Voils 2007) in the integration of qualitative research findings. Of course, this research stream has been growing since the 1970s with the establishment of meta-analytical research techniques by Glass (1976). However, there is much more that needs to be accomplished in the analysis of research findings that could contribute to a more evidence-based approach to meta-level research (Petticrew and Roberts 2006; Littell et al. 2008), taking into account broader conceptions of evidence than those often defended on the basis of restricted and one-sided methods like double blind test series (Chandler and Torbert 2003).

The fields of meta-theory, meta-method, meta-hermeneutics and meta-data analysis and synthesis together describe the interacting key branches of an overarching meta-studies. While there has been some tradition to the meta-theory branch of this field, little work has been done on raising awareness about the other three branches, and still less on the complex interactions between these different meta-studies branches on the one hand, and between the meta-layer and the other layers on the other hand. In identifying this overall scheme we hope that a greater awareness of the boundary-crossing possibilities for connecting streams of meta-layer research is made possible.

The meta-studies framework described here is not without its precedents and several similar models have been proposed in the areas of sociology (Zhao 1991), healthcare (Finfgeld 2003; Paterson, Thorne, Canam and Jillings 2001), business marketing (Leong 1985), knowledge management (Gadomski 2001), and in the history of science studies (Holton 1973, 1975).

Most of these approaches are smaller in scope in that they focus on narrower disciplinary interests and include only two or three of the four branches of learning/knowledge development. The meta-synthesis model of Paterson and her colleagues for example, proposes a meta-layer integration of qualitative health research that includes meta-theory, meta-methodology and meta-data-analysis but leaves out meta-hermeneutics.

To sum up, integral meta-studies are particular forms of boundary-crossing meta-layer science in that they:

1. Attempt to develop overarching frameworks that are meta-disciplinary in their scope—that is, they move across disciplinary boundaries and are not confined within mainstream demarcations;
2. Utilize meta-layer resources such as other meta-theories and meta-methodologies in the building and testing of their products; and
3. Often (but not necessarily) overtly identify themselves as belonging to an 'integral/integralist' or 'transdisciplinary' tradition in or across philosophy, history, sociology, psychology or spirituality.

Integral meta-studies make explicit reference to (1) the goal of raising consciousness in the sense of Abbott (2001: 5) recalling that 'we should become explicit about what is implicit in our practices'; (2) to the enunciation of emancipatory goals (as stressed by Bhaskar 2002; Dussel 2002; Giri 2006a; Wilber 2000a, among others); and (3) to the central place of self-critical awareness in performing research in terms of collective reflexivity in truth seeking (Maton 2003).

Conclusion

> Indeed, knowledge acquired on knowledge becomes a means of knowledge shedding light on the knowledge which allowed to acquire it. We can . . . now step from one layer of knowledge to the next and the other way round. At the same time we can envisage a transformative development in which the elaborative knowledge tries to know itself on the basis of the knowledge it elaborates, and which thus becomes collaborative.
>
> — EDGAR MORIN (1986: 232).

Interestingly, the three basic attitudes towards knowledge-building that we have discussed in this chapter (namely, bounded specialism, boundary-crossing integration and deconstruction) seem to have been in contention for a considerable period of time, as the following quote shows, and will most likely continue to do so:

Evidence from the fourth century BCE reveals not one but a broad range of exegetical attitudes, all of which would reappear in some guise in later periods of textual growth: exegetes heatedly defending or attacking the integrity of single traditions or 'schools'; high-level syncretists ... fusing traditions with abandon; and, at the opposite extreme, anti-text radicals, reacting to the 'clamour of the schools', some of whom eventually turned into scepticism on human knowledge in general. . . . These movements tended to rise and fall. . . . (Farmer et al. 2000: 69–70)

Today, the 'single traditions' mentioned in this quote can be identified with the disciplinary or interdisciplinary research paradigms and the sub-disciplinary research fields keen to defend and extend their influence by attacking their adversaries in endless science and paradigm wars (Flyvbjerg 2001; Oakley 1999) in their competition for reputation and limited resources. The 'high-level syncretists' appear as advocates of integrative meta-approaches whereas the deconstructive postmodernists correspond fairly well to the radicals trying to pull the rug out from under the feet of both, the intra- and the cross-boundary scholars. From a self-reflective meta-perspective each of these attitudes has its specific role to play. They are actually correcting each other's onesidedness. If an overall balance is maintained the sceptics stimulate reflexivity and creativity in those attempting to construct knowledge systems. The sceptics are, in turn, prevented from becoming nihilists, the syncretists get rich material to draw from the others while being prevented from gliding down the dangerous path of totalizing reality (see Weinstein and Weinstein 1992), whereas the specialists can make their enclaves livable and healthy through an openness to the provisions that come from outside their particular specialties. This receptiveness will safeguard them from the dangers of conceptual inbreeding and disciplinary autism (Gasper 2004). As Giri (2002: 107) puts it bluntly:

A transcendental perspective makes us aware of the contingent nature of our locations but in order that these contingent locations are not left unattended to degenerate into closed ponds where the water is stagnant and stinky, it requires the art of establishing connection among different contingent locations.

None of these three types of positions, practices and trajectories could and should dominate the other two if there is to be a strive for processual optima in knowledge generation. As long as one of them is weak—as are meta-studies programmes today in institutional terms—the overall capacity of the human endeavour of making sense of the world, of each other and of oneself is severely hampered, as also our collective capacity to transform our societies towards sustainable living. We are convinced that each scholar can take great advantage in training her/his ability to adopt and alternate between these three vantage points, and so do research groups, institutes, research traditions and systems of higher education (Molz 2010).

Overall, regarding the priorities of funding of research projects, recruitment of scholars and training of young researchers, the scholarship of integration across boundaries based on variants of integral meta-studies needs to become as fully developed and recognized as the scholarship of discovery inside specific fields. By far, this is not yet the case. On the contrary, until today there remains a widespread ignorance and neglect of traditions of boundary-crossing, meta-perspective reflection and pluralistic integration within the (social) sciences. This is due to the almost exclusive organization of research in compartmentalized specialties (Russell 2005), to which, sometimes, active though partly ill-informed institutional opposition is added (Ritzer 1992). In the context of global crises, boundary-crossing initiatives to which meta-studies belong, instead of being considered as the spearheads of innovation, which they actually often are, and as core for the future-building capacity of research and higher education, are among the areas most threatened by cuts in funding (Gasper 2004; Turner 2000). Only collective action and coordination between integral, transdisciplinary and boundary-crossing researchers, far-sighted research administrators and progressive funders can change the hyperdominance of bounded empirical and middle-layer research. For these reasons, and many others, meta-studies can and must not only cross boundaries between disciplines and cultures but also the theory-practice line regarding its own institutionalization.

In this chapter we have outlined the place we see for meta-layer research in the overall landscape of the social sciences and other disciplines and interdisciplinary domains. We provided a rough sketch of how research from a meta-perspective could be legitimated and enhanced along the lines of an integral meta-studies. The framework for integral meta-studies has been structured on the basis of deep universals of human embodied cognition, action and sociality. The intention has been to catalyse the further development of (social) research generally, of integral sciences more specifically, and the active involvement of meta-layer research in real-life future building activities. This is an open proposal, a call. We are well aware that integral meta-studies in the social sciences, and actually in all sciences, is at its very beginning. It can only be developed as a larger collective undertaking—a joint undertaking of researchers with a balanced array of cultural and disciplinary roots. But the promise in opening up the richness of these sense-making tools is that they can inspire visions and become a rich practical resource for boundary-crossing integrative research, not only for social scientists but also as a cultural heritage of humanity. As Galtung and Inayatullah (1997: 164) write regarding macro-historians:

Each thinker emerges from a particular discourse and . . . attempts to create new categories of the social and the transcendental that create the possibilities of new discourses. In this sense, their new categories cease to belong to the original thinker. Rather, they become part of the historical collective intellectual space.

And Edgar Morin (1986: 25) too reminds readers that:

the knowledge of knowledge shouldn't be constituted as a privileged domain for privileged thinkers, as a competency of experts, as a speculative luxury for philosophers: this is a historical task for everyone and for all of us. It should go down if not to the streets then into the heads, even though this probably requires a revolution in the heads.

In an atmosphere of dramatic global changes of all kinds, the generation of young people growing up at this time is subject to both unprecedented potential and unprecedented threat. Creative and critical sense-making is crucial in this new axial era and it requires a broad, informed and appreciative openness as well as a playful, joyful attitude towards humanity's diverse scientific heritage—an attitude that can move beyond rigid identifications and closed-down discourses. How can such an integral understanding encompassing the entire range of dimensions of sense-making make inroads into education and research more widely? How can they become a meeting place between philosophers, researchers and activists in transformative social movements (Giri 2006a)? These questions will need to be addressed on multiple fronts and one of those fronts will be the development of integrative research streams. Towards that goal, we have proposed here an intermediate, catalytic step and a methodically feasible means which consists in collectively investing in the further deployment of integral meta-studies in a pluralistic and dialogical understanding. We offer this approach as a response to the 'call for a trans-civilizational dialogue on our foundational presuppositions about self, culture and society' (Giri in this volume).

References

Abbott, A.D. (2001), *Chaos of Disciplines*, Chicago: University of Chicago Press.

Aerts, D. et al. (2007), *World Views: From Fragmentation to Integration*, Internet Edition, Retrieved 31 July 2014 from http://pespmc1.vub.ac.be/CLEA/Reports/WorldviewsBook.html.

Ashmore, M. (1989), *The Reflexive Thesis: Wrighting Sociology of Scientific Knowledge*, Chicago: University of Chicago Press.

Bahm, A.J. (1980), 'Interdisciplinology: The Science of Interdisciplinary Research', *Nature and System*, vol. 2, pp. 29–35.

Barrow, J.D. (1999), *Impossibility: The Limits Of Science and the Science Of Limits*, Oxford, NY: OUP.

Bateson, G. (1972), *Steps to an Ecology of Mind: Collected Essays in Anthropology, Psychiatry, Evolution, and Epistemology*, Chicago: University of Chicago Press.

Beck, U. (2002), 'The Cosmopolitan Society and its Enemies', *Theory, Culture & Society*, vol. 19, no. 1, pp. 17–44.

Bendle, M.F. (1996), 'Logics of Integration and Disintegration in Contemporary Social Theory', *Journal of Sociology*, vol. 32, no. 3, pp. 70–84

Bhaskar, R. (1999), *Roy Bhaskar interviewed*, Retrieved 31 July 2014 from http://www.raggedclaws.com/criticalrealism/archive/rbhaskar_rbi.html.

———(2002), *The Philosophy of Meta-Reality: Creativity, Love and Freedom*, New Delhi: Sage.

Bhaskar, R., M. Archer, A. Collier, T. Lawson and A. Norrie (1998), *Critical realism: Essential Readings*, London: Routledge

Boyer, E.L. (1990), *Scholarship Reconsidered: Priorities of the Professoriate*, Princeton, NJ: Carnegie Foundation for the Advancement of Teaching.

———(1994), 'Scholarship Reconsidered: Priorities for a New Century', in *Universities in the Twenty-first Century*, ed. G. Rigby, London: National Commission on Education.

Chandler, D. and B. Torbert (2003), 'Transforming Inquiry and Action, Interweaving 27 Flavors of Action Research', *Action Research*, vol. 1, no. 2, pp. 133–52.

Christopher, J.C. and M.H. Bickhard (2007), 'Culture, Self and Identity: Interactivist Contributions to a Metatheory for Cultural Psychology', *Culture & Psychology*, vol. 13, no. 3, pp. 259–95.

Cilliers, P. (2005), 'Knowledge, Limits and Boundaries', *Futures*, vol. 37, no. 7, pp. 605–13

Clark, B.R. (1995), *Places of Inquiry: Research and Advanced Education in Modern Universities*, Berkeley, CA: University of California Press.

Colomy, P. (1991), 'Metatheorizing in a Postpositivist Frame', *Sociological Perspectives*, vol. 34, no. 3, pp. 269–86.

Creswell, J.W. (2009), *Research Design: Qualitative, Quantitative, and Mixed Methods Approaches*, 3rd edn., Thousand Oaks, CA: Sage.

Davies, M.L. (2003), 'Thinking Practice: On the Concept of an Ecology of Knowledge', in *Breaking the Disciplines: Reconceptions in Knowledge, Art, and Culture*, ed. M.L. Davies and M. Meskimmon, London: I.B. Tauris, pp. 9–34

Dupré, J. (1995), *The Disorder of Things: Metaphysical Foundations of the Disunity of Science*, Cambridge: MA: Harvard University Press.

———(2003), *Human Nature and the Limits of Science*, Oxford, UK: OUP.

Dussel, E. (1985), *Philosophy of Liberation*, New York: Orbis Books.

———(2002), 'World-system and 'trans'-modernity', *Nepantla–Views from South*, vol. 3, no. 2, pp. 221–44.

———(2009), 'A New Age in the History of Philosophy: The World Dialogue between Philosophical Traditions', *Philosophy and Social Criticism*, vol. 35, no. 5, pp. 499–516

Eckensberger, L.H. (2002), 'Paradigms Revisited: From Incommensurability to Respected Complementarity', in *Between Culture and Biology: Perspectives on Ontogenetic Development*, ed. H. Keller, Y. H. Poortinga and A. Schölmerich, Cambridge, UK: CUP, pp. 341–83

————(2003), 'Wanted: A Contextualized Psychology: Plea for a Cultural Psychology Based on Action Theory', in *Cross-cultural Perspectives in Human Development*, ed. T.S. Saraswati, New Delhi: Sage, pp. 70–101

Edwards, M.G. (2008), 'Where's the Method to Our Integral Madness? An Outline of an Integral Meta-studies', *Journal of Integral Theory and Practice*, vol. 3, no. 2, pp. 165–94.

————(2010), *Organisational Transformation for Sustainability: An Integral Metatheory*, New York: Routledge.

Engeström, Y. (1987), *Learning by Expanding: An Activity-Theoretical Approach to Developmental Research*, Helsinki: Orienta-Konsultit.

————(2009), 'The Future of Activity Theory', in *Learning and Expanding with Activity Theory*, ed. A. Sannino, H. Daniels and K.D. Gutierrez, New York: CUP, pp. 303–26.

Esbjörn-Hargens, S. (2006), 'Integral Research: A Multi-method Approach to Investigating Phenomena', *Constructivism in the Human Sciences*, vol. 11, no. 1, pp. 79–107.

Esbjörn-Hargens, S. and K. Wilber (2006), 'Toward a Comprehensive Integration of Science and Religion: A Post-metaphysical Approach', in *The Oxford handbook of Religion and Science,* ed. P. Clayton and Z.R. Simpson, Oxford: OUP, pp. 523–46.

Farmer, S., J.B. Henderson and M. Witzel (2000), 'Neurobiology, Layered Texts, and Correlative Cosmologies: A Cross-cultural Framework for Pre-modern History', *Bulletin of the Museum of Far Eastern Antiquities*, vol. 72, pp. 48–90.

Finfgeld, D.L. (2003), 'Metasynthesis: The State of the Art– So Far', *Qualitative Health Research*, vol. 13, no. 7, pp. 893–904

Fiske, D.W. and R.A. Shweder, eds. (1986), *Metatheory in Social Science: Pluralisms and Subjectivities*, Chicago: University of Chicago Press.

Flick, U. (1992), 'Triangulation Revisited: Strategy of Validation or Alternative?', *Journal for the Theory of Social Behaviour*, vol. 22, no. 2, pp. 175–97.

Floriani, A. (1993), 'Negotiating what Counts: Roles and Relationships, Texts and Contexts, Content and Meaning', *Linguistics and Education*, vol. 5, pp. 214–74.

Flyvbjerg, B. (2001), *Making Social Science Matter: Why Social Inquiry Fails and How it Can Succeed Again*, Cambridge: CUP.

Foley, K.J. (2005), *Meta management*, Sydney: Standards Australia.

Fuchs, S. (1992), 'Relativism and Reflexivity in the Sociology of Scientific Knowledge', in *Metatheorizing,* ed. G. Ritzer, Newbury Park: Sage, pp. 135–50.

Gadomski, A.M. (2001), 'Meta-knowledge Unified Framework', http://erg4146. casaccia.enea.it/Meta-know-1.htm, accessed 31 July 2014.

Galtung, J. and S. Inayatullah (1997), *Macrohistory and Macrohistorians: Perspectives on Individual, Social, and Civilizational Change*, Westport, CT: Praeger.

Gasper, D. (2004), 'Interdisciplinarity: Building Bridges and Nurturing a Complex Ecology of Ideas', in *Creative Social Research: Rethinking Theories and Methods*, ed. Ananta Kumar Giri, Oxford: Lexington Books, pp. 308–44

Giddens, A. (1987), *Social Theory and Modern Sociology*, Stanford: Stanford University Press.

Giri, Ananta Kumar (2002), 'The Calling of a Creative Transdisciplinarity', *Futures*, vol. 34, no. 1, pp. 103–15

————(2006a), 'Creative Social Research: Rethinking Theories and Methods and the Calling of an Ontological Epistemology of Participation', *Dialectical Anthropology*, vol. 30, pp. 227–71.

————(2006b), 'Cosmopolitanism and Beyond: Towards a Multiverse of Transformations', *Development and Change*, vol. 37, no. 6, pp. 1277–92.

————(2009), *Learning the Art of Wholeness: Integral Education and Beyond*, Chennai: Madras Institute of Developmental Studies

Glass, G.V. (1976), 'Primary, Secondary, and Meta-Analysis of Research', *Educational Researcher*, vol. 11, pp. 3–8.

Gülerce, A. (1997), 'Change in the Process of Change: Coping with Indeterminism', in *Process of Change and Indeterminism,* ed. A. Fogel, A. Lyra and J. Valsiner, Hillsdale, NJ: Plenum, pp. 39–64.

Gusdorf, G. (1977), 'Past, Present and Future of Interdisciplinary Research', *International Social Science Journal*, vol. 29, no. 4, pp. 580–600.

Heron, J. (1996), *Co-operative Inquiry: Research into the Human Condition*, London: Sage.

Holton, G. (1973), *Thematic Origins of Scientific Thought: Kepler to Einstein*, Cambridge, MA: Harvard University Press.

————(1975), 'On the Role of Themata in Scientific Thought', *Science*, vol. 188, no. 4186, pp. 328–34.

Hutcheon, L. (1993), 'Beginning to Theorize Postmodernism', in *A Postmodern Reader*, ed. J.P. Natoli and L. Hutcheon, Albany, NY: SUNY Press, pp. 243–72.

Jantsch, E. (1972), 'Towards Interdisciplinarity and Transdisciplinarity in Education and Innovation', in *Interdisciplinarity; Problems of Teaching and Research in Universities*, ed. L. Apostel, G. Berger, A. Briggs and G. Michaud, Paris: CERI/OECD, pp. 97–121.

Kagan, J. (2009), *The Three Cultures: Natural Sciences, Social Sciences, and the Humanities in the 21st Century*, Cambridge: CUP.

Kolb, D.A. (1984), *Experiential Learning: Experience as the Source of Learning and Development*, Englewood Cliffs, NJ: Prentice Hall.

Lakoff, G. (1990), 'The Invariance Hypothesis: Is Abstract Reason Based on Image-Schemas?', *Cognitive Linguistics*, vol. 1, no. 1, pp. 39–74.

Lakoff, G. and M. Johnson (1999), *Philosophy in the Flesh: The Embodied Mind and its Challenge to Western Thought*, New York: Basic Books.

Leong, S.M. (1985), 'Metatheory and Metamethodology in Marketing: A Lakatosian Reconstruction', *The Journal of Marketing*, vol. 49, no. 4, pp. 23–40.

Littell, J.H., J. Corcoran and V.K. Pillai (2008), *Systematic Reviews and Meta-Analysis*, New York: OUP.

Lyotard, J.F. (1993), *The Postmodern Explained: Correspondance, 1982–85*, Minneapolis: University of Minnesota Press.

Lyotard, J. (1984), *The Postmodern Condition*, Manchester: Manchester University Press.

Masterman, M. (1970), 'The Nature of a Paradigm', in *Criticism and the Growth of Knowledge*, ed. I. Lakatos and A. Musgrave, Cambridge: CUP, pp. 59–89.

Maton, K. (2003), 'Reflexivity, Relationism & Research, Pierre Bourdieu and the Epistemic Condition of Social Scientific Knowledge', *Space & Culture*, vol. 6, no.1, pp. 52–65.

Mingers, J. (2006), *Realising Systems Thinking: Knowledge and Action in Management Science*, New York: Springer.

Mohanty, J.N. (2000), *The Self and its Other: Philosophical Essays*, New Delhi: OUP.

Molz, M. (2010), 'Contemporary Integral Education Research: A Transnational and Transparadigmatic Overview', in *Integral education, New Directions for Higher Learning*, ed. S. Esbjörn-Hargens, J. Reams and O. Gunnlaugson, Albany, NY: SUNY Press, pp. 317–30

Morin, E. (1986), *La méthode 3. La connaissance de la connaissance*, Paris: Seuil.

Nicolescu, B. (2002), *Manifesto of Transdisciplinarity*, Albany, NY: State University of New York Press.

Oakley, A. (1999), 'Paradigm Wars: Some Thoughts on a Personal and Public Trajectory', *International Journal of Social Research Methodology*, vol. 2, pp. 247–54.

Overton, W.F. (2007), 'A Coherent Metatheory for Dynamic Systems: Relational Organicism-Contextualism', *Human Development*, vol. 50, pp. 154–9.

Paterson, B.L., S.E. Thorne, C. Canam and C. Jillings (2001), *Meta-study of Qualitative Health Research: A Practical Guide to Meta-Analysis and Meta-Synthesis*, Thousand Oaks, CA: Sage.

Peirce, C.S. (1891), 'The Architecture of Theories', *The Monist*, vol. 1, no. 2, pp. 161–76.

Petticrew, M. and H. Roberts (2006), *Systematic Reviews in the Social Sciences*, Malden, MA: Blackwell.

Reich, K.H. (2002), *Developing the Horizons of the Mind Relational and Contextual Reasoning and the Resolution of Cognitive Conflict*, Cambridge, UK: CUP.

Rescher, N. (1999), *The Limits of Science*, Pittsburgh, PA: University of Pittsburgh Press.

Ritzer, G. (1991), *Metatheorizing in Sociology*, Lexington, MA: Lexington Books
——— (1992), 'Metatheorizing in Sociology: Explaining the Coming of Age', in *Metatheorizing*, ed. G. Ritzer, Newbury Park: Sage, pp. 7–25.

Ritzer, G. and S. Goodman (2006), 'Postmodern Social Theory', in *Handbook of Sociological Theory*, ed. J.H. Turner, New York: Kluwer/Plenum, pp. 151–69.

Ritzer, G., S. Zhao and J. Murphy (2006), 'Metatheorizing in Sociology: The Basic Parameters of the Potential Contributions of Postmodernism', in *Handbook of Sociological Theory*, ed. J.H. Turner, New York: Kluwer/Plenum, pp. 113–31.

Robbins, D. (2003), 'Vygotsky's Non-Classical Dialectical Metapsychology', *Journal for the Theory of Social Behaviour*, vol. 33, no. 3, pp. 303–12.

Rodgers, S., M. Booth and E. Joan (2003), 'The Politics of Disciplinary Advantage', *History of Intellectual Culture*, vol. 3, no. 1, pp. 1–20.

Russell, A. (2005), 'No Academic Borders? Transdisciplinarity in University Teaching and Research', *Australian Universities Review*, vol. 48, no. 1, pp. 35–41.

Salthe, S.N. (1985), *Evolving Hierarchical Systems*, New York: Columbia University Press.

Sandelowski, M., J. Barroso and C.I. Voils (2007), 'Using Qualitative Metasummary to Synthesize Qualitative and Quantitative Descriptive Findings', *Research in Nursing & Health*, vol. 30, no. 1, pp. 99–111.

Scharmer, C.O. (2007), *Theory U: Leading from the Future as it Emerges*, Cambridge, MA: The Society for Organizational Learning.

Shweder, R.A. (1984), 'Anthropology's Romantic Rebellion against the Enlightenment, or there's More to Thinking than Reason and Evidence', in *Culture Theory: Essays on Mind, Self, and Emotion*, ed. R.A. Shweder and R.A. LeVine, Cambridge: CUP, pp. 27–66.

———(2001), 'A Polytheistic Conception of the Sciences and the Virtues of Deep Variety', *Annals of the New York Academy of Sciences*, vol. 935, pp. 217–32.

Skinner, Q., ed. (1985), *The Return of Grand Theory in the Human Sciences*, Cambridge: CUP.

Slingerland, E.G. (2008), *What Science Offers the Humanities: Integrating Body and Culture*, Cambridge: CUP.

Snow, C.P. (1958), *The Two Cultures*, Cambridge: CUP.

Sorokin, P. A. (1958), 'Integralism is My Philosophy', in *This is My Philosophy*, ed. W. Burnett, London: Ruskin House, pp. 180–9.

Stenmark, M. (2008), 'Science and the Limits of Knowledge', in *Clashes of Knowledge*, ed. P. Meusburger, M. Welker and E. Wunder, Dordrecht: Springer, pp. 111–20.

Sternberg, R.J. (1984), 'Toward a Triarchic Theory of Human Intelligence', *The Behavioral and Brain Sciences*, vol. 7, pp. 269–315.

Szostak, R. (2004), *Classifying Science: Phenomena, Data, Theory, Method, Practice*, Berlin: Springer.

Törnebohm, H. (1971), 'Reflections on Scientific Research', *Scientia*, vol. 106, pp. 225–43.

Torbert, W. (1991), *The Power of Balance: Transforming Self, Society, and Scientific Inquiry*, Newbury Park, CA: Sage.

Tsoukas, H. and C. Knudsen (2003), 'Introduction: The Need for Meta-theoretical Reflection in Organisation Theory', in *The Oxford Handbook of Organisation Theory*, ed. H. Tsoukas and Knudsen, Oxford, UK: OUP, pp. 1–36.

Turner, J.H. (1991), 'Developing Cumulative and Practical Knowledge through Metatheorizing', *Sociological Perspectives*, vol. 34, no. 3, pp. 249–68.

Turner, J.H. and D.E. Boyns (2006), 'The Return of Grand Theory', in *Handbook of Sociological Theory*, ed. J.H. Turner, New York: Kluwer/Plenum, pp. 353–78.

Turner, S. (2000), 'What are Disciplines? And How is Interdisciplinarity Different?', in *Practising Interdisciplinarity*, ed. N. Stehr and P. Weingart, Toronto: University of Toronto Press, pp. 46–65.

Valsiner, J. (2000), *Culture and Human Development: An Introduction*, London: Sage.

Van Gigch, J.P. (1991), *System Design Modeling and Metamodeling*, New York: Plenum.

Van Valen, L. (1972), 'Laws in Biology and History: Structural Similarities of Academic Disciplines', *New Literary History*, vol. 3, no. 2, pp. 409–19.

Wallerstein, I. (1995), 'What are We Bounding, and Whom, When We Bound Social Research', *Social Research*, vol. 62, no. 4, pp. 839–56.

Weingart, P. (2000), 'Interdisciplinarity: The Paradoxical Discourse', in *Practising interdisciplinarity*, ed. N. Stehr and P. Weingart, Toronto: University of Toronto Press, pp. 25–41.

Weinstein, D. and M.A. Weinstein (1992), 'The Post-Modern Discourse of Metatheory', in *Metatheorizing*, ed. G. Ritzer, Newbury Park: Sage, pp. 135–50.

West, C. (1993), 'The New Cultural Politics of Difference', in *Social Theory*, ed. C.C. Lemert, Boulder: Westview Press, pp. 577–89.

Wilber, K. (2000a), *The Collected Works of Ken Wilber: Sex, Ecology, Spirituality*, vol. 6, Boston: Shambhala.

———(2000b), 'Introduction to vol. 7', in *The Collected Works of Ken Wilber*, vol. 7, ed. K. Wilber, Boston: Shambhala.

Zhao, S. (1991), 'Metatheory, Metamethod, Meta-Data-Analysis, What, Why, and How?', *Sociological Perspectives*, vol. 34, no. 3, pp. 377–90.

4

B E T S Y   T A Y L O R

Body-Place-Commons: Reclaiming
Professional Practice, Reclaiming Democracy

In opening new pathways of creative social research, Ananta Kumar Giri continues his important efforts, over many years, to reground theory. In this chapter, I engage his call for an 'ontological epistemology of participation' in four ways. First, I look at the concrete political ecology that results from what he describes as 'one-dimensional epistemic violence'. The dominance of global market forces under neo-liberal globalization is crucially enabled by what I have elsewhere called 'logics of fungibility' (Reid and Taylor 2003, 2006, 2010). These are systems of knowledge that reduce persons, creatures and earth to the infinitely interchangeable. Academic professions and government regulatory bureaucracies are deeply complicit in legitimating these logics of fungibility. This chapter tries to explore the connections between this violence and the reduction of knowledge to narrow epistemic protocols that Giri so powerfully describes. Second, I look at the narrowing of knowledge to epistemology as a problem of power and social relationships among professionals. Third, I critique postmodern social theory that tries to overcome the one dimensionality of epistemic violence by denying dimensionality itself. Finally, to respond to Giri's call, I briefly suggest ways to reground theoretical practices in embodied, placed care for the commons—as Reid and I propose in our recent book, *Recovering the Commons: Democracy, Place, and Global Justice.*

The Role of Experts in Chronotopic Reframing of Citizen Concerns and Debates

I have come to these concerns about neo-liberalism and transdisciplinarity through a long loop outside academe. I have sat through many grassroots meetings over two decades (on topics ranging from strip mining, water quality, public health, community forestry, cultural heritage and identity, toxins, air quality, biodiversity, local food economies, etc.) In such meetings, questions about science keep coming up. Particularly astonishing were similarities between different parts of the world in questions citizens raised about the scientific frameworks that they encountered in regimes of social and environmental planning that affected their lives. Such regimes brought together academic and professional forms of knowledge with official government systems of regulation and management. Whether sitting in a community hall in rural southern USA or a women's self help group in north-east India, I have heard echoes of the similar concerns—suggesting that something structural is going on, a grass roots interrogation of the limits and negative consequences of forms of knowledge built into current forms of the nation state.[1]

On one hand, grass roots citizen's organizations argued for kinds of knowledge that are place-based and integrative. On the other hand, regulatory and policy systems often appear to them to be on trajectories of increasing fragmentation, at least in terms of the causal and spatio-temporal frameworks that government applied to assessment, management and planning. This happens across three dimensions: causality, space and time— creating big gaps between grass roots and official ontological frameworks for constructing the objects under contestation (whether local watersheds, forests, children's bodily health, etc.) I have argued that grass rooted civic action and discourse tends to frame questions and solutions as multi-causal, multi-scalar and multi-temporal—out of concern for real-world risks and consequences that might affect them and the places and people that matter to them (Taylor 2009). However, government action and discourse, at its best, often appears in public contestation to narrow and fragment the spatio-temporal and causal frameworks around questions and solutions. At its worst, these constrictions of space, time and causality can be seen as ways to shut out citizen voices, and empower economic elites—by creating a kind of shell game in which the matter under discussion is continually reframed within space-time frames that exclude real-world causal patterns and consequences and pressing questions of habitability and life stewardship. Diverse grass roots imaginaries can show similar high levels of anger when official perspectives fracture community concerns—as if holding a shattered mirror up to realities that the communities experienced as integrative.[2]

This shattering of matrices for time, space and causality compound the difficulties citizens face in conceptualizing, deliberating and acting on collective concerns, hopes and possibilities. To engage in contestation about the well-being of their bodies, places and the commons on which they depend, citizen organizations typically have to develop 'counterexpertise' (Fischer 2000) to match the specialized skills and mandates of the government agencies with which they deal. Again and again, it has been observed that citizen organizations must do an exhausting amount of intellectual labour to break multi-causal local realities into component issues, reconstruct them into appropriate technical or bureaucratic languages, and reframe and repackage their analyses according to the contradictory and limited time frames of disparate government agency planning protocols. Contrary to the displacing ideology of most official science, grass roots concerns about the lack of accurate and sufficiently field-tested science arises directly from the place-based nature of these struggles. Place-based matrices of political action do not necessarily oppose feeling and reason. Rather, they can provide durable chrono-topic frameworks for weaving feeling and reason together with laboriously gathered scientific understanding.

Professions, the Fragmentation of Knowledge and Displacement from Particularity

Professions rose in the late nineteenth century based on guild-like systems for certifying the calibre of individuals and programmes in their ranks. The great strength of this system came from its democratic nature, insofar as it encouraged excellence through lateral identity formation among peers. It also, remarkably, created large numbers of stable, middle-class jobs that were, to a significant extent, organized around logics of the commons. Despite recent enclosure of ideas as private property in heavily corporatized parts of the contemporary university, most of academe, most of the time, has treated the knowledge it produces as an intellectual commons— accessible to other scholars and the general public (with appropriate recognition of authorship) in support of intellectual inquiry and public interest. Despite their competitiveness, the daily practices of professional life within such a commons-centred livelihood have, at their most democratic, produced a fabric of intersubjectivity that nurtures subjects with capacity for, and pleasure in, plurality—open-ended speech among peers engaging a world-in-common with courage, creativity and a sense of personal security. As Peirce insisted, the freedom and integrity of scholarly inquiry can only arise from, and be secured by, a 'community of inquiry' (Westbrook 2005).

Despite its vicissitudes in an era increasingly dominated by private interest ideologies, professionalism still retains ideals that promise a measure of personal dignity, and, meaningful work for something greater than one's private interests. A democratic and mutually empowering fabric of life based on labour for an intellectual commons also provides certain kinds of security for professionals as workers, that most workers lost when they were displaced from the civic and environmental commons that supported other livelihoods. Professional bodies have been able to secure high wages through archaic guild strategies vis-à-vis the state, including monopoly control of whole sectors of more or less artisanal work—although this negotiating power has plummeted in recent decades in professional sectors not connected with high capital accumulation industries. The increasing vulnerability of professions and expert knowledge to enclosure within logics of fungibility is directly proportional to the collapse of stewardship of the commons, and public assets, as a key role for government.

Having noted democratizing features of professionalism, it is now necessary to turn to negative tendencies. Foremost in most discussions of modern knowledge systems is the problem of fragmentation. The proliferation of disciplines and sub-disciplines based on ever increasing methodological and epistemological specialization has had the effect of chopping up the world into bits—which are then divided up among disciplines in a way not unlike the European scramble for Africa. Critical social theory has produced large and eloquent literature critiquing these trends, from Husserl's last anguished book (1970) through the efforts in recent decades to found interdisciplinary social theory and cultural studies programmes. Never successful in shifting the centres of power and funding streams, inter- and transdisciplinarity continue as guiding goals for many efforts within academe.

In addition, to this fragmentation of the world, there are ways in which displacement and disembodiment were unfortunately (and unnecessarily) built into professional subject formation. This creates an unworlding of professions, a tendency towards post communal identity (Reid 2001). In important ways, the intersubjectivity of professional disciplines was made out of the shared 'stuff' of common methodological training and evaluation and common disciplinary objects of investigation. Professional expertise then produces, as a sort of by-product, a chronic haunting by a collective subject—the imaginary community of others who use this expertise and before whom this expertise is performed. It also, as many have noted, reconstructs the world according to the logic of one's own expertise—a sort of spectral collective object, predefined according to one's own intellectual tools.

This pushes towards professional practices that have the internal logic of fungibility, even against the conscious intention of practitioners. When disciplinary epistemologies freeze into non-pluralist, fixed protocols, then the collective disciplinary subject is hooked into a mimetic relationship with a collective disciplinary object—which has displaced 'world'.[3] The relationship between Collective Disciplinary Subject and Collective Disciplinary Object then is in danger of losing precisely that slippage which is constituted of plurality, and the best of modernity. At its best, modernity allows a kind of playing around in the relationship between subject and object—as Giri and Strydom both suggest in this volume. The doubt of modernity is best when it is not completely systematic, a sort of serious play within self-conscious (self-disciplined) boundaries—a messing about, trying now this, and now that in aligning, un-aligning and mis-aligning subject and object: 'How do things look if I (we) move from this perspective to that?', 'What happens if this factor is added (or subtracted), emphasized (or backgrounded)?'. This is a non-dualistic play between distancing and re-alignment of subject and object. However, when disciplinary epistemologies or methodologies become fetishized rituals in the court of the Collective Disciplinary Subject, free enquiry becomes more lever than hinge. 'World', remade as Collective Disciplinary Object becomes just something that is predesigned for expertise to move according to its own constitutive and predesigned logic. This evinces the arrogance of Western modernity at its worst—like the grand claim of Archimedes that he could move the world if he had a lever large enough and could find a place to stand. It also embodies the logic of fungibility, whether or not the disciplinary world-levers involved are quantifying or positivistic. The interpretive humanities and social sciences can fall into this as easily as the hard sciences—when they, as collective bodies, are levered into the world in such a way as to reduce the world into constituent elements, and, to containerize and circulate those elements. And, this reduction of the Collective Disciplinary Object inevitably involves a reduction in the Collective Disciplinary Subject as their mimesis binds them into a hall of mirrors without slippage. Husserl pointed to such a dynamic, when he said, 'Merely fact-minded sciences make merely fact-minded people' (Husserl 1970). On the other hand, professional disciplines can reclaim the best of modernity by re-placing and re-embodying themselves and their labour within emergent global justice movements to reclaim the right to steward the commons. As Tim Luke puts it, 'populist resistances are about recollectivizing people and things by finding alternative modernities in modernity to serve more people more fairly more locally' (Luke 1999: 237).

The ideal of professionalization was to create protected zones around communities of enquiry to protect the sovereignty of open-ended, critical discovery. Insofar as disciplines have been able to function as something like democratic republics organized around stewardship of a defined intellectual commons, this has worked well. At its best, the fabric of mutuality in a community of enquiry nurtures plurality which in turn produces methodological and epistemological pluralism, criticality and creativity in work.[4] These features of subject/ world relationship are integrally related to forms of (inter)subjectivity that discourage servility and arrogance, and encourage a passion for thinking. It is important to note how emotion affects intellectual agency. The best guarantee that thinkers will not grovel their talents before Power and Money comes when the pleasures of thought and the joys of conversation among thinkers are strong and relatively free of the fears endemic to chronic self-abasement and self-reconstruction before a spectral Collective Disciplinary Subject or before a boss in an unsatisfying and scary job.

If there is a freezing of the playful distantiations of modernity, and, a chilling of the open-ended and pleasurable mutualities of egalitarian plurality and shared world, the Collective Disciplinary Subject falls head over heels into the paradoxes of sovereignty. This is the result of a distinctively modern vicious circle: no system of order can ground itself, yet modernity recognizes no system of authority except itself. Arendt says that the 'predicament of all modern political bodies, their profound instability [is] the result of some elementary lack of authority' (Arendt 1965: 159). The result, Arendt says, is a distinctively modern need for distinctively modern absolutes. The absolutism she describes in politics is analogous to absolutism in knowledge. If the Collective Disciplinary Subject stakes its rights to define the Collective Disciplinary Object, in the perfection of its epistemic world-levers, it is perilously close to the dynamics Arendt imputes to the French Revolution. The absolutism of the decapitated Sovereign reappears in the absolutism of revolutionary self-founding (Arendt 1965).

One of the successes claimed for modernity has been the production of knowledge, which has improved the lot of humans and improved the world. But this progressivist picture changes if one applies a 'through-put analysis', asking as ecological economists ask of industry, 'But, what happens to it after it is produced?' A tragic by-product of the insulation of academics from public life is inattention to the ways in which epistemologies circulate once they leave academe, and, the way in which they provide conceptual equipment for enframing public deliberations to decrease pluralistic and real world of deliberation. If one looks at environmental and social planning structures from the point of view of people and places affected, the fragmentation of knowledge discussed above becomes a significant political problem.

Social Theory, Flatness and the Critique of Meta-Levels and Unitary Selves

From its beginning, social theory has questioned whether hierarchical regimes of knowledge and power were hidden behind the apparently democratizing Reason of Western modernity. A recurrent concern has been that universalizing knowledge produces multiple layers of knowledge—as abstraction and generalization (seem to) generate meta-levels of thought of ascending degrees of orderliness, clarity and law-likeness. One concern has been that this multi-levelled ontology creates hierarchical and imperializing epistemologies—as when positivist science sidelines or forecloses more hermeneutic, messier epistemologies by claiming ascendancy based on greater clarity and order. But another concern has been that this cognitive hierarchy has elective affinities with other hierarchies (gender, race, ethnicity, caste, etc.) and forms of domination such as those of state, empire and market.

Two kinds of complicities in power and knowledge hierarchies are particularly relevant here. First, I agree with those who argue that régimes of expert knowledge are complicit with rationalizing State and corporate bureaucracies that facilitate the global circuitry of markets that now produce greater inequality than earlier imperialisms. Second, problematic kinds of subject formation are complicit with these systemic patterns. Social theory has given much thought to how the meta-levels of universalizing Reason hide within apparent objectivity a universal Subject—the God's Eye view positioned to surveil messy particularities—which carries covert meanings of male, whiteness, sovereignty, escape from nature and the body. This empowers certain social actors by disempowering others. It also hardwires the subject/object dualism into multiple channels in the circulations of power and authority. Martin Jay describes Merleau-Ponty's critique of the *pensée au survol* as suspicion of that 'high altitude thinking which maintained the Cartesian split between a distant, spectatorial subject and the object of his sight' (1989: 52–3).

In reaction against entangled hierarchies of knowledge, state, market and empire, some social theory, especially in the last several decades, tries to dismantle levels within epistemology and ontology, for fear of meta-levels which purport to control and to transparently encompass and sublate 'lower' levels. Closely related to this, are efforts to dismantle the notion of the 'subject' out of fear that a notion of unitary selfhood requires the perfect adequation of the *pensée au survol*—selves that author themselves from some Archimedean vantage point like an ideal cartographer, and selves that can be known because they are adequated to their objects. All of these concerns have led to an interest, in social theory, in flatness—theories of knowledge that put knowers and known in common ontological scale.

The historical development of the Periodic Table of the Elements exemplifies the efficacy of logics of fungibility—and continues to lend them prestige and legitimacy. By demonstrating that there is a viewpoint from which one can reduce matter to discrete elements, it legitimated a certain kind of essentialization—the attribution of an essence to substances such that they can be pre-known as necessarily displaying a fixed array of traits. This was joined to two other processes. First, this essentialization was a kind of brick-making factory for the reconstruction of 'nature' as machine regulated by a layered hierarchy of 'natural laws'. Second, the mechanistic reconstruction of nature begun in the seventeenth and eighteenth centuries flowed into extraordinary increases in human productive capacity in the nineteenth century and first half of the twentieth century. Husserl's point is still relevant that the success of mechanistic and positivist world views in popular culture had to do with '[t]he exclusiveness with which the total worldview of modern men, in the second half of the 19th century, let itself be determined by the positive scientists and be blinded by the "prosperity" [he uses the English word] they produced' (Husserl 1970: 6). It is an historical accident that logics of fungibility were constructed at the convergence of these three different processes—essentialization by predefinition of traits, hierarchical causal laws, economic and technological transformation. It is crucial to differentiate between the three because they pose different ethical and political challenges.

One may start with the problem of 'essentialization', since social theory has expended much effort, over the past three decades, in combating 'essentialization' as a prime force of domination. The linguistic turn in social theory led to an unfortunate conflation of the positivist essentialization and metalogics discussed earlier with any naming of any entity as enduring over time. Derrida and others drew on Saussure to argue that the relationship between signs and their referents was arbitrary, labile and driven by immanent characteristics of language. Unfortunately, the problems of linguistic representation engulfed reflection about whether there are unitive and durable beings (including 'selves') and what 'stuff' might constitute them. In much social theory, the unmasking of 'essences' became equated with the labour to demonstrate that no one entity can be zipped into one word with nothing hanging out and no room to move and change. But, to say this is to argue from within the logic criticized. Who ever thought that language was a set of pre-labelled, pre-measured body bags? Well, really only positivism in its extreme form. But, positivism is a strong example of the long tendency in Western modernity that Adorno critiques as trapped under the 'law of identity' requiring adequation of subject and its object (Adorno, 1983, 1997). Unfortunately, the battle against 'essentialization' has increasingly and unnecessarily become a debate about representation in general—a 'baroque' (Sanbonmatsu 2004) debate that is displaced and disembodied from sensuous living struggles to attend and tend to the particularity alimenting and secreted by sensuous living creatures.

To say that the problem is how things are named, is to skip over what is distinctive and most dangerous about logics of fungibility. The power of fungibility is the way in which it constructs a label for a 'thing' that guarantees that it is an entity that bears a fixed repertoire of traits. These traits are not just any sort of characteristic. A trait is selected because it is an indicator that the 'thing' will behave in a predictable way. In other words, such a trait is really a marker of repetitive dramas that one can definitely provoke the 'thing' to 'do'. Hydrogen is hydrogen because (1) it can be identified as that which has a set of characteristics that (2) are predictive of hydrogen-like reactions to (3) other 'things' with traits that similarly predict patterns of reaction. This way of essentializing could best be called 'elementalizing' because it reduces things to entities that can be put onto a common grid of mutual interactivity like the Periodic Table of the Elements. The form of the grid and the qualities of its elements construct each other. Nothing can be put into the grid that does not already embody its terms. Because elementalization is produced by reduction, it naturally produces hierarchies of law like regularity. It is the same process run in the opposite direction.

This hierarchy matters not simply because it is a metalogic, but because of its extraordinary power to turn complex beings into fungible items by provoking controlled dramas. It is here that technocratic science, markets and bureaucratic government conjoin. It is for this reason that the political ecology of fungibility poses far more urgent ethical and political dilemmas than questions about 'representation' posed as a general feature of human engagement in the world. The key problem of the modern age is not so much that things are slippery and cannot be easily or safely lassoed by words. The key problem is the political economy in which markets, technocracy and bureaucratic governance displace democratic public space with hegemonic regimes of interlocking and ever expanding grids that pre-label things and beings according to elementalizing categories that ontologically containerize them as entities that are infinitely exchangeable and substitutable—and which kick anything that does not act according to a small repertoire of actions off the game board. It is not a panopticon of observation so much as the construction of a game board which one can navigate only through mimetic obedience to a grid whose logic is not accessible from one's position within it. To cast this only as a problem of representation, or as a problem with the metalogics of modernist 'science', is to overlook the social relations that determine who gets to play the game, and who makes the board it is played on (Latour 2004).

It is this absolutism, that is the mainspring of the *pensée au survol*. To try to undo this absolutism by decapitating anything that sticks its head up and which appears 'meta' is to set up a process, metaphorically speaking, which keep barricading the doors against Sun Kings, while Bonapartes crawl in the windows. It is the cult of epistemic levers that sucks one into the paradoxes of sovereignty—in which Subject is always dualistically opposed to Object (or vice versa). The opposition of self/object should be replaced and re-embodied with the surrounding world from which a particular being arised. If that cannot be done, academe will literally be fiddling while the planet burns. To hold fast to disciplinary epistemic levers, will be to trap oneself in an endless process of self-understanding based on how the world is enframed.

There are two dangers. One is the 'blueprint' thinking in which a reductive academic model is projected onto the world. At best, the 'blueprint' will be both wrong and irrelevant so that it does not affect anything much. At worst, it will remake the world in its own image. One of the horrors of the moonscapes of the post-industrial devastated earth, is the sensation that one is looking into the face of the Collective Disciplinary Subject of technocratic science and neo-liberal economics. But the second danger is the danger of what Sanbanmatsu calls 'baroque theory' (Sanbonmatsu 2004). This is the theory that uproots itself from world, and repots itself in carefully and consciously delimited theoretical frameworks. Unable to move beyond the limits of its pot-bound epistemic base, it implodes in hypertrophy of entangled forms—ever more elaborate twists entrapped in too small and rigid a framework for its forms of life.

Body-Place-Commons

In *Recovering the Commons: Democracy, Place and Global Justice*, Herbert Reid and I turn away from flat ontologies and epistemologies (Reid and Taylor 2010). We feel they do not grapple with important, constitutive forces of domination. Rather than a flat ontology, we propose a folded ontology, in two senses. We propose body-place-commons[5] as ruly and unruly generative matrices which are manifolds of ontologies—multi-levelled, flat, but mostly curved/ing and (un)folded/ing. We call for:

…a rescaling and reclaiming of social being that pivots on the very complex temporalities and spatialities of re-inhabitation—rebuilding infrastructures of embodied being, in particular places, in sedimented and emergent dependencies within ecological matrices and given limits of the non-human surround and placed histories. Body-place-commons is the name we are giving to these chronotopic infrastructures—a theoretical notion developed to try to describe the pivot of social and ecological being which the global justice movement struggles to reclaim. (Reid and Taylor 2010)

Body-place-commons has imminent architectonics which provide something like a meta-level, a certain kind of life-world logic, but one that provides purchase, not vantage, on its mostly wild, occasionally domesticated, heterogeneous, constituent ontologies—what Latour might call 'pluriverse' (Latour 2004). Reid and I argue that body-place-commons provides a site from which to think about the folding, unfolding and enfolding of manifold ontology that is not at all like the *pensée au survol*. Several political, intellectual and moral possibilities follow. We argue that, as a way to kilter multiple knowledges, the architectonics of body-place-commons is immanently dialogical and open in texture—giving it elective affinities with democracy, empowerment and tolerance. Second, as a way to understand across, and with, many differences, body-place-commons is transversalizing not universalizing in the traditional sense. In part, this is because it is in the pragmatist genealogy of 'good enough' truth rather than perfect truth— lessening needs to dominate differences it moves between. It comprises habitational logics, which look for simple recurrent patterns in the mutual transformations of creatures inhabiting worlds and worlds transmuting under the tooth of time. The simplicity and recurrence of these patterns give them a kind of cognitive power—a power that outweighs its fuzziness as merely 'good enough' truth. Third, this approach argues for new alliances between social theory and science. In many ways, social theory emerged over a century ago as a repudiation of Science's claims to *pensée au survol*. Our argument is for a turn toward science, but a critical turn. We urgently call urgently for building far stronger institutional and intellectual alliances between social theory, the field sciences and public arts and humanities, and, between local and professionalized knowledges—in movements for civic and ecological renewal arrayed against conjoined hegemonies of technocracy, scientism and globalization.

Notes

1. For more detail on these processes, see my ethnographic explorations of grass roots social and environmental activism (Taylor 2009).
2. For discussion of similar dynamics of what Mary Hufford calls 'clashing epistemologies' in community/government relations in Appalachia, see Hufford (2001) and McNeil (2007).
3. In our recent book, Reid and I define 'world' as '...that dynamic mesh of relationships among creatures and their ambient surround that provide durable and livable architectonics for creaturely action and environmental sustenance...' (Reid and Taylor: 2010: 8). This definition draws on Arendt's understanding of 'world' but expands it to non-human creatures and processes. We say, 'Hannah Arendt might not have agreed with this extension of world to nonhumans, but our understanding of world draws directly from her thinking about humans. Arendt emphasizes that world is a strange mixture of history as residue from past action and history-in-the-making as sheer openness of new possibilities for action' (Arendt 1958). Human world arises in, and out of, history, with all its particularity and on rush, as people find their lives to be at stake in what happens around them. And so, historical events pile up in traces of meaning and matter— forms of intelligible speech, conscious remembrance, unconscious habit and

ecological engagement. And, world is where this piling up happens, and, where it becomes available for people to make and remake individual and collective life in its particularity. 'Human world is that durable architectonics of engagement that creates the background which actors need to illumine future and present as coherent settings for action, and, into which acts can transmute into remembrance (or habit) that avails past for future action. (Reid and Taylor 2010: 8).

4. I draw on Hannah Arendt's of 'plurality' but expand it to non-humans. In *Recovering the Commons*, Reid and I describe this greening of the structure of feeling which Arendt saw as crucial to democracy, when we say, 'Plurality for Arendt suggests a complex social and cultural field between humans in which there is a non-dualistic relationship between individuation and listening to the other. Plurality is the stuff of democracy—the generative space within public life that catalyses conversations that are open-ended, and, in which persons relate to each other as peers, creating a field of intersubjectivity that cultivates originality of individual being (or what we call particularity in chapter 6). This book struggles to understand what cultural and political frameworks encourage and sustain plurality. We emphasize that plurality must not simply be understood as social or intersubjective. It must not be only framed as dyadic relationships between persons. Rather, we understand plurality as communication that illuminates the worlds that are the generative conditions of personhood—including ecological matrices. This is a greening of Arendt's notions of plurality and democracy.' (Reid and Taylor 2010: 13).

5. We follow Kelso and Engstrøm, who propose the tilde or 'squiggle' (~) as the 'symbolic punctuation for reconciled complementary pairs'—signifying non-dualistic reconciliation of human/nature, mind/body (Kelso and Engstøm 2006).

References

Adorno, T.W. (1983), *Against Epistemology: A Metacritique: Studies in Husserl and the Phenomenological Antinomies*, 1st MIT Press edn., Cambridge, Mass.: MIT Press.

————(1997), *Negative Dialectics*, New York: Continuum.

Arendt, H. (1965), *On Revolution*, Compass Books edn., New York: The Viking Press.

Fischer, F. (2000), *Citizens, Experts, and the Environment: the Politics of Local Knowledge*, Durham: Duke University Press.

Hufford, M. (2001), 'Stalking the Forest Coeval: Fieldwork at the Site of Clashing Social Imaginaries', *Practicing Anthropology*, vol. 23, no. 2, pp. 29–32.

Husserl, E. (1970), *The Crisis of European Sciences and Transcendental Phenomenology*, tr. D. Carr. Evanston, Ill.: Northwestern University Press.

Kelso, J.A.S. and D.A. Engstøm (2006), *The Complementary Nature*, Cambridge, Mass.: MIT Press.

Latour, B. (2004), *Politics of Nature: How to Bring the Sciences into Democracy*, Cambridge, Mass.: Harvard University Press.

Luke, T.W. (1999), *Capitalism, Democracy, and Ecology: Departing from Marx*, Urbana and Chicago: University of Illinois.

McNeil, B. (2007), 'Mountaintop Removal, Bureaucracy, and the Spaces of Disaster', 'Unnatural Disasters', Annual Meetings of the Society for the Anthropology of North America, University of New Orleans, New Orleans, LA, April, pp. 19–21.

Reid, H.G. (2001), 'Democratic Theory and the Public Sphere Project: Rethinking Knowledge, Authority, and Identity', *New Political Science*, vol. 23, no. 4, pp. 517–36.

Reid, H.G. and B. Taylor (2003), 'John Dewey's Aesthetic Ecology of Public Intelligence and the Grounding of Civic Environmentalism', *Ethics and Environment*, vol. 8, no. 1, Special Issue on 'Art, Nature and Social Critique', pp. 74–92.

———(2006), 'Globalization, Democracy, and the Aesthetic Ecology of Emergent Publics for a Sustainable World: Working From John Dewey', *Asian Journal of Social Science*, vol. 34, no. 1, pp. 22–46.

———(2010), *Recovering the Commons: Democracy, Place, and Global Justice*, Urbana & Chicago: University of Illinois Press.

Sanbonmatsu, J. (2004), *The Postmodern Prince: Critical Theory, Left Strategy, and the Making of a New Political Subject*, New York: Monthly Review Press.

Taylor, B. (2009), '"Place" As Pre-political Grounds of Democracy: An Appalachian Case Study in Class Conflict, Forest Politics and Civic Networks', *American Behavioral Scientist*, vol. 52, no. 6, Special Issue on 'Democracy in an Age of Networked Governance: Charting the Currents of Change', ed. Joyce Rothschild and Max Stephenson, Jr., pp. 826–45.

———'Terrains of Justice: Economic Globalization in Appalachian America and the Scaling of Democratic Public Space', Unpublished manuscript.

Westbrook, R.B. (2005), *Democratic Hope: Pragmatism and the Politics of Truth*, Ithaca: Cornell University Press.

5

Kairos and an Ethics of Space: Towards Reconceptualizing Conversations and their Loci

SCOTT SCHAFFER

Ananta Kumar Giri's provocative opening essay in this volume gives us a great deal of material to consider when thinking about the direction social theorizing must take in order to adequately address the problems our globe faces today. In that piece, Giri calls on us to consider new ways of interacting with, communicating with, and acting with those who are Other to Us in ways that not only transcend the traditional subject/object dualism present in social science research, but also enable us to approach other people in ways that go beyond the typical rule-bound approaches offered to us by the usual conceptions of ethics. Implicit in the voluminous development of his notion of 'creative social research' is a twinned ethical conception of 'compassion and confrontation'; that is, Giri calls on us to act with compassion, or 'passion with', those in our social space, and to act in such a way that we confront the barriers and gaps that prevent us from acting in precisely this manner (Giri 2017).

There are to my mind three specific elements of Giri's call that allow us to envision what it is he means by 'creative and critical social research' and which enable me to contribute to this unique conversation about the future of social science research. In particular, I refer to Giri's conceptions of 'ontological sociality' (2017), the 'ontology of autonomy and interpenetration' (2017), and the possibility of social engagement through what Giri calls 'pathways of partial connections' (2017). The first of these, ontological sociality, refers to the idea that our reality is that of sociality; above all else, we are not simply individuals (and institutions are not simply 'society'), but rather we are inherently self-developing creatures who operate within a social, institutional, and interactive context (Giri 2017). By transcending the individual/society divide—and I believe that Giri intends this to be moving beyond this dichotomy in a dialectical manner, preserving both while overcoming the artificially constructed schism between them—we are thereby able to also understand our reality as one in which we not only work to develop ourselves as autonomous self-determining creatures in accordance with some plan for our existence (see Schaffer 2004), but are also penetrated by and impact upon the other human beings with whom we act and interact in our social spaces (Giri 2017), developing a deeper understanding of ourselves through the impacts others have on and with us, and likewise comprehending those around us more thoroughly through this process. Understanding this more thoroughly, Giri seems to argue, will not only provide us a more reflexive understanding of ourselves vis-à-vis and with others, but will also enable our social-scientific research to more closely parallel the experience of being a member of society. This sociology that would be characterized by the exploration of 'pathways of partial connections' would enable us to surpass the dichotomies that have characterized the development of Northern sociology in ways that would grant us a fundamentally different basis for comprehending the social world, one which would allow us to engage with others—in both our role as researcher and our position as member of the social order—in ways that would further the ethic of compassion and confrontation.

What is missing from the ethic of compassion and confrontation, to which I believe Giri is working to bring us, is a claim about the extent to which one should pursue this ethic; or, to put it in the more pragmatic language with which Giri is working in this volume, how far does one go in pursuing this normative call in the furtherance of our research? Do the methodological changes Giri asks for in his opening essay compel us to only attempt to understand and engage with the local, whether in the intimately anthropological sense or that of comparative sociology? Do they prevent us from doing macro-level types of work that might allow us to more fully critique and creatively transform the process of globalization and corporatization that trouble our planet? And, do they depend upon a particular understanding of the present within which we work, whether as fellow-travelling social agents or scrutinizing sociologists? To my mind, I believe that an understanding of how we conceptualize the present is crucial for comprehending and implementing the normative claim to which Giri calls us. In particular, I believe that Giri's methodological, ontological, and normative claims depend upon a conception of the present as a social space—a different notion from the temporal notion with which we currently operate in our social lives. In adding this conception to Giri's formulations of ontological sociality and autonomy and interpenetration, I believe that we can develop not only a better approach to living sociology and sociological living, but can also begin to act more ethically with those others in our space, responding to what Max Scheler called kairos, or the 'ethical demand of the hour.' It is to the development of this reconceptualization of the loci of these 'global conversations' that I now turn.

Temporal Conceptions of 'The Present'

In examining the way in which the present gets talked about, it is interesting to note that the present is generally viewed as a member of a temporal continuum or triad—that of the past, the present, and the future. Implicitly, there is within conceptions of the present that are bound with the other couplet a notion that there can be no 'present' without the other two members. Any discussion of the 'present' without the other two members tends to be synchronic; that is, it takes the present as a 'snapshot' of some larger scheme or continuum, or, as Mead put it, the 'knife-edge' of time, a moment cut out of the temporal continuum, taken from its context. In this section, I will explore four different conceptions of the present and ways of beginning to think about what their parallel social orders would appear to be. These four conceptions of 'the present' are placed implicitly on a continuum, ranging from the 'ecstatic unity' of Merleau-Ponty's existentialism, wherein the past, present and future are all simultaneously bound together, separated only by the agent's intentionality, to synchronic 'stop-point' snapshots of the world. I do this to provide for consideration a variety of ways of temporally conceptualizing the present.

However, there is within this welter of constructions of time a lack of a strong conception of the present, one which can be oriented to without recourse to longing for the revenants of the past or the future. (Derrida 2006). This is, I would argue, the root of the insecurity, foundationlessness, and anxiety with which the 'postmodern' era is plagued (Bauman 1993), because without a strong conception of the present there can be no strong formulations of or relations to the past or the future. Hence, I want to end up with a different picture of the present, one which is not so much temporal as it is spatial; that is, I want to take Derrida's conception of 'the here and now', and use it to construct a sense of the present as a space upon which the human being can exert some agency in response to a kairos, or what Scheler acknowledged as 'the ethical demand of the hour'. Using this conception, I want to construct a conception of a present- or spatially-ordered social situation, one which, if we take analyses of the dispersed and fragmented 'postmodern' subjectivity seriously, will provide a way in which to develop a stronger orientation not to some 'imagined community' (to take Benedict Anderson's [1991] term), but rather a community within which the human agent is embedded at any particular time.

The 'Ecstatic Unity':
All Good Times, Bound into One

In an existential conception of time, such as that of Merleau-Ponty, the present is still existent; however, there is no longer a need for borders around 'the present,' as both 'the past' and 'the future' are bound up within— or more accurately, are only existent within—the present. The conception of time as an 'ecstatic unity' has as its fundamental premise the notion that time forms the infrastructure of human consciousness. Because the human being, that is, the being-for-itself, has the ability to transform 'non-beings,' such as ideas, into being, it has at its most fundamental level a sense of time that guides its consciousness. The non-being (of the idea, for example) is the not-yet existent, something which, through the work of the human being-for-itself, can be brought into being. This occurs through an intentional process through which something is 'partially manifest' in the present becomes, through the work of the human being, more fully manifest, in order to be worked or to do work upon the human being. Within this process, then, there is a 'character of wholeness', one which anticipates a 'more perfectly (but never completely) manifest' state of affairs (Merleau-Ponty 1963: 165; Whiteside 1988: 48).

This character of wholeness is not merely limited to the analytic relationship of the intentional being-for-itself to the object or idea in becoming, but is also apparent in the conception of time that goes along with this process. As the relationship between what would generally be called 'object' and 'subject' is a dialectical rather than a causal one (Merleau-Ponty 1963: 149; Whiteside 1988: 50), the temporality that goes along with this relationship is one in which the past as well as the future are always present within any setting. That is, that which the 'object' (the thing which is being worked on) was is always present within that which it is; and the relationship between the 'subject' (that which is doing work on the 'object') and the 'object,' this relationship of intentionality, has always within it the possibility of the 'more perfectly manifest' future. In other words, the present has within it the 'what was' as well as the 'what can be', which is always dependent upon the work done within the present.

Furthermore, the past that is within the present is always dependent upon the orientation of the intentional being; that is, the relevance of the past to the present is a result of the intentionality of the relationship between the thinking being and the past it explores. In other words, the past is 'always "present" in the form of primal structures acquired in a social setting' (Merleau-Ponty 1964: 80; Whiteside 1988: 114) Hence, within the present there is both the past basis for it as well as the future for which it will become the basis of; and work done on the present affects both the meaning of the past as well as the possibilities for the future.

The social order that parallels this conception of time is one in constant process. That is, within the present manifestation of it there are 'pressures and instabilities' that have broken down previous instantiations of the order and that are also breaking down the present form of it. The breakdown of the current form of the social order provides the prefigurement of the future form of the order, so that within what could be called 'the present social order' there are the previous forms of it as well as the tensions which prefigured the present version of the social order, in addition to the conditions for a future form of the community (Merleau-Ponty 1962: 449; Whiteside 1988: 113). Taken together, these form what Merleau-Ponty calls a sens, a gestalt that includes both the meaning of the perceived social order as well as the direction it takes in its historical progression (Merleau-Ponty 1962: 428). The object of the sens of the social order provides a structure by which humans can understand their relations with other humans within the community. More specifically, the cultural objects that help constitute the sens of the community—the structures with which humans in the community perceive the world around them—are constituted through a 'meaning-saturated milieu that it creates for itself and that it transmits to its members', one which requires that these same members work to perceive the behaviour of other persons by understanding the intentions with which they perceive and work on the world (Merleau-Ponty 1962: 348; Merleau-Ponty 1963: 163; Whiteside 1988: 75).

The manifestation of the social order in 'the present', then, requires that individual members of the community take the 'meaning-saturated millieu' that they inherit from past members and work with it so as to maintain their own individual and particular membership in the community, guaranteed by understanding the intentions with which other members come to the community. Hence, the community is oriented both towards the past, in the sense of understanding the tools with which it is founded and has changed, and to the future, in the work required for the preservation of the community. The present, then, only appears as the locus at which the community works to understand its past and maintain itself into the future, both of which appear within the always partially-formed perceptions of the present. There is no independent conception of the purpose of the present that can be understood without recourse to either the past or the future, thanks to the 'ecstatic unity' that the three form. The 'present' can only be conceived of as processual work, which members of the community engage in to preserve their community for the future, as well as to understand the past sens from which they come.

The Present As 'Sedimented':
Tracing the Past and the Future

The conception of time as an 'ecstatic unity', within which all phases of time are dependent upon each other, is similar to the idea, attributable to George Herbert Mead, that time is a result of the passage of the 'event'. Within this conception, only the present is existent, and therefore in the realm of the 'real'. Both the past and the future have what Mead calls a hypothetical status in relation to the present; that is, the meaning of the past is always able to be rewritten in regards to the present from which it is being regarded; as well, the future determines the possibilities for action (Mead 1959a: 637; Mead 1959b: xvii–xviii). The present, in this formulation, is marked by 'its becoming and its disappearing' (Mead 1959b: 1), and is brought into relationships with its past, which is determinative but not causal, as well as a future, both of which are denied existence by Mead, in that they can only be lived through the present. A particular present will have an 'irrevocable past' (Mead 1959b: xvii), the past that determines that present; however, as this relationship is not a causal one, a different present can have a different past, which can only be worked out within that present. It is only the meaning of that past in relation to the present from which it is being regarded that changes; the actual events of that past never change. (Mead 1959b: 11) As Mead notes, 'The present is a passage constituted by processes whose earlier phases determine in certain respects their later phases. Reality then is always in a present' (1959b: 28). But this present is always a 'recipient' present; that is, it has no meaning-content of its own, but is instead sedimented with its relationship to its past and to the future possibilities of the event of the present.

This conception of the present as being sedimented by the determining factors of the meaning of the past and the hypothetical nature of the future bears within it a conception of social order which depends upon the ability of the human to step outside their own limited perspective. Our status as 'selves' within this social order is determined by our relationship to others; in this sense, difference within a 'system' is what characterizes the individual (Mead 1959a: 654–5). The system maintains its coherence and order through the capacity of individuals to be 'social', meaning their ability to step out of their own limited perspective and have the perspective of others, most generally in the gaze of others upon themselves (Mead 1959b: 49, 193; Baert 1992: 57). Change occurs thanks to the unheimlich state of humans within their present social situation; that is, we do not feel secure within our social order because we always feel a need for salvation as a social being:

As social beings we are not at home in the world because we demand a different social situation and a different environment. We may project that into a world to come, or back to a Golden Age, but the social order in which we are actually existing is not one in which the self, as such, is at home. (Mead 1959a: 475–6)

Mead is unclear as to the source of this apparent 'grass is always greener' syndrome that seems to be at the root of the human condition. I would argue that this is a result of the 'recipient' nature of the present. Because the present has no content of its own, but rather is the existent manifestation of the sediments of the past oriented to the possibilities of action foreseen in the future, there is no reason for humans to be at home in the way that things are. Again, the lack of a stable conception of the present, one that can stand apart from, or at least be identifiable without recourse to, the past and the future, makes it so that there is an insecurity or anxiety about the lack of possibility of understanding our position within the social order. In this conception of the 'recipient present', where any social order is maintained through 'sociality', or the ability of the members of the system to transcend their limited perspectives and take on those of others, the reflexivity of the knowledge required to gain this perspective (see Baert 1992: 78) further undermines the possibility of a present, as it requires that the cogito dredge up the sediments of past performances, either by the cogito or by others, and translate them, in the face of future possibilities of action, into a course of activity that is oriented to this end. In this sense, then, there is again no conception of the present as such, leaving the individual to suffer with their lack of a stable position within the present.

The Present as 'Bracketed' by the Past and Future

Conceptualizing the present as a segment of a temporal continuum which is bracketed by the past and the future would seem, at first glance, to put us back earlier in the discussion to Derrida's conception of time. For Derrida (2006), the only way to have a proper consideration of 'the present' as a temporal segment would be to erect impermeable borders around it, marking it off as qualitatively different from the past and the future. However, there can be no impermeable borders around 'the present', given that the movement of the revenant, the spectre, can come to us either from the past or from the future. This movement, furthermore, is completely out of our control; that is, messages from the past or from the future can come to us in a variety of ways, the inheritance and the promise being two of them, and their time schemes show that a conception of the present which can be asserted against its other cannot happen. The inheritance and the promise, while both being performative moments having a particular singular time (that is, a time in which they happen), also have a dualized moment, both times of which we cannot know—the moment of the bequeathment or the promise, and the moment at which the memory of the deceased is upheld as such or that when the promise is fulfiled or 'kept'. Both of these moments are always already present; that is, the inheritance and the promise are kept always with the agent, even though they are only actually 'active' when recalled by that agent. So, then, there can be no impermeable border around 'the present', as there are moments at which moments from the past and/or the future, intrude upon the temporal ground marked off as 'the present'.

However, it is still possible to conceive of a temporal ordering that brackets off 'the past' and 'the future' from the present. One way could be seen in the way in which formal theory talks about the social agent (see Heise 2000). The agent in this view is one who, with regards to a present problem, takes information gained in the past and works on the present problem in line with some future-oriented strategy. In this conception, the agent takes information from the past and applies it to the present in order to achieve something in the future. Here, that which is oriented to most strongly (though not in itself) is the present problem—that for which a solution is being sought. However, the solution must be in line with a future-oriented strategy, and must necessarily draw from information gained in the past. In a repeated-move game situation, the solution to this move then becomes part of the past block of information, a new problem is posed by the countermove of the other, and the future-oriented strategy will still be maintained.

The brackets around the situation of the present in this scenario are, admittedly, rather weak. That is, they are only a matter of orientation to the information contained within each of the temporal segment under consideration: the present is seen as a problem, with which information learnt within the past can be used to solve with respect to a strategy oriented to the future. Information from the past and future passes through the borders that bracket the present, if only to aid in solving the problem that is the present. However, this is the least of concerns here. Again, the conception of the present as a problem which needs to have work done on it lends itself to a view of a better 'present' which would no longer be a 'problem', one in which the problem of the present has been solved. As Baert notes, 'Reflective intelligence refers to the ability to solve present problems in the light of possible future consequences and on the basis of past experience. So, what it means to be human is not only to live in the present, but also to break out of it' (Baert 1992: 78). There is, then, again more of an orientation away from the present, in that the goal of 'human' activity is to 'break out of' the present within which we are all immersed. The brackets around the present serve only to mark it off as a problem, and direct the agent's attention to other temporal segments for the information on how to solve this problem. To bring Mead's terminology back into this: 'Reflective knowledge is to be considered a 'span', a durée: that is, a stream of interpenetrating states of consciousness each of which involves a representation of both the past and the future' (Baert: 83).

Another way of understanding the bracketing of the present in favour of the past and the future might be Benjamin's notion of historiography. Benjamin sought to explore or recollect the past in such a way as to retrieve the possibility of paths not taken in the past, so as to help redeem the future (Benjamin 1968: 253–64; Dallmayr 1993: 30). The present is bracketed off here only as the temporal locus of this work; all work is done with the intention of preserving those redemptive aspects of the past via 'the "time of the now" which is shot through with chips of Messianic time' (Benjamin 1968: 263) in order to save the future. These 'chips of Messianic time' are treated, in their crystallization in the present, as the key to redemption in the future, the Nichtjetztzeit, the not-yet-time, that can be saved through a historical materialist analysis of the present, which finds the lost potentialities of the past in the present and highlights them as paths of action for the future. Again, bracketing the present (Benjamin 1968: 254, 255), in this case as an object of historical analysis, is only engaged in so as to retrieve 'untapped potentials' (Dallmayr 1993: 30) in order to bring about a sense of a 'state of emergency' (Benjamin 1968: 257) by which to shock humanity into redeeming that which it once had the opportunity to implement. The reflexive knowledge required in both of these attitudes towards the present is, as some would have it (cf. Rabinow 1986), a requirement in postmodernity; and this reflexivity requires a movement outside of (and, therefore, a weak relation to) the realm of the present into those of the past and future. As Dallmayr puts it, 'Seen in this light, postmodernity heralds neither a "brave new world" nor a regressive primitivism, but rather a peculiar meshing of the temporalities of past and future: the intersection of these temporalities marks the terrain of the present' (Dallmayr 1993: 31).

All of these conceptions of temporality, because they have no strong conception of the present outside of the other terms of the triad, are also fundamentally weak when it comes to considering their parallel social orders. Within the temporal 'ecstatic unity' that Merleau-Ponty noticed, the present is the only existent; however, it becomes the 'playground' upon which the meanings of the past and the potentialities of the future are worked out. The sens of this 'playground' is in continual flux, as the tensions of the past are worked upon in the present in light of the potentialities of the future, and all of this is engaged in for the preservation of the community. Hence, the ethos of this conception of time is one, that is always geared towards the perpetual improvement of the human social condition. The sedimented conception of the 'recipient present', in Mead's view, also functions in this way; that is, there is always a perpetual process going on by which humans, who ontologically have a conception of a better social order, do work upon the present so as to make themselves more 'at home' in their world. And conceptualizing the present as being bracketed off from the past and future also has a sense of the nature of the present as a 'problem' that must be solved. All of these conceptions—between which the distance is not great, and is primarily a matter of nuance—leave the present with a sense of insecurity, anxiety, or Unheimlichkeit, one which requires work to be done upon the present in order to eliminate it by making things in the temporal, as well as the social, worlds manageable or controllable. There is fundamentally a feeling that, as Derrida puts it, of postmodern insecurity (Bauman 1999: 14)—that "'The time is out of joint": something in the present is not going well, it is not going as it ought to go' (Derrida 2006: 23); and I would argue that it is the lack of control, removed because of the lack of a strong conception of and relation to the present, that is at the root of this. I turn now to conceptualizing the present synchronically as an attempt to counterbalance this absence of a present in more continuum-based conceptions of time.

Synchrony and the Elimination of the Present

The final conceptualization of time which I wish to discuss here is one in which the present is treated as a synchronic stop-point in time. In this view, life is only a series of presents: because there is no past or no future that can be directly experienced, there can only be the present. Yet, as Roquentin points out in Sartre's *Nausea*, even that which has only just been completed is in the past, and cannot be reexperienced, meaning that it is no longer existent (Sartre 1964: 130). There is nothing that can persist, even for a short moment, so it is indicative of the human condition that we are doomed to exist only in the present (Crosby 1988: 63). Life, then, is a series of presents, in which we futilely act, only to have our actions and the things which we act upon pass out of existence into that which we call 'the past'. There is no way to retrieve that which disappears into the past; even 'memory', which we think brings those things that have passed into the present, cannot resurrect the moment, as each attempt to do so further distorts the lived actuality of that moment, and inevitably makes it something which it was not, leaving us in the position of not being able to distinguish fact from fiction (Crosby 1988: 64). There can also be no future in this view, as 'future moments have no reality until they enter the present and then… vanish irrevocably into the past' (Crosby 1988: 65). Hence, it is the human condition that we are doomed to live in nothing but the present. This, however, means that the construction of a social order is nearly impossible.

Social order, by most definitions of it, involves some recourse to, if not tradition and a common cultural millieu (something which Merleau-Ponty rightly claims that the early Sartre ignores; Whiteside 1988: 112; cf. Schaffer 2004), then at least to 'values'. In this synchronic view of the present and its subsequent construction of time as a series of presents, values are constructed ad hoc, only in relation to the current conditions of existence, and may be uncreated as quickly and as easily as they were created by the actor (Crosby 1988: 41, 258, 300). In this view, the only social order that could be constructed is one in which all members of it could be counted on to commit to it for a lengthy period of time, something which this conception of time prohibits.

The absurdity of placing value on anything that appears in the present in this conception of time means, again, that no stable conception of a social order can be produced. As well, there can be no stable conception of the present. While 'the present' is definitionally marked off as 'that which occurs now', the present which is produced through this synchronic view of existence is one in which there can be no consistent view of the social actor, nor any conception of what a social order might appear to be. Because there is no room in this view for a conception of those things which make a social order possible, such as tradition or habits (which even Merleau-Ponty argues are the result of 'favoured interpretations that sustain the goals of the individual and the needs of the "social group"', Whiteside 1988: 114), the social agent is nothing more than a solipsistic agent, acting upon the whims of the immediate situation. There can also be no consistent notion of the actor, because the mere notion of 'consistency' requires some sense of permanence; as Sartre, for example, argues contra this notion, 'life decides its own meaning because it is always in suspense' (1964: 664), that is, something only has meaning in the moment it is lived, and once it is gone it can no longer have any meaning.

There is, then, no possibility for a conception of the social order within the present, at least not in this sense. Having as the only existent conception of time 'the present', which necessarily passes out of existence, never to have an effect upon the world again, makes every present have no meaning except in the moment at which it exists (Mead 1959b: 1). Because, in the synchronic view of the present that I have laid out here, everything is but 'the present'—that is, anything in existence can only exist in the present, and the past and future can have no bearing upon the existent in the present—there can be no present. This would leave the possibility of constructing a social order in the present seemingly impossible.

I would argue, then, that conceptualizing 'the present' as a temporal category might be at the root of the problem that I have identified here. That is, attempting to develop a strong temporal conception of the present, one which could stand on its own as the object of an ethical relation, falls flat because there can be no stable conception of the present on its own.

Conceptualizing 'the present' as a temporal entity grants it either the instability that comes with the inability of members of the social order to orient to it in itself, or that instability that comes with the elimination of the present as a whole. This instability leads to an insecurity about one's place within the social order, one which provides the occasion at which 'nobody quite knows what "the right time and place for everything" might be' (Harvey 1989: 239). This ambiguity about action leads to an inability to act, for there can be no knowledge about what the ethical mode of action might be. The social order in late capitalism is one characterized by the suppression of proximity, thanks to the lack of a strong relation to the present in a temporal sense. Hence, I see exploring 'the present' as a spatial concept—in a way not dissimilar to Derrida's 'the here and now'—as a viable way in which to begin reconstructing a social order founded upon an ethical relationship. Within this social order—not to be taken as a social structure—human agents respond to what Scheler calls the kairos, the ethical demand of the situation, in order to construct through their social acts communities within which the intentionality of the actors for Others within the community is not dependent upon any past tradition of loyalty or fealty, nor any future expectation of return or reward, but is instead dependent solely upon the strong relation to the call of the kairos. In this sense, the individual has a strong relation to the present in their performance of an ethical act that responds to the calling that is the kairos.

'The Present' as a Space

Part and parcel of the instability, insecurity, and anxiety that comes in the 'postmodern condition' with the lack of a strong conception of the present is a suppression of proximity. That is, as conceptions of time become crowded, not unlike the way in which Derrida describes, conceptions of space become more dispersed. The technologies, which, as Poster notes (1995: 30), make necessary the qualified 'real time' (as there are other possible times, as well as other realities, such as 'virtual reality'), also contribute to or exacerbate a lack of physical proximity between humans. Distances between individuals are already quite large, but these technologies make physical closeness unnecessary in order to maintain some sense of sociality. Derrida observes that, similar to the spectral effect that occurs with regards to time, there is also a spectral effect in regards to space, which parallels the decline of a pre-modern morality that depends upon proximity (2006: 63, 169). Space as well as time, then, becomes the site for a lack of security, especially with regard to the old morality, which depends upon proximity for its action (Bauman 1993: 83). Social and moral regulations ensure that there need be no closeness between members of a community, as they artificially guarantee the regularity and predictability of social transactions between members, who may never enter into a social transaction until such a time as the Law is invoked. This, though, is no guarantee of personal security, as crime can enter the home as swiftly as a bullet, and even less violent transgressions of the Law can occur without any recourse by the social regulators. In other words, there can be no security in the realm in which there is no strong relation to the present as a temporal category, nor to regular physical proximity as a socio-spatial relation.

Conceptualizing the present as a space, then, counteracts both of these tendencies with the 'postmodern era'. Taking the present as Derrida did 'the here and now' above, the present can be described as that which a human actor can exert their agency over. In other words, the realm within which an individual human being can act in a measurable sense shall be taken as 'the present'. There is obviously a temporal component to this, as the agent cannot act over this space, which may be as small as a kitchen or as large as a country, in any other time but 'the (temporal) present'. I will return to a discussion of the relation of temporality to this spatial conception of the present later; however, suffice it to say for now that my conception of the present is unichronic, that is, it is the area that an agent can do work upon in the moment.

Within this conception of the present as a space, we can begin to see the value of eliminating the relevance of time, or more accurately, detemporalizing the present. By conceptualizing the present as a space upon which work can be done, the insecurity that comes from not being able to orient to a time frame is removed.[1] In this conception of the present, it is easier to orient to a space within which an individual can do some work, regardless of its Cartesian size. For example, the Prime Minister of Canada, who can easily do work upon the Cartesian space known as 'Canada' in one fell swoop (by passing a law, for example, though this work would be mediated by the body of social regulations known as the Law), while someone no less important, such as my mother, can do work upon her three-room living space in the same amount of time. In both cases, the primary orientation of each actor's agency is to the social space within which each works and can be or needs to be done within that space in the moment. Furthermore, analytically this version of the present is easier to identify than a temporal version of the present; as Scheler writes, 'The present, however, is originally that wherein we are actually operating and working' (1973: 341), and it would be relatively easy analytically to enter into the space of a set of practices and operations, much as in the way in which ethnography would work.

To further delimit the space I am talking about here, I would argue that the space of the present can be seen as the social space of being with others, a space which must constantly be constructed at the moment of its delimitation (Bauman 1993: 185). In this sense, actors within this present have within them an intentionality, in that individuals doing work within this present-space are always oriented towards others; i.e. there is within this work an a priori orientation towards to Other (Bauman 1993: 50). Hence, the present becomes that space within which an individual can do some work that is intended for or toward others.

Kairos and Ethical Agency

As I have said earlier, agents working within this spatial conception of the present have an orientation towards Others within this same present. Remember that this present-space, because it has no determinate time (but rather is unichronic), is constructed through the acts of a human agent that are oriented towards Others, and is therefore processual, in the sense of being a result of the action of agents. There is no traditional sense of a 'social structure' in this view, as a social structure tends to regiment and regularize interactions between actors, as well as institutionalize the suppression of proximity and render actions morally indifferent (Bauman 1993: 123, 125). Rather, the social space that follows this spatial conception of the present is one which is a result of the ethical intention of the actors involved: 'What we are learning, and learning the hard way, is that it is the personal morality that makes ethical negotiation and consensus possible [and therefore the social order], not the other way round' (Bauman 1993: 34). Granted, this is rather shaky ground upon which to stake a social order. However, given that, in the social orders which parallel temporal conceptions of the present, the social order is predicated upon predictable regularities of individual action, most of which are enforced by others, and few of which are entered into willingly or invested with much moral significance, I would argue that predicating a social order oriented to the present-as-space upon the intentionality of individuals to be moral actors is much more relevant. This version of the social is easier to develop a strong relationship to, as it becomes manifest not in the begrudging acceptance of enforced social norms, but rather in the social practices which the individual actor engages in that are always, even if not directly, oriented toward Others.

But what is it that causes this intentionality on the part of the actor? I would argue that it is what Scheler identified as kairos, or 'the ethical demand of the hour'. This essential category of ethics, Scheler argued, finds itself manifested in the call to the individual to engage in ethical action, or what Scheler called 'das An-sich-Gute für mich', the 'good-in-itself-for-me'

(Deeken 1974: 115–16). This is not a 'good' in a solipsistic or egoistic sense, but rather a good that is 'directed to a specific subject calling it to moral action'. The historical development of an individual within social spaces defined, in my view, by this conception of the present-space allows the individual to experience certain ethical calls, i.e. calls to certain moral tasks and actions, that may or may not be directed merely at them.

There exists the possibility of an insight into a good which contains in its essence and value-content a pointing to an individual person. It also possesses a corresponding oughtness that emerges as a 'call' to this person and to this person alone, regardless of whether or not the same 'call' is also addressed to other persons. . . . [The good in question] is the good-in-itself for me in the sense that in the particular material content of this good-in-itself (descriptively said) lies a pointer to me, an experienced hinting, which emerges from this content and points toward me. It says and whispers, so to speak, 'For you.' Thus, this content offers me a unique place in the moral cosmos. (Scheler 1973: 482)

Instead of insisting upon a universal set of ethical codes to which all members of a social order must hold, this view allows for the possibility of subjectively experienced callings to engage in certain actions; these callings may quite possibly be the same as those which are experienced by other members of the social group. This 'good-in-itself for me' that characterizes kairos is matched just as vigorously by the intentionality of the actors within this model. This means that, within this present-space, individuals engaging in actions that are intended towards Others—because, as Bauman points out, we may be alone as moral actors, but as social creatures we are always surrounded, even if there is no one around (Bauman 1993: 60)—are interested in preserving their relationship, their ethical proximity to these Others. Unlike a temporal conception of the present, within which individuals are concerned either with the future payoff of actions or with the ramifications of not following through on earlier or traditional promises of loyalty, those within a social order formed by the present-space have no foundation upon which to premise their actions intended towards Others. To be more precise, there is no 'practical foundation' to this ethics: there is no expectation of future reward or reciprocation, and the good within this is in orienting to the Other, regardless of their orientation (Bauman 1993: 48; Deeken 1974: 67).

I am for the Other whether the Other is for me or not; his being for me is, so to speak, his problem, and whether or how he 'handles' that problem does not in the least affect my being-for-Him (as far as my being-for-the-Other includes respect for the Other's autonomy, which in its turn includes my consent not to blackmail the Other into being-for-me, nor interfere in any other way with the Other's freedom). Whatever else 'I-for-you' may contain, it does not contain a demand to be repaid, mirrored, or 'balanced out' in the 'you-for-me.' My relation to the Other is not reversible; if it happens to be reciprocated, the reciprocation is but an accident from the point of view of my being-for. (Bauman 1993: 50)

There is, then, only one reason to engage in this form of intentional action—to engage in this intentional, ethical action. The call of the kairos, which I argue drives individuals to this intention towards the Other within this present-space, is the only drive necessary in this formulation. It is only through our being moral in our action that any sort of society can be formed; in other words, society does not breed morality, but rather vice versa. This would make sense, given the problems with conceptualizing a social order in regards to a temporal conception of the present; the inability of any member of the social group to be sure of the Other's intentions in that view lends itself to a fundamental insecurity about one's place within the social order. By reconceptualizing the present as present-space, we can see that one's place within the social order, that is, their relation to the other members of the community, is constructed not through the perceptions of the Ego by Others, but rather through the actions of the individual.

By starting from Giri's position of ontological sociality, which recognizes 'an ontological reciprocity of individual and society' (Giri 2017), we are able to understand the social order as a 'space for self-development of individuals' (Giri 2017), one which at the same time requires us to recognize that that very process of self-development demands our action and interaction with others, giving 'simultaneously an autonomous and relational existence' (Giri 2017), both as social science practitioners and as members of society. Membership within this social order, unlike that of a temporal-present social order, is not a fixed quality of those who participate within it. So, to fall in line with the various ways in which individuals today define themselves, there is no set criterion by which membership is defined.

In previous conceptions of social orders, membership in a community is often defined on the basis of one particular aspect of a dispersed identity, so that someone who identifies themselves by a number of identities would become a member of potentially competing communities. In a conception driven by the idea of the present-space as the boundaries of the community, membership is fluid, and is marked only by one's activity in response to the 'good-in-itself for me'. One way of understanding what this might look like in a practico-ethical sense is through the process of 'serial reciprocity', which sociologists are only now beginning to explore. Rather than a dyadic form of reciprocity, wherein one person repays a gift or debt to the person from whom they received it, serial reciprocity occurs 'when people reciprocate for what they have received—for example, from a parent, a friend, a mentor, an anonymous stranger, a previous generation—by providing something to a third party, regardless of whether a return is also given or makes its way back to the original giver' (Moody 2008: 132). Borrowing from Simmel, Moody develops this notion of serial reciprocity and recognizes that this form of reciprocity is unidirectional and exists not in the structure of the exchange relationships, but rather in the meaning with which people intend these exchanges (2008: 136).

However, while Moody privileges the discussion of temporality in serial reciprocity (2008: 135–6), arguing that 'serial reciprocity links the past to the future sometimes over long periods of time', I believe it more fruitful to understand this form of social interaction spatially. This social act reflects an obligation an actor feels they have to someone with whom they shared a social space, and is an instance where the actor 'pays forward' that obligation to someone within the social space they exist in the moment. Ultimately, its function may be as Moody indicates, to link the past with the future; however, recognizing the spatial dimension of serial reciprocity gets us closer to understanding what a practical version of Giri's ontology of autonomy and interpenetration might look like. Within serial reciprocity, we act autonomously, yet we do so on the basis of having been penetrated by the generosity of another, and act in such a way as to further that impact towards an other within our space.

To sum up, then, I would argue that conceptualizing of 'the present' as a space instead of as a time frame improves the ability of the human agent to orient to and develop a strong relation with the social order and makes for a stronger ethical order in what some have called the 'postmodern era'. Whereas social orders that have a temporal orientation to the present have the problem of producing insecurity, anxiety, and the sense of Unheimlichkeit that plagues this 'postmodern era', a social order that has a spatial orientation to the present takes hold of this ambiguity and argues that, while being a part of existence as a moral actor (Bauman 1993: 12), it is more a result of the inability to know if one is being moral enough, rather than knowing if the perceptions of others grant one membership in this community. As such, the social order of the present-space is one predicated not upon the maintenance of borders by social legislators but rather is dependent upon the actions of moral agents within it, so that the call of the *kairos* instead of the machine-gun of the border guard is the motivating factor for action. The picture of a spatially-oriented social order that I have developed here is one that can rescue the notion of a voluntary community, as well as a social agent that has some agency.

Importantly, Giri has asked to reflect in this volume on the nature of social relations, both between social scientist and their research subjects and those between people. I believe that the crucial highlights of his call—the notions of ontological sociality, the ontology of autonomy and interpenetration, and our engagement in our social world through what he calls 'pathways of partial connections'—all indicate a reconceptualization of the social realm that facilitates the practice of an ethics that is truly ethical. To my mind, it is important that this reconceptualization enables us to envision the present as a space within which we work, rather than a particular temporal moment among other temporal moments. I believe that it is only by seeing the present spatially that we can really begin to respond to the kairos, the ethical demand of the moment, in ways that fully reflect the human capabilities each of us in the world possess and the dignity each of us deserves.

Note

1. The suggestion to detemporalize the present does not forget that there are aspects of our existence that precede us or will outlast us; in other words, I am not suggesting that we forget social and cultural traditions, nor any sense of pursuing action projects that will make life for our descendants difficult or impossible. Rather, the suggestion here is to address the question, what is to be done now for and with those around me? It is a question that has both a temporal aspect (action in the here and now) and a spatial aspect, making it possible to better address, for example, the ethical problem of facing a homeless person.

References

Anderson, Benedict (1991), *Imagined Communities: Reflections on the Origins and Spread of Nationalism*, London: Verso.

Baert, Patrick (1992), *Time, Self, and Social Being: Temporality Within a Sociological Context*, Aldershot: Avebury.

Bauman, Zygmunt (1993), *Postmodern Ethics*, New York & London: Routledge.

———(1999), *In Search of Politics*, Stanford: Stanford University Press.

Benjamin, Walter (1968), 'Theses on the Philosophy of History', in *Illuminations*, ed. Hannah Arendt, New York: Schocken Books, pp. 253–64.

Crosby, Donald (1988), *The Specter of the Absurd: Sources and Criticism of Modern Nihilism*, Albany NY: State University of New York Press.

Dallmayr, Fred (1993), 'Modernity in the Crossfire: Comments on the Postmodern Turn', in *Postmodern Contentions: Epochs, Politics, Space*, ed. John Paul Jones, Wolfgang Natter and Theodore Schatzki, New York: The Guilford Press.

Deeken, Alfons (1974), *Process and Permanence in Ethics: Max Scheler's Moral Philosophy*, New York: Paulist Press.

Derrida, Jacques (2006), *Specters of Marx: The State of the Debt, the Work of Mourning, and the New International,* New York: Routledge.

Giri, Ananta Kumar (2017), 'Pathways of Creative Research: Rethinking Theories and Methods and the Calling of an Ontological Epistemology of Participation', in *Pathways of Creative Research: Towards a Festival of Dialogues*, ed. Ananta Kumar Giri, Delhi: Primus Books.

Harvey, David (1989), *The Condition of Postmodernity*, London: Basil Blackwell.

Heise, David R. (2000), 'Thinking Sociologically with Mathematics', *Sociological Theory*, vol. 18, no. 3, pp. 498–504.

Mead, George Herbert (1959a), *The Philosophy of the Act*, Chicago: University of Chicago Press.

———(1959b), *The Philosophy of the Present*, Chicago: Open Court Publishing Company.

Merleau-Ponty, Maurice (1962), *The Phenomenology of Perception*, tr. Colin Smith, London: Routledge and Kegan Paul.

———(1963), *The Structure of Behavior*, tr. Alden Fisher, Boston: Beacon Press.

Moody, Michael (2008), 'Serial Reciprocity: A Preliminary Statement', *Sociological Theory*, vol. 26, 2 June, pp. 130–51.

Poster, Mark (1995), 'Postmodern Virtualities', in *The Second Media Age*, ed. Mark Poster, London: Polity Press, pp. 23–42.

Rabinow, Paul (1986), 'Representations are Social Facts: Modernity and Post-modernity in Anthropology', in *Writing Culture: The Poetics and Politics of Ethnography*, ed. James Clifford and George Marcus, Berkeley: University of California Press, pp. 234–61.

Sartre, Jean-Paul (1964), *Nausea*, tr. Lloyd Alexander, New York: New Directions Publishing.

Schaffer, Scott (2004), *Resisting Ethics*, New York: Palgrave.

Scheler, Max (1973), *Formalism in Ethics and Non-formal Ethics of Values: A New Attempt Toward the Foundation of an Ethical Personalism*, Evanston, IL: Northwestern University Press.

Vandenberghe, Frédéric (2008), 'Sociology of the Heart: Max Scheler's Epistemology of Love', *Theory, Culture & Society*, vol. 25, no. 3, pp. 17–51.

Whiteside, Kerry (1988), *Merleau-Ponty and the Foundation of an Existential Politics*, Princeton: Princeton University Press.

6

Configurational Dialectics

BOIKE REHBEIN

Poststructuralism, postmodernism and postcolonialism have convinced us to appreciate difference, multitude and tolerance. At the same time, empirical research in the global South has shown the social world to be much more complex than classical Eurocentric sociology suggested.[1] What can be made of this? Has it become unacceptable to strive for—one—truth? Are concepts as rationality, consensus, science merely expressions of a totalitarian, hegemonic logic? Should all unifying endeavours be discarded in favour of contingency and otherness? In a way, yes. However, this essay argues that these questions are flawed in themselves. It proposes an idea towards the solution of the dichotomy of Eurocentrism and post-Eurocentrism—of totalitarianism and arbitrariness, of unity and multitude, of identity and difference.

Postcolonial thought has moved through three phases that are also three different paradigms while Eurocentric thought has basically failed to react to this critical movement. In the first phase of postcolonial thought, anticolonialism was the driving force. This, of course, implies that postcolonialism was negatively tied to colonialism, which is expressed by the fact that this phase relied heavily on Marxism—or on a dialectic. The simple dialectic was only criticized by the third phase of postcolonial thought, whereas the second phase was characterized by the attempt to establish alternative modernities, authentic identities and a non-Eurocentric thought. This phase corresponded to the factual liberation from colonialism and the creation of an industrial base in postcolonial societies. The third phase recognized that neither anti-colonialism nor non-colonialism truly liberates from the colonial heritage. At the same time, it was acknowledged that there is no pure colonialism and no pure indigenous authenticity. However, unlike the second phase this third phase drew mainly on Western traditions, especially poststructuralism and postmodernism, and many of its proponents hold chairs in the Anglo-Saxon world.

The critical impulse of poststructuralism, postmodernism and postcolonialism should be regarded as a necessary condition to study the social world and to act in it. The impulse consists of a critique of authoritarian attempts at unification, universalism and domination. It is no sufficient condition for research and action because forms of life and knowledge do not exist in an isolated manner. Especially in a globalizing world, they influence, limit and contest each other. Contingency and arbitrariness are no sufficient ways to deal with this multitude, as each form of life and knowledge has to react to others and actively alter them. To just acknowledge this as a fact means to preclude active learning.

Therefore, I wish to argue for a post-postcolonial, post-postmodern and post-poststructuralist thought focusing on the social sciences. If the redoubled 'post' reminds of Hegel's dialectic, this reminiscence is intended here. However, the simple dialectic of the first phase of postcolonial thought, which is basically an adapted version of Hegel's and/or Marx's dialectic, has been overcome by the third phase. There is no way back to this dialectic. For this reason, I wish to propose a 'post-ly' informed dialectic that I specify as configurational.[2] In the first section of the chapter, I will outline a few characteristics of Eurocentric thought. The second section delivers some empirical criticism of Eurocentric thought, while the third section summarizes a couple of theoretical aspects of postcolonial critique. In the fourth section, the idea of a configurational dialectic is proposed.

Eurocentric Theory

Grossly generalizing, I wish to reduce the social sciences to a paradigm that I call Eurocentric theory. Eurocentric theory is characterized, among others, by: an ethnocentric writing of history, a linear evolutionism, a container model of society, a deductive theory of science and the concept of totality. These characteristics are linked to the conditions of the emergence of the social sciences. This emergence occurred at the same time as Europe's rise to dominance in the world. The social sciences were born into a world with only one dominant civilization, which was that of Europe. Therefore, they sought to explain that European society seemed to be the only remaining civilization in the world. Voltaire still began his *Histoire générale* (1756) with a discussion of China instead of Europe. Ever since Kant and Hegel, China signifies underdevelopment and plays no major role in the historical narrative. Europe is the telos and fulfilment of history. With Tocqueville and Marx, discussions began of whether the United States should be regarded as a perfection of European civilization or its perversion but the general picture of history and the contemporary world remained unchanged. It is still the picture that Western children learn at school.

According to Europe's ethnocentric writing of history, the history of civilization did begin in the East, in Mesopotamia and Egypt. However, the

East passed on the torch of historical development to Greece and Rome. After the interlude of the Dark Ages, the Olympic torch reappeared in north-western Europe that came to dominate the world on the basis of enlightenment. This picture is advanced in a very straightforward manner by such diverse thinkers as Hegel (1970) and Fukuyama (1992). It emerged with European expansion in the Renaissance and is reflected by the transformation of European maps of the world during that period (Hodgson 1993: 3–6). They divide the world into five continents with Europe in the centre. However, it may be argued that Europe is neither in terms of geology nor in terms of size a continent. Furthermore, its location in the centre is purely arbitrary.

The picture of geography and history corresponded to an evolutionism in the social sciences. According to this evolutionism, the world was sound asleep until European modernization began its civilizing mission. Marx (1974) regarded most of the world as primitive and Asia as an 'Oriental despotism' characterized by an 'Asian mode of production' coupled with subsistence farming. Weber (1978) regarded most of the world as underdeveloped and as lacking the conditions for a modernizing development that were only present in Europe. Much of the literature in the social sciences has dealt with these conditions. However, it remained established consensus that the world outside Europe was underdeveloped and had to be developed by imitating modern European history (e.g. Marx 1974; Weber 1972; Rostow 1960; Fukuyama 1992).

Evolutionism went well with a deductive theory of science that had been applied successfully in the natural sciences for several centuries. Carl Gustav Hempel (1965) has argued that sciences explain a phenomenon by applying a law and describing the boundary conditions. According to Hempel, the only difference between social and natural sciences consists in the fact that an explanation in the social sciences has merely a statistical probability while in the natural sciences it is entirely deductive. This conception suggests that science should seek for laws and for reduction of empirical phenomena to laws. In an ideal case, the world can be explained by applying a small set of universal laws and thereby be predicted in its future and technologically manipulated.

Eurocentric social sciences chose societies as their units of analysis. Societies were studied according to the European present, which was characterized by the existence of sovereign nation states. Ulrich Beck (1997) has called this the 'container model of society'. Social relations and structures are confined to a closed container.[3] This model has been dominant in sociology, especially in the analysis of social structure—from Marx's class struggle to sophisticated models (Hradil 2004: 14) and even to the elaborated theory of Pierre Bourdieu (e.g. Vester et al. 2001).

Eurocentric theory is based on provincialism and chauvinism. The provincial perspective never became fully accepted in area studies and was heavily attacked by scholars studying the 'underdeveloped world'. Departing from dependency theory, Immanuel Wallerstein (1974) attempted to replace Eurocentric theory by a global perspective. However, he did not abandon the afore-mentioned four characteristics of Eurocentric theory. According to Wallerstein, societies have always been linked to each other. Therefore, one should look at the network of societies, which he calls a 'world system'. A world system is an interregional division of labour, which does not have to encompass the entire globe. Wallerstein characterizes the world system almost exactly as sociologists before him had defined national societies. The modern world system, which according to him is a capitalist world economy, was a result of European expansion and capitalism from 1450 to 1650. That was the time when modern capitalism became the dominant force in north-western Europe. After this, it spread across the globe. Wallerstein neglects the interregional exchange systems before Europe's rise. And he defines the modern world system as a container comprising three classes, adding a moderating middle class between Marx's two classes. Apart from the four characteristics of Eurocentric theory, world systems theory perfectly exemplifies the fifth characteristic, which is the concept of totality. As Adorno has put it, nothing is allowed to remain outside. To scientifically grasp a totality, the theory has to be so abstract as to be virtually devoid of content. This is true for Wallerstein's theory as well. It is not possible to study Asia on the basis of his theory. Neither is it possible to arrive at an adequate picture of contemporary reality, which contains many forms and phenomena that cannot be reduced to an overarching logic. This has already been argued by Marx (2002: 390).

The five characteristics of Eurocentric theory should be abandoned. First, European or Western modernity cannot be considered the telos of history any more. Second, the linear evolution is a misguided or at least overly simplifying framework to interpret history. Third, deductive explanations are either trivial or too limited in their explanatory force in the social sciences. Fourth, the container model of society is only applicable to the Western European nation state and an economically biased view of society. Fifth, no object of the social sciences can be considered a totality, not even a globalized world, because any object refers to an Other (nature, history, biology, etc.).

The Study of Asia

The postcolonial critique of Eurocentric theory exerted an impact on the mainstream only in the first decade of the twenty-first century. The influence is due to the number of strands in theory that have adopted elements of poststructuralist thinking, such as feminism, subaltern studies and critical aesthetics. However, it is very difficult for the Anglo-American-European mainstream to appreciate the significance of these studies of 'otherness' as its focus remains ethnocentric. If presuppositions gained from the study of Europe are applied to the study of Europe they are logically convincing. Therefore, the greatest impact of post-colonialism will most likely come from Asian studies. The late André Gunder Frank was partly responsible for the revision of Eurocentric theory in world systems theory on the basis of a study of Asia. This revision is partly due to the rise of Asia, i.e. to developments in the real world rather than theoretical reflection. At first, Asia's rise came as a surprise to politicians as well as to sociologists. With the Asian crisis of 1997 it appeared to be short-lived, but more extensive research has shown that the rise of India, China, and South-East Asia in the early twenty-first century is neither surprising nor new (Frank 1998; Hobson 2004).

The consensus about Asia's underdevelopment has been eroded by recent research. Frank has shown that the historic norm has in fact been a multi-centric world, with a slight gravitation towards Asia (Frank 1998). The centre of long-distance trade has always been in Asia, except during the two short phases of European domination in antiquity and recent modernity.[4] The centre lay in the triangle of the Middle East, India and China, at least until 1750 (Pomeranz 2000; Hobson 2004). Until 1750, China had a higher per-capita income than England, until 1850 a higher gross national product, and until 1860 a greater share of the world's production of goods. In 1750, China's share of world production was 33 per cent, which exceeded the United States' share in the 1990s (Hobson 2004: 76). Printing, gunpowder and the compass—according to Francis Bacon the most important inventions in history—were all invented in China. Although Westerners usually assume that these inventions were not used for industrial purposes but for toys such as fireworks, China already had steel tools, firearms, paper money, a credit system and agricultural subsidies at the time of the European Middle Ages.

One thousand years ago, China enjoyed the same international status that it is regaining today. The same is true for India and South-East Asia. Indian steel was cheaper and better than English steel well into the nineteenth century, Indian textiles were sold across the Eastern hemisphere in bulk, and the financial system was more developed than in Europe (Hobson 2004). According to Marco Polo, whenever a ship entered the harbour of Alexandria, 100 Chinese vessels sailed into the harbours of South-East Asia. At these ports, Chinese merchants did not merely sell goods and pick up raw materials, they bought agricultural products that were specifically produced for the market (Reid 1993: 7–12). The growing volume of European trade in the seventeenth century corresponded to the internal weakness of China at the end of the Ming dynasty, heralding the hegemony of Europe over China and India. Europe moved to the centre of world trade in the eighteenth century. Japan and the United States became new centres in the twentieth century. Today, the centre undoubtedly lies in the United States, but an increasing number of other significant centres have emerged around the globe, China even challenging the central position of the US (Nederveen Pieterse/Rehbein 2008). The historic norm of a multi-centric world has been reinstalled.

Post-colonial Theory

The recent rise of Asia has implications for Eurocentric theory because if Asia pulls level with Europe or even takes the lead it is logically incoherent that it should follow the European model of modernization. It is not likely that any region will be the exclusive model for the others in the future. Hegemony has only existed for very brief periods and has never attained all places and social phenomena on the globe. The multi-centric world was even characteristic of pronounced world systems in the past, such as South-East Asia 1400–1700 (Reid 1993) or the Middle East 800–1600 (Abu-Lughod 1989; Hodgson 1993) or even ancient Mesopotamia around 3000 BC (Stein 1999). This means that the five above-mentioned characteristics of Eurocentric theory do not fit any reality apart from Europe 1700–2000. There is not one historic ethnocentrism but each region develops its own, which may accidentally become dominant if the region acquires dominance. No region ever experienced a linear evolution without cycles, backlashes, rearrangements and variations. The container model only applies to the modern European nation state. Universal historical laws are either too general or inadequate. Finally, no unit of analysis can be delimited as a totality.

This criticism is not new. It has been proposed in different variations by post-colonialism. The first phase or paradigm of post-colonialism was basically anti-colonialism and corresponded to the liberation struggle of the colonies. It was inspired by Marxism, especially by the successful Soviet revolution. Dialectical thinking and particularly the master-slave-chapter in Hegel's *Phenomenology of the Spirit* (1970: 113–20) were corner stones of the liberation movements all through the twentieth century. In 1926, Ho Chi Minh wrote that Lenin was the first to denounce colonialism and to encourage the liberation struggle of the colonies (Ho 1971). After the dissent between China and the Soviet Union, Lenin's ideas became more ambivalent but the master-slave-chapter continued to be an important inspiration. On Algeria, Frantz Fanon (1959) wrote that the white man makes the Negro but the Negro makes the negritude, i.e. a counter-picture to white domination. In Brazil, Paulo Freire (1989) made full use of Hegel's dialectic by claiming that the oppressed have to liberate not only themselves but also their suppressors. According to Hegel, the slave has to labour and to fight the master, while the master remains idle. Therefore, the slave gains insight into reality and the will to freedom. On this basis, he is able to construct an epistemologically and practically better world by ousting the master. Freire repeats this line of thought and thereby introduces an element of reconciliation into the dialectic that is absent from Ho's and Fanon's theory. This element also inspired the freedom struggle of Nelson Mandela in South Africa.

The second phase or paradigm of post-colonialism is linked to successful liberation. The aim shifts from ousting the master to defining oneself. This often translated into nationalism and ethnocentrism. Sometimes the master was now the bad guy, while the slave was the good guy, the origin and telos of development. The initial anti-colonialism was reiterated with a contrary evaluation. Both paradigms have their origin in colonialism and continue to exist. In India, one might consider the thought of Rammohun Roy in the early nineteenth century and of Vivekananda in the late nineteenth century already comparable to Freire's motivation, while Manabendra Roy and Bhimrao Ambedkar in the twentieth century pursued a much more pronouncedly anti-colonial view. Their contemporaries Radhakrishnan and Nehru might be considered more representative of the second paradigm. They emphasized the superiority of Indian spirituality over European science. However, their goal transcended Indian nationalism and aspired an international solidarity of all beings (Nehru 1946: 510–15). Radhakrishnan advanced a critique of materialist dialectic in order to argue that the 'light of the world' originates in Indian spirituality (Radhakrishnan 1947: 25–46). The anti-Eurocentric search for a superior authentic tradition within the own ethnocentric realm is exemplified in India by K.M. Panikkar (1954), who argued after Indian liberation that a weak Europe at the periphery of the civilized world was only able to conquer a well-meaning, unsuspicious and culturally far superior Asia through a combination of treason and violent force.

Most versions of both paradigms share a universalism, an evolutionism and a container model of society with Eurocentric theory. However, the first paradigm criticizes the Eurocentric writing of history, while the second paradigm adds the critique of the deductive theory of science. The third paradigm follows up with a critique of universalism, evolutionism and the container model. Edward Said (1978) has analysed the opposition of good and bad as the main heritage of colonialism. Under colonial rule the slave was bad and the master good, while after liberation the relation was reversed. This mere reversal is the focus of the third phase or paradigm of post-colonialism, which may have its origin in Said's work. The third paradigm dissolves concepts like good and bad, history, modernity, unity, universalism, rationality or domination into a multitude of related concepts. An example is Homi Bhabha's concept of hybridization. According to Bhabha (1994), Said drew a misleading picture of the colonial relation because it is too unified itself. Any discourse presupposes intermediate categories and spaces. Therefore, a fertile post-colonialism cannot be anti-colonialism but has to look at intermediate categories and spaces. These are hybrids with no determined value. Their ambivalence can be used to interpret modernity differently.

Configurational Theory

All three paradigms of post-colonialism are justified and render insight into shortcomings of Eurocentric theory. There is no way back to a colonial Eurocentric theory. However, I wish to briefly return to colonial Eurocentric dialectic in order to arrive at a diagnosis of the precise philosophical aspects of its shortcomings and to draw conclusions for a post-colonially inspired dialectic. This line of thought will lead from Hegel and Marx to Adorno and Wittgenstein. From there I will turn to a discussion of the concepts of configuration and understanding.

Hegel (1970) interpreted reality as the historical unfolding of the spirit from the simple to the complex. The insight into the entire history and into the entire history of interpretation of history was supposed to constitute 'absolute knowledge' or the complete insight of the spirit into itself (434 passim). This was gained by Hegel himself. The driving force of history and knowledge was supposed to be the contradiction, as everything is coupled with its negation. For example, there is no master without slave, such as there is no one without many. The full exploration of both parts of a contradiction leads, according to Hegel, to its resolution. Both parts are found to define each other and to be identical in everything else (31). Therefore, the contradiction is overcome by posing a new problem on a different level without forgetting the former contradiction. The new problem is once again a contradiction that is resolved in the same manner but relates to something else, to another content.

In his *Critique of Political Economy*, Marx basically followed Hegel in his conception except for one basic distinction. According to Marx, reality was not the unfolding of the spirit but practice to be distinguished from knowledge. For this reason, the unfolding of knowledge is not identical with the unfolding of history. Marx describes the unfolding of knowledge exactly like Hegel as a dialectical movement from the most abstract and general category to the complex totality of the present (2002: 386). For

Marx, the movement of thought may correspond to real history but usually this is not the case. He defines the most abstract and general category as the one that defines or dominates the present. Its inherent contradiction has to be unfolded, whereby new categories and contradictions unfold, until the entire present is explained. According to Marx, this is only possible if the present is fully developed, i.e. when it has reached a full realization of its defining contradiction.

Bourgeois society is the most highly developed and most highly differentiated historical organization of production. The categories which serve as the expression of its conditions and the comprehension of its own organization enable it at the same time to gain an insight into the organization and the relationships of production which have prevailed under all past forms of society ... The anatomy of the human being is the key to the anatomy of the ape. But the intimations of a higher animal in lower ones can be understood only if the animal of the higher order is already known (390).

For Marx (unlike for Hegel) history does not end in his own knowledge of it as the present still contains pronounced contradictions. The main contradiction of bourgeois society according to Marx is that of capital and labour. Its critique enables him to go beyond this form of society and to occupy a position which renders bourgeois society and the entire preceding history intelligible. This history of course is the Eurocentric narrative outlined in the first section of this essay. Marx repeats the story and then proposes the structure of a future work (which in the end became The Capital): 'first, the general abstract definitions which are more or less applicable to all forms of society ... Secondly, the categories which go to make up the inner organization of bourgeois society ... Thirdly, the organization of bourgeois society in the form of the state . . . Fourthly, the international organization of production . . . Fifthly, the world market and crises' (2002: 392 passim).

This structure nicely reflects the container model, the evolutionism and the concept of totality that I listed as characteristics of Eurocentric theory. Less evident is the deductive theory of science—because dialectic is not deductive in the strict sense but rather conceptual. This is one of the reasons for me to propose a configurational dialectic. Was this its only advantage, one could abandon it. Postmodernism has suggested abandoning the idea of a dialectic, precisely because it incorporates most of the characteristics of Eurocentric theory. In fact, Hegel has been the main target of poststructuralism and postmodernism from Deleuze to Lyotard. Their critique of Hegel— along with Kant and Marx—is pointedly summarized from a postcolonial perspective by Gayatri Spivak (1999).

This critique of dialectic was advanced by a dialectic thinker before poststructuralism and postmodernism were born. In his *Minima Moralia*,

Adorno demands we think dialectically and undialectically at the same time (1979: 98). Dialectical elements are critique, the recognition of the whole in the part and the negation of anything independent. Undialectical elements are the negation to resolve any contradiction into an affirmation and the commitment to the singularity. Just like Bhabha, Adorno is looking for phenomena that elude Hegel's and Marx's narrative—that do not fit the unfolding of categories. Just like Marx and unlike Hegel, he claims that history has not reached its telos in contemporary society but contrary to both of them he denies that one can find any position beyond contemporary society. It is well known that Adorno's approach ends up in an aporetical situation. On the one hand, he criticizes the shortcomings of contemporary society from the 'perspective of salvation', while on the other hand he admits that this perspective is inaccessible from contemporary society (1979: 153).

Adorno's aporia resembles the postcolonial situation, which comprises a denial of universals and claims that go beyond the singularity at the same time. In my opinion, both do not acknowledge the particular. Adorno recognizes the general immediately in the singular without contrasting either with other aspects of reality. It may be said that, there is no hermeneutical process or there is no test against the resistance of reality. Of course, Adorno was aware of this. He was looking for a method that is neither description nor historical explanation. Many aphorisms in his *Minima Moralia* pursue this method—while others do not. Adorno calls the method a 'constellation' or a 'configuration'. Looking at a problem as a constellation presupposes that the causal chains and relations of objects are in principle endless or at least countless (1975: 263). Causality implies an identity of the object and linear cause-effect-relations. The construction of a constellation attempts to seek relations of the object to other objects and its history in order to destroy the apparent independence of the object and its concept, while proving its determination by the totality (Adorno 1975: 164).

Adorno's construction of constellations is an alternative to his immediate—or unmediated—relation of the general and the singular. However, he does not abandon the concept of totality, mainly because he interprets society within the framework of the container model. This, along with his commitment to singularity, has to be abandoned in order to make Adorno's dialectic a feasible one. Other aspects of his configurational method can be built upon: first, the search for relations of the phenomenon, second, the search for relations to its history, and third, the destruction of its independence. The configurational dialectic consists in determining the concept of a phenomenon by relating it to its history and other phenomena. Each relation also relates to something more general and historically previous but in most cases not to 'a society' and never to the totality. It is not possible to determine the concept so fully that it only applies to a singularity. Furthermore, it is not possible to determine any concept through one relation—a contradiction—but there is always a web of relations. This means that I do not agree with Adorno's 'undialectic' elements of his thinking (1979: 98; see earlier). In fact, I agree just as much with Marx's method, while contradicting him in every detail. Marx describes a method that is rather close to a configurational dialectic but comprises the characteristics of Eurocentric theory (2002: 392; see above). He posits evolutionism, an ethnocentric history, a container model and a totality. In addition, he bases his dialectic on the concept of contradiction, which still dominates Adorno's thought. I wish to argue that a contradiction is only one possible relation among others and a very abstract one, which does not contribute much to the determination of a concept. It should be replaced by the concept of a web of relations.

One has to situate deductive explanations within this method. The problem with explanations in the social sciences is that there is a countless number of possibilities to describe the boundary conditions—or, in Adorno's words, a countless number of causal chains and relations. Consequently, there are a large number of possibilities to explain an identical phenomenon through general laws. Each level of explanation, each interest, each disciplinary background, each method and almost every look at the phenomenon results in a different description of the phenomenon, even if it does not change in itself. This leads to the multitude that is characteristic of postcolonialism—and to the alternative to either reduce the multitude to rather abstract general laws or to let multitude persist in an arbitrary way. The concept of configuration seems to offer a third way beyond this alternative. This concept confounds law and boundary condition. According to Hempel and nineteenth-century science, a law is valid independently of the phenomena. I wish to argue that laws emerge historically in conjunction with the phenomena. This would mean that all laws have specific realms of application or validity. This is the particular. There are laws that are applicable to a very large number of cases, while others only apply to a few cases. But none applies to all or one. Therefore, Hempel's explanations are merely statistical in the social sciences.

The configurational method consists in constructing histories and relations of phenomena in order to find more and less general statements and to describe the configurations more or less adequately. The goal is neither to find general laws nor to describe the singularity nor to look at the entire history but to show links, relations and similarities. More precisely, the goal is to establish family resemblances (Wittgenstein 1984a). It is not possible to subsume the objects of the social sciences under overarching general concepts because they are not determined by general categories, except in a very abstract sense. Wittgenstein uses the example of a family to explicate this point. The members of a family do not have one trait in common, some share the height, others the colour of the eyes, and yet others the temper—but no two share exactly the same (Wittgenstein 1984a: 67). 'We see a complicated net of similarities that overlap and criss-cross'. (Wittgenstein 1984a: 66; translation mine).

Striving for the general or universal means to exclude most of the knowledge and reality from the social sciences. The problem of the social sciences is not little but too much knowledge. However, limiting oneself to the singular or individual means to be arbitrary and reckless. A phenomenon cannot be interpreted in an arbitrary manner for two reasons. First, social reality is not arbitrary but has definite and often brutal limits. Second, the interpretation has to be acceptable to others. The limits of social reality have been referred to by Hegel and Dilthey as 'resistance'. Wittgenstein called them 'form of life'. 'True or false is what people say; and people agree in their language. This is no agreement of opinions but one of the form of life' (Wittgenstein 1984a: 241; translation mine). Life is 'there', it cannot be altered at will or interpreted arbitrarily (Wittgenstein 1984b: 559). Forms of life are precisely the objects of the social sciences.

Neither Wittgenstein nor Adorno paid much attention to other human beings as co-subjects. The object of the social sciences may contradict a scientific statement—which is not the case in the natural sciences. If the social scientist attributes a certain characteristic (thought, language, lifestyle, etc.) to a human being, he or she may not accept this and there may be an argument about the interpretation. What is more, the object may even contradict the social scientist on a reflexive level by suggesting a different perspective on the object or even another paradigm. This again has been acknowledged by postmodernism and post-colonialism. However, this does not mean that any interpretation or any perspective is equally valid but that the social sciences require understanding—in a double sense. The object has to be understood and between different perspectives an understanding has to be sought. In neither sense a consensus is required but in the first sense some form of testing and in the second sense some form of acceptance is necessary.

The object is another human being. Trying to understand another human being one precisely focuses on 'being'—or 'Dasein'. I have called this type of understanding an 'existential understanding' (Rehbein 2008). Existential understanding is no empathy and no change of perspective but a construction like any type of knowledge. One could say that one fantasizes or dreams of another's being there. If observations of the other's behaviour on the basis of one's own experience fit plausibly to his/her fantasy of the other's being there, then that person has a justified impression of understanding him or her. This is an intellectual and constructive act involving hypotheses and reflection. It differs from other types of knowledge in at least two ways. First, its material is lived experience. Second, its result is not true or false but more or less adequate or plausible. In order to adequately understand another human being, one needs to obtain a certain mastery of his or her symbolic universe and of his or her everyday life. This mastery does not have to be real but may be to a certain extent virtual. We understand another being on the basis of our own being—which includes our personal life course, our historical times, our language, our knowledge and our being in the world. It is possible to acquire full mastery of another language game and form of life and still not understand any other human being in this form of life. On the other hand, it is perfectly possible to know nothing about a certain form of life and still to understand another human being in this form of life plausibly and adequately. There is no ready recipe for understanding. Understanding contributes more than illustrations and verifications to explanations in the social sciences. This would only be the case if the perspective of the social scientist were as objective as in the natural sciences. It is not, as the social scientist is in many ways entangled in the social world, which is his or her object. In a way, social science is merely one point of view on the social world among an endless amount of other points of view (Bourdieu 1999). If these other points of view are to be taken seriously in any way, there is no other access to them except through existential understanding.

Any understanding in the second sense should be based on existential understanding. I would call this second type a 'mutual understanding'. If a person wants to move beyond provincial forms of life and social science, he/she has to actively look for challenges to their own perspective. One has to use one's imagination to reconstruct them, understand people with a point of view different from their own and reach a mutual understanding with them. Ultimately, mutual understanding refers to a common form of life on this planet, which becomes a necessity under the conditions of globalization. As forms of life differ, points of view, standards and actions differ greatly as well. Each is a dialectical structure in itself and cannot be objectively or universally judged. Whenever two forms of life meet, it will not be possible to reach a consensus about all points of view, standards and actions unless one adapts in principle to the other. However, understanding leaves open the option of learning without a consensus. one may learn about a different point of view and accept it without adopting it. In my opinion, this is precisely what understanding is about.

Conclusion

A configurational dialectic differs from Eurocentric theory in abandoning four of its afore-mentioned characteristics. The fifth characteristic, the deductive theory of science, is accorded an unimportant place within the endeavour to construct configurations—webs of relations to other phenomena in the sense of family relations and to history in the sense of more general determining factors. Each configuration is regarded as particular—but neither general nor singular. It refers to something more general but not to an all-encompassing totality that would determine all other configurations in the same way. Finally, the construction of a configuration implies understanding in a double sense. Therefore, I regard it as very important to support Ananta Giri's (2008) programme of 'sociology as conversation'.

Many social scientists have made use of some sort of configurational dialectic closely related to the thoughts advanced in this essay. Marshall Hodgson called the object of his research a 'configuration' (1993: 17). Each new relation alters the entire configuration and results in new relations, while each new perspective opens up new relations as well. In a similar vein, Victor Lieberman has called for a configurational approach. 'I therefore argue less for a single lock-step pattern than for a loose constellation of influences whose local contours must be determined empirically and without prejudice' (2003: 45).

Notes

1. As a matter of convenience, I will subsume the entire Anglo-Saxon world under the term 'Eurocentrism'. For the sake of my argument, the significant difference between Europe and the United States does not play any major role.
2. I apologize for the inconvenient term, especially for the composition of a Latin and a Greek term. However, the expression 'configurational dialectic' seems to capture my intentions best.
3. This container in turn is mainly defined by economic structures. In contemporary society these are subsumed under the term 'capitalism'.
4. In both cases, the rise of Europe may have been based on this intrusion into the Asia-centred trade.

References

Abu-Lughod, Janet L. (1989), *Before European Hegemony, The World System, A.D. 1250–1350*, New York/Oxford: OUP.

Adorno, Theodor W. (1975), *Negative Dialektik*, Frankfurt: Suhrkamp.

———(1979), *Minima Moralia*, Frankfurt: Suhrkamp.

Bhabha, Homi (1994), *The Location of Culture*, New York: Routledge.

Bourdieu, Pierre (1999), *The Weight of the World*, Cambridge: Polity Press.

Fanon, Frantz (1959), *L'an V de la révolution algérienne*, Paris: Maspero.

Frank, André Gunder (1998), *ReOrient*, Berkeley: University of California Press.

Freire, Paulo (1989), *Learning to Question*, Geneva: WCC.

Fukuyama, Francis (1992), *The End of History*, London/New York: Free Press.

Giri, Ananta Kumar (2015), 'Spiritual Cultivation for a Secular Society', in *Religion und die Modernität von Traditionen in Asien*, ed. Judith Schlehe and Boike Rehbein, Münster: LIT., pp. 77–113.

Hegel, Georg W.F. (1970), *Phänomenologie des Geistes*, Frankfurt: Ullstein.

Hempel, Carl Gustav (1965), *Aspects of Scientific Explanation and Other Essays in the Philosophy of Science*, New York: Free Press.

Hobson, John M. (2004), *The Eastern Origins of Western Civilization*, Cambridge: CUP.

Ho Chi Minh (1971), *Ecrits 1920–1969*, Hanoi: Editions en Langues Etrangères.

Hodgson, Marshall G.S. (1993), *Rethinking World History, Essays on Europe, Islam, and World History*, Cambridge: CUP.

Hradil, Stefan (2004), *Die Sozialstruktur Deutschlands im internationalen Vergleich*, Wiesbaden: VS.

Lieberman, Victor (2003), *Strange Parallels: Southeast Asia in Global Context, c. 800–1830*, Cambridge: CUP.

Marx, Karl (1974), *Grundrisse der Kritik der politischen Ökonomie*, Berlin: Dietz.

——— (2002), 'General Introduction to the Critique of Political Economy', in *Selected Writings*, 2nd edn., OUP, pp. 380–400.

Nederveen Pieterse, Jan and Boike Rehbein, eds. (2008), 'Emerging Powers and Global Inequality', *Futures*, October (Special Issue).

Nehru, Jawaharlal (1946), *The Discovery of India*, London: Meridian Books.

Panikkar, Kavalam Madhava (1954), *Asia and Western Dominance*, London: Allen & Unwin.

Pomeranz, Kenneth (2000), *The Great Divergence*, Princeton/London: Princeton University Press.

Radhakrishnan, Sarvepalli (1947), *Religion and Society*, London: Allen & Unwin.

Rehbein, Boike (2007), *Globalization, Culture and Society in Laos*, London/New York: Routledge.

——— (2008), 'Cosmopolitanism and Understanding in the Social Sciences', in 'Cosmopolitanism and Beyond', ed. Ananta Kumar Giri, Manuscript.

Reid, Anthony (1993), *Southeast Asia in the Age of Commerce*, vol. II, New Haven/London: Yale University Press.

Rostow, Walt W. (1960), *The Stages of Growth: A Non-Communist Manifesto*, Cambridge: CUP.

Said, Edward (1978), *Orientalism*, New York: Pantheon Books.

Spivak, Gayatri Chakravorty (1999), *A Critique of Postcolonial Reason*, Cambridge, MA: Harvard University Press.

Stein, Gil J. (1999), *Rethinking World-Systems. Diasporas, Colonies, and Interaction in Uruk Mesopotamia*, Tucson: The University of Arizona Press.

Sugimoto, Yoshio (2003), *An Introduction to Japanese Society*, 2nd edn., Cambridge: CUP.

Vester, Michael von Oertzen et al. (2001), *Soziale Milieus im gesellschaftlichen Strukturwandel*, Frankfurt: Suhrkamp.

Wallerstein, Immanuel (1974), 'The Rise and Future Demise of the World Capitalist System: Concepts for Comparative Analysis', *Comparative Studies in Society and History*, vol. 16, pp. 387–415.

Weber, Max (1978), *Gesammelte Aufsätze zur Religionssoziologie*, 3 vols., 6th edn., Tübingen: Mohr.

Wittgenstein, Ludwig (1984a), 'Philosophische Untersuchungen', *Werkausgabe Band 1*, Frankfurt: Suhrkamp: Philosophische Inter Suchunger, pp. 252–80.

———— (1984b), 'Über Gewissheit', *Werkausgabe Band 8*, Frankfurt: Suhrkamp, pp. 113–257.

7

Creative and Social Research:
Ideas from Discourse Analysis and
Creative Thinking

DES GASPER

Ananta Kumar Giri's essay 'Pathways of Creative Research' proposes to bring '"ontological cultivation"—deeper reflection about be-ing—to the discourse and practice of social research' (Giri 2017). It advocates an epistemology that stresses wide participation, on grounds not only of participation's direct instrumentality for identifying and testing diverse knowledge-claims, but in light of what he terms human persons' ontological sociality. I think these emphases are shared to some degree—greater or lesser, openly or tacitly—by various streams in innovative present-day social research, not least in parts of action-oriented, participatory and interpretive research; including for example some of the strands surveyed by Denzin and Lincoln (2005), Reason, Rowan and Heron in various works and in their own model of cooperative or collaborative enquiry, and Yanow and Schwartz-Shea (2006). This is perhaps a more optimistic impression than given by the opening of Giri's chapter, yet at the same time these streams are indeed not mainstreams.

Other obstacles need to be looked into—educational, logistical and socio-political—that are faced by these approaches, not solely at the obstacles set by widespread philosophical presumptions. For example, centralized power breeds a demand for generalized forms of knowledge claim. Concepts are inevitably limited, which limits the strength of generalized theory, certainly in the social sciences; yet centres of power typically prefer generalizing methodologies, that declare themselves to be objective and sufficient to sustain clear-cut performance rankings which can be used to publicly justify resource allocations and policy decisions. Approaches that stress the limited validity of broad general claims may be more scientifically adequate but less politically welcome and consequently less funded.

Such types of obstacle may imply that ways forward are more likely to be found through examination of examples of effective research practices—effective in sustained extensive use as well as in principle—than through general theorizing on ontology and epistemology, though that has a supportive role to make sense of and give heart to the practices. This judgement is consistent with Edward de Bono's advice that one is more likely to change people's behaviour by examples that change their perceptions—how they focus, frame and visualize a situation—than by logic alone or by trying directly to change their values. Logic is in danger of rushing one to a conclusion, without stopping to think that there are other ways of viewing and responding to the situation than the ones that have been presumed. When each person acts in this way, but from their own set of presumptions, conflict becomes almost guaranteed (de Bono 1985a). Giri's own work has given valuable attention to examples of effective research practices supported in particular social milieux (e.g. in Giri 2004).

I would like to refer to two aspects or areas in research practice that are not highlighted in Giri's chapter, namely, discourse analysis and creative thinking, which embody themes that he raises, and then go further in certain respects. First, I try to connect discussion of creative research to the work on effective creative thinking more generally. Second, while 'ontological sociality' can be explored from many angles—for example, in the work of the 'social quality' movement in Europe (van der Maesen and Walker 2012; Gasper et al. 2015)—the angles provided in discourse analysis, such as on 'subject positions', can be very helpful. Within discourse analysis one of the ways of getting into other people's minds, in both teaching and research, is through intensive text analysis. I will outline a relatively simple and widely accessible method that adds value to the widely known variant used by Wayne Booth and others for structuring research projects (Booth et al. 2008).

Parallel and Creative Thinking

'What is sharp, cool and soft?'

—KHANDWALLA

'When faced with two alternatives, always choose the third'

—Jewish proverb

Creative research is not primarily generated by knowledge of philosophy of science or of standard techniques. It calls instead for fertile imagination. Pradip Khandwalla, a leading figure in the study of innovative public management in India and internationally, shows in his books *Fourth Eye: Excellence Through Creativity* (1988) and *Lifelong Creativity* (2004) that faced with a variety of structures of problems a variety of types of (and stages in) problem solving is required. In particular, techniques of creative thinking are needed in addition to those for deductive reasoning. Most education deals with convergent thinking, the mechanisms of thought for clarifying given problems, analysing them in detail, synthesizing and selecting and refining a solution. Skills are also required for divergent thought: novel thinking that looks for unexpected approaches and solutions; for example, policy responses that do not correspond to identified causes. Creative, divergent thinking requires engagement of other parts of the brain than does convergent thinking. Edward de Bono remarks that at school students are unfortunately trained only in how to interpret given information, not in what to do when there is little information. As a result younger children typically have more ability to create new ideas than do older ones, who lose much of their creativity and require ways for rekindling it. Suggestions in the general creativity literature include diverse ways to stimulate divergent thinking, far different from staring at computer screens and printouts; for example, by musing during a shower or going for a walk.

By referring to de Bono I undertake, in his terms, a provocative operation, a PO. De Bono largely inhabits the world of large corporations, the global centres that advance and enforce the simplistic, non-participatory reasoning of the logic of money power. He pens his pieces in a single draft during his first-class flights to and from super-remunerated speaking engagements. Still his work has much to offer. Belying its airline bookstall manner, it goes deeper than most of the creativity literature.

De Bono's scientific training was in physiological psychology, and his research concerned the physical mechanisms through which people think. This helped him to recognize types of thinking, which people can do but computers cannot. Starting from physiology rather than philosophy, de Bono underlines the imperfect, constructed character of concepts. One must not rely exclusively or even heavily on the unchanging, simplified partitions of experience that are given by standard concepts, and one should look instead at systems, relations and processes (de Bono 1993). Becker (1998: 44–5) warns similarly that one should not, for example, automatically take people as the units of analysis; sometimes activities are the more appropriate unit. But thinking is normally dominated by already-existing categories and concepts, for the human brain is a pattern-seeking and pattern-reproducing mechanism. Each use of a concept reinforces the tendency to see similar situations only in terms of that concept. Special devices are needed to transcend this domination and avoid being trapped by old concepts and habits or by premature and stifling categorization.

De Bono's package of devices for this purpose has several aspects. The earliest part is called lateral thinking, and has enjoyed prominence from the late 1960s onwards (de Bono 1970). It goes much further than brainstorming, the uninhibited search for relevant ideas. For it systematically prompts that search, by use of visual images and Provocative Operations (de Bono 1992); for example, by considering the implications of reversing one of the assumptions about a case. Similarly, it favours interruptions as a method of spurring creativity; they allow one to re-start in a different way.

Edward advises using lateral thinking when there is a focus on purpose—[a preoccupation with set objectives; so think instead about what happens if you] distort it, reverse it, exaggerate it, change it—and [he advises using] random entry [throwing into the discussion at random a word from a quite different context, to see what suggestions this generates] when there is nothing to challenge, nothing to reverse, and in stagnant situations where you keep coming back to the same ideas (Dudgeon 2001: 112).

More generally, de Bono stresses that thinking involves not only inborn intelligence but also learnable skills, to help make the most of whatever inborn intelligence one possesses. Nearly everyone needs training in generic thinking to give 'operacy', which is needed in addition to literacy and numeracy. Like other work on creative thinking, de Bono highlights that various activities within thinking should be distinguished, even if the activities can overlap; and he goes on to make them memorable and communicable by use of vivid standardized titles and acronyms. His CORT (Cognitive Research Trust) family of thinking activities has been used worldwide. The CORT activities are no surprise but the set serves to distinguish, highlight, label, and thus 'institutionalize' them:

- AGO – (specify) Aims, Goals and Objectives
- FIP – look First at Important Priorities
- CAF – Consider All Factors; in other words, gather information. It overlaps with the other activities.
- APC – (specify) Alternatives, Possibilities, Choices. This can include attention to constraints.
- C & S – (specify) Consequences & Sequel, the effects of making a particular choice
- PMI – list the Pluses, then the Minuses, then the other Interesting features of an idea. Don't form an attitude about the idea from looking only at one side.
- OPV – consider Other People's Views. This is a novel element in the CORT list, compared to much advice on reasoning. Reasoning becomes placed in a social context.

Since these different styles of thought involve rather different mental states, they need to be separately recognized and used. Otherwise some are neglected and others overused. For example, the PMI (Plus, Minus, Interesting) method does not consist of a general brainstorming to generate ideas about a topic and then a sorting of the ideas into three boxes—Plus, Minus, Interesting. Instead, one separately concentrates first on one of those three themes, then on the second, then the third, for each involves different skills, different mental circuits. Similarly, brainstorming and argument analysis should be distinct stages; judgement must be suspended while one tries to generate new ideas. CORT has been used with substantial measured beneficial impacts in thousands of schools in many countries, such as China, Malaysia and Singapore; with business executives in many companies, including IBM; with job-seekers; with extra-gifted children, who often need help to rush less in their thinking; and with the mentally handicapped and autistic, who are helped by becoming more self-conscious about thinking (Dudgeon 2001). At one time it was compulsory in schools in Venezuela. In the late 1990s elements of CORT were adopted in the British schools curriculum.

From the mid 1980s on, de Bono introduced a more vivid and— important for this discussion—more social characterization of different thinking activities. He distinguishes 'Six Thinking Hats'. These metaphorical hats can be and are used by individuals alone, but are used mainly for the productive organization of analysis in and by groups. When wearing a White Hat one obtains and digests information, specifies facts; wearing a Red Hat one expresses feelings and intuitions; wearing a Green Hat one identifies and generates alternative possible responses to a situation; wearing a Yellow Hat one identifies advantages and benefits, and gives praise; wearing a Black Hat one finds weaknesses and costs, and makes criticisms; and wearing a Blue Hat one manages the group's processes of thinking and investigation, including by deciding on in which sequence to use the other Hats (which could involve using them several times each). Different tasks will require different combinations and sequences. By highlighting the differences between types of thinking, through the image of 'hats', de Bono encourages one to use them all and use them separately and therefore seriously (de Bono 1985b).

The Six Hats method combines elements from CORT and lateral thinking in a more vivid format. It upgrades CORT's advice to think separately and comprehensively about many issues, for it adds awareness of vital psychological, political, and organizational aspects. For example, feelings are often central motivators for finding (or evading) arguments and alternatives and in making choices. Serious advice on thinking has to incorporate attention to feelings. Of the CORT elements listed above, only 'Other People's Views' (OPV) potentially has that awareness. OPV is tacitly built into the Six Hats system inasmuch as Six Hats is primarily a method for organizing group discussions; OPV may also be seen as one White Hat activity. But if attention to feelings is not highlighted then it is easily overlooked or done too casually. Hence one of the Six Hats is Red.

Similarly important is how to make argumentation probing without being hurtful. Open criticism of other people's views is often difficult, especially in some cultures; and it risks destroying working relationships even in more debate-oriented cultures. Thus in the 'Delphi technique' diverse relevant parties are consulted but are kept apart from each other. A coordinator sends a set of questions to the relevant parties, makes a synthesis from their responses (the synthesis report sometimes includes extracts), receives their reactions to the synthesis and then sends them a new round of questions; and so on, until a concluding synthesis is achieved. The Delphi arrangement avoids unproductive conflict but loses the direct personal interaction that can stimulate and enrich thought and learning. The Hats method has a potential to combine both benefits. The use of separate hats turns discussion into a team effort, during which everybody works together in construction, and in criticism, and in the other activities, rather than having personalized duels as too easily occur otherwise. The group's thinking capacity flows into each of the required thought activities in turn, with members thinking in parallel rather than at cross purposes. Avid and ambitious individuals now cannot shine by attacking other people; instead their energies flow into finding relevant alternatives, during that stage, and into finding their advantages, finding their disadvantages, and so on, each at its own moment. Potentially, each of the activities becomes more effective, none is elided, and time is not lost in battles of ego and status. Dudgeon (2001: 256–64) reports how in Cambodia, a society with traditions of strong hierarchy and unwillingness to lose 'face' by making a statement in public that might be wrong, a large NGO programme adopted and adapted the Six Hats approach with great success.

De Bono sees a connection between a combative/defensive, ego-based, self-righteous approach in argumentation and a traditional essentialist conception that there is one, absolute, truth. But mistaken epistemology is not the only cause of the I Am Right, You Are Wrong syndrome (de Bono 1990). To escape from argumentation as combat one may often need to escape altogether from the mode of argumentation as dispute, into the 'parallel thinking' that the Six Hats method exemplifies (de Bono 1994). The workgroup attacks each facet of a problem jointly; they are never allowed to turn to attacking each other. People can get gratification and fulfil their desires to be noticed and to shine, but not by attacking others, for that destroys the impact of much argumentation and is not always conducive to developing new ideas. Instead individuals can shine in each of the six stages, each of which is conducted by all participants jointly ('in parallel') as cooperators not as rivals. Everyone 'owns' the whole process. Non-rivalrous approaches to argumentation have been feared as likely to bring sleepy complacency and 'groupthink' (see, e.g. Janis 1972). But in Six

Hats Thinking people can try to co-own and jointly undertake also the activities of critical attack and of control of the whole procedure.

Parallel thinking embodies themes relevant for creative and participatory social research. First, a commitment to downgrade ego and, second, to operate collegially, with broad involvement. These themes are supported by two further ideas: avoidance of any expectation of absolute and universal correctness; and recognition of a variety of necessary thinking styles and skills.

Suggestions from Innovative Policy and Project thinking

Within policy analysis there has been much work on creative thinking. In social science research methodology it may perhaps receive less attention. As a result, to rephrase Henry Kissinger, the disputes in social science academe are so bitter, partly because the toolkits that are used, and not only the stakes, are on each side so small. Themes from both the general creative thinking literature and the creative policy analysis work can be helpful then in social research. Often the themes are the same. The popularity of Wayne Booth et al.'s The Craft of Research stems from a profound incorporation of a number of such ideas. Other authors—like Howard Becker (1998), Michael Patton (1987) and Gareth Morgan (1993)—show further connections from creative thinking to research methodology. I will highlight four such themes.

1. A common piece of advice in policy analysis theory is: deal with causes not symptoms. For example, one should prioritize preventive above curative health programmes, and conflict prevention above pouring 'relief' resources into conflict situations; and should provide public support to stressed families, children and communities rather than only belatedly try to deal with symptoms such as crime, middle-class flight and burnt-out teachers. The role of creative thinking here becomes to support a broader-ranging problem analysis that helps one to see that what is focused on as a problem is only the symptom. This theme does not directly apply to research, but a more general version of the principle of broad-ranging analysis does apply: focus on goals rather than on familiar methods. In this way one may identify new methods for reaching the research goals, and compare alternative methods and alternative uses of inputs. The Craft of Research applies this principle to research planning, to help researchers clarify their different levels of objectives and decide which are only means and which are the main

TOPIC →	RESEARCH → QUESTION	RATIONALE/ → MOTIVATED QUESTION	*[PRACTICAL SIGNIFI- CANCE]*
'I study X' [A research area]	'I am studying X because I want to find out why/ how/whether Y (happens)' [This clarifies a research question/ focus/problem]	'I am studying X because I want to find out how/why/ whether Y, so that I can then understand how/why Z' [Z provides the *rationale*. It can be an intellectual purpose or part of some practical real-life problem. If the former, then its practical *significance* may arrive in a 4th column]	*'I am studying X because I want to find out…Y, so that I can then understand how/ why Z, so that we will be able better to arrange/do/ choose about practical issue P'* [A more complex rationale]

Example 1 of a proposed study rationale: 'I am studying Foucault, because I want to learn about how discourses can dominate behaviour; so that I can better understand how a Northern economics model of society dominates in the world, so that I can then contribute to the development or use of alternatives.'

Example 2: 'I am studying women textile workers in Dhaka and London,/because I want to find out why they choose to work in factories or at home,/so that I can then more generally understand women's labour market behaviour,/so that I can then [amongst other uses] assess arguments that factory textile produce from Bangladesh is unethical and forms unfair competition with Northern textiles production and so should be kept out of Northern markets.' (Based on Kabeer 2000.)

FIGURE 7.1: THE KEY SKILL OF FORMULATING A RELEVANT AND FEASIBLE QUESTION FOR INVESTIGATION

Source: Author, using ideas from Booth et al. (1995).

intended ends. Figure 7.1 summarizes the structure of thinking that they advise a researcher to aim for when formulating his or her study.

2. In policy planning this sort of clarification of levels of objective is commonly done through an interactive workshop, a format that potentially can generate both imaginative thinking and rigorous testing (Chambers 2002; Honadle and Cooper 1990). Workshops also have a potential for building shared commitments and teamwork (White 1990). The same principles apply in research planning, not least for action research. Workshops are subject to several dangers too. They can

become exclusively playshops, for example; though to work best they should indeed be partly playful.

3. A second danger in workshops concerns excessive in-group bonding and out-group 'othering'. Each work group within a workshop can come to believe that its solution is best, and that it can and must demolish the work of the other groups. In my experience, each work group assigned to make a choice of water supply methods for a heterogeneous rural area, out of a menu of technical alternatives, typically opts after a complex process of assessment for just one of the alternatives, which it then vigorously advocates. The complexity of the assessments exceeds the care given to initial formulation: the work groups have not been told that the technical alternatives cannot be combined, but they nearly invariably presume that one cannot or should not combine. They think inside a mental 'box' created or inherited by themselves, not directly given. Yet a combination of the methods would allow drawing on the strengths of each of them and would respond better to the diversity of needs. Such group formation and deformation indicates possible advantages of thinking instead in parallel.

    The same 'both-and' principle applies in much research design. Set to prepare a research design for a given question and context, and provided with a menu of 'pure' design alternatives, researchers often busy themselves in the convergent thinking task of weighing the advantages and disadvantages of each approach—for example, conversation analysis, interpretive repertoire analysis, critical discourse analysis and Foucauldian discourse analysis (Wooffitt 2006)—and then selecting and advocating one, while neglecting the divergent thinking task of asking what set of alternatives, including combinations, is really available. Designs containing a combination of approaches can often be best. To achieve that notional optimum requires a technical grasp of each approach, but other things too: avoidance of destructively exclusive group identity formation amongst people educated and socialized into a single approach or discipline; capability for divergent thinking and transcending mental boxes; and a group process that promotes these features. Much evidence shows that engaging in 'boundary work' (Star and Griesemer 1989) at the intersections between different intellectual worlds can be more creative and fruitful than work within those worlds (Dogan and Pahre 1990). The role for parallel thinking and its functional equivalents is clear.

4. Thinking afresh about concepts. Of all themes in creative policy thinking, centremost is the periodic reconsideration of key concepts

that have come to be taken for granted. Jeff Gates (1998) describes the rise of employee participation and the reconceptualization of business ownership as being not only the exclusive domain of 'the employer'. I examine whether in public planning contexts work should be classified only as a cost—the viewpoint taken by a capitalist employer—even though much work is felt as fulfilling (Gasper 2009). Money itself can be re-conceptualized, for example in relation to Local Exchange Trading Systems (LETS); so too can the nature of banking, creditworthiness, and access to funds, as seen in the work of Grameen Bank.

Where can acute, conceptually questioning, box-transcending, creative thinking come from? Discourse analysis can be one contributor. I will try to illustrate this with a particular form of argumentation analysis. My students and I have found helpful a package approach that further adapts and extends the Toulmin format of argumentation structure, which Booth et al. (2008) adopted in The Craft of Research, and that marries it to a format for exploration of meanings and interconnections derived from the work of Michael Scriven (1976). The approach helps one to clarify and test positions and think creatively about improving them or finding alternatives. Particularly important, it is accessible for a wide range of users.

Discourse Analysis, via Text Analysis

As warned by de Bono, classical European rhetoric is antagonistic, 'non-parallel thinking', a battle between viewpoints—as in the debating chamber, the law court, the Western-style parliament, the election. For, the aim is to try to convince a third party—audience, judge and/or jury, electorate—by any and every means that will work (Fahnestock and Secor 1996). In contrast, discourse analysis with a priority to understanding tries to get into the mind of an author, to explore. It typically finds unexpected depths and strengths, and builds respect, even if not agreement.

Consider for example the Rogerian approach to argumentation, based on the ideas of the American humanistic psychologist Carl Rogers, the founder of 'person-centred therapy' (Young et al. 1970). In Rogerian argumentation one pays as much attention to others' ideas as one would like them to pay to one's own. One states one's own viewpoint only after having stated the position of one's debating partner as clearly and carefully as possible, in a way that they can accept. A Rogerian protagonist might proceed as follows: Step 1: 'Your position is Y', presented in a systematic way (such as via the Scriven-Toulmin model); Step 2: 'It's valid when A, B and C'; Step 3: 'My position is M and it's valid when A, S, T and U'; Step 4:

'Your position will gain if it absorbs (parts of) my ideas, in the following way' (Brent 1996). In contrast to the gladiatorial format of classical rhetoric, where the aim is to persuade a third party rather than to convince an opponent, in Rogerian argumentation one tries to convince a counter-claimant or tries to move to an agreed joint position. The format is dyadic and dialogical. Step 1 is the vital step, essential for establishing a mutual willingness to listen and communicate.

Some elements of the Rogerian approach are found in the approaches of Michael Scriven and Stephen Toulmin. Their formats appear at first sight monological—an analyst seeks to assure herself about what is the best representation of a position (as in Rogers's Step 1) and what is the best argued position—but they contain a dialectical, and thereby pragmatic, orientation. For, they hold that positions are to be understood and evaluated within their social, discursive context, including in comparison with the alternative arguments available (see, e.g. Lunsford 2002).

A synthesis of the Scriven and Toulmin approaches uses two main tables for investigation (Gasper 2000a, 2002, 2004a). The first table (see Fig. 7.2) is for understanding more clearly the components and meanings of what you or someone else says. It adapts the method of argument analysis provided in evaluation specialist Michael Scriven's classic textbook *Reasoning* (1976). The second table (see Fig. 7.3) adapts the format for viewing arguments from Stephen Toulmin's even more influential *The Uses of Argument* (1958). This is for clarifying the structure of arguments, how and how well their components fit together. Only if meanings are clarified, as in the first part, can one be ready to check logic and adequacy, in the second part. Further, following de Bono's principle of differentiation of types of thinking, the description and specification of arguments must be separated as far as possible from their ultimate evaluation. Admittedly, when specifying the implicit assumptions of arguments, one has choices between stronger

THE TEXT	COMMENTS ON MEANINGS	A REWORDING OF KEY COMPONENTS	MAIN CONCLUSIONS AND ASSUMPTIONS IDENTIFIED IN THE TEXT
Section 1			
Section 2			
.....			

FIGURE 7.2: TEXT ANALYSIS TABLE

I Claim [this conclusion],	given this Data (empirical facts)	and this Principle (or principles = theoretical and/or value statements);	Unless (/except when) one or more of these counter-arguments applies
Conclusion 1	Data 1.1, (1.2, ...)	Principle 1.1, (1.2, ...)	Rebuttal 1.1, (1.2, 1.3, ,...)
Conclusion 2	Data 2.1, (2.2, ...)	Principle 2.1, (2.2, ...)	Rebuttal 2.1, (2.2, 2.3, ,...)
.....	....	......	......

FIGURE 7.3: TEXT SYNTHESIS TABLE

and weaker—more and less defensible—formulations. Here Scriven advises that stronger formulations be adopted and evaluated, for this leads to judgements that are less easy to criticize and that produce more collective insight.

In the first part of the method a selected key text or passage is looked at closely, line-by-line and word-by-word (see Fig. 7.2). After reading the whole of it carefully:

- The text is placed in the first column of a table and divided into sections, to examine in detail. This helps to both get close to a position and carefully look at all its parts, and to take distance and think about it in a detached way.
- In the second column keywords and phrases are identified and commented upon, including the major images and metaphors, for these can help to reveal choices of assumptions and framing; also the language which hints at praise or criticism and, thus, gives a pointer towards both the value premises and the conclusions of the piece.
- Becker recommends attention too to emphatically asserted clear-cut distinctions. The phrase "'That isn't photography [science/research/...]" ...is a good diagnostic sign of someone trying to preserve a privilege, something they have and don't want to share' (1998: 158). He advises that one look for the unstated premises behind these claims, the motives and roles for such arguments, and why their premises remain unstated.
- Sometimes it is useful to have a column in which one takes keywords and phrases and rewords them more neutrally or with an opposite evaluative load. This helps to clarify the conclusions that the actual choice of words led towards; and it can suggest possible counter-arguments, other ways of viewing the same situation, against which the text should be compared when it is judged overall.

- In the final column, after the second and detailed reading of the whole text, one then identifies the main conclusions and assumptions, both the stated ones and those unstated or hinted at.

Identification and analysis of the figurative constructions is one way to 'open eyes' and generate new ideas. De Bono suggests, for example, that to think of the sources of one's thinking or identity as 'roots' gives too fixed an image; instead, the image of tributaries flowing into a river is less restricting and more appropriate (Dudgeon 2001: 206, 293). Attention to the metaphors used in the rhetoric of research is particularly important; such as the engineer's language of design or the explorer's language of discovery of the mysterious and unforeseen. Economists favour adjectives like 'solid', 'elegant' and 'neat', and metaphors of battle and the jungle. Examination of the typical imagery and rhetoric of economics, led by Deirdre McCloskey (e.g. 1994) and Philip Mirowski (e.g. 1989), has been revelatory.[1] McCloskey shows how models are particular types of metaphor, for models say that A (a complex phenomenon) is like B (a simplified model), at least in the aspects that are considered important. Even a production function is a metaphor, argues McCloskey: by using which it is accepted that the production process can be spoken of as if it were a mathematical function. Creators of such ideas knew they are metaphors but modern users have forgotten, which sometimes leads to misuse.

Becker (1998) raises more general doubts about the imagery and associated logic of social research that tries to estimate the separate impact of each of a set of causes as if they were separate weights to be placed in a weighing scale. Other causal factors are held constant and then the highlighted hypothesized causal factor is varied, to see what (if any) impact this produces on the effect-variable (the weighing scale's dial). If one considers that an alternative image fits the case better, an image of clapping hands together, it will be concluded that it is futile to ask how much of the contribution is due to the left hand, how much to the right. Becker's chapter on logic proceeds to offer an alternative way of thinking for social research.

Hunting for value-premises has an important role too. This does not depend on an ontological assertion of a strong fact-value distinction. (An ontology of strict fact-value division would anyway not entail an epistemological stance that declares value knowledge to be impossible.) Instead, the procedure of seeking to identify and comment on values has a methodological justification: that it deepens understanding in several ways, regardless of whether facts and values are fully separable or not (Gasper 2008). From a pragmatist viewpoint for example, one can—with de Bono— be sceptical of the strength of most broad concepts and of one's ability often to sharply distinguish facts and values, and yet one will treat the adequacy of distinctions as dependent on particular contexts and purposes, and will stress how attention and understanding are in important ways guided by values, which should thus be consciously considered. One may add that values of caring are not promoted by avoiding value discourse; and that creativity depends on motivation, and thus connects to caring.

The second part of the method builds on the results from the first. In Figure 7.3, the synthesis table, for each important conclusion identified in the first table one specifies the basis on which it is proposed: the asserted or assumed data and principles. The possible counterarguments (rebuttals) that are also specified can either be direct doubts about the identified data and principle(s), or other doubts or exceptions concerning the claimed conclusion. Often it is found that the Claim in one row reappears in another row as a declared Principle or Datum, as part of a multi-step argumentative structure (see, e.g. Roldan and Gasper 2011).

Seeking the principle(s)—in Toulmin's language the Warrant(s)—that are used, explicitly or more usually implicitly, in moving from given Data to a proposed Claim/conclusion helps to 'show how an argument is connected to the wider social context and [to show] the traditions and social practices that sustain the credibility of the argument' (Gold et al. 2002: 375). Gold et al. report how identification of the warrants within their practice-stories helps managers to reflect on 'why they had drawn on a particular discourse or social language', and leads them into 'questioning three topics: current organizational practice (e.g., Why do I/we do things this way?); identity and life history (e.g. Why am I like this?); and relationship to "experts" and others in authority (e.g. Why do I consider this person to be correct?)' (2002: 379). When the managers whom Gold and the other authors taught began to apply argument analysis, they started to engage in major elements of critical thinking, including 'critique of rhetoric', in the sense of questioning 'the assumptions, logic and general credibility of their [own] arguments' (2002: 382); and second, 'critique of tradition': 'in particular a questioning of who they are and a critique of their own and others' practices. This critique of tradition was principally achieved through a careful examination of the warrant. Through this process managers could focus on how their arguments relied on a particular understanding or way of speaking' (2002: 383). Third, some of the managers arrived at 'critique of authority': 'Argument analysis provided a means to examine the reasons for their suppressed voice and their perception of the nature of authority . . . [We] found managers questioning the validity of their own position, attending to the perspectives of others and looking to find areas of mutual agreement as a way of taking things forward' (Gold et al. 2002: 383). They found also in some managers a shift towards 'a more contextualized form of epistemological understanding' (2002: 383). In sum, argument analysis can generate reflective identification of the habitual discourses that agents have accepted as authoritative.

Thinking Outside Boxes, and Inside Humane Perspectives

The overall procedure for text analysis that I have just described combines element-by-element examination with reflection on structural roles, assumptions, possible counterarguments and alternative formulations. It embodies a principle of both getting close and taking distance, in order to see more and to move 'outside the box'. It nearly always provides interesting new insights about what is being said and how, and a helpful basis for then evaluating and if necessary changing. This sort of detailed text analysis, involving fresh and close examination, helps us, first, to avoid being the prisoner of preconceptions. Many errors are missed when proofreading, especially one's own work. Since the mind is used to operating in terms of familiar patterns, often only that which is expected to be seen is seen. Becker warns similarly that usually mental 'scripts' are too readily available in one's head and these are superficially used to 'explain' cases of which one has little or no knowledge. It is too easy, on the basis of a few facts and almost no deep knowledge of a case, to compose a picture or story about what is going on, by using a mass of tacit 'stereotypes [which] my own experience of society has provided me with' (Becker 1998: 13). Detailed observation and description of a case 'helps us get around conventional thinking. A major obstacle to proper description and analysis of social phenomena is that we think we know most of the answers already' (Becker 1998: 83). In the same way, ordinary reading usually misses many significant aspects in a text. Detailed specification of the text's components and structure of presentation and argumentation helps to counteract prejudgement concerning the content and quality of its arguments.

The prejudgements involved are non-random. Frequently they come from dominant societal 'scripts', master discourses. Equally, such scripts may structure the texts. Close attention to texts helps one to see better the choices that were involved in making them, and the impacts on meanings and conclusions from having followed those choices rather than some alternative; and it leads one to consider what were the influences on those choices. Examining the impact of different choices of words, and of different warrants, data, etc., helps one to build counterarguments and 'counter scenarios' to compare against the original argument and representation. The search for an accurate, thoughtful picture of texts can thus have a radical, emancipatory implication: it leads one to think independently in relation to existing power hierarchies. Becker points out

(1998: 90–1) that often one does not look in a fresh, independent way at a situation because of the assurance given by the people in power that this is unnecessary; e.g. educators may typically advise that one should study students and their weaknesses and failings, and, implicitly, should not study the educators. By highlighting alternatives and the roles of power, text analysis can help to build the power of alternatives.

Various stages and roles have been identified, including argument generation, argument specification and argument evaluation. It is important to keep these separate. In each of those stages one can sometimes use parallel thinking. Thus something can be added to Giri's call for an ontological epistemology of participation. Since various types of thought are each important, there is no one proper stance for the social researcher, whether as scholar-activist or detached sociologist. Rather, there exists a range of distinct, necessary roles (Gasper 2000b; 2004b). One needs to alternate, and combine, close involvement and cool detachment. Research, like policy analysis, needs to be sharp and cool and soft (one answer to Khandwalla's conundrum stated near the opening of this paper)—creatively sharp-witted, critically cool-headed, caringly soft-hearted. Text analysis is one way to facilitate this and train for it. Its humanistic roots—and in this case one can affirm that metaphor—may help to ensure that 'the freedom that thinking brings' (Dudgeon 2001: 297) becomes a freedom used for humane and caring ends, rather than a Nietzschean fest of creativity for selfish and cruel ones.

Parallel thinking, and text analysis of the type I have sketched, leading into discourse analysis, can contribute to bringing the ideals of Giri's project further into practice.

Note

1. See for example McCloskey's 'How to do a Rhetorical Analysis, and Why' (1994), available with most of her other published works at: http://www.deirdremccloskey.com/articles/index-php. Recommended also are, e.g. her 'Storytelling in Economics' and 'Towards a Rhetoric of Economics'.

References

Becker, Howard (1998), *Tricks of the Trade: How to Think About Your Research While Doing It*, Chicago: University of Chicago Press.

de Bono, Edward (1970), *Lateral Thinking: A Textbook in Creativity*, London: Jonathan Cape.

———(1985a), *Conflicts: A Better Way to Resolve Them*, London: Harrap.

———— (1985b), *Six Thinking Hats*, New York: Little, Brown, and Co./revd. edn., 2000, London: Penguin.

———— (1990), *I Am Right, You Are Wrong*, New York: Viking.

———— (1992), *Serious Creativity*, London: Harper Collins.

———— (1993), *Water Logic*, New York: Viking.

———— (1994), *Parallel Thinking*, New York: Viking.

Booth, Wayne, Gregory Colomb and Joseph Williams (1995), *The Craft of Research*, Chicago: University of Chicago Press, 2nd edn. 2003; 3rd edn. 2008.

Brent, Doug (1996), 'Rogerian Rhetoric: Ethical Growth through Alternative Forms of Argumentation', in *Argument Revisited, Argument Redefined*, ed. B. Emmel et al., pp. 73–96.

Chambers, Robert (2002), *Participatory Workshops*, London: Earthscan.

Denzin, Norman K. and Yvonna S. Lincoln, eds. (2005), *The Sage Handbook of Qualitative Research*, Thousand Oaks, CA: Sage.

Dogan, M. and R. Pahre (1990), *Creative Marginality: Innovations at the Intersections of Social Sciences*, Boulder, CO: Westview.

Dudgeon, Piers (2001), *Breaking Out of the Box—The Biography of Edward de Bono*, London: Hodder.

Emmel, B., P. Resch and D. Tenney, eds. (1996), *Argument Revisited, Argument Redefined*, Thousand Oaks, CA: Sage.

Fahnestock, J. and M. Secor (1996), 'Classical Rhetoric: The Art of Argumentation', in *Argument Revisited, Argument Redefined*, ed. B. Emmel et al., Thousand Oaks, CA: Sage, pp. 97–123.

Gasper, Des (2000a), 'Structures and Meanings—A Way to Introduce Argumentation Analysis in Policy Studies Education', *Africanus*, vol. 30, no.1, pp. 49–72, Longer version at http://adlib.iss.nl/adlib/uploads/wp/wp317.pdf.

———— (2000b), 'Anecdotes, Situations, Histories: Reflections on the Use of Cases in Thinking about Ethics and Development Practice', *Development and Change*, vol. 31, no. 5, pp. 1055–83, Earlier version at http://biblio.iss.nl/opac/uploads/wp/wp300.pdf.

———— (2002), 'Fashion, Learning and Values in Public Management: Reflections on South African and International Experience', *Africa Development*, vol. 27, no. 3, pp. 17–47.

———— (2004a), 'Studying Aid: Some Methods', in *Ethnographies of Aid: Exploring Development Texts and Encounters*, ed. J. Gould and H.S. Marcussen, International Development Studies, Roskilde University, Denmark, pp. 45–92. Also at http://biblio.iss.nl/opac/uploads/wp/wp382.pdf.

———— (2004b), 'Interdisciplinarity', in *Creative Social Research*, ed. Ananta Kumar Giri, Lanham, MD: Lexington Books and Delhi: Sage, pp. 308–44.

———— (2008), 'From "Hume's Law" to Policy Analysis for Human Development', *Review of Political Economy*, vol. 20, no. 2, pp. 233–56. Earlier version at http://biblio.iss.nl/opac/uploads/wp/wp451.pdf.

———— (2009), 'Capitalism and Human Flourishing?', in *Global Social Economy: Development, Work and Policy*, ed. John B. Davis, London: Routledge, pp. 13–41.

Gasper, Des, Thanh-Dam Truong, Laurent van der Maesen and Alan Walker (2015), 'Human Security and Social Quality: Contrasts and Complementarities', in *New*

Horizons of Human Development, ed. Ananta Kumar Giri, Delhi: Studera Press, pp. 229–56.

Gates, Jeff (1998), *The Ownership Solution*, Harmondsworth: Penguin Books.

Giri, Ananta Kumar, ed. (2004), *Creative Social Research*, Lanham MD: Lexington Books and Delhi: Sage.

——(2017), 'Pathways of Creative Research', in this volume.

Gold, J., D. Holman and R. Thorpe (2002), 'The Role of Argument Analysis and Story Telling in Facilitating Critical Thinking', *Management Learning*, vol. 33, no. 3, pp. 371–88.

Heron, J. (1996), *Cooperative Inquiry: Research into the Human Condition,* London: Sage.

Honadle, G. and L. Cooper (1990), 'Closing the Loops: Workshop Approaches to Evaluating Development Projects', in *Methods for Social Analysis in Developing Countries*, ed. K. Finsterbusch et al., Boulder, CO: Westview, pp. 185–202.

Janis, Irving (1972), *Victims of Groupthink; A Psychological Study of Foreign-policy Decisions and Fiascoes*, Boston: Houghton Mifflin.

Kabeer, Naila (2000), *The Power to Choose—Bangladeshi Women and Labour Market Decisions in London and Dhaka*, London: Verso.

Khandwalla, Pradip (1988), *Fourth Eye: Excellence through Creativity*, New Delhi: Wheeler Publishing.

——(2004), *Lifelong Creativity*, New Delhi: Tata McGraw-Hill.

Lunsford, Karen (2002), 'Contextualizing Toulmin's Model in the Writing Classroom', *Written Communication*, vol. 19, no. 1, pp. 109–74.

McCloskey, Deirdre (1994), 'How to Do a Rhetorical Analysis, and Why', in *New Directions in Economic Methodology*, ed. Roger Backhouse, London: Routledge, pp. 319–42.

Mirowski, Philip (1989), *More Heat than Light: Economics as Social Physics; Physics as Nature's Economics*, Cambridge, MA: CUP.

Morgan, Gareth (1993), *Imaginization: The Art of Creative Management*, Newbury Park, CA: Sage.

Patton, Michael (1987), *Creative Evaluation*, 2nd edn., Newbury Park, CA: Sage.

Reason, P., ed. (1995), *Participation in Human Inquiry,* London: Sage.

Reason, P. and J. Rowan, eds. (1981), *Human Inquiry: A Sourcebook of New Paradigm Research*, London: Wiley.

Roldan, Bernice and Des Gasper (2011), 'The Global Forum on Migration and Development: "All talk and no action", or "a chance to frame the issues in a way that allows you to move forward together?"', in *Transnational Migration and Human Security*, ed. T-D. Truong and D. Gasper, Heidelberg: Springer.

Scriven, Michael (1976), *Reasoning*, New York: McGraw Hill.

Star, S. and J. Griesemer (1989), 'Institutional Ecology, "Translations" and Boundary Objects', *Social Studies of Science*, vol. 19, pp. 387–420.

Toulmin, Stephen (1958), *The Uses of Argument*, Cambridge: CUP.

Van der Maesen, Laurent and Alan Walker, eds. (2012), *Social Quality: From Theory to Indicators*, Basingstoke: Palgrave Macmillan.

White, Louise (1990), *Implementing Policy Reforms in LDCs: A Strategy for Designing and Effecting Change*, Boulder: Lynne Rienner.

Wooffitt, Robin (2006), *Conversation Analysis and Discourse Analysis*, London & New Delhi: Sage.

Yanow, Dvora and Peregrine Schwartz-Shea, eds. (2006), *Interpretation and Method: Empirical Research Methods and the Interpretive Turn*, New York & London: M.E. Sharpe.

Young, Richard E., Alton L. Becker and Kenneth L. Pike (1970), *Rhetoric: Discovery and Change*, Harcourt, Brace & World.

8

Research as Searching for Nescience

PETER HERRMANN

Control and its Loss:
Reconsidering the Social Dimension

It is quite common to see the social dimension of control solely in its politico-economic meaning, leaving perhaps a small portion to social work and (social) pedagogy. There are surely good reasons for such perspective—not least the fact that political control and economic power relationships play such a prominent role in the (modern and still industrialist) societies, leaving only small, adjudicate spaces for control to 'individuals themselves' as citizens.[1] Control, moreover: the question of control is thus segmented, on the one hand seen as matter of individual life and as such very much a matter of self-control; on the other hand it is seen as a matter of 'transcending' social sphere, supposing to be more a question of structures. Already this formulation suggests that the problematic is actually about something else. There is a need to look for the underlying soci(et)al developments and structures: socio-political control, political practice and (social) science apparently lost their sound reference to the actuality of the social. And this means as well, that they lost any foundation on which creativity can be based. This means that control emerges as more or less oppressive power, political practice moves towards short-term oriented executism and science develops as utilitarian instrumentalism. Thus, the search for pathways towards creative research has to concern itself with looking for wide roads rather than just pathways, if it is right to understand the latter as narrow openings. Nevertheless, these wide roads, possible new highways will have to be pathways as it is not just about seeking to simply replace the existing

*I am grateful to Laurent van der Maesen and Yitzhak Berman for the inspirations arising from frequent discussion. Also I want to express my thanks to Brigitte Kratzwald and Hans F. Zacher—ongoing communication with them had been surely meaningful in the context of the work on this contribution.

approaches. Instead, the aim has to be to weave a new network of access routes that can serve as facilitator of new research and cognizance.

Integrity, Dissolution and Transcendence

INDIVIDUALIZATION: LOSS OF INTEGRITY

Science, including social science, can be seen as one of the foundations and also one of the consequences of Western enlightenment. Seeing it as foundation is very much a matter of linking it to the emergence of the individual in today's understanding, as

[a]n image of individualist self-identity must be situated within the context of individualism itself; within the web, adduced earlier, of a world in which each person thinks of himself as his own maker, as his own telos. In such a world, according to the political scientist Steven Lukes, four basic values prevail: 'the dignity of man', or the person as an end in himself; the autonomy and self-direction of the person; privacy, or personal sovereignty over the domain of self; and self-development, the imperative to allow the self to pursue its own 'genius'. Therefore, the individualist self is the referent of a person who speaks about and values his own and other persons' identities as independent, autonomous units—'selves'—who have a hand in crafting their separate and there individual destinies.

– MASCUCH (1996: 20).

The specific ambiguity is clear; although the general development is one of increasing control through human action, the emerging pattern had been at the very same time one of loss of practice: action developed towards being conceptualized in a more or less shallow way as increasingly utilitarian, 'purposeful' action.

Considering practice as different from action, the deeper meaning that is lost may be seen: connections and links between individual acts are in this perspective only established ex post, by a process of socialization that is comparable with—and actually ontologically derived from—capitalist production itself. Production occurs as individual act, only in the hope of being later valued on the market. And even on the market—in the case that value-confirmation and thus socialization occurs—a genuine social process is not found but only process of socialization that is mediated by commodities, in their most abstract form: money. Accepting these presumptions by no means is a naturalist and trans-historical approach suggested. The concern is with the fact that abstract labour can become the measure of value only to the degree that a specific kind of human labour—wage labour—becomes general (Harvey, [1982] 2006: 15).

Then value, on the one hand being a social relation, is inextricably bound to the commodity form which itself is depending on exchange that takes place after production by individuals.[2] On the other hand it has to be accepted that the following complex relationship is indissociably interwoven with this presented pattern.

The extension of exchange puts producers into relations of reciprocal dependency. But they relate to each other by way of the products they exchange rather than directly as social beings. Social relationships are expressed as relationships between things. On the other hand, the things themselves exchange according to their value, which is measured in terms of abstract labour. And abstract labour becomes the measure of value through a specific social process. (Harvey, [1982] 2006: 17)

Actually, complex relationship can also be seen in another way; the social relationship itself, its genuine character is now fundamentally undermined and its complexity is reduced. Fetishism goes hand in hand with alienation, and is actually in several regards nothing else than a specific form of alienation itself. And, as such, it runs like a kind of general thread through all social relations: the capitalist process of production as social construct; the capitalist exchange with its immanent drive to permanently redefine even the most useless use-values as actually especially useful (for instance by 'branding'); the increasing integration and subordination of genuine social relations into and under the process of commodification; and of course it importantly determines, serves and underlies also the development of socially constructing scientific work (be it as educational process or as matter of research).

Importantly, another point needs to be kept in mind: as much as one is confronted with personifications of economic relations and moreover with the penetration of all fibres of life by capitalist principles, one has to consider that this is a hugely contradictory process. This means not only that certain aspects of life are still 'exempted' but it also means that one has to look at the concrete patterns by which the relationships are realized. Valuation is as much an economic category as it is a social category, concerned with the socio-economic recognition of things and processes and the human beings themselves in a given society, and that means today: in a society of which the rationality is following the crude rules of the capitalist mode of production.

For research—and in particular for research that does not accept a limitation of research practice on permanent replication of existing fundamental knowledge by its application to 'new data' or at most 'new realities'—this poses obviously a major challenge. There is a need to develop a truly iterative pathway that combines practice, an understanding of the substantial objectivity of reality and its 'evaluation' based on and oriented towards the intervention into reality. Figure 9.1 tries to visualize this.

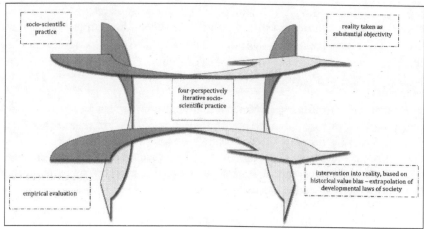

FIGURE 8.1

SCIENTIFICATION: LOSS OR GAIN OF CONTROL?

On the second level, science is seen as a consequence. To the extent to which one can take enlightenment as matter of shifting responsibility towards individuals—accompanied by the loss of practice, replaced by the orientation on action—one is also confronted with a shift of disjoining or dissolving meaning.[3] Rather than being a matter of personalities as 'whole, content entities', merged with the environment—two entities that are integrated in themselves and mutually in each other—one is now confronted with just the opposite: two themselves disintegrating, even decomposing entities, separating from each other and moreover developing in to contradictions of each other.

This finds various expressions and many social science analysis is importantly impeded by the fact that even the analysis of the process of disembedding is based on the presumption of some kind of disembodied-ness. So at this point, distinct debates are found, especially (1) on secularization, looking for the patterns and meaning of processes around the loss of previously integrated systems of 'meaning' and (2) on economic patterns as apparently technical, non-social processes.

The paradox is the increasing capability of acting in terms of influencing issues on the surface—the gain of reach—going hand in hand, with and depending on the decreasing capability of maintaining practice as a matter of depth. The Luhmann's dictum that everything could be different but that humans are not able to change anything (Luhmann 1969: 44) translates into the increasing orientation on superficiality of life and the equally increasing feeling of loss and respective search for meaning. It is important to acknowledge this as a matter of development, thus allowing an understanding that is found somewhat in waves, the reoccurrence of the fundamentally same complaints: the persistence of the loss of confidence and a permanency of fin de siècle sentiments.

The actual paradox is this: it is seen at least in general, on the one hand, the lament about development which is again and again perceived as alienation; nevertheless celebrated development as an 'abstract form' is also, then captured as an expression of individual (sic) self-realization by way of absolute reunification; the absolute idea (sic) as absolute independence and also as absolute transcendence. One may well consider this interpretation of development as being seen as a kind of reification or objectification; although people, individuals, surely play a role as 'rational beings', being able to make choices, they are nevertheless also very much personifications of economic relations. Leaving the inherent contradiction aside, here too is seen a re-emergence of natural right theories. To the extent to which the absolute idea is suggested to be a way of regaining integrity of humankind and rejoining humanity and nature, it paradoxically follows the laws of nature, the laws inherent in the processes themselves rather than giving rise to history as being a consciously controlled and designed process.[4]

While this may seem to be very 'abstract', its immediate relevance is reflected in terms of socio-political analysis in Hegel's considerations around social class, distinguishing between peasantry, the middle classes of the burghers and the business class. It is important to keep in mind that:

[f]or Hegel, classes always remain estates, in the sense that they represent a legitimized differentiation (interestingly enough, Hegel uses the term 'class' only when referring to those directly involved in labour). Each estate stands for a different mode of consciousness: the principle of immediate trust and obedience is represented in the peasantry, the principle of law and order in the middle classes, and the principle of universality in the bureaucracy, the universal class. (AVINERI 1971: 113)

Of course, this is then consequently translated into his interpretation of the state, seen in terms of the 'universality of political power' (Avineri 1972/1994: 42).

To quote Hegel:

An act issued by the public authority is a general act and in virtue of its generality it carries in itself the rule for its application. The matter it affects is general, homogenous. The act of the public authority varies in itself a free and general determinacy and its execution is at the same time its application. (AVINERI: 181)

Hegel, though importantly pointing out some central matters of the development of class and the transcendence of humankind, the blasting of the fetters of instinct-led behaviour, remains caught in or even reinforces the dichotomization of ethical principals. He acknowledges the need for transcending the bourgeois in the form of the 'higher developed' citoyen, asking Bildung in the understanding of formation and more importantly development of personality to take the role of facilitator of such process. But he fails to acknowledge the need of such transcendence going beyond a simple 'merger by harmonization' or 'merger by finding a common minimum denominator'. Hegel's understanding of Aufhebung, being concerned with sublation and supersession, remains a matter of maintaining the dichotomy which then finds its expression for instance, in the two forms of ethics: Moralität as individual ethics and Sittlichkeit as social ethics. The only way of fundamentally solving this contradiction is by defining the dichotomy as what it actually is—a fundamental contradiction of two systemic elements, the separation of production and consumption as it is interwoven with the separation of use value and exchange value which can be seen in some way as dissolution of an abstract category of value. The latter can be presumed to the extent to which it is accepted that value is primarily a socio-historical category.

However, this creates a serious problem in the process of social science research and subsequently also with a major limitation of socio-political (i.e. soci[et]al) practice. A fundamental loss is faced of the social as a matter of human practice. The human being is confronted with the social as apparently independent, objectified reality, later considered by Émile Durkheim as social facts of which he writes that they exist separately from the individual and as a coercive force upon them.

Taking a broader historical perspective, and basing this on the mainstream thinking, mainly referring to Hegel's work, it is interesting to bring three strands together.

Hegel's View on Class Hierarchy

Hegel presumes three main classes in modern societies. Hegel's view is here of special importance as he is not concerned with the immediate position of different classes in the economic system, i.e. the process of production. Instead—and surely not least somewhat complementing a Marxist perspective—he is looking at how the different classes relate to nature and the processes of appropriation. This results in attributing to each of the three classes a particular 'ethical lifestyle', i.e. a specific relation to the different dimensions of ethical life. This had been earlier briefly explored.

Hegel's View on Ethical Life

With respect to ethical life one finds a fundamental—dialectical— dichotomization that sets social and individual ethics aside from social ethics. Hegel, in the German original, speaks of Moralität in the first case and Sittlichkeit in the second case. There is now confronted with a 'double-triangularization', which can be seen as replication of the class division. First, ethical life in general terms strongly refers to 'will' and is as such a matter of how nature is related to—the 'external' nature that is seen all around but also and not least the inner nature in form of instincts and the question of domesticating these forms of immediate expression now subordinated under various mechanisms of control. Looking, then, at 'will' the unconstrained, instinct-based will of taking crude possession is found, hierarchically followed by a reflected will—though limited in the reflection by the individual referring to him/herself and the immediate (social) environment and being expressed as individual ethics, i.e. Moralität. It is supposedly only on the third level that a higher plane of ethical life is found, namely, Sittlichkeit—Hegel suggests this as a matter of a complex relationship between the individual who considers him/herself consciously as part of a relationship or even relationality. On the one hand, she/he is gaining independence from immediate individual will (overcoming instincts), on the other hand this conscious engagement, by transcending him/herself, is able to relate on a higher level with the physical environment.

Hegel's view on Sittlichkeit

This higher plane, Sittlichkeit, is now itself triangularized

1. Natural spirit; the family;
2. The civil society, or spirit in its dual existence and mere appearance;
3. The state, or freedom, which, while established in the free self-dependence of the particular will is also universal and objective. This actual and organic spirit [a] is the spirit of a nation, [b] is found in the relation to one another of national spirits, and [c] passing through and beyond this relation is actualized and revealed in world history as the universal world-spirit, whose right is the highest.

– Hegel (1820: 33).

This can be understood by looking at Russian nesting dolls, in some way parallel to their hierarchical interlacing—class-organization and division of society, being the container for morality, which is itself in some way a container for ethical life (Sittlichkeit); and saying that it is a container 'in some way' refers to the fact that it can be seen as the procrustean bed, providing the higher ethical echelon; and it also shows the Hegelian understanding of society as dialectical tension of Aufhebung.

All this can be seen as a reflection of the principal limitation of traditional thinking, permanently reproducing some form of closure, which is based on hierarchical principles. Furthermore, it is not least the unconscious penetration by the Christian Trinitarian formula, aiming at defining a way between or balance of the

- 'actual ideal reality' as a given socio-political economy;
- its 'exclusionary' character of being a 'society' that is not even for its members in a position to fulfil the complete 'civic state'; and
- the absolute ideal: the integrated 'state' as the absolute idea, a representation of an ideal representation of the general interest, be it understood as objectively and 'externally/eternally' given or be it understood as 'negotiated sum total' of the citizens.

The challenge is, especially in connection with the challenge of defining fundamental and social rights, that such undertaking cannot be approached—either as a matter of definition or of implementation—if and when such rights are not 'accepted' and borne by the people; in other words, they will be voided if and when they are imposed from above.

With this arises a fundamentally important question with two dimensions, the first being concerned with power and the second a matter of property.

One may begin with the frequently-stated and widely-accepted presumption that the state is by and large a body mainly concerned with the protection of property. On this general level this does not necessarily claim any specific form of property and can thus be communal or private. Actually, it is necessary to start from another dimension rather than looking at the legal status of property. At stake is to develop an understanding of property as process—the process of appropriation. Understood this way, there seems to be a push towards some form of communal property. That and the way in which appropriation depends on labour as the actual process of appropriation—a process that links and interweaves human individuals with each other—is in the same respect relevant for the constitution and design of the relationship between humankind and nature ('confronting' nature with individuals, groups and societies alike), and finally constitutes not least social relationships, i.e. the relationship between groups and classes respectively.

The ménage à trois thus gains, so to say as a fourth moment and its buttress, the 'social dimension' that requires and maintains[5] the individual relationships by providing direction but is by no means an external force. It gains its existence from the permanent interaction of conditional, constitutional and normative factors. It is only this permanent interaction that establishes its existence and defines it at the very same time as immanent socio-historical moment of practice rather than as social fact, external and independent from practice, only reifying it.

Linking property and process this way directs one smoothly towards rethinking power, highlighting that it is fundamentally concerned with control and appropriation. However, an effort to overcome the general negative notion which is linked to political and personal control—very much as matter of 'limiting the other'—as default has to be made. The reference then is the 'notion of an appropriation of nature by human beings in order to satisfy 'their wants and needs' (Harvey 1982: 5) which Harvey defines as 'basis of Marx's conception of the world'. This may easily misinterpreted as anthropocentric. To avoid such anthropocentrism one may, however, introduce on the one hand the consideration of appropriateness and on the other hand the notion of (cap)ability. With this the human beings and nature actually enter the processes of relationality as it had been presented earlier. And it can also be seen that relationality gains a time perspective, which can only be grasped by a truly dialectical understanding of the permanent interaction of conditional, constitutional and normative factors. A further dimension to this is that a clear distinction between development and growth is necessitated. This goes much beyond the current debate on qualitative growth and developing measuring tools that go beyond GDP. It is not about a return to any romanticized historical past. But at least one needs to keep in mind that

before the emergence of the industrial revolution, which had been also a revolution concerned with fossil fuels, there had not been any or any major growth. Again: Before the emergence of capitalismó before the separation of wage work and capital, before the transformation of fossil fuels in work related energy, before the emergence of the societally guiding principle that a surplus product has to provide surplus value there had not been growth. Zelik and Altvater (2009: 26)

This brings one to another orientation, the need to replace growth by development concerned with quality of relationships rather than quantities of supply.

Social Services: Contradiction in Terms

Using this background as a way to approach a closer understanding of the social, it will here and now be necessary to concentrate on social services, a particularly important issue in terms of today's policy debates and also an area that allows especially well to understand the relevant tensions.

Speaking of social services means to some extent dealing with a contradiction in terms, the social commonly being defined by matters of mutuality, 'equal-relationality', complex relations of acting together whereas service carries a general notion of hierarchical relationship, one-sidedness and activity of providing something for somebody.

In other words, in the one case one is employed by a pattern of complex relations whereas in the second case the relationship is at least in tendency one-sided, determined by the 'provider' who, though showing openness, remains a hegemonic instance.

A possible solution to this tension is to orient attention towards a strong, i.e. ontological relationality of which Brent Slife says

[s]trong relationality ... is an ontological relationality. Relationships are not just the interactions of what was originally nonrelational; relationships are relational 'all the way down'. Things are not first self-contained entities and then interactive. Each thing, including each person, is first and always a nexus of relations. (2004: 159).

Building on this, I propose a shift in thinking in four steps:

1. from self-centred, reflexive considerations to a referential approach, i.e. an approach which considers explicitly that—and in which way—identity is dealing with issues of demarcation, defining identity by differentiation, as matter of being different from 'the other';
2. moving from such self-referential approach to weak relationality;
3. then moving from weak relationality further to strong relationality;
4. and finally from strong relationality to multiple strong relationality, adding explicitly to the before mentioned dimension the aspect of time and space. Rather than talking about multiple strong relationality The term strong relational integrity may also be used, aiming by this to advance an understanding that allows grasping time and space also as fundamentally social matters.[6]

Relationality

There are at least three important dimensions to this when it comes to substantial terms determining this kind of relationality: first, concern is with a productive process and the understanding of productive is going back to Hegel's understanding where he speaks of labour as complex engagement that is linked to appropriation and the development of 'power' by Bildung, a matter of developing increasing 'control', distancing oneself from crude needs and from being occupied solely by 'nature' and 'basic needs'. This is surely also of central focus for social policy, when employment is put into the centre of many approaches; labour has not least a socializing character. However, seeing it this way means not least to acknowledge that the actually important part is the quality of work rather than just getting people into a job. Quality of work in the perspective of such socializing character of labour means not least that it is a matter of property building—not, however, following Hegel's conclusion that property, namely, private property is not only instrumental but an essential moment for developing and maintaining belonging and recognition. Instead, and this has been already briefly mentioned above. The exact opposite point should be made:

to the extent to which property is based on labour, it can only be common property—a kind of social service that provides the hardware for the socialization and is at the same time its product. Importantly a concept of practice can from here be underpinned and also a concept that puts both, the understanding of the social and of social services, on the basis of practice. This means that one's understanding cannot be based on dealing with a simple combination of individual activities or actions. This has, of course, a fundamental consequence for research, as it requires a renunciation of methodological individualism. This will be taken up at a later stage, suggesting as alternative a methodological relationalism.

Second, this labour as relationality is also about the embodiment of personality. Potentially this has two sides. On the one hand—and this is Hegel's point—the individual leaving an imprint in and on the environment, and then being a private matter, a matter of private property and also a matter of dominance. On the other hand it is a matter of 'universalization' and in this context allowing to develop needs, also to refine them and to contribute to developing independence from nature, from crude needs of existence and instincts.

Third, relationality is then not least about tackling the four dimensions of (1) individuals relating to themselves, developing a self; (2) people relating to each other with the general dimension of 'relationships within humankind' and 'relationships within groups and classes'; (3) classes and groups relating to one another and (4) humans appropriating nature—to be precise: not appropriating nature in terms of subordination and exploitation but appropriating nature as matter of finding a relationship that is appropriate, reflecting needs and potentialities of both sides. Marx points to this factor when he emphasizes in 'Manuscripts' that human beings are themselves part of nature (passim).[7] It is worth mentioning here that the work by Norbert Elias can importantly guide to further considerations as they allow investigating the tension between individual and society as question of developing social space.

This leads one to believe in some kind of 'general interest' not only in today's debates much more so during history, in particular with the historically recent emergence of the modern state. All the theories of social contracts have to be seen in this perspective, highlighting different aspects, providing different interpretations and still suggesting by and large a general interest, a will of all, being real or imagined.

Disengagement: The Dissolution of the Social

One can find different references—in the history of soci(et)al development and the view taken on this history—that point out that in soci(et)al development something like disengagement can be found. Some of the perspectives may be briefly highlighted as follows:

Descartes refers to the separation of body and mind,

Descartes' ethic, just as much as his epistemology, calls for disengagement from world and body and the assumption of an instrumental stance towards them. It is of the essence of reason ... that it push us to disengage. What is meant by that? Disengagement means standing apart from each other as external, as mere object. The key is in the word instrumental: we use the other as an instrument, as the mere means for realizing our will, and not as in some way integral to our being. It has its heart in the technocratic attitude: the view that the world is there to do with exactly as we choose. Its other sideóand I give an extreme viewóis that we do not seek in the world for what is true and good and beautiful, but create our truth and values for ourselves. (Gunton 1993: 13 f).

The decisive moment here is the instrumentalism that comes up and that is later reflected by Niklas Luhmann by the following considerations, showing the immediate relevance for the topic of social services:

This way one arrives at a systematized positive law, defined by rules and principlesóand one can be content with this. Consequently, the traditional question concerned with justice loses any practical meaning. It cannot be added as third wayóaside of justice and injustice, nor does it link into one of the programs of the systemóas if there would be alongside with planning and building law, road traffic law, inheritance law and copyright law a just law (gerechtes Recht). (Schmid (1981: 16 f). translation P.H.)

Against this background it is emphasized that morality has to be consulted in order to find out about the justice of law.

This is not alone an ontological issue. It is also a matter of the social reality which had been on one stage strongly marked by a general process of politico-social differentiation: the emergence of the state, as complement and opposite of civil society, as emergence of the public sphere standing against the private sphere of the 'utilitarian' and 'individualist' civil society of the bourgeois, pursuing their own interests. The citoyen, representing an all-encompassing ideal of the general interest, transcending from instinct and also transcending from individual needs–satisfaction and refinement, is different from the bourgeois and his limitations.

Of course, in real history this means that the two spheres are developing differently, one compensating for what the other cannot provide. And not least, here a space for social services develops not only as social space but also as space for a special economy—the social economy and a kind of social capital in its true sense.

It is important to see that this politico-social differentiation is also part of a wider process of social and socio-economic differentiation. Much has been written on the sequence and causal links between the forms of differentiation and their mutual meaning. This discussion is at the moment not of any interest. What is important is that—not least with industrialization—'the social' gains a completely new meaning. Derived from the Latin, originally being concerned with general relations to society or community, the meaning changes in the middle of the nineteenth century and the meaning is now geared towards the 'social question', meaning the workers question as matter of the challenges of integrating specifically the industrial proletariat (see Fournier and Questiaux 1978; Robert 1975; Geck 1957).

First and foremost it is important to note that such a perspective on the 'pre-capitalist social'—surely in many respects questionable, not least because of an engrossed social romanticism—points out that the distinction between social and societal (more precisely in Ferdinand Toennies's terminology Gemeinschaft and Gesellschaft) does not exist, at least not to the same extent to which it is known from later stages of development. As said earlier there is some form of social-romanticism involved in such a view. At the same time it is important to acknowledge that this interpretation follows a strict sequential dichotomization: Gemeinschaft is followed by Gesellschaft and the latter is simply considered as a 'higher', 'more advanced' stage of development—a position that I questioned on another occasion, proposing that societal stages emerge as forms of perpetuated socialization, providing a foundation for a new push towards societalization (cf. Herrmann 2009). Notwithstanding this, the divisions of and separations between different groups and classes in pre-capitalist societies had been based on different grounds, namely, on political violence and social constructions rather than on 'rational grounds' of the capitalist economy of utilitarian calculability and consequently lacked genuinely social considerations.

This meant, in consequence that the social emerged now as a matter of binary contractual relationships rather than complex socio-productive relationships. Ontological relationality itself had been 'utilitarianized' and reformulated as technicality. Ananta Kumar Giri makes one aware of this reference to William Connolly with the following.

Another assumption of modernity that social research reflected was modernity's primacy of epistemology and the neglect of ontology which short-circuited 'ontological issues by assuming that once the right procedure for attaining truth as correspondence or coherence is reached, any remaining issues will be either resolved through that method or shown to be irrelevant' (Connolly 1995: 6). In the modernist mode, social research was considered only an epistemic engagement, a project of knowing about the world with proper procedure and scientific method. But this only embodies a questionable 'social ontology' which in its 'empiricist version . . . treats human beings as independent objects susceptible to representation, or at least, a medium in which the designative dimensions of concepts can be disconnected rigorously from the contexts of rhetoric/action evaluation in which they originate' (Connolly (1995: 6), quoted in Giri's opening essay in this volume)

Of course, this was nothing else but the very consequence of the changes in social reality; the split between classes, the explicit definition of gender inequality as social rather than as biological issue, the singling out of social policy and its redefinition as mater of social philanthropy, subsequent to modernization and emerging capitalism had been the actual basis that required denouncing disengagement, losing any kind of questionable, politically enforced 'general interest', separating morality and economy[8] and also splitting up ethical life itself.[9] It may also be said more forcefully, the shift from political control to purely economic division of labour and tendency of a disentanglement of exchange value from its utility value had been equally cause and effect of the separation of bourgeois and citoyen.

One finds here the foundation of many shortcomings of today's definitions of social policy and social services as 'provisions for somebody' rather than approaching relevant issues as part of a much wider process of socialization. Here is also found the ground of a social policy concept that is oriented towards distinct groups or individuals 'in need' rather than understanding itself as part of this wider process. Instead of blaming individuals for failing to take a wider perspective, one has to blame soci(et)al development for dealing with new modes of regulation which had been answering the requirements of the new mode of production and adapting to the concrete accumulation regimes. This can, to a large extent, be seen as result of what Ananta Kumar Giri highlights: the need for 'ways of rethinking society and subjectivity and . . . for a frame of ontological sociality' (Giri, in this volume). What in the present contribution is highlighted as matter of relationality, links closely Giri's quest for rethinking the position and role of the subject within the entirety of 'engagement in activism and creative understanding, fieldwork and philosophical reflections, ontological self-cultivation and epistemic labour of learning'.

Social State and the Emergence of 'Dissolved Social Services'

In some respects one may see what had been said before as a long-winded introduction. This approach was necessary, however, to show an underlying thread (and actually threat) in Western societies' social or welfare state and what is globally taken as a model for the rest of the world—the term 'developmental welfare state' gives broad evidence of it. In the broad way in which it is here approached, the following discussion, linked to what had been said before, can actually show that the social/welfare state structurally limited—for instance by the lack of finances that is most needed during phases of least means, etc. Moreover, it is fatally linked to a way of destructive thinking that undermines both its own foundation of being a control and corrective instance, complementing capitalism; and ways of constructive criticism, oriented towards improving societies in the interest of the citizens and cosmopolitan orientation. In other words, the history of thinking welfare is to a large extent the history of undermining a true welfare state. And the capitalist social policy system is very much a way of destroying a constructive, creative way of dealing with society building.

People tend to refer to the things known, to conventions taken as unquestioned and even unquestionable, a reference that pretends to refer to a clear understanding and that nevertheless contributes factually to some degree in maintaining ignorance. One issue in question is that WE not only refer to a rather ahistorical understanding of the state, taking it simply for given without considering the fact that it is in today's form historically only a very recent invention, going back at most to about the renaissance/ enlightenment period—systems dating back to earlier times cannot be considered as comparable. It is important in this context to note that the role of the political as means of system-steering changed fundamentally over time (political rule being dominant mechanisms before the emergence of the modern capitalist state) being on the one hand replaced by economic mechanisms as regulators and at the same time much more effectively complemented by political steering through an appropriate mode of regulation (see in this context discussions by and in Herrmann 2010b). Furthermore, another issue is concerned specifically with what is called the welfare state, which can actually mean two things. The term usually refers to the politico-institutional system that emerged after the Second World War. As such it is characterized in particular by three broad features:[10]

- The first feature is the traditional, pre-capitalist concern of social intervention: poor relief being maintained though possibly being transferred in respect of agency. However, although some changes are found in the institutional setting one can nevertheless also see continuities, for instance, the church playing a major role in many countries but perhaps more importantly moral grounds serving as point of departure and reference for definitional efforts.
- The second feature is the 'social question' or 'workers question'— establishing new institutional answers as part of an overhaul of the politico-economic system. Whereas previously the social had been part of a 'harmonious socio-economic system', of course harmonious

only in the sense of of political and economic control being fully 'integrated' and in the same hand and definitely not harmonious as it had been by and large a matter of violence, including the use of physical violence. Looking at agency by and large there is found to be a shift from individual and direct relations to institutional provisions and indirect, not least commodity-defined, relations.[11] Looking here as well at the point of departure and reference for definitional efforts moral grounds are seen being pushed aside, replaced by rational, technical considerations, based in 'utilitarian ideals', emerging from methodological individualism.

- The new pattern of the welfare state, and a pattern that gains a dominant role in the definition of the system, is the strong orientation on general patterns and needs of social integration or moreover social integrity. In this perspective, largely inspired by Keynesian economic thinking, the guiding idea is actually to a large extent Hegelian: the assumptions of a general interest that considers the class question as being irrelevant. The modern 'public estate' is seen as neutral power, the Beamte—as later presented by Max Weber—is seen as 'personality without personal interest', fully committed to 'neutral fulfilment' of duties. Social policy and social services are now guided by reference to the status of a citizen. Tom H. Marshall (1992), in this context, emphasizes a development that reflects a claim of completing citizenship and stating 'completed modernity'. If, and in that case to what extent, this is true may be left open—and only one remark may point to some doubts: the fact that rights are in Marshall's understanding 'granted', i.e. being 'handed down' rather than a matter of true relationality. This means as well that actually the juridification of rights—as important as it is in a protective perspective—entails the danger of segmenting and 'technicizing' the question of rights. In other words, rights are now only considered as legal rights, as matter of procedures and as part of contractual relationships. This, of course, turns the entire concept of citizenship and social policy alike fundamentally upside down. At least three moments have to be highlighted: (1) the juridical securitization of rights as somewhat neutral development, with possible positive and possible negative consequences; (2) the interpretation of such securitization in contractual terms, going hand in hand with an individualization of rights as means that opens as well the door to disciplinary measures; (3) the reinterpretation of welfare in a somewhat communitarian light, though communitarian does in this context not refer to the libertarian (in particular, though not only) American tradition.[12] It is more employed by the idea of a welfare society that guarantees, by strong responsibility, a care-taking role and consequently, by and large interventionist approach, a cohesive system that is more focused on integrity rather than integration. Actually, the foundations had been established before the British version had been put into reality; the most pronounced example is Swedish folkhemmet. In its specific character it can also be seen as an attempt to Aufhebung—abolish and maintain—communitarian principles within a state system. Looking again at agency another shift is found (leaving differences in the concrete shape aside). To recall: the emergence of the social state meant a development from individual and direct relations to institutional provisions and indirect, not least commodity-defined relations. Now, with the emergence of the welfare state as a kind of successor of the social state one finds the development of direct, though institutionally established provision of social policy and service provision, defined by and linked to citizenship rather than being linked to and defined by employment status and commodification. This also meant a broadened orientation, this policy-realm now very much middle-class rather than working-class oriented. Recalling the point of departure and reference for definitional efforts in the case of the development of the social state, this had been shifting from primarily moral grounds towards rational, technical considerations, based in 'utilitarian ideals', emerging from methodological individualism. This changes now with the welfare state towards some forms of moral entrepreneurship. Although one has to be extremely cautious when it comes to putting forward concepts of corporate social responsibility (see Herrmann 2010a), one should never forget that there is an increasing notion of social entrepreneurial engagement, the increasing (though not necessary lasting) awareness of the capitalist class that it is necessary to employ some form of 'productive role of social policy'. And as such it is linked to a weak form of methodological relationalism.

- One can talk with some justification of an even more recent development, seeing a service state complementing and replacing the welfare state. To the extent to which this is a valid reflection of reality, it is about a re-emergence of direct relations between individuals, however, now not based on kinship but on a different status, professional knowledge on the one side and 'modern–patriarchal relationship' on the others. Personal dependencies, based on precarity, for instance of members of the modern middle classes, migrants and others[13] are points of entries for 'service relationships'. From here emerges a bizarre mix of professionalism, personal dependency and commodified relationship. The definitional dimension first changed with the development from the social to the welfare state from technicist, utilitarian thinking towards moral entrepreneurship. With the development of the service state there is again a re-emergence, now as renaissance of some forms of new princedoms: foundations, benevolence and voluntarist political orientations are emerging as search for ways of how to deal with the new modes of production. While the industrial structures are changing, the mode of regulation and in particular the mode of social integration has also to look for mechanisms of adaptation.

It is important to consider the relationship between these strands, as there is a certain tension between them. On the one hand this relationship may be seen as a sequence, from dealing with the excluded and marginalized, looking after 'people in need' and thus reflecting the fact that this pre-capitalist system did not refer to the dominance of economic self-steering. The first stage of development in capitalist systems is the old 'workers question' or 'social question', the system as it had been established in particular in the German system of workers-related insurance systems. Dealing with people in need can be considered as resting outside the realm of this system. Greatly like the much later European social policy system, the early social state had been a workers-only provision. Whereas the later European orientation would deal with securing the freedom of movement, however, the earlier Bismarckian system had been established in order to secure exploitation. The later welfare state developed as a child of the Second World War, being closely related to the foothold Keynesian thinking gained in economic thinking—in some way it can also be seen here as a re-emergence of the dominance of the political. Early capitalism had been based on pure 'economic thinking', i.e. a governance that followed the laws of a utilitarian ideology—individualist, rational and oriented along the line of self-regulation on the grounds of assuming individual. To the extent one could justifiably make the simplifying statement that the social state was a system that was established in order to secure exploitation, the welfare state may be referred to as a system established in order to secure exploitability. The emergence of the service state—even with the emphasis on services as an increasingly important part of the social one faces, the search for ways of dealing with the loosening ties within the capitalist economy: historical forms of inclusion by way of kinship and immediate personal bonds—was replaced by the utilitarian individualist-rationalist system of socialization. Although they were to a large extent exclusive, defining social policy and social services largely as 'combating exclusion', they could secure a system that had been based on fixed rules. With loss of such fixed rules societies are now confronted with the need of finding a new framework, and possibly even the need of finding a new basis for securing socialization. This surely requires not least a reconsideration of what the social actually is and how it can and has to go beyond the aggregation of individuals. And it has also to watch out for ways that not only go beyond GDP but also go beyond relying on moral sentiments.

Notes

1. Leaving elections and other formal, large-scale mechanisms of democracy out of consideration—though they are in no way meaningless they are surely problematic in terms of offering sound mechanisms of control over political and societal structures.
2. Be it 'real individuals' or individuals brought together in enterprises within which production is coordinated but between which production is not let alone that it is in definite terms foreseeable how this translates into exchange.
3. One word or caution may be appropriate: looking at what had been said as 'mainstream' and dominant development there is also another move, pursuing a course of renaissance and in search for integrated and holistic concepts. The 'Bildungsansprueche', the claims for all-encompassing formation, including the 'formation' of personalities, plays an important role and leads in particular in Germany to the emergence of a somewhat specific social group: the Bildungsbuergertum, probably best grasped by the translation into citoyenitée on grounds of humanist education and knowledge.
4. This is in an ongoing topic of classical Western philosophy connected with names such as Epicure, Zenon, Kues, Aquino, etc.
5. Maintaining does not (necessarily) mean perpetuation of the existing. It can equally mean changes of the weighing of factors (for instance, changes in the hegemonic position of one class), questioning the role and importance of elements (for instance, the debate on protection of the environment), the 'detection' of the previously unrecognized (for instance, the recognition of [the use of] language as—though unconsciously used—instrument of power).
6. To be clear, it is not meant in a constructivist understanding.
7. Of course, this could be further subdivided, looking at the relationship in general and then specifically in the perspective of groups/classes.
8. In this context an important question is actually concerned with how the economic theory and the moral philosophy are related to each other; see for instance Ellen Frankel Paul (1979).
9. The assumption of a bifurcation of Moralität and Sittlichkeit as it is explored by Hegel.
10. It is important to keep in mind that these are extrapolations of main features rather than pure realities.
11. Even decommodification has to be seen as commodity-defined.
12. Referring to traditions leaves the discussion of current concepts, as for example the British 'Big Society', aside.

13. In most of the cases, it is not the 'traditional poor' being dealt with, as qualification plays an important role.

References

Avineri, Shlomo (1971), 'Labor, Alienation, and Social Classes in Hegel's Realphilosophie', *Philosophy & Public Affairs*, vol. 1, no.1, pp. 96–119.

———(1972 [1994]), *Hegel's Theory of the Modern State,* Cambridge: CUP.

Connolly, William (1995), *The Ethos of Pluralization*, Minneapolis: University of Minnesota Press.

Fournier, Jacques and Nicole Questiaux (1978), *Traité due social, situations*, luttes politiques, institutions, Paris: Dalloz.

Geck, Adolph (1957), *Zur Sozialreform des Rechts*, Stuttgart.

Giri, Ananta Kumar (2017), 'Pathways of Creative Research: Rethinking Theories and Methods and the Calling of an Ontological Epistemology of Participation', in this volume.

Gunton, Colin E. (1993), *The One, the Three and the Many. God, Creation and the Culture of Modernity*, The Bampton Lectures 1992, Cambridge: CUP.

Harvey, David (1982 [2006]), *The Limits to Capital*, London/New York: Verso.

Hegel, Georg Wilhelm Friedrich (1820), *Philosophy of Right § 33*, Online version: http://www.marxists.org/reference/archive/hegel/works/pr/printrod. htm#PR33 - 11/04/2011.

Herrmann, Peter (2009), 'Gemeinschaft der Gesellschaft—die Suche nach einem Definitionsrahmen für Prekarität', in *The Fragilisation of Socio-structural Components/Die Fragilisierung soziostruktureller Komponenten*, ed. Rolf Hepp, Bremen: Europaeischer Hochschulverlag, pp. 76–107.

——— (2010a), 'CSR: Corporate Social Responsibility versus Citizens Social Rights Or: On Regaining Political Economy', in *Corporate Social Responsibility and Ethical Aspects of Business*, ed. Grazyna O'Sullivan, Janusz Torunski and Henryk Wyrebek, Zeszyty Naukowe Akademii Podlaskiej, Warsaw: Wydawnictwo Studio Emka, pp. 41–59.

———(2010b), 'Prolegomena. Encore Citizenship: Revisiting or Redefining?', in *World's New Princedoms. Critical Remarks on Claimed Alternatives by New Life*, ed. Peter Herrmann, Amsterdam: Rozenberg Publishers, pp. 17–75.

Luhmann, Niklas (1969), 'Komplexität und Demokratie', in *Politische Planung. Aufsätze zur Soziologie von Politik und Verwaltung*, ed. Niklas Luhmann, Opladen 1971).

Marshall, Tom H. (1992), 'Citizenship and Social Class', in *Citizenship and Social Class*, ed. T.H. Marshall and Tom Bottomore, London: Pluto Press.

Mascuch, Michael (1996), *Origins of the Individualist Self: Autobiography and Self-Identity in England*, Stanford: Stanford University Press.

Robert, Paul (1975), *Le Petit Robert. Dictionnaire*, Paris: Dictionnaire Le Robert.

Schmid, Felix (1981), *Sozialrecht und Recht der Sozialen Sicherheit. Die Begriffsbildung in Deutschland, Frankreich und der Schweiz*, Berlin: Duncker & Humblot.

Slife, Brent F. (2004), 'Taking Practice Seriously: Toward a Relational Ontology', *Journal of Theoretical and Philosophical Psychology*, vol. 24, no. 2, pp. 157–78.

Zelik, Raul and Elmar Altvater (2009), *Vermessung der Utopie. Ein Gespräch über Mythen des Kapitalismus und die kommende Gesellschaft—Statement by Altvater*, München: Blumenbar Verlag.

9

The Power of Uncertainty: Reflections on the Nature of Transformational Initiatives

MIHIR SHAH

I spent the last 20 years of my life living and working with the tribal people of central India, trying with them to forge concrete solutions to some of the most difficult challenges of today—of water and livelihood security. Over the past 10 months, I have been working as Member, Planning Commission handling Rural Development, Water Resources and Panchayati Raj. This chapter is an attempt to put together some of my reflections as a participant in the struggle for change, to share some of what I have learnt in this process.

My central question in this chapter is one that has repeatedly arisen over the years and with even greater urgency in the recent past—what is the way to act in a world beset by fundamental uncertainty? If uncertainty (of many kinds, as I will elaborate) is at the heart of the knowledge of the world that is possible for all, what implications does this have for transformational initiatives, whether by government, social activists or citizens? The question gains renewed attention thanks to the grave crisis the world economy has just been going through; and also due to the emergence of climate change as a central issue defining the modern times. This is, therefore, as opportune a moment as any to revisit some of the most fundamental questions regarding Economics as a Science. I will reflect on the nature of knowledge that Economics provides by inter alia drawing upon the work of some of the greatest economists the world has ever seen. I will, therefore, be speaking today as an economist but will also perforce draw upon insights from other disciplines, without which I believe full justice cannot be done to the questions on hand.

Three Kinds of Uncertainty

UNCERTAINTY RELATED TO TIME

The natural starting point for an economist dealing with uncertainty is Knight (1921) who introduced the distinction between risk and uncertainty.

Briefly understood, risk describes a future outcome whose probability can be reasonably determined, while uncertainty refers to an event whose probability cannot be known in advance. It could even be called a distinction between calculable and incalculable uncertainty.

The most important text that took uncertainty seriously was Keynes's *General Theory*. But Keynes's clearest statement on the matter is to be found in an article in the *Quarterly Journal of Economics* in February 1937, which he wrote in response to critics of the *General Theory*:

> our knowledge of the future is fluctuating, vague and uncertain. . . . By 'uncertain' knowledge, let me explain, I do not mean merely to distinguish what is known for certain, from what is only probable. The game of roulette is not subject, in this sense, to uncertainty. Or, again, the expectation of life is only slightly uncertain. Even the weather is only moderately uncertain. The sense in which I am using the term is that in which the prospect of a European war is uncertain or the price of copper and the rate of interest twenty years hence. About these matters there is no scientific basis on which to form any calculable probability whatever. We simply do not know.

It is stunning to read perhaps the greatest economist of the twentieth century affirm radical uncertainty in no uncertain terms! Of course, Keynes laid the foundations of the modern welfare state whose interventions he saw as correcting the fallibility of the market mechanism.

Arguing from the opposite end of the ideological spectrum but agreeing with Keynes fundamentally on the nature of knowledge in Economics was Friedrich von Hayek. In his classic 1945 piece *The Use of Knowledge in Society,* and his 1974 Nobel Lecture 'The Pretence of Knowledge', Hayek questions the very possibility of rational calculation by central planners. Hayek was highly critical of what he termed scientism—a false understanding of the methods of science, which has been forced upon the social sciences—such as the view that all scientific explanations are simple two-variable linear relationships. Hayek points out that much of science involves the explanation of complex multi-variable and non-linear phenomena. Of course, the irony is that Hayek had a touching faith in the power of unrestrained markets, assigning them near omniscience, quite ignoring his own insights into the nature of knowledge and also ignoring the fundamental revolution in Economics inaugurated by the work of Keynes.

Perhaps the economist who captures most beautifully the insights of both Keynes and Hayek is the relatively unsung G.L.S. Shackle. In a much more radical position, he questions both Hayek's naiveté about markets and Keynes's simplistic optimism about state intervention. Shackle introduces the notion of inceptive choice, where the person who chooses cannot 'foreknow what the sequel of his present choice will be, for if his own choices are inceptive, if his own choices are non-implicit, in some degree, in their antecedents, so are the choices of others and so are all the choices-to-come of himself as well as others' (Shackle 1975: 23). Since 'the ultimate permissive condition of knowledge is the repetition of recognizable configurations' (Shackle 1972: 6), this limits the possibilities of knowing the courses of action that will be chosen in future. Shackle criticizes his teacher Hayek for not fully acknowledging the implications of the decision-maker's 'unknowledge' for the possibilities of self-regulation in a market economy.

Shackle's work potentially takes economics into novel territory such as the role of imagination to assess the plausibility of alternative outcomes while taking economic decisions. But the very freedom that is the basis for imagination makes perfect knowledge an impossibility. Shackle, therefore, posits a fundamental hiatus between freedom and knowledge, as also between time and reason. In an incredibly insightful, though very short, Chapter 2 of his work *Epistemics and Economics* titled 'Time, Novelty, Geometry', Shackle writes:

> Time is a denial of the omnipotence of reason. Time divides the entirety of things into that part about which we can reason and that part about which we cannot. Yet the part about which we cannot reason has a bearing on the meaning of the part that is amenable to reason. The analyst is obliged to practice, in effect, a denial of the nature of time. For he can reason only about that which is in effect complete; and in a world where there is time, nothing is ever complete. (1972: 27)

It must immediately be recognized, however, that Shackle's work has remained on the fringes of mainstream economic theory. The standard response to uncertainty in Economics can be traced to von Neumann and Morgenstern's (1944) expected utility theory, which led on to Nash's (1951) non-cooperative equilibrium and game theory, Savage's (1954) reformulation of expected utility theory and climaxed in Arrow and Debreu's (1954) derivation of the necessary and sufficient conditions for existence and optimality of general equilibrium under uncertainty. Of course, these formulations were challenged by Allais (1953), and Arrow (1963) himself acknowledged the empirical implausibility of the relevant necessary and sufficient conditions in the face of uncertainty. Indeed, even more recently, Arrow has warned that 'vast ills have followed a belief in certainty, whether historical inevitability, grand diplomatic designs or extreme views on economic policy. When developing policy with wide effects . . . caution is needed because we cannot predict the consequences' (Arrow 1992: 46).

Over the last 40 years, but especially following the work of psychologist and 2002 Economics Nobel Laureate Daniel Kahneman with Amos Tversky on prospect theory, the expected utility hypothesis has been under attack and alternatives proposed. Here however, it is important to recognize that all of this work is concerned with one project—finding probabilistic solutions aimed at taming uncertainty, attempting to collapse the radical distinction between risk and uncertainty first postulated by Knight and later developed by Keynes and Shackle. As Keynes said, 'The calculus of probability was supposed to be capable of reducing uncertainty to the same calculable status as that of certainty itself. Actually, however, we have, as a rule, only the vaguest idea of any but the most direct consequences of our acts' (Keynes 1937).

Before going on to elaborate the other sources of this inescapable uncertainty, I will close this section with a most telling example of the point I am making. Long-Term Capital Management (LTCM) was a US hedge fund founded in 1994, with 1997 Economics Nobel Laureates Myron Scholes and Robert Merton on its Board of Directors. LTCM used complex mathematical models to take advantage of trading strategies such as fixed income arbitrage, statistical arbitrage and pairs trading, combined with high leverage. LTCM was initially highly successful with annualized returns of over 40 per cent. But it lost $4.6 billion in less than four months in 1998 and collapsed by early 2000. The failure of LTCM is a classic case-study of the impossibility of accurately anticipating unforeseen and relatively unforeseeable events such as the 1997 East Asian financial crisis and Russia's 1998 default on its sovereign debt. LTCM collapsed despite having the best economists on its Board because it mistakenly thought it could conjure away an uncertain and unknown future by turning it into a set of calculable risks (Lowenstein 2000). Similar mayhem has occurred across the world in the latest economic crisis.

UNCERTAINTY RELATED TO CONTEXT

Apart from the 'time' dimension of uncertainty, which has found recognition in Economics, there is a need to also acknowledge the existence of a contextual element in uncertainty, which disciplines like Anthropology have best brought to the fore. The question they ask is: how to understand the 'Other'? Or, what happens when one tries to understand the other? One of the most evocative treatments of this question is to be found in the work of the Brazilian anthropologist Eduardo Viveiros de Castro.[1] As de Castro explains:

The real problem lies in knowing which are the possible relations between our descriptive practices and those employed by other peoples. There are undoubtedly many possible relations; but only one impossible relation: the absence of a relation. We cannot learn these other practices—other cultures—in absolute terms; we can only try to make explicit some of our implicit relations with them, that is, apprehend them in relation to our own descriptive practices (2003: 11).

De Castro cautions against 'the fantasy of an intellectual intuition of other forms of life "in their own terms", for there is no such thing. "Their terms" are only determined as such in relation to "our terms", and vice-versa. Every determination is a relation. Nothing is absolutely universal, not because something is relatively particular, but because "everything" is relational' (2003: 11).

One of the richest descriptions of this relationality is to be found in the work of the German philosopher Hans-Georg Gadamer. In his magnum opus *Truth and Method*, Gadamer expresses the matter through his notion of the fusion of horizons:

> What do we mean by 'placing ourselves' in a situation? Certainly not just disregarding ourselves. This is necessary, of course, in that we must imagine the other situation. But into this other situation we must also bring ourselves. Only this fulfils the meaning of 'placing ourselves'. This placing of ourselves is not the empathy of one individual for another nor is it the application to another person of our own criteria but it always involves the attainment of a higher universality that overcomes not only our own particularity but also that of the other. To acquire a horizon means that one learns to look beyond what is close at hand, not in order to look away from it, but to see it better within a larger whole and in truer proportion. Understanding is always a fusion of horizons which we imagine to exist by themselves. (1960: 271–3)

Knowledge thereby loses the certainty of its own voice by acknowledging the need to listen to and understand the knowledge produced by the other whose situation one claims to be trying to transform. Thus, the acknowledgement of the otherness of the other demands recognition of at least five different elements that shape knowledge:

1. The context where intervention is tried is not a blank canvas or as the Roman legal term goes, *terra nullius* ('land belonging to no one' or 'empty land'). These are situations and contexts with a dynamic of their own. The impact of what is done is mediated through the ongoing dynamic of the context where the initiative rolls out. There is a need to study and understand this dynamic.[2]
2. What is more, there is a great diversity to this dynamic across the contexts, which are intervened. So all initiatives need to be sensitive to the variety of dynamics that is encountered.
3. These contexts also have knowledges of their own that are often paradigmatically different from those of others and from each other. An appreciation of these and an effort to understand them will greatly benefit the course of a person's own initiative.
4. Whether one likes it or not, however unaware one may be of this, interventions are not unidirectional or omnipotent. They, willy-nilly, transform those who seek to bring about change—beyond their

wanting, doing or even knowing. Change will, therefore, never flow univocally from one direction.

5. The presence of the other also compels the question: who is the calculator? Is there at all a decision-maker acting in pristine isolation and autonomy? What is the meaning of studying the calculation of the individual, atomistic homo economicus, in a world characterized by deep interdependencies?

6. Finally, one needs to recognize that transformational initiatives are generally located in contexts of deep inequalities and discrimination, some historically inherited, others created anew, whether based on gender, caste, ethnicity, race, community or class. Every intervention inhabits a contested terrain and itself becomes a site for further contention and contestation. This makes outcomes profoundly uncertain and indeterminate. It also demands an understanding of questions of power and justice and the articulation of an appropriate approach towards them.

UNCERTAINTY RELATED TO NATURE

Nature has its own dynamic and autonomy that circumscribes and shapes human action. The current crisis of global warming is an example of what happens when one acts as if Nature does not matter. The roots of the crisis may be traced to the way Economics has sought to conceptualize itself and its relationship with Nature.

The founders of neo-classical economics, on their own testimony, aspired to create a science patterned exactly on Newtonian Mechanics. Newtonian Mechanics could visualize change only as locomotion, which is both quality-less and reversible. The economic process is seen here as a circular flow between production and consumption, with no outlets and no inlets. This flow is isolated, self-contained and ahistorical, neither creating nor being affected by qualitative changes in the natural environment within which it occurs. Keynesian macro-dynamics (starting with Harrod) and all its concepts of national income, investment and incremental capital-output ratio also find no place for physical entities. Even the Classical Political Economy of Ricardo expressly saw land as a factor immune to qualitative degradation ('the original and indestructible powers of the soil'), and though Marx was centrally concerned with dynamics, viewing the economic process as essentially historical and qualitative in character, he also did not integrate natural resources into his main analysis. It is true that Marx speaks of labour as a 'process between man and nature' (1976: 283), but the terms of this interaction are that 'man, through his own actions, mediates, regulates and controls the metabolism between himself and nature' by working on 'objects of labour that are spontaneously provided by nature' (1976: 284).

This dual conception of 'free gifts of nature' and the imperative to exercise 'control over nature' runs through the entire gamut of thinking in Economics. Progress is seen as co-terminus with the conquest of nature.[3] Allied to this is the presumption that unlimited quantities of waste can be without cost dumped into the bottomless sink of the environment. Along with the assumption of free gifts goes also the assumption of free disposal.

Following Debreu (1959), the neo-classicals posited the 'rational expectations hypothesis'[4] which presumes that decision-makers in the market know the probability distribution of future outcomes, the future being visualized as stationary and stochastic (Davidson 1982: 182).[5] 'At the initial date there should exist a complete set of forward, contingent commodity markets, on which it is possible to buy or sell goods for delivery in any future time-period and state of the world' (Dasgupta and Heal 1979: 472). Such an approach can provide accurate predictions only if the stochastic process is ergodic—but that is ruled out when one is dealing with irrevocable ecological phenomena which produce a whole range of effects unobservable by the price system.[6] As Shackle has shown there are a range of phenomena for which no 'pre-image' exists in one's mind. There are no previous observations on the basis of which probability distributions can be constructed since the phenomena being dealt with are unprecedented. This means that there can be no 'omni-competent classificatory system' for listing hypothetical scenarios which are endless and beyond human imagination (Shackle 1972: 18).[7]

Another neo-classical device of dealing with the problem of uncertainty is to discount the future. This approach could be said to derive from the contributions of Gray (1914) and Hotelling (1931).[8] The market mechanism supposedly mirrors the preferences of individual economic agents while allocating resources efficiently. When the problem is inter-generational, one runs into the ontological difficulty that many of the relevant economic agents are not yet in existence to be able to express their willingness to pay.[9] And in discounting the future it is assumed that the future will be brighter than the present. But a high rate of discount will also imply a faster rate of depletion,[10] which could mean that the growth path becomes unsustainable and that the future ends up being bleaker than today. The key problem here is again uncertainty. For 'the discounting of time is at one and the same time the discounting of uncertainty' (Perrings 1987: 116), the latter being an increasing function of time. And the higher the discount rate, the more will be depleted an exhaustible resource while raising the level of economic activity. This will imply higher disposals into the ecosystem, that will in turn, bring about environmental changes, raising the level of uncertainty. This will once again raise the discount rate and so on. Thus, the device meant to tackle the problem of uncertainty only ends up aggravating it.[11]

Following the publication in 1971 of Nicholas Georgescu-Roegen's *The Entropy Law and the Economic Process* what is called for is a revolution in economic thinking, nothing short of a Kuhnian paradigm shift, which compels the abandonment of the mechanistic dogma by forcing the realization that qualitative and irrevocable changes necessarily characterize the environment of which economic processes are a part—that both the assumptions of free gifts and free disposal are untenable, there being a dynamic, two-way interrelationship between the economy and the environment. One must see the macro-economy as an open subsystem of the finite natural ecosystem and not as an isolated circular flow of abstract exchange value.[12]

Viewed in the light of the Entropy Law, the economic process is, in fact, not circular, but unidirectional, involving a continuous transformation of the flow of low entropy received from the environment into high entropy or irrevocable waste which is returned to the environment. This is a one-way flow, not a circular one. The flow of blood is to the circulation of exchange-value as the digestive tract is to the unidirectional entropic flow, beginning with environmental resources and energy, through firms and households, and ending with high-entropy waste into environmental sinks.[13]

What is more, this entropic flow has a continuously degrading impact on the environment from which the economy must incessantly draw its low entropy. Each qualitative transformation of the environment within which the economy operates, demands a re-adaptation from the economy. Thus, the very sustainability of the economic process depends on its ability to so adapt. No model that seeks to understand the economy can be complete if it ignores the broader ecosystem of which the economy is a part, and the co-evolutionary path of the subsystem and its parent.[14] The changes in the environment are both exogenous and, increasingly in this high-entropy age, caused by the interaction of the global economy with the environment.[15]

One could say that it is the pace at which low entropy is pumped from the environment into the economy that limits the pace of economic development. Constantly, therefore, the economic process calls upon human beings, much like Maxwell's demon,[16] to filter and direct environmental low entropy towards the satisfaction of economic goals. Based on such a vision, one could describe the challenge of economic development as not merely the multiplication of the filtering mechanism based on existing sieves, but much more as the imaginative task of the innovation of finer sieves (technologies) to filter and thereby reduce the proportion of low entropy ending up as waste.

In such highly complex and highly coupled systems, characterized by both intricate interconnections, as well as novelty, uncertainty has a deep presence. For there still are significant levels of ignorance about upcoming threats, most severely highlighted by the current context of climate change, that are at best poorly understood and at worst completely unknown.

Before going on to the theme concerned with teasing out the implications of uncertainty for the nature of transformational initiatives, let me try and summarize in yet another way the three kinds of unknowns that one is typically likely to encounter.

		META – LEVEL	
		Known	Unknown
PRIMARY LEVEL	Known	Known knowns	Unknown knowns (tacit knowledge)
	Unknown	Known unknowns (conscious ignorance)	Unknown unknowns (meta-ignorance)

FIGURE 9.1: WHAT WE KNOW AND WHAT WE DO NOT KNOW

Source: Bammer et al. 2009.

The most straightforward kind of uncertainty arises from what may be called conscious ignorance or those matters, which one knows one does not know enough about. But there can be two other kinds of unknowns as well. One, which may be called tacit knowledge describes, for instance, the improvizations of a Hindustani classical musician who knows what she sings but may find it hard to describe, explain or exactly pin it down. The same applies to intuitions that arise sometimes about timing and tactics in politics or in the management of people in an organizational context. And, of course, there are several issues where one does not know what one does not know. Typically, these arise in the context of an interface with Nature, in phenomena, which exhibit what Shackle calls 'surprise' or what Georgescu-Roegen has called 'novelty by combination'. The emergence of the HIV virus is one such example. The entire range of phenomena related to global warming is another.

Implications for Action

The inescapable presence of what may be termed irreducible uncertainty in knowledge of the world has thus been established.. The many sources and ramifications of this uncertainty have also been understood. The question now is—how is one to act given the nature of the human predicament? Does the recognition of these multiple uncertainties lead to confusion, enfeeblement, non-action? Does it paralyse? Or does it define a particular course of action, with certain defining characteristics that derive from recognition of the ineluctable presence of uncertainty? These are large philosophical, existential questions. But to these I propose to give very specific, concrete answers, which are based on what I have learnt from and will illustrate through the work I have done as part of Samaj Pragati Sahayog, living in a tribal village over the last 20 years and also by reference to my early work in the Planning Commission over the past 10 months. I summarize the principles that need to guide and features that must characterize transformational initiatives under uncertainty and exemplify these through particular instances. I find it useful to divide the implications for action into four sections:

1. The Approach
2. The Interface with Nature
3. Handling Conflict and Contention
4. Institutional Implications

THE APPROACH

- Uncertainty is the best corrective to fundamentalism. The biggest contribution of a recognition of uncertainty as an essential feature of human knowledge about society is that it leads to a rejection of the notion of a single truth or the correct path. What saves science from degenerating into a dogma is the acknowledgement of the limits of knowing. This liberates one from the tyranny of certainty, whose claim is a part of the arrogance of power and the aspiration for which leads to a suppression of dissent, enquiry and the sense of wonder and mystery that has to be the beginning of all science. Uncertainty demands humility, the non-presumption of the arrogance of complete knowledge or certainty. It calls for a non-assertion of the definitive correctness of one's own viewpoint—an acknowledgement that truth resides in a matrix, not in any one location. That it flows from multiple directions and is embodied in relationships.

- Uncertainty demands nimble-footedness. Uncertainty requires an openness to mid-course correction as new knowledge is acquired over time. This means an abandonment of the heavy-handed inflexibility, which characterizes so many development interventions.

- Uncertainty calls for dialogue. The loss of certainty opens up the possibility that one must also look elsewhere, to other sources for help and support in his/her quest for knowledge. Uncertainty, therefore, necessitates deep listening and the building of common ground across differences, respecting a diversity of approaches and standpoints regarding the same problem. It calls for an attempt to learn from the context where change is being attempted—an open and rich dialogue, a true engagement, which is both transparent and participatory. For it is transparent and participatory processes that are also more accountable and open to mid-course correction. They also facilitate the building of social trust, which is a powerful and often indispensable resource in situations of uncertainty (Luhmann 1979).

- This dialogue neither romanticizes nor devalues so-called people's knowledge. It would be a mistake to valorize any one form of knowledge over another. A corrective is needed to the stridency of both the bottom-up activist and the top-down planner. Neither by itself is appropriate or adequate. What matters, what enlightens, is deep dialogue, an engagement from which something quite un-anticipatable, something novel emerges and guides action.

- Uncertainty demands a fusion of horizons à la Gadamer in at least 3 senses—historical, embracing different stakeholders and across multiple disciplines. Since attempted change in a specific context and this context has a unique history, is characterized by a range of stakeholders and requires an understanding of issues that reside in a multiplicity of disciplines, effectiveness of action demands that the requisite effort be made to bring together diverse perspectives in each of these three dimensions.

INTERFACE WITH NATURE

- One must weave interventions into the contours of Nature. Once the contours defined by the balances in Nature are recognized, the entire approach needs to shift from an attempt to control Nature towards a creative weaving of interventions into the flows and dynamics of natural processes. This requires a new imagination, to use Shackle's term, to visualizing the future. The best positive examples of this are the watershed approach and the move towards organic farming. The most significant negative illustration is the interlinking of rivers project. In a country like India, which gets seasonal rainfall from monsoon, the periods when rivers have 'surplus' water are generally synchronous across the subcontinent. Further, given the topography of India and the way links are envisaged, it might totally bypass the core dryland areas of central and western India, which are located on elevations of 300+ metres above median sea level. It is also feared that linking rivers could affect the natural supply of nutrients through curtailing flooding of the downstream areas. Along the east coast of India, all major peninsular rivers have extensive deltas. Damming the rivers for linking will cut down the sediment supply and cause coastal and delta erosion, destroying the fragile coastal ecosystems. Most significantly, the plan could threaten the very integrity of the monsoon system. The presence of a low salinity layer of water with low density is a reason for maintenance of high sea-surface temperatures (greater than 28°C) in the Bay of Bengal, creating low-pressure areas and intensification of monsoon activity. This layer of low saline water controls rainfall over much of the subcontinent. A disruption in this layer consequent upon massive interlinking of rivers, which would curtail the flow of fresh river water into the sea, could have serious long-term consequences for climate and rainfall in the subcontinent, endangering the livelihoods of a vast population.

- The unity and integrity of natural cycles must compel giving up the silo-based approach to transformation. No solution to India's water crisis can be found unless one comes out of the silos into which water has been and take a holistic view of the hydrologic cycle. There is now a situation where the left hand of drinking water (under the Department of Drinking Water Supply located within the Ministry of Rural Development) acts as if it does not know what the right hand of irrigation (within the Ministry of Water Resources) is doing. Today groundwater is both the single largest source of rural drinking water (over 80 per cent) and irrigation (over 60 per cent). Both tap the same aquifer without any coordination whatsoever. Indeed, one is close to entering a vicious infinite regress scenario where the proposed solution (deep drilling by tube wells) only ends up aggravating the problem it seeks to solve. If one continues along the same lines, the initial problem will recur infinitely and will never be resolved. This regress appears a natural corollary of what has been termed 'hydroschizophrenia'[17], which entails taking a schizophrenic view of an indivisible resource like water, failing to recognize the unity and integrity of the hydrologic cycle. This is the central message emerging from the Mid-Term Appraisal (MTA) of the Eleventh Plan just completed.

- Interventions need to be location-specific reflecting every element of diversity—social, cultural and physical. Since intervention is done in very diverse contexts, there is a need to give up the bureaucratic one-size-fits-all, monocultural approach. All across the country, India is faced with multifarious variations—in rainfall received, in soil and rock type, in slope and contour, in animal forms, in kinds of vegetation, crop or forest—and each of these and each combination of these, has different implications for the possibilities of striking, harvesting and storing water as also the possible forms of livelihood. Many of these variations occur even within a small micro-watershed. And this natural diversity has a complex interplay with the socio-cultural-economic tapestry of these regions. That includes values regarding life-goals, priorities (e.g. security in view of pervasive, inherent uncertainty), understanding of and relationship with natural forces and resources, development of markets, etc., which have evolved over centuries, if not millennia. This canvas of differentia specifica poses a unique challenge to the development planner, the scientist, the social worker. Those who seek to intervene in any context, but especially in one with such diversity and potential fragility, cannot do so on the basis of a notion of mastery over nature and society. With mastery and control, comes the resort to simple tech-fixes—monocultural, unilinear, indiscriminate. Irrespective of the specific challenges of each situation, an unthinking, insensitive bureaucracy seeks to impose its own pet solution—tube wells, eucalyptus, soya bean, Holstein Friesian. Appropriateness does not matter. Sustainability is of no concern. Dialogue is not attempted. History is given a go by—with disastrous consequences.

Unfortunately in development programmes, there has been an attempt to impose simplistic answers, top-down, without making the effort to understand the context, in all its diversity and complexity. One has been narrowly pre-occupied with single variables like aggregate income, neglecting completely the entire range of issues involved in eco-system resilience and stability. Disciplines, narrowly defined through specialization, have not interacted each other. Nor have they interacted the people in whose name solutions are sought to be developed. They have not been mindful of the balance that must be retained if interventions are to be sustainable. Nature and society are not to be mastered or subdued. They are, rather, to be deeply understood so that all interventions can be woven in a creative manner into their delicate fabric. Consistently learning each step of the way—light, nimble and innovative in tread.

The MTA of the Eleventh Plan attempts a corrective in this direction. There are many examples of this. I will limit myself to only a few. One of the limitations of the Total Sanitation Campaign (TSC) that has been identified is the narrow range of technology options offered in a country with such immensely diverse geographic, hydrologic, climatic and socio-economic conditions (high water table, flood prone, rocky ground, desert/water scarce areas and extreme low temperatures). This has led to many problems, including non-acceptance by local communities, water pollution in shallow water table regions and waste of public funds. There is an urgent need to broaden the range of models permissible under TSC and offer an initial menu of alternatives derived from detailed consultations with experts and practitioners.

Similarly, the MTA highlights the fact that problems surrounding groundwater overuse are not just a matter of the share of extraction in annual replenishment. The relationship between extraction and replenishment is complex and depends upon the aquifers from which groundwater is extracted.[18] The foundation of good groundwater management is a clear understanding of aquifers, which requires knowledge of geology—of rock types and rock structure. For groundwater availability is dependent on the water storage and transmission characteristics of these underlying geological strata. The geological diversity in India makes aquifer understanding challenging, but all the more important because the local situation dictates the approach to managing groundwater. Moreover, these local situations also determine how groundwater overuse, droughts, floods, etc., impact drinking water security. The vulnerability of different hydrogeological settings to the level of groundwater development is different.

About 54 per cent of India (comprising mainly the continental shield) is underlain by formations usually referred to as 'hard rocks'.[19] Groundwater resource in hard rocks is characterized by limited productivity of individual wells, unpredictable variations in productivity of wells over relatively short distances and poor water quality in some areas. The initial thrust of irrigation by tube wells following the Green Revolution was restricted to India's 30 per cent alluvial areas, which are generally characterized by relatively more pervious geological strata. But from the late 1980s, tube well drilling was indiscriminately extended to hard rock regions where the groundwater flow regimes are extremely complex. Deeper seated aquifers often have good initial yields, but a tube well drilled here may be tapping groundwater accumulated over hundreds of years. Once groundwater has been extracted from a deeper aquifer, its replenishment depends upon the inflow from the shallow system or from the surface several hundred metres above it. The path this water has to traverse is characterized by relatively unfavourable media, which greatly slows down the rate of groundwater recharge. This poses a severe limit to expansion of tube well technology in areas underlain by these strata. Similarly in the mountain systems, which comprise 16 per cent of India's land area, effects of groundwater overuse do not take very long to appear. As the processes of groundwater accumulation and movement are vastly different in different geological types, the implications of any stage of groundwater development will vary significantly across types of geological settings. Clearly, therefore, a much lower level of groundwater development across 70 per cent of India's land area (hard rock and mountain) could be as 'unsafe' as a comparatively higher level in alluvial settings.

• Factoring in uncertainty demands creation of more resilient systems. Location-specific interventions, deeply cognizant of diversity necessarily give rise to polycentric, diverse and deeply interconnected systems, which are more resilient in the face of external perturbation. The best example of this is provided by the recent moves towards bio-farming.

The internal stability of an agro-ecological system could be defined as its elasticity towards any sort of external perturbation (Tiezzi et al. 1991). This stability is a function of the network of links that can be forged between various components of the system. Such links typically break down when mono-cultural production practices are adopted as in the Green Revolution or due to processes of environmental destruction such as deforestation and infringement on the domain of common property. These interventions weaken the internal linkages of the system, making it increasingly dependent on external energy subsidies (such as fossil fuels-based chemical fertilizers, pesticides, etc.). This makes the system vulnerable to external shocks and market fluctuations, which cause a further decline in stability. On the other hand, an integrated agro-ecological system, such as a bio-farm, characterized by energy conservation and material recycling, is considerably more stable. In this system, several new links are forged within the elements of the natural resource base (climate, rain-fed agriculture, wastelands, forests, crop residues, animal and human wastes and decentralized energy sources). With soil and water conservation technologies, surface run-off is minimized which improves the level of soil moisture. Loss of essential soil nutrients is also reduced. And harvested run-off is recycled to agricultural land through water harvesting structures. Part of the crop residues is returned to the soil through microbial decomposition. Animal wastes are directed to biogas plants, from which bio-energy is supplied to households for cooking. The organic residues from the biogas plant (digested slurry) go to enrich the soil as nitrogen-rich fertilizer. The biomass surplus generated from land, as a consequence of water and nutrient recycling, in turn,

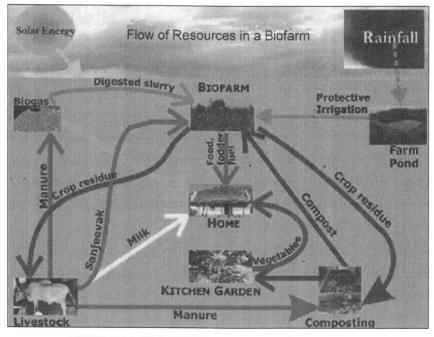

FIGURE 9.2: FLOW OF RESOURCES IN A BIOFARM

supplies more residues, supports more livestock and creates an expanding decentralized energy base within the agro-ecological system.

HANDLING CONFLICT AND CONTENTION

• Uncertainty related to Conflict—Power, Justice, Love. The fruits of India's development have been shared very unequally, especially in certain geographies (Adivasi enclaves, drylands, hills) and with specific social groups (Dalits, Muslims). In recent years India has witnessed the fastest growth of high net-worth individuals worldwide. In the same period in the 'other India', across 200 districts, lakhs of people have committed suicide or taken to the gun. Martin Luther King, Jr. suggests a different response to injustice—the path of love. But the love he spoke of was no ordinary love. King (1958) elaborates the very different meanings of three words for love in the Greek New Testament. Eros, in Platonic philosophy, means the yearning of the soul for the realm of the divine. It has come now to mean a sort of aesthetic or romantic love. Philia signifies the intimate love between friends, a reciprocal love, where one loves because one is loved. But the love King advocates is best expressed in the Greek word agape. Agape implies understanding. It intimates a creative, redeeming goodwill for all, an overflowing love, which seeks nothing in return. Agape is not a weak, passive love. It is love in action (King 1957).

  Through a profound inversion of Nietzsche's critique of Christianity, King provides a reconceptualization of the relationship between power and love. Nietzsche sought to determine the conditions of a new affirmation of life by overcoming what he regarded as the nihilistic despair produced by Christian values. King interrogates the very terms of this problematique by providing a radical restatement of his own spiritual tradition. He questions the legacy of viewing love and power as polar opposites, where love appears as a rescinding of power, and power as a rejection of love. King argues that 'power without love is reckless and abusive, and love without power is sentimental and anaemic' (1967: 247). And this new understanding of power helps King positively formulate the unbreakable bond between love and justice: 'power at its best is love implementing the demands of justice, and justice at its best is power correcting everything that stands against love' (1967: 247).

  Love must necessarily take on the larger structures of injustice that stand in its way. This love includes but goes well beyond isolated acts of kindness. At the same time, because it is a weapon, it is sought not to defeat anyone and try not to end up humiliating those positioned against us. For the struggle is not against persons, it is for transformation of the opponent's view and the system of oppression. And even more for the self-renewal of those who work for change. As King says, 'to retaliate with hate and bitterness would do nothing but intensify the hate in the world. Along the way of life, someone must have sense enough and morality enough to cut off the chain of hate. This can be done only by projecting the ethics of love to the centre of our lives' (1958: 19).

Such an organic link between inner transformation of the individual and larger social change is invariably missing in politics. But there is more. In pursuit of structural change one cannot overlook the immediacy and enormity of suffering. Sadly, this has been the record of many movements for justice. The millennial quest, based on various teleological certainties of the dynamic of History has often led to people being treated as cannon fodder. The finiteness of their lifetimes appears to have little import for leaders who invariably belong to classes quite distinct from those who suffer injustice. As a result, the desperation for finding tangible solutions appears much less evident in leaders than for the masses they lead.

One is confronted with a paradox. Narrow preoccupation with daily issues results, for example, in the sterile 'economism' of the working class. But the quest for millennial goals of a distant Shangri-la means a striking lack of concern for real-time solutions and an unyielding 'protest for the sake of protest'. The former reflects a complete absence of broader vision, the latter a cruel neglect of immediate anguish. The challenge of creative politics is to strike an imaginative balance between the two, without disadvantaging either.

Conflict must stop being viewed as an arena of victory over the 'other'. It is better regarded as a problem in search of a solution. A conflict needs not so much a victory, as a resolution. Indeed, a 'defeat' that moves society forward on the moral landscape, that empowers the disadvantaged and sensitizes those in power, deepening democracy in the process, could even be preferred to a 'victory' that fails to achieve any of these.

A key to moving forward in this direction is to give up the antediluvian unitary and insurrectionist conception of Revolution. The unique appeal of 'scientific socialism' was its claim to have discovered the 'laws of motion of society' that definitively predicted the inexorable coming of a new dawn. This teleology has ended up becoming the chief weakness of Marxism. If change is visualized in these terms, means-ends questions will be run roughshod over and horrors of the Stalinist kind will continue to be perpetrated.

The standpoint of agape love finds strong support in recent advances in Neuroscience and Economics, both of which have traditionally been bastions of selfishness as the central motive of human behaviour. Neurobiologists like Donald Pfaff (2007) marshal a new understanding of genes, neuronal activity and brain circuitry to explain concern for the other. The path-breaking work of economists like Samuel Bowles questions standard textbook assumptions of the selfish homo economicus and emphasizes the role of altruism in the very survival of humankind in the difficult years ahead.

A one-track, single-event notion of revolution must also be discarded because it leads to complete neglect of crucial nitty-gritty detail that forms the heart of the transformation dreamt of. It is this dry spadework that also contains solutions to immediate distress. Running mid-day meals in schools under active supervision of mothers, local people managing sanitation and drinking water systems, social audits in vibrant gram sabhas, participatory planning for watershed works, women leading federations of self-help thrift groups and workers running industrially safe, non-polluting factories as participant shareholders—all these and many more are the immediate, unfinished, feasible tasks of an ongoing struggle for change. Unfortunately, activists typically push these questions into a hazy future, to be all answered after the revolution, so to speak. These are difficult questions that necessitate intricate answers. And there is a need to begin looking for these here and now, in the living laboratories of learning of the farms and factories, villages and slums. Not in some imaginary distant future after a fictitious insurrection.

- Social mobilization of the weak and voiceless essential part of any intervention. If uncertainty related to a context of contention and conflict is to be adequately recognized one needs to dedicate specific time, human and financial resources to the social mobilization of the disadvantaged in each development intervention. In the MTA of the Eleventh Plan, I have tried to provide a road map for this in the specific context of various development initiatives such as the Mahatma Gandhi National Rural Employment Guarantee Act (MGNREGA), sanitation and drinking water supply. The Parthasarathy Committee had already outlined this approach for the watershed programme and this has been incorporated into the Common Guidelines issued during the Eleventh Plan. One has to resist the rush to universalize without adequate preparation so that quality outcomes with genuine inclusiveness can be attained.

- Uncertainty flowing from contention also demands inclusive approaches to the land question. Land acquisition initiatives such as the Special Economic Zones (SEZ) Act and the proposed Land Acquisition (Amendment) Bill (LAAB) portend a serious conflict in India's countryside. The fact that the Supreme Court has held that the state is the 'trustee of all natural resources' must be regarded as posing a challenge to the doctrine of eminent domain, for it qualifies the assertion of absolute sovereign power by the state over natural resources. The inclusion of labourers, SC/ST families, vulnerable persons (disabled, destitute, orphans, widows, unmarried girls, abandoned women, or persons above fifty years of age, without alternative livelihoods) and the landless, is a very significant provision in the R&R Policy, which must become part of the LAAB. The LAAB and the SEZ Act also appear inconsistent with land ceiling laws and do not incorporate the special protection for Scheduled Tribes in the Indian Constitution, whether those under Schedules V and VI, the Panchayats (Extension to the Scheduled Areas) Act, 1996 or the Scheduled Tribes and Other Traditional Forest Dwellers (Recognition of Forest Rights) Act, 2006.

It needs to be clearly understood that the process of industrialization or infrastructure development in rural India cannot be sustained in the long-run if opposition by Project Affected Families (PAFs) continues unabated or and they are not made the very first beneficiaries of its outcomes. It has been estimated that 70 per cent of 190 infrastructure projects in the pipeline have been delayed due to land acquisition problems. Enlightened state policy aimed at ensuring long-term sustainability of the process must gain decisive ground over a short-sighted recourse to available legal loopholes. There are many possibilities here that need to be regarded as very small investments that ensure the long-term sustainability of the development process. One is to provide land in the command area of irrigation projects, as mentioned in the R&R policy. The other is to utilize the long period that separates project initiation and land acquisition as also the gap between first notification, displacement and project construction to train PAFs in skills that could be used on the project. Facilities and products created by the project could be made available to PAFs. Compensation could also be tied more closely to future valuations is an inflation-adjusted monthly pension combined with a savings bond. The pension could be partially tied to the profits of the project. The best route could be to make PAFs shareholders in the proposed project given their contribution to a key element of share capital. The safest way to disincentivise land acquisition from degenerating into a real estate proposition (as it has, reportedly in quite a few cases) is to resort to leasing or temporary alienation, which will not sever the relationship of the landowner with her land. This would mean that if the project does not take off or shuts down or comes to a close, the land would be returned to the original landholder.

Each of these initiatives can help restore the faith of people in the democratic process, which is under strain in the remote hinterlands of India. The way forward is to move away from the vision of 'subjects' inherent in the eminent domain doctrine towards that of citizens, whose rights are guaranteed under the Constitution. Ultimately, it is necessary to go beyond narrow legality to seek broader legitimacy. This demands giving a cutting edge to many provisions of the R&R Policy, making each of them mandatory and not reducing them to—what they are in effect—conditionalities without consequences (Ramanathan 2008). But it also requires an unequivocal commitment to imaginatively exploring ways of rebuilding the livelihoods of those adversely affected by development projects.

INSTITUTIONAL IMPLICATIONS

• Uncertainty demands forging of partnerships. Certainty is the requirement and characteristic of top-down, unilinear visions of change. Rejecting the illusory certainty of a single voice is a liberating, enriching, inclusive experience. It potentially provides the benefits of multiple perspectives and standpoints, each of which has a unique value. One needs to recognize that a multidimensional, multi-stakeholder, multi-directional and multidisciplinary matrix of relationships governs the dynamics of change in a deeply interconnected way. While one may never fully fathom the depths and intensities of these interconnections (which is the residual uncertainty that ineluctably characterizes interventions), the more a person is cognizant of these and the more he/she forges partnerships that bring all of them together, harnessing their respective strengths and insights, the more sustainable interventions will become (in social, ecological and financial terms). Emerging from iterative, consultative, inclusive processes, they will also, therefore, be both more richly informed and more widely acceptable. What is needed, therefore, are consortia or partnerships of players and agencies each of which are poles of change. Both civil society and the state need to be open to and be prepared for such partnerships. By prepared I mean not only willingness but also a degree of prior preparation for what would in most cases be a novel and certainly demanding experience. As so many examples already illustrate, no real change is possible without that.[20] However, above all what I have learnt of living and working in the tribal areas of central India for 20 years is that the people of this country will need to be prepared to activate themselves. Democracy ultimately is a lot of hard work that demands one to move way beyond the victim mode. Neither waiting passively for the state to deliver nor activating ourselves only to fight for one's rights can bring about real change. Transformational initiatives will succeed only if they are energized by the active participation of the people themselves. The space for this needs to be created by the state, which has to also facilitate this participation by building people's capacities and supporting their initiatives in this direction. I illustrate this point in a minute through the example of MGNREGA.

• Recognition of uncertainty calls for and enables the growth of new kinds of organizations. An acknowledgement of uncertainty in all the dimensions explicated creates the conditions for the evolution of lean, learning organizations based on partnerships. This kind of nimble-footed organization is engaged in a process of continuous self-transformation even as it facilitates learning by its members.[21] It pledges itself to building partnerships with other organizations, which show a similar commitment to remaining lean and open to learning from others. Rather than unilinear 'command and control' strategies, it follows 'adaptive management' practices where surprises are expected and learning through experience and evolving knowledge is built into the organizational DNA (Kasperson 2009).

Following Schapiro (1988) and Thompson (2008), these could even be described as 'clumsy institutions', in which 'contestation is harnessed to constructive, if noisy argumentation' (Thompson 2008: 172). Clumsiness is preferable to its alternative elegance, which would seek optimization around just one of the definitions of the problem and a unique solution, thereby silencing other voices. Clumsy institutions are agile and flexible enough to facilitate adaptability to turbulent environments. They can absorb plural perspectives and frames of reference found in inter-organizational partnerships.

- A new definition of reform. Such an institutional design hints at a completely new definition of 'reform' for the neglected parts of India.

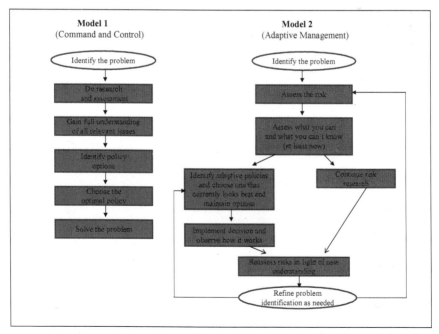

FIGURE 9.3: ADAPTIVE MANAGEMENT IN THE FACE OF UNCERTAINTY

Source: Kasperson 2009.

Over the last 20 years, reform has been restricted to the corporate sector. But the large mass of this country will not benefit till reforms are extended to the public sector in rural development. It is here that there is a need for new institutional designs that will make the poorest people of India active participants in the development process. Perhaps the best example is provided by what is being attempted through MGNREGA, which is clearly the most radically new programme ever conceived in the history of independent India.

The MGNREGA has given rise to the largest employment programme in human history and is unlike any other in its scale, architecture and thrust. Its bottom-up, people-centred, demand-driven, self-selecting, rights-based design is new and unprecedented. MGNREGA enjoins the state to provide a guarantee of employment to each rural household that demands work. But it also demands of the people that they participate actively in the design and implementation of the programme. For, only then will it realize its true potential. Thus far, the programme has suffered because it continues to rely on the same ossified structure of implementation that has failed rural development for six decades. The programme demands a new imagination to be brought to bear on its institutional design. The main implementing agency, the Gram Panchayats (GPs), needs to be empowered with the requisite personnel and build their capacities so that they can make people aware of their entitlements, as also the unique demand-driven character of the programme. And people need to be moved beyond their long-held belief that they will get work only when government decides to 'open' work. There is also a need to build GP capacities to enable them to develop detailed micro-plans that truly reflect the needs and aspirations of the people. Without this effort what is truly new about MGNREGA will not come into play. This empowerment initiative is what will strengthen the roots of democracy in India and place rural governance on a completely new and stronger foundation. This demands lively partnerships with civil society organizations and research institutions that can provide critical inputs in each of these vitally important aspects.

MGNREGA is also exciting because it has a self-limiting character, which has not yet been adequately recognized. The ultimate potential of MGNREGA lies in a renewed focus on improving the productivity of agriculture and convergence to engender allied sustainable livelihoods. Millions of small and marginal farmers are forced to work under MGNREGA because the productivity of their own farms is no longer enough to make ends meet. Among agricultural labour households in India, the percentage of those who own land is around 50 in Rajasthan and

Madhya Pradesh, 60 in Odisha and Uttar Pradesh and over 70 in Chhattisgarh and Jharkhand. And if there is a focus on tribals, the proportion shoots up to as high as 76–87 per cent in Chhattisgarh, Jharkhand and Rajasthan. MGNREGA will become really powerful when it helps rebuild this decimated productivity of small farms and allows these people to return to full-time farming, thereby also reducing the load on MGNREGA. There are many such examples to be found under MGNREGA, although they still remain small in number. For example, the First Annual Report of the National Consortium of Civil Society Organizations on MGNREGA (2009) reports that earthen dams on common land have recharged wells of thousands of poor farmers who earlier worked as labourers to build these dams. These farmers are now busy making a series of investments to improve their own farms. Rising incomes also improve capacity utilization and happier expectations act as incentives for more investment. Under MGNREGA, farmers have come back to land they long abandoned, as increased output, in an atmosphere of renewed hope, spurs further investment. Converging MGNREGA with other programmes for rural livelihoods would carry this momentum forward in a positive upward spiral, which will broad-base the growth process via downstream multiplier-accelerator effects (Shah 2009).

The endeavour has to be to not merely help MGNREGA realize its full potential but to carry that positive momentum forward in a redesign on similar (though necessarily different and specific) lines of all other development initiatives.

Conclusion

The totalitarian state, the invisible hand of the market and science and technology—these were the three main bastions of certainty in the twentieth century. As the century ran its course, each one of them, at different points of time, palpably and demonstrably reached their limits. It is in the space created by their dethronement that the power of uncertainty has the potential to flower. It is only this fracturing of fundamentalisms that has forced each of these fulcrums of power to seek answers to unresolvable challenges in other domains. It is now the time to seize the moment by showing the requisite imagination and creativity in very concrete terms to harness the possibilities created by this unleashing of the insuperable recognition of uncertainty.

This needs to be very carefully understood. For, there is a very real possibility in precisely the opposite direction. So overwhelmed by the collapse of these certainties, one could allow oneself to be gripped by the worst cynicism and despair, an alarmist fear of cataclysmic consequences leading either to an extremist stance of counter-violence or a giving up, translating in its most desperate form, into large-scale suicide. Both of these responses are in evidence in contemporary India. Both can, in one sense, in a large swathe of compassion, even be understood. But neither serves any useful purpose whatsoever. Violence, as is already evident, only incites the draconian character of the state. And surely there can found a better option for farmers than their swallowing the poisonous fluid.

The challenge is not to allow oneself to be overwhelmed by the undeniable darknesses of the time but to seize the light that still shines within so many endeavours, small, unsung but powerful, many outside the government but also several within it. And envision the forging of strong alliances among them. I speak today of a hope in this direction. Where the imagination is exercised to creatively utilize the spaces that democracy is perforce obliged to provide its citizens, exemplified in recent years, after the watershed General Elections of 2004, by the Right to Information Act, the MGNREGA, the Forest Rights Act, the Right to Education Act and the upcoming National Food Security Act. These have resulted from an acknowledgment of the need to forge new instruments once the certainties of old had all run their course.

But one should be reminded that these are spaces that have as yet only been just created. To realize their full potential will require all the resourcefulness available. That will give reform a completely new, intricate and powerful meaning. That will demand forging of new kinds of institutions and partnerships. Building these will not mean a denial of the state, markets or science and technology. Rather, it will mean a harnessing of their respective strengths in a completely new alignment of forces.

The Prime Minister has described the Planning Commission as 'an essay in persuasion'. The word essay has an incredible range of meanings that includes trial, test, effort, attempt, especially an initial tentative effort and the result or product of an attempt. My aim as Member, Planning Commission is an 'aagraha' (an attempt to persuade) with key players in the Central and State Governments, as also in civil society and academia across disciplines, to forge partnerships with each other that would help roll out a wide range of best practices that are already in place in isolation but need to be mainstreamed at scale without the customary loss of quality that such scaling normally entails. This would require a joint endeavour, deeply cognizant of one's own individual, discrete limitations but fully aware of the enormously powerful potential of the coming together.

Notes

1. I thank Mekhala Krishnamurthy for guiding me to this reference.
2. Much of the devastation wrought by colonial settlers in their assignation with the aboriginal/indigenous people across the globe had to do with the presumption of *terra nullius*. Many of the mistakes made in the Adivasi areas also have a similar origin.
3. 'It is the necessity of bringing a natural force under the control of society, of economizing on its energy, of appropriating or subduing it on a large scale by the work of the human hand, that plays the most decisive role in industry' (Marx 1976: 649).
4. The hypothesis entails 'supposing that the entire sequence of future prices will be "announced" at the initial date in order that the inter-temporal equilibrium is sustained' (Dasgupta and Heal 1979: 337). They deploy the hypothesis despite an awareness that 'we simply do not know how expectations are formed. But we do know that rational expectations yield tidy formulations. These are easy to work with. This forms the motivation for the constructions that follow. But it is worth bearing in mind that as a description the rational expectations hypothesis is likely to be way off the mark here' (Dasgupta and Heal 1979: 337). Quite clearly, considerations of neatness and ease weigh more heavily than those of accuracy of description.
5. A stochastic process is stationary if the random variables are well-defined for all points in time and if their cumulative probability distributions are independent of time.
6. After their analysis is complete, Dasgupta and Heal add with complete honesty: 'it is clear that the foregoing construction is of very little use for analyzing resource markets in the world we know' (1979: 349). At another point they say, 'the rational expectations hypothesis . . . is so far-fetched. Each individual is required to possess the correct theory of how the economy behaves in order to make the hypothesis credible. Such a requirement is, however, not credible' (1979: 436).
7. Methodologically, this leads Shackle to advocate an exciting diachronic approach for unravelling the 'broad current of self-determining, or organically evolving history' (1979: 436).
8. Right from the start, however, there was a lively recognition of the fact that the whole procedure entailed serious ethical problems, because of which it was not found acceptable by most economists till as late as the 1960s. Ramsey was the first and most trenchant critic: 'we do not discount later enjoyments in comparison with earlier ones, a practice which is ethically indefensible and arises merely from the weakness of the imagination' (1928: 543). Harrod regarded it as 'a polite expression for rapacity and the conquest of reason by passion' (1948: 30). See also Pigou (1932) for similar observations.
9. See Martinez-Alier (1987: ch. 11) for a brilliant exposition of the consequences of methodological individualism for the inter-generational allocation of resources. Standard discounting procedures do little more than ensuring a 'trickle ahead' for future generations. See Norgaard and Howarth (1991).

10. In his Richard T. Ely Lecture (1974), Solow expresses the judgement that 'the market will tend to consume exhaustible resources too fast' (1974: 12).

11. In a study of the twin implications for environmental preservation of uncertainty and irreversibility, Arrow and Fisher concede: 'if we are uncertain about the pay-off to investment in development, we should err on the side of underinvestment ... Given an ability to learn from experience, underinvestment can be remedied before the second period, whereas mistaken overinvestment cannot, the consequences persisting in effect for all time' (1974: 317). The authors cite 'extinction of a form of life, the destruction of a unique geo-morphological phenomenon, the toxicity and the persistence, indeed the increasing concentration, of the hard or non-degradable pesticides' (Arrow and Fisher 1974: 319) as examples of irreversible changes in the environment produced by economic activity.

12. Alfred Marshall in his magnum opus *Principles of Economics* suggests 'The Mecca of the economist lies in economic biology' (1920: xii). 'The forces of which economics has to take account are more numerous, less definite, less well known, and more diverse in character than those of mechanics; while the material they act upon is more uncertain and less homogeneous. ... economics, like biology deals with a matter, of which the inner nature and constitution, as well as the outer form, are constantly changing. . . economics has no near kinship with any physical science. It is a branch of biology broadly interpreted' (Marshall 1920: 637; emphasis mine). However, in Marshall's own body of work, the influence of these insights can be said to be virtually non-existent. This could be because he saw himself as writing only the Foundations, which in his view, 'must give a relatively large place to mechanical analogies' (1920: xii).

13. This corresponds to what biologists call the 'metabolic flow' through which a living organism sustains its highly ordered structure by sucking in low entropy from the environment to compensate for the continuous entropic degradation it is subject to (see Erwin Schrodinger 1944).

14. Co-evolution is once again a biological concept, which describes the reciprocal relationship between two closely interacting species (see Norgaard 1984).

15. 'The virtue of the thermodynamic approach to evolution is its ability to connect life ecologically to the rest of nature through shared matter and energy flows' (Wicken 1988: 442).

16. James Clerk Maxwell (1871). A fabled minuscule demon posted near a microscopic swinging door separating two gases A and B of equal temperature. The demon would allow only faster molecules to go from A to B and only slower ones to move in the reverse direction, thus raising the temperature of B relative to A, defying the Entropy Law.

17. R. Llamas and P. Martinez-Santos (2005). 'Intensive Groundwater Use: Silent Revolution and Potential Source of Water Conflicts', in *American Society of Civil Engineers Journal of Water Resources Planning and Management*, vol. 131, no. 4.

18. An aquifer is described as a rock or rock material that has the capacity of storing and transmitting water such that it becomes available in sufficient quantities through mechanisms like wells and springs.

19. Hard rock is a generic term applied to igneous and metamorphic rocks with aquifers of low primary intergranular porosity (e.g. granites, basalts, gneisses and schists).
20. One of the most striking of these is the partnership between the Government of Andhra Pradesh and the Mazdoor Kisan Shakti Sangathan for NREGA social audits.
21. M. Pedler, J. Burgogyne and T. Boydell (1997), *The Learning Company: A Strategy for Sustainable Development*, 2nd edn., London: McGraw-Hill.

References

Allais, M. (1953), 'The Behaviour of the Rational Man Faced With Uncertainty', *Econometrica*, vol. 21, no. 4.

Arrow, K.J. (1963), 'Uncertainty and the Welfare Economics of Medical Care', *The American Economic Review*, vol. 53, no. 5.

Arrow, K.J. and G. Debreu (1954), 'Existence of an Equilibrium for a Competitive Economy', *Econometrica*, vol. 22, pp. 265–90.

Arrow, K.J. and A.C. Fisher (1974), 'Environmental Preservation, Uncertainty and Irreversibility', *Quarterly Journal of Economics*, vol. 87, pp. 313–19.

Bammer, G. and M. Smithson, eds. (2009), *Uncertainty and Risk: Multidisciplinary Perspectives*, London: Earthscan.

Bammer, G. et al. (2009), 'The Nature of Uncertainty', in *Uncertainty and Risk: Multidisciplinary Perspectives*, ed. G. Bammer and M. Smithson, Earthscan.

Carvalho, F. (1983), 'On the Concept of Time in Shacklean and Sraffian Economics', *Journal of Post-Keynesian Economics*, vol. 6, no. 2, pp. 265–80.

Cernea, M. and H.M. Mathur, eds. (2008), *Can Compensation Prevent Impoverishment?*, New Delhi: OUP.

Costanza, R., ed. (1991), *Ecological Economics: The Science and Management of Sustainability*, New York: Columbia University Press.

Dasgupta, P.S. and G.M. Heal (1979), *Economic Theory and Exhaustible Resources*, Cambridge: CUP.

Davidson, P. (1982), 'Rational Expectations: A Fallacious Foundation for Studying Crucial Decision-making Processes', *Journal of Post Keynesian Economics*, vol. 5, no. 2, pp. 182–98.

de Castro, E. Viveiros (2003), '"AND", After-dinner speech at "Anthropology and Science"', The 5th Decennial Conference of the Association of Social Anthropologists of Great Britain and Commonwealth, 14 July, published in Manchester Papers in Social Anthropology, vol. 7.

Debreu, G. (1959), *Theory of Value: An Axiomatic Analysis of Economic Equilibrium*, New Haven: Yale University Press.

Gadamer, Hans-Georg (1960), *Truth and Method*, New York: Continuum.

Georgescu-Roegen, N. (1971), *The Entropy Law and the Economic Process*, Cambridge: Harvard University Press.

Gray, L.C. (1914), 'Rent under the Assumption of Exhaustibility', *Quarterly Journal of Economics*, vol. 28, pp. 466–89.

Harrod, R.F. (1948), *Towards a Dynamic Economy*, London: Macmillan.

Hotelling, H. (1931), 'The Economics of Exhaustible Resources', *Journal of Political Economy*, vol. 39, pp. 137–75.

Iyer, R.R. (2009), 'A Slow But Sure Step Forward', *The Hindu*, 7 August.

———(2007), 'Towards a Just Displacement and Rehabilitation Policy', *Economic and Political Weekly*, July 28.

Kahneman, D. and A. Tversky (1979), 'Prospect Theory: An Analysis of Decision Under Risk', *Econometrica*, vol. 47, no. 2.

Kasperson, R.E. (2009), 'Coping with Deep Uncertainty', *Uncertainty and Risk: Multidisciplinary Perspectives*, ed. G. Bammer and M. Smithson, Earthscan.

Keynes, J.M. (1936), *The General Theory of Employment, Interest and Money*, London: Macmillan.

———(1937), 'The General Theory of Employment', *Quarterly Journal of Economics*, February.

King, Martin Luther (1957), 'Non-violence and Racial Justice', in *A Testament of Hope: The Essential Writings and Speeches of Martin Luther King Jr.*, ed. J.M. Washington, New York: Harper Collins.

———(1958), 'An Experiment in Love', in *A Testament of Hope: The Essential Writings and Speeches of Martin Luther King Jr.*, ed. J.M. Washington, New York: Harper Collins.

———(1967), 'Where do we go from here?', in *A Testament of Hope: The Essential Writings and Speeches of Martin Luther King Jr.*, ed. J.M. Washington, New York: Harper Collins.

Knight, F.H. (1921), *Risk, Uncertainty and Profit*, Boston: Houghton-Mifflin.

Lowenstein, Roger (2000), *When Genius Failed: The Rise and Fall of Long-Term Capital Management*, Random House.

Luhmann, N. (1979), *Trust and Power*, John Wiley, UK.

Marshall, A. (1920 [1890]), *Principles of Economics*, 8th edn., London: Macmillan.

Martinez-Alier, J. (1987), *Ecological Economics*, Oxford: Blackwell.

———(1991), 'Ecological Perception, Environmental Policy and Distributional Conflicts: Some Lessons from History', in *Ecological Economics: The Science and Management of Sustainability*, ed. R. Costanza.

Marx, Karl (1976), *Capital*, vol. 1, Harmondsworth: Penguin.

Maxwell, J.C. (1871), *Theory of Heat*, Longmans.

Nash, J. (1951), 'Non-cooperative Games', *Annals of Mathematics*, vol. 54, pp. 286–95.

Norgaard, R.B. (1984), 'Coevolutionary Development Potential', *Land Economics*, vol. 60, pp. 160–73.

Norgaard, R.B. and R.B. Howarth (1991), 'Sustainability and Discounting the Future', in *Ecological Economics: The Science and Management of Sustainability*, ed. R. Costanza, New York: Columbia University Press.

Perrings, C. (1987), *Economy and Environment: A Theoretical Essay on the Interdependence of Economic and Environmental Systems*, New York: CUP.

Pfaff, D.W. (2007), *The Neuroscience of Fair Play*, New York: Dana Press.

Pigou, A.C. (1932), *The Economics of Welfare*, 4th edn., London: Macmillan.

Ramanathan, U. (2008), 'Eminent Domain, Protest and the Discourse on Rehabilitation', in *Can Compensation Prevent Impoverishment?*, ed. M. Cernea and H.M. Mathur, Delhi: OUP.

Ramsey, F.P. (1928), 'A Mathematical Theory of Saving', *Economic Journal*, vol. 38, pp. 543–59.

Savage, L.J. (1954), *Foundations of Statistics*, New York: Wiley.

Schapiro, M. (1988), 'Judicial Selection and the Design of Clumsy Institutions', *Southern California Law Review*, vol. 61, no. 3.

Schrodinger, E. (1944), *What is Life?* Cambridge: CUP.

Shackle, G.L.S. (1975), *Time and Choice,* Oxford: OUP.

———(1972), *Epistemics and Economics*, Cambridge: CUP.

Shah, M. (2009), 'Multiplier Accelerator Synergy in NREGA', *The Hindu*, 30 April.

Slovic, P. (1993), 'Perceived Risk, Trust and Democracy', *Risk Analysis*, vol. 13, pp. 75–82.

Solow, R.M. (1974), 'The Economics of Resources or the Resources of Economics', *American Economic Review* (Richard T. Ely Lecture), vol. 64, pp. 1–21.

Thompson, M. (2008), 'Cultural Theory, Climate Change and Clumsiness', in *Contested Grounds*, ed. A. Baviskar, New Delhi: OUP.

Tiezzi, E., N. Marchettini and S. Ulgiati (1991), 'Integrated Agro-Industrial Ecosystems: An Assessment of the Sustainability of a Cogenerative Approach to Food, Energy and Chemicals Production by Photosynthesis', in *Ecological Economics: The Science and Management of Sustainability*, ed. R. Costanza, New York: Columbia University Press.

von Neumann, J. and O. Morgenstern (1944), *Theory of Games and Economic Behaviour*, Princeton: Princeton University Press.

Washington, J.M., ed. (1986), *A Testament of Hope: The Essential Writings and Speeches of Martin Luther King*, Jr. New York: HarperCollins.

Weber, B. et al., eds. (1988), *New Perspectives in Physical and Biological Evolution*.

Wicken, J.S. (1988), 'Thermodynamics, Evolution and Emergence: Ingredients for a New Synthesis', in *New Perspectives in Physical and Biological Evolution*, ed. B. Weber et al., Cambridge, MA: MIT Press.

PART THREE

NURTURING EXPERIMENTAL CREATIVITY: GANDHI, ILLICH, VYGOTSKY, PANIKKAR AND BEYOND

10

Global Movements, Gandhi and the Progress of Humanity

ÅSE MØLLER-HANSEN

We will not build a peaceful world by following a negative path. It is not enough to say we must not wage war. It is necessary to love peace and sacrifice for it. We must concentrate not merely on the negative expulsion of war but the positive affirmation of peace. We must see that peace represents a sweeter music, a cosmic melody, that is far superior to the discords of war. Somehow, we must transform the dynamics of the world power struggle from the negative nuclear arms race, which no one can win, to a positive contest to harness humanity's creative genius for the purpose of making peace and prosperity a reality for all the nations of the world. In short, we must shift the arms race into a peace race. If we have the will and determination to mount such a peace offensive, we will unlock hitherto tightly sealed doors of hope and transform our imminent cosmic elegy into a psalm of creative fulfilment.

— MARTIN LUTHER KING JR., *Nobel lecture 1964*

It may seem that my teaching means nothing
It describes the infinite, so of course it means nothing
If it meant something, it would long since have been refuted

Yet I have three treasures which I follow and commend to you
The first is compassion, by which one finds courage
The second is simplicity, by which one finds strength
The third is humility, by which one finds influence

Those who are fearless, but without mercy,
Powerful, but without restraint,
Or influential, yet not humble,
cannot endure.

— the *Tao Te Ching* (Dao De Jing), chapter 67

In Ananta Kumar Giri's 'Pathways of Creative Research', he highlights important aspects to social research, aspects that hopefully can contribute to a more distinct direction for social science in a time with severe global challenges.

In Giri's essay there is a quote from Wallerstein: 'Human arrogance has been humanity's greatest self-imposed limitation. In all these arrogances we have betrayed first of all ourselves, and closed off our potential'.[1]

Maybe the worst of these arrogances is the Western hegemony, the self-imposed leadership on religion, economics, science, that has treated other cultures as objects and not as subjective voices in a global, open dialogue. We are living in a globalized world, but not in an inclusive world, and this is part of the problem.

A question that concerns many people, young and old in the civil society is this: 'How can we create a better world for everyone?' It has been said so many times, for so many years, that it sounds like a cliché.

In spite of this, many young people still go into sociology, philosophy, social-anthropology and a wide range of disciplines to search for solutions to global challenges; ecological disturbances, conflicts and war, unjust distribution of resources: problems that seems to increase rather than decline.

These years of learning give valuable insights and knowledge, tools to analyse the world and new perspectives to approach the world and the political and distributive problems of our time. Others are learning by travelling the world, working in aid-organizations and so forth.

Just a small minority continue working at the university, becoming scientists and researchers. The majority go out into the 'real world' with their degrees as masters and bachelors, working in schools, museums, governmental agencies and newspapers, earning their daily bread, but the questions that once brought them in to the social sciences are still there.

What is wrong with our civilization? How can we change an unfair world? How can we take care of the environment? How can we create peace in a conflict-and war torn world where 1200 billion dollars[2] are spent each year on military expenditures (Sipri 2006).

Former students are thus becoming students of life, still searching for creative solutions, in solitude or through networking with people.

This is the kind of creative research I want to reflect upon. The quest for hope, knowledge and necessary action—at the grass roots.

Social Forums: New Public Spaces

Different kinds of grass roots-initiatives and social forums offer new possibilities for learning. Social forums can be everything from small local forums, national forums, regional forums and even World Social Forums, which have taken place in Porto Alegre, Mumbai and Nairobi. The forums are open for everyone, and most of the participants are activists from a multitude of grass roots-movements, Non-governmental organizations (NGO), unions, religious groups and feminist groups.

These forums are unique arenas for learning. One example is the European Social Forum 2004, where 20,000 people from nearly 70 countries across continents gathered to gain more knowledge about a wide range of issues, to find strategies for change and to strengthen the movements. Participants gathered at Alexandra Palace in north London and Bloomsbury in central London to hear over 2,500 speakers at over 500 meetings and to discuss with passion how to make 'Another World Possible'. Key themes of the forum were war and peace, social justice and solidarity, environmental crisis, equality and diversity and neo-liberalism versus sustainable society. These forums are new public spaces to listen and learn, to share knowledge and experiences, to build networks and find strategies for social and political action.

The teachings are usually on a high level, but it is not value free research. Values like peace, fair distribution of wealth, equality and sustainable development are at the core. This is the common denominator, though there are passionate discussions about the right political analysis or strategies.

Speakers come from all over the world to the big forums to share their own research and life experiences. Union leaders from Columbia and India had two of the presentations on a meeting called 'Privatisation for aid money: the third worlds' deadly compromise', a medical doctor and politician from Jerusalem spoke about how Palestine was becoming a Bantustan, a bunch of connected little islands. Two young conscientious refusenics from the Israeli army spoke about the situation for Israeli conscientious objectors and about their own decision to refuse to do service in the West Bank. An environmental NGO-leader from Malaysia spoke about WTO and the consequences for local people and the ecology of the area. This is just a glimpse of the magnitude and possibilities. Towards the end of the forums there were meetings where the aim was to draw knowledge from the meetings and make conclusions and strategies for further action.

So is this research? It is possible to say both yes or no to this question, but it is definitely a public space to learn, to strengthen the hope and to find active solutions and strategies.

Internet

Around 1987 a sociology professor told his students: 'soon we will have access to a new kind of media, a huge database where you can search for a name or a concept, and you will have access to a magnitude of different sources of information'.

Now in 2007, especially in the affluent countries, many of us have next to unlimited access to information. These days you can sit in the outskirts of Reykjavik and read the daily news and comments in newspapers from South Africa, Canada or India. If you also want to go behind the news, you can for instance read reports about peace-research in Sweden, Japan and Iran on quality-internet sites.

In some countries, you can even follow the footnotes and search in a national library database that give access to all the libraries, and if you are lucky, you can get the book in your nearest library just a few days later.

Last but not least, you can stay in touch with other seekers of humanity and share some of the knowledge you have gained and may be reflect on it together.

The point is that there is a greater interesting flow of high-quality information now, than in earlier days, when it might have been difficult to find information outside the universities and academic circles.

All this together have created new situations and possibilities in the search for knowledge, hope and pathways for change.

Limitations

Some are in a position to implement change more than others are. The social movements are at the grass roots. They create undergrowth, and they can grow stronger, or they can decline.

Just a minority are recognized as formal experts, with positions, and there is a trend that you shall not speak out about serious matters if you are not an expert, at least not in the mainstream media, the political areas and the powerful institutions.

The activists have knowledge, enough hope to sustain their spirit, at least for a while and they have some strategies. In the affluent countries, some are changing their lifestyles, trying to live a simpler, calmer and more sustainable life, and they try to share their knowledge in a busy society, through media, film, art, exhibitions, demonstrations, NGO-campaigns and so on.

Some are also trying to build bridges, between groups that are expected to be antagonistic to each other. In the Middle East, young Palestinians and Israelis work together to create a better future for all.

In 2006, a group of Iraqi women Sunnis, Shias and Kurds who had all lost family members under the invasion, together visited USA and Code Pink, an American Peace movement.

These meetings of bridge building are unfortunately not big news. They do not get much attention. The solutions are expected to come from negotiations at the macro-level in society.

The social movements are moving on though. It is a wave, and people are using their spare time and energy struggling to get the message through. They are not the professionals. They are the grass roots.

Who has the responsibility?

Can we, the minor citizens, contribute at all? Should we not expect the politicians to turn the tide? I am afraid though, that many of them are caught in the Western 'rapid economic growth'-paradigm, sometimes moving in a very narrow field, limited by neo-liberal trade rules and laws, accepted truths, global economic dogmas and the struggle to solve day to day problems in the society. They have no time for the deep questions and global challenges of our time.

So what about the United Nations (UN)? The General Assembly with the 192 member states has created a range of fair and good resolutions, but they lack the necessary force to get the resolutions through. What about the Security Council then? We know for instance that the five permanent members of the Security Council together provide the world with 90 per cent of the weapons.[3] They will meet themselves at the door, and they are not at all representative of the global society. I am afraid we cannot put our faith in them either.

Still, I think that the UN as a system with all the different institutions is the best we have, even with all its limitations. Unfortunately, after 62 years, it still has not been able to implement the good intention of making this planet a better place for all children of the world.

So who can make the necessary changes? Journalists are reaching out to society, sometimes with profound and useful information, but they cannot make the necessary changes alone; waves maybe, but rarely big movements. What about the photographers? It is said that the picture of the young girl fleeing from a napalm attack in her village in 1972, was one of the factors that led to an end of the Vietnam War. At least it showed the true face of war, and that made a deep impact on world opinion.

What about the scientists, the social researchers, scholars who view the world from a peak of wisdom. They are employed to uncover the reality and share their knowledge with students and the broader society and help us to get a deeper understanding of this complex global society.

Many of them have shed a light on how things are connected or unconnected and given us brilliant tools to analyse the world, though one sometimes gets a feeling that there is a glass ceiling between the academic spheres and the grassroots spheres.

They seem to never get tired of deconstructing each other's concepts and work, playing a kind of never-ending game with intricate thoughts, not easy available for ordinary people who have not had the time and interest to follow the whole discussion.

Another problem is that there seems to be thick walls between the different disciplines. You can only be an expert on your own limited field, but the problems of the world are connected. They are holistic in nature. The field of economics is in reality very closely connected to the field of ecology and to sociology and ethics, as also mentioned in Giri's references to Van Stavern's research. The question of transcending disciplinary boundaries is more elaborately discussed in Giri's book *Conversations and Transformations*.[4]

E.F. Schumacher, the author of the famous book *Small is Beautiful*, depicted economics as a science with severe limitations, because it dealt with money and economic growth alone, and not with values like a good society and sustainable development, and he asked for a meta-economics that was concerned about the well-being of people and the beauty of nature.

The economists though, seem to rule most of the world today, both developed and developing countries with their 'rapid economic growth-paradigm', a paradigm in which people, animals and nature itself are reduced to input-factors in production, and where citizens are most interesting as consumers. Powerful global and regional institutions as World Trade Organization (WTO), the World Bank and big multinational corporations are reinforcing this development. Trade agreements are serving the rich corporations and their shareholders and not the majority of the people.

Some of the justification for this, is what Margaret Thatcher claimed as 'There is No Alternative', the faith in the invisible hand of the market, the free market ideology that is expected to sooner or later solve the poverty problems of the world. The economists though, seem to be busy looking elsewhere, at profits and the rise and fall in the stock markets.

All this is of course partly true and partly false. In all the mentioned areas there are many great thinkers and actors, with vision and integrity, who are dealing creatively with global and local problems that have to be solved, comprising economists, politicians, social scientists and journalists. Many of them give strong and valuable contributions to the quest of making a better world, but still many of the global and local predicaments are rapidly increasing, not declining.

The questions are still not answered. How can we make a better world? Who can make a better world?

Before I try to make a modest conclusion, I would like to introduce a particular person. At university we heard interesting presentations and discussions about Marx, Hegel, Kant and Habermas to mention a few, but there was never one word spoken about this person in lectures of sociology and political philosophy.

His name is Mohandas Karamchand Gandhi, later given the name Mahatma.

Was he not relevant in the discussions of ethics, change, power, dialogue? Giri has an interesting point when he writes about the Eurocentric academic dialogue and the need for transcivilizational-dialogue.

Gandhi is just a conspicuous example. What about scholars from the Muslim world?

Is Gandhi the missing link in the evolution of mankind?

This is not a question about our enigmatic past but about a new humanity.

Though it might seem quite overstated, it is a relevant question. The major challenges of the world today are, as we know closely connected.

Increasing materialism, poverty, illiteracy, hunger, conflicts over resources, lack of dialogue, arrogance, terrorism, military globalization, destruction of the environment, more hunger, these are vicious circles where all aspects are linked together.

If these problems are ever to be solved, knowledge is necessary, also political and social action and we also need hope to move forward.

Gandhi had deep wisdom related to all these aspects, to critical reflection, to political action, and wisdom related to hope. (I use the word wisdom here, because knowledge connected with heart is called wisdom.)

After returning to India from South Africa in 1915, Gandhi travelled around India for a year and met the people in the villages, experiencing their realities, listening to their stories, learning about the life of the downtrodden people in this country and what was going on in the villages. He gained an important foundation for his further political and social work.

Gandhi contributed with theories to the many aspects of life and society: to politics, economics, ecology, inter-religious dialogue, conflict-solving and ethics. There was another very important aspect too; he showed us with his own life and action that his theories were working.

Martin Luther King Jr. once said: 'If humanity is to progress, Gandhi is inescapable. His life, thought and action are inspired by the vision of a humanity evolving towards a world of peace and harmony. We may ignore him at our own risk'.[5]

If we in the affluent parts of the world really want fair shares for the global family, to reach the UN Millennium Goals before 2015, and if we really want to re-allocate intellectual and material resources from military development to human and sustainable development, we could learn several important things from Gandhi's life and theories, and also from his sources of inspiration.

Gandhi's concept of non-violence goes much deeper than what meets the eyes at first glance. It has deep spiritual implications. At the core of his thinking were at least two concepts that we miss in the Western languages. *Satyagraha* (Gandhi's concept of active non-violence) literally means holding on to truth and it also implies soul force.

The other concept is *ahimsa*, which also means non-violence, but even more than non-violence. The concept is wider and deeply rooted in Hindu, Buddhist and Jain traditions, carrying strong elements of love and care and respect for all sentient beings, including nature itself. It also implies that we are all parts of a much higher entity, a divine creative, unseen power, and this gives a non-dual approach to other living beings and nature.

This is a way of thinking that is far from the Western scientific and so-called rational thinking, but this thinking is alive especially at the grass roots in many parts of the world.

There are signs of a growing awareness of Gandhi's relevance in the world today. He is an important source of inspiration for many NGOs and religious groups, peace movements and solidarity movements

Visionary leaders such as Martin Luther King, Nelson Mandela and Dalai Lama have all been deeply influenced by Gandhi's life and thinking.

There are also European scientists whose research has not been value-neutral, like Johan Galtung (peace studies), Arne Naess (deep ecology) and E.F. Schumacher (meta-economics), who over many years have drawn inspiration from Gandhi.

According to Radhakrishnan[6]:

There is a belief that Gandhi's philosophy of non-violence humbles the arrogance of modern civilization and values. Pioneering work to delineate non-violent ways of intervention for peace and human rights is gaining acceptance. The question 'what is the way to peace' is sought to be answered in Gandhian dictum 'There is no way to peace, peace is the way'. Getting this message across is not easy in a milieu where even peacekeeping is militarized and Gandhian social and political values are ignored as archaic. But that is precisely what the whole political revival and intellectual ferment is about.

Many aspects of Gandhi's knowledge were gained from his experiments with truth.

In particular he held non-violence as a basic ethical tenet and creed, and his life was living proof that his 'active confronting non-violence' was capable of making changes on many levels, from self to interpersonal level and to relations between states.

Gandhi experimented also with himself in many ways. He renounced many things in life that most people in his position would take for granted. He had few personal belongings and lived a very simple life, by limiting his wants. This had at least two aims: to identify with and live in solidarity with the poorest in society and to gain spiritual strength, soul force.

He also said that these renunciations brought him closer to God.

Gandhi's concept of God is worth a much closer look than it is possible to give here. The following quotes are just small glimpses:

'I do dimly perceive that whilst everything around me is ever changing, ever-dying, there is underlying all that change a living Power that is changeless, that holds all together, that creates, dissolves, and recreates. That informing power or spirit is God'. [7]

'The essence of all religions is one. Only their approaches are different'. [8]

'Let me explain what I mean by religion. It is not the Hindu religion which I certainly prize above all other religions, but the religion which transcends Hinduism, which changes one's very nature, which binds one indissolubly to the truth within and whichever purifies'. [9]

'I recognise no God except the God that is to be found in the hearts of the dumb millions.'[10]

Gandhi had, as we can see, a strong spiritual dimension in his life, a practical spirituality that was political in its nature but also a more metaphysical aspect.

The metaphysical aspects of life as an existent reality have through the years been rejected by mainstream Western science, since it cannot be measured or verified. I wish to discuss this briefly before I approach conclusion.

Non-Material Aspects of Life

According to Henry Bergson, 'Science first started with the material aspect. In 300 years it has not been occupied with another object'.[11] This is for the West.

Allan W. Watts, the author of *The Way of Zen* (1957),[12] was concerned about the difficulties in communicating his experiences of Zen Buddhism, which can be called an eastern science of the mind. He writes: 'Zen is above all an experience, nonverbal in character, which is simply inaccessible to the purely literary and scholarly approach. To know what Zen is and especially what it is not, there is no alternative but to practice it, to experiment with it in the concrete so as to discover the meaning which underlies the words' (preface xii).

To write about Zen is, therefore, as problematic for the outside 'objective' observer as for the inside 'subjective' disciple. In varying situations I have found myself on both sides of the dilemma. I have observed and studied with the 'objective' observers and I am convinced that for all their virtues they invariably miss 'the point and eat the menu instead of the dinner' (preface xiii).

It should be added here that the practice of Zen usually involves meditation as a way to development of mind and heart.

Though Western science is still not very open to the existence of a transcendent reality, people at the grass roots though, are experiencing this on their own. In every modern bookstore there is a well assorted department of literature on self-development and spirituality, and there is a growing interest.

A recent international survey showed that Norway was one of the very few countries where for the first time more people would prefer to call them selves spiritual rather than religious. [13]

In another survey,[14] the spiritual group was classified into two groups, one group labelled 'new-age' and the other 'spiritual'. The new age group was characterized by preoccupation with phenomena like astrology, reincarnation, prophecies and articles about supernatural phenomena. They ranked lower on educational variables than the average population.

The spiritual group ranked high on questions about meditation, the wish for a richer spiritual life, inner experiences and they were concerned about political values like environmental protection, equalization and extended democracy. Their educational level was higher than the average in the population.

Some further reflections on civil society and the quest for peace

Concerned spirituality that is not dogmatic, but animates values such as gratitude, solidarity, non-dualism and peace seems to have a potential to unite people from different religions.

In the 75th year anniversary of Gandhi's salt march, people from different countries and religions joined together in a march called 'The International Walk for Peace, Freedom and Justice'. In this march was also a group of 92 Pakistani students and elders. They told the press that they were overwhelmed by the reception accorded by ordinary Indians. 'Common people on both sides want peace. It's only the politicians and fundamentalists who keep us apart. If both countries reduced their defence budgets and concentrated instead on development, we would both prosper', one said. 'The sacrifices our ancestors made should not go in vain. Both Gandhiji and Bacha Khan fought imperialism, and we should follow their path.' [15]

People in civil societies all over the world want peace to blossom in this world. Spiritual values like love, peace and frugality are common for all religions. These values might unite us, but they have to be cultivated in each and every person, in each and every society. Education, sharing of knowledge and hope, is essential in this respect.

Hopefully, in the future, more social scientists will include and have openness for the spiritual aspect of reality. Spirituality is not supernatural, but something natural that lies as a potential in every being. One has to be open to it and experience it. It could have the potential to be a natural antidote to the greed, destruction and conflicts that are riding our world today.

How can we create a better world?

This is a huge and complex question, and of course, no one has the whole answer. We have to find new paths of creative research and rejuvenate our knowledge, our hopes and our actions.

At the personal level, we have to take more responsibility, by limiting our own consumption, be aware of what kind of goods we buy and consider our ecological footsteps: how much waste and pollution our lifestyle generates.

If we also over time could develop a non-violent, loving approach to our less fortunate co-beings this would generate a global atmosphere of more well-being and hope.

But this is not enough. One of the bigger challenges is to make radical changes in the economic and political system, so it becomes more including, more democratic and less destructive. This is a task where the professional actors, like politicians, advisers, journalists and scholars have to play a stronger role.

For this task we need a more open, democratic and inclusive global dialogue, a trans-civilizational dialogue that includes the magnitude of grass roots movements.

As Giri points out: 'A new architecture for producing and sharing knowledge about globalization could provide the foundations of a pedagogy that closes this gap and helps to democratize the flow of knowledge about globalization itself. Such pedagogy could create forms of dialogue between academics, public intellectuals, activists, and policymakers in different societies.'

In the flow of knowledge about globalization, Gandhi's legacy could hopefully give more direction in the important discussions about

- Inter-religious dialogue and ethics
- Sustainable development
- Inclusive economies

- Conflict-solution and non–violence
- The art of democracy

There are many beautiful sources of wisdom from all over the world that could inspire us in our quest for peace and justice, many of which are of spiritual origin.

We have enough statistical knowledge to know that a radical change is needed, and we can be a part of the destruction or part of the healing. It is our choice.

Notes

1. Ananta Kumar Giri, 'Creative Social Research: Rethinking Theories and Methods and the Calling of an Ontological Epistemology of Participation', this volume.
2. Sipri (2006), Stockholm International Peach Research Institute.
3. Coordination Office for the Decade to Overcome Violence, World Council of Churches, Geneva (2005).
4. Ananta Kumar Giri (2002), *Conversation and Transformations: Towards a New Ethics of Self and Society*, Lanham, MD: Lexington.
5. N. Radhakrishnan (2003), *Gandhi in the Globalized Context*.
6. Ibid.
7. Gandhi (1928), *Young India*, 11 October.
8. *Gandhiji's View of Life* (1954:158).
9. Gandhi (12 May 1920), *Young India*.
10. *Harijan* (11 March 1939).
11. Henry Bergson(1977), *The Two Sources of Morality and Religion*.
12. Alan W. Watts (1957), *The Way of Zen*.
13. RAMP (Religious and Moral Pluralism) data collected in 11 European countries in (1998).
14. International Social Survey Programme (2000).
15. 'Dandi in the time of globalisation' Dionne Bucher in *Frontline*, 23 April–6 May, India.

11

Towards an Organic Process of Substantial Sociology

KARL-JULIUS REUBKE

When Thomas Aquinas wrote his first great opus 'Summa contra Gentiles' 750 years ago, he could talk about the creation of substances without matter (*quaedam creaturae non habent materiam, sicut substantiae intellectue*).[1] For Thomas it was evident, that creation cannot start by giving forms to matter—matter has to be created as well and out of nothingness. And not only matter had to be created, but also intellect, which is closer to god and therefore had to be created before matter. Therefore, according to Thomas, there needed to be something substantial without matter, a 'being' or 'ens' as Thomas would say without matter and, therefore, also without form. Since all matter requires form, matter is thus 'controversial' (*contrarium habent*) and therefore 'corrupt'. In his time the reality of substantial beings transcending matter (*Substantiae enim intellectuales secundum suum genus transcendunt omnem naturam corpoream*) was not only taken as evident but also as a requirement for the functioning of the world. The world at that time was looked at in a holistic way, as one being, created and organized by the One. But it was not taken as only matter. Today we dare to speak about an 'intellectual substance' only metaphorically since nothing without matter is regarded as 'substantial'. There is no consent about how the world came to be, the idea of creation and of 'substance without matter' has long been dispelled. To understand the world and more so the working of human society I believe it necessary to take into account the 'intellectual substances' again. Only sociology aware of the reality of these can deal with the substantial needs of a community, a social unit.

Looking at sociology as a chemist though leaving the materialistic point of view of that science behind, I was interested in the chemistry of the formation and transformation of social entities. Reading about social problems in a globalized world I realized that quite often an approach as genius as the Einsteinian physics is adopted: solve the problems by starting from beautiful theories stemming from one enigmatic observation, try to find a unified world formula and leave the experimental proof to the less illustrious future. Very often these theories work quite well for some time and only after a certain period there is an awakening to some unwanted side effect. Recently many doubts as to the 'doctrines' of these approaches have succinctly been put up, for example in 'Rethinking Nature and Society' (Macnaghten and Urry 1998). Theory enters already into the kind of collection of data to build models for change. Not surprisingly desirable results are rarely obtained applying the models. Chemists of my generation are sceptical about 'ab initio' theories along the lines of theoretical physics and still like to start from some observable and reproducible experimental results. Is there something like such a 'chemical' approach to social problems? —I started to wonder.

One day in 2002, I got an invitation from Rajagopal, the founder of the Indian people's movement Ekta Parishad, to join the Jeep-Yatra through Chhattisgarh. I went there, motivated a young filmmaker to make a documentary, translated a booklet on this Yatra and finally wrote a book about the experience involving a lot of questions which I could not even classify as to which fields of science would most properly treat them: sociology, anthropology, environmental science, economy, etc. I will describe just one experience in short.

There was a meeting in a large village, where one third of the families had left to seek for employment somewhere else in a neighbouring state. A drought for some years, missing irrigation and severe interference of the forest department in the collecting of non-wood products of the forest had created a disastrous situation of famine and unemployment causing migration. The villagers had gathered in a big crowd. Rajagopal invited them to tell him their problems. From the various descriptions a detailed picture of the situation slowly formed and questions by the visitors were answered in a way to add some more and clear contours and shades to this picture. Finally, Rajagopal asked: 'What should be done, what can be done.' Again the villagers knew some of the answers quite well, they suffered and had been thinking and probably discussing the issues at length for a long time. And again in this huge congregation a picture was painted of things to do. The next question 'And what can you do?' produced a deep silence and slowly some quiet and timid suggestions were made until one villager pronounced: 'Only if all of us together join in the effort to change our situation some change may be possible.'

At this point I was reminded of some chemical experiments: one has a clear solution of some complex mixture of substances, one drops in a tiny little crystal and up shoots a lot of large, fast-growing crystals producing astonishing heat. I felt in this village congregation: the germ of a new 'substance' of community had been thrown in. I could feel a kind of warmth. What would crystallize here? Could it lead to the formation of a new organized social organism?

In some of the cases this happened. A new 'substance of community' was formed and the villagers started to work towards a betterment of their social situation, quite often with astonishing results. I realized that this is an organic process and as such this 'substance of problem solving community' has a lifespan of defined length, depending on the task ahead.

This lifespan is a common feature of any organism, also of a social organism. The notion of a social organism refers to an idea common in old times and probably not wrong though a little disregarded today. For a long time now it was more scientific to speak of systems. Systems are obtained by cutting them out of their surrounding for the sake of better understanding and planning and according to operational requirements. When planning failed some scientists (like C. West Churchman 1979) turned to open systems, others, like Nicanor Perlas,[2] turned to the ideas of Austrian philosopher Rudolf Steiner,[3] who based his arguments on the understanding that a world for humans should best be shaped in harmony with the human being. The human organism is as such not constructed from parts, nor is it divided into compartments, but clearly it is structured. A new approach to social life could well reflect on this 'organized' way of interaction of relatively independent members. In practice this happened just on the lowest step in some of the villages I visited with Ekta Parishad.

Two years later I was again on a Yatra in Chhattisgarh. It was a particularly hot day of the Nautapas period All were tired and close to 100 activists had gathered under some trees in the shade. And there, Rajagopal invited some young women to tell the group, why and how they came to be with us, since they had come all the way from Kerala. In the tsunami-relief work organized by some Ekta Parishad activists they had experienced how it had transformed them from mourning victims into actively creating members of a 'substantial' community. They were enthusiastic about the 'heart-warming' experience and, therefore, had come to share this feeling of empowerment with the people suffering from a manmade catastrophe of a less publicly sensationalized kind.

I realized that this was actually a second step in creating civil society. The first can be described as getting awareness and understanding into action, this second step is creating a feeling of emotional togetherness, which is strong enough to act in a larger context.

During the travels with Rajagopal on the Yatras in India as well on some of his journeys in Europe I was fortunate to learn some of the Gandhian philosophy this 'social practitioner' has developed out of the Mahatma's life. One of the fundamental statements of Gandhi is 'My life is my message' which implies that everything has to be related to the life itself, not to theory. On the other hand Gandhi was making up his mind all the time, trying to understand, to find and formulate relations as an approach to the next 'experiment'. This requires a perfect presence of mind, since 'experiments' have to be carefully controlled or else they go the wrong way—as chemists know well.

Slowly I realized a third step in the development of civil society, the observing scientific mind, which shuns the fallacy of theory. Only this kind of experimental approach actively creating a substance of understanding can avoid the dangers of ideologies, whether scientific, religious or political.

One day in May 2004, Rajagopal met Nicanor Perlas in Germany for the first time and it was a touching experience to see how the two great social workers discovered their common aims. They exchanged their experiences in the field of social work in India and the Philippines for hours and finally came to call each other spiritual brothers.

As I reflected on this meeting and how and why these two very different men understood each other so well, I came to realize, that the idea of 'threefolding' as Nicanor Perlas terms it in his book, is reflected in a very simple and straightforward manner in the work of Rajagopal: a nucleus of community is formed out of a concerted action in the field of daily needs, a networking of helping cooperation is formed between those many nuclei on the basis of a feeling of relatedness and the whole is structured by individual independent and problem related thinking. There is no division but a structuring like in an organism with its organs.

When Ananta Kumar Giri invited me to discuss practical spirituality in education I was reminded of this experience. Practical spirituality, I thought, has to do with bringing activity into the spiritual life of thinking. This will bring the thinking process out of the abstract description of existing 'systems' and avoid the 'Environmental Fallacy' as C. West Churchman (1979) termed it in the late 1970s—one could call it the ontological approach—as well as out of the normative dominance of so called 'science'—which might be closer to the epistemological approach.

When Ananta Kumar Giri uses the 'black-white' term 'ontological epistemology'—some will hold ontology and epistemology as opposing strategies of the underlying philosophical approach—I think he has not fallen back into the old Indian habit of using a 'dvandva' like 'sukha-dukha' 'joy-misery' and much less wants to add another shade to the grey theory of descriptive or normative sociology, but is trying to focus the attention on a completely new and more 'practical' approach of the 'being' or 'evolving' society which is still in need of its own understanding. A very similar point of view is expressed by Michael Singleton (2004), the socio-anthropologist 'misunderstood even in France', who also speaks of 'onto-epistemology'. He describes his experience in social work in the sub-title of his book: 'Du missionaire anthropophage à l'anthropologue post-développementiste' ('From Man-eater Missionary to Post-Development Anthropologist') which indicates well, how his approach painfully changed from a viewpoint of the superior helping hand to a yet undefined vision of something new out of the contradicting duality of ontology and epistemology into a middle position.

Both personalities realize that creation of a better world involves the author. He cannot stay back describing societies but also not prescribing what should be. Neither criticizing what is wrong nor awarding what seems to be right is a process of creating 'social substance'. Civil society after Gandhi is about this. Sociology of substantial civil society involves the sociologist as an active part of this society. Rajagopal with Ekta Parishad is just one example of this kind of new 'substantial sociology'.

It requires courage to speak about such 'substance without matter' and it requires much more to help such a substance to come into being in social life—but it seems to be very much needed.

Notes

1. Thomas Aquinas (2005), *Summa contra gentiles*, Latin–German, ed. Karl Albert, Paulus Engelhardt, Leo Dümpelmann, 2nd edn., vol. 2, Darmstadt, pp. 114, 474
2. Perlas was awarded the Right Livelihood Award in 2003, is president of the Centre for Alternative Development Initiatives (CADI), a civil society organization based in Metro Manila, Philippines.
3. The idea of 'threefolding' was first developed at the end of the First World War by Rudolf Steiner (1861–1925), Austrian philosopher and founder of Anthroposophy, an approach expanding science from the natural to the spiritual dimension.

References

Churchman, C. West (1979), *The Systems Approach and Its Enemies*, New York: Basic Books Inc.

Macnaghten, Phil and John Urry (1998), *Contested Natures*, London: Sage Publications, See chapter 1, 'Rethinking Nature and Society'.

Perlas, Nicanor (1999), *Shaping Globalization: Civil Society, Cultural Power and Threefolding*, Centre for Alternative Development Initiatives (CADI) and Global Network for Social Threefolding (GlobeNet3), 2000.

Singleton, Michael (2004), *Critique de l'ethnocentrisme—Du missionnaire anthropophage à l'anthropologue post-développementiste*, Paris: Parangon.

12

Pathways of Creative Research:
Ivan Illich's Regenerative Methodologies

TRENT SCHROYER

Who Was Ivan Illich?

Every one of Ivan Illich's genealogies of modern certainties are a critique of what is taken for granted as modern institutional certitudes, e.g. schooling, development, energy, etc. Yet those who read Illich's *Deschooling Society*, *Tools for Conviviality*, *Gender*, etc., were not fully informed by the texts themselves about Illich's intentions. He wrote, not affirmatively about god, but to indicate how the social relations described in these books were not consistent with an ecclesiological ideal community. All his books from 1971 till 2002 were written to enable people to understand the pathologies of modernity so that they might acquire the inner dispositions to live more in conscious relations within community and have a decent life on this earth.

Until his last posthumous book Rivers North of the Future, only those close to Illich understood that all of Illich's writing after 1971, when he stopped functioning publicly as a Catholic priest, till this last book, were exercises in Apophatic negative theology.[1]

Domenico Farias, a long time friend of Illich, asserts that Illich went beyond Apophatic theology and actually aspired to an Apophatic anthropology. While masking his continued vocation Illich was also radically open to other traditional practices. Apophatic anthropology is the rigour of not talking about God, but actually loving as Christ enfleshed had done. It is the practice, not the theology that matters.

Ivan Illich's Regenerative Methodologies

Illich's early theological interest was ecclesiology, or the study of the mystery of faith and the mystical body of Christ. In secular terms, what the Church conceived as the ideal community. His genealogies use early Christian ecclesiology as an actual evolving historical practice, to show how choices made by the later Roman Church and modernity lose these practices. As Illich notes, ecclesiology is twenty times older than modern social science and as a critical hermeneutics may have more depth.

Results of his genealogy were an understanding of how the Church's gradual substitution of power for faithful free choice resulted in more and more comprehensive regulations for Christian life. Each of these attempts to further stabilize and institutionalize grace, over time became perversions that led to loss of the freedom that Christ brought into the world. Specific losses include the criminalization of sin, the perversion of hospitality into service, the rise of value orientations that undermines contextual judgements of the Good, and the creation of the needy and isolated modern individual. The Western Roman Church distorted its relation to local vernacular domains[2] when it took over educational functions that empowered professionals to dominate the cure of souls and standardize pastoral services that had hitherto been worked out locally. The Church's pastoral care model weakened the autonomy of self-limiting vernacular domains. These genealogies are examined below.

Illich's 'regenerative methodology' is also stated as continuous with the ancient Greek Epimethean quest for prophetic reappropriations of the past. The term 'Epimetheus' in classical Greek meant 'hindsight' and Illich seeks to uncover the truth of the past in his historical reconstructions in order to respond to the present. One could also read his radical doubt of the certainties that are central to modernizing institutions—such as schooling, 'resources', 'development', 'need', 'life', 'communication' from this Epimethean perspective.

His interest was to deflate these conceptual certitudes in order to liberate the imagination and open the reader to surprise and new discoveries in everyday life. His interest was also to illustrate how it has been done and can be done in vernacular realms of ordinary community behaviour. Simultaneously, it is to recover the spontaneity and unpredictability of human existence and form a resistance to the technical terms that would distort this quality of living.

This method might be seen as a traditionalist parallel to the Hegelian-Marxist 'immanent critique', or the critical analysis of the existing social relations in terms of their intrinsic norms. However, the institutional certitudes that Illich deconstructs are not just pseudo-necessities of false ideological consciousness that yield greater actions potentials. Also exposed are the technical abstractions that empower experts who have come to be masters of specific social technologies and spheres of human interaction. Illich's interest is not to dissolve false causality but to show how they shrink the competences and learning capabilities of passive bodies or consumers.

It is not the deeper understanding of the objective situation which is the point, but rather releasing the motivations of persons to use their imagination and insight to find solutions. Ultimately it is the trust in human resourcefulness, hope and creativity of nature that guides Illich's 'critiques, not reflections on class war or psychic struggle. It is insight, not reflective knowledge.'

Thus, Illich's critical methodology differs from modern social science efforts to keep social order in step with progress, as in positivism, or critique the socially unnecessary forms of domination with an emancipatory intention, as in critical theory. His intention is to be regenerative in the interests of recovery of greater capacity for practical judgements of the good and right proportion in common sense living in convivial worlds. Or to participate in Christian Freedom in the sense expanded below.

But one has to venture behind the epistemological breaks that emerged from the thirteenth to the seventeenth centuries in the West to understand that Illich's seemingly secular frames of critique also derive from an intent to recover the sacred in everyday life. However, he does not profess theological frames or idealize religious traditions. Instead he focuses on the historical turns that distort the self-regulation of convivial communities—or Christian Freedom.

He shows, he does not say.

Ecclesiology as Critical Regeneration Theory

Illich shares the research interest of Gerhard Ladner in giving a historical account of what Christ brought into the world. Ladner, in *The Idea of Reform* (2004), documents that man's reformation towards his original image-likeness to God was of central importance to early Christianity. In the first six centuries after Christ the idea of 'reform' was a guide for monastic practices where transformation of self in penitential rituals were expressions of inner 'reform'.

The possibility of reform was seen as part of the original liberty of man and his liberation from external domination. Christian Freedom stands above legal necessity as a precondition for striving towards liberation from social and moral pressures.

The good Samaritan answers the question, 'Who is my neighbour'? by expanding the boundaries of community as his freely made loving choice. The parable is not about an obligatory 'ought', which would be a legalization of conscience, its meaning is free choice of inclusion. Ultimately, the choice expresses the spiritual telos of humanity; it is not a normative imperative as in Kantian ethics.

All of Illich's works presuppose this radical notion of Christian reform as a departure point in seeking to help people find a way back to the renunciations that are essential to rise above the pathologies of modernity. To represent the contemporary meaning of the idea of reform, one must describe what is necessary to step outside of the existing world and have confidence in forgiveness, mercy and love. Ultimately this comes down to living with the least contamination of flesh, eyes, and language.

What it takes to renew the church and community today, in an age of systems, is the capacity to renounce the illusions of power and recognize the gift of Christ and 'radical contingency' (discussed below). Jesus brought a new idea of friendship into the world, one that differs from civic culture in the classical sense. Illich's gambit, since faith in God has been obscured, is the hope for a new society spread by the vocation of friendship; people are led to discover God in each other. The coldness of turning away was revealed by Christ as sin, as betrayal of love.

Ivan Illich often called himself a historian but he actually does history as a traditionalist in special ways. Accurately viewed as a negative, Apophatic, theologian-philosopher, he researches history in order to critique existing social orders by showing that 'this is not it'; i.e. a fulfilment of the Christian escathon in this world. His early theological focus was upon ecclesiology, or the study of what the Church has conceived as the ideal community since the fourth century.

The application of ecclesiological thinking involves critical reflections into the mission and internal liturgical rituals and practice of the church and how it is situated within the surrounding community. These reflections resulted in monastic movements as indicted by periodic reforms—such as the Benedictine reform, the Alcuin reform, the Clunic reform and finally the Gregorian reform, which Illich sees as the watershed that finally spawned modernity.

As Gerhard Ladner has shown the idea of 'reform' that emerged from the history of Christian monasticism begins with the meaning of transformation of self in crucial penitential rituals—as public expressions of inner 'reform'. In the Gregorian reform the Roman Church finally takes over this penitential territory from the communities and monasteries and empowers the priest to officiate in the confessional, breaking with the Eastern Church which refused to benefit from the new theological mapping of purgatory and its escape options.

Origins of Modernity in Perversions of Roman Church 'Reforms'

Illich shows how the western Roman Church distorted its relation to vernacular domains when it began to take over educational functions that empowered its spiritual 'professionals' to dominate the cure of souls and the pastoral services that were heretofore defined within the vernacular world itself. The Church's pastoral care model weakened the autonomy of self-limiting vernacular domains—especially that of vernacular gender.

This genealogy is further developed in an essay on 'The War against Subsistence' where Illich shows that the fundamental ideologies of the industrial age are derived from the monastic reforms from the ninth to the thirteenth centuries where the personal pastoral services of the professional priests were more and more asserted to be essential for salvation. He says:

The idea that there is not salvation without personal service provided by professionals in the name of an institutional mother church is one of the formally unnoticed developments without which, again, our own age would be unthinkable. True, it took 500 years of medieval theology to elaborate on this concept. Only by the end of the Middle Ages would the pastoral self-image of the church be fully rounded. And only in the Council of Trent (1545) would this self-image of the Church milked by clerical hierarchies become formally defined. Then in the Constitution of the Second Vatican Council (1964) the Catholic Church, which had served in the past as the prime model for the evolution of secular service organizations, aligns itself explicitly in the image of its secular imitations. (1981: 60)

In addition to the discovery of Roman Church professional monopoly over the new spiritual territory of 'purgatory', the emergence of the image of the Church as a 'Mother' who has responsibility over the *eductio prolis*—the upbringing of Christians—is the key perversion. The Catholic priest, now a curate, was upgraded from a celebration of sacramental liturgical blessings to the administration of the sacraments which had expanded in the eleventh century. So, too, expanded the services performed and technical instruments used by the Church. Along with professionalization of the priesthood, new technological innovations, such as the organ and the Church clock, increase the religious institutions dominance over the vernacular domain. Again these were resisted by the Eastern Church.

Other technifications of the cure of the now genderless Catholic soul by the curate included new manuals and language for the confessional. Compulsory confessional once a year presided over by a male professional using written rules for the cure of souls and the creation of a schooled conscience overshadowed the gender specific vernacular practices that had balanced the vernacular domain in the early church communities. All these professionalizations prepared the 'universal' Catholic soul for the rule of written law and universal education. All of these regulations reduced Christian Freedom and its practice. These are also the conditions essential for modern state formation and they change the reciprocity of monastic practices and surrounding communities in ways that excluded vernacular traditions and wisdom about learning that they contained.

In the past, inclusion of regional vernacular traditions into monastic practices were how monastic and church centred villages influenced mutually stabilizing influences upon the aristocratic warrior cultures and slave-owning empires. But that changed as the Church consolidated its power and simultaneously the power of the state.

From Mother Church to Mother State

The Papal Revolution of 1075 created a professionalization that separated the regular priests from the secular clergy who were organic to the communities and not connected to the emergent corporate entity of the professional priesthood. This professionalization, emergent from the Clunic reform, turned the 'spiritual ones' (in opposition to the laity) into the first trans-local, trans-feudal, transnational class in Europe to achieve political and legal unity. One could say the first international corporation.

The Papal Revolution rapidly sponsored the first Crusade (1096–1099), the second (1147) and the third (1189). These increased the power and authority of the papacy, but also turned the Mediterranean Sea into a route for Western expansion. This correlates with the explosion of the resettlements of towns and cities, massive immigrations to new parts of Europe and commercial trade expansions. The first universities that emerged subjected theology, jurisprudence and philosophy to systematization, and Latin now constituted the scholarly language.

The Church in disembedding itself from vernacular society formed a new system of law to execute its hierarchical administrative functions and showed the way to the creation of new social institutions. Most significant was a disembedding of law from the customs of communities that legitimated strong central authorities, both sacred and secular. The Church's new organizing principles differed from those of previous centuries. It established arrangements that are being repeated in many places around the world today—as traditional communities are pulled into modernizing and globalizing dynamics.

As Roman Church becomes a centralized 'mother church' in the Middle Ages, it represented itself as an all-caring authoritarian teacher and sovereign order. The internal debate about the dual authority, Pope or King, raged throughout medieval Christendom, swinging from those who justified papal supremacy, e.g. Gregory the VII, Becket, John of Salisbury, to state supremacy, e.g. Dante, William of Ockham, Thomas Aquinas. Ilich claimed that the actual institutionalizations of the modern state was modelled on the Papal State.

A historian of law, Morris Berman, also interprets the Papal Revolution of 1075–122 as establishing the first legal state—which thereafter became the model for state formation throughout Europe. This revolution had many complex consequences—to state just a few of them that are assumed in Illich's earlier analysis:

'Freedom of the Church' became a cry that meant not only wresting power from the kings to appoint bishops but also freedom from the laity too—it represents a disembedding of the Church from other institutional orders that had mercantile consequences and broke the Benedictine monopoly over religious life.... the collective clergy became a unified corporation for the first time—the first model of a transnational corporation;... the codification of Church Canon law, essential to justify the papal revolution, was systematized in ways that could be integrated with secular laws.(Berman 1983: 404ff)

The revolutionary character of this 'reform' gave out a new sense of the possibility of effecting change in this world and this new-found glory was embodied in gothic Cathedrals with soaring spires and vaulted arches. This revolution also represented the irreversible separation between the western and eastern Church's as well as contributing to the formation of modern individualism; discussed below.

Cultural Colonization of Vernacular Speech

A significant case of utilizing the new state power was Queen Isabelle of Spain who tried to create an administrative state, by calling in the Office of the Inquisition to get rid of useless nobles and replace them with lawyers and technicians. She was confronted with two enormous projects in the same year 1492: Columbus's quest for Cathay and Nebrija's proposal for the 'marriage of empire and language' (Illich 1981: 37).[3] She wanted to govern, not simply rule, in the traditional sense with the usual tolerance for vernacular diversity in Spain.

Consequently, Spain became the first European state to develop a formal grammar—or a taught mother tongue. With Nebrija's new systematization of Castilian Spanish all verbal expressions of Spaniards would have the stamp of the state in their linguistic practice. This new precise Spanish required formal teaching of the mother tongue. A new form of state control over the wild untaught vernacular diversity was beginning. Moving from artificial Castilian to Latin would then be an easier step. In retrospect, it may be that Nebrija's project provided more unity to the state than new world wealth; the printing press and bureaucratic control were reigned in and the wild expression of many vernacular hybrids and multilingual styles put in their place.

What Illich is documenting is the formalizing of language as a commons that turns it into a 'need that cannot be met by vernacular life'.

Dependence on formal teaching of the mother tongue is the paradigm for all other dependencies created in an age of commodity-defined existence. The general framework implied here is that every attempt to substitute a universal commodity for a vernacular activity 'has led, not to equality, but to a hierarchical modernization of poverty' (1981: 63, 73).[4]

What Marx was struggling to understand in his reflection on the fetishism of commodities is given a more general and deeper cultural interpretation here. Step by step the war against subsistence has defined as commodities that which is essential for living communities and in each case the result has been new hierarchies and new forms of domination.

Perversions of the Contingency Axiom that 'Reformed' the Church

Illich's last book *Rivers North of the Future* begins with reflections on the crucial Christian notion of 'contingency' that expresses the ontic state of a world, which has been created from nothing, is destined to disappear, and is upheld in its experience through divine will. This point involves the theological philosophical debates that led to modern instrumental reason.

The final point of this analysis is that contingency did not have to devolve to where nature's laws became independent of God's will and nature lose its living qualities. Consequent theological elaborations of the axiom of contingency led to imagining a set of 'intermediaries' considered necessary for heavenly movements (e.g. angels), as well as operational instrumentalities deemed necessary for reforming church practices. In the context of an emergent, denied and yet latent dualism, the radical contingency meaning of these 'intermediaries' faded from memory and they became a sub-category of Aristotle's *causa efficiens* and then, effectively, tools for human self-assertion. A human regime of will and human self-assertion replaces a cosmos of gratuity, or gift.

Illich notes that 'intermediaries' present in the cosmological writings of Aquinas were screened out in translations by contemporary theologians who knew these notions would not be acceptable to a scientific ethos.[5] When macro-micro intermediaries became viewed as instruments, it put the world into human hands and led to replacing the spirit of contingency with a spirit of tools and technology. This opened the age of technology, which Illich claims lasted for 700 years until the age of systems emerged about 1980.

Intermediaries, as reforms of church administration, changed the social and spiritual relations of church and community in multifold ways. For Illich, these instrumental reforms were consolidations of the church powers in this world and erased felt senses of appropriateness unique to localities, replacing them with universal rules for the faithful. Blessings were expanded to seven sacraments that only certified churchmen could use as divine instruments. Legal oath taking, forbidden by the New Testament (Mathew 5), became legal foundations for all levels of a feudal hierarchy—family, city and macro political orders. For Illich these reforms brought the legal mentality back into the heart of love, and sin, as a turning away from the Holy Spirit, was turned into a regulated legal crime. What for the good Samaritan was a gut-driven act of love is turned into an obligatory norm of conscience, losing the quality of Christian Freedom.

New Fears and new Psycho-Spiritual Pathologies

Illich relates these perversions of the reformed church order to new pathologies of sensibility and psyche of the 'organized' faithful. Fears created by the newly-defined inner forum of conscience, subject to juridical review by self, priest and state, carve out a more vulnerable and internally fearful form of selfhood.

A Christian response, in the light of the incarnation, to a face, a person or an icon, brings with it a sense of awe about seeing the infinitely good. But after a formalized criminalization of sin a confusion arises in non-public, privatized forgiveness—one enters into a new psychic topography. The inner forum, the new sphere of conscience, and individuated responsibility to a confessional priest as magistrate, opens up a non-communal inward experience of fear, dread, aloneness, abandonment and despair. Rather than being supported in an ethos where the 'I' is always surrounded and supported by the 'we', the believer now is more fearful of temptation by hidden cosmic powers. Fear of demons, witches and magic are the results of new experiences in institutions that would regulate grace.

While fear of losing the bond with God or being excluded from loving is a reality of human life, the fear that is released after the criminalization of sin is compatible with the rise of the docile believer who is manipulated by the new juridical order and 'fatherland' and, therefore, easy to mobilize for crusades, both then and now. As Charles Taylor remarks in the 'Foreword' to *Rivers North of the Future*, the new polite civilized order is 'the Christian order'. The 'polite', 'civilized' moral orders of Protestant England, Holland, and later the American colonies, lost much of their 'transcendental' content in being domesticated to accept state legitimacy.

Transformations of church liturgical procedures were central to changing relations between the church and local communities. Some of these changes created conditions leading to the Church's domination of vernacular life and the emergence of a spiritual, legal, political and economic individual.

Illich interprets the socio-genesis of Western individualism as beginning in transformations of perception and disembodiment of the senses in the practice of liturgical reading. Reading sacred texts was originally a speaking event where the reader pronounces the undivided line aloud in order to recreate a pilgrimage through the text. Reading was an oral activity in which the page is a vineyard, where the reader tastes the words that are plucked from the page (see Illich 1993). The pilgrimage of reading leads towards the light and to contemplation and prayer.

Early in the twelfth century, the lines become divided and sub-headings appear, as well as an indexed and numbered sequence of paragraphs and sub-paragraphs. These seemingly minor transformations in mental space ordering actually changed the cultural uses of memory and the practices of relating the eye to the ear, seeing to hearing. What was once a public hearing by voice and action became transformed into a 'writ', an external object outside of sensual experience.

The communitarian public-ness of vowing in marriage, or positioning in land, became a hard copy writ with huge impacts upon lay literacy. The relations of perception and imagination were altered and created a superficial confusion of 'appearing signs' (writs) with reality. This confusion of virtual mappings has continued to expand and now charts, graphs and statistical probabilities are seen as actualities. For Illich, the productive role of imagination is to form metaphoric images of the invisible and not get misled by taking abstractive theoretical frames as 'real'. One loses the ability to read the 'flesh of the world' and instead orient all attention to virtualities.[6]

Certifications of individual 'identity' became a new social expectation that overwhelmed local customary practices. These new symbolizations of the 'individual' provided a new metaphor of the inner conscience-as-text that could be read by authoritative priests, inquisitors and of course God and the Devil. Institutionalization of these expectations into juridical processes empowered the monopolies of the Papal Church, and the emerging city and nation states, in ways that made the local associations incapable of providing what the new individual needed. The new 'needy individual' empowered these radical monopolies against communal-vernacular associations and fostered perceptions of scarcities that communities cannot provide. The implications of this transformation are multifold.

Formalized credentialed frames became essential for individual orientations to wider political and economic exchanges, local reciprocities were no longer enough. The institutionalizations of 'identity' expectations were the origins of the colonization of local cultures and became preconditions for what Marx later called 'the fetishism of commodities'.

From this perspective on colonization one can appreciate why Illich sees the last 500 years as a 'war against subsistence' and presents a research programme focused on what he called 'the history of scarcity'.[7] Comprehending the origins of scarcity becomes the counter research programme to the Marxist critique of capitalist exploitation.

Disembodiments of Modern Sensibility; How Modern Virtualities Eclipse Actualities

Secularization produces extraordinary disembodiments that lose the phenomenological density that the felt body acquired after Christ. The mystery of the incarnation, of God becoming flesh and man becoming divinized, meant that Christian hope was oriented not only to hearing the gospel but also to the vision of God's face. The gaze of the believer is a homesickness for the beyond, for the grace of the face of God. This results in seeking the face of God in the face of everyone, developing an inner sense that is a source of felt body experience in this world.[8] Faith, for Illich, is rooted in the flesh of the body; the tendency to accept modern abstract virtualities as reality loses touch with this sensuous felt body and its intuitive sensing of the sacred.

For Illich, modern sensibility has been profoundly disembodied; the gaze is no longer a willed action subject to one's moral decisions. The early Church's images in frescoes and icons were linkages of the visible and invisible; gateways and thresholds to what is in heaven. The inner eye sees the inner image. In later scholasticism the visual cone was inverted with the object radiating an image of itself that is secularized. Seeing is now a passive reception and digestion of images from outside; the eyes are now cameras that receive information. Illich reminds one that many ascetic traditions talk about the guarding and training of the eye, since appropriate seeing is a virtue.

Secularization means the poetic, performative qualities of the world are erased and forgotten in field after field; a world of fitting proportion and appropriateness is replaced by a mechanical world where integrations of common sense are replaced by value assessments of risks and cost-benefits. While local festival and pageantry continue everywhere, the integration of these into a self-understanding of the modern individual is not easy to do. Lost is the aesthetics of liturgy—of bringing beauty, music and dramatized experience of the Holy Spirit together in ritual service.

The unique practical interest of Illich's spiritually grounded method can be shown by contrasting it to Catherine Pickstock's supposed 'Liturgical Critique of Modernity'. Pickstock presents an account of Catholic Liturgy that argues that only within this practice is the ethical and the aesthetic, the private and the public, held together and human life participates in a meaningful cosmos. Only in the ensemble of music, architecture, and liturgical performance does beauty and transcendence come to create an event of participation in the sacred. She argues that modernity, having broken with liturgical traditions, is only able to construct pseudo-liturgies such as the art-as-life opposition to universalizing commodifications. In this sense she claims that only traditional communities governed by liturgical patterns are likely to be the sources of resistance to capitalism or bureaucratic norms. Specifically she holds that the Catholic hierarchy is a needed expertise to enable these linkages and provide the events that release this insight.

Whereas this reflection is a significant critical traditionalist effort, she has not presented a concrete remembrance of the operations and practices of the Church itself and how it relates to this 'transcendence'. So it has no immanent critique of the evolution of the Church or any implications for wider concrete models for socio-economic practice here or around the world.

So too does Illich's celebration of liturgical drama depart from an image of the liturgy of the Church as a womb out of which the mystical community comes into the present. But his reflections on the history of the Church imply that this has been done in a controlling and this worldly consolidation of power. When the Church over-extended hospitality into corporate service or over-stabilized the parish in ways which controlled neighbourliness, the practices of the Church were not life affirming. But it is ultimately the change of the nature of promise or bondedness from an early conspiratio to legalized oath taking that turns freedom into law breaking. These insights focus on the failure of the Church to realize its community ideals in ways that suggest how to reorient Church and community.[9]

For Illich, modern evils are best discerned through the eyes of faith because modernity has been 'dis-eviled' by secularizations which override the felt body's sensibility and substitutes abstractions that sacrifice the present to virtual futures—such as 'progress', 'development', 'globalization', etc., Illich sees these future-oriented categories as 'man-eating idols'.

The contaminations of techno-globalization are the increasing power of multimedia and visual imaging that substitutes virtual experience for actualities. Most persons today get their signs, symbols and images as consumers of a growing industry of commercial and ideological image producers. Contemporary human consumer sensibility is deepening participation in virtually-created 'worlds'.

These image fabrications have specific interests guiding their construction and do not express living and felt social 'worlds'. Image-information services are disproportionately consumed and controlled by the powerful corporations or states and constitute ever new versions of social control, manipulation and propaganda consumption.

But the logics of the new disinformation systems have evolved in sinister ways:

In pronouncements by the military in the US and United Kingdom, 'full spectrum information dominance' begins with 'weaponizing of information'. The goal is to put a positive spin on all information in order to degrade any dissent. The 314–page US Army manual on information was issued November 2003. It begins with the premise that 'information is an element of combat power' which goes beyond propaganda construction and distribution. What is now relevant is 'mastery of the situation' and the goal is to 'have our way and nothing done can make any difference'. What is not seen by the public is development of a systemic capacity to deny, degrade and destroy unfriendly information. This is a partial answer to why President George W. Bush (and corporate interests) continued to deny everything that might cast official policies in a bad light. The concern is not for truth, the concern is that nothing stop the execution of their policies. (Trent et. al. 2006: 91)

The world today is involved in a crisis of truth—exacerbated by the nexus of corporate PR and disinformation, for example Exon's denial of global warming, the propaganda state, the weaponization of information, etc.

Current economic ideologies—such as 'economic freedom'—are constructed via these virtual techniques and presented by the reigning powers as social 'necessities'. Only in this way is it possible to explain how deeply flawed projects—such as neo-liberal economic development or the Iraq war—can be sustained against the tide of negative information and experience that constantly feeds back from these inhuman actualities. Only in this way is it possible to understand why the majority of watchers of Fox News continue to believe that Iraq conspired with the 9/11 conspirators. A recent book by Ron Suskin—*The Way of the World: A Story of Truth and Hope in an Age of Extremism*—brings this crisis home to the US White House too.

Creating Vernacular Free Spaces

Illich claims that 'today in addition to "who gets what" two areas of choice have always been and are now become non-expert, or "lay", issues: the legitimacy of local judgement about the appropriate means for production (e.g. traditional agriculture not imposed chemical agriculture) and the selection of forms of community or regional intermediary structures that foster common sense forms of self-reliance' (Illich 1981: 11). For example, the participatory budgeting process in Brazil increases local participation in political decision making in ways that have made a great deal of difference in the poorest neighbourhoods of Brazilian cities. Or community support for agriculture in the US can support the remaining small farmers before all choice for local food production disappears.

Those are public choices oriented to subsistence use of common environments that would protect local livelihoods and foster public debates about trade-offs between growth and freedom. For example, the communities of western Pennsylvania that came together to exclude agribusiness overuse of water and soil resources that would disrupt local small farming.

Such choices have been exercised in various political ways since time immemorial. But since 'development' has become the means-end logic of national economic 'planning' local resistances are usually viewed as quaint and not 'productive' for the national aggregate of growth or efficiency, unless local groups and municipalities get very imaginative about getting their interests protected. Because such choices are always context specific and take a variety of forms that cannot be generalized, they are rejected by experts as not productive. Alternatives mean local varieties of the inversion of 'development' in that they would replace consumer goods by personal action, or industrial tools by convivial tools.

This does not mean a return to the past. As Illich says: 'I do not oppose growth-oriented societies to others in which traditional subsistence is structured by immemorial cultural transmissions of patterns. Such a choice does not exist. Aspirations of this kind would be sentimental and destructive' (Illich 1981: 105).

No bipolar oppositions are implied, the point is to attempt to secure political or participatory space for forms of governance that enable exceptions to national/international forced development or ideally maximize this option in today's complex national-international systems.

Greater options for communities result from promoting self-defined work and creating local community institutions for local economies—in opposition to the totalities of the left and right ideology. In the context of the recognition of globalization as colonization, there may be an emerging common ground for some left and right agreements about small scale local self-regulating autonomy. On the other hand, critics from both right and left charge that such vernacular arrangements have co-existed with slavery, serfdom and other forms of enforced dependence. But vernacular free spaces are only where it is possible for workers to be owners of their tools and resources in interaction with agreements about the use of the local commons. That would mean today the achievement of arrangements for sustainable communities—a project that many corporations would like to help with in the form of partnerships that guarantee them profits; when it is no longer profitable then is the test of 'partnership'.

Behind these reflections is a unique perspective and methodology for recovering what is being lost in modernity, and painfully being recovered every day by groups struggling all over the world. The following is an attempt to understand this methodology which begins with the central notion of the vernacular domain.

The vernacular domain is the sensibility and rootedness that emerges from shaping one's own space within the commons associations of local-regional reciprocity. It is the way in which local life has been conducted throughout most of history and even today in a significant proportion of subsistence and communitarian oriented communities. It is also central to those places and spaces where people are struggling to achieve regeneration and social restorations against the forces of economic globalization. A vernacular way of being, doing and making is historically illustrated by subsistence villages, classical cities as well as self-governing municipalities and city regions during most of history.

Convivial Living as a Post-Industrial Society Practices

In *Tools for Conviviality*, Illich extends the anti-development vision that stresses community and subsistence logic into formulations that can be applied to all in post-industrial service societies. These principles are aimed at orienting people to enlarge the range of each person's competence, control and initiative in commodity-intensive consumer societies. Aware persons practising these principles would be able to select modern technologies that serve political related individuals rather than hierarchical managers from state or corporations. Illich's vision is that where tools are responsibly limited, a quality of playful gracefulness permeates personal and communal relations—as against the competitive or feigned solidarity's of modern capitalist or socialist societies.

Use of collections of social organizations as a form for restoring communities is what Polanyi calls regenerative social restoration and Illich calls convivial reconstructions. In a world dominated by the quasi-religion of economic freedom this perspective should be taken seriously, especially those who are advocates of sustainability and who have not yet accepted market as the real decider.

Illich focuses on the scale and structure of 'tools'—which can be machines, institutions, techniques—and presents criteria to guide research into the dis-economies of destructive logics of over determined engineering of the human and natural world. Where tools expand beyond limits they become radical monopolies that transform the free use of natural abilities into dependencies or robot like repetitions of other defined work.

The following are negative design criteria to guide the sustaining of a multidimensional balance of human relations to tools and to the environment:

OVERGROWTH VERSUS BIOLOGICAL BALANCE

Where there is a presumption that humans can be fitted into a world conceived as a technological whole, the earth's ecologies become unlivable and the natural scales and energies essential to maintain social reciprocities are disturbed. Illich put this out in 1973, long before ecological economics said it systematically.

OVER–INDUSTRIALIZATION VERSUS CONVIVIAL WORK

Dominance of industrial process can make people prisoners of welfare and enforced compulsory consumption. This does not promote a balance between what people can do for themselves and what anonymous institutions can do for them.

OVER–PROGRAMMING FOR THE INDUSTRIAL ENVIRONMENT VERSUS SUSTAINING THE POWER OF CREATIVE IMAGINATION TO CREATE MEANING

Tools that become too specialized and centralized exclude convivial learning that is derived from the primary involvement of people and balancing the knowledge mix so that independent learning is possible. Mass production models have since Adam Smith's 'pin factory' stressed productivity rather than innovative creativity. In recent decades, flexible specialization has emerged to form an alternative to industrial specializations.

ECONOMIC PRODUCTIVITY VERSUS THE RIGHT TO POLITICAL PARTICIPATION

Centralization of power and idealization of growth creates imbalances that render people helpless to choose the option of greater happiness at lower levels of affluence. Fevered development strategies emerge to protect local jobs while simultaneously blocking open discourse about alternatives that would create work opportunities from differing production arrangements, e.g. Michael Shuman's assertion of the returned relevance of import substitutions.

ENFORCED OBSOLESCENCE VERSUS THE
RIGHTS TO TRADITION

People lose shared places and memories and established judgements on precedents when unlimited rates of change are forced adjustments. This devalues shared normative pasts that are essential to establish cultural limits in place.

Each of these above defines essential balances to be preserved if people are to cooperatively act to create and protect convivial living. This does not mean abolition of industrial or service productions but a reduction of compulsive learning and a protection for individuals and communities to choose their own styles of life through smaller scale renewals. Otherwise radical monopolies emerge that force the 'materialization of values' by means becoming coercive ends. Therefore, they release blind envy as augmentations of self-interested economic 'progress'.

The unique milieu essential to sustain self-defined work, liberty and autonomy in tools and self-governance, presupposes what German phenomenology calls the *lebenswelt*. That is a taken for granted sphere that is not permeated by excessive technical idealizations or the authority of professional cognitions deriving form centres of power in every institutional sphere. But it is much simpler to call it the 'vernacular domain' which is essential to sustain human liberty and meaning and to critique the forces and hierarchical powers.

Converging with what Habermas calls 'internal colonization', it also objectifies how language and sensibility is forced to be submissive to dominations by technical language justifying coercive force. Habermas sees that the 'economistic form of understanding undermines cultural meanings, but he does not recognize that ordinary language must be used to resist the destruction of everyday interactions. Only in this way can critical reflections become part of everyone's everyday life and not require an army of professional critical philosophers and sociologists to tell people what is happening to them or how they can seek "emancipation".'

Loss of Vernacular Gender as
Condition for Economism

Illich claims that feminist research has uncovered truths that changes the way modern category of 'work' is understood and at the same time revitalizes the notion of 'gender'. Illich appropriates these perspectives and adds to them a historical perspective that changes one's understanding of the origin of modernity too. In contrast to human beings having a 'sex',

Illich was persuaded that gender was always culturally determined because one never sees a 'human', non-gendered body, or hears an asexual voice.

Against the sphere of subsistence activity Illich contrasts wage labour—a new form of work that emerges and becomes normative for the formal economy. Citing E.P. Thompson and others, Illich points to how resistant crowds were to the undermining of the traditional food security norms that protected the poor and starving from the intervention of police and goons from crown corporations. When police tried to incarcerate the poor who were not able to pay their bills, the 'moral economy' intrinsic to the subsistence domain resulted in spontaneous crowd refusal of coercion for what was customary practice in situations of hunger. Formalizations of the commodity logic were applied to food security, first by Adam Smith, despite that the 'right to live' was protected by subsistence custom and it took massive restructuring of social life to make this change happen.

How, to use Marx's formulation, did the capacity to create use values turn into the commodity value of exchange values; or in his terms the exchange value of labour power? Marx's analysis of the fetishism of commodities is a formal one of the development from simple reproduction of exchange to expanded exchange sequences, but it does not explain the actual historical transformations that rupture the vernacular domain and usher in the work ethic and wage labour and the genderless economic individual. This is done by Illich in his book *Gender* (1982).

The necessary transformation was turning the economic division of labour into a productive and unproductive kind, and that was first enforced through the domestic enclosure of women. The subsistence domain is a commons maintained by a gendered division of labour, where 'labour' is not the same as 'work' as Hannah Arendt has sharply argued. Loss of vernacular gender and the emergence of genderless sex is the 'universal' precondition for the emergence of the regime of scarcity.

But for this major disruption of the subsistence domain several other cognitive transformations had to come together, such as:

Gender in the subsistence domain is an asymmetrical duality that takes different shapes in different contexts. Here it is important to distinguish patriarchy, which uses gender to justify male dominance and power from a more balanced regime of gender complementary. (Illich 1982: 33)

Imaging of the woman as literally a 'home-body' whose nature was to support the wageworker is what Illich calls 'Shadow Work'. This confuses the gender specific roles of subsistence domain with the particular bifurcation of work in the nineteenth century when the wageworker and shadow worker emerged together. The point that Illich argues is that wage-labour requires more and more supportive shadow work to maintain and that this is an index to the counterproductivity of the regime of scarcity.

Self-limiting social communities evolved envy protections that are symbolic ceremonial evasions of violence. Subsistence-oriented institutions, such as cycles of ritual feasts, pageants, dramas, etc., are oriented to the reduction of invidious individualism and envy. These associations can also be distorted by disruptive interventions of empires and hierarchical interventions. But the purpose of these events is to neutralize the dangers that emerge from the unequal accumulations of wealth by economic individuals (Illich 1982: 12–13). Such techniques are forgotten in communities where the display of private accumulations and cultural imitating of consumer lifestyles become the norm.

Truth-Seeking Presupposes Friendship: Illich and Gandhi

Illich demonstrates how truth-seeking presupposes friendship, philia, and that creativity is improved in such an ethos. He asserts, like Gandhi, that institutions of learning have lost this social and moral dimension and have become radical monopolies that control learning rather than facilitate autonomous self-reliant forms of learning.

Illich's own learning style was to set up a minimal form of inclusive monastic life wherever he lived and share this vocation with friends invited to the table, just as Gandhi established seven ashrams that modelled inter-religious solidarity. In this way both Illich and Gandhi's inclusive practices of freedom challenge all modern academics and politico's failure to aesthetically unify insight and action. Their acceptance of voluntary poverty, affirmation of powerlessness and spontaneity as well an insistence on playful graciousness as the best response to purposive control systems state that these practices yield a different 'truth'.

In the end they both reveal different sacred paths to human enlightenment that, in a secularizing age, converge more than they differ. Both identify those things that are non-secular like friendship and human dignity while acting in a secular world. In doing so, they demonstrate that the sacred is present in a secularizing world in new ways.

Their lives were their message.

Notes

1. Apophatic means denial or negation; what God is not. Explicated in Lee Hoinacke, 'Why Philia?', lecture given at 'Conversations: The Legacy of Ivan Illich' at Pitzer College Clarmont, California on 26–28 March 2004.

2. Illich defines 'vernacular' as an old term that can be used 'to denote autonomous non-market related actions through which people satisfy everyday needs . . . (in a way) that they give specific shape' (Illich 1981: 38). In this sense, oldest forms of penance tended to be public the Berman (1983: 68 ff).
3. Illich 1981: 37.
4. In a similar way, the Nazi state tried to formalize its language in an effort to solidify its elite control.
5. Illich tries to show that Aquinas ultimately held a radical contingency view despite his theology also reinforcing that of the Franciscans—Bonaventure, Duns Scotus, and Francis—whose views stressed God's freedom and more directly created the dualism. Illich cites Theodor Litt (1963), to document the elimination of angels as the 'instrumentalis' for dealing with heavenly bodies. He comments that Jacques Maritain and Etienne Gilson also do this.
6. Here Illich continues to assume Aquinas's idea of revelation as a 'special illumination of the intellect in which the imaginative interpretation of external signs, the recognition of these signs as revelatory, and the inner transformations of the soul were all one single indivisible occurrence' (Milbank et al. 1999: 5).
7. See Illich (1981), especially chapter 3, 'The War Against Subsistence' and a later Illich inspired collection edited by Wolfgang Sachs The Development Dictionary (1992), which contains the beginnings of this 'history of scarcity' project. *The Subsistence Perspective* (1999) by Veronika Bennhodt-Thomsen and Maria Mies also picks up the same subsistence perspective logic and cites Illich.
8. Behind this perspective is an incredible amount of research into ocular phenomenon and Church history of discourse about icons. See Ivan Illich 'The Scopic Past and the Ethics of the Gaze: A Plea for the Historical Study of Ocular Perception', http://www.pudel.uni-bremen.de/100en_startseite.htm.
9. To me this is done by Illich in a way that goes beyond the Christian community and images the conditions under which human life be affirmed in any context. It seems to be extremely relevant for post-secular and inter-religious discourse of every faith.

References

Bennhodt-Thomsen, Veronika and Maria Mies (1999), *The Subsistence Perspective*, London: Zed Books.

Berman, Harold J. (1983), *Law and Revolution: The Formation of the Western Legal Tradition*, Cambridge, Mass.: Harvard University Press.

Hoinacke, Lee (2004), 'Why Philia?', Lecture given at 'Conversations: The Legacy of Ivan Illich', Pitzer College Clarmont, California, 26–28 March.

Illich, Ivan (1981), *Shadow Work*, Boston: Marion-Boyers.

———(1982), *Gender*, New York: Pantheon Books.

———(1992), *The Development Dictionary*, ed. Wolfgang Sachs, London: Zed Books.

———(1993), *In the Vineyard of the Text: A Commentary to Hugh's Disdascalicon*, Chicago: The University of Chicago Press.

Ladner, Gerhart B. (2004), *The Idea of Reform: Its Impact On Christian Thought and Action in the Age of the Fathers*, Eugene, Oregon: Wipf and Stock Publishers.

Litt, Theodor (1963), *Les corps celestes dans L'universe de saint Thomas d'Aguin*, Paris: Lowen.

Milbank, John, Catherine Pickstock and Graham Ward, eds. (1999), *Radical Orthodoxy*, London: Routledge.

Schroyer, Trent and Tom Godilik, eds. (2006), *Creating a Sustainable World*, Apex Press.

13

'What Else Could it Be?': Recovering the Human Good in the Age of Systems. Reviving Illich's 'Gandhian' Proposal for Personal Knowledge in a Post-Industrial World

PAUL SCHWARTZENTRUBER

> The replacement of the good by the idea of value begins in philosophy, and is then expressed in an ever-growing economic sphere within which my life becomes a pursuit of values rather than a pursuit of what is good for me, which can only be another person. What else could it be?
>
> — IVAN ILLICH (2005: 63).

> Homo educandus represents the historical emergence of a new kind of human being: who needs education in order to learn or live well. Homo educandus radically differs from homo sapiens or homo faber.
>
> — MADHU SURI PRAKASH and GUSTAVO ESTEVA (2008: 17).

> There's nobody in my audience without one foot in the age of instrumentality. And they are barely aware of the fact that they have passed over into the age of systems. . . in which you can't speak about the instrument anymore.
>
> — IVAN ILLICH (2005).

This essay is inspired by the project of re-envisioning social science research 'in an ontological way where our whole self—not just the inquiring mind—is involved with research, . . . where research becomes a time and space of laying open oneself and a realization of co-being' (Giri 2017). That project seeks to move beyond mere critiques of modernity and its programme of epistemically controlled engagement towards creative and 'transformational theories and methods'. Such hope-filled envisioning of the possibilities of a new engagement or rather, re-engagement of human understanding with the world at a deeper level than the merely 'critical' is an unquestioned and timely good—indeed, to paraphrase Illich, 'what else could it be?'

It is also a project that is fraught with difficulties and complexities. I want to reflect on the character of this project and its mythos (or 'fundamental narrative' shape) from directions theological and cultural, offering some thoughts on the metaphors of 'moving beyond', 'recovery of the excluded', 'holistic' and 'transformational theory' that are central to it.[1] This will allow for some general reflections on one's placement in the post-critical, postmodern context and the nature of one's hope to 'transcend' it. My touchstone for these reflections will be the work of one of the keenest critics of this 'post-modern' context, Ivan Illich.

Illich provides a good guide, I will argue, precisely because he has followed the modernist project through to its proper end in the often unquestioned postmodern outcomes of 'values, needs and systems'. Thus, his critique is acute and unsparing because it is not cut short by the false claim of the 'post' in postmodern but rather 'goes the distance' in its critical endeavour before it begins to hope again.[2] From this point of view, it raises some important points for further critical reflection on the project to 'recover ontology'. In the light of that critique, I want to present and appraise Illich's own proposal for a 'post-industrial' transformation of method towards 'personal learning' and 'convivial tools' aided by what he called 'counterfoil research'. It is especially worth revisiting this 'marginal' proposal in the light of the appeal to Gandhi as a model of the 'personal'. As I will argue below, Gandhi 'interrupts' the post-enlightenment discourse about 'the transformation of method' in a very critical way and with disturbing claims about the priority of both the practical experience of the good and personal transformation through 'service to other'. With regard to both these issues, Illich very much had his 'ear to the ground' and persists as an important 'Gandhian' partner in the dialogue. Thus, I take up this task in the positive spirit of that other metaphor invoked here, namely, the 'festival of dialogues'.

The Mythos of Modernity

Let me begin by identifying some of the metaphors used in this project's self-description. The mythos or narrative shape of a project is expressed in and through metaphor. Indeed, in this case, one might say that this project arises from the 'productive imagination' as a kind of narrative that Paul Ricoeur would call a 'sustained metaphor aimed at the re-description of reality'.[3]

The first metaphor central to the project is that of 'transcending' or 'moving beyond' the strictures of a too limited (modernist) method and its assumptions. Thus, in its wish to 'move beyond/transcend' the critical, epistemological norms of science (as well as the ongoing critiques of that model), this project hopes to embody a shift of the fundamental paradigms of self and world, understanding and event. Moreover, the central axis of this paradigm shift clearly involves 'moving beyond' the modernist privileging of epistemology and 'method' over ontology and 'self' and that move is aptly portrayed—again, metaphorically—as a 'recovery' of something that has been 'lost or excluded' in modernity.[4] Such a project of 'recovery', the narrative of this project argues, would not only correct the hidden and distorting assumptions of the modernist project of science (e.g. nationalism/colonialism/patriarchy/individualism/dualism), but would fundamentally transform the engagement of episteme by including in the knowing, the 'the whole self' of the knower and thus its potential for self-transformation. The 'wholeness' of this self is another of the benefits of the recovered ontology; the potential self-transformation, in turn, becomes a new dimension of the episteme itself and gives it a mutuality that is also 'holistic' (rather than dualistic). Thus, the original metaphor of 'moving beyond/transcending' is aligned in a single narrative plotline with those of 'recovering the excluded' dimension (ontology) and 're-engaging' with the world on its more 'holistic (non-dualistic) terms', namely, the 'co-being' (ontological and epistemological interdependence) of the self and other (researcher/social actor).

If one turns from this to what might be called the deeper narrative of the project, one can say that it portrays the relationship between the modernist project (here primarily scientific method and its claims to 'critical' methodology) and the postmodernist critiques as one of necessary antagonism—seeing the later as an articulation of the voices of those excluded. Thus, modern social movements have given rise to 'critiques of the disciplines by interrogating notions of normality and pathology around which conceptual distinctions have been organized' (Giri 2017). Moreover, as this deeper narrative implies, the antagonism has not yet been a fruitful one because the values of the critiques—embodied largely in the form of activist social movements—have not been integrated into the theoretical discussions of the social sciences and contributed to a transformation of method. Here again the project has its metaphor for a solution to the modernist-postmodernist stalemate—'interpenetration':

The worlds of scholarship and critical social actions have their own autonomies but they are also related to each other in a spirit of embodied interpenetration. To be a scholar-activist is to realize this logic of autonomy and interpenetration in one's own vision and practice, ontology and epistemology, embodying a labour and love of learning. (Giri 2017: 16)

Especially from the side of the scholar, this requires an openness to participation 'in the ongoing negotiation of sociality (social relationship)' (Giri 2017: 16) and above all, a commitment to an ongoing revision of 'methodology' as it is informed (through 'interpenetration') by action. In short, it means a shift from abstract principles to a commitment to praxis (rather than closed, deductive method) and ongoing—creative—transformation of theory.[5] This transformation is portrayed as a transformation of the nature of theory itself,[6] and an abandonment of the 'theoretical arrogance lying at the heart of modernity', in favour a 'situated universality' that is 'relational and perspectival' (Giri 2017: 28). Finally, this acceptance of irreducible diversity (championed by postmodernism) can be integrated into the theoretical realm precisely by re-conceiving 'universality' in ontological (rather than epistemological) terms on the basis of the 'co-being' or 'co-presence' of all reality in the form of 'emergent totalities'.[7] Again, then, the 'recovery of the excluded' ontology and its claim to a renewed 'integration' of theory and practice, self and world is the metaphor for the overcoming of both dualism and the antagonism between modernity and postmodernism. Such an integration, it suggests with creative insight, might have the form of 'an ontological epistemology of participation' (Giri 2017: 46ff).

★ ★ ★

One further dimension of this narrative is crucial to its argument: it gives a very suggestive, concrete character to the 'integration' of theory and practice through the personae of Heidegger and Gandhi. Thus, this project locates itself not simply within the larger Heideggerian proposal for the 'recovery of the excluded' ontology, but at a point where that proposal has itself been critiqued and balanced. Thus, it proposes to

supplement Heidegger with Gandhi, not only in politics but also in epistemology, thus rescuing us from complicity with any politics of mastery in the name of the resoluteness of Dasein and making Dasein and self an involved and emergent participant in learning. (Giri 2017: 49)

In these terms, Heidegger's proposal provides a historical context for the metaphor of the 'recovery of the excluded' as well as for the ontology of 'holistic' and 'co-being'; while that of Gandhi provides the context for the metaphors of the epistemic 'transformation' of theory and 're-engaging the world' through participatory praxis (where knowing and action can coincide) in a holistic way.

Clearly, this Gandhian 'supplement' is a crucial one for it grounds the 'recovered ontology' in a transformed (non-dualistic) form of epistemology, one that is personal and practical in that it is conceived 'in the spirit of a journey and evolution' (Giri 2017: 49). Thus, Gandhi suggests the essential suture between ontology and epistemology, theory and practice, subject and object; he does this not simply in the form of a split off subjectivism but rather in the form of his personal self-engagement through practice in the quest for 'Truth', (a kind of 'concrete universal'), and as 'an involved and emergent participant in learning' (Giri 2017: 49). It is the Gandhian self-engaged openness and 'experimentation with truth' that promises to heal the 'absolutism' of both method and ontology and to reintegrate again the 'value' of 'knowing' with that of 'acting'.

'What else could it be?'

I want now to return to the echo of Illich's question and develop his very contrasting account of modernity and its outcomes. By doing so, I open a space for a dialogue of creative challenge.

Illich's hypothetical question suggests a very different mythos about modernity. It begins by setting up a contrast between 'the pursuit of values' and 'the pursuit of the [human] good' that is uncompromising. Though a life spent 'in the pursuit of values' might now seem incontrovertibly good, the rhetoric of Illich's question implies that it is in fact a perversion of the human good ('which can only be another person'). Moreover, he implies, this perversion has been so 'systemic' and complete that one is no longer even aware of it. Indeed, he argues that, the 'replacement of the idea of good by the idea of value' in the theoretical realm has become so encompassing that in the concrete (economic) realm 'my life becomes a pursuit of values rather than a pursuit of what is good for me'. Thus, the 'perversity' of the situation; the 'replacement' has been effected so subtly and completely that the obvious 'good' has disappeared from view and 'value' can freely masquerade as the good, unquestioned by any of us.

Like any good drama, this raises some fundamental questions. What could possibly be wrong with the pursuit of values? How could it be a perversion of the good? To answer this question and grasp the meaning of Illich's 'values rather than. . . what is good', it is necessary to examine the metaphor of perversion more closely.

The metaphor of 'perversion' (as 'overturning' and 'subverting') is indeed central to Illich's narrative about modernity (and postmodernity) and it is encapsulated in his use of the phrase 'corruptio optima quae est pessima'—the corruption of the best is the worst.[8] Thus, the beginning should be with the best. Illich traces the beginnings of modernity to the emergence of a radically new understanding of human freedom emerging in Christian claims about the human being, an ability—by one's choice to love—to transcend 'the traditional basis for ethics, which was always an ethnos, an historically given "we" which precedes and pronunciation of the work "I"'.[9] Emblematic of this individual freedom is the act of the Samaritan in the parable of the 'good Samaritan':

The suggestion in this story [is] that are creatures that find our perfection only by establishing a relationship, and that this relationship may appear arbitrary from everybody else's point of view, because I do it in response to a call not a category, in this case the call of the beaten-up Jew in the ditch (Illich 2005:).

Illich identifies two implications of this story; the first has to do with the character of the 'good' and the second with its potential for 'perversion':

This has two implications. The first is that this 'ought' is not, and cannot be a norm…. It aims at some body, but not according to a rule. . . . The second implication…is that with the creation of this new mode of existence, the possibility of its breakage also appears. And this denial, infidelity, turning away, coldness is what the New Testament calls sin, something which can only be recognized by the light of this new glimmer of mutuality. (2005: 52)

For Illich, this 'denial' and 'infidelity' to the 'new glimmer of immortality' is to be found first and foremost within the Christian Church itself as it tries 'to manage, and eventually, to legislate this new love, to create an institution that will guarantee it, insure it, and protect it by criminalizing its opposite' (2005: 47). Thus, along with the good of this new kind of love there emerges its perversion in 'an entirely new kind of power, the power of those who organize Christianity and use this vocation to claim their superiority as social institutions' (Illich 2005: 47). 'This power', Illich argues, is not only claimed by the Church 'but later by the many secular institutions stamped from its mould' and therein, lay 'the roots of modernity' (2005: 48).

As Illich traces the transformation of the call to 'love of neighbour' into an 'ideology and an idealism' (i.e. a theology and a moral code) in late Roman Christianity and then again into the institutionalized (and economically enriching) forms of the medieval Church's welfare programmes and institutions, he argues that the original good of a freely given 'hospitality' is transformed into the quite different form of the ideal of 'service'.[10] Modernity, for him, arises not essentially as a break from this Christian world but as a kind of 'extension' of it. On the other hand, he continues, 'we have immediately perverted it'.

The personal freedom to choose who will be my other has been transformed into the use of power and money to provide a service… It…creates an impersonal view of how a society ought to work. It creates needs, so-called, for service commodities, needs which may will never be satisfied—is there enough health yet, enough education?—and therefore a type of suffering unknown outside of Western culture with its roots in Christianity.

The type of suffering to which Illich refers is the suffering of a constantly perceived 'scarcity' or 'unsatisfied needs for service'. This is, for him, the inner (and perverted) dimension, which corresponds to the unlimited drive of modernity (and postmodernity) toward progress, development and growth. Just as there can never be enough 'growth' in the economy or 'development' in the world, so there can never be enough 'education' or 'knowledge' or 'health' or 'values' to sate the sensed, inner scarcity of the human beings who identify themselves primarily through their needs.[11] Thus, as 'charity' becomes 'service' in modernity it engenders—quite logically—a series of professionally trained elites to provide for those needs (all with their appropriate scientific methodologies). These elites then establish control over areas of previously 'natural competence' and create compulsory modes of consumption that Illich would later call 'radical monopoly'.[12] Thus social life is reshaped around institutions (education, medicine) and new modes of living (motor vehicles, centralized planning) that increase dependence and reduce autonomy. Looking outward from the pinnacle of those social 'developments' in industrial Europe, it is easy enough to see the logic and rationale of colonialism and from there it is but a short step to 'underdevelopment' and indeed, to globalization itself (where no boundaries or cultures stand in the way of the claim of 'universal' human needs/rights/values).

By identifying this inner dimension of *homo educandus* (the being in need of education), Illich opens up the possibility of taking the critique of modernity's ideals of 'progress, development—and the manipulative control of knowledge by theory'—to a much deeper level. Yet he also allows for identifying the fact that this same 'systemic' enclosure of the human world (through the inner needs, values and growth) in an institutional/elite professional matrix of 'service' continues to obtain in postmodernity. The optimism is gone, to be sure, but the words and, above all, the 'system' remain: the dark side of unlimited and unregulated growth and development. To be sure, more humane institutions have been created. To be sure, better international standards have been deployed to guarantee the 'needs' and 'rights' of all human beings. But all of these developments unfold and continue to have their meaning within the total social 'system' of service—needs. In other words, there are more and better versions of what feeds the ever-consumptive anthropology over which there now falls a vague sense of the shadow of the limit to it all, and—'they are barely aware of the fact that they have passed over into the age of systems...in which you can't speak about the instrument anymore'.

What does the postmodern passage into the age of systems mean? The vanishing of *homo faber* and *homo sapiens*, indeed, but the illusion of control, control of the instrument, of the method, of the knowledge, of the self remains. By contrast to this, it is now a truism that is experienced daily: 'when you become a user of the system you become a part of the system'. The Earth becomes an 'eco-system' and the human being an 'immune system'. And so, as David Cayley observes, 'systems incorporate their users—they have no outside, no privileged standpoint' (2005: 40). Until there is no possibility even of raising the question 'What else could it be?' This, finally, returns one to the metaphor of perversion:

Illich points to a new kind of evil that appears only when the good is replaced by measurable values and transmogrified into an institutional output. In this case the good is not just temporarily forgotten, it is rendered imperceptible; and this reversal, whereby the greatest good opens a door to the extinction of the good, is what Illich calls the mystery of evil (2005: 43).

The Vanishing of the Good in Illich's alternative Mythos of modernity

An admittedly very small and targeted element in Illich's large body of work has been outlined. Yet the mythos of modernity as a 'perversion of the good' is a central element of his mature thought and connects directly with the detailed elaborations (on education, health, instrumentality, gender, systems) that occur throughout his corpus. It brings into view a quite distinct account of 'secularization', as Charles Taylor notes approvingly.[13] But above all it identifies that re-imagination of the human being (as *homo educandus*, the 'being of needs') which underlies modernity's social order and ideals (the 'servicing of needs' and 'development of resources'). And since perversion means the disappearance of the alternative, postmodernity now rises into view as the complete legitimation of that disappearance, the encompassing 'system' from which the 'excluded' has been banished entirely, displaced. *Homo educandus* becomes *homo programmandus*.[14]

Before returning to the task of dialogue, it will prove 'valuable', no doubt, to articulate the claim of that banished and displaced 'good'. Here is Illich:

As far as I can understand, I live in a world, which has lost the sense for good, the Good. We have lost the certainty that the world makes sense because things fit together, that the eye is made to grasp the sunlight, and is not just a biological camera which happens to register this optical effect. We have lost the sense that virtuous behaviour is fitting and appropriate for human beings...Good is absolute: the light and the eye are simply made for each other, and this unquestioned good is deeply experienced. . . .

The good is or is not, like a perfect fifth in music...This loss of proportionality points to the historical uniqueness of modernity, its incomparability. The poetic, performative quality of existence was erased in field after field.... (2005 : 63, 136)

The sense of 'fit' and 'fittingness', 'belonging', 'appropriateness' and 'proportion', 'this unquestioned good [which] is deeply experienced'—all this carries with it the echoes of an ontology, a sense of the gratuity of being and the co-being (fitting correspondence) of all things. Yet that sense of 'being' resides not in theory but rather in experience. Thus, it is primarily embodied in the practical dimension, in 'the poetic, performative quality of existence', a 'common sense...of what fits, what belongs, what is appropriate'.[15] It is an 'experience of the world' and of ourselves in it.

The loss of this, means the loss of an understanding of the intrinsic connections between things and therefore, the loss of the understanding of their 'limits':

Today, can think of a world of objects, of persons, of social constellations to which nothing corresponds. It is not only a wombless world, it is a world in which the idea of frontier, of limit has a meaning [previously]...inconceivable. Until that time, if you spoke of a limit, a horizon, the word itself implied that you spoke of a frontier leading to a beyond. A frontier with no beyond is something profoundly new, something which affects all our daily dealings, and makes us so different from all other persons, other cultures, worlds, languages. (Ilich 2005: 137)

The vanishing of the 'beyond' in the limits/frontiers of things (or of their intrinsic connectedness with all other things) is the concrete form of the banishment of the good itself. It is what allows and compels one to create meanings, values and relationships among things, arbitrarily and ad hoc according to individual 'needs'. 'Limit' only refers to the present capacity to do this, to manipulate the materials of the 'wombless world'. This, it must be added, is also the point at which theory passes out of the realm of wonder/thaumazein and into the realm of data control.

Contrasting Reading of Modernity

After such an extensive and uncompromising a critique of the systemic 'perversion' of knowledge and understanding, self and world, it is not surprising that Illich's own positive proposal is modest and self-limiting in nature. Indeed, as Richard Kahn has observed, Illich was wedded to a kind of 'impractical practicality', a 'hope for post-industrial conditions' in which human beings would rediscover the use of '"convivial tools"', that is, tools that represent the obverse of rampant technocracy and the globalization of corporate development' (Kahn 2009: 42–3). The possibility of that, in turn, hinged on a rediscovery of human limits, or more importantly, of the ability to self-limit, as Illich argues in *Tools for Conviviality*; in this context, it must be noted that this strategy, bears a striking resemblance to the Gandhian ideals of *aparigraha* (restraint from possessiveness), *brahmacharya* (control of self) and *swaraj* (self-governance/determination).[16] There will be a return to that intriguing connection in the following pages.

Before turning to examine this 'counter-proposal' that arises out of Illich's critique of modernity and postmodernity, however, I want to develop the contrast between that critique and the one on which the project for a 'recovered' 'ontological epistemology of participation' is based. There are important and mutual-illuminating parallels between the two narratives and these can provide the basis for a positive and creative dialogue.

Since the two accounts of modernity are not symmetrical, the task of comparison has to do with coordinating the points for a potential dialogue.

We may begin with the root metaphors: Illich's metaphor about the 'perversion' of the good raises a series of questions for the possibilities claimed in the metaphor about the project of a 'recovery' of the 'lost/ excluded' dimension of ontology. For example, it would question whether this ontological dimension has been 'excluded/lost' only or primarily in the methodological realm, i.e. by the privileging of epistemology in the sciences. By Illich's account, this methodological shift to privilege epistemology merely reflects the already accomplished 'displacement' of the good from the realm of practical and common experience by virtue of the intense commodification of things as needs/values/meanings in a 'service-society'. So the first question for Illich becomes, how can ontology be recovered methodologically if it is not recovered in lived experience (individual and social)? Moreover, since for him postmodernity is an intensification of this perversion and a systemic exclusion of the good, it becomes clear that the social order itself excludes the good and hence the ontological possibility: 'It is impossible to teach joyful renunciation in a world totally structured for higher output and the illusion of declining costs' (Illich 1973: 57). Clearly, on the level of metaphor, 'perversion' implies a more extensive and complex problem than 'exclusion/loss'; what has been 'displaced' cannot simply be 'recovered' and 'added to the mix'. Rather, the 'perverted' and distorted process and elements must be purged in practice and the human being freed from their grip to shape experience. Thus, for Illich, no method or theory could unlock the 'narrow gate' leading back to the good or being; without a self-renunciation of the 'use' of things (including knowledge) for one's needs/values/meaning, the experience of the good simply cannot reappear within contemporary culture. Without some such practical experience, in turn, the knowledge and 'method', which arise out of and participate in this sociality and its systems, could not 'recover' the good or ontology, except perhaps as archaic notion, impractical and 'use-'less.

In more positive terms, it might be said that this line of critical questioning from Illich may help to clarify the significance of the appeal to Gandhi in the project to recover and reintegrate ontology. This appeal to Gandhi relates to a second point of coordination between the positions. While it has been suggested that Gandhi's self-involvement and experimentation with the truth provides an exemplar for a new form of 'engagement' with the world, one might ask, with Illich, whether it is simply this personal dimension that opens the way to the holistic transformation that is sought. Is it not more true to say that Gandhi's holistic praxis consists in his linking of this personal dimension to a socially transformative, lived experience of the good and 'the Truth' through service? And that lived experience of the good (expressed essentially in the project of ahimsa) is, in turn, based precisely on Gandhi's personal commitment to 'limit' himself and achieve active non-attachment (*brahmacharya/aparigraha*) in the use of things.[17] Thus, it is Gandhi's self-limiting praxis of service to others that allows the good, the 'Truth' and the 'co-being' of all reality to become visible, and, through his social movement, to become a force capable of social transformation.[18] In and through this praxis, Gandhi restores the claim of the good and being but in the form of 'holistic and transformative' method of a 'cognitive minority' (i.e. *satyagraha* as 'clinging to the truth'). The rationale for this appeal to Gandhi is also clear: the perversion of the good into needs/values/uses is too dense, too inculturated into both personal identity and sociality to be overcome by mere thought or theory (which have been themselves shaped by this perverse inculturation and its systemic reach). A radically personal act of self-awareness and praxis (from which a new identity unfolds) will alone suffice to effect transformation.

The ethical act of self-denial/self-limitation on the model of Gandhi may provide a 'privileged point' outside of this systemic perversion for an experience of the good, but can that lived experience of the good provide the basis for a 'transformed' theory and method of knowledge? Can this self-limiting renunciation of the 'use' of things—in order to allow their ontological reality to reappear—be the basis of a transformed method of research? Can ethics provide the ground for knowledge—especially in this radical form? This ethical askesis and self-denial is, to say the least, a considerable extension of the notion of 'participatory' research as well as of the notion of 'research as a time and space of laying open oneself'.

These questions bring one to a third and final point of dialogue between the two narratives. The project which sees a 'necessary antagonism' between the 'theoretical arrogance lying at the heart of modernity' (in its abstract universal claims about normality) and the claims (to diversity and 'perspectival' universality) articulated in the practice of the critical social movements of postmodernity, proposes to solve this antagonism through an 'interpenetration' and ultimate 'integration' of theory and practice (ontology and epistemology). This integration will be both practical and theoretical, personal and methodological; in this sense, it will involve the creative transformation of theory towards 'situated universality' and a non-dualistic (participatory) epistemology. In this act of 'concretizing of the universal' claims of knowledge, the personal self-involvement of the individual researcher will play a crucial role, it is suggested. This intuition about the need to 'personalize' knowledge (and thereby creatively transform methods and practice) is, I think, essentially correct and a very important avenue for reflection—especially if what is meant by 'personal' is not simply 'individual' in the Cartesian sense but rather something that is explicated in the richer and denser sense of the Gandhian model of personal praxis.[19] I would like to reflect on this, again taking Illich's contrasting critique as a foil. In that context, the fundamental question is can the methods of knowledge be transformed (as researchers) without truly entering into transformative experience (as persons)?

Since Illich is skeptical about the claims of 'post-modern' social movements to have broken free of the 'system and theory' model through their appeal to concrete 'experience', he does not see the problem in the form of an 'integration' of theory and practice, or an 'interpenetration' of method and experience. The issue for him, rather, is that knowledge in its institutionalized form of 'education' (whether inspired by abstract theory or the many critical theories) is essentially depersonalized and disempowering; it embodies the same 'development' goals, professionalized 'management' methods, and unjust structures of power as are at work in the society.[20] And, it excludes the personal. Within this systemic context, learning remains 'an institutional enterprise rather than a personal activity' and its product a 'knowledge without limits' or human regard. In that form, obviously, 'methods' cannot truly be 'transformed' nor can knowledge ever become transformative. On the contrary, knowledge produced by compulsory education remains a 'commodity' and schooling, a 'ritual' of disempowerment that 'hampers people's ability to decide for themselves and then undermines their belief that they can decide' (Illich 1973: 72). But what, by contrast, can learning 'as a personal activity' mean? And how can a true transformation be brought to the methods of knowing?

Rediscovering convivial tools in an age of system

It has been noted above that Illich's positive proposal was really a 'hope' for 'post-industrial' conditions in which people might discover the use of 'convivial tools' and move towards a convivial social order. This proposal may now be outlined briefly in order to clarify the notions of 'personal knowledge' and 'transformed method'.

In *Tools for Conviviality* (1973), Illich proposed 'the concept of a multidimensional balance of human life which can serve as a framework for evaluating [the hu]man relation to [their] tools'; 'in each of several dimensions of this balance' he argued, 'it is possible to identify a natural scale':

When an enterprise grows beyond a certain point on this scale, it first frustrates the end for which it was originally designed, and then rapidly becomes a threat to society itself. These scales must be identified and the parameters of human endeavors within which human life remains viable must be explored.

These notions of a 'multidimensional balance of life' and 'a natural scale' of growth in a technology that can be identified and accepted as a 'limit', lead Illich to his central definition of the relationship between the human being and their tools as 'convivial':

We must come to admit that only within limits can machines take the place of slaves; beyond these limits they lead to a new kind of serfdom . . . Once these limits are recognized, it becomes possible to articulate the triadic relationship between persons, tools, and a new collectivity. Such a society, in which modern technologies serve politically interrelated individuals rather than managers, I will call 'convivial'. (Illich 1973: 3)

The use of the term 'persons' may be especially noted here that arises as the proper coterminus to the 'convivial (naturally limited) tool'. 'Person' reflects the possibility of a human being acting in 'post-industrial' social/ political conditions, namely, with a 'competence, control, and initiative, limited only by other individuals' claims to an equal range of power and freedom' (Illich 1973: 2). Therefore, also 'tool'—as something scaled to human use and reflecting its intentional self-limitation—becomes possible, even in the systems. This is to identify the re-empowered possibility of human beings who have been liberated from the 'specialization of functions, institutionalization of values and centralization of power [which] turns people into the accessories of bureaucracies or machines'.

The re-empowerment of personal 'competence, control and initiative' is clearly central to the restoration of the 'personal' in a post-industrial society. Yet Illich is not speaking in a purely utopian sense; he is trying to imagine how the 'recovery' of this personal dimension might take place in the concrete and that means, in the shadow of an industrial culture in crisis (1973: 72). In this sense, he argues that the 'crisis' created by industrial civilization will need to be met both with a restoration of 'the homeostatic balance which constitutes human life' (Illich 1973: 72) but also by the 'acceptance of inevitable self-limitations'.[21] With regard to the restoration of balance between 'personal' and institutional/social forms, Illich identifies a potential restoration of this balance in five different dimensions: control of nature, institutional function, learning, social mobility and the rate of innovation (1973: 72). The focus here will only be on 'learning' because it leads to Illich's attempt to articulate a transformed method of research.

Since learning in the industrial and post-industrial context has become 'education' and in that form, an 'institutional enterprise' that is 'disempowering and depersonalizing', a restoration of balance can only be sought by invoking a second kind of knowledge 'that is the result of the creative action of people on their environment'.[22] Illich argues that this kind of learning has been displaced by the 'trivialization' of the human being in the 'manufactured milieu'. Though this form of 'purposeful and programmed training' has produced the vast body of knowledge that characterizes modern civilization, it is essentially 'imbalanced' because of its methodological exclusion of the 'personal', the 'primary involvement of people with each other' and above all, the empowered human need to learn creatively by interaction with others and the environment.[23] It is only this kind of learning that can restore an 'ethical balance' to the human knowledge that has been developed in the drive for unlimited growth, exploitation of nature, institutionalization of processes and innovation. That balance will have to do essentially with asking about the human 'uses' of knowledge and its 'implications' for human life; it will be a shift from knowledge as commodity, to knowledge as a human tool. It is at this point that Illich proposes his notion of a 'transformed method' of research, namely, 'counterfoil research'.

Since, for Illich, the essential threat to the human good lies in the perverted relationship of the human being to their 'tools', whereby the tools 'are used to contract, eliminate, or replace human functions' and thereby disempower the human person by reducing the 'range of choice and motivation':

Survival depends on establishing procedures that permit ordinary people to recognize these ranges and to opt for survival in freedom, to evaluate the structure built into tools and institutions so they can exclude those which by their structure are destructive, and control those which are useful. (1973: 72)

Thus, Illich proposes a change in the direction of research that would turn it away from its fundamental orientation in an industrial-consumerist society to the discovery of 'breakthroughs to the better production of better wares and general systems analysis concerned with protecting man [*sic*] for further consumption' (1973: 65) A 'counterfoil research', which is ethically directed towards the preservation of personal knowledge, would have, Illich proposes, 'two major tasks: to provide guidelines for detecting the incipient stages of murderous logic in a tool; and to devise tools and tool systems that optimize the balance of life, thereby maximizing liberty for all' (1973: 65).[24]

Illich's notion of this counterfoil research not only involves the incorporation of the ethical dimension of analysis that asks method to become 'self-critical', it also shifts the focus of research from 'data' in a context of industrial/consumer uses to the diverse contexts of the human social environment and their 'natural scales':

It seems obvious that each person lives in several concentric social environments. To each social environment there corresponds a set of natural scales. This is true for the primary group, for the production unit, for the city, the state, and the organization of men on the globe. To each of these social environments there correspond certain characteristic distances, periods, populations, energy sources, and energy sinks. In each of these dimensions tools that require time periods or spaces or energies much beyond the order of corresponding natural scales are dysfunctional. They upset the homeostasis, which renders the particular environment viable. At present we tend to define human needs in terms of abstract goals and treat these as problems to which technocrats can apply escalating solutions. What we need is rational research on the dimensions within which technology can be used by concrete communities to implement their aspirations without frustrating equivalent aspirations by others. (1973: 65)

What is perhaps most striking in this context is the notion of research that is refocused on 'human social environments' and their 'natural scales'; clearly here, research has taken an 'ontological turn' while at the same time moving towards the concrete context of the human being and its intrinsic needs (rather than the 'abstract goals' which attract 'escalating solutions'). In this second sense, it may be said that research has taken a turn towards 'socio-critical praxis' in the Gandhian sense.

Research at the service of 'concrete communities' is necessarily 'self-limiting', Illich implies, since it will be driven by 'well-being' rather than 'growth': 'Counterfoil research is concerned first with an analysis of increasing marginal disutility and the menace of growth. It is then concerned with the discovery of general systems of institutional structure which optimize convivial production' (1973: 69).

In the context of an industrial system in crisis, then, this research will be both socio-critical and an activity of transformative social praxis— dramatizing the problems implicit in tools, the scarcity of resources, the victims of exploitation of resources, and the necessity for a free political discourse.[25] Above all, it will ally itself with those who recognize the 'crisis of an over-productive society' and are searching for its convivial alternative.[26] In this sense, it can become an expression of the 'confidence of an emerging group of clear-thinking and feeling people' intent on an 'institutional revolution . . . whose goals emerge as they are enacted'.[27]

Finally, it must be stressed that all of this socially-critical praxis articulates, for Illich, an essential transformation of the method and nature of research, because it is rooted in the personal ethical transformation of the researcher. That transformation is not something that can be 'taught' or acquired through 'education'; it must be learned by the praxis of 'living active and responsible lives'; the call to a personally-grounded knowledge is the true alternative to a life of research within the institution where, Illich suggests, many 'will perish—passive though well-informed, frustrated yet resigned' (1973: 57).

Hospitality and the Recovery of the Personal Nature of Truth

Illich's proposal for 'counterfoil research' from *Tools for Conviviality* was enhanced in a highly personal way by his subsequent studies of medical practice, work, gender, tradition/obsolescence and the shift from text to computer/technology.[28] In all of these areas, he himself attempted to practice 'counterfoil research' as he had proposed it. More importantly, perhaps, his own life became an eloquent articulation of the possibility and character of research as critical social praxis and a highly personal expression of the quest for truth. As Illich came more to focus on the systemic character of the perversion of the good in his last years, his sense of this essentially personal and concrete context of knowledge came to be more and more highlighted. In an address titled 'The Cultivation of Conspiracy' (1998), Illich spoke eloquently about 'learned and leisurely hospitality' and 'the commitment to friendship' as the necessary basis for the 'quest for truth':

Learned and leisurely hospitality is the only antidote to the stance of deadly cleverness that is acquired in the professional pursuit of objectively secured knowledge. I remain certain that the quest for truth cannot thrive outside the nourishment of mutual trust flowering into a commitment to friendship. (235)

Still later, in a talk given at the Oakland Round table in 2000, he is heard to be contrasting abstract 'space' with the concrete sense of place 'which is between you and me' and wondering whether 'our addiction to thinking in spatial terms destroys our sense of place'.[29]

This concrete and personal place 'which is between you and me' is, for Illich, the only point at which the integration of knowledge and action, method and practice, subject and object can occur. It is the pivotal point at which the Samaritan—for reasons not formulated or even imagined in any theory or ethical code—crosses the road and responds to the call of the beaten Jew in the ditch. It is the 'privileged point' outside the system for a recovery of both the good itself and the possibility of imagining its place in the human realm again. Within the 'spacious' (but place-less) worlds constructed by 'the deadly cleverness' of knowledge, the recovery of such concrete places marks the possibility of new beginnings. From a starting point in this lived ontology of the good, research might again root itself in 'a pursuit of what is good for me, which can only be another person'.

Indeed, 'what else could it be?'

Notes

1. As will be clearer below I am using the term 'mythos' primarily in the sense given to it in the work of Paul Ricoeur, as a shaping or configuration which creates an intelligible whole out of disparate parts, i.e. 'mythos' as emplotment. (Ricoeur 1984: 53ff).

2. I refer to Illich's own metaphorical narrative on Prometheus and Pandora at the end of Deschooling Society: 'The history of modern man [*sic*] begins with the degradation of Pandora's myth and comes to an end in the self-sealing casket. It is the history of the Promethean endeavour to forge institutions in order to corral each of the rampant ills. It is the history of fading hope and rising expectations. To understand what this means we must rediscover the distinction between hope and expectation' (1972: 105ff).

3. Ricoeur (1991: 117), Ricoeur argues that the aesthetical grasping of the world in the literary narrative can be compared to the epistemological grasping of the world by scientific models. Both are words of the 'productive imagination'.

4. Giri (2017): '"Another assumption of modernity that social research reflected was modernity's primacy of epistemology and the neglect of ontology which short-circuited ontological issues by assuming that once the right procedure for attaining truth as correspondence or coherence is reached, any remaining issues will be either resolved through that method or shown to be irrelevant" (Connolly 1995: 6). In the modernist mode, social research was considered only an epistemic engagement, a project of knowing about 'the world with proper procedure and scientific method'.

5. Paolo Freire (2000: 75), 'Praxis involves engaging in a cycle of theory, application, evaluation, reflection, and then back to theory. Social transformation is the product of praxis at the collective level.'

6. Giri (2017): 'Now theory has to be thought of in a new way as our companion rather than as a master, as a moving beacon which gives possible direction in the sea of complex reality, rather than as a fixed star. It involves a critique of "theoreticist theory"—a "theoretical logic" which is not grounded in a concrete research practice' (Bourdieu and Wacquant 1992: 32).

7. According to Roy Bhaskar, 'The critique of postmodernism involves accepting the emphasis on uniqueness and differentiation without throwing out our concepts of universality and connection. Indeed the ground-state and cosmic

envelope are just precisely the concepts we need to understand differentiation within a unity. But these aspects of being, on which all other aspects ultimately depend, are precisely those which through the generalized theory of co-presence, allow us to see that everything is implicitly enfolded or contained and may be brought to consciousness, implicit or explicit, in everything else, so that anything can be traced or manifest in anything else' (Giri 2017).

8. The phrase is the leitmotif of the work The Rivers North of the Future (2005). The phrase first emerges in a talk given in 1987: 'This central reality of the West is marvelously expressed in the old Latin phrase: Corruptio optimi quae est pessima—the historical progression in which God's Incarnation is turned topsy-turvy, inside out. I want to talk about the mysterious darkness that envelops our world, the demonic night paradoxically resulting from the world's equally mysterious vocation to glory' (29). Illich expands on this by reference to the parable of the Good Samaritan (47–63).

9. 'A new dimension of love has opened, but this opening is highly ambiguous because of the way in which it explodes certain universal assumptions about the conditions under which love are possible. Before I was limited by the people into which I was born and the family in which I was raised. Now I can choose whom I will love and where I will love' (Illich 2005: 47).

10. Illich, (2005: 55–6): 'But as soon as hospitality is transformed into a service, two things have happened at once. First, a completely new way of conceiving the I-Thou relationship has appeared. Nowhere in antique Greece or Rome is there evidence of anything like these new flophouses for foreigners, or shelters for widows and orphans. Christian Europe is unimaginable without its deep concern about building institutions to take care of different types of people in need. So there is no question that modern service society is an attempt to establish and extend Christian hospitality.'

11. See Illich, (2005: 103): 'With the beginning of capitalist production in the spinning and weaving shops of the Florence of the Medicis, a new type of human being was engendered: needy man, who has to organize a society, the principal purpose of which is to satisfy human needs. And needs are much crueler than tyrants.'

12. 'Radical monopoly exists where a major tool rules out natural competence. Radical monopoly imposes compulsory consumption and thereby restricts personal autonomy. It constitutes a special kind of social control because it is enforced by means of the imposed consumption of a standard product that only large institutions can provide' (Illich 1973/online edn: 43).

13. 'Illich's understanding of our modern condition as a spinoff from a 'corrupted' Christianity captures one of the most important historical vectors that brought about the modern age and allows us to see how good and bad are closely interwoven in it. Ours is a civilization concerned to relieve suffering and enhance human well-being, on a universal scale unprecedented in history, and which at the same time threatens to imprison us in forms that can turn alien and dehumanizing' (Illich 2005: see Foreword, xiii).

14. See Richard Kahn, (2009: 42): 'Illich went on in his later work to insist that, in a highly professionalized and commoditized media culture all aspects of life

either promote themselves as educative or increasingly demand some element of training as a cost of unchecked consumption. Under such conditions, the being possessing wisdom—homo sapiens—becomes reduced to homo educandus, the being in need of education. Then, in an age when the computer becomes the 'root metaphor' of existence, this reduction becomes further processed and networked into the cybernetic reality of homo programmandus'.

15. 'Common sense, as this term was used of old, meant the sense of what fits, what belongs, what is appropriate. It was by common sense, for example, that a physician understood the limits of what he could and should do' (Illich 2005: 137).

16. 'People must learn to live within bounds. This cannot be taught. Survival depends on people learning fast what they cannot do. They must learn to abstain from unlimited progeny, consumption, and use. It is impossible to educate people for voluntary poverty or to manipulate them into self-control. It is impossible to teach joyful renunciation in a world totally structured for higher output and the illusion of declining costs' (Illich 1973/online edn: 57).

17. 'In working our plans for self-restraint, attention must not for a single moment be withdrawn from the fact that we are all sparks of the divine and, therefore, partake of its nature, and since there can be no such thing as self-indulgence with the divine it must of necessity be foreign to human nature. If we get a hard grasp of that elementary fact, we should have no difficulty in attaining self-control, and that is exactly what we sing every evening. You will recall that one of the verses says that the craving for self-indulgence abates only when one sees God face to face' (Gandhi 2008: 58).

18. Gandhi's cognitive claims were based on his practical claims of service. 'Truth is impossible without a complete merging of oneself in and identification with this limitless ocean of life. Hence for me there is no escape from social service . . . Social service here must be taken to include every department of life. In this scheme there is nothing low, nothing high. For all is one, though we seem to be many' (Gandhi 2008: 64–5).

19. For this distinction between the personal and individual, I refer to the important work of Thomas Merton. New Seeds of Contemplation, (1972) 'The object of salvation is that which is unique, irreplaceable, incommunicable—that which is myself alone. This true inner self must be drawn up like a jewel from the bottom of the sea, rescued from confusion, from indistinction, from immersion in the common, the nondescript, the trivial, the sordid, the evanescent . . . The person must be rescued from the individual. The free son of god from the conformist slave of fantasy, passion and convention. The creative and mysterious inner self must be delivered from the wasteful, hedonistic and destructive ego that seeks only to cover itself with disguises' (38).

20. Illich, (1937: 71) 'Above all, political discussion is stunned by a delusion about science. This term has come to mean an institutional enterprise rather than a personal activity, the solving of puzzles rather than the unpredictably creative activity of individual people. Science is now used to label a spectral production agency, which turns out better knowledge just as medicine produces better

health. The damage done by this misunderstanding about the nature of knowledge is even more fundamental than the damage done to the conceptions of health, education, or mobility by their identification with institutional outputs. False expectations of better health corrupt society, but they do so in only one particular sense. They foster a declining concern with healthful environments, healthy life styles, and competence in the personal care of one's neighbour. Deceptions about health are circumstantial. The institutionalization of knowledge leads to a more general and degrading delusion. It makes people dependent on having their knowledge produced for them. It leads to a paralysis of the moral and political imagination.'

21. 'The crisis I have described confronts people with a choice between convivial tools and being crushed by machines. The only response to this crisis is a full recognition of its depth and an acceptance of inevitable self-limitations. The more varied the perspectives from which this insight is shared by interest groups and the more disparate the interests that may be protected only by a reduction of power within society, the greater the probability that the inevitable will be recognized as such' (Illich 1937.: 90).

22. Illich, (1937: 53): 'The balance of learning is determined by the ratio of two kinds of knowledge in a society. The first is a result of the creative action of people on their environment, and the second represents the result of man's "trivialization" by his manufactured milieu. Their first kind of knowledge is derived from the primary involvement of people with each other and from their use of convivial tools; the second accrues to them as a result of purposeful and programmed training to which they are subjected'.

23. Illich, (1937: 53): 'The transformation of learning into education paralyzes man's poetic ability, his power to endow the world with his personal meaning. Man will wither away just as much if he is deprived of nature, of his own work, or of his deep need to learn what he wants and not what others have planned that he should learn'.

24. Also 'Counterfoil research must clarify and dramatize the relationship of people to their tools. It ought to hold constantly before the public the resources that are available and the consequences of their use in various ways. It should impress on people the existence of any trend that threatens one of the major balances on which life depends' (Illich 1937: 69).

25. 'Counterfoil research must clarify and dramatize the relationship of people to their tools. It ought to hold constantly before the public the resources that are available and the consequences of their use in various ways. It should impress on people the existence of any trend that threatens one of the major balances on which life depends. Counterfoil research leads to the identification of those classes of people most immediately hurt by such trends and helps people to identify themselves as members of such classes. It points out how a particular freedom can be jeopardized for the members of various groups which have otherwise conflicting interests. Counterfoil research involves the public by showing that the demands for freedom of any group or alliance can be identified with the implicit interest of all' (Illich 1937: 69).

26. 'Forces tending to limit production are already at work within society. Public, counterfoil research can significantly help these individuals become more cohesive and self-conscious in their indictment of growth they consider destructive. We can anticipate that their voices will acquire new resonance when the crisis of over-productive society becomes acute. They form no constituency, but they are spokesmen for a majority of which everyone is a potential member' (Illich 1937: 86–7).

27. '[T]he transformation of catastrophe into crisis depends on the confidence an emerging group of clear-thinking and feeling people can inspire in their peers. They must then argue that the transition to a convivial society can be, and must be, the result of conscious use of disciplined procedure that recognizes the legitimacy of conflicting interests, the historical precedent out of which the conflict arose, and the necessity of abiding by the decision of peers. Convivially used procedure guarantees that an institutional revolution will remain a tool whose goals emerge as they are enacted; the conscious use of procedure in a continually anti-bureaucratic sense is the only possible protection against the revolution itself becoming an institution' (Illich 1937: 89).

28. See respectively, Medical Nemesis (1975), Shadow Work (1981), Gender (1982), In the Mirror of the Past (1992), In the Vineyard of the Text (1993) and Blasphemy: A Radical Critique of Our Technological Culture (1995).

29. 'The Oakland Table' In Conversations Between Ivan Illich and Friends. Notes by Debbie Moore at http://www.davidtinapple.com/illich/

References

Freire, Paolo (2000), *Pedagogy of the Oppressed*, New York: Continuum.

Gandhi, M.K. (2008), *The Essential Writings*, ed. Judith M. Brown, Oxford: OUP.

Giri, Ananta Kumar (2017), 'Pathways of Creative Research: Rethinking Theories and Methods and the Calling of an Ontological Epistemology of Participation', in present volume.

Illich, Ivan (1972), *Deschooling Society*, London: Boyars.

———(1973), *Tools for Conviviality*, Online edition at/clevercycles.com/tools_for_ conviviality.

———(2002), 'The Cultivation of Conspiracy', in *The Challenge of Ivan Illich*, ed. Lee Hoinkacki and Carl Mitchum, Albany, NY: SUNY Press.

———(2005), *The Rivers North of the Future, The Testament of Ivan Illich as told to David Cayley*, Toronto: Anansi.

———'The Oakland Table', Conversations between Ivan Illich and Friends, Notes by Debbie Moore at http://www.davidtinapple.com/illich/

Kahn, Richard (2009), 'Critical Pedagogy takes the Illich Turn', *The International Journal of Illich Studies*, vol. 1, no. 1.

Merton, Thomas (1972), *New Seeds of Contemplation*, New York: New Directions.

Prakash, Madhu Suri and Gustavo Esteva (2008), *Escaping Education. Living as Learning within Grassroots Cultures*, 2nd edn., New York: Peter Land.

Ricoeur, Paul (1984), *Time and Narrative*, vol. 1, tr. K. McLaughlin and D. Pellaver, Chicago: Chicago University Press.

———(1991), 'The Function of Fiction in Shaping Reality', in *Reader: Reflection and Imagination*, ed. A Ricoeur, Harvester Whitesheaf.

14

Pathways of Creative Research: Creating Zones of Proximal Development

LOIS HOLZMAN

When discussing the essential role of play in early child development, Vygotsky remarked, 'In play a child always behaves beyond his average age, above his daily behaviour; in play it is as though he were a head taller than himself' (1978: 102). In this chapter I will explore that marvellous metaphor 'a head taller' in the context of investigating the mundane creativity that is and produces human development and learning. In other words, my focus here is on the collective activity of creating. I am interested in how social units create environments in which they qualitatively transform themselves and their environments. I propose an understanding of creativity as socially imitative and completive activity. I have come to this understanding from immersion in a quarter-century of intervention research that actualizes the 'head taller' experience for people across the life span by allowing, inviting and guiding them to create zones of proximal development (ZPDs). This research, serving only as a backdrop for the present discussion, is discussed in other writings, the most recent being *Vygotsky at Work and Play* (Holzman 2009).

A ZPD is a ZPD: or is it?

Even though Vygotsky's ZPD is essential to his understanding of the relationship between development and learning and play, it has become, today, more narrowly associated with learning and the school-like acquisition of knowledge and skills. Part of what I want to do in this discussion is restore the complexity, radicalness and practicality of Vygotsky's discovery of the ZPD.

The ZPD is important in Vygotsky's rejection of the popular belief that learning follows and is dependent upon development, and in his related criticism of traditional teaching: 'Instruction would be completely unnecessary if it merely utilized what had already matured in the developmental process, if it were not itself a source of development' (Vygotsky 1987: 212).[1] Rejecting the view that learning depends on and follows development, Vygotsky put forth a new relationship between these two activities: 'The only instruction which is useful in childhood is that which moves ahead of development, that which leads it' (211) ... 'pushing it further and eliciting new formations' (198). In other words, for Vygotsky learning leads to development. In previous works, I refer to this discovery as not merely a new relationship but as a new kind of relationship (at least for psychology)—the dialectical unity learning-leading-development. I do this to capture the way Vygotsky sees learning and development as a totality, and change as qualitative transformation of the whole (Newman and Holzman 1993; Holzman 1997).

The question of how learning leads development depends, at least in part, on how one understands what the ZPD is. As the most popularized concept stemming from Vygotsky's writings, the ZPD has been given multiple interpretations by educational researchers, psychologists and others. Different meanings can be traced, in part, to different translations of his writings (Glick 2004) and from the numerous contexts in which Vygotsky wrote about the ZPD. In briefly reviewing some of these contexts, understandings and implications that follow from them, I will bring together Vygotsky's comments from diverse sources and provide the backdrop for the view I am putting forth.

INDIVIDUAL

A common understanding of the ZPD is that it is a characteristic or property of an individual child. This understanding stems from passages like the following:

The psychologist must not limit his analysis to functions that have matured. He must consider those that are in the process of maturing. If he is to fully evaluate the state of the child's development, the psychologist must consider not only the actual level of development but the zone of proximal development. (Vygotsky 1987: 208–9)

To some educational researchers this translates into the ZPD being—or producing—a measure of a child's potential, and they have devised alternative means of measuring and evaluating individual children (e.g. Allal and Pelgrims 2000; Lantolf 2000; Lidz and Gindis 2003; Newman, Griffin and Cole 1989; Tharp and Gallimore 1988).

DYADIC

In other passages, however, the ZPD plays a key role in Vygotsky's argument that learning and development are fundamentally social and form a unity.

Joint activity and collaboration in children's daily life are also implicated, as in the following passage:

What we call the Zone of Proximal Development . . . is the distance between the actual developmental level as determined by independent problem solving, and the level of potential development as determined through problem solving under guidance or in collaboration with more capable peers. (Vygotsky 1978: 86)

Perhaps it was the phrase more capable that led to the conceptualization of the ZPD as a form of aid—termed prosthesis by Shotter (1989) and Wertsch (1991) and scaffolding by Wood, Bruner and Ross (1976).[2] This conceptualization has become so popular that the typical college textbook equates the ZPD with scaffolding and (incorrectly) attributes both terms to Vygotsky (for example, Berk and Winsler 1995; MacNaughton and Williams 1998; Rodgers and Rodgers 2004). Moreover, despite Vygotsky's mention of 'peers' in the passage above, most empirical research with this perspective takes 'the aid' to be a single, more capable individual, most often an adult (termed 'expert' in contrast to the 'novice' child).

In keeping with this dyadic interpretation of the ZPD, it is common for 'social level' and 'interpsychological' to be reduced to a two-person unit in the following oft-quoted passage:

Every function in the child's cultural development appears twice: first on the social level and later, on the individual level; first between people (interpsychological), and then inside the child (intrapsychological). This applies equally to all voluntary attention, to logical memory, and to the formation of concepts. All the higher mental functions originate as actual relations between people. (Vygotsky 1978: 57)

COLLECTIVE

At other times Vygotsky emphasized more clearly that the socialness of learning-leading-development is collective, that the ZPD is not exclusively or even primarily a dyadic relationship, and that what is key to the ZPD is that people are doing something together. For example, 'Learning awakens a variety of internal developmental processes that are able to operate only when the child is interacting with people in his environment and in cooperation with his peers' (1978: 90).

The necessity of collective activity that Vygotsky attributes to the learning-development relationship is at the forefront of his approach to special education. His writings on this subject (collected and published in English as *Fundamentals of Defectology,* 1997) argue that children with abnormalities such as retardation, blindness or deafness can indeed develop. They should not be written off or remediated, nor should these children be segregated and placed in schools with only children like themselves.

Vygotsky made the point that qualitative transformation (as opposed to rote learning) is a collective accomplishment—a 'collective form of "working together"' he called it in an essay entitled 'The Collective as a Factor in the Development of the Abnormal Child' (Vygotsky 2004: 202). In this same essay he characterized the social, or inter-psychological, level of development (in the quote above, p. 4) as 'a function of collective behaviour, as a form of cooperation or cooperative activity' (Vygotsky 2004: 202).

I like that phrase, 'a collective form of working together'. It seems a good fit with my experience as researcher, teacher and trainer. I read Vygotsky here as saying that the ZPD is actively and socially created. This is beyond and perhaps other than the popular conception of the ZPD as an entity existing in psychological-cultural-social space and time. For me, the ZPD is more usefully understood as a process rather than as a spatio-temporal entity, and as an activity rather than a zone, space or distance. Furthermore, I offer the ZPD activity as the simultaneous creating of the zone (environment) and what is created (learning-leading-development).

Creativity

The concept of ZPD activity provides a new way to understand human development that puts creativity centre stage. Not creativity as typically understood, however. For in both everyday and psychological discourse creativity is taken to be an attribute of individuals. Further, creative individuals are understood to produce special things—original, novel, unique, and perhaps extraordinary or extraordinarily significant—relative to others who are 'not creative'. The kind of creativity I am talking about in relation to ZPD activity is not an attribute of individuals but of social units (e.g. dyads, groups, collectives and so on), and it is not special or extraordinary, but ordinary and everyday. (Yet, while mundane, it is also magical!)

How do social units create ZPDs? More importantly one must be capable of doing what one does not know how to do, either individually or collectively. Human beings learn and develop without knowing how or not realizing that it is already known. In other words, 'we become epistemologists without employing epistemology'. Vygotsky recognized this seeming paradox of human life, at least in its early childhood version. He understood that developmental activity does not require knowing how, as when he identified 'the child's potential to move from what he is able to do to what he is not' (Vygotsky 1987: 212) as the central characteristic and creative activity of learning leading development.

Further, he understood that for young children, knowing how to do a particular thing does not require knowing that they are doing this particular thing. As he put it, 'before a child has acquired grammatical and written language, he knows how to do things but does not know that he knows.... In play a child spontaneously makes use of his ability to separate meaning from an object without knowing that he is doing it, just as he does not know he is speaking in prose but talks without paying attention to the words' (Vygotsky 1978: 99). This thread of Vygotsky's thought has, to my way of thinking, been neglected, not only in the study of early childhood but also in its implications for understanding and fostering development throughout the life span. If children do not need to know, why do the others? (Holzman 1997; Newman and Holzman 1997). This question has been debated vigorously by postmodernists, of course, but very little by cultural historical activity theorists—a situation I have tried to remedy (see, for example, Holzman 2006).

Inspired by Vygotsky's insights on how very young children and children with disabilities go beyond themselves qua selves and participate in ZPD activity (creating environments for learning-leading development and simultaneously learning-leading-development), my work has been to expand this creative methodology through collaboration with others in building 'ZPD-creating-head taller' therapeutic, educational and organizational practices and simultaneously studying the practices that have been built. Development, from this perspective, is the practice of a methodology of becoming—in which people shape and reshape their relationships to themselves, each other and to the material and psychological tools and objects of their world.

Imitation

Thus far, I have suggested that from a developmental and educational perspective it is useful to understand ZPDs as actively created, that the creators are social units rather than individuals, and that the creative ZPD activity is a non-epistemological methodology of becoming. What is this methodology? In other words, what does being a head taller look like?

The answer requires taking a new look at imitation. Along with not knowing, imitation has been overlooked by socio-cultural researchers, in my opinion. And as with not knowing, I suggest that imitation is necessary for creativity in general and for creating ZPDs in particular. In relation to ZPDs, I take my cue from Vygotsky: 'A full understanding of the concept of the zone of proximal development must result in a reevaluation of the role of imitation in learning' (1978: 87).

As part of his re-evaluation, Vygotsky discounted an essentially mechanistic view of imitation that was 'rooted in traditional psychology, as well as in everyday consciousness. He was also wary of the individualistically biased inferences drawn from such a view, as for example, that the child can imitate anything' and that 'what I can do by imitating says nothing about my own mind' (Vygotsky 1987: 209). In its stead, Vygotsky posited that imitation is a social-relational activity essential to development: 'Development based on collaboration and imitation is the source of all specifically human characteristics of consciousness that develop in a child' (1987: 210).

Children do not imitate anything and everything as a parrot does, but rather what is 'beyond them' developmentally speaking and yet present in their environment and relationships. In other words, imitation is fundamentally creative, by which I mean that it helps to create the ZPD. The kind of language play that typifies conversations between very young children and their caregivers can perhaps provide clarity on this point. Here is one of Vygotsky's many descriptions of early childhood language development. It is a difficult passage, one that I have to re-discover the meaning of each time I read it.

We have a child who has only just begun to speak and he pronounces single words... But is fully developed speech, which the child is only able to master at the end of this period of development, already present in the child's environment? It is, indeed. The child speaks in one-word phrases, but his mother talks to him in language which is already grammatically and syntactically formed and which has a large vocabulary. . . Let us agree to call this developed form, which is supposed to make its appearance at the end of the child's development, the final or ideal form. And let us call the child's form of speech the primary or rudimentary form. The greatest characteristic feature of child development is that this development is achieved under particular conditions of interaction with the environment, where this . . . form which is going to appear only at the end of the process of development is not only already there in the environment . . . but actually interacts and exerts a real influence on the primary form, on the first steps of the child's development. Something which is only supposed to take shape at the very end of development, somehow influences the very first steps in this development. (Vygotsky 1994: 348)

Both developed and rudimentary languages are present in the environment, Vygotsky tells us. In that case, what is environment? If both forms of language are present, then environment cannot be something fixed in space and time, nor separate from child and mother. Rather, it seems that environment must be both what is—the specific socio-cultural-historical conditions in which child and mother are located—and what is coming into existence—the changed environment being created by their language activity. In other words, this environment is as much activity as it is context. In their speaking together, very young children and their caregivers are continuously reshaping the 'rudimentary' and 'developed' forms of language.

It is this activity, I suggest, that is and creates the ZPD—and through which the child develops as a speaker, meaning maker and language user.

Completion

Along with imitation there is another activity taking place in the creating of the language-learning ZPD—completion. This idea is based in Vygotsky's understanding of the relationship between thinking and speaking, in which he challenged the expressionist view of language (that one's language expresses one's thoughts and feelings). Speaking, he said, is not the outward expression of thinking, but part of a unified, transformative process. Two passages from *Thinking and Speech* are especially clear in characterizing his alternative understanding:

The relationship of thought to word is not a thing but a process, a movement from thought to word and from word to thought . . . Thought is not expressed but completed in the word. We can, therefore, speak of the establishment (i.e. the unity of being and nonbeing) of thought in the word. Any thought strives to unify, to establish a relationship between one thing and another. Any thought has movement. It unfolds.

The structure of speech is not simply the mirror image of the structure of thought. It cannot, therefore, be placed on thought like clothes off a rack. Speech does not merely serve as the expression of developed thought. Thought is restructured as it is transformed into speech. It is not expressed but completed in the word. (Vygotsky 1987: 250–1)

Instead of positing a separation into two realms—the private one of thinking and the social one of speaking—there is just one: speaking/thinking, a dialectical unity in which speaking completes thinking. Vygotsky was delineating the thinking-speaking process for individuals, but his conceptualization can be expanded in the following way. If speaking is the completing of thinking, if the process is continuously creative in socio-cultural space, then the 'completer' does not have to be the one who is doing the thinking—others can do it (Newman and Holzman 1993; Holzman 2009). Think about it. Would children be able to engage in language play/conversation before they knew language if thinking/speaking were not a continuously socially completive activity in which others were completing for them?

The ongoing activity of completion can be seen in the conversations that very young children and their speaking caregivers create, as in caregivers' typical responses to the single words and phrases of toddlers (e.g. Child: 'Cookie!' Adult: 'Want a cookie?' [getting cookie and giving it to child] Child: 'Mama cookie.' Adult: 'Yes, Mommy's giving you a cookie.'). Like the child's imitations, completion is also a dominant activity of creating the language-learning ZPD.[3] Together, imitation and completion comprise much of the language play that transforms the total environment, a process out of which a new speaker emerges.

The current culture too often loses sight of what I have presented—not its detail but its general common sense notions. Children do not learn language nor are they taught language in the structured, systematic, cognitive, acquisitional and transmittal sense typical of later institutionalized learning and teaching. They develop as speakers, language makers and language users as an inseparable part of joining and transforming the social life of their family, community and culture. When babies begin to babble they are speaking before they know how to speak or that they speak, by virtue of the speakers around them accepting them into the community of speakers and creating conversation with them. Mothers, fathers, grandparents, siblings and others do not have a curriculum, give them a grammar book and dictionary to study, nor remain silent around them. Rather, they relate to infants and babies as capable of doing things that are beyond them. They relate to them as fellow speakers, feelers, thinkers and makers of meaning—in other words, as fellow creators. This is what makes it possible for very young children to be as though a head taller.

Play

It is time to return to play, the activity to which Vygotsky attributed the 'head taller' experience. His writing on play concerned young children's free play of fantasy and pretense, and the more structured and rule-governed playing of games that becomes frequent in later childhood.

All play, Vygotsky believed, creates an imaginary situation and all imaginary situations contain rules. It is the relationship between the two that changes with different kinds of play. In the game play of later childhood, rules are overt, often formulated in advance, and dominate over the imaginary situation. The elements of pretend are very much in the background and rules are instrumentally necessary to the playing (Vygotsky 1978). Think of basketball, video games, and board games.

In the earlier play of very young children—the rich meaning-making environment of free and pretend play—the imaginary situation dominates over rules. The rules don't even exist until the playing begins, because they come into existence at the same time and through the creation of the imaginary situation. In Vygotsky's words, they are 'not rules that are formulated in advance and that change during the course of the game but ones that stem from an imaginary situation' (Vygotsky 1987: 95). That is, they are rules created in the activity of playing.

When a young child takes a pencil and makes horse-like movements with it, in creating this imaginary situation s/he is simultaneously creating the 'rules' (keep jumping, make whinnying sounds, don't write on the paper) of the play. When children are playing Mommy and baby, the new meaning that the imaginary situation creates also creates the 'rules' of the play (for example, how Mommy and baby relate to each other 'in character'). In these examples, at the same time as new meaning is being created with pencil, self and peer, the 'old' meanings of horse, pencil, Mommy and baby are suspended from these objects and people. Both the old and the new meanings are present in the environment. This is analogous to creating language-learning ZPDs just discussed, in which environment is both the specific socio-cultural-historical conditions under which children play, and the changed environment being created by their play activity. Here, as in that case, environment is as much activity as it is context.

It is these elements of free or pretend play that, for Vygotsky, distinguish the play ZPD from that of learning-instruction ZPD:

Though the play-development relationship can be compared to the instruction-development relationship, play provides a much wider background for changes in needs and consciousness. Action in the imaginative sphere, in an imaginary situation, the creation of voluntary intentions, and the formation of real-life plans and volitional motives—all appear in play and make it the highest level of preschool development. (Vygotsky 1987: 102–3)

In making this distinction, to my way of thinking Vygotsky makes too sharp a break between playing and learning-instruction. Can't play be the highest level of preschool development and still be developmentally important cross the life span? I think so. I think that Vygotsky overlooked some continuity between the two ZPDs, in part because he was so concerned with learning in formalized school contexts. This continuity, which I have come to believe has significance for later childhood and beyond, relates to the characteristics of creativity in ZPD activity that I have been discussing.

Learning Playfully Outside of School

It is a feature of the Western culture (and most other cultures) that one relates to very young children as creative. I mean that both in the sense of creativity I have introduced here—their participation in creating ZPDs— and in the more conventional sense of appreciating their individual products (scribbles, phrases, songs, dances and so on). And this gradually stops as they get older. Learning and playing is bifurcated, trivializing play in the process, and have creating institutionalized structures to maintain that bifurcation and trivialization. The concept of work is introduced. In nearly all schools the elements of ZPD-creating—freedom from knowing, creative imitation and completion—are absent.

The imitative activity of very young children is also thought of as creative in both the mundane and the appreciative senses. And one gradually stops doing that as they get older. Imitating becomes copying. What once gave delight is to be avoided. A child of three or four years is likely to be told she is clever or smart (or at least cute) for creatively imitating. In nearly all schools, a child of seven or eight is likely to be told she is cheating and shouldn't copy.

In the extreme, schooling transforms not knowing into a deficit; creative imitation into individualized accomplishments, rote learning and testing; and completion into correction and competition.

This is the current situation. This is what schools do and don't do. I am as concerned as the next person about it, but I am equally concerned with bringing outside of school learning to the forefront of dialogue and debate among educators, researchers, policymakers and the public. This is because that is where creativity still lives. Putting on a play or concert and playing basketball as a team require the members to create a collective form of working together. Unfortunately, doing well in school does not. My reading of the literature on outside of school programmes, along with my own intervention research, shows that outside of school programmes (in particular, those involving the arts or sports) are more often than not learning-leading-development environments, methodologically analogous to early childhood ZPDs in a manner appropriate to school-aged children and adolescents.[4] Whether deliberately or not, they continue to relate to young people as creative, in both mundane and appreciative senses.

These kinds of cultural outside of school programmes share important features, most notably, those that foster activities that create ZPDs: freedom from knowing and socially imitative and completive activity. First, children come to them to learn how to do something they do not know how to do. Maybe they want to perform in a play, make music videos, play the flute, dance or play basketball. They bring with them some expectation that they will learn. They are related to by skilled outside of school instructors, often practitioners themselves, as capable of learning, regardless of how much they know coming in to the programme. Thus, while there are of course differences in skills and experience that young people bring to outside of school programmes, the playing field is more level than in school. Really good programmes, in fact, use such heterogeneity for everyone's advantage (Gordon, Bowman and Mejia 2003; Holzman 2006, 2009).

Second, in these programmes it is acceptable to imitate and complete. In fact, it's essential. The presumption is that how one becomes an actor, music producer, musician, dancer and athlete is by doing what others do and building on it. From the fundamentals through advanced techniques and forms, creatively imitating instructors and peers—and being completed by them—is what is expected and reinforced.

I have come to view outside of school programmes that have these features as learning environments created by, and allowing for, learning playfully. They are, in this sense, a synthesis of Vygotsky's ZPDs of learning-instruction and of play, not as spatio-temporal zones but as mundane creative activity. For, as in the free or pretend play of early childhood, the players (both students and instructors) are more directly the producers of their environment-activity, in charge of generating and coordinating the perceptual, cognitive and emotional elements of their learning and playing. Most psychologists and educators value play for how it facilitates the learning of social roles, with socio-cultural researchers taking play to be an instrumental tool that mediates between the individual and the culture and, thereby, a particular culture is appropriated (as in the work of Nicolopoulou and Cole 1993; Rogoff 1990; Rogoff and Lave 1984; Wertsch 1985). Through acting out roles (play-acting), children try out the roles they will soon take on in 'real life'. I am sympathetic to this understanding and yet I think there is more that play contributes to development than this. Being a head taller is an ensemble performance, not 'an act'. After all, one does not say the babbling baby is acting out a role.

I see play as both appropriating culture and creating culture, a performing of who the individuals are becoming (Newman and Holzman 1993; Holzman 1997, 2009). I see creative imitation as a type of performance. When they are playing with language very young children are simultaneously performing—becoming—themselves. In the theatrical sense of the word, performing is a way of taking 'who we are' and creating something new—in this case a newly emerging speaker, on the stage a newly emerging character, in an outside of school programme a skilled dancer or athlete—through incorporating 'the other'.

In his essay on the development of personality and world view in children, Vygotsky wrote that the preschool child 'can be somebody else just as easily as he can be himself' (Vygotsky 1997: 249). Vygotsky attributed this to the child's lack of recognition that s/he is an 'I' and went on to discuss how personality and play transform through later childhood. I take Vygotsky to be saying that performing as someone else is an essential source of development, at the time of life before 'I'.

Early childhood is the time before 'I' and the time before 'I know'. The type of lived activity out of which learning-leading-development occurs and 'I' and 'I know' are created, can never be replicated—nor should there be a desire to do so. But outside of school programmes, to the extent that they are spaces and stages for creativity (mundane and otherwise), appear to support young people's learning-leading-development through revitalizing play and performance. Such programmes are precisely the kind of support schools need, for as long as schools continue to discourage creativity.

Notes

1. Vygotsky used the Russian word 'obuchenie', which refers to both teaching and learning. It is usually translated as 'learning'.
2. Lantolf and Thorne (2006) note this misunderstanding and make a worthwhile distinction between scaffolding and development in the ZPD.
3. What I am describing as completion would be identified in language acquisition and linguistics literature by other terms, such as expansion or contingency, which are located within a cognitive framework. My expansion/liberal interpretation of Vygotsky's terms is not.
4. Reports on the advantages of culturally-based outside of school programmes, including arguments that they can help close 'the achievement gap' are many. See for example, Arts Education Partnership, 1999; Bodilly and Beckett 2005; Childress 1998; Heath 2000; Heath, Soep and Roach 1998; Carnegie Council on Adolescent Development 1992; Gordon, Bridglall and Meroe 2005; and Mahoney, Larson and Eccles 2005.

References

Allal, L. and A. Pelgrims (2000), 'Assessment of or in the Zone of Proximal Development', *Learning and Instruction*, vol. 10, no. 2, pp. 137–52.

Arts Education Partnership (1999), *Champions of Change: The Impact of the Arts on Learning*, Washington, DC: Arts Education Partnership.

Berk, L.E. and A. Winsler (1995), *Scaffolding Children's Learning: Vygotsky and Early Childhood Education*, Washington, DC: National Association for the Education of Young Children.

Carnegie Council on Adolescent Development (1992), *A Matter of Time: Risk and Opportunity in the Nonschool Hours*, Carnegie Council Monograph, http://www.carnegie.org/ccadpubs.htm, accessed December 2007.

Childress, H. (1998), 'Seventeen Reasons Why Football is Better than High School', *Phi Delta Kappan*, vol. 79, no. 8, pp. 616–20.

Glick, J. (2004), 'The History of the Development of Higher Mental Function', in *The Essential Vygotsky*, ed. R.W. Rieber and D.K. Robinson, NY: Kluwer Academic/Plenum Publishers.

Gordon, E.W., C.B. Bowman and B.X. Mejia (2003), *Changing the Script for Youth Development: An Evaluation of the All Stars Talent Show Network and the Joseph A. Forgione Development School for Youth*, Institute for Urban and Minority Education, Teachers College, Columbia University.

Gordon, E.W., B.L. Bridglall and A.S. Meroe (2005), *Supplementary Education: The Hidden Curriculum of High Academic Achievement*, Latham, MD: Rowan and Littlefield.

Heath, S.B. (2000), 'Making Learning Work', *Afterschool Matters: Dialogues in Philosophy, Practice and Evaluation*, vol. 1, no. 1, pp. 33–45.

Heath, S.B., E. Soep and A. Roach (1998), 'Living the Arts through Language and Learning: A Report on Community-based Youth Organizations', *Americans for the Arts Monographs,* vol. 2, no. 7, pp. 1–20.

Holzman, L. (1997), *Schools for Growth: Radical Alternatives to Current Educational Models*, Mahwah, NJ: Erlbaum.

———(2002), *Young People Learn by Studying Themselves: The All Stars Talent Show in Action,* NY: East Side Institute for Short Term Psychotherapy, DVD.

———(2006), 'Activating Postmodernism', *Theory & Psychology*, vol. 16, no. 1, pp. 109–23.

———(2009), *Vygotsky at Work and Play*, Routledge: New York and London.

Lantoff, J.P., ed. (2000), *Sociocultural Theory and Second Language Learning,* Oxford: OUP.

Lidz, C.S. and B. Gindis (2003), 'Dynamic Assessment of the Evolving Cognitive Functions in Children', in *Vygotsky's Educational Theory In Cultural Context*, ed. A. Kozulin, B. Gindis, V.S. Ageyev and S.M. Miller, New York: Cambridge University Press, pp. 96–116.

MacNaughton, G. and G. Williams (1998), *Techniques for Teaching Young Children: Choices in Theory and Practice,* French Forests, Australia: Longman.

Mahoney, J.L., R.W. Larson and J.S. Eccles, eds. (2005), *Organized Activities as Contexts of Development: Extracurricular Activities, After School and Community Programs*, Mahwah, NJ: Erlbaum.

Newman, F. and L. Holzman (1993), *Lev Vygotsky: Revolutionary Scientist,* London: Routledge.

———(1997), *The End of Knowing: A New Developmental Way of Learning,* London: Routledge.

Newman, D., P. Griffin and M. Cole (1989), *The Construction Zone: Working for Cognitive Change in School,* Cambridge: CUP.

Nicolopoulou, A. and M. Cole (1993), 'The Generation and Transmission of Shared Knowledge in the Culture of Collaborative Learning: The Fifth Dimension, its Play World, and its Institutional Contexts', in *Contexts for Learning: Sociocultural Dynamics in Children's Development*, ed. E.A. Forman, N. Minick and C.A. Stone, New York: OUP, pp. 283–314.

Rodgers, A. and E.M. Rodgers (2004), *Scaffolding Literacy Instruction, Strategies for K-4 Classrooms*, Portsmouth NH: Heinemann.

Rogoff, B. (1990), *Apprenticeship in Thinking: Cognitive Development in Social Context*, New York: OUP.

Rogoff, B. and J. Lave, eds. (1984), *Everyday Cognition: Development in Social Context*, Boston: Harvard University Press, pp. 95–117.

Shotter, J. (1989), 'Vygotsky's Psychology: Joint Activity in the Zone of Proximal Development', *New Ideas in Psyhcology*, vol. 7, pp. 185–204.

Tharp, R.G. and R. Gallimore (1978), *Mind in Society*, Cambridge, MA: Harvard University Press.

————(1987), *The Collected Works of L.S. Vygotsky*, vol. 1, New York: Plenum.

———— (1988), *Rousing Minds to Life: Teaching, Learning and Schooling In Social Context,* Cambridge: CUP.

————(1994), 'The Problem of the Environment', in *The Vygotsky Reader*, ed. R. van der Veer and J. Valsiner, Oxford: Blackwell, pp. 338–54.

————(1997), 'The Historical Meaning of the Crisis in Psychology: A Methodological Investigation', in *The Collected Works of L.S. Vygotsky*, ed. R. van der Veer and J. Valsiner, vol. 3, NY: Plenum, pp. 233–343.

————(2004), 'The Collective as a Factor in the Development of the Abnormal Child', in *The Essential Vygotsky*, ed. R.W. Rieber and D.K. Robinson, NY: Kluwer Academic/Plenum Publishers, pp. 201–19.

Wertsch, J.V. (1985), *Vygotsky and the Social Construction of Mind*, Cambridge, MA: Harvard University Press.

————(1991), *Voices of the Mind: A Sociolcultural Approach to Mediated Action*, Cambridge MA: Harvard University Press.

Wood, D., J. Bruner and G. Ross (1976), 'The Role of Tutoring in Problem Solving', *Journal of Child Psychology and Psychiatry*, vol. 17, pp. 89–100.

15

Cultural Innovation Through a New Hermeneutic of Reality

L. ANTHONY SAVARI RAJ

Introduction

One of the typical traits of postmodernism is its attempt to demolish the firm construction of self-sufficiency, reason and progress[1] and point to a dwelling place where plurality, especially plurality of cultures, is possible, desired and will even feel at home. In fact, when postmodernism 'speaks of culture, it prefers to speak of cultures' (Lemart 1997: 22).

But with all its thrust on difference and diversity[2] can plurality be still equated with pluralism?

To be sure, plurality does represent best the spirit of pluralism. Yet, pluralism, I submit, requires more than mere acknowledgement of multiple cultures and a desire for unity.[3] It stands, further, for the experience of contingency of cultures which makes one realize that one is not a monolithic whole and that one essentially and constitutively needs the other for existing, growth and fulfilment. In other words, it presupposes that cultures are neither isolated nor enclosed, but each is really a dimension of the other.

Is this experience and explication of contingency a postmodern priority? My essay enquires further into this, focusing, of course, on the issue of development.

It may be fitting here to make an exploration into the notion of cultural innovation as a pathway of creative learning, being and co-living of cultures.

By cultural innovation, I understand the following:

Each tradition, inasmuch as it is not stagnant, has to innovate, transform and regenerate itself not only from within but also from without, i.e. by accepting inspiration, influence and even correction from outside. But this external stimulus will become effective only when a tradition is able to find a resonance and acceptance of what it receives in its very heart.

The myth of progress and development—one of the pillars of modernity—which postmodernism critiques and even desires to deconstruct and demolish, offers a wonderful opportunity to enquire about the priority and function of cultural innovation, which I am just indicating.

Before I make a few submissions, I would like to indicate three presuppositions that form the basis for my considerations:

1. In today's contemporary cross-cultural human situation, the mutual fecundation of cultures has become a cultural imperative.
2. In this new situation, cultures do influence each other and, therefore, a positive symbiosis is possible.
3. This positive symbiosis may assist in meaningful and creative ways of being.

Let me begin my consideration with a story.

In an ashram in north India, an American engineer was criticizing the backwardness of India, in front of a guru and his disciples squatting on the ground. 'We have put a man on the moon,' he said.

'But do you know whom you've sent?' was the prompt reply of the guru.

Well, reaching the top of the world is certainly a great sign of development. But getting to the centre of one's being and existence could equally signal significant progress.

In today's cross-cultural human situation it may be realized that both these forms and directions of development, though important, are insufficient to ensure human and cosmic welfare. Perhaps both need to serve as 'external stimulus' and even as 'pressure points' to one another, so that an intermediary space may be created by their mutual criticisms and mutual concessions.

Let me come to the heart of the problem by providing an example— the analogy of the net.

Traditional cultures, I believe, have overstressed and overstretched the net (kinship, hierarchical structure of society, the function to be performed, the role of each part in relation to the whole, and so on)—so much so that the knot has been suffocated and not allowed sufficient free-space for its own self-identity, human flowering and development.

On the other hand, modern cultures, it seems to me, have stressed too the knots much (individual free will to choose any option, the automization of society, and so on)—so that often the knot has been lost in loneliness and solipsism, alienated by its own social mobility, wounded or killed in competition with other, more powerful knots.

Perhaps an interplay between the knots and the net, symbolized best in the notion of person, could provide a starting point for the cultural innovation that I am hinting at. Cultural innovation, therefore, would imply discovering the sense of life through mutual collaboration and recognizing the possibility of human fulfilment without imposing upon one another any one parameter of civilization or culture and, of course, in the context of the present discussion—the parameter of development.

A proper understanding of culture becomes crucial here.

Culture is not just one more dimension of society, alongside economy, politics, science, technology, philosophy, religion and so on. It is the existential reality of peoples and communities in a society in which religion, philosophy, politics, science and so on, are 'Cultural Areas'. Therefore, if an innovation is brought about in any of these cultural areas, it would automatically amount to and stand for a cultural innovation.

For the moment, I choose and highlight very briefly just three cultural areas: the area of politics, science and philosophy, and in presenting each of these areas, I shall be guided by three considerations:

1. to offer a cultural critique;
2. to make a cross-cultural comment; and
3. to indicate a possible cultural innovation in the area under reflection.

A New Hermeneutic of Reality

Before I highlight the cultural areas cross-culturally, I would like to insert and introduce the holistic and creative vision of Raimon Panikkar—one of the leading intercultural thinkers of today, which may well serve as the basis of the new and creative pathway, which is being searched for. Panikkar's vision offers not only a new hermeneutic to the issue of development, but also, more basically, proves a good starting point for a fresh way of approaching and understanding reality.

Coining the word 'cosmotheandric' Panikkar brings to light the three irreducible dimensions of reality: Cosmos, Theos and Anthropos (Earthly, Divine and Human). He discerns the inseparable nature of these dimensions, though a distinction between them could easily be made. 'Inter-relatedness', 'inter-dependence', and 'inter-independence' are the chief characteristics of anything that exists. In a word, whatever 'is' is relational (Podgorski 1996: 107).

Panikkar has given different expressions to his cosmotheandric vision of reality in his writings. I recall here only some of them. 'The times begin to be ripe now to gather again the broken pieces of these partial insights into a new holistic vision: there is no matter without spirit and no spirit without matter, no world without Man, no God without the universe, etc. God, Man and World are three artificially substantivized forms of the three primordial adjectives which describe Reality' (Panikkar 1978: 206). 'There is a kind of perichoresis, "dwelling within one another" of these three dimensions of reality,—the Divine, the Human and the Cosmic—the I, the you and the it' (Panikkar 1979: 217).

The cosmotheandric principle could be stated by saying that the divine, the human and the earthly—however we may prefer to call them—are the three irreducible dimensions, which constitute the real, i.e. any reality inasmuch as it is real. . . What this intuition emphasizes is that the three dimensions of reality are neither three modes of a monolithic undifferentiated reality, nor are they three elements of a pluralistic system. There is rather one, though intrinsically threefold, relation, which expresses the ultimate constitution of reality. Everything that exists, any real being, presents this triune constitution expressed in three dimensions. I am not only saying that everything is directly or indirectly related to everything else: the radical relativity or pratityasamutpada of the Buddhist tradition. I am also stressing that this relationship is not only constitutive of the whole, but that it flashes forth, ever new and vital, in every spark of the real. (Panikkar 1979: 74)

These formulations indeed clearly indicate the non-dual character of reality. God, World and human beings are not totally separate beings, as one might have thus far imagined and led a person's thinking about his/her life. No reality is devoid of the cosmic, human and divine dimensions or aspects. All the three dimensions are interwoven. Of course, the divine may be stressed in God, the human dimension may have a focus in human persons and the cosmic dimension has its thrust on the world. But no matter what the accent is, all the three dimensions are constitutively related (Panikkar 1977: 4). Here I very briefly elucidate Panikkar's understanding of each of these dimensions.

Panikkar considers the cosmic dimension as the body dimension of reality, which is tangible, concrete and objectifiable. Perhaps this is the dimension, which can easily be understood as well as affirmed, for whatever is, including all living beings, comes from the Cosmos. Everything is earth-related and earth-bound. Every being partakes of the World and participates in the secular dimension. Matter matters, and it matters very much, because every day-to-day experience shows that there is nothing which comes in touch with human consciousness that is not associated with the World. Joining St. Thomas and the Scholastics, it can even be said that the starting point of all knowledge of God is sense experience. The concepts and terms that are employed to speak of God apply first and foremost to objects of the world and sense experience. Rightly so, Panikkar states: 'a metaphysical truth—whatever this may be—is only true if it is really kata-physical (1977: 78). And furthermore, it may even be said that 'God without the World is not a real God, nor does he exist' (1977: 79).

Panikkar elucidates the divine dimension as another dimension of one's very self and the World and not as the 'Totally Other'. Here it is seen how the transcendence of God is perceived and interpreted more in terms of the transparency of the world and the human. Panikkar discerns the divine dimension as 'the infinite inexhaustibility of any human being, its ever-open character, its mystery—if the word is allowed in this connection—its freedom, another language might prefer' (1977: 79). Again, this is not so much a question of bringing down the Divine to the level of the matter and the human, as an attempt to make the Divine feel more at home here on earth and to discover the real worth of nature and the human. One needs only to be open to discover this immeasurable and 'ever-more' dimension that is ever present and ever-eluding within every being and within every experience. It is also Panikkar's contention that this element of 'ever-more' in every reality can never be fully brought into the strictures of human reason and attempts to do so have brought enough problems today.

Panikkar describes the human dimension in terms of consciousness. But this consciousness—a trait, which has been mostly associated with and only confined to human personality—is perceived in a better and broader perspective. In this vision, every real being is connected with Man's awareness by the very fact that every being is thinkable. Whatever said or thought of, positively or negatively, is always tinged with an element of consciousness. 'The waters of human consciousness wash all the shores of the real—even if man cannot penetrate the terra incognita of the interior—and by this very fact, Man's being enters into relation with the whole of reality' (1977: 76). Or again, if growth only in terms of space is the qualifying mark of life, then, that which doesn't grow in space will be non-living as such. But if growth in terms of time is determined, then everything becomes living, as there is nothing which is not growing in time. Everything is living and conscious as the humans (Panikkar 1993: 139–42).

Cosmotheandrism, in short, represents an effort and a vision where there is a happy marriage between the secular and the sacred, which Panikkar calls 'Sacred Secularity' (Panikkar 1973: 9). In this, the secular is sacredly secular and the sacred is secularly sacred. By the same token, this insight also overcomes the separation between time and eternity. In this new vision, time is the symbol of eternity, where there is neither time nor eternity but 'tempiternity'. 'I have created the word tempiternity to express that which overcomes the scheme of time here and eternity later. I think that the entire reality is tempiternal, that is, temporal and eternal in one and the same time in a non-dualistic relation' (Panikkar 1982a: 25).

In the backdrop of Panikkar's new hermeneutic of reality, as presented above, let one may explore how an innovation can come about in the cultural areas of politics, science and philosophy.

THE AREA OF POLITICS: POLITICAL INNOVATION

The political area, which most urgently needs an innovation, is the issue of 'development'. Speedy processes of globalization are the result of contemporary technological, economic, political and conceptual developments. People, materials, money and ideas are carried by means of communication and transportation, which have tremendously progressed in speed and efficiency. Development of consumer goods has reached phenomenal heights.

This developmental project, however, while being very successful for some countries and classes, has not been conducive and beneficial at all to most of humanity exposed to poverty and misery. Though in the post-Second World War era 'International Development' proposed to help 'backward' countries 'catch up' with the industrialized world, the poor did not benefit much from it. Many maintain that, even today, development is subservient to the rich and powerful. The poor and powerless are left out of the process (see Escobar 1995; Berkeley 2001).

No wonder that the UN Millennium Development Goals in 2000 proposed to 'halve, by the year 2015, the proportion of the world's people whose income is less than one dollar a day and the proportion of people who suffer from hunger and, by the same date, to halve the proportion of people who are unable to reach or to afford safe drinking water' (United Nations 2000: pt 9).

As I have indicated, the dominant vision of development may be compatible with some cultures, but not with all. The development ideal seems to be a continuation of the monocultural and messianic syndrome of the Western culture, which desires one mode of development everywhere. Furthermore, not all cultures have the same sense of life as progress and as an orientation of a future goal. The anthropology, which underscores the idea of development, is not so very adequate to the majority of mankind (see Nobn 2002). To quote Panikkar:

The idea of development has an underlying anthropology which sees Man as a bundle of potential needs which require only development in order to make life happy and meaningful. Development is the anthropological counterpart to the biological theory of evolution. Man develops in the same manner as the universe is set on evolution. This is an empirical proof that something is fundamentally wrong with the ideology of development. (1995: 3)

In other words, this idea of development is not conducive to those traditional visions, which allow no separation between the goal and the way. These visions stand for discovering the destination in the way itself. If not, one can well imagine the consequence: alienation, that may never feel at home if always preoccupied with the goal of development in future. Life can be lived in fullness, even when a person is not sufficiently 'developed'.

Moreover, the goal of development seems to deprive the element of freedom as well. It is in this context, that I like to situate Amartya Sen's proposal of Development as Freedom, a freedom much further from an economic-centric orientation. He explains why development should be regarded as providing more levels of freedoms to the people: 'Freedoms are not only the primary ends of development, they are also among its principal means' (Sen 1999/2000: 10). He also thinks of development as 'a momentous engagement with freedom's possibilities' (Sen 1999/2000: 298), suggesting thereby that the quality of a person's life should be measured not by the wealth, but by the freedom he/she enjoys. An attention to capability dimension may perhaps pave the way for development in all directions and also assign place to other choices: 'The perspective of human capability focuses, on the other hand, on the ability—the substantive freedom—of people to lead the lives they have reason to value and to enhance the real choices they have' (Sen 1999/2000: 293).

Or again, the developmental ideal appears inadequate from a cosmological point of view. It leads to an alienation of the human also from the earth. 'The unrestrained dominance of corporate capitalism and its commodifying values would be catastrophic not only for human communities but for the entire biosphere' (Laoy 2004: 100).

In other words, the ideal of development assumes that matter is dead, and is meant only for resources to be tapped for human advancement. But the consequences have just begun to be seen, since

technological system in which most of us live, any technological micro-progress implies a macro-regress, sociologically-speaking. Any little thing which is an improvement here will have somewhat negative repercussions somewhere else. Antibiotics produce population explosion, subsidies to European agriculture lie at the root of famines elsewhere. The reason is very simple: once the rhythms of the earth are broken and once we have reached the limits of the planet in all aspects, then any increase here will result in a decrease somewhere else. (Panikkar 1992: 30)

The political innovation suggested, therefore, seems to operate on another word which Panikkar calls 'awakening', people 'on the way to awakening'. 'Awakening would suggest a new awareness concerning the meaning of life, the reality of the earth, and the sense of the divine. Awakening could amount to perceiving better with one's ears and eyes and mind, discovering the invisible dimension of things. It is not the privilege of the few who have "made it" because they are developed' (Panikkar 1992: 34). Needless to say these inspiring words come alive in the context of the mutual fecundation of cultures. They also do 'justice' to the experiences of more than one culture.

THE AREA OF SCIENCE: SCIENTIFIC INNOVATION

The second area, that needs an innovation is the field of science and technology which emerged as the 'New God' of today (see Hawk 2004). Though this century also has other gods such as the Market, Military Might, and so on, it is technology that powers the Market, Consumerism, Wars and other secular religions.

Of course, war against terrorism seems to be the primary preoccupation of modern age. Yet, there is a war waged by the technocratic culture on practically everything everywhere. Consider the use of war, even in language, e.g. trade wars, fashion wars, war on poverty. War has come to be a new way of being. The divine gods were once attributed with the higher power. Today, the military and political leaders have assumed this power making themselves the real, secular gods of War (Hadley 2004: 198–203). All this is achieved through the 'blessings' of technology. 'The scientific caste today has accumulated a power on life and death immensely superior to any other caste of any other period of human memory' (Panikkar 1995: 6).

This only shows that science has not maintained its original purpose of being a 'saving knowledge'. In this sense it has become perverse (Panikkar 1995: 4; also see Nandy 1988). Besides being perverse, modern science also does violence to life: life of nature, of women and of the poor (see Amaladoss 1997: 50–1). Besides the violence of abstracting each element from its natural and historical circumstances, modern science also performs a violence by interfering with its normal function.

This process of objectification through analysis, experimentation and quantification ultimately functions through a creation of dichotomies: between nature and God, nature and human, human and human, and man and woman. This brings about an instrumentalization of nature, which also spills over onto humans, especially of their bodies. Obviously, the women are the targets here. There is no better example than the dehumanizing advertisements and contemporary biotechnological experiments (Siva 1993: 138–9).

No wonder the rape of the earth is linked with the rape of women. This extreme form of instrumentalization manifests in the dehumanization of the poor and their cultures without any sense of feeling.

Science has no feelings. One can produce and sell weapons of mass destruction that maim and diminish people and engage in war games without worrying about their human consequences—feelings do not enter into the process. One can promote production and development without bothering about the consequences to poor peasants, tribals or fisherfolk. One can play the market, hoping it will adjust itself, without worrying about its impact on the oppressed. (Amaladoss 1997: 51)

Here Panikkar's idea of techniculture can be situated. 'Techniculture suggests the civilization of the machine, which, being inanimate, can only be the object of human exploitation for human benefit or rather profit' (Panikkar 2002: 109). Besides dealing only with an aspect of reality, science inflicts violence on life through its exclusive mechanical approach to nature and people.

Modern science, and more specifically, technological science owing its origins to the West, has also helped the West's economic development and expansion. It is not, therefore, neutral and universal (ETH Zurich 1996: 205–9). In this connection Panikkar makes a distinction between human invariants and cultural universals. While techne is a human invariant, a kind of a common denominator, technology is not. The latter is a construct of the West. Moreover, 'for techne, we need spirit (in-spiration), for technology, we need a special cognitive "know-how" (techno-logos)' (ETH Zurich 1996: 207). To quote Panikkar again:

The difference between technique or techne and technology is patent in the word itself. Techne is art, it is the human capacity of instilling human spirit into matter and giving life to matter. The author of techne is the artist who has to be inspired in order to produce a work of art. The spirit, the pneuma is the real creator. Technology is the substitution of the spirit by ratio; reasoning reason is its author. Technology is not there to make a pot, but to produce thousands of pots in the minimum of time and cost—otherwise there is no point in having the thousand pots. In the language of the above-made distinction, technological society is an organization and not an organism. (Panikkar 1982b: 32)

This also indicates that the values of technology are not universal and further, seem to be at loggerheads with those of the traditional cultures, especially in their visions of matter, life, space, time and so on. The contact of the technological vision with other cultures has produced what Panikkar terms as a 'conflict of cosmologies' (Panikkar 2002: 106).

The scientific innovation, therefore, will first of all reduce modern science to its proper limits. 'Not all epistemology is "scientific"; not all cogniton measurable; not all knowledge is covered by "Science". Modern Science cannot be said to know the world or to have penetrated the nature of Reality' (Panikkar 1996b: 52). Though it is through technological science that economic and other developments and expansion have come about in the Western societies, yet modern-day Western scientific culture is not the only scientific culture possible even in the West. Furthermore, its suppositions are not universal and are not shared by other cultures and ways of life in other parts of the world.

The non-separation between the human and the nature, the recognition of non-rational or mystery dimension to reality, the desire to forge a communion with nature, and so on are the thrusts of non-Western cultures. These values perhaps assist the technological culture in relativizing its values, and suggest that there are other ways of approaching and leading life.

The traditional cultures, through their vitalistic cosmology, experience the universe not as a mechanical or sophisticated organization, but as a living organism, which requires a holistic and creative participation and collaboration (Panikkar 2002: 113). On the other hand, there is also a need for the traditional cultures to simultaneously turn towards the spirit of the new situation of humanity and assist, assimilate and effect a transformation within in ways that are needed and possible.

THE AREA OF PHILOSOPHY: PHILOSOPHICAL INNOVATION

Philosophical innovation would stand for a re-assessment of the dominant mode of time, which operates behind all belief in history and progress. It is the historical mode of time, that is, in fact, at the basis of the idea of development and the scientific enterprise.

Development presupposes an attainment of a goal in future and science has at its heart a sense of linear time. While development implies a future fulfilment, science pays attention also to the beginning of time. But both of them share in the common idea of not finding fulfilment in the present time. Marching towards the future is the paradigm and goal of life for both of them. A preparation and living for the future seem to be the model of an ideal education and life. The present life is only an intermediary stepping-stone for the one to come in the future. The goal is never here and now, it is always to be found later. History means not merely a narration of the past, but it is mainly a hopeful and at times hopeless parade towards a known or unknown future destination.

The destination of this parade may be indecisive and not very clear, but not so its motivation. It is an ambition towards 'success'. Success is not the only thing, it is everything and has to be measurable and monetizable. Progress is the modern mantra. Work is the modern way of finding salvation. This salvation can come about only if one keeps running (working) all the time, even if it brings only alienation and total restlessness. Any temporary progress now is only a glimpse of a greater thing to come in the future. Panikkar observes:

Modern life is preparation for later, for the time to come. Credit, growth, education, children, savings, insurance, business—all is geared for later, oriented toward the possibilities of a future which will forever remain uncertain. We are always on the go and the quicker the better, in order to gain time. Without planning, strategy, preparation and purpose for the future, our lives are inconceivable. Temporality haunts modernity; the time factor is the aspect of nature to be overcome. Acceleration is the great discovery of modern science. Individually and collectively, our lives are all bent forward, running toward the goal, the prize, in unrelenting competition, heading toward the 'Great Event'. Soteriology has become eschatology, sacred as well as profane. (Panikkar 1996b: 39)

The philosophical innovation, therefore, would consist of reassessing the idea of history and progress in light of other cultural perceptions and orientations. If history and progress are the measurements of human life and experience, then obviously a greater part of humanity would not be able to fit into this scheme.

And yet, for millennia, these cultures have nourished millions of people, even when they could not 'make it' according to the dominant economic paradigm. Even in the hardest times and in the face of the greatest survival struggles, people could face life with joy and dignity precisely because they have been sustained by hope.

This hope, however, is not merely of the future, but in the 'invisible dimension of reality', a kind of 'tempiternal hope'. 'For the majority of the peoples on the earth, the aboriginal people, the slaves, the outcasts, the starving people, the sick, the oppressed, the women all too often, true hope cannot be of the future; it has to be of the invisible, of another dimension which makes life worth living even if I live five years under exploitation. To make of the necessity a virtue may not be sociologically advisable, but for the oppressed people it is the only chance of keeping their human dignity. It is certainly not a vice (Panikkar 1995: 7).

This dimension may be ever-eluding, or ever-escaping, but ever-present as the ever-more dimension of reality. Panikkar would call it a transcendental attitude,

which does not necessarily mean an explicit belief in transcendence. It means an awareness accompanying every action, that life on earth, is only a kind of 'comedy', 'divine' or not, a sort of play, a re-enactment of something bigger than ourselves and yet taking place within ourselves. Rebirth and transformation, heaven and moral responsibility, whatever religious underpinnings they may have, entail a firm sentiment that we are not private proprietors of our life, but actors and spectators of it. We live as if we were performing a role, which is greater than us, transmitting a little worse or a little better of the life, which we have received. (Panikkar 2002: 110)

In other words, it is this 'cosmic confidence' that does not allow people to be totally crushed by circumstances, however inhuman they may be.

On the other hand, the philosophical innovation would also represent the effort of the traditional cultures to revitalize themselves as they come into contact with the dominant modern culture. This effort may be seen in their serious attitude towards history and progress and identification and attempt to overcome all the traditional notions and elements, which have not been so very helpful to a fuller flowering of authentic human life.

More concretely this would mean to pay greater attention to the questions of human rights, poverty, a degeneration that has come about in the caste structure and all the conditions that deny a 'normal' human life to millions of people (Wilfred 2005: 23–45). Pressing problems such as lack of food, housing, healthcare and education would need immediate attention. In other words, the traditional cultures should do a reassessment of their traditional values in the light of human welfare, particularly of the oppressed and downtrodden.

As already noted, this reassessment would be greatly stimulated, complemented and enhanced by the dominant modern culture with its focus on the human dimension and blossoming.

Notes

1. See, for instance, Jean-François Lyotard (1984) for the rejection of grand narratives, the dethroning of discursive reason and the rejection of a privileged centre.
2. Of course, the connected issues of 'plurality of cultures' are: the end of the colonial era, radical critique of positions and methods of enquiry, the awareness of cultural conditioning, the sense of history, the recognition of the bias of science and technology, the affirmation of the non-rational in a person's life, and so on.
3. Lemart distinguishes 'strategic postmodernism' from 'radical postmodernism'. He writes: 'strategic postmodernism believes that modernity is too clever, too subtle in its workings, for anyone to be able to criticize it from the point of view of its own ideas. Yet, this position also believes that there is no sensible choice but to use modern culture, that is: to subvert the culture, to overcome its denial of differences, its deceptive deployment of power/knowledge, its self-denying ideologies' (1997: 53).

References

Amaladoss, Michael (1997), *Life in Freedom: Liberation Theologies from Asi*, Maryknoll, New York: Orbis Books.

Berkeley, Bill (2001), *The Graves are Not Yet Full: Race, Tribe and Power in the Heart of Africa*, New York: Basic Books.

Escobar, Arturo (1995), *Encountering Development: The Making and Unmaking of the Third World*, Princeton, NJ: Princeton University Press.

ETH Zurich (1996), 'Europe-Asia: Science and Technology for their Future', *Forum Engelberg*, 26–28 March.

Hadley, Michael L. (2004), 'The Ascension of Mars and the Salvation of the Modern World', in *The Twenty-first Century Confronts its Gods: Globalization, Technology and War*, ed. David J. Hawkin, New York: State University of New York Press.

Hawkin, David J., ed. (2004), *The Twenty-first Century Confronts Its Gods: Globalization, Technology, and War*, New York: State University of New York Press.

Lemart, Charles (1997), *Postmodernism is Not What You Think*, Malden, MA & Oxford: Blackwell.

Loy, David R. (2004), 'The West Against the Rest?: A Buddhist Response to the Clash of Civilizations', in *The Twenty-first Century Confronts its Gods: Globalization, Technology and War*, ed. David J. Hawkin, New York: State University of New York Press.

Lyotard, Jean-François (1984), *The Postmodern Condition: A Report on Knowledge*, Manchester: Manchester University Press.

Nandy, Ashis (1988), *Science, Hegemony and Violence*, Delhi: OUP.

Nolan, Riall (2002), *Development Anthropology Encounters in the Real World*, Boulder, CO: Westview Press.

Panikkar, R. (1973), *Worship and Secular Man*, London: Orbis Books.

———(1977), 'Colligite Fragmenta, For an Integration of Reality', in *From Alienation to At-Oneness*, Proceedings of the Theology Institute of Villanova, ed. F. A. Eigo and S.E. Fittipaldi, Villanova.

———(1978), 'Philosophy as Life-Style', in *Philosophers on Their Own Work*, ed. A. Mercier and M. Svilar, vol. IV, Berne.

———(1979), 'The Myth of Pluralism: The Tower of Babel—A Meditation on Non-Violence', *Cross Currents*, 29 Summer.

———(1982a), 'Alternative à la Culture Modèrne (Texte II Dialogue)', *Interculture*, vol. 15, October–December.

———(1982b), 'Cross-Cultural Economics', *Interculture*, vol. 15, no. 4, cahier 77.

———(1992), 'Philosophical Investigation of Sustainable Development: Fundamental Issues', in *Proceedings of the International Conference: Living with the Earth. Cross-Cultural Perspectives on Sustainable Development: Indigenous and Alternative Practices*. Montreal: Intercultural Institute of Montreal (30 April–3 May).

———(1993), *The Cosmotheandric Insight: Emerging Religious Consciousness*, New York: Orbis Books.

———(1995), 'Ecosophy', *New Gaia*, vol. 4, no. 1, Winter.

———(1996a), 'The Contemplative Mood: A Challenge to Modernity', *Interculture*, vol. 29, no. 1, Winter, issue no. 130.

PART FOUR

CULTIVATING PATHWAYS OF
NON-DUAL REALIZATIONS AND
NEW HORIZONS OF ONTOLOGICAL
EPISTEMOLOGY OF PARTICIPATION

16

The Ontology of Humanities and Social Sciences: A Gadamerian Perspective

BINOD KUMAR AGARWALA

Everyone self-evidently belongs to the world, society and history. That was the presupposition of all knowledge from antiquity to the end of the medieval period. With the advent of the modern period, came the condition in which one ceased to presuppose that he belonged naturally to the world. One ceased to accept that he is at home in the world and one's situation in the world came to be characterized as that of alienation (*Fremdheit*). Subject and object separated and precipitated out simultaneously from the primordial unity of man's being at home in the world due to this presupposition of the condition of alienation of man in the world. The subject with a will, who no more belonged to the world, tried to control and dominate the world through knowledge conceived as acquired through some empirical method of enquiry, i.e. sciences.

The ideas of subject-object dichotomy and the ideal knowledge acquired through controlled empirical method of enquiry were not confined to the natural world. They were extended to the social and historical world too. When man takes the stance of the subject, i.e. conceives himself as the subject to get methodic empirical knowledge of society, and in turn, conceives society as the object of knowledge, then he reflects himself out of the society, out of all social relations, to maintain the duality of subject and object. So the subject must conceive himself as a being no more belonging to the society. That is to say, when man conceives himself

---

* The subtitle of this essay is meant to indicate that the understanding of the mode of being of the social, cultural and historical world is in terms of the ideas explicated by Hans-Georg Gadamer in his writings including his magnum opus *Truth and Method* (2004). Since Gadamer's philosophical hermeneutics is more ontological then epistemological, I am sure his views are congenial to the concerns of the present volume, i.e. ontological sociality.

as the subject of the knowledge, which has society as its object, he conceives of himself as an individual who can exist independently of society. Such a man by taking the stance of subject reflects himself out of all social relations, he also conceives all men as a subjects, and reflects them out of all social relations, and hence conceives them all as individuals and not belonging to society any more. So the logic of the subject–object dualism applied to society leads inevitably to the collapse of society, i.e. the society is reflected out of existence as no one belongs to it. This is the reason why modernity cannot admit the ontological autonomy of society and admits only the primacy of existence of individuals, and thereby begets metaphysical individualism in philosophy. Together with society, by similar arguments, both tradition and history also get dissolved as no one belongs to tradition and history. The concept of individuals standing in no social relations to each other, and also without tradition and history, is the concept of the state of nature of political philosophy. In the early modern period, philosophers like Hobbes, Locke and Kant followed this line of thinking and arrived at the idea that the natural condition of mankind is not a condition of civil society, rather civil society is an artificial construction from the state of nature through social contract made by the exercise of will by subjective individuals. Thinkers devoted themselves to designing the ideal society that would be constructed artificially from state of nature and the favoured ideal was a liberal society of one form or another incorporating rights, liberties, equality, justice, etc.

From nineteenth century onwards, when some branches of humanities self-consciously adopted the method of natural sciences and conceived themselves as social sciences, they dropped one of the assumptions of the philosophers described above. The social scientists dropped the assumption that every man has become or conceives himself as a modern subjective individual to gain objective knowledge of society. This dropping of the crucial assumption made it possible to make available the object of their study. For social scientists, most of mankind still belongs to society, history and tradition and hence society, tradition, history are available to them for objective study methodologically. It is the privilege of the social scientist that they have acquired the capacity to objectify society and investigate society objectively through empirical methods as they are the only subjects who can acquire such knowledge by bracketing their own subjectivity from objective knowledge of society.

The objective knowledge of sciences—whether of natural or social sciences—is knowledge of causalities, tendencies, trends, and statistical correlations operating in the objects of their investigations. Hence, scientific knowledge is geared to control and dominate the object. The projected theories in sciences are conceived in terms of the will to dominate what exists. While natural sciences are geared for technology, social sciences are geared for social engineering piecemeal or wholesale. Sciences, through modern education, have turned everyone into *homo fabers*, both in the natural and social sphere, standing apart from both but trying to transform both to satisfy their goals. With the coming of modern sciences men have ceased to be *homo sapiens* 'wise men', and have ceased to be *homo ludens,* they have turned into *homo fabers* 'men the makers' who make things artificially—including their dwellings, families, societies, and also intervene artificially to modify the surrounding environment, society, nature and everything they fancy.

Here social sciences have landed Man in a double contradiction, i.e. in theory and practice. In theory: whatever theories are proposed in social sciences are based on assuming every member of society to be a subjective individual constituting society through inter-subjective interaction while the object of their study is made available to them for empirical and methodical investigation by dropping this assumption. In practice: the ideals for social transformation are conceived by assuming every member of society to be a subjective individual while the knowledge of social engineering is achieved by dropping this assumption.

This double contradiction of social sciences is taking a toll on people. Even in the eighteenth century, there were prophets for transformation of society to suit their fancied ideals in Europe. But the massive supporting forces of European culture, Christianity, humanism, the heritage of antiquity, and the old forms of political organization being decisive contained the effects of attempted transformation. If one thinks of transformation unleashed by the French Revolution, whereby a new lower estate, the third estate, entered decisively into social life, it was not so revolutionary, for this third estate too lived for the most part as conditioned by religion and tradition. The destruction of social solidarity was still postponed. But now having become *homo fabers*, awareness has been pervaded by a new expectation. Everyone now expects to rationally reorganize society and economy by intentional planning with knowledge of social engineering and resolute application of technological capacity to social life. For this experts are needed as an indispensable figure of society. Man has become beholden to experts for practical, social and political decisions. But due to the double contradiction in the knowledge of the social experts, they cannot fulfil everyone's heightened expectations from them. And yet these experts have come to play a decisive role in public opinion formation through technologies of information. On the other hand, as people have abandoned their judgement in favour of guidance from experts, more and more people are manning the social apparatus and fewer and fewer are making the decisions. This is social irrationality built into the very assumption of social sciences as double contradictions as explained above, leading to the destruction of social solidarities, pitting one people against another and which is not only making universal the condition of alienation (*Fremdheit*) but also intensifying it through the passage of time, making the problem of alienation more acute.

To overcome this social irrationality and to rehabilitate reason and judgement in social practices, the primordial being needs to be recovered at home in the world. One needs to belong to the world. To fulfil this demand, some sociologists have tried to use Husserl's idea of lifeworld to which all belong. Edmund Husserl introduced the concept of the lifeworld in *The Crisis of European Sciences* (1970 [1936]):

In whatever way we may be conscious of the world as universal horizon, as coherent universe of existing objects, we, each 'I-the-man' and all of us together, belong to the world as living with one another in the world; and the world is our world, valid for our consciousness as existing precisely through this 'living together'. We, as living in wakeful world-consciousness, are constantly active on the basis of our passive having of the world . . . Obviously this is true not only for me, the individual ego; rather we, in living together, have the world pre-given in this together, belong, the world as world for all, pre-given with this ontic meaning . . . The we-subjectivity. . . [is] constantly functioning.

The lifeworld is only an inter-subjective world where individuals are still characterized with subjectivity. Husserl could not rise above the subject object dualism, nor did the two sociologists Schütz and Habermas who made use of the idea of lifeworld following him.

II

It is needed to think afresh as to the mode of being of the world, especially the social, cultural, historical world to which one belongs. My starting point, in an earlier essay (Agarwala 2004), was the concept of play, as one aspect of the mode of being of the world is the mode of being of play. The mode of being of player does not allow the player to behave towards play as if it is an object and he the subject.[1] Rather the player is absorbed in the play as he loses himself in the play. Play proper is in-being when the player plays seriously. Play has its own essence, independent of the consciousness of players. Play proper exists when players do not conceive of themselves as being-for-itself of subjectivity, and where they do not behave 'playfully' as subjective individuals. Players are not the subjects of play; instead play merely reaches presentation (*Darstellung*) through the players. Play is to-and-fro movement that is not tied to any goal that would bring it to an end. Since the movement of playing has no goal that brings it to an end, it renews itself in constant repetition. The movement backward and forward is central to the definition of play and it makes no difference who or what performs this movement. The movement of play as such has, as it were, no substrate. It is the game that is played, it is irrelevant whether or not there is a subject who plays it. Play is the occurrence of the movement as such. Hence, the mode of being of play is not such that, for the game to be played, there must be a subject who is behaving playfully. Play is not to be understood as something a person does. The actual subject of play is not the subjectivity of an individual who, among other activities, also plays but is instead the play itself. The *primacy of play over the consciousness of the player* is fundamental in this phenomenological understanding of play. Play represents an order in which the to-and-fro motion of play follows of itself. It is part of play that the movement is not only without goal or purpose but also without effort. It happens, as it were, by itself. This does not mean that there is no effort by the players rather it refers phenomenologically only to the absence of strain, felt by players, as relaxation. The structure of play absorbs the player into itself, and thus frees him from the strain of taking the initiative. Hence, the spontaneous tendency to repetition emerges in the player in the constant self-renewal of play. All playing is a being-played. The game masters the players. It is this fact that constitutes the attraction of a game. The fascination the game exerts consists precisely in the fact that whoever 'tries' is in fact the one who is tried. The real subject of the game is not the player, but instead the game itself. What holds the player in its spell, draws him into play, and keeps him there is the game itself. Every game has its own proper spirit, by which it suffuses the players. Games differ from one another in their spirit. The to-and-fro movement that constitutes the game is patterned in various ways due to difference in the spirit of the game. The particular spirit of a game is partially manifested in the rules and regulations that prescribe the way the field of the game is filled with to-and-fro movements. The playing field, on which the game is played, is set by the spirit of the game itself. It is defined far more by the structure that determines the movement of the game from within by its spirit than by the external boundaries of the open space that it comes up against, limiting movement from without. Play sets off the sphere of play as a closed world, one without transition and meditation to the outside world, i.e. outside of play. The world of play is a self-contained whole. All play is playing something, where the ordered to-and-fro movement of the game is determined as one kind of comportment (*Verhalten*) among many other possibilities of comportment.[2] Every game presents the man who plays it with a task. He cannot enjoy the freedom of playing himself out without transforming the aims of his purposive behaviour into mere tasks of the game and adopting the tasks of the game as his own aims. And yet the purpose of the game is not really solving the task, but ordering and shaping the movement of the game itself that comes about in solving the task. One can say that performing a task successfully 'presents it' (*stellt sie dar*). Here, fulfilling the task does not point to any purposive context. Play is really limited to presenting itself. Thus, its mode of being is self-presentation. As self-presentation is a universal ontological characteristic of nature, play is natural. The self-representation of human play depends on the player's conduct being tied to the goals of the game set for him, but the 'meaning' of these goals does not, in fact, depend on their being achieved. Rather, in spending oneself on the task of the game, one is in fact playing oneself out. The self-presentation of the game involves the player's achieving his own self-presentation by playing, i.e. presenting, something. What has been noticed in the mode of being of play also holds good with respect to the mode of being of all social, cultural historical world.[3] But it is just one aspect of the mode of being of world. There are other aspects in the mode of being of the world.

III

The second aspect of the mode of being of the world, from which science attempts to abstract an objective world in itself, is that the world is profoundly verbal in nature (see Gadamer 2004: 436–52). The social, cultural historical world is sustained in language. As every individual member grows into a language, which maintains an independent existence, it introduces him to a particular orientation and relationship, i.e. comportment to the world. Yet language has no independent life apart from the world that comes into presentation in it. The world is a world only insofar as it comes into representation in language, and at the same time language, too, has its real being only in the fact that the world is presented in it.

'To *have* a world' means to have an orientation or comportment towards it. The orientation towards the world that amounts to having a world, allows one to keep oneself so free from what one encounters of the world that one can present it to oneself as it is. It is this capacity for freedom from the world that is at once a capacity to have a world and to have language. Wherever language and people exist, there is not only a freedom from the pressure of the world, but this freedom from the world is also freedom in relation to the language. That is to say, that it is freedom to present the same world in different languages. The verbal constitution of the world does not amount to Man being imprisoned within a specific verbally schematized environment. Because of the freedom from the world, man has a multiplicity of diverse languages, as well as a general verbal relationship to the world. Since man can always rise above the particular environment in which he happens to find himself, and because his speech brings the world into language, he is, from the beginning, free for variety in exercising his capacity for language and world views.

The free, distanced orientation, that man has to world, which is linguistic through and through, is realized in language as unique *factualness* (*Sachlichkeit*) of language. It is matter of fact (*Sachverhalte*) that comes into presentation in language. That a thing behaves (*eine Sache verhalt sich*) in various ways permits one to recognize its independent otherness, which presupposes a real distance between the speaker and the thing. That something can foreground itself as a genuine matter of fact and become the content of an assertion that others can understand depends on the free distanced orientation of man to the world. In the structure of a matter of fact that foregrounds itself, there is always a negative aspect as well. To be this and not that, constitutes the determinacy of all beings. Fundamentally, therefore, there are also negative matters of fact. What is thus conceived of as existing is not really the *object* (*Gegenstand*) of statements, but what 'comes to language in statements'. But the factualness of language misleads one into thinking that the essence of language is statement and statements are about objects (*Gegenstand*).

Here it must be understood that language has its true being only in dialogue, in *coming to an understanding*. That is to say language is not to be understood as a system of signs that sets up a means of communication for the purposes of coming to an understanding. Coming to an understanding is not a purpose. Coming to an understanding is a life process in which community of life is lived out. Hence human language must be thought of as a special and unique life process, that manifests itself in dialogue, and in which a 'world' is disclosed. Reaching an understanding in language places a subject matter before those discussion partners like a disputed object set between them. Thus the world is the common ground, trodden by none and recognized by all, uniting all who talk to one another. Every human community is a linguistic community. Since, language is by nature the language of conversation; it fully realizes itself only in the process of coming to an understanding. That is why language is not a mere means in the process of coming to an understanding.

Hence, invented artificial system of signs for communication is never a language. Artificial sign systems, such as systems of mathematical symbols, always presuppose a prior agreement, which is that of natural language. It is known that the consensus by which an artificial language is introduced necessarily belongs to another language, a natural language. In a real community of language, on the other hand, one does not first decide to agree on language but are always already in agreement, the language already exists even before one decides to agree. The object of understanding in dialogue is not the verbal means of communication as such but rather the world that presents itself in common life and that embraces everything about which understanding can be reached. Agreeing about a language is not the paradigmatic case but rather a special case of agreement. The so called agreement on a language is nothing but agreeing about an instrument, a system of signs, which does not have its being in dialogue but serves as a means rather to convey information. Hence the objective world in itself represented through the artificial mathematical sign system of modern sciences sustained by the prior natural language that discloses a common world. The verbal world in which one lives is not a barrier that prevents knowledge of being-in-itself, but fundamentally embraces everything in which one's insight can be enlarged and deepened.

Even though each particular linguistic and cultural tradition presents the world in a different way from other traditions, even though the historical 'worlds' that succeed one another in the course of history are different from one another and from the world of today, the world presented by every tradition is verbally constituted. As verbally constituted, every such world is of itself open to every possible insight and hence to every expansion of its own world picture, and is accordingly available to others and others are available to it.

The verbal worlds of different traditions are not relative in the sense that one could oppose them to the 'world in itself'. There is no such right view from some possible position outside the human, linguistic world that could discover world in its being-in-itself. It is part of the meaning of every human, linguistically constituted view of the world that the world can exist without man and perhaps will do so. In every world view the existence of the world-in-itself is intended. But this world-in-itself intended in every verbal world is only the whole world that is never grasped as a whole but aspired to be grasped as a whole in language. In Gadamer's words:

every word breaks forth as if from a center and is related to a whole, through which alone it is a word. Every word causes the whole of the language to which it belongs to resonate and the whole world-view that underlies it to appear. Thus every word, as the event of a moment, carries with it the unsaid, to which it is related by responding and summoning. The occasionality of human speech is not a casual imperfection of its expressive power; it is, rather, the logical expression of the living virtuality of speech that brings a totality of meaning into play, without being able to express it totally. All human speaking is finite in such a way that there is laid up within it an infinity of meaning to be explicated and laid out. (2004: 454)

The multiplicity of these world views does not make the 'world' relative. Rather, the world is not different from the views in which it presents itself. The 'world-in-itself' of verbal world view is nothing but the continuity with which the various linguistic perspectives on world shade into one another. Each shading of verbal world views potentially contains every other one within it, i.e. each worldview can be extended into every other. It can understand and comprehend, from within itself, the 'view' of the world presented in another language. That a person's experience of the world is bound to language does not imply an exclusiveness of perspectives. The verbal experience of the world has the capacity to embrace the most varied relationships of life.

A person who opposes 'world-in-itself' to these 'aspects' must think either theologically—in which case the 'world-in-itself' is not for him but only for God—or he will think like Lucifer, like one who wants to prove his divinity by the fact that the whole world has to obey him and the whole world is amenable to his will. In this case the world's being-in-itself is a limitation of and resistance to the omnipotence of his imaginative planning. The world of objects that science knows, and from which it derives its own objectivity, is one of the relativities embraced by language's relation to the world. In it the concept of 'being-in-itself' acquires the character of a *determination of the will*. What exists in itself is independent of one's own willing and imagining. But in being known in its being-in-itself, it is put at one's disposal in the sense that one can reckon with it, i.e. use it for one's own purposes. What exists 'in itself' in the sense of object of study of modern science allows for the possibility of certain knowledge, which permits one to control things. The certified facts are like the object (*Gegenstand*) and its resistance (*Widerstand*) consists in that one has to reckon with them. What exists in itself, then, is relative to a particular way of knowing and willing. This does not imply that some particular science is concerned in a special way with dominating what exists and, on the basis of this will to dominate, determining the real meaning of being-in-itself. The world model of mechanics is related in a special way to the capacity to make things, but the knowledge of all the natural sciences is 'knowledge for domination'. Even social sciences aim at getting knowledge that will enable it to dominate and make it the society imagined. It is an error of science to think that the world is a world of being-in-itself where all relativity has been surpassed and where knowledge can be called an absolutely certain knowledge. The very concept of an 'absolute object' is a contradiction in terms. The being-in-itself towards which research, whether in natural or social sciences, is directed is relative to the way being is posited in its manner of enquiry. There is not the slightest reason, beyond this, to admit science's metaphysical claim to know being-in-itself. Each science, as a science, has in advance projected a field of objects such that to know them is to control them.

As against objective world in itself posited by sciences, in language the world itself presents itself. Verbal experience of the world is prior to everything that is recognized and addressed as existing. That language and world are related in a fundamental way does not imply that world is the object of language. Rather, the object of knowledge and statements is always already enclosed within the world horizon of language. That human experience of the world is verbal does not imply that a world-in-itself is being objectified. When man's relationship to the world is considered as a whole, as it is expressed in language, a different situation is discovered. The world that appears in language and is constituted by it does not have, in the same sense, being-in-itself, and is not relative in the same sense as the object of the natural and social sciences. It is not being-in-itself, insofar as it is not characterized by objectivity and can never be given in experience as the comprehensive whole that it is. But as the world that it is, it is not relative to a particular language either. For to live in a linguistic world, as one does as a member of a linguistic community, does not mean that one is placed in an environment as animals are. The linguistic world cannot be seen from above in this way, for there is no point of view outside the experience of the world in language from which it could become an object. None of the sciences—natural or social—provides this point of view, because the world, i.e. the totality of what exists, is not the object of research and calculation of any of the sciences. Nor does comparative linguistics, which studies the structure of languages, have any nonlinguistic point of view from which one could know the in-itself quality of what exists and for which the various forms of the linguistic experience of the world could be constructed, as a schematized selection, from what exists in itself—in a way analogous to animal habitats, the principles of whose structure are studied Rather, every language has a direct relationship to the infinity of beings. To have language involves a mode of being that is quite different from the way animals are confined to their habitat. By learning foreign languages men do not alter their relationship to the world, like an aquatic animal that becomes a land animal; rather, while preserving their own relationship to the world, they extend and enrich it by the world of the foreign language. Whoever has language 'has' the world.

If this is kept in mind, the factualness (Sittlichkeit) of language will no longer be confused with the *objectivity (Objektivität) of science*. The distance involved in a linguistic relationship to the world does not, as such, produce the objectivity that the sciences achieve by eliminating the subjective elements of the cognitive process. The distance and the factualness of language, of course, are also genuine achievements and do not just happen automatically. It is known how putting an experience into words helps cope with it. It is as if it is threatening, even annihilating, immediacy is pushed into the background, brought into proportion, made communicable, and hence dealt with. Such coping with experience, however, is obviously something different from the way science works on it, objectivizing it and making it available for whatever purposes it likes. Once a scientist has discovered the law of a natural or social process, he has it in his power. No such thing is possible in the natural experience of the world expressed in language. Using language by no means involves making things available and calculable. It is not just that the statement or judgement is merely one particular form among the many other linguistic orientations—they themselves remain bound up with man's life orientation. Consequently, objectivizing science regards the linguisticality of the natural experience of the world as a source of prejudices.

When the linguistic nature of world is joined with its play nature, what emerges is the nature of world as language game, as conceived by Wittgenstein. Gadamer writes, '*Language games* exist where we, as learners—and when does one cease to be that?—rise to understanding of the world' (2004: 484).

IV

The third aspect of the world is its radical temporality. Section II of the chapter ended with the idea that play, as well as the world, is a self-presentation of itself. All presentation is potentially a representation for someone, i.e. the spectator. The mode of being of play is not determined merely by the fact that players are completely absorbed in it, but also by the fact that they play their role in relation and regard to the whole of the play, in which not they but the audience is to become absorbed. The spectator has methodological precedence in that when the play is presented for him, the meaning that the play bears within itself is understood and that can therefore be detached from the behaviour of the players.

When play comes to its true consummation in being understood by the spectator, the play undergoes *transformation into structure* (Gadamer 2004: 110). Only through this transformation does play achieve ideality, and emerge as detached from the representing activity of the players and consist in the pure appearance (Erscheinung) of what they are playing. Now play is in principle repeatable and hence permanent. In this sense it is a structure (Gebilde). In relation to the players, the play has an absolute autonomy. In being presented in play, what 'is' emerges. Audience is supposed to recognize what it 'is'. It is this aspect of the play when related to language appears as the factualness of language. Freedom from the world and the factualness of language depend on the capacity to be spectators of the play.

There is another aspect of transformation, that emerges when it is contrasted with change. Transformation is not change, even a far-reaching change. Change always means that something in what is changed also remains the same and is maintained as such. However totally it may change, only something changes in it. To put it in philosophical jargon all change is change of quality, i.e. of an accident of substance, but the substance remains the same. But transformation means that something is suddenly and as a whole something else, that this other transformed thing that it has become is its true being, in comparison with which its earlier being is nothing. There cannot here be any gradual transformation leading from one to the other, since the one is the denial of the other. Thus transformation into structure means that what existed previously exists no longer. But also that what now exists, what represents itself in the play, is the lasting and true. This gives the term 'transformation into structure' its full meaning. The transformation is a transformation into the true. In being presented in play, what is emerges. It produces and brings to light what is otherwise constantly hidden and withdrawn. Audience is supposed to recognize what it 'is'. This refers to the speculative structure of play, which will be analysed later in the essay.

Here there arises a possible objection. How can a person's being-in-the-world be interpreted as the engrossment of the player and spectator in the play? Player is playing on the stage while the spectator cannot enter the stage, his entering the stage would destroy the play. So engrossment in *the world* cannot be of the mode of *player* and *spectator* simultaneously since it is contradictory. How can one get out of this contradiction? Being in the world, with engrossment in it as *players* and *spectators,* is radically temporal in nature. This temporal and historical nature of one's being-in-the-world helps in avoiding the contradiction mentioned above. Every person is the spectator of the past of his/her play. The temporal difference and distance ensures the condition of the *spectators*, he/she cannot go back to the past to interfere in it. They are players of the play that is going on now. Hence there is no contradiction. This condition of historicity of being-in-the-world has to be understood properly. The *spectators* of the *play* that has taken place in the past, are themselves would-be players of the play that is continuing. Since there is no *telos* of the play outside itself, the players cannot organize their activities with reference to it to participate in the *play*. Hence, the would-be players become spectators of the *past of the play* to learn how to continue the *play* themselves. But this radical temporality of play of the world displays other ontological features of the world also.

'Transformation into structure' that takes place for the spectators of the play points to the ideality, repeatability, and permanence of the play. Play is structure—this means that despite its dependence on being played it is a meaningful whole, which can be repeatedly represented as such and the significance of which can be understood. But structure is also play, because it achieves its full being only each time it is played. No doubt there is a differentiation between 'what is being represented' in the play from the representing activity of players who are presenting the play, but play as structure, play as understood, play as what is presented does not exist anywhere independently of the representing activity of players. To put it another way, even though a distinction is made between a play and its performance, yet play has its being in performance. What has been called a structure is one insofar as it presents itself as a meaningful whole of what is presented in performance.

The variety of the performances or realizations of such a structure are not subjective variety of conceptions of the same play. Rather, these multiplicity of performances are play's own possibilities of being that emerge as the play explicates itself, as it were, in the variety of its aspects. Hence there cannot be any canonization of a particular representation as a correct representation of the play. A 'correctness' striven for in this way, to look for a unique correct representation of the play, would not do justice to the true binding nature of the play, which imposes itself on every player immediately, in its own way, and does not allow him to make things easy for himself by simply imitating a so-called correct model. In the socio-cultural world there is no such unique correct model of any socio-cultural world to be imitated or preserved. Every age has to understand one's own socio-cultural world in a different way, every linguistic community articulates the world in different ways.

The 'freedom' of interpretative choice is not external and marginal phenomena, rather the whole performance is both bound and free. It is bound because it is an interpretation of the play, but it is free in that there can be multiplicity of interpretation. In a certain sense performance probably is re-creation, but this is a re-creation not of the creative act but of the play itself, which has to be brought to representation in accord with the meaning the player has found in it as spectator.

In view of the finitude of man's historical existence, it would seem that there is something absurd about the whole idea of a unique, correct interpretation. Here the obvious fact that every interpretation tries to be correct serves only to confirm that the non-differentiation of the performance from the play itself is the actual experience of the play. The distinction between the play and its performance is available only where the interpretation breaks down. In other words, when the performance does not become, as such, thematic, then the play presents itself through it and in it.

It is interesting to note that the world presents its multifarious views in multiplicity of languages, as play presents its multiple possibilities of interpretation and performance for different spectators in different situations. And yet neither the world nor the play loses its identity in being dissolved into their multiple possibilities. Rather all the possibilities belong to the same world and the same play.

There is a need to ask what this identity of the play and the world is that presents itself so differently in the changing course of ages and circumstances. It does not disintegrate into the changing aspects of itself so that it would lose all identity, but it is there in them all. They all belong to it. They are all *contemporaneous* with it. Thus, it is necessary to understand the radical temporality of play and the world, i.e. it is necessary to understand the world in terms of time. This takes one to the next aspect of the world.

V

Fourthly, the world has being in celebration, to use a metaphor, as it does not exist as an object in itself (*Gegenstand*). This emerges from the understanding of radical temporality of the world. The being-of-the-world is contemporaneous of every time. This kind of temporal structure is exhibited by festivals. It is in the nature of periodic festivals, at least, to be repeated. It is called the return of the festival. But the festival that comes round again is neither another festival nor a mere remembrance of the one that was originally celebrated. The time experience of the festival is rather its *celebration*. From its inception—whether instituted in a single act or introduced gradually—the nature of a festival is to be celebrated regularly. Thus its own original essence is always to be something different (even when celebrated in exactly the same way). An entity that exists only by always being something different is temporal in a more radical sense than everything that belongs to history. It has its being only in becoming and return. A festival exists only in being celebrated. This is not to say that it is of a subjective character and has its being only in the subjectivity of those celebrating it. Rather, the festival is celebrated because it is there. The same is true of play and the world: it must be presented for the spectator, to be understood, and having understood what it is that is being presented, present it himself in his time as a player. This is how the play exists in understanding playing of the play in one's own time.

There is a need to understand how this happens. The being of the spectator is determined by his 'being there present'. Being present does not simply mean being there along with something else that is there at the same time. To be present means to participate. If someone was present at something, he knows all about how it really was. It is only in a derived sense that presence at something means also a kind of subjective act, that of paying attention to something. Thus, watching something is a genuine mode of participating. This idea lies behind the original Greek concept of *theoria*. *Theoros* means someone who takes part in a delegation to a festival. Such a person has no other distinction or function than to be there. Thus the *Theoros* is a spectator in the proper sense of the word, since he participates in the solemn act through his presence at it. In the same way, as Greek metaphysics conceives the essence of theoria and of nous as being purely present to what is truly real, for others too the ability to act theoretically is defined by the fact that in attending to something one is able to forget one's own purposes. But *theoria* is not to be conceived primarily as subjective conduct, as a self-determination of the subject, but in terms of what it is contemplating. *Theoria* is a true participation, not something active but something passive (pathos), namely, being totally involved in and carried away by what one sees. That is to say, the spectator engrossed in play is not to be conceived as the self-conscious subjective observer standing over against the object to observe it methodically.

There is also an essential difference between a spectator who gives himself entirely to the play of world and someone who is merely a curious onlooker. It is characteristic of curiosity that the onlooker is as if drawn away by what he looks at, that he forgets himself entirely in it, and cannot tear himself away from it. But the important thing about an object of curiosity is that it is basically of no concern to the onlooker; it has no significance for him. There is nothing in it, which he would really be able to come back to and which would hold his attention focused permanently. It is the formal quality of novelty, i.e. abstract difference that makes up the charm of what one looks at out of curiosity. One becomes bored and jaded when the novelty wears off after some time. In contrast that which presents itself to the spectator as the play of world does not simply exhaust itself in momentary transport, but has a claim to permanence and the permanence of a claim. The 'claim' is very significant here.

A claim is something lasting. Its justification (or pretended justification) is the primary thing. Because a claim lasts, it can be enforced at any time. A claim exists against someone and must therefore be enforced against him; but the concept of a claim also implies that it is not itself a fixed demand, the fulfillment of which is agreed on by both sides, but is rather the ground for such. A claim is the legal basis for an unspecified demand. If it is to be answered in such a way as to be settled, then to be enforced it must first take the form of a demand. It belongs to the permanence of a claim that it is concretized in a demand. (Gadamer 2004: 123)

So the play of the world has a permanent claim and a claim of permanence that needs to be concretized as a demand by being understood. Here there is no distinction of is and ought. The play of the world is moral and ethical like the *sittlichkeit* of Hegel and *ethos* of Aristotle. This explains why player has to be spectator and spectator has to be player. This is the permanent claim always needing to be concretized, placed by the world on the person to which he/she belongs.

Thus, contemporaneity is not a mode of givenness of an object to a subjective consciousness, but a task and an achievement that is demanded of one as a claim of the world to which one belongs. It consists in holding on to the world in such a way that it becomes 'contemporaneous', which is to say, 'contemporaneity' does not mean 'existing at the same time'. Rather, it names the task that confronts one, the task of understanding as a spectator and playing as a player in the world, so that the moral and ethical world continues to be in being permanently.

VI

The fifth aspect of the mode of being of the world is that *belonging* refers to the transcendental relationship between being and truth. For *belonging*, knowledge is conceived as an element of being itself and not primarily as an activity of the subject. That knowledge is incorporated in being is the presupposition of belonging to the being. Here thought does not start from the concept of a subject that exists in its own right and makes everything else an object. In this thinking there is no question of a self-conscious spirit without world, which would have to find its way to world: both belong originally to each other. The relationship of belonging together is primary. Hence, to belong to being thinking must always regard itself as an element of being itself. Parmenides considered this to be the most important signpost on the way to the truth of being. In thinking what thought experiences is the movement of the thing itself. One needs to recover and learn this kind of thinking which is the self giving of the being to thought, if he/she wants to recover concept of belonging and wants to go beyond the idea of the object and the objectivity of modern scientific knowledge towards the idea that subject and object belong together, i.e. to the world. One's involvement in the play of world as spectator and player ensures that the understanding belongs to the being understood.

For this one needs to understand the figure of spectator of the play of world and the distance from the world that it implies even when he belongs to the world. In the context of lived world experience of spectator is the nature of occurrence, i.e. in the experience of the lived world something occurs. Seen from the point of view of the spectator belonging to the lived world, 'occurrence' means that he is not an active knower seeking an object, 'discovering' by methodological means what was really meant and what the situation actually was, though slightly hindered and affected by his own prejudices. Here there is an element of passivity of thought that needs to be acknowledged. The actual occurrence is made possible only because the word of the lived world that has come down to one as tradition and to which he is to listen really encounters him , and does so as if it addressed him and is concerned with him, and this occurrence defines correctly the meaning of belonging as it pertains to his experience of the lived world. From tradition, one cannot actively control what addresses a person and how he/she is addressed. This condition of belonging to the world is ensured by one being a spectator of the world's past due to temporal distance. The temporal distance from the past ensures that one cannot control that which addresses one from the past.

On the other side, that of the thing, this occurrence means the coming into play, the playing out, of the content of tradition in its constantly widening possibilities of signification and resonance, extended by the different people receiving it. Inasmuch as the tradition is newly expressed in language, something comes into being that had not existed before and that exists from now on. As noted when the play transforms into structure by being understood by the spectator, this ideality of play that is understood is not something subjective but the very possibility that is of the play itself, that is there henceforth, which was not there before this understanding. Here understanding of the spectator is not a methodic subjective activity of the spectator, but the activity of the play itself that the spectators suffer in which what is represented in the play emerges into being henceforth.

Methodic activity of the scientific observer is based on the model of seeing the alienated object standing over against him. But the idea of belonging (*Zugehörigkeit*) to the world is related to the idea of *hearing* (*hören*) also. 'It is not just that he who hears is also addressed but also that he who is addressed must hear whether he wants to or not' (Gadamer 2004: 458). It is a moral and ethical demand. When one looks at something, he can also look away from it by looking in another direction, but one cannot 'hear away' in this way. Because of this difference between seeing and hearing, the latter has primacy as the basis of belonging. 'There is nothing that is not available to hearing through the medium of language' (Gadamer 2004: 458). All the other senses have no immediate share in the universality of the verbal experience of the world. They only offer the knowledge of their own specific fields, but hearing is an avenue to the whole because it is able to listen to the logos. It is needed to recover the ancient insight into the priority of hearing over sight to recover the idea of belonging. Since, the language heard is universal, in the sense that everything can be expressed in it, in contrast to all other experiences of the world, language opens up a completely new dimension, the profound dimension from which tradition comes down to those now living. Tradition's addressing one brings about belonging. Everyone who is situated in a tradition—including even the man who considers himself free from all history like the social scientist—must listen to what reaches him from it. The truth of tradition is like the present that lies immediately open to the senses.

And yet the mode of being of tradition, and hence that of lived world, is not sensible immediacy unlike the case with mode of being of objects of science. It is language, and in interpreting its texts, the hearer who understands it relates its truth to his own linguistic orientation to the world.

This linguistic communication between present and tradition is the event that takes place in all understanding.

This structure of the hermeneutical experience, experience of the lived world totally contradicts the idea of scientific methodology. It itself depends on the character of language as event of conversation. Language as event means among other things that the use and development of language is a process of conversation, which has no single knowing and choosing consciousness standing over against it to guide it, unlike what happens in artificial technical language of science. The other more important point is that what constitutes the hermeneutical event proper, the coming into language of what has been said in the tradition. This is an event that is at once appropriation and interpretation. This event is not one's action upon the thing, but the act of the thing itself.

The modern scientific method that dealt with the objective thing in itself is alien to it and it is only an 'external reflection'. The true method was an action of the thing itself. This assertion does not mean that hermeneutical cognition is not also an activity, or an effort. But this activity and this effort consist in not interfering arbitrarily with the immanent necessity of the unfolding of thought unlike what happens when one latches onto this or that ready-made notion as it strikes one. Certainly, the thing does not go its own course without one's thinking being involved, but thinking means unfolding what consistently follows from the subject matter itself. It is part of this process to suppress ideas 'that tend to insinuate themselves' and to insist on the logic of the thought. In all thought, only pursuing what consistently follows from the subject matter can bring out what lies in it. It is the thing itself that asserts its force, if the entire reliance is on the power of thought and there is disregard for obvious appearances and opinions. The hermeneutical experience of the world is an activity of the thing itself, an action that, unlike the methodology of modern science, is a passion, an understanding, an event that happens to one.

The hermeneutical experience of the world requires rigour of uninterrupted listening. A thing does not present itself to the hermeneutical experience without an effort special to it, namely that of 'being negative toward itself'. A person who is trying to understand a text has to keep something at a distance—namely everything that suggests itself, on the basis of his own prejudices, as the meaning expected—as soon as it is rejected by the sense of the text itself. The experience of reversal (which happens unceasingly in talking) has its presence here. Explicating the whole of meaning towards which understanding is directed forces one to make interpretive conjectures and to take them back again. The self-cancellation of the interpretation makes it possible for the thing itself—the meaning of the text—to assert itself. The movement of the interpretation is dialectical not primarily because the one-sidedness of every statement can be balanced by another side—this is, as shall be seen, a secondary phenomenon in interpretation—but because the word that interpretatively fits the meaning of the text expresses the whole of this meaning, i.e. allows an infinity of meaning to be presented within it in a finite way.

VII

The sixth aspect of the world is that in its being it is speculative. The word 'speculative' here is derived from 'speculum', i.e. mirror (see Gadamer 2004: 453–69). That is speculative which has the structure similar to that of something being reflected in the mirror.

Being reflected involves a constant substitution of one thing for another. When something is reflected in something else, say, the castle in the lake, it means that the lake throws back the image of the castle. The mirror image is essentially connected with the actual sight of the thing through the medium of the observer. It has no being of its own; it is like an 'appearance' that is not itself and yet allows the thing to appear by means of a mirror image. It is like a duplication that is still only the one thing. The real mystery of a reflection is the intangibility of the image, the sheer reproduction hovering before the mind's eye. (Gadamer 2004: 461)

Every possibility of the play that is reflected by being understood by the spectator is like an image that is thrown back on the original. It is the image in which the original itself emerges. Every world view that comes to the language is just an image of the world, the image that belongs to the world, as it is the same world that appears in the multiplicity of languages.

Hence, speculative means the opposite of the dogmatism of everyday experience. The world, as experienced in its coming to be in language, overturns one's previous experience. Every understanding of the world articulated by different linguistic communities is a reflection of the world. Each reflection of the world depending on the nature of medium of reflection that is language is different. Yet as reflected images of the world they all belong to the same world. The very speculative nature of the being of the world requires that multiplicity of linguistic articulation belong to it as its own possibility. There are two other interrelated aspects of the speculative: first, in the speculative thinking presentation is no adventitious activity but the emergence of the thing itself, and second, the representation is not the reflection of something pre-given rather it is the coming into language of a totality of meaning which exists henceforth. So understanding is not a methodic activity of the subject that masters the pre-existent object, but as something that the thing itself does and which thought 'suffers'. This activity of the thing itself is the real speculative movement that takes hold of the speaker. To come into language does not mean that a second being is acquired. Rather, what something presents itself as belongs to its own being and it has its being henceforth as it appears. This was also noticed in the context of the transformation play into structure when that, which is being represented in play, is understood by the spectator. Thus everything that is understood in language has a speculative unity: it contains a distinction, that between its being and its presentation of itself, but this is a distinction that is really not a distinction at all as explained before. Only by a secondary thematization of two things is it possible to make this kind of differentiation. The social world, cultural world, world of economy is not fixed beings in themselves. All these are linguistic worlds with a speculative structure as described above. What appears in the social scientist's study of these worlds is not a reflection of something pre-existent, rather what appears in the study exists from now on which did not exist before. Every study of the social scientist has a backfire effect on the subject matter of its study. Hence, it is naive to believe that a social scientist's study can be objective and ethically neutral. It is peculiar to the subject matter of study of humanities and social sciences that it has its being in its presentation, that it is to be understood in its significance. Self-presentation and being-understood belong together in the subject matter of humanities and social sciences.

The objectifying procedure of natural science and the concept of being-in-itself, which is intended in all knowledge, is only an abstraction when viewed from the medium of language. Abstracted from the fundamental relation to the world that is given in the linguistic nature of experience of it, science attempts to become certain about entities by methodically organizing its knowledge of the world. Consequently, it condemns as heresy all knowledge that does not allow of this kind of certainty and that therefore cannot serve the growing domination of being. But precisely this kind of heretical knowledge is needed to belong to the social world. What exactly is the nature of knowledge, understanding and thinking that belongs to the being understood, which enables one to belong to and to participate in social world uncovering social solidarities? What is the element of happenstance in the speculative thinking, which amounts to the activity of the thing itself that the understanding mind suffers? What is the discipline that needs to be exercised in the effort needed for the happening of understanding? These are questions that will be taken up in another essay.

Notes

1. Here I follow the phenomenological description of play given by Gadamer in *Truth and Method* (2004: 102–10) and *Relevance of Beautiful and Other Essays* (1980: 22–31).
2. Roger Caillois has distinguished at least four basic comportments in the games—agon: competition; alea: chance; mimicry: simulation; ilinx: vertigo in his *Man, Play, and Games* (1961). Translated from the French and with an Introduction by Meyer Barash, New York: The Free Press of Glencoe, Inc., 1961.
3. That nature of culture in its entirety shares in the nature of play and the fact that play is not just part of culture has been noticed by Johann Huizinga (1970), Jacques Ehrmann (1968) and Gadamer (2004: 102–10, 1980: 22–31).

References

Agarwala, Binod Kumar (2004), 'Humanities and Social Sciences in the New Millennium: Theorization in/for Society as Play', in *Creative Social Research: Rethinking Theories and Methods,* ed. Ananta Kumar Giri, Lanman MD: Lexington Books, pp. 253–72.

Caillois, Roger (1961), *Man, Play, and Games,* tr. and with an Introduction by Meyer Barash, New York: The Free Press of Glencoe, Inc.

Ehrmann, Jacques (1968), 'Homo Ludens Revisited', *Yale French Studies,* no. 41, *Game, Play, Literature,* pp. 31–57 (is 'Game, Play, Literature' the title of the Yale French Studies vol.).

Gadamer, Hans-Georg (1980), *Relevance of Beautiful and Other Essays,* tr. Nicholas Walker, Cambridge: CUP.

———(2004), *Truth and Method,* 2nd rev. edn., translated and revised by Joel Weinsheimer and Donald G. Marshall, London, New York: Continuum.

Huizinga, Johann (1970), *Homo Ludens: A Study of the Play-Element in Culture,* London: Paladin.

Husserl, Edmund (1970), *The Crisis of the European Sciences,* Chicago: Northwestern University Press.

17

Ontology Today: Social Science as Discursive Practice Participating in World Creation

PIET STRYDOM

In *Pathways of Creative Research*, Ananta Kumar Giri pursues the highly commendable goal of providing an outline for a new synthetic philosophy of social science attuned to the demands of the times. His strategy is to bring together various late twentieth and early twenty-first century trends and proposals in an attempt to overcome a series of debilitating philosophical assumptions, which have not only reigned in social science for a considerable period, but also contributed to the pathogenesis of modern society. Who could possibly disagree with such an endeavour to open up a space for creative social scientific research that could play a constructive role in the coming into being of a globally expanding social world of legitimately regulated interpersonal relations within the context of a cared for nature?

Yet, there are many things on which it would be worthwhile to linger. A comprehensive discussion of Giri's proposal is impossible, of course, as the ground he covers is too extensive. I propose instead to single out a few matters where his discussion, in my view, could benefit from a little more stringency or rigour. More importantly, I do not think that he has succeeded at every point in his argument in articulating his envisaged balanced position sufficiently clearly. On the one hand, he gestures towards a pluralist philosophy of social science, but on the other he stresses mainly an interpretative philosophy. If his tentative acknowledgement of the potentially fruitful co-existence of the 'quantitative', 'qualitative' and 'critical' approaches marks the first, then the profusely used concept of 'ontology' stands for the second.

Needless to say, it is in this latter respect that the most serious question arises: what is the appropriate way to understand 'ontology' in contemporary philosophy of social science? To make it manageable, I propose to take as my reference point Giri's key concept, 'ontological epistemology of participation'.

'Ontological Epistemology'?

To begin with, it is difficult on first encounter to resist the impression that 'ontological epistemology' is a rather awkward concept. Is it not the case that every epistemology necessarily and unavoidably has its ontology, whether more limited or more expansive, and vice versa? If this is so, then it implies that the expression 'ontological epistemology' is vacuous, for what is required is a more precise or more substantive indication of the type of ontology intended. As against positivism or logical empiricism's one-dimensional ontology of directly observable things and/or events, for instance, Giri obviously has an expanded ontology in mind. Following his text, names such as those of Bergson, particularly Heidegger and also the later Bhaskar, all cited with strong approval, indicate the direction of this expansive move.

To my mind, however, the expression 'ontological epistemology' in association with these names signals that the concept of ontology is used here in a tendential and inflationary way. Witness the extreme proliferation of the adjective 'ontological' in the text. This uncontrolled growth must be curtailed by a specification of the kind of ontology Giri needs in order to qualify the epistemology he has in mind. What potentially redeems his proposal is the fact that, rather than unequivocally joining for instance Heidegger (1963) and Gadamer (1972) in rejecting methodology out of hand in favour of elevating ontology to the be all and end all, he in principle moves within the elastic boundaries of the philosophy of social science and context-sensitive, creative, social scientific research. If he indeed does so in all earnest, however, then he would have to admit that the different social scientific approaches do not only have distinct methodologies, but also their own epistemologies and corresponding ontologies, and in addition he would have to clarify the relations among them. In this latter respect, the expression 'ontological epistemology' could perhaps begin to make sense.

Heideggerian Interpretative Social Science and its Other

Giri's account of creative research is to a significant degree inspired by what Paul Rabinow and William Sullivan (1979) called the 'interpretative turn' in social science. The principal contact point here, however, is Heidegger's hermeneutic phenomenology and some of its offshoots that resonate with Indian, especially Gandhian, thought rather than for instance the linguistic or pragmatic turn or the broad range of creative sociologies. This line of development indeed made a very important contribution, although built on an incomplete and hence shaky foundation. Drawing on Dilthey, Bergson, Husserl, Nietzsche and others, Heidegger (1953, 1963, 1975) not only consolidated the nineteenth-century reversal of the Kantian shift of emphasis from ontology to epistemology but undercut philosophy itself— including the philosophy and methodology of science—by arguing that it is an outcome of Western metaphysics gone wrong. Ironically, this allowed him, and more explicitly still Gadamer (1972), to advance the seminal thesis that all scientific activity and knowledge presuppose an interpretative punctuation of the whole complex of relations with the world. Although Giri hardly mentions Gadamer's name, concepts, which he constantly uses such as 'ontology', 'interpretation', 'dialogue', 'participation' and so forth, all remind one of the German hermeneutic philosopher. I take it that this hermeneutic-phenomenological residue goes a long way towards making clear what Giri's key concept of 'ontological epistemology of participation' is intended to mean.

There are some critical observations that need airing, however. First, considered within the context of the philosophy of social science, ontologically deepened epistemology[1] is so fundamental that it allows one to justify a range of different approaches rather than simply coinciding with a particular, e.g. a positivist or an interpretative approach. Giri's account tends to move the reader in the latter one-sided direction instead of the more plausible pluralist one (see Delanty and Strydom 2003; Strydom 2008). An indication of this tendency is, for instance, his proposal for rethinking theory. To want to replace theory as 'a body of prescriptive and predictive rules' by interpretative theory, whether conceived as 'grounded' theory or as a 'conditional, non-systematic mode of theorizing', is to advocate a narrowing of perspective to only one type of theory among a range of legitimate, albeit in their own ways limited, types in social science. Among the latter, besides interpretative theory, are those types that play a central role in quantitative and in critical social science.[2] Second, this interpretative one-sidedness in turn is closely related to the marked partiality from which the Heideggerian line itself suffers. Even if one ignores Heidegger's ugly Nazi past (and his persistent refusal to acknowledge his mistake?), as Giri counsels, then one cannot overlook the fact that there is a decisive divide in the history of philosophical, social and political thought which, like other chasms, cannot simply be ignored since it is not without consequences for the creation and organization of social life.

From Hegel, who ambivalently set the tracks for the nineteenth-century reaction to Kant, there also stretches besides the right-Hegelian strand, which prepared the ground for Heidegger, a left- or young-Hegelian heritage represented for instance by Marxism (e.g. Marx 1967) and pragmatism (e.g. Peirce 1992, 1998) which graphically shows up the limits of the former. Ontology should not be understood in terms of Heidegger's idealistic pretension to a kind of superior knowledge, which supposedly allows one to escape from modernity. Rather, it must be grasped with reference to the multidimensional world of complex relations in which one lives—a world having, in addition to its pathogenetic characteristics, much stronger features of contingency, openness, ambivalence, uncertainty, self-criticism, self-corrective learning, potentialities and realizable possibilities than the reductive straw-man concept of modernity so fashionably bandied about nowadays gives to understand.

Against this background, some serious unresolved tensions in Giri's account become apparent. First, on the one hand, with Heidegger he believes he has the key to an exit route out of modernity through, for instance, the cultivation of particularistic identities, spiritualization and re-enchantment. On the other hand, he stresses the need to engage with contingencies, while—note well—at the same time failing to recognize that the most outstanding characteristic feature of modernity is precisely that it is the only form of life which is aware of its own contingency and tries to live with it. Second, is it not self-contradictory to insist that it is untenable to subject whole forms of life to criticism and then, nevertheless, to go ahead repeatedly to criticize 'modernity' in exactly this manner, as though it consists of or is exhausted by 'the primacy of epistemology', 'the neglect of ontology', 'theoretical arrogance', 'egoism', 'anthropocentrism' and so forth? Surely, the burden of the critic would be to specify which authors, traditions or directions are guilty of these errors and to acknowledge the disadvantaged and victims rather than tarring everyone with the same brush. Is it not precisely the task of social science, creative social research, to account both for the way the world is and why people want to change it, are able to and, in fact, engage in doing so?

Multidimensional Cultivation of the Self

A major thrust of Giri's argument is that traditional social scientific approaches neglect the vital dimension of the cultivation of the self which is well represented in Indian thought and, lately, has been adopted only hesitantly by Western authors. Behind his position, obviously, stands Heidegger's (1953 Section 64) critique of traditional epistemological theories of the self from an existential and ontological perspective. The young-Hegelian Søren Kierkegaard (e.g. 1992), of course, articulated this very type of interpretation well before the German philosopher, making a responsible and authentic life the formal requirement for every individual. Adding his characteristic qualification, Giri repeatedly speaks of the 'ontological cultivation of the self'. Formulated in a way relevant to the current context, this can be taken to mean that the social scientist, the creative social researcher, while engaging in research, must at all times be aware of resolutely having to live a meaningful life within the larger complex of relevant relations and of being oriented towards the possibility of realizing an authentic form of life. Such an orientation indeed makes sense to me, but a few critical observations are in order here.

First, I am not convinced that such an understanding has been altogether lacking in Western social science. Let just one example be taken—that of the pragmatist George Herbert Mead (1974; Chriss 2005). For him, the self is a social structure that arises in stages in and through communication and the experience of both others and objects, and is then affirmed, modified and transformed in the ongoing process of the constitution and reconstitution together with others of a shared social world which under propitious conditions is understood as universalizing. The conventionally emphasized bare theoretical structure of the 'I' and the 'me' involved here should not be allowed to detract from the depth of Mead's contribution. Not only did he keep the issues of moral validity and ethics at the forefront of his thinking, but more basically still he resolutely took ownership of the self and afforded his work a unity through his lifelong commitment to ethical reciprocity, social reform, the emancipation of blacks and women, and efforts to advance human cooperation at the global level beyond communities and nation states. At one point, Giri mentions Habermas's notion of 'post-conventional moral consciousness', which is closely related to Mead's position. This concept, as is well known, goes back to Jean Piaget (1983) who articulated the idea in the context of the very same early twentieth-century international debate in which Mead developed his understanding. Surely, it must be clear to everyone that, for Habermas too, this is not just some sterile epistemological idea serving mere argumentation or 'techno-praxis'—as it is dismissively put—that is without any consequences for his own self-understanding and relation to himself, to others and the shared social world which is jointly being brought into being? In fact, he stresses throughout his work that one of the normatively significant dimensions of modernity is precisely the requirement of 'self-directed individuation' in the form of an autonomous yet dependent and abstract, flexible but responsible ego-identity (Habermas 1987b: 345; 1979b: 93–4) and, further, that it is directly related to the quality of the social world being brought into being.

Second, Giri's emphatic treatment of the 'ontological' cultivation of the self gives rise to the question whether the cultivation of the self is exclusively a matter of ontology. Several aspects come into purview here. To begin with, there can be no doubt about the importance of the cultivation of the self, as already implied, irrespective of whether it is individual, communal, national or eventually, perhaps, global cosmopolitan identity that is at issue. Given the concurrent phenomenon of in-group/out-group relations, however, particularly the relation between the inner morality of ethnocentric groups and the complementary projection and displacement of latent internal group aggression and conflict on to outside groups, the problem of how the difference between internal and external morality can be bridged is, considering the current challenge of intensifying cultural and civilizational conflict, one of the most urgent tasks of contemporary social science. Giri indeed demands an 'embodied striving for eudaimonia' and a 'spiritualization of practice' in the name of the 'realization of beautiful and dignified worlds', on the one hand, and calls for a 'transcultural and transcivilizational dialogue' between such worlds, on the other. But while he commendably gestures towards 'contestation, conversation and learning', especially 'learning from each other in a transgressive manner' or 'mutually transforming border crossing' involving a 'moment of creative discovery' and thus 'transcendence', he does not systematically link these to the problem of the tension-laden relation between particularlism and universalization.

What needs to be done is that the mechanisms involved be investigated and specified. My point is now that a crucial part of this is epistemological rather than just ontological. This is what Mead (1974) and especially Piaget (2001) analysed—with the latter discovering a parallel development also in Husserl's phenomenological epoché—and what Habermas (1979b) appropriated. The cultivation or formation of the self, whether individual or collective, involves a differentiation of levels in the activities of the subject and their interrelation. Starting from activity in which its concern is with itself, the subject gets taken up into the stream of internal and external events and becomes strongly influenced by the emergent configurations, with the result that its concern diversifies. Above and beyond ontological cultivation but by no means excluding it, the subject is transformed through concern with the general conditions of its activity and the forms of combination, which make possible the coordination of the different levels of the self as well as its relations with objects, others and the encompassing world. Both, the intelligence and conscience, as well as even the emotions are structured by these forms of coordination which relate to the epistemic subject and equally belong to the cultivation task of the self. Insofar as Giri takes on board the notion of post-conventional moral consciousness, as it appears he does, he effectively acknowledges that the formation of subjectivity involves more than ontological cultivation. And insofar as he adds learning to that, which he also seems to suggest, he moves on to a plane that, considering the challenges of the times, should be central to creative social research and, therefore, requires more serious attention than he affords it.

This is perhaps also the appropriate place to register my objection to Giri's uncharitable and, indeed, incorrect characterization of critical social science as lacking 'sufficient acknowledgement of the transcendental dimension of our co-present reality' and suffering from an 'anxiety to distantiate [itself] from any engagement with transcendence'. This comes across like a description of positivism, not of critical theory. As regards the first point, which in the case of social scientific research, can be understood in the sense of social, subjective and natural conditions of possibility, critical theorists like Karl-Otto Apel and Jürgen Habermas, for instance, are more than clear. Apel (1996) stresses what he calls the 'communication community' as the 'transcendental presupposition' of social science, while Habermas elaborates not only on the 'transcendental fact that subjects capable of speech and action, who can be affected by reasons, can learn' (2003: 8), but also on 'natural evolution as a process analogous to learning [which] ensures that structures that have evolved naturally and make our learning processes possible themselves have cognitive content' (2003: 29; see also 2005). As regards the second point, authentic critical social science, which is characterized by its young-Hegelian heritage, from its start in Marx and throughout its elaboration up to Habermas and Axel Honneth (e.g. 2000), has been precisely about transcendence, i.e. meta-level oriented, non-arbitrary learning, transformation and change on the level of the individual, institutions, culture and society aimed at a closer approximation to an authentically lived, reasonable and humane social form of life beyond what one is familiar with at present. The social ontology of critical social science, unlike that of both quantitative and qualitative social science, explicitly includes the understanding of society as an always incomplete phenomenon that emerges from living experience, the historical development of expanding societal relations and conditions within the horizon of the future, and hence from the tension between the real and the possible. Society is by no means exhausted by actuality, since it is simultaneously potentiality, including unfulfilled real possibilities. Moreover, an acute awareness of one's dependence on something unconditional (e.g. Habermas 2003: 99) and, indeed, 'unconditionable' (e.g. Habermas 2005)[3] is to be found in all the major critical theorists. The question that is raised by Giri's criticism, however, is what the appropriate understanding of 'transcendental' and 'transcendence' is. Unfortuntely, I do not find his use of the concepts sufficiently clear to be able to pursue the argument.[4] On reading his text, I sometimes get the faint yet perturbing impression of a connotation of the privileged possession of special knowledge about the unconditional which is directly relevant to social science.

A final point I want to raise about the problematic of the cultivation of the self concerns its sense in the face of one of the central challenges of today. In his exhortation that contemporary social scientists should resolutely engage in the cultivation of the self, Giri proceeds from the assumption of the long-standing understanding of anthropological constants. Under current conditions shaped by the life sciences and biotechnology combined with computer-based information technology, however, there are several signs that the traditional self-understanding of the human species is being transformed (Habermas 2001; Strydom 1999a, 2002). People are today in the process of quite rapidly acquiring the ability not merely to intervene extensively and intensively in nature, but in fact modify and create their own human nature themselves. A new field is being opened up in which anthropological constants are being transformed into biotechnologically manipulable variables and, consequently, previously unquestionable assumptions about the *conditio humana* are becoming progressively invalidated. Is this disturbing phenomenon not indicative of a novel form of cultivation of the self, indeed, ontological cultivation in quite a different sense than that intended by Giri, which also requires urgent and creative social scientific attention?

Participation

Before being somewhat more specific about ontology and, in that context, about transcendence, a few reflections on Giri's concept of 'participation' are in order.

Giri speaks consistently of the 'ontological epistemology of participation'. Considering his various critical observations on the traditionally dominant strand of social science, one could surmise that he understands participation in opposition to objectivism largely in terms of interpretative social science. This intuition is confirmed by his emphasis on the significance for the social scientist who studies, say, a social movement of engaging in 'participation in the dreams and struggles of the activists'. That he nevertheless counters the tendency to go completely native or to become uncritical is borne out by his further demand that both 'sympathetic participation' and 'critical understanding' should be brought into play in social scientific practice. This is, of course, a well-known demand in late twentieth-century social science which, for instance, Habermas (1987a: 153) captured by means of the notions of the 'participant perspective' adopted in the performative attitude, whereby access is obtained to the social world as a meaningful world, and the 'observer perspective' characterized by the objectifying attitude necessary for gaining distance and a critical foothold. Giri himself mentions the well-established concept of 'participant observation', which, if pursued adequately, could possibly achieve what Habermas presents analytically. But this is where the thrust of Giri's proposal becomes apparent. For him, the standard procedure is far too bland in that it does not include an acknowledgement of the 'ontological work on oneself', which could and should give it depth. The social scientist is required to participate in the production of knowledge in such a way that he or she concurrently engages in 'ontological nurturance' aimed at the growth of subjectivity.

The apparent presumption that such participation could benefit not only the self, but also social science and perhaps even the social world is certainly borne out by social scientists who have ethically and politically opposed unjust domination and contributed, however small, to political and social transformation. Yet, participation can be understood still more broadly—a point I want to make with reference to a young-Hegelian insight which was particularly clearly articulated by Charles S. Peirce. Giri's references to Bhaskar's notions of 'cosmic envelope' and 'identification' may contain an echo of it, but it is very faint and, in any case, he neglects to relate it to participation. According to Peirce (1992; Apel 1981), the semiotic pragmaticist, the production and employment of knowledge is a process in which signs mediate between reality and those who experience as well as interpret signs and engage with reality. All three moments are at all times involved in the temporal semiotic process.[5] Far from being simply an imaginary concatenation of figments of the mind, signs are an essential element in the process of evolution and hence the constitution of the universe. It is incumbent on us, the sign interpreters, therefore, to use signs correctly and appropriately, and to learn to do so is to acquire the ability to participate responsibly in the process of evolution, both social and natural.

For his part, Giri invokes the Indian spiritual tradition and Gandhi to provide backing for his idea of ontological participation, and he even contrasts Gandhi's position with that of pragmatism, suggesting that the latter is inferior to the former. I tend to think, however, that Peirce made available the framework for a position that is more adequate than the one Giri puts forward. For one, it is based on a theory of sign mediation that not merely allows greater multidimensional logical rigour, but also facilitates the appreciation at one glance, as it were, of the relations among knowledge, reality and the self or, differently, among epistemology, ontology and subjectivity. Moreover, he is fully alive to the role that transcending 'real generals' (e.g. Peirce 1998: 343) play. Consequently, Peirce's acute understanding of participation not only captures Giri's sense, but at the same time also places the self-reflective, learning, self-critical and responsible sign interpreting subject within the broader framework of an unfolding natural and social process with its penumbra of potentialities and real possibilities. As such, it clears the way for a discussion of creatively practised social science in relation to the process of world creation.

The Contemporary Interpretation of Ontology

Finally, I wish to venture a few brief words on what I regard as the appropriate way to interpret ontology in the context of the philosophy of social science today.

To begin with, social science ontology concerns the nature and character of social reality as it is understood for the purposes of fulfilling the task of social science. Since there are different types of social science which are aimed at producing knowledge for different purposes and hence audiences, however, social reality is open to being interpreted in correspondingly different ways (Strydom 2008, 2011a). This means that social science ontology appears in the plural. If one accepts the co-existence of quantitative, qualitative and critical approaches, as Giri seems to do, then one has to acknowledge the distinction between ontologies trained on things and/or events, on beliefs, intentions, actions and/or their products, and on hidden forces and/or deformed cognitive and symbolic structures which can be identified only in the light of immanently-rooted yet context-transcendent conceptual structures, respectively. In practice, it is of course possible to interrelate or triangulate the different epistemological-methodological approaches, which Giri also seems to accept, but since only one of them could possibly determine the overall purpose of the research, the guiding ontological emphasis would ultimately nevertheless still be partial, limited to one of the available options. One thing is certain. However central and important the interpretative social science ontology is, and there is no doubt about this at least after Gadamer's hermeneutic philosophy, it is not possible to generalize this particular ontology to all of social science, as Giri tends to do. In my view, the critical theoretical ontology is the most adequate and justifiable social-scientific ontology available.

But there is of course more to Giri's understanding of ontology than just the ontology of social science. Social science as such, like all science, is in principle incomplete. It is in fact completed by being embedded in social relations and this de facto completion has to be reflexively ratified. But such reflexivity is by no means achieved exclusively by science, since it requires a much wider societal practical discourse in order to make sense of what counts as the world. Science is not just about knowledge. Science has its starting point in practices, and, therefore, it has to be brought back eventually to the world of practices and be subjected to assessment and appropriation within that context. The appropriation of scientific knowledge takes place in and through a practical discourse in which relevant scientific knowledge is incorporated into a much wider historically specific social, moral, ethical and political framework. Here ontology is touched upon in the extended sense relevant to social science, that is, the larger complex of relations within which social science stands. Generally speaking, one could conceive of it as a continuing process not just of problem solving but more generally of world creation, which itself presupposes natural historical or evolutionary processes with which it is also in interaction. Being inescapably implicated and involved in it, social science participates in this process, making a contribution as a process of the flow of information, communication and critical meaning creation in the form of a discursive practice (Strydom 2000, 2002; Delanty 2005).

This process of world creation is generated and carried by a plurality of actors and agents who are guided by their own normative codes and corresponding world models, and accordingly seek to bring into being their own distinct worlds (see e.g. Strydom 2009, 2011b, 2012). Taking the current process of the construction of a global society as an example, they include corporations, states, global institutions, non-governmental organizations, global social movements, and so forth. Some of these agents pursue a global private law and free trade society and others either a world government, multi-level world governance, a theocratic world state, a global civil society, a communicatively constituted world society spanned by a global public sphere rooted in particular civic communities, a universal human community or a closed theocratic community. Through their competition, contestation and conflict, but also intercultural and trans-civilizational communication and cooperation, these actors and agents get embroiled in inter-subjective communicative and discursive contexts in which a variety of learning processes (Strydom 2009) take place on which the formation of the currently emerging society feeds. Among these are at least four types of learning processes relevant to social science: aggregative learning that renders individuals and organizations able to pursue their own interests more effectively; institutional learning that allows institutions to fulfil their particular missions to their clients, customers or the citizens; associational learning that makes possible the formation of voluntary groupings and social movements as collective actors as well as collective action; double contingency learning through which, for example, corporations and/or states on the one hand conflict with social movements on the other, leading to accommodation between the parties; and, finally, triple contingency learning, a discursive form of societal learning, made possible by the emergence of personalities capable of intercultural and trans-civilizational communication, discourses, public spheres and publics able to observe, evaluate, judge, opinion formation and commentary, in which the competing protagonists take account of each other via a reference to the public who has constitutive significance for the emergent, jointly constructed social reality (see Strydom 1999b). It is in this latter type of learning that transformative moments of discovery and transcendence occur through the unforeseeable and unexpected creative combination of forces, cognitive structures and symbolic forms. It is undoubtedly the most improbable kind of learning, which is what makes it also the most interesting, but it does actually take place, as is borne out by the South African case for which Nelson Mandela (1994) for instance provides much illuminating evidence in his autobiography. This kind of learning, the very vehicle of transcendence, it should be pointed out, has become the central concern of recent critical social science (e.g. Miller 1986, 1992, 2002; Eder 1996, 1999, 2002; Strydom 1987, 2000, 2002, 2008).

As a discursive practice, social science plays a part in practical discourses in and through which communicative-discursive processes of learning and world creation such as those mentioned above occur. But it is far from laying claim to a direct relation between theory and practice—as though the application of social scientific knowledge will immediately lead to the desired state of affairs, or of being the epistemic authority to which all and sundry has to submit—as though social scientists know beforehand and throughout what ought to be the case. Social science is but one among a number of participants in a much wider collective learning and world creation process, which is itself characterized by a non-linear mode of unfolding. As a participant, it does not simply identify with the intentions, values, normative code, goals or identity of any one of the other participants, but rather takes into account the whole plural range of participants without any tendency to favour or value any one above the others. To adopt such an identificatory or legitimationist procedure, for instance identifying with a favoured social movement considered as good as against some corporate or political actor regarded as bad, would not only be prejudicial of the latter's contribution to life support systems, but would also render any critique of the former impossible. In relation to each and every one of the participants, social science must retain and exercise its ability both to understand through participation and to distantiate itself through objectivation and, if necessary, critique. Its contribution to the process of learning and world creation is to assist in opening communication processes, which support discursive reflection on the implications, consequences and side-effects of the full spectrum of social practices. And its aim is to locate starting points for and identify steps towards potentially transformative inter-subjective learning experiences, which could move one toward less problematic and more adequate conditions of existence. For this reason, social science ultimately has to remain open to the possibility of the transformation of cultural, moral, ethical, social, and political assumptions, structures and symbols—a transformation which is, more likely than not, in some way connected with our relation to nature. This requires nothing less than creative research.

From the earlier reasoning I am convinced it is possible to conclude that to regard social science, which has creative social research at its very core, as a discursive practice participating in the process of world creation, is the most appropriate perspective to take towards ontology today. To my mind, it is at the same time also the most charitable reading of Ananta Kumar Giri's proposal in *Pathways of Creative Research*.

Notes

1. Consider, for example, the ontological turn in the philosophy of language spearheaded by John Searle's (1972) speech act theory and Habermas's (1979a) radicalization of this ontological turn that eventuated in the formulation of formal pragmatics embracing the three objective, social and subjective world-concepts that themselves are unified by the reflexive concept of world.
2. On theory in critical theory, see Strydom (2011a).
3. See the German word *Unverfügbarkeit* in the title of the cited chapter.
4. On 'immanent-transcendence' as the key concept of contemporary critical theory, see Strydom (2011a).
5. For an explication of the tripartite sign-mediated or communication methodology of critical theory, see Strydom (2011a).

References

Apel, K.O. (1981 [1967, 1970]), *Charles S. Peirce: From Pragmatism to Pragmaticism*, Amherst, MA: University of Massachusetts Press.

———(1996 [1977–1994]), *Selected Essays*, vol. II, New Jersey: Humanities Press.

Chriss, J.J. (2005), 'George Herbert Mead', in *Encyclopedia of Social Theory*, ed. G. Ritzer, vol. I, Thousand Oaks: Sage, pp. 486–91.

Delanty, G. (2005), *Social Science: Philosophical and Methodological Foundations*, Maidenhead: Open University Press/McGraw Hill.

Delanty, G. and P. Strydom, eds. (2003), *Philosophies of Social Science: The Classic and Contemporary Readings*, Maidenhead and Philadelphia: Open University Press/ McGraw Hill.

Eder, K. (1996), *The Social Construction of Nature*, London: Sage.

———(1999), 'Societies Learn and Yet the World is Hard to Change', *European Journal of Social Theory*, vol. 2, no. 2, pp. 195–215.

———(2002), 'Zwischen evolutionärer Anpassung und kognitiver Selbstorganization', *Sozialer Sinn*, vol. 3, pp. 423–7.

Gadamer, H.G. (1972 [1960]), *Wahrheit und Methode: Grundzüge einer philosophischen Hermeneutik*, Tübingen: Mohr.

Habermas, J. (1979a [1974]), 'What is Universal Pragmatics?', in *Communication and the Evolution of Society*, ed. J. Habermas, London: Heinemann, pp. 1–69.

———(1979b [1974]), 'Moral Development and Ego Identity', in *Communication and the Evolution of Society*, ed. J. Habermas, London: Heinemann, pp. 69–94.

———(1987a [1981]), *The Theory of Communicative Action*, vol. 2, Cambridge: Polity Press.

———(1987b [1985]), *The Philosophical Discourse of Modernity: Twelve Lectures*, Cambridge: Polity Press.

———(2001), *Die Zukunft der menschlichen Natur: Auf dem Weg zu einer liberalen Eugenik?*, Frankfurt: Suhrkamp.

———(2003 [1999]), *Truth and Justification*. Cambridge: Polity.

———(2005), '"Ich selber bin ja ein Stück Natur"—Adorno über die Naturveflochtenheit der Vernunft. Überlegungen zum Verhältnis von Freiheit und Unverfügbarkeit', in *Zwischen Naturalismus und Religion: Philosophische Aufsätze*, ed. J. Habermas, Frankfurt: Suhrkamp, pp. 187–215.

Heidegger, M. (1953 [1927]), *Sein und Zeit*, Tübingen: Niemeyer.

———(1963 [1950]), 'Die Zeit des Weltbildes', in *Holzwege*, ed. M. Heidegger, Frankfurt: Klostermann, pp. 69–104.

———(1975 [1954, 1961]), *The End of Philosophy*, London: Souvenir Press.

Honneth, A. (2000), *Das Andere der Gerechtigkeit: Aufsätze zur praktischen Philosophie*, Frankfurt: Suhrkamp.

Kierkegaard, S. (1992 [1843]), *Either/Or*, London: Penguin.

Mandela, Nelson (1994), *Long Walk to Freedom*, London: Little, Brown and Company.

Marx, Karl (1967 [1844–46]), *Writings of the Young Marx on Philosophy and Society*, ed. and tr. L.D. Easton and K.H. Guddat, New York: Doubleday.

Mead, G.H. (1974 [1934]), *Mind, Self, and Society*, Chicago: University of Chicago Press.

Miller, M. (1986), *Kollektive Lernprozesse: Studien zur Grundlegung einer soziologischen Lerntheorie*, Frankfurt: Suhrkamp.

———(1992), 'Discourse and Morality: Two Case Studies of Social Conflicts in a Segmentary and a Functionally Differentiated Society', *Archive Européennes de Sociologie*, vol. 33, no. 1, pp. 3–38.

———(2002), 'Some Theoretical Aspects of Systemic Learning', *Sozialer Sinn*, vol. 3, pp. 397–421.

Peirce, C.S. (1992 [1867–93]), *The Essential Peirce*, ed. N. Houser and C. Kloesel, vol. 1, Bloomington: Indiana University Press.

———(1998 [1893–1913]), *The Essential Peirce*, ed. Peirce Edition Project, vol. 2, Bloomington: Indiana University Press.

Piaget, J. (1983 [1932]), *The Moral Judgement of the Child,* Harmondsworth: Penguin.

———(2001 [1965]), *Insights and Illusions of Philosophy*, London: Routledge.

Rabinow, P. and W.M. Sullivan (1979), *Interpretative Social Science*, Berkeley: University of California Press.

Searle, John (1972), *Speech Acts*, Cambridge: Cambridge University Press.

Strydom, P. (1987), 'Collective Learning: Habermas' Concessions and Their Theoretical Implications', *Philosophy and Social Criticism*, vol. 13, no. 3, pp. 256–81.

———(1999a), 'The Civilisation of the Gene: Biotechnological Risk Framed in the Responsibility Discourse', in *Nature, Risk and Responsibility: Discourses of Biotechnology*, ed. P. O'Mahony, Basingstoke: Macmillan, pp. 21–36.

————(1999b), 'Triple Contingency: The Theoretical Problem of the Public in Communication Societies', *Philosophy and Social Criticism*, vol. 25, no.1, pp. 1–25.

————(2000), *Discourse and Knowledge: The Making of Enlightenment Sociology*, Liverpool: Liverpool University Press.

————(2002), *Risk, Environment and Society: Ongoing Debates, Current Issues and Future Prospects*, Buckingham and Philadelphia: Open University Press.

————(2008), 'Philosophies of Social Science', UNESCO Encyclopedia of Life Support Systems, Oxford: Eolss Publishers.

————(2009), *New Horizons of Critical Theory: Collective Learning and Triple Contingency*, New Delhi: Shipra.

————(2011a), *Contemporary Critical Theory and Methodology*, London: Routledge.

————(2011b), 'The Cognitive and Metacognitive Dimensions of Social and Political Theory', in *Routledge International Handbook of Social and Political Theory*, ed. G. Delanty and S. Turner, London: Routledge, pp. 328–38.

————(2012), 'Modernity and Cosmopolitanism: From a Critical Social Theory Perspective', in *Routledge International Handbook of Cosmopolitan Studies*, ed. G. Delanty, London: Routledge, pp. 25–37.

18

Three Ontological Contributions to Knowing About Praxis

WENDY OLSEN

Ananta Kumar Giri has taken a big problem and given a short answer to it. His problem is what the foundational assumptions should be for praxis (useful action) in late modernity. His answer is complex, as expected. He argues:

1. epistemology should not be the primary issue in social science knowledge gathering practices.
2. social movements create an important scene (or canvas) upon which we should ground any theoretical work that we do (or any painting we paint).
3. the researcher as a social actor, who is an embedded agent having what Giri calls 'ontological sociality', is a source of knowledge deeper than one can ever hope to achieve under methodological individualist assumptions. The single 'me' is given up in favour of a relational approach to knowledge.

What a good idea! I share these suppositions and I have drawn upon critical realism in some earlier writings to find out how to explore the world—and good action in the world—from this perspective. What I found brought me to question some of the most basic assumptions that those around me at my workplace carry and exhibit in their habitual behaviour: that valid facts are the aim of science, that people are isolated units, and that a holistic view of peaceful cooperation is an ideal not a reality. These three false assertions need to be challenged.

In tracing through this kind of argument, Giri first notes that these are fundamentally ontological starting points. Let me give a succinct summary of the argument in each case:

1. claims about the possibility of knowledge depend upon a confidence that we can make reference to the world, that there is a world to be known, that knowing is possible, and thus that our ontological

assumptions are workable enough to be going on with. Aspects of truth and validity, which are often thought to be central to epistemology, need to be put into the background to make space for good-enough knowledge which is 'right' in more fundamental ways than ever before under the pre-positivist and empiricist paradigms.

2. the agent in late modern society is not an isolated individual but a relational co-mutual being who only 'thinks' s/he is alone! What a reassuring thought Giri offers us. It should be comforting. If you are not used to thinking in post-individualist ways, however, it can be unsettling. Those with spiritual, religious or theistic convictions may find it easier to accept. They may have experienced the weaknesses of language when words are used to represent the relatedness of us-to-all. The mistranslation of the word 'Allah', the key hermeneutical interpretation of the concept 'God' as meaning a person-like Deity in christianities, and many other misunderstandings arise as a result. But upon reflection, thinks the spiritually minded person, let us focus on that which is beyond words. Let these reflections on perfection, on timeless Being, on nature as including-me-us-all, give comfort where modern theories of 'happiness' do not. Collective meditation, private worship, prayer, whatever—they all recognize that one must go beyond words to find some kinds of truths. Realists would argue you find reality when you search like that, but even realists are now split between those who would interpret that-which-can-be-discovered in secular versus. Soulful terms. The secular interpretation, by the way, would be that 'the social is in myself, and when I transform my thoughts I make a new possibility of transforming the social of which I am a part'.

3. The knower and that which is known are not just separate-but-related; they are part of a single whole, too. This ontic point differentiates 'ontology' from 'ontic being', in my view. The ontological argument is that we need to conceive of people in non-individualistic ways. It would be good to do so. A depth ontology, for example, starts us off much more clearly (Layder 1993). But the levels or layers of a depth ontology cannot be seen as just separate-but-linked. They are part of that same whole! This whole is our being, and the word 'ontic' is used to refer to the being-aspect of the world. Time is another a dimension that can be collapsed into that greater whole. That way our 'being' and our 'well-being' is not only social but historical. Our future death as individuals is inevitable, but our future life as a socio-natural whole is certain. The mystery that starts to strike us in the face, as knowers, in trying to comprehend

this vast 'reality' is not easily knowable. But for Bhaskar, who Giri
cites repeatedly in part of his argument, to know something is not
to exhaust it, not to be able to forecast it, not totalizing, not value-
free. The awe, the sharing of splendour, the positive affect that
arrives in us when we contemplate the skies at night are a small
reflection of the greatness of that great whole. Ontology leads
towards comprehension of the ontic, the awesome, the complex,
that which has parts that inevitably change because they are all part
of the One. Whilst our knowledge of this One cannot exhaust it
(nor get outside it to get a 'view' of it), it leads us towards a self-
reflexive awareness of our being as an overlapping subcomponent
of that system. Since it is an open system, which is undergoing
organic transformation like other organic systems, we ourselves are
part of the power that can change the universe. We are no longer
small. We are effective agents. Our consciousness and our 'selves' are
not the same. Our pitiable little voices that say 'I want to . . . I need
. . .' are not the same as that 'self' which is great and which drives
us forward.

To illustrate: I remember that after about 10 years living in Salford,
Manchester, I drew up a summary of my group of friends. We all met in
pubs, and then we all went camping with campfires and long walks. Then
camping took precedence over pubs and clubs. At present, having had lots
of children, some of the gang still do drugs and the rest don't. But we are
all still anti-racist at our core. That is the one overriding commonality of
this whole gang of friends, this social network, this web that I live in. That's
my story. That's the 'me' of 'me in Salford'. But I also have another group
of politically active acquaintances, and we do progressive acts of social
inclusion and so on. After 18 years living here I became a school governor.
Now I have another new gang of people who care. If the racist electoral
party, British National Party (BNP), ever get elected in this area I know
who I will turn to for implacable opposition to add to my own.

This is a trajectory of thought that Giri has led us down merely by
pointing out that the ontic reality demands us to widen our ontological
perspective to encompass it.

There are some problems with the framework of ontology that Giri has
mapped out. I will deal with three of them briefly before concluding. First,
the 'oneness/God' problem and the way it has defused Bhaskar's real-world
energy. Second, the weaknesses of Giri's diagrams. Third, he didn't say
enough about the Hardt-Negri phenomenon—the two authors who
theorized imperialism in its new unilateralist American-led form.

First, quoting Bhaskar on 'transcendental identification' is a little
problematic. In the third point made earlier I have tried to do justice to part

of the argument but I would not want to call it identification. The verb 'to identify'—analysed in detail by Jenkins (2004) and in social context by Crossley (2002)—could lead to individualistic misunderstanding. Let us be specific and pare down the argument to its bare bones.

1. The duality Bhaskar refers to is 'me' vs. 'the world'.
2. Non-duality is basic to life.
3. The ideal and practice of transcendental identification is necessary for daily acts.
4. We are enfolded into the larger reality even when we imagine that we take individualistic or techno-practical action.
5. Therefore without knowing it we are doing the work of the Inevitable Whole whether we sit doing nothing, plan a grand riot against the state, or vote British National Party!

This argument has some weak points and can be represented to show these premises that I would question.

2–i. The duality Bhaskar refers to is a possessive individual actor 'me' vs. 'the world' as a separate entity.

2–ii. Non-duality is basic to life, thus these two components of reality (the 'me' and 'the world') imply each other.

X 2–iii. Non-duality implies that humans cannot act as independent agents.

X 2–iv. Non-duality being basic to life, there are no hard boundaries between an individual agent and the rest of the world. (This statement creates ontological confusion. If the word 'duality' has any purchase then it refers to hard boundaries separating 'self' and 'other'. But then the phrase non-duality become ambiguous. Does it mean that there is no distinction between 'self' and 'other'?)

X 2–v. The ideal and practice of transcendental identification is necessary for daily acts of individual humans

2–vi. We are enfolded into the larger reality even when we imagine that we take individualistic or techno-practical action as individuals.

2–viii. We also are part of larger realities—including stuctures, institutions, and agents—when we act as people within larger co-mutual agencies.

X 2–ix. Therefore, without knowing it we are doing the work of the Inevitable Whole whether we do nothing or do a lot.

2–x. Whether we know it or not, our actions and inactions both contribute to shaping the future.

2–xi. 'We' in the present are a part of the timeless whole of our socio-nature through all of time. It is a self-congratulatory trick of consciousness that 'we' think 'we' are so powerful that our decisions will shape the End of Human History. Whilst actions are causally efficacious and do generate causal mechanisms that influence future events, there is real complexity in how those later outcomes evolve from early ones. The mysteries seen in slides under a microscope should convince anyone of the myriad possibilities for our future evolution.

What is left of Bhaskar's argument when the false or poorly framed (marked with 'X') premises are removed from the series of claims? Some of the mystery drops away. Instead of being 'quasi-magical' (Bhaskar 2002: 248), the powers and liabilities of agents in human society are simply susceptible to scientific scrutiny. Religious and spiritual ideas are open to contestation, just like other claims. The 'One' need not be seen as a cosmic envelope or as invoking invisible or magical qualities, either (Bhaskar 2002: 257–8). However, conscious human agents can have a reasoned discussion about what is the best action, the best theory, the best data for a given task or purpose. And we are back to doing good social science, but having gained a rich ontology. We might also have more sympathy and co-feeling with religious people and less of a secular urge to silence them than we did before.

I have critiqued and developed the argument Giri makes about transcendental identification. I suspect he wants us to further develop such a concept. If it is a vague concept it may help us develop our sensitivity. When it becomes more concretized, it may not be as stimulating or as unnerving. But my series of premises and propositions didn't have anything about identity or identification. So what does the word 'identification' add to the simple concept, 'our transcendental being'?

The discussion of epistemological richness that follows in Giri's text, after the diagrams, is excellent and I would not argue against it. I also like the ideas shared with us by Flyvbjerg which are summarized aptly by Giri here.

But I have another problem. To my mind Giri is too kind to Hardt and Negri (2000). Giri rightly points out a logical flaw in their argument against God (i.e. it is an incomplete argument; see Morgan 2001). But there are more points at issue here in taking up such a serious and large corpus of work as Hardt and Negri's. I have backed away from this myself, because it is work that is highly theoretical and because I can't see see how engaging with their work is going to push forward my own engagements. Yet I think that if Giri is ready with both welcoming and critical points on a variety of fronts of the Hardt-Negri corpus, then that should be written up in full. And since social movements are one of the serious competitors to global neoliberal ideology, we need to clarify the role and praxis of ideology-making so that we don't make the same mistakes that social democracy and Soviet state socialism made before.

So, we need to ask for more detail from Giri after all this!

Write another book. I have enjoyed them all so far. The present one introduces three contributions to praxis. Each one is 'ontological' in the sense of helping us to re-perceive our being in ways that are enriched through a sense of connectedness. The three points—(a, b, and c, as I have labelled them here) deserve more work and practical application. Many practitioners know them intuitively. Ontology gives us words to help us discuss these things.

Thank you Ananta Kumar Giri for this gift full of life, liveliness, realism, and critical participation. It is an excellent work right up to the closing pages.

References

Bhaskar, R. (1993), *Dialectic: The Pulse of Freedom*, London: Verso.

Crossley, N. (2002), *Making Sense of Social Movements*, Buckingham: Open University Press.

Hardt, M. and A. Negri (2000), *Empire*, Cambridge, MA/London: Harvard University Press.

Jenkins, R. (2004), *Social Identity*, London: Routledge.

Layder, D. (1993), *New Strategies in Social Research*, Cambridge: Polity Press.

Morgan, J. (2001), 'The Soul: Plausibility and Persuasiveness in Realism', *Journal of Critical Realism*, vol. 5, no. 1.

19

Critical Distance and Dualism: A Tangential Response

ANDREW SMITH

Introduction

Ananta Kumar Giri in his opening essay provides a dense, provocative, but above all open-minded series of considerations with regard to practices of social scientists in the modern world. The response that I offer below is probably best thought of as marginalia, as comments scribbled beside the lines of Giri's text, addressed more to the particular themes which strike me as a reader than to the overall argument of his essay. In this respect, what follows is marginal in a double sense. First, because a response of this sort is inevitably somewhat idiosyncratic. Second, and more positive, because margins are also places of meeting or touching. My comments are undertaken, 1 hope, in the same spirit of dialogue that marks out the original discussion. More than anything else, I take from this essay the lesson that search for answers must always remain perpetually qualified by an invitation to response. It is equally incumbent on the respondent, therefore, to keep that invitation open.

Critical Distance

One of the ways in which one might begin to imagine a 'new vocation of social research', Giri suggests at the beginning of his essay and throughout, is by dismantling the conventional distinction between academic reflection, on the one hand, and activism or engagement, on the other. His argument is that one should recognize that an adequate sociology is not predicated on a cold-blooded detachment from its object of analysis. If the established model of social scientific thought assumes critical distance as the basis for an appropriately objective consideration, Giri proposes instead what might be called a model of critical involvement. Underlying this claim is a more fundamental one, that is to say, the claim that human beings have identities or meaningful selves only in and through the existence of relationships with others. Sociologists and anthropologists are called, therefore, to 'participate in the lifeworlds of actors' not merely because there are insights to be gained 'on the ground' as much as there are in an aloof contemplation of events, but also because it is a mistake to understand the life of others as being essentially cut off from one's own. One is, ineluctably, part of the world that is studied. To deny this, Giri argues, involves not just a methodological mistake, but also an ontological one.

In many ways these are important and necessary reminders, and one should be glad to hear them again. I have written elsewhere of my own experience teaching courses on African literature in an extra-mural educational setting (Smith 2000). One of a number of profound lessons that my interlocutors in that context taught me was precisely the understanding that the conventional academic coupling of 'critical' ability and 'distance' is mistaken. In the essays written at the end of these courses, student after student offered a response to the novels they had read which took the form of a retelling of the original narrative. In their retellings or re-plottings of these novels, the students corrected those aspects of the original work that they disliked and added speculative extra branches of plot concerning the characters they felt were particularly significant. In this respect the students, of course, wholly failed to exhibit that emotional detachment from the narrative, which is considered to be the hallmark of good critical practice in orthodox literary studies. Nevertheless, these retellings, which precisely sought to eradicate the 'distance' that separates a reader from a text, were full of critical understanding: each retelling of a story that inserted newly invented material about a female character, or sought to alter the emphasis of a narrative sequence to downplay the role of a patriarchal character, for example, implied a very real criticism of the text as it stood. In non-elite, or non-academic popular culture, as a range of studies have pointed out, the transmission or repetition of a narrative or motif always entails an act of critical revision. Moreover, such acts are inescapably collaborative; within them the seemingly self-evident high cultural distinction between author and audience collapses (Barber 1997; Burke 1978: chapter 4). In this respect, then, I am entirely in agreement with Giri's point. One needs to be continually reminded that the detachment vis-à-vis the object of analysis which is conventionally demanded of scholars in a wide range of disciplines may well tell more about the middle-class dispositions of academics than it does about any necessary condition for truly critical understanding.

As I have suggested, this claim in Giri's essay seems to me to be underpinned by his more general invitation to social scientists to 'rethink subjectivity' in new, non-dualist manner, attentive to the subtle connections between subjects and between what he calls 'parts of reality', while maintaining an awareness of 'disjunction and antimonies' between the same. Here again there is another important reminder. I write from a European context in which the conceptual binaries—'Africa and Europe; Islam and the West' 'democratic and barbaric'—that supported imperial practices in an earlier era can be seen returning daily, with a weirdly revenant glow, in the stories told by the mainstream media and by the politicians. A responsible social science can only respond to this with a willingness, as Giri urges, to transcend those categorical modes of thought that sustained previous injustices and which are being heated over to the same purpose today. In much the same way, what Marx mocked as the 'Robinsonades' of nineteenth century political economy, the 'unimaginative fantasy' (1973: 83) of the isolated and perfectly rational economic actor, has returned in an all too obvious neoliberal reincarnation. In the face of this one embraces Giri's call to 'go beyond the false dichotomy between individual and society', a call which is perhaps not quite as new as the author implies: Marx's own response to the nineteenth-century version of this 'twaddle', for example, was to remember the same, fundamental fact that 'the human being is in the most literal sense a Ζωον πολιτικον [a political animal] not merely a gregarious animal, but an animal which can individuate itself only in the midst of society' (1973: 84).

In these respects, it is necessary to seek to reiterate the lessons of what Giri calls 'ontological sociality'. Yet, it also seems to me that there are reasons here for moving carefully. Those of us who are academics have the privilege of being able to speak in certain ways that are legitimated, or given force, by virtue of our their positioning within a particular social field; a field whose conditions of operation and distinctiveness are themselves the product of long historical struggle objectified in various institutional and intellectual forms. This is, of course, a description borrowed from Pierre Bourdieu, and it seems to me that one needs to follow Bourdieu in thinking through its implications. Although, in a range of detailed studies, Bourdieu sought to demonstrate the inequalities that affect outcomes in the various fields of cultural and intellectual practice (e.g. 1984, 1993), he also repeatedly defended the autonomous practices of those fields. Paradoxical as this may seem, as he makes clear in a striking coda to *The Rules of Art* (1996), he recognized that it is the existence of these fields that continue to make possible an analysis of the social world not beholden to the rationales of the reigning economic and political regimes. In a British context, universities are increasingly represented as commercial organizations; whereas, with a corresponding assumption that their first concern should be their to make a strategic contribution to the national economy.[1] Hence there is all the more in the face of pressures of these kinds, it seems to me that there is, an urgent need to preserve those shared assumptions about 'what matters' the purposes and intentions of academic endeavour. Additionally, a need to and a corresponding need to preserve those defend the particular institutional spaces and practices which make possible the work and interventions by of scholars. Certainly, in a British context in which universities are increasingly represented as commercial organizations whose first concern should be their strategic contribution to the national economy,[1] one feels all the more urgently the need to preserve those assumptions about 'what matters' along with those particular institutional spaces and practices which make possible our work and our interventions as scholars. If one is 'called' to anything, it is to this simultaneous engagement on two fronts: on the one hand, the need for continual self-criticism, for criticism of the deep injustices within, replicated by, and sustaining the structures in which one spends his/her working lives; on the other hand, the need to vigorously defend what Giri calls the 'autonomies' of those very structures. What is crucial, in my opinion, is that the awkward tension between these two imperatives is not defused. One does not need to agree with Adorno's claim that 'for the intellectual, inviolable isolation is now the only way of showing some measure of solidarity' or of sharing in 'the sufferings of men' (1974: 26), in order to recognize how easily calls for a renewed intellectual engagement, for a public sociology, might diminish to a merely 'policy relevant' social science that has surrendered the very things which sustained its critical and interventionist impulse in the first place.

I have to admit, here, to being unclear what Giri means when he says that 'the worlds of scholarship and critical social actions have their autonomies but they are also related to each other in a spirit of embodied interpenetration'. The inescapable fact that social identities are corporeally lived out might perhaps be taken to mean that one has the possibility of transcending or even playing with the various kinds of subjectivity authorized by particular social fields. This, at least, would be one gloss on Giri's sentence. If it is accurate to the author's intended meaning, it becomes hard to reconcile the claim (which refers to the implicit possibilities of bodily experience) with the preceding claim that social movements themselves 'embody' the 'self-transcendence of culture' in a fundamentally new way. In any case, what is clear is that this argument is intended to support Giri's more specific call for a 'transgressive' practice; a practice in which actors leave off guarding their identities as scholars or activists and 'strive to embody the vision and practice of both'. The danger, it seems to me, is that this call for transgression ends up collaborating, entirely without intending this, with the forceful ongoing attempts to dismantle the autonomy of the field that supports scholarly investigation. In the neoliberal context, there is surely a renewed need to guard, if not personal identities as scholars, then at least the conditions of possibility for the social identity of 'the scholar'. Of course, this does not mean that one should cease to think reflexively and critically about the inequalities written into the production of that social identity. Nor does it mean that he/she should fall into the old romanticist celebration of a kind of cloistered academic detachment as a good thing in itself. Nor, for one moment, does it preclude a person's involvement in political protest. What it does mean, is recognizing that there are many things that one can do working *through* the identity of the scholar that could not be done by seeking to transgress or get beyond that identity. The field of academic production exists by virtue of an autonomy, which should be both critiqued and defended at once. If transgression of that field is made more important than a guarding of its own logic of practice and forms of value, then there is the risk of forfeiting the peculiar space for critical consideration, which it supports. Moreover, bodily practices—habits, gut-level responses, instincts—express slowly learnt recognition of what are recognized as meaningful or appropriate ways of acting and expressing 'a sense of self', within the contexts defined by particular social fields. This means, on the one hand, that transgression of this bodily 'second-nature' is not easy. It also means, on the other, that it is not inconsequential. The bodied selves are *in themselves* one line of defence for a social identity that makes possible certain kinds of critical engagement that are not possible otherwise.

Dualism

I find myself in similarly qualified agreement with what I take to be the proposition, which, in many respects, underlies the argument discussed above: i.e. Giri's invitation to move 'beyond dualism' towards what he calls 'a multi-valued logic of autonomy and interpenetration' (15). Giri argues that this 'non-dual sensitivity' should inform a wide-ranging reconsideration of sociological method entailing, among other things, a searching for (even 'an aesthetics' of) the various 'threads of connections' between elements of the social world. In this respect, linear causality, so long a key component of the social scientist's conceptual toolbox, is to be replaced by an approach which is alive to connections, but also to the 'provisionality' of judgement and to the presence of slippages, lack of fit, and disruptive unpredictability, not only in the social scientific models, but equally in the social life they seek to model. This, at least, is how I understand what is argued in much of the 'rethinking methods' section of the essay. Such arguments are very much in harmony with a great deal that has been written in this discipline over the last quarter of a century, from the attempts to rethink human migration in terms of contemporary scientific understandings of 'turbulence' (e.g. Papastergiadis 2000), to Arjun Appadurai's famous emphasis on 'disjunction' in global economies of wealth and knowledge (1990, 1996). Most of all, of course, Giri's call chimes with the now more or less orthodox view that one needs to move towards an understanding of social identity that transcends the binary logic of 'either/or'.

As I have suggested earlier, there are many reasons for welcoming this intellectual shift. Indeed, the way in which dualisms of various sorts have been made explicit and subsequently deconstructed has to be seen as one of the genuinely significant achievements of contemporary social criticism, especially of the feminist, postmodern, and postcolonial varieties. One should unquestionably be grateful for this work, and for ongoing endeavours in this direction such as are presented here. Nevertheless, here again it seems to me that there is good reason why discrimination in response should be exercised—since, it should not be forgotten that oppositional thought, as it may be called, has been centrally important to many of the most progressive political struggles of the modern world. As Benita Parry argues in an important essay with a provocative subtitle—'Two Cheers for Nativism'—a profound mistake is made if one dismisses out of hand those forms of political mobilization, which are premised on the assertion of a duality. Addressing, in particular, the context of anti-colonial struggle, she notes that figures such as Frantz Fanon and Aime Cesaire understood this fact only too well. Both writers, she argues, affirmed:

the invention of an insurgent, unified black self, acknowledge[d] the revolutionary energies released by valorising the cultures denigrated by colonialism and, rather than constructing the colonial relationship in terms of negotiations within the structures of imperialism, privileged coercion over hegemony [in order] to project it as a struggle between implacably opposed forces. (1996: 91)

In a context such as that of the Algerian war of independence it is certainly difficult to imagine how a different conceptualization could have been adequate. This does not mean, as even a cursory reading of his work makes clear, that a thinker like Fanon believed in the possibility of recovering some pristine, unsullied and wholly unified pre-colonial African identity. Nor does it mean that Fanon believed in some objective 'African identity' understood as a *thing* that was capable of being recovered. There is, however, a cautionary reminder here with regard to the very prominent contemporary critique, which argues that political struggles based around the deployment of dualist identities are indelibly flawed. And the reminder is that the maintenance of this position is a privilege of one's retrospective detachment from the struggles that necessitated the assertion of these identities. Such arguments, as Parry puts it, rely on an abstraction of 'resistance from its moment of performance' (1996: 91). Moments of performance, of course, contain their ironies and their paradoxes. Nevertheless, in the face of urgent political necessities, there can be a need for conceptualizations that will enable those involved in struggle to recognize the homologies of position which they share with others—those forms of allegiance whose possibility lies latent in the social structure—and which project an unequivocal 'struggle between implacably opposed forces'.

Moreover, it seems to me that one needs to be alert to a somewhat fatalistic note in the fashionable condemnation of dualist thought. Even in the very different (and very valuable) discussions of Anthony Kwame Appiah (1992), on the one hand, and Hardt and Negri (2000) on the other, one finds an implication that the contemporary crisis in Africa, for example, can be understood as a direct consequence of the 'bad thought', i.e. the dualist logic, adopted during the anti-colonial struggle. This account makes ideology the overriding factor in the course of historical events, overlooking the economic and political conjunctions that have done so much to undermine the social viability of many postcolonial nations. At the same time, the power of this argument rests on a more or less un-remarked collapsing of dualism into determinism, as if every way of conceptualizing social relations in terms of an opposition requires that the categories it deploys are necessary, non-negotiable, essential. One knows that those who hold social power often do propose seemingly inescapable dualities as a means of corralling support and silencing dissent. These, however, are strategies of power, not statements of sociological necessity. When Marx, for example, makes use of an explicitly dualistic notion of class in his exhortatory publications he does so not because he is unaware of the disjunctions that an advanced division of labour is likely to produce in terms of social outlook, and certainly not because he believes that class position somehow reflects essential characteristics, but because he is seeking to provide his audience with a means of conceiving of their social position which may make possible action to move beyond that position. In Marx's use, class offers a dualistic explanation of social processes, but a profoundly anti-essentialist explanation: class is precisely intended as a means beyond class.[2] In much the same way, Fanon referred to assertions of Algerian nationalism as 'the people's own lie' (1965: 87), a phrase which puts on open display the constructed nature of nationalist identities even as Fanon acknowledged that the historical and contemporary actions of the colonists forced that lie on to the people.

Dualist models, in short, have been hugely important in promoting critical consideration of the status quo and of the position of individuals and groups within it. Such models are quite capable of exposing their own provisionality, even of inviting those who make use of them to recognize that they are in a sense degradable, that they offer ways of understanding position and alliance which are used up in the struggle to overcome the very things which initially make them necessary. Although Carole Boyce Davis (1999), and many others, have attacked this kind of politics because it smothers difference in the name of political objectives, Bourdieu is right to point out that acts of social classification are politically potent precisely because they allow such equations to operate (1987). This kind of categorical thought is always, in a sense, too simple or too presumptuous. But it may also, for those whose daily social experience is one of fragmentation, alienation and vulnerability, reveal the dynamics of social power in an empoweringly simple way, as well as making conceivable a community that might contest those dynamics.

In short, my response to Giri's essay is to offer a defensive 'two cheers' for theoretical models which propose oppositional dualism, and not just for these, but also for the theories of causality and determination, which are asked to make way for newer models premised on contingency and indeterminacy. One needs to keep in view at all times the potential 'openness' of history to the actions of human agents, but sometimes models which propose a causal explanation of the world as it is are peculiarly effective at breaking history open in this way. Globalization, for example, presents a tremendously complex and proliferating series of relations and interconnections within and across the boundaries of language, belief and state power. Across the world, popular responses to this condition and to its attendant inequalities have sought explanation or refuge in a range of renovated magical practices, conspiracy theories and fatalisms (Moore and Sanders 2001; Meyer and Pels 2003; West and Sanders 2003; Comaroff and Comaroff 2000). To respond to this, as social scientists, with a demand for theoretical models that mimic those complexities, or which embrace the magicality of 'a re-enchanted world' (15), seems to me to be a misstep. Apart from anything else, such a response leaves one *more* distanced and detached from possible interlocutors outside of the academy than models that sought to explain causality or represent social oppositions ever did. Provisionality, contingency, complexity are words with which scholars are more than comfortable, indeed they express perfectly the detachment from worldly affairs and the discursive instincts of the academic habitus. One needs to recognize that when they are made central to attempts to 'think the world', in a sense it is like trumpeting the privileges of having attained 'academic habitus'. It seems to me, therefore, that in truly seeking a renewed conversation with a wider public, what may be incumbent is to seek to 'think the world' in ways that are uncomfortable, and that this may mean— among other things—accepting that oppositional politics has its place.

Conclusion

This is, as I suggested at the start, an ad hoc and rather tangential response to an essay, which is panoramic in its range of reference and consideration. *Pathways of Creative Social Research* is instructive, not only in its suggestions, but also in the gracious way in which the author frames his argument and invites response. One should be grateful for these lessons, and for the call to reconsider what it means to have social science as one's profession—not merely in the limited modern sense of this word, but in the older and more profound sense: a mode of reflecting upon life in which one has faith, and to which one commits one's self.

Notes

1. As argued, for example, by the head of the Scottish Chamber of Commerce, in a widely publicized attack on the country's higher education sector (*Sunday Herald*, 23 September 2007).
2. That is to say one should not collapse a critique of dualism into a critique of essentialism. I take Marx's whole project to be premised on a non-essential view of human life, in his assertion of the fundamental capability of men and women to change themselves, their circumstances and their understandings—his profound faith in this potential creativity, which can be destructive as well, seems to me to underlie his world view. But this does not prevent him asking his readers to see the world in a very clearly dualistic way, and for important ethical reasons. Indeed, one could argue that he felt that it was only by clarifying the fundamental antagonism between those who wielded economic power and those who did not that the real creative energies of humankind could be released. For me this suggests that dualism is not simply to be dismissed, and that it has its political uses, and that it can itself work to deeply anti-essentialist ends.

References

Adorno, Theodor (1974), *Minima Moralia: Reflections on Damaged Life*, London: Verso.

Appadurai, Arjun (1990), 'Disjunction and Difference in the Global Economy', in *Global Culture: Nationalism, Globalization and Modernity,* ed. M. Featherstone, London: Sage.

———(1996), *Modernity at Large: Cultural Dimensions of Globalization*, Minneapolis: University of Minnesota Press.

Appiah, Kwame A. (1992), *In My Father's House: Africa in the Philosophy of Culture*, New York: OUP.

Barber, Karin (1997), 'Preliminary Notes on Audience in Africa', *Africa,* vol. 67, no. 3, pp. 347–62.

Bourdieu, Pierre (1984), *Distinction: A Social Critique of the Judgement of Taste*, London: Routledge.

———(1987), 'What Makes a Social Class?', *Berkeley Journal of Sociology,* vol. 22, pp. 1–18.

————(1993), *The Field of Cultural Production: Essays on Art and Literature*, Cambridge: Polity.

————(1996), *The Rules of Art: Genesis and Structure of the Literary Field*, Cambridge: Polity.

Boyce Davis, Carole (1999), 'Beyond Unicentricity: Transcultural Black Presences', *Research in African Literatures*, vol. 30, no. 2, pp. 96–109.

Burke, Peter (1978), *Popular Culture in Early Modern Europe*, London: Temple Smith.

Comaroff, Jean and John Comaroff (2000), 'Millenial Capitalism: First Thoughts on a Second Coming', *Public Culture*, vol. 12, no. 2, pp. 291–343.

Fanon, Frantz (1965), *Studies in a Dying Colonialism*, New York: Monthly Review Press.

Hardt, Michael and Antonio Negri (2000), *Empire*, Cambridge, Mass.: Harvard University Press.

Marx, Karl (1973), *Grundrisse: Foundations of the Critique of Political Economy*, Harmondsworth: Penguin.

Meyer, Brigit and Peter Pels, eds. (2003), *Magic and Modernity: Interfaces of Revelation and Concealment*, Stanford: Stanford University Press.

Moore, Henrietta L. and Todd Sanders, eds. (2001), *Magical Interpretations, Material Realities: Modernity, Witchcraft and the Occult in Postcolonial Africa*, London: Routledge.

Papastergiadis, Nikos (2000), *The Turbulence of Migration: Globalization, Deterritorialization and Hybridity*, Cambridge: Polity Press.

Parry, Benita (1996), 'Resistance Theory/Theorising Resistance or, Two Cheers for Nativism', in *Contemporary Postcolonial Theory: A Reader,* ed. P. Mongia, London: Arnold.

Smith, Andrew (2000), 'Imaginative Knowledge: Scottish Readers and Nigerian Fictions', *African Research and Documentation*, vol. 83, pp. 23–36.

West, Harry and Todd Sanders, eds. (2003), *Transparency and Conspiracy: Ethnographies of Suspicion in the New World Order*, Durham and London: Duke University Press.

20

Beyond Boundaries: Dualism, Non-Dualism and Creative Research

JENS SEIFFERT

'I do not look for a way out of the philosophical problems, but a way into the philosophical problems.' [translation by the author]

— MITTERER (1992: 13)

'The dawning of the millenium witnesses a visible increase in the complexity and interconnections of human life.'

— HOYT ET AL. (1999: 379)

Introduction

Being raised in a scientific world that itself was built upon a specific scientific tradition, one finds it hard to emancipate what has made oneself grown. Thinking in terms of formal logic has been one of the key qualities of social researchers since the emergence of social sciences at the end of the nineteenth century. Nowadays it seems that the social scientific tradition comes more and more into what Giri calls the 'crisis of European sciences'. The 'project of knowing about the world with proper procedure and scientific method' (Giri 2017) has been object of criticism by 'socio-cultural movements and critical discursive movements and new movements (that) challenged the modernist paradigms of pathology and normality as well as distinction between ontology and epistemology' (Giri 2017).

At the beginning of the twenty-first century, the need for new answers to the questions that are brought up by the processes of globalization, regionalization or the global climate change (to name a few) arose in all societies world-wide. Social research, grounded in the tradition of what Beck called 'methodological nationalism' (Beck 2002), seems more and more unable to provide such answers.

This contribution to a festival of dialogues wants to put Giri's proposals to overcome that crisis by the development of creative research, and into a broader view of science characterized by revolutions, as described by Kuhn (1976). It is argued that the idea of creative social research might be the next revolutionary stage of social research to overcome the 'crisis' of normal science.

Therefore, a new paradigm of social research needs to be developed, a paradigm that forms plurality out of unity by differentiation, and overcomes distinctions by reflecting the own usage of distinctions.

The Use of Dualism in Normal Science

> Any scientific theory, however well it has been verified empirically, will always have infinitely\many rival theories that fit the available evidence just as well but that make different predictions, in an arbitrary way, for yet unobserved phenomena.   − MAXWELL (2000)

Being a young science, 'Western' sociology has already created a wide bunch of theories that try to make sense out of reality, or the other way round. Even in the very young discipline of communication research, Weber identified almost twelve framing theories (Weber 2005: 19f.), postmodernism, marxism, pragmatism, constructivism, and so on, that offer an understanding compared to what Kuhn called 'Weltsicht' (1976).

Giri regards the Western social scientific tradition, which describes the world over the dualism of dichotomies, as causal for its own crisis. As a matter of fact, the idea of abstracting the operations of social systems into a binary code, as proposed by the systems theory, was, and is still, the guiding idea within the main meta-theories of social research. No matter if materialism, idealism, relativism or essentialism, 'distinctions like language and reality, descriptions and objects' (Weber 2002: 33) are to be found everywhere and rule the discourse. No matter what kind of theory is focused on, they all create dichotomical distinctions.

With regard to communication research being compared to sociology, the use of distinctions has worked out well, so far.

The first ideas of communication processes used the distinctions between sender and audience, as expressed in the stimulus-response model. The model itself became one of the most way-guiding models in communication research, not because of the theoretical brilliance standing behind it, but for creating a myth of providing a dominant paradigm for the discipline. Brosius and Esser show that the Stimulus-Response-Model (S-R-Model) was more or less cultivated by science itself (Brosius and Esser 1998: 347), based upon an essay by Lasswell about propaganda where he states that 'the strategy of propaganda can readily be described in the language of stimulus-response' (Lasswell 1927: 630). In fact, this short essay by Lasswell can be regarded as the take-off point for modern communication research: the cause-effect chain between sender and audience was born.

The simplifying model of stimulus-response dominated the scientific discourse about the effects of media and Denis McQuail picked up the S-R-Model as dominating the first phase in his history of media effect research (1977).

Whatever the position of a researcher was towards the S-R-Model, it was regarded as a paradigm that structured scientific communication research and implemented a certain kind of thinking in cause-effect chains that still seems to dominate communication research nowadays. As a matter of fact, Brosius and Esser discovered a gap between perception and the reality of communication research, since most scientists did not refer to the S-R-Model at all, refusing it because of its simple and deterministic nature (Brosius and Esser 1998). Nevertheless, the S-R-Model made a 'career' that is of interest for this dialogue because of three reasons.

First, the S-R-Model introduced a dichotomy into communication science, namely, stimulus and response, sender and audience, cause and effect. This dichotomy is, of course, today already regarded to be too simple. Nevertheless, the terms are still in use and the shift from a uni-/bidirectional idea of communication to a multidirectional theory hasn't taken place yet (Weber 2002: 35).

Second, the S-R-Model provided a kind of paradigm[1] that enabled 'normal science' (Kuhn 1976: 37) to develop itself within the boundaries of the paradigm. The workings on the basis of the S-R-Model and the scientific controversy around it, created a bunch of new ideas, theories and models that brought communication research forward.

And third, closely connected to the second point, research within the paradigm of cause-effect chains as introduced by the S-R-Model brought up the conclusion that the paradigm itself gives many answers, but by far not all that is looked for. The awareness arose that a change in thinking would be needed for future research.

Thereby, the first conclusion and thesis of this essay is that dualism is part of non-dualism. The brief description of the role of the S-R-Model in communication research showed the use of dualism in what Kuhn called 'normal science' and the need for a non-dualism at the same time.

Contrary to the Kuhnian perspective on science as an on-going alteration between normal science and revolution, the idea of non-dualism seems to lead the way a stage of research as a permanent revolution. If Kuhnian theory of scientific research is correctly applied to Giri's idea, normal social research as one knows it, has come to its boundaries in dissolving scientific riddles and the revolutionary paradigm would be the creation of non-dualist research.

To deal with this idea of new creative social research it is now needed to deepen the thesis that dualism is part of non-dualism by regarding the (non-) dichotomy of dualism and non-dualism.

Dualism vs. Non-Dualism—A New dichotomy?

> Systems with integrated reflexion are forced to abstain from absolutenesses.
> [translation by the author]   − LUHMANN (1996: 656)

On the one hand, the consideration that rational science, operating by distinguishing the communication about the phenomena it researches into dichotomies, leads into a crisis of a lack of understanding.

On the other, it can be argued that the same system of Western science provided the openness for concepts such as Giri's idea of an ontological shift to a science that makes its researchers create a sphere of 'learning and self-cultivation'.

The central question is whether Giri proposes a change in the way researchers learn, namely, to go beyond the borders of their scientific realm without erecting new borders just within another, wider context. Or is the idea of a multi-rational science just a new meta-story that guides scientific research, by simply setting the borders at a different place?

If dualism is regarded as the key reason for social sciences being unable to put up theories, giving answers on questions, than it is necessary to consider what a shift to non-dualism would mean.

Let us, therefore, consider tie in with Giri's quote of Elias who tells us that 'the individual person is able to say "I" because he can at the same time say "we"' (Elias 1991: 61). By stating that 'I' always contains an unspoken 'we', we must realize that the thinking of a non-dualistic science must always include a dualistic science as well. To abandon dualism would mean to create a paradox, by puting one way of research into a normative higher position than the other. Or to describe it with a dualism: the one way of research would be good, the other one would be bad. As I understand Giri, the quest for a creative social research is not to place a new meta-story above another, not just to redefine what is right and what is wrong.

Dualism, therefore, would be part of a new paradigm that places the abstraction into dichotomies within a new realm of non-dualism research. Overcoming the disjunction means to accept it as a part of reality in research to gain the ability to look behind. To strive towards knowledge by adopting a non-dualistic, self-reflecting point of view would mean to create a totally new type of researcher.

Researchers would be in the need to break new grounds by thinking of theory in a new way. Luhmannian systems theory might be an example for the challenges that are ahead of us.

The central paradigm of Luhmannian systems theory is the difference between system and environment (Luhmann 1996: 242). To make a difference means finally to set up a distinction between the self and the other, to make a difference as they are expressed through key differentiations like true/not true or power/non-power.

But regarding systems only by setting a dual distinction would mean to underestimate the potentials of difference. One of Giri's main concerns seems to me the embodiment of 'methodological pluralism'. It is, to use the words of Bhaskar, 'to understand differentiation within a unity' (2002: 248).

The key consideration would therefore be that differentiation within a unity leads to pluralism. Only by making a difference, by setting up distinctions, can one be aware of the plurality of being.

The proposal of Luhmannian thinking would be to understand research as the study of observation, an observation of second order (Luhmann 1998: 76). The realization thereby would be that the distinction in ability to realize at all is just an abstraction that only exists within ourselves. The one who observes is by the act of observing tied to the 'object' of observation. The subject observing the object thereby becomes part of the object, and the object turns into the observing subject. In other words, observation constitutes a social system in discriminating system to environment by differentiation. But by that process the distinction between the subject observing the object is no longer existent because subject and object enter a state of interaction.

'It is not about the reflection of the relationship of subject and object, rather about the reflection of the introduction, the argumentative use and the significance of the use of the distinction of subject and object [translation by the author]' Weber (2005: 15).

If Weber is to be rightly understood, then future research would not any longer refer to the relation between subject and object, but to the reflection of introduction, argumentative use and sense of the usage of that differentiation.

Finally, Weber's ideas, referring to Mitterer, question the use of the classical term of truth in social research (2005: 17): 'Would it be an alternative to be geared to >Change<, to the alteration of realit(ies)?' (2005: 16).

Non-Duality as an Answer on Complexity

The story of humankind seems to be a story of growing complexity (Hoyt et al. 1999). Telling stories is by far one of the most important abilities of humans (Baskin 2004) and regarding the number of stories told, and regarding their extent, it can be argued that one is living in a world that becomes more complex day by day.

In my view, researchers are people who are concerned with stories in a certain way; asking what is told, how it is told and why it is told. In understanding the importance of asking questions and trying to find an answer to them, lies the relevance of research for humankind. One may argue that the development of science was one kind of response (among others) to the growing complexity of human societies. The differentiation of social systems in general, and the creation of a scientific social system in particular, were, according to Luhmann, grounded in the need to reduce complexity by discriminating what is true and not true in scientific terms (Luhmann 1998: 9).

By constructing social science as the ongoing search for answers, it may be argued, as has been done already in the previous chapters, that science has come to a point, which Giri calls the 'crisis of European sciences'. Growing complexity has brought social science to a point where answers more and more seem to be unsatisfying.

With his works on non-dualism and distinction-theory, Stefan Weber puts the question into discussion if there is a model imaginable that leaves the controversy between realism and constructivism behind (Weber 2002: 33). Realizing that dualism is part of non-dualism, a possible pathway for creative research has already been drawn. But the question why there is a need for such creative research still needs to be answered besides stating a crisis within the system of science—and the answer is: complexity.

Luhmann argues that complexity demands complex systems, because 'only complexity can reduce complexity' (1988: 49). The logic behind this idea is simple but ingenious. The more complex a system is, the more it is able to cope with complexity.

That the world is growing more complex day by day can hardly be denied. What follows from this process according to Jarchow, is that the 'cause-effect chains disintegrate into circles of alternating prerequisites' (Jarchow 1992: 53). The story of research as a linear quest for truth could vanish because of its inability to cope with complexity.

It seems to be obvious that research work with a plural concept of its own is able to cope better with complexity than one based upon distinctions.[2]

Very briefly, the relationship of dualism and non-dualism have been discussed and thereby worked out that creative research as non-dualist research contains dualism, but is able to go beyond. The example of communication research showed us the use of dualism in realizing the use of non-dualism, namely, not to replace one dualism by another, one truth by another. Second, I argued, that non-dualism is adequate to complexity and seems more able than the dualistic tradition of research to reduce this complexity under the conditions of growing complexity.

Now let us have a last brief look at the problem that creative pathways of social research might confront us with.

Standing on the Shoulders of Giants

Pigmaei gigantum humeris impositi plusquam ipsi gigantes vident.

— SIR ISAAC NEWTON

Isaac Newton said that he was able to see further, because he was standing on the shoulders of giants. Although the saying was already known before Newton used it,[3] he gave it its modern meaning of using past created works for gaining future intellectual understanding.

Newton gives an idea of the task that confronts one on the way to creative social research. I have already referred to Kuhn and his paradigm of scientific revolutions.

As a matter of fact, the proposals made by Giri, and thereby the whole idea of shifting to a non-dual view on social research, would mean even more than a revolution, it would mean to change the way of thinking in general.

The question for me is how to unite two different ways of thinking to create a new one that benefits from both, Western logical (analytical, linear, rational) and Eastern pre-logical (holistic, associative, affective) thinking (Maletzke 1996: 64). According to Maletzke, there are four dimensions of thinking expressed in dichotomies:

- logical or pre-logical
- inductive or deductive
- abstract or concrete
- alphabetical or an-alphabetical[4]

These distinctions show the problem that confronts one on a journey to creative social research. For Western researchers, logical thinking is not only part of their education, it is already implied within their language, their culture as a whole. It was Paul Feyerabend who stated that terminology used by Western researchers is interfused by objectivistic ideology.

'Our terminology is that much interfused by objectivistic ideology, that one paradoxically must use it to describe different kind of views' [translation by the author] (Paul K. Feyerabend quoted in Mitterer 1992: 48).

In other words, the language that researchers nowadays is structured for dual philosophy, and thereby dual thinking. Works like those of Josef Mitterer's on development of a non-dualistic speech (1992: 49) need to be taken further and received by social researchers.

Now one starts to realize that climbing on the shoulders of giants goes beyond everything experienced in social research so far. The shift in thinking needs a shift in speaking as well, as Mitterer proposes with his non-dualized way of speech (1992: 49). The self-emancipation of researchers from their research tradition is not something easily achieved.

As Giri proposes Gandhi as a source of inspiration for that journey, I would like to introduce another great thinker into this festival of dialogues. Born 469 BC, Socrates is one of the most influential philosophers of the ancient world, inspiring Occidental thinking until today. The famous saying attributed to Socrates that 'I only know that I don't know',[5] might serve as a guide in striving towards non-dualism, self-reflection and self-cultivation of social research. 'Probably indeed neither of us knew anything fine and good, but he thought he knew something he didn't know, whereas I, just as I didn't know, didn't think I knew. I seemed likely therefore to be wiser than him by virtue of a small thing, this very point, that what I didn't know I didn't think I knew either' (Socrates quoted in Stokes 1997: 496).

Besides the wisdom of Socrates in realizing that 'the highest form of Human Excellence is to question oneself and others' (Coppens 2008), he might be a useful teacher from another point of view, namely, as an intellectual interconnection between East and West. Helmut Uhlig states that Buddha and Socrates, being two inspiring thinkers of their civilizations, are at least at two points very close in their position; their 'estimation of life and their attitude towards death' (Uhlig 1996: 108).

Without giving further evidence for the thesis that there is much more in common between Oriental and Occidental thinking than one might realize, we can argue that the philosophical closeness of Socrates and Buddha might be a bridge we should travel on our pathways to creative research. It might show us that the question of creative research is not what divides us or what unites us, but what divides us and unites us.

Conclusion

In this essay I have, very briefly, discussed the thesis that a future non-dualistic research needs to integrate the current tradition of dualistic thinking in order to avoid a new distinction and to take into account the usage of dualistic thinking for social research so far. The crisis in 'European science' might be a fallout of the ongoing process of growing complexity in societies worldwide, and the call for creative social research thereby is a possible pathway to cope with that complexity.

However such a non-dualistic, creative research will be shaped in the future world, creating a sphere of 'learning and self-cultivation', the calling for 'an Ontological Epistemology of Participation' confronts social research with a massive challenge, mainly in changing thinking and speaking from duality to pluralism and non-dualism. Although there is blueprint for the pathways to creative research, realizing the need to ask for what divides us and unites us might bring us a step closer to answering the questions we are asking ourselves.

Notes

1. I say kind of, because the S-R-Model has never been formulated as a theory in the sense of the term (Vgl. Brosius/Esser 1998). Unfortunately, to investigate the emergence of the S-R-Model within communication research would fill an essay on its own.
2. Non-dualist research includes distinctions as well, but is able to go beyond the boundaries set up by dichotomies to see the world in a holistic manner.
3. A very interesting discussion of the emergence of that saying gives Merton in his book *On the Shoulders of Giants* (Merton 1965). The phrase itself is said to have been first used by Bernard of Chartres in the twelfth century.
4. Maletzke himself relativizes this distinction by saying that they have to be understood as scales with many intermediate states (Vgl. Maletzke 1996: 63).
5. As a matter of fact, Socrates never used that term. But nevertheless it became a common phrase that is credited to Socrates (Vgl. Stokes 1997).
6. Vgl. Stokes 1997: 49.

References

Beck, Ulrich (2002), 'The Cosmopolitan Society and its Enemies', *Theory, Culture and Society*, vol. 19, nos. 1-2, pp. 17–44.

Bhaskar, Roy (2002), *Reflections on Meta-Reality: Transcendence, Everyday Life and Emancipations*, New Delhi: Sage.

Brosius, Hans-Bernd and Frank Esser (1998), 'Mythen in der Wirkungsforschung: Auf der Suche nach dem Stimulus-Response-Modell [Myths in Effects Research: In Search of the Stimulus-Response Model]', *Publizistik*, vol. 43, no. 4, pp. 341-61.

Coppens, Philip (2008), 'Socrates, that's the question', Feature Articles—Biographies, PhilipCoppens.com., Zugriff am 13.6.2008 – 13.56, Uhr.

Elias, Norbert (1991), *The Society of Individuals*, Cambridge, MA: Basil Blackwell.

Giri, Ananta Kumar (2017), 'Pathways of Creative Research: Rethinking Theories and Methods and the Calling of an Ontological Epistemology of Participation', this volume.

Hoyt, Elizabeth Gutierrez et al. (1999), 'Bridging Established and Emerging Directions in Communication Research', *Communication Research*, vol. 26, Jg.: 379–84.

Jarchow, Klaus (1992), *Wirklichkeiten—Wahrheiten—Wahrnehmungen. Systemtheoretische Voraussetzungen der Public Relations*, Bremen: WMIT.

Kuhn, T.S. (1976), *Die Struktur wissenschaftlicher Revolutionen*, Frankfurt am Main: Suhrkamp.

Lasswell, Harold (1927), 'The Theory of Political Propaganda', *The American Political Science Review*, vol. 21, pp. 627–30.

Luhmann, Niklas (1996), *Soziale Systeme. Grundriß einer allgemeinen Theorie*, Frankfurt and Main: Suhrkamp.

————(1998), *Die Wissenschaft der Gesellschaft*, Frankfurt and Main: Suhrkamp.

Maletzke, Gerhard (1996), *Interkulturelle Kommunikation: zur Interaktion zwischen Menschen verschiedener Kulturen*, Opladen: Westdeutscher Verlag.

Maxwell, N. (2000), 'A New Conception of Science', *Physics World*, August, pp. 17–18.

McQuail, Denis (1977), 'The Influence and Effects of Mass Media', in *Mass Communication and Society,* ed. James Curran, Michael Gurevitch and Janet Woollacott, London, pp. 70–94.

Merton, Robert K. (1965), *On the Shoulders of Giants. A Shandean Postscript*, Free Press.

Mitterer, Josef (1992), *Das Jenseits der Philosophie. Wider das dualistische Erkenntnisprinzip*, Wien: Passagen Verlag.

Stokes, Michael C. (1997), *Apology of Socrates*, Warminster: Aris & Phillips.

Uhlig, Helmut (1996), *Buddha und Jesus. Die Überwinder der Angst*, Bergisch Gladbach: Bastei-Lübbe.

Weber, Stefan (2002), 'Konstruktivismus und Non-Dualismus, Systemtheorie und Distinktionstheorie', in *Systemtheorie und Konstruktivismus in der Kommunikationswissenschaft,* ed. Armin Scholl, Konstanz: UVK, pp. 21–36.

————(2005), *Non-dualistische Medientheorie. Eine philosophische Grundlegung*, Konstanz: UVK.

21

Shifting Boundaries in the Process of Self and the Process of Coming to Know

INGRID DASH

In this chapter my intention is to share my understanding of two aspects of an ontological epistemology of participation as proposed in Ananta Kumar Giri's *Pathways of Creative Research*.

These aspects have relevance to research in education of mathematics and I want to emphasize the importance of exploring and developing these both in research as well as in teaching practice.

1. Both the researcher/teacher and the informant/pupil participate in a learning process, where ontological assumptions are contested rather than pre-determined. A multi-valued logic underlines that in a statement there are more or less differentiated meanings.
2. An intercultural perspective not only means a continuous change in perspectives and shifts in taken-for-granted dualisms, it also underpins a creative research approach/teaching approach, which includes an intercultural sensitivity to how meanings are created and identities (here, learning identities) are constituted in different contexts.

Flexibility in Knowing School Mathematics

In my doctoral dissertation (Dash 2009) the research deals with a quality of learning, specifically the flexibility in how pupils understand whole and part-whole-relationships in the process of working with mathematical problems.

I conducted observations and teacher-pupil interviews in one class of a school in southern Sweden and a similar one in a school in Odisha (a state in eastern India). I explored modes of knowing and from the analysis emerged three categories of knowing:

Associative flexible experiencing
Compositional flexible experiencing
Contextual flexible experiencing

Associative flexible experiencing means separation of aspects from each other, with a continuously changing focus on what distinguishes the parts and the discernment of wholes. Importantly, the parts are not focused in relation to each other, but selected on the basis of what momentarily is focused.

In compositional flexible experiencing the focus is on compositions, part-whole-relationships, which sometimes are view-turned. The compositions can be used in several different tasks.

Contextual flexible experiencing means a focus on what the part-whole-relationships mean in different contexts, mathematical or reality-based. The dominating mode of knowing was the compositional flexible experiencing.

The underlying assumption is that knowing is relational, which means that a person understands the world through her experiences of the world. This view opens a horizon from which one can look at learning not only as a purely cognitive activity, but as one that engages the whole being. To have knowledge in mathematics is, in other words, neither seen as an inherent quality of the learner, nor is empowerment of the learner an outcome of only possessing mathematical knowledge.

The process of coming to know mathematics is seen as a learner's engagement with ontological issues and epistemological issues, which often are not recognized in mathematics education. The process of Self, here specifically the cultivation of a learner identity, is intertwined with the process of working with the nature of mathematics and the constitution of meaning of the mathematical content. As a consequence of this relational and intentional view, communication in mathematics classroom ceases to be basically performative.

If ontology (of Self and of mathematics) is considered parallel to epistemology (the knowledge content and meaning), communication on mathematics in the classroom becomes participatory and real empowerment can be achieved. Burton found in her research on mathematicians' ways of knowing mathematics that five categories, based on philosophical, pedagogical and feminist literature, could define what it means to know mathematics:

1. its person—and cultural/social relatedness
2. the aesthetics of mathematical thinking it invokes
3. its nurturing of intuition and insight

4. its recognition and celebration of different approaches particularly in styles of thinking
5. the globality of its applications (1995: 287)

Knowing school mathematics could embrace four dimensions, which can be part of a creative teaching approach (Dash 2006):

Formal and objective
Aesthetic
Socio-cultural
Mythopoetical

The formal and objective dimension is the one often dealt with in school mathematics. This dimension hides the dialogical and multicultural origin of the mathematical work under an apparently unified logic. The contextual meanings of the mathematical models, which have been created at different localities and with different purposes in interaction between different people, are disguised under the formalization of mathematical symbols.

The socio-cultural dimension of mathematics re-situates mathematics into human experience and deals with questions of how mathematical models carry different meanings in different disciplines such as physics, biology, economy, art and social science. What were the original questions to these mathematical models? Who posed them? Why? And in what context? It also recognizes the mathematics used by people who are not mathematicians. A critical examination of mathematics and its multicultural origin can give a more holistic view and a sense of appreciation for mathematics as a language among others (Joseph 2000).

The aesthetic dimension recognizes that mathematicians mostly strive for beauty and simplicity. To explore how mathematics can be expressed in shapes and forms in art, architecture, astronomy, physics and in computer design is exciting.

The mythopoetical dimension has been forgotten slowly through a change in society from an emphasis on verbal transmission of knowledge to text-based information. (Dahlin et al. 2002). The magical relationships between numbers can be, and has been, presented in a narrative way. Pythagoras formulated the relationship in friendship in this way: friends are related to each other as the numbers 220 and 284. If one takes the sum of all prime numbers in 220, one gets 284, and similarly with 284.

A creative teaching approach requires that school mathematics is presented not as hierarchical, logically consistent, and rule-based, as at present, but as idea-based. Hence, one needs to negotiate on shared ideas of mathematics and encourage surprise and joy, Neyland writes (2004). But, as Stigler and Hiebert (1999) concluded, there is a need to give challenges to the pupils so that they can experience frustration and struggle.

A Multi-valued Logic: the Process of Constituting Self and an Object of Knowledge

The dialogue model developed by Anderberg, Alvegård, Johansson and Svensson is in educational research used to explore the gap between what meanings the informants give the content and the language use. The interview follows the following structure (Anderberg et al. 2006: 2–3):

The original question
Analysis of the function of expressions and meanings used
The original question

The first phase of the interview is where the mathematical content is presented by the researcher in the form of a question. Here, time is spent exploring how the interviewee understands the content. During the second phase, the focus is on the expressions (in the present studies, both verbal and mathematical) that have been used by the pupil to describe the understanding of the content. The pupil is invited to reflect upon these key formulations. The interview finishes by returning to the question addressed at the beginning. Here the researcher takes time to verify that there is a correspondence between the pupil's statements, and the researcher's own interpretations of the pupil's understanding. The use of the dialogue-model made it possible to explore modes of knowing and to make a preliminary analysis. In asking questions about a mathematical problem or a theme, I wanted to explore:

Which aspects the pupils were focusing on.
What meaning they gave these aspects.

What they understood of these aspects in relation to how they understood the problem/theme/mathematics.

During the interviews and analysis, I continuously needed to reflect upon my preconceptions of what I found. My background as a mathematics teacher and my experiences of living and working in both the localities have created a sensitivity of the cultural context, which was helpful when I gained access to the field, as well as when I collected the empirical material. Mohanty (2000) has described interpretation as a process, which leads to an overlapping of understanding:

Interpretation is, and should be, a many-layered path. If A interprets B, B also should simultaneously interpret A. As a matter of fact, a correct understanding presupposes a much more complicated multi-layered process. B can interpret A's interpretation of B. So A can also do the same, that is, interpret B's interpretation of A. Such a multi-layered process and the consequent synthesis of 'overlapping' can lead as much to a better self-understanding as to a better understanding of the other (122).

During interviews or classroom communication there is a possibility to negotiate meanings and intentions for participation that can be useful in order to promote understanding of mathematics.

An Intercultural Perspective

An intercultural perspective helped me to find out what meanings of expressions are related to, how the person understands the mathematical content and constitutes her/his learner identity.

Pupils in the Swedish school talked about the ontology of mathematics in positive terms. They compared how 'before when mathematics was a competition and a matter of being the fastest'—when they did things without knowing what it was. The documentation of the thematic project work gave them a possibility to 'return' and to 'see' and remember the material. The fallibilist classroom discourse and its clear goals and structure encouraged the pupils to reflect on mathematical and verbal language use, and about their reasoning. During interviews, though, there was an emphasis on retelling what they had done and what the steps were.

The pupils in the Indian study struggled to work with the mathematical tasks. The students considered repetition for meaning and memorization to be two sides of the same coin. There is a perceived circularity between creating meaning and memorization, as well as between mathematical work and mathematical truth. The work process is equal to the process of understanding content. All the pupils in the study expressed that they should understand mathematics more than memorize it. At the same time, work meant attentive effort with patience, concentration and focus, as well as memorization and a 'perception' of when the solution is complete in detail.

Superficially there were clear differences between the two studies. The teacher in the Swedish school class context used a variety of methods and let the pupils discuss among themselves and encouraged them to contribute plausible reasoning. The teacher in the Indian school class context dominated the presentation of the content from the textbook and used the blackboard during the whole lesson. Beyond and beneath these differences, it appeared to be crucial for the learners how they were encouraged to be authors of their own knowledge and how they used these possibilities for authorship.

Authorship (Burton 2004; Holland et al. 1998) includes the 'what' and the 'who', and the process of Self and the process of coming to know are parallel. In the Swedish school I saw that the pupils were encouraged to work with reflections, to express themselves and to make a picture of their understanding. The content was as much as possible put in a context of pupil's own reality.

In the Indian school the pupils experienced themselves as learners with responsibility to develop patience, exactness and concentration. They repeated and practised the mathematical content in detail and that demanded of them to choose different aspects of a task each time it was repeated. The classroom talk encouraged the pupils to develop reflection, as the teacher's questions implicitly demanded of the pupils to ponder on what to answer next. The work process was considered as a process for achieving understanding, and in order to understand one has to memorize and understand simultaneously.

The kind of authorship the pupils chose to develop depended on what possibilities for it were offered. At the same time, the authorship was related to the way the pupils approached the knowledge object.

Shifting Boundaries

An extension of the view that the researcher cannot mirror a person's statements in her/his meanings of the expressions, is that every expression and meaning has to be interpreted and re-interpreted. When mathematical ideas are the focus in mathematics education, there opens a space for reflection over the origin of the ideas, the conditions for the ideas, as well as a cultivation of a mode of being a learner, which is empowered.

Furthermore, think of it this way: scientific 'truth' comes at the end of inquiry, but where is the end of enquiry? So when one says that science gives one the 'truth' about the world, one is referring to ideal science, completed science—which has not been achieved yet. So scientific truth is the goal, not what the scientists discover every day. It is a goal, an ideal that is mistaken for an achievement (Mohanty 2002: 65–6).

If a creative teaching approach strives to encourage learners to learn how to make enquiries and how to follow them up in an argumentative way, it can make ground for pupils to participate in their own learning. Likewise, researchers can, with a creative research approach, come to understand and value the interviewee's own lived experiences as objective 'truths'.

References

Anderberg, E., C. Alvegård, T. Johansson and L. Svensson (2006), 'The Phenomenographic View of the Interplay between Language Use and Learning',

Theoretical report from the research project: 'The interplay between language and thought in understanding problems from a student perspective', Department of Education, Lund University, Sweden.

Burton, L. (1995), 'Moving Towards a Feminist Epistemology of Mathematics', *Educational Studies in Mathematics*, vol. 28, no. 3, pp. 275–91.

———(2004), 'Learning as Research', in *International Perspectives on Learning and Teaching Mathematics*, ed. B. Clarke et al., Göteborg, Sweden: National Centre for Mathematics Education, Göteborg University, pp. 283–98.

Dahlin, B., R. Ingelman and C. Dahlin (2002), *Ensouled Learning (Besjälat lärande)*, Studentlitteratur AB.

Dash, I. (2006), 'Intercultural Mathematics: What is Meant by That? (Interkulturell matematik: vad är det?)', in *Intercultural Perspectives: Pedagogy in Multicultural Learning Environments (Interkulturella perspektiv. Pedagogik i mångkulturella lärandemiljöer)*, ed. B. Bergstedt and H. Lorentz, Lund, Sweden: Studentlitteratur.

———(2009), *Flexibility in Knowing School Mathematics in the Contexts of a Swedish and an Indian School Class*, Lund, Sweden: Department of Education, Lund University.

Holland, D., W. Lachicotte, D. Skinner and C. Cain (1998), *Identity and Agency in Cultural Worlds*, Cambridge, MA: Harvard University Press.

Joseph, G.G. (2000), *The Crest of the Peacock: Non-European Roots of Mathematics*, London: Penguin.

Mohanty, J.N. (2002), *The Self and Its Other. Philosophical Essays,* New Delhi: OUP.

Neyland, J. (2004), 'Towards a Postmodern Ethics of Mathematics Education', in *Mathematics Education within the Postmodern*, ed. M. Walshaw, Greenwich, Connecticut: Information Age Publishing, pp. 55–73.

Stiegler, J.W and J. Hiebert (1999), *The Teaching Gap: Best Ideas from the World's Teachers for Improving Education in the Classroom*, New York: Free Press.

22

Neither Theos Nor Logos:
Indic Divine Mother Beyond 'Ontotheology'

NEELA BHATTACHARYA SAXENA

Introduction

The term 'plane of immanence' has taken up quite a lot of philosophical space via Deleuze and more recently through Agamben's commentaries that revive a Spinozan understanding of a divine reality that is deeply embedded in the world. Yet, since the ghost-like presence of the name of the Father informs and influences most ideas in the Western world, the gender implications of the idea of immanence which has traditionally been associated with Nature and the feminine from which the transcendental patriarchal God rescues the rational man, are never made quite clear. Notions of both Theos and Logos, at least in their exoteric presentation, imply a creator God, quite decidedly masculine and outside creation. India is probably the only civilization that resisted the one-sided theology of the Father God and retained multiple faces of the divine feminine in myriad manifestations; she who is at once immanent and transcendent cannot be contained within these binary categories; likewise philosophical musings on Being cannot hint at her presence as she is also absent from the frame of ontotheological discourse. In this essay in a spirit of this 'festival of dialogue', I would like to present this Indic Mother God and explore the possibilities she opens for one's understanding of self, culture and action.

Although the Indic Mother God has been of serious interest to Indologists as an object of study, she is little known within Western social sciences because she has often been summarily dismissed as irrelevant to feminist purposes, and useless for spiritual needs as she has been, like every other tradition, sometimes been appropriated by patriarchal or nationalistic forces. Yet she must be spoken of in an age when return of the Mother God has been heralded by feminist theologians, environmentalists, alternate spiritualists and feminist philosophers as an answer to a world crisis deepened by hyper-masculinist ideologies and religiosities. This writer locates her spirituality of the not-self in the Great Goddess Kali of her childhood and would like to show how such a tradition of Gynocentric spirituality grounded in the tantric[1] path presents alternative ways of understanding the world and the self. It is also the contention of this writer that mystical traditions of most world religions reveal a veiled Divine Feminine who nullifies the small, circumscribed selves, erasing distinctions that are merely based on external and so called rational understanding of everyday reality.[2]

Yet it is extremely difficult to cut across the 'epistemic violence' and psychic conditioning that years of hyper-masculine imperial discourses have forced on peoples of the world. I would contend that an intense form of 'epistemic violence' caused by colonial enterprises has been an attempt to dislodge the feminine divine by simply dismissing her as irrelevant to women, also within a Hegelian march of history, merely a relic of primitive times; nonetheless, resistance in India to such attempts have been quiet but effective. Giri's comments about assumptions of modernity behind sociological studies are relevant here because modernity in its universalist pretensions paradoxically wants to redeem people from antiquated 'religion' but in the process imposes hyper-masculine ideologies on colonized people. In India where the demarcations between sacred and profane were never quite clearly drawn, the concrete presence of the Great Mother has suffused all spaces with a kind of sacrality that is not an abstract and distant principle.

To Dipesh Chakrabarty's argument in *Provincializing Europe: Postcolonial Thought and Historical Difference* (2000) that reading 'other' places such as India through the European lens of modernity and historical time is problematic, I will add that European hegemonic discourse cannot be dislodged, and which non-Westerners cannot afford to ignore in any case, without dislodging the Name of the Father as a psychic reality that stands behind practically all 'Eurocentric' thought, even, including, and I would claim, especially modernist or atheistic discourse, that had relegated the spiritual to the irrational and feminine end of the mind/body binary. As a Shakta (from Shakti, the active feminine force in the universe as exemplified in this Gynocentric[3] religiosity that has traditionally resisted androcentric currents within Brahminic Hinduism) lover of Kali, the fiercest manifestation of the Great Goddess of India, I will contend that the tantric tradition she represents contributes to a different structuring of the psyche through her presence in the cultural self understanding, however problematic some of its socio-political manifestations might have been.

I am calling for a woman's reading and reclaiming of the Shakta tradition of India to resist the androcentric and exclusivist ways that are threatening to swallow up all spiritual horizons. I present in this essay the Great Goddess of India as neither theos nor logos who severs with her sword all imaginary attachments to a phenomenal ego, opening up to the infinite potential and real possibility of a radical transformation. I invoke here the paradox of a so called 'violent' Goddess to behold the reality of violence within and propose a difficult but real transformation of being that may be strategically utilized by women, feminists, and others who are committed to sustainable transformation and radical social justice. Ananta Giri's call for an 'ontological epistemology of participation' can be truly realized when full divinity is accorded to the body of the woman who equally participates in the socio-political as well as spiritual realms. While spirituality is not the exclusive realm of women or any particular religious tradition, often the spiritual core of most religions reveal the intimation of a Divine Feminine who as the totality of Being or as Wisdom incarnate marks humanity as it plunges in the dark depths of her womb and realize the not-self as one's true 'identity'. But it is necessary to posit a different relationship between the self and the other in order to access that reality.

Self/Other Dialectic

Before going into the spiritual comportment of the Divine Feminine, one should examine how the self/other relationship within a master narrative affects the way the self and others are viewed. The hegemonic West posited the Hegelian master/slave relationship as the prime site of the march of a Spirit that engulfs all others in its way to a totalizing unity. Within the hierarchically opposed dualisms that have been posited by Western metaphysics, such a figure is often gendered as a rational masculine self triumphantly conquering a feminized and irrational slave/other. The teleological march of Spirit puts all other histories in the 'waiting rooms' awaiting enlightenment. In such an ideology the self triumphantly returns to itself in a synthesis that is an unashamedly homogenizing force, rooted in the colonizing rationalizations, on the one hand and philosophies of sameness on the other. Ironically, worlds under the gaze of the master have been repeating the self same pattern in mimicking the master narrative. India too has not been left behind in resurrecting a regressive Hindutva that wants to outperform the master in its hyper-masculinist posturing.

On the other side of the coin, missionary crusades of 'democracy' and its resistance by jihadist impulses of every kind have kept the world in a militaristic stranglehold that speak of 'flammable' sealed off identities leading to a 'clash of civilizations' (Huntington 1996), however misguided the writers of such clash ideologies may be. Perhaps it is time to change the dynamics of such antagonistic discourse and bring two other figures, one of a mother and child and another the dance of dualities of Shakti and Shiva as markers of relationality, constructing a playful and borderless self in relation to an 'other'. Such a self does not threaten the other into submission, assimilation, or annihilation but is able to playfully engage each other soul, body and mind. Such a self is also deeply aware of the cosmos itself as *lila* or play of the Divine Mother. Shakti and Shiva mingled in *ardhanarishwar* image is posited in the tantric paths to denote a person's psychic bi-unity and as a model for male and female equality in a microcosmic and macrocosmic dance of dualities that sustains both the social and spiritual universes.

I claim that both models arise out of an acknowledgement of the Divine Feminine that envelops women's beings in a numinosity that the Name of the Father of traditional Western religions denies her. Tzvetan Todorov (1996) in 'Living Alone Together' had suggested the mother/child model as a solution to the problem of living together. Carol Ochs (1983) in *Women and Spirituality* develops the spiritual significance of motherhood. I will discuss their formulations and add the dancing dualities of Shakti and Shiva that could resist dueling dualities inherent in the battle of the sexes. I argue that neither can one leap outside of the hegemonic androcentric religious ideologies, nor can they change the master/slave dialectic without acknowledging the Divine Feminine as the erased unconscious yet of the West where the Name of the Father remains paramount often in its secular guise.

On the other hand, one must reveal the persistence of the Divine Feminine in alternate spiritualties such as native traditions and in places like India where she remains an integral part of most people's lives in spite of patriarchal forces' efforts to dethrone her or to assimilate her into power structures. Gynocentric spirituality must be grounded in a different dialectic; or humans are condemned to repeat histories of violence that has been the hallmark of revolutionary histories marked by a binary opposition between a bounded self and his rival other. Recognizing the power struggle inherent in the master/slave dialectic, Tzvetan Todorv argues, 'The existence of the individual as a specifically human being does not begin on a battlefield but in the infant's solicitation of his mother's gaze' (1996: 12), and he concludes that though the master/slave description

is not false, but its claim to universality is exorbitant. The reality of human relationships is infinitely richer... The human world is much more polymorphous than the 'master/slave dialectic,'. . . The extraordinary diversity of demands and grants of recognition is here reduced to the monotony of a conflict over power. Barely explored, recognition is seen to be brought back to a single one of its variations, and practically merged with that other weary tenant of Western philosophy, the permanent war of everyone against everyone else. It is this self-mutilating limit that we today must overcome. (1996: 14)

But mother/child relationship cannot be a model in a discursive world that is mesmerized by a strict variation of scientific rationalism, which relegates nurturing and regeneration to the passive feminine realm within the mind/body split. This is not to diminish reason but only to critique its reductive and instrumental applications. Such an ideology that accompanied the philosophical justifications of colonialism has had a curious effect in producing new misogynists. Recounting the story of a Bengali intellectual Dilipkumar Ray's 'conversion to rationalism and atheism', Dipesh Chakrabarty writes that this was 'accompanied by his immediate discovery that the women of the household—his aunt and his grandmother in particular—were the "irrational" people whose company he needed to avoid. Ray's misogyny is typical of the history of the "scientific temper" in modern Bengal' (2000: 238).

This is a new kind of misogyny that could bolster homegrown ascetic ideals that marked woman as the one who presides over the cycle of *samsara* that must be overcome, an ideology resulting from a simplistic reading of *Advaita Vedanta* that saw the world as illusion or *maya*. But the Indic traditions never trusted Master Reason; plus, since the Mother God has reigned supreme in every manifestation of the dharma traditions, the physicality and nurturing aspects of the Mother God were always acknowledged side by side with her powerful annihilating aspects. Tantra and its supreme 'Gynocentrism' of course would bring the body and materiality at the centre of its spiritual transformation. The Mother God also presides over diversity as the Divine Dyad engendered from her body resists the homogenizing impulse of monotheisms. Name of the Father from Carol Ochs's point of view:

The male God is a spiritual (not physical) progenitor and an external judge of creation. . ... God's own non-physicality makes the physical suspect, if not absolutely evil. If God, the perfect Creator, creates in a nonphysical way (by word alone), then our nonphysical creations are more divine than our physical creations...and procreation is certainly not viewed as a central spiritual experience. The world itself, so material, so physical, and so sexual, is viewed as unreal and as a potential trap for the would-be seeker of God. (1983: 21)

I have described such transcendentalizing adventures in most world religions as androcentric that have denied materiality its numinosity. It is quite interesting that wherever the Mother God has presided over the religious psyches of the people, such rabid other worldly focus has been missing; examples abound in Native American, Shamanic, and Chinese traditions as well as the pre-Christian Western religions from Mesopotamia to Greece. God the Father of Western religions began to lose his religious powers somewhat within European history due to a severely violent history of Christian institutions resulting in the Age of Enlightenment, but he remained paramount in the guise of Reason, and his presence was imposed on all 'others' of the West through the proselytizing and civilizing missions of colonialism that saw the Mother God as a remnant of primitive religions.

Neither Theos nor Logos

It is important to recognize that the Divine Feminine in all her manifestations points to a different 'ontology' if that word can even be used, or more as a 'deontology' since praxis and ethics is central to her traditions rather than dogma and moralizations. Here I posit the Great Goddess of India as neither Theos nor Logos and its implication; in essence she belongs to the non-theist traditions of India although she too like many other forms is worshipped as an *ishta-devata*. I show her presence in a poor village within the eastern tantric belt in Odisha before presenting a textual reading. Making use of the extraordinary anthropological work of Frédérique Apffel-Marglin (1996) that does not treat people as 'objects' of study, I will show how the existence of the Great Mother in a so called pre-modern setting differently constructs the psyche of both men and women who do not see spirituality through an other worldly prism. It is vital here to suspend Western essentialism and constructivism debate which maybe somewhat valid in its reasoning but is not applicable everywhere. Personally, I do accept the premise of a difference, albeit a fluid one, between men and women, or there will be no revolutionary potential left to feminism in its spiritual realm.

Apffel-Marglin, who argues in her essay for a different kind of cognition, describes in detail *raja-parba* or the menstruation festival of the Goddess Harachandi; her work also shows that there is a kind of continuity between the Great Goddess and the village practices of mostly low-caste women and men. During this festival, for three days, women stay in the village resting and men rest from their regular work celebrating with other men the annual menstrual cycle of the Goddess. In Apffel-Marglin's interviews, a woman from the village clearly identifies herself with the Goddess and finds continuity between her body and the 'body' of the Goddess. Sisulata explains how men must leave the women alone during this festival: 'This festival is almost like our menstruation . . . we follow the same rules as during our menses since we are of the same kind as her . . . We are parts [*ansa*] of her.' Then a man, Bhikari Parida from another village who participates in the festival, explains the difference between men and women, but he identifies the Goddess beyond the play of difference:

Women are *prakriti*, the creative energy [*srusti sakti*] and we are *purusa* [male] and we come here to worship the greater energy [*adisakti*], the Mother [*ma*]. . . . The Mother, the earth, and women are the same thing in different forms. . . . When the Goddess is bleeding we stop all work in the fields, and not only we farmers but all other men, blacksmiths, carpenters, potters, washermen, barbers, etc. It is incumbent upon us that we should please the Goddess and women at this time. Young women [i.e. pre-menopausal] celebrate Raja because they are at the centre of creation and we want to make them happy and please them. (1996: 161)

It is important to notice that the tantric substratum to which the Oriya tradition belongs has a different attitude towards menstruation than the oft quoted Brahminical pollution idea, which too is more complex and varied than it often appears in analysis. Also, the notion of untouchability during menstruation has a different connotation within the tantric reading and does not connote pollution but sacred power that must not be disturbed. Having seen my widowed grandmother celebrate a similar festival called *ambubachi*, in a Brahmin household, I can attest to the fact that traditions of the Goddess permeate Brahmin and non-Brahmin worlds.

The fact that men take up similar roles of menstruating women during the festival when they give up their regular work, rest, and celebrate as they cook and share meals together, reveals that in such a non-modern ethos the strict separation between rational male world of the mind, and irrational female world of unreflective subjectivities does not exist. To designate such a world as primitive and in need of modernist developmental intervention so that they could participate in 'progress' and capitalist production and reproduction is to fall into the trap of universalism which hides its imperial persona behind the mask of benevolence. This is not to say that the poverty of these villagers should not be alleviated, but as most of the modernist projects like the Narmada dam show these projects are not meant to remove poverty but the poor from their land and ways of subsistence.

I designate such a world as primarily Gynocentric. It is not condescension to or privileging of village women, but in the spirit of participation in this volume, I will venture to say that one needs to listen to and learn from villagers such as these, both women and men. Instead of patronizing attitudes that most elite feminists bring to such 'third world' women, one needs to participate in their modes of resistance steeped in their spiritual understanding of their world, which does not separate the material world from the spiritual. I will also argue that solidarity cannot be based on a supposed ideology that 'all women are oppressed' and need to unite to fight the enemy—the male of the species. There is a need to steer clear of agonistic models of the self, or one will remain locked in conflict models for all time. Revitalizing the Shiva/Shakti model for all concerned may be a useful *upaya*, or skillful means of transformation.

Without denying the reality of oppressive structures, one must resist them in ways that produce wholesome results. In fact, only by recognizing the complex interplay of historical formations of particular patriarchies in conjunction with imperialist and capitalist modes of production and modernist ideology that women experience particular kinds of oppression, that can actually begin to be transformed as work is done towards a more equitable world for all. In neither idealizing nor denouncing their ways of life, the immense diversity of human knowledge systems and spiritual paths can be recognized.

Apffel-Marglin's theoretical conclusions from her fieldwork posits a different cognitive model. Following the school of 'enactive cognition' which is a 'mode of being, acting, or thinking where there is no ontological gulf between the mind and the world or body', Apffel-Marglin shows how the villagers enact a creative activity which emerges 'out of a particular interactions between humans and the world. . . . It is therefore not an imitation of nature but a creative, intelligent activity motivated by our embodied condition' (1996: 171). There is a seamless connection between everyday life of the villagers and the ritual action of the festive times that suffuses their embodied existence with the spirit of the Divine Mother, marked by an understanding of the self and the universe which saves them from that radical alienation which afflicts modernity. But one is enamored of one's own 'way of life' to such an extent that he/she wants to bring it to everyone around the world whether they like it or not. If they reject the neat geometries of rationalist calculations that will give them all the plastic 'necessities' they can manufacture in the sweatshops, they are branded as ignoramuses incapable of instrumental rationality. Fortunately, environmental crisis is bringing in a new consciousness that resists mindless development.

The better known aspects of the Goddess needs a closer look to recognize how she avoids easy identification either as Theos, a creator deity outside of creation or Logos, the word identified in reason. The Divine Feminine has been present within the Indic horizon from time immemorial. Patriarchal traditions could not dethrone her as exclusive male deities supplanted the Goddess in the West. The Great Goddess's re-emergence in the later Indic textual horizon in the fifth-century text *Devi Mahatmya* has been testified and argued over by many writers. A fellow Shakta writes:

In the *Devi Mahatmya*, various conceptions of the feminine principle (*prakriti, maya, shakti*) combine with the notion of an ultimate reality to create a Great Goddess who is the power inherent in creation and dissolution, the primordial material substance (*mula-prakriti*), as well as the creative impulse, formless yet the matrix of all forms, transcendent as well as immanent. . . . An important development in this text is its departure from the normative understanding of shakti as an aspect of a male supreme divinity; here, the feminine principle has self-agency and complete autonomy. She is not merely the power of the Absolute, She *is* the Absolute. (Dasgupta Sherma 2000: 33)

Goddess and Violence

Since then the Great Goddess as the one beyond both the categories of transcendence and immanence (that are after all categories arising out of a binary logic) has enveloped the Indic world with great benevolence for the devotee. She appears differently to the one desirous of real freedom and her iconic meaning speaks to her multi-vocal absent presence. One of the ways that the Great Goddess of India especially Kali has been understood and devalued in some Western scholarship and popular media is that she is a 'violent' Goddess, or in psychoanalytic speak a 'castrating mother'. It requires a considerable leap of imagination for people from traditions that have thoroughly erased the feminine from the space of the Divine to understand the unique tradition that proclaims that the active force in the universe, Shakti, is feminine. Her garland of heads has created serious anxieties among Western male scholars (Kripal 2000) leading to all kinds of psychoanalyzing impulses. The symbolic meaning of Kali's icon has been elaborated by other western scholars who did not feel threatened by the image. (Kinsley 1997)

Yet the idea of a violent goddess remains prevalent in Western writings. In response, discussing the demon slayer Durga's story, Madhu Khanna explains:

the gory mythological episode expresses the multiple personality of the demon, Mahisha, who is gradually divested of his many 'egos' by Durga/Kali's relentless fury. His ability to transmute and advance a new threat in diverse guises depicts the split image as a root of violence. In contrast, the goddess's doubly violent role has been interpreted as a demonstration of the 'masculinized mother', a frenzied, almost psychotic state when she throws her femininity to the winds, and reverses her gender role. While the elemental powers of wrath, fury, anger and destruction are considered demonic or even dangerous in the Judeo-Christian tradition, the Hindu perception does not split these two aspects but views them as part of an integral totality of the divine feminine. The energy of the goddess is a seamless continuum of conscious force, which, when aroused, flows forth as violence or benign beneficence. The forces of opposition between militant masculinity and acquiescent femininity are not so sharply defined. (Unpublished paper. 7)[4]

I argue that without facing Kali's *bhayankari rupa*, fear-evoking, ferocious form, there is no access to her *abhaya mudra*, the gesture that assures 'be not afraid'.

Her transcendent function is to help her devotee leap out of the bounded ego, through the visual imagery of a severed head, and awaken to an ecstatic recognition that the world is immanently divine because it is her body, and she is both within and beyond the linguistic, or imagistic forms created to bring her to one's conscious understanding. To communicate the symbolic meaning of Kali here I will cite Ajit Mookerjee's detailed description in *Kali: The Feminine Force*:

The image of Kali is generally represented as black: 'just as all colours disappear in black, so all names and forms disappear in her' (*Mahanirvana Tantra*). In tantric rituals she is described as garbed in space, sky-clad (*digambari*). In her absolute, primordial nakedness she is free from all covering of illusion. She is Nature (Prakriti), stripped of 'clothes'. She is full breasted; her motherhood is a ceaseless creation. She gives birth to the cosmos parthenogenetically, as she contains the male principle within herself. Her disheveled hair (*elokeshi*) forms a curtain of illusion, the fabric of space-time which organizes matter out of the chaotic sea of quantum-foam. Her garland of fifty human heads, each representing one of the fifty letters of the Sanskrit alphabet, symbolizes the repository of knowledge and wisdom, and also represents fifty fundamental vibrations in the universe. (1988: 62)

Sometimes she is imagined simply as a compassionate mother without the complex psycho/spiritual symbolism. Multi-vocal meaning of an icon is meant to invoke different aspects of the Great Goddess in different people as they take what makes sense to them within their own spiritual paths, but in the path of knowledge, the emphasis has always been on the mind. The iconic and ritual practices are meant to lead to inner meditations. Indic traditions that recognized that the mind itself is the root of all troubles turned profoundly inward in its precise understanding of the way the mind works. Whether it is the most ancient substrata of the Yoga tradition manifested textually in Patanjali's *Yogasutra* where non-violence is the first commandment, or the Buddha's recognition of the truth of suffering, observation of the mind has been the first step in all meditation practices. Tantric traditions recognize some aspects of violence as a fact of life and its manifestations, and therefore teach the adept to visualize the shakti of the Goddess in her annihilating form in order to face it ritually and erase its destructive power within. Ahimsa, after all, is to annihilate the thought of violence from the mind, which is more difficult to do than simply avoiding its external manifestations.

Masculinity, Violence, and Motherhood

Whether violence is fundamentally masculine is a matter of debate, but as masculinity studies are pointing out, it definitely and persistently manifests itself in the arena of the male. I will not depict violence itself as masculine, but contend that it speaks of a breakdown within cultures where power as aggression is worshipped in every form. In Loren Pederson's insightful study *Dark Hearts: The Unconscious Forces that Shape Men's Lives* (1991), he writes about the movement of consciousness understood as primarily feminine in matrilineal periods to the understanding of consciousness as more masculine in modernity.

While science and technology have thrived under this excessively masculinized ideology of progress, born out of the Cartesian split in the

West, it also led to the most violent of all centuries, the twentieth one and continuing to the present, with warring nations at the brink of destroying all life on earth. Unfortunate side effects of this hyper-masculinity that gets its energy from a truncated divinity are quite apparent in everyday life too. Calling this particular phenomenon as the dark side of consciousness, Pederson writes, 'We are becoming more aware of this dark side in terms of damage to the environment, the nuclear problem, the centuries of war that have been waged by men, and the harmful effects of domineering attitude toward women' (1991: 5).

From the Indic Shakta perspective, without bowing to the Great Goddess who both creates and destroys, a male adept cannot face the turmoil within and transcend it; without such clear confrontation of human reality, one can only wish for a heaven beyond the violence of the earth and its association with maternity and materiality that leads to a misogynist spirituality that must deny life processes. It is perhaps no accident that the *asuras* or demons that the Great Mother destroys are always male, but they do not symbolize the masculine principle imaged in the deep quiescence of Shiva, rather the hyper-masculine with his inflated ego that must be sacrificed so that the self recognizes its Shiva nature. The role of a teacher who guides one through the psychic processes are central in the tantric tradition, and the Shakta path that is deeply cognizant of the feminine force and the troubled male, recommends a woman guru whom the man must recognize as the image of the Great Goddess. This helps him recognize the Goddess within him who remains hidden under masculine pretensions of aggressive power. Recognition that she is the source of all, one who creates and destroys her own maya, allows the shakti within to rise.

It must be said that ironically women's traditional roles that have definitely kept her under patriarchal power as far as social and political realms are concerned, have also generally kept her from perpetrating serious violence on others although she has borne the brunt of male violence. Woman, whose primary role in most societies has been as a mother, may be able to overcome the turmoil within through the rituals of motherhood, but this is no automatic panacea for overcoming all violence within and without. Carol Ochs thoroughly examines motherhood in *Women and Spirituality* and demystifies its passive, container status and suggests that 'mothering—with its complex relationship to another person, its ever-changing roles, and its deep concern, all coupled with vast areas beyond control—may be an ideal context within which to explore spirituality' (1983: 29). She argues:

the insights that occur naturally in the course of mothering—the need to give oneself over completely, for a time. . .. the need to endure some discipline... the necessity to love the child not as a possession but as belonging to itself; and perhaps the most difficult insight of all, the necessity of letting go—complement and correct the insights of traditional spirituality. (Ochs 1983: 32)

There is a direct relationship between annihilating the divided and bounded self and the flowing of *karuna* or compassion symbolized in the flowing milk of the mother. Sexuality and violence have to be squarely confronted, as Kali the feminine force commands—after all, no commandment against murder or sexual transgression has worked. The Indic tantric tradition recognizes this fundamental fact; instead of hiding behind repression, escape and denial, it faces the facts and creates rituals to confront the power of desire and death. Although there have been abuses of power among tantric men, that does not invalidate the tradition itself which is deeply satisfying to women as a philosophy. In the Shakta tradition a woman herself through meditative and ritual practices has to first realize her own power, and in being the proper guru of her companion, she helps him through the process of self-realization. At the same time she can learn from male teachers who have recognized their identity with the Divine Feminine. It is vital to recognize that within Gynocentric spiritualties, there is no devaluation of the masculine, but the woman adept marvels at the beauty that the male of the species brings to creation as she invites him to their conjoined spiritual path. Miranda Shaw, who in her book *Passionate Enlightenment* (1994) exposed the Western male bias in tantric scholarship to reveal a wealth of female teachers and adepts within tantric Buddhism, writes in her essay 'Is Vajrayogini a feminist?':

Clearly Vajrayogini is a strong supporter and champion of women, but she does not promote this philosophy at the expense of men. A woman on this path does not seek to dominate or exploit the man or crush him into submissive service. In Vajrayogini's version of ideal relationships, the women who manifest her presence in the world are to dispense kindness, happiness, bliss, insight, and sakti, or spiritual nourishment, helping men overcome their arrogance, intellectual pride, and alienation from life. (2000: 171–2)

Dancing Dualities

There is a possibility of a relationship between men and women that arises in such a tradition that can be called dancing dualities where each retain their difference and are able to dance together, emblematized in the Tibetan tantric Buddhist images of yub/yum. In the Hindu Shakta tantric world, such a duality of energies appears as Shakti and Shiva and is represented as the playful dance of the twosome. There are considerable differences how Shakti and Shiva are viewed in different Indic ways. It is important to recognize that these different valuations and emphases reveal the tension between more masculine or more feminine traditions within Indic history; however, no matter what pole of these formulations a particular sect identifies with, Shakti as a dynamic and active principle without which the masculine principle remains inert is quite prevalent across all Indic traditions, and there has always been a tantric substratum present within hugely diverse and complex Hindu, Buddhist, Jain and Sikh ways.

Individual men and women through visualization, meditative and ritual practices, as prescribed by both tantric Buddhism and its correspondent tantric Hinduism, harmonize these forces within them to ultimately unite with the *Brahman* or dissolve in *Shunyata* in a blissful merger with the infinite. In the Shakta tradition along with Vajrayana Buddhism with its Gynocentric emphasis on Prajna Paramita and Vajrayogini tradition bring the feminine principle at the centre to effectually counter hyper-masculine forces imaged as *asuras* in the myths about Durga. Miranda Shaw writes:

Part of the Tantric methodology of deconstructing the ordinary self is to replace it with a divine self. In Tantric union, the self, as a deity, unites with a partner who is simultaneously conceived as a deity. To experience the divinity of the partner is the touchstone of Tantric vision. One cannot divinize oneself while abusing, degrading, or dehumanizing the other person, because the partners mirror each other. (1994: 204)

I claim that without recognizing the presence of the Divine Feminine in the realm of the psyche, and her transformative role in a spiritual path, relationships between men and women remain locked within the logic of a power struggle, a battle of the sexes to grasp limited power positions and fast vanishing natural resources.

Such a battle keeps feminism within a vertical and individualistic domain of struggle since the only option available is the upwardly mobile movement to wrest power from the dominant master, and the slave must turn the dynamic upside down and subjugate the master within such a hierarchical structuring of dualities. The Shiva Shakti model presents dancing dualities[5] to resist the dueling dualities that permeate the political realm. Such a model of relationality between the sexes is different from the mind/body split model resulting in the master/slave dialectic. I will argue that the dancing dualities and mother/child model that Todorov and Ochs prescribe may effectively present an alternative to never-ending agonistic modes that Western ideologies present.

At this point, postmodern resistance to Enlightenment subjectivities in critical theory has its own vast discursive history and French feminists such as Luce Irigaray have been looking at the feminine philosophically to recognize the revolutionary potential of the Divine Feminine. In *Between*

East and West: From Singularity to Community (2002), Luce Irigaray looks at Yoga and what she calls feminine cultures of India, and identifies more integral Greek traditions that the West has forgotten: 'For the masters of the East, the body itself can become spirit through the cultivation of breathing. Without doubt, at the origin of tradition—for Aristotle, for example, and still, and still more for Empedocles—the soul still remains related to the breath, air. But the link between the two was then forgotten, particularly in philosophy' (7).

Philosophical Goddess and Mystical Awareness

Irigaray's observation brings me to my last point, that deep within most traditions sleeps the Divine Feminine, and it is a worthwhile project to unearth that layer for the beneficial effects on human psychic and spiritual health.[6] Feminist theologians have been long engaged in recovering the lost feminine divine. But she must also be understood philosophically to resist the phallic economy of thought. I will posit that 'Forgetting of Being' that Martin Heidegger (1968) laments in his philosophy can be compared to the Forgetting of the Feminine in theology. Heidegger shows that Greek thinking as in gathering of thought became mere ratio as Western metaphysics turned towards mere rationality (139). It is significant that post Heideggerean thought emblematized in Derrida and Deleuze is moving towards the feminine as Derrida's reading of Plato's Khora reveals.[7] It can be said that without recognizing the Divine Feminine, theology and philosophy both remain truncated and imprisoned in a halfway house that does not honour the complete being.

While the Divine remains beyond the borders of conceptual thought and therefore beyond gender, language requires form and whenever an effort is made to speak of the Divine, masculine language limits that divinity, not because it is masculine but because the presence of the female divine is unimaginable within the Judeo-Christian tradition, as many of my colleagues and students have attested. But even within these traditions, when the mystical paths of a Meister Eckhart or a Hildegaard are looked into, the hidden feminine presence is discovered. Amy Hollywood, who has studied contemporary interest in mysticism and bodily experiences in *Sensible Ecstasy: Mysticism, Sexual Difference, and the Demands of History*, shows how mystical has always been the site of the feminine and 'Eckhart, often taken as the greatest of speculative mystics. . . was profoundly influenced by women...'(2002: 8).

To further understand her 'Being' as neither Theos nor Logos, whose divine maya, her creative principle delights one into the play of life and death, eros and thanatos, as well as liberates us from our too close an association with life's ever-changing flux that we misread, we need to understand her as a philosophical goddess. She does not promise a heaven, but her sword cuts the delusion of our own projection that prevents us from direct perception of reality. It must be remembered that Greek thinkers (from whom the West traces its philosophical pedigree) did their thinking under the aegis of many powerful goddesses. Thomas McEvilley's insight into Greek and Indic paths is helpful here which must be considered and cited in detail. Comparing Greek *doxa* with Sanskrit *maya* which is 'conceived as either a cosmic force or an individual delusion', he writes:

Both concepts connect to Goddess-religions. Like Parmenides' goddess of *doxa*—Ananke, or Necessity, who sits within the wheels and gears of the illusion and manipulates them—*maya* is conceived as performing a philosophical version of the mother goddess role.... She is on a different ontological level from the Homeric and Hesiodic gods. As Xenophanes had said, the gods of the polytheism are creatures of *doxa*, living within the illusion; but Ananke makes the illusion work, and is outside and above it.... Mediating between One and Many, she echoes ancient goddesses both of fertility, who bring the Many into being, and of destruction, who return the Many into One. (McEvilley 2002: 55)

Arguing 'that association of monistic philosophy with goddess-worship was common', he mentions besides Parmenides that Pythagoras's house was turned into a temple of Demeter, and Heraclitus offered his book to the Ephesian Artemis. A form of her also 'sits at the center of Plato's universe in the Republic (616c–7b), spinning out time like a thread upon her spindle'. McEvilley shows the Indian parallels, noticing 'Indian monistic schools also favored goddess imagery—*maya,* the bewitching cosmic dancer whose dance *is* the stream of events; Kali, the devourer with necklaces of skulls around her neck, simultaneously engaged in sexual intercourse with Siva and in drinking brains from human skulls, and others' (McEvilley 2002: 56). To his reference of Sankara 'the unqualified monist and "Indian Parmenides"' as a Kali worshipper, I will add Abhinavgupta, the tenth-century Shakta-Shaiva tantric thinker and the better known second-century Nagarjuna, the Mahayana Buddhist, the non-theist whose Prajna Paramita texts are centred on another version of the Divine Feminine. Miranda Shaw in her recent book *Buddhist Goddesses of India* cites the following verse from *Astasahasrika Prajnaparamita Sutra*, or *8000–Line Perfect Wisdom Scripture*:

She is the Perfect Wisdom that never comes into being
And therefore never goes out of being.
She is known as the Great Mother...
She is the Perfect Wisdom who gives birthless birth to all Buddhas.
And through these sublimely Awakened Ones,
It is Mother Prajnaparamita alone
Who turns the wheel of true teaching. (2006: 166)

Shaw explains that 'In the foundational body of Mahayana literature known as the Prajnaparamita or Perfection of Wisdom texts, the highest metaphysical principle—the energy, glory, and radiance of enlightened wisdom—is envisioned as a cosmic female, the mother of knowledge, the source of all Buddhas' (2006: 166). She further argues for this deity figure's femaleness:

Although Prjnaparamita, like her namesake wisdom, is said to transcend all categories and to be beyond form…femaleness is central to her character. . .. Her femaleness, however, has an internal logic that goes beyond mere linguistic coincidence. There are deep metaphoric resonances between motherhood and the matrix of wisdom and reality she represents. If gender is to be assigned to a generative principle, the feminine gender is a logical choice, for the womb is the most tangible source of generation in human experience. (2006: 167)

I conclude that a truncated spirituality marked by the master narrative of the Father God is philosophically accompanied by the master narrative of a truncated Reason. I also claim that Heidegger's questioning and attempted overthrow of Western metaphysics remain incomplete without recognizing that the Forgetting of Being is perhaps a Forgetting of the Woman/Mother, and in order to 'decolonize the divine' it is necessary to re-instill both the Divine Feminine and Philo-Sophia as the proper name of the unnamable whose transcendent function is to suffuse the world with her immanent presence, transforming the material with an indwelling presence that will help resist the consumerist gods.

Conclusion: Feminist Projects and the Goddess

Perhaps future historians writing about past worlds will marvel at the remarkable revolutions brought about by women's movements worldwide and be amazed at the quiet transformation of public spaces with massive presence of 'free' women. Today, young women living in the economic comfort zones of the world (whatever the political marking—first or 'third'—of that world may be) take for granted their freedom to have a career and some collective political and social voice that would at least attempt to safeguard their rights as human beings.[8] The struggle continues to include more women in that economic comfort zone which remains monumental in many parts of the world, but economic freedom remains elusive and problematic as globalizing forces promise women freedom and pay them mere pittance in the sweatshops around the world.[9]

As they write their histories, the world my imagined future historians[10] will not 'see' is the inner worlds, the minds and souls of women and men that are, consciously or unconsciously, in search of a power within, that would truly free them from the most oppressive of all forces, the inner shackles. While there is no question that without political, economic and social freedom women's collective and individual lives in this new millennium remain severely truncated and under patriarchal forces of all shapes and sizes, in a world torn apart by violence of every kind, where even feminist gains in the political realms often replicate the hegemonic power structures, ultimately it is spiritual freedom that will provide the strength, resilience, and inner quiet necessary to sustain the struggle and enhance the real 'quality' of life for most people.

One may argue that feminist projects even spiritual activism, can be done without invoking the Divine Feminine. Yes, of course, but I claim that radical change comes from going into the psychic roots of oppression, and reclaiming traditions that have been erased or appropriated. If the divine has been a marker of value for humanity, it cannot be a truncated divinity. On the other hand, if the spiritual heritage of the Divine Mother is not claimed, hyper-masculinist fundamentalists will forever wound the Divine, and a reductive materialism in the form of consumerism will hold sway. Rita Gross has trenchantly asked 'what can more effectively undercut the humanity of women than to regard femaleness as unworthy to symbolize the sacred?' (2000: 107). She has argued 'against some western feminists' that 'Hindu goddesses can promote the humanity of Hindu women by providing the psychological well-being that positive female imagery brings' and that 'the first function of goddesses is not to provide equal rights or high status, but to provide psychological comfort, and nothing is more basic to psychological comfort than the presence of positive female imagery at the heart of a valued symbol system' (Gross 2000: 107). I will go a step further and say that the presence of the Great Goddess in the symbolic sphere and the recognition of her different ontological status in her transcendent immanence are vital to curb the excessive masculinization of the social and the body politic leading to incessant wars.

My perspective is spiritual and philosophical rather than socio-political, not in opposition to but as supplement to the work of feminist activists. Without acknowledging that symbol systems, ideologies and unspoken beliefs construct one's unconscious self, one is in danger of falling prey to their power; therefore, eternal vigilance by right minded women and men is vital to resist such ultra-masculinist projects that even some women can fall prey to. Without dismantling the Name of the Father in its most destructive aspect of instrumental rationality there is no access to the numinosity of the Divine, and that is possible only when the acknowledgement has been made of the dual nature of the Divine in her phantasmagoric appearance in the world as both female and male. Primacy must be given to the mother/child relationality, only then the dancing dualities and the playfulness of the original being can be revealed. Both Greek and Indic 'thinking' traditions arose when thinkers were psychically attuned to the Divine Feminine and could perceive the depth of the Divine Mother's *lila*.

Once recognizing the transcendent immanence of her presence, one can then free oneself from the acute self-centred action of the small self in its possessive grasping and observe the violence within that engenders the violence without. While the Indic God the Mother remains philosophically complex, above all she shows our relatedness to the world. She also severs any excessive attachment to the same world and hence excessive immanence that mere materiality brings about. Since the feminine opens the way to a not-self like Afro Surinamese idea of 'odo'[11] where the borders between human and divine are porous to the point that it marks a different epistemology and ontology, identification with the feminine may inaugurate a different way of being leading to a less violent world. If a philosophical turn is seen towards the plane of immanence, the worldwide appeal of the recent film *Avatar*, however stereotyped and binary in its presentation of a hyper-masculine West vs. a 'feminized' non-West steeped in mother deities may be, is a popular marker. People, at the brink of an ecological disaster, may recognize the need for asserting the divinity of the body, the woman, and the mother earth. Thus this festival of dialogues has an urgency in today's world since the balance between dualities have been severely skewed; in order to work towards harmony and restore relative peace, it is important to revitalize the feminine in her pristine suchness so that both women and men as dancing Shakti/Shiva can become actors in her *lila* beyond mere self-knowledge.

Notes

1. Tantra has been defined in various ways but the meaning most associated with it is that which extends knowledge. It is at once a body of texts, a *sadhana/* practice methodology as well as a philosophy. Tantra situates spirituality within the body, especially in the body of the woman and attempts to realize the non-dual thought in the ecstatic union with the Divine Feminine.
2. I had written elsewhere that once a devotee has been devoured by Kali, she had nothing to fear, so I was delightfully surprised to hear about Gloria Anzaldua's discussion of her being 'devoured' by Coatlique, the serpent goddess of her Mesoamerican tradition (cited in Fernandes 2003: 42). Scholars have yet to do comprehensive cross-cultural studies about the connection between goddesses and the idea of a not-self.

3. In my book *In the Beginning IS Desire* I use the word Gynocentric with a capital G to denote Shakta perspectives of a spirituality marked by the Divine Feminine.

4. I thank Madhu Khanna for permission to cite this paper 'The Goddess at War: A Hermeneutical Interpretation of War and Peace in Hindu and Tantric Myths' presented at World's Religions After 11 September conference in Montreal, September 2006.

5. The yin/yang icon in its circularity and interpenetrating positioning of polarities also represents a more harmonious and non-hierarchical model. It is important to remember that such a model too like Shiva Shakti acknowledges the presence of the other within each and does not necessarily subscribe to a watertight and 'essentialized' model that cannot cross the boundaries of the other that hierarchized models represent.

6. Elinor Gadon's *The Once and Future Goddess: A Symbol for Our Time* (1989) heralds the coming of the Goddess spirituality in the modern world.

7. See Ilse Bulhof's essay 'Being Open as a Form of Negative Theology' where she writes: 'Khora is something different, not even transcendent; it is removed or near. Khora is on one side mother and nurturer, and on the other side virgin. She/It is not a link to the father. She/It has no descendants, children. She/It is not fertile, overflowing with goodness' (2000: 213).

8. Julia Kristeva in 'Women's Time' states that the benefits ensuing from women's movements, which originated in 'the socio-political life of nations' are quite extensive and 'these have already had or will soon have effects even more important than those of the Industrial Revolution.' (1989: 197).

9. Writing about the maquiladoras, June Nash says: 'Women are drawn to the border by illusory promise of secure jobs and access to consumer goods beyond their dreams' (2005: 153).

10. I use the idea of history with caution and with playfulness as historicism itself is implicated in the world order mapped by the Enlightenment which ignores the inner world and relegates it to the irrational in its march of a progressive worldview that will bring European modernity to 'civilize' the irrational 'others', including women as they too belong to the irrational pole of the equation. See Dipesh Chakrabarty (2000) for his critique of historicism.

11. Gloria Wekker's description of Afro-Surinamese 'odo' 'suggests that the subject is made up of various instances, including gods and spirits of ancestors, and that all of these need to be acknowledged and held in harmony' (quoted in Fernandes 2003: 40).

References

Apffel-Marglin, Frédérique (1996), 'Rationality, the Body, and the World: From Production to Regeneration', in *Decolonizing Knowledge: From Development to Dialogue,* ed. Frédérique Apffel-Marglin and Stephen A. Marglin, Oxford: Clarendon Press.

Bulhof, Ilse N. (2000), 'Being Open As a Form of Negative Theology: On Nominalism, Negative Theology, and Derrida's Performative Interpretation of "Khora"', in *Flight of Gods: Philosophical Perspective on Negative theology*, ed. Ilse Bulhof and Laurens ten Kate, New York: Fordham University Press, pp. 195–222.

Chakrabarty, Dipesh (2000), *Provincializing Europe: Postcolonial Thought and Historical Difference,* Princeton: Princeton University Press.

Cixous, Helene (1989), 'Sorties: Out and Out: Attacks/Ways Out/Forays', in *The Feminist Reader: Essays in Gender and the Politics of Literary Criticism,* ed. Catherine Belsey and Jane Moore, New York: Basil Blackwell.

Desmond, William (2005), *Is There a Sabbath for Thought?: Between Religion and Philosophy*, New York: Fordham University Press.

Fernandes, Leela (2003), *Transforming Feminist Practice: Non-Violence, Social Justice and the Possibilities of a Spiritualized Feminism*, San Francisco: Aunt Lute Books.

Gadon, Elinor (1989), *The Once and Future Goddess: A Symbol for Our Time*, New York: Harper.

Gross, Rita M. (2000), 'Is the Goddess a Feminist?', in *Is the Goddess a Feminist?: The Politics of South Asian Goddesses,* ed. Alf Hiltebeitel and Kathleen Erndl, New York: New York University Press.

Heidegger, Martin (1968), *What is Called Thinking?,* tr. Fred D. Wieck and J. Glenn Gray, New York: Harper and Row.

Hollywood, Amy (2002), *Sensible Ecstasy: Mysticism, Sexual Difference and the Demands of History*, Chicago: Chicago University Press.

Huntington, Samuel (1996), *The Clash of Civilizations and the Remaking of World Order,* New Delhi: Penguin.

Irigaray, Luce (2002), *Between East and West: From Singularity to Community*, tr. Stephen Pluhacek, New York: Columbia University Press.

Kant, Immanuel (1784), 'What is Enlightenment?', http://www.english.upenn.edu/~mgamer/Etexts/kant.html.

Khanna, Madhu (Unpublished paper), 'The Goddess at War: A Hermeneutical Interpretation of War and Peace in Hindu and Tantric Myths'.

Kinsley, David (1997), *Tantric Visions of the Divine Feminine: The Ten Mahavidyas,* Delhi: Motilal Banarasidass.

Kripal, Jeffrey J. (2000), 'A Garland of Talking Heads for the Goddess: Some Autobiographical and Psychoanalytic Reflections on the Western Kali', in *Is the Goddess a Feminist?: The Politics of South Asian Goddesses,* ed. Alf Hiltebeitel and Kathleen Erndl, New York: New York University Press.

Kristeva, Julia (1989), 'Women's Time', in *The Feminist Reader: Essays in Gender and the Politics of Literary Criticism,* ed. Catherine Belsey and Jane Moore, New York: Basil Blackwell.

McEvilley, Thomas (2002), *The Shape of Ancient Thought: Comparative Studies in Greek and Indian Philosophies,* New York: Allworth Press.

Mookerjee, Ajit (1988), *Kali: The Feminine Force,* Rochester, Vermont: Destiny Books.

Nash, June (2005), 'Women in Between: Globalization and the New Enlightenment', *Signs: Journal of Women in Culture and Society,* vol. 31, no. 1, pp. 145–67.

Ochs, Carol (1983), *Women and Spirituality,* Totowa, NJ: Rowman and Allanheld.

Pederson, Loren (1991), *Dark Hearts: The Unconscious Forces That Shape Men's Lives*, Boston: Shambhala.

Saxena, Neela Bhattacharya (2004), *In the Beginning is Desire: Tracing Kali's Footprints in Indian Literature*, New Delhi: Indialog.

Sherma, Rita Das Gupta (2003), ' " Sa Ham—I am She": Woman as Goddess', in *Is the Goddess a Feminist?: The Politics of South Asian Goddesses,* ed. Alf Hiltebeitel and Kathleen Erndl, New York: New York University Press.

Shaw, Miranda (1994), *Passionate Enlightenment: Women in Tantric Buddhism*, Princeton: Princeton University Press.

Shaw, Miranda (2000), 'Is Vajrayogini a Feminist?: A Tantric Buddhist Case Study', in *Is the Goddess a Feminist?: The Politics of South Asian Goddesses,* ed. Alf Hiltebeitel and Kathleen Erndl, New York: New York University Press.

Shaw, Miranda (2006), *Buddhist Goddesses of India*, Princeton: Princeton University Press.

Todorov, Tzvetan (1996), 'Living Alone Together', *New Literary History,* vol. 27, no.1, pp. 1–14.

23

Sociality and Subjectivity:
An Ontological Return to the Other

PRASENJIT BISWAS

The idea of 'sociality' as a foundational notion of human relationship assumes the role of a ground or basis of all possible forms of human relationships—ethical, aesthetic and intellectual. But such an idea in its concrete shape produces a genealogy of belonging to a tradition or culture in which every shift is considered as a 'internal' historical episode. Such episodes of shifting valuational and epistemic framework are attributed to interplay between reason and consciousness that always formed a basis or a ground. Hegel's reading of Kant's notion of Consciousness as noumenal being, a being that is in-itself and also a being of in-itself expounds the latter 'in-itself' only as a being-for-consciousness, which radically alters the very character of consciousness as a being-toward in-itself of the Consciousness (Hegel 1977: 55–6). Such a being is 'being' of conscious facts, as in psychology, while at the same time it remains a being that possesses such conscious facts. Such a being cannot anymore be the being of 'in-itself' as in-itself is now altered into the 'being' of in-itself, which is Consciousness itself. Although Hegel considers this transformation of in-itself into consciousness, which is no longer a being-in-itself, which rather is a being-for-itself as dialectical, yet one has to probably make a distinction between transcendental dialectic and immanent dialectic. The transcendental dialectic concerns itself with the independence of being, while the immanent dialectic concerns itself with interplay between being and consciousness in order to situate the outcome of this play. Kant can be credited with maintaining a distinction between analytic of judgements and the function of pure reason, though he didn't venture into how such a distinction itself is possible because of the dialectical character of consciousness that overcomes the duality between transcendental and empirical/sensible. This combination of 'immanence' and 'overcoming' the diversity of phenomenological datum about consciousness assumes the role of a 'metaphysical substance' that belongs to a definite 'opening in the space' (Derrida 1982: 133). Such an opening is 'multiple' as its origin does not lie in causal or normative sources. Rather it is an opening to the Subject within the instability of the singular omnipresence of History, which belongs to the infinite regression or progression of events and situations, counted as one in the interest of a presumed unity between thought/subjectivity and its conditions of possibility. For a post-Kantian Hegelianism of this sort, the overcoming of the duality between 'transcendental' and 'empirical' lies in being-in-the-situation, which is a collation of multiple possibilities that gives an ontological force to the will-to-know in order to count the multiple as one cardinal entity. Such an ontological force is explained by Heidegger when he says, 'Metaphysics, insofar as it always represents only beings as beings [das Seiende als das Seiende vorstelt], does not recall Being itself [das Sein selbst]' (1975: 275–6). This annulment of Being in order to respond to the call of being, which is an ontological situation of naming Being as no-thing or void, which at the same time is the difference between beings and being-as-such. The description, 'being-in-the-situation' is the mark of this differences such that the event as present(ed) 'belongs to that-which-is-not-being-qua-being' (Badiou 2005: 189–90). But such a difference is the predominance of one signifying order over other, one can call it a 'presentation' of the presented as different from that which is present—an ontological duality that simultaneously denies the limits of presentation as well as transgression of the limit. In Heidegger's words,

What is distinctive about man resides in the fact that, as the one whose essence it is to think, open toward Being, he is placed before the latter, remains related to Being and thus corresponds to it. Man properly is this relation of correspondence, and he is only this. 'Only': this does not mean a limitation, but an overabundance.

In man, there prevails a belonging to Being, a belonging, which listens to Being, because it is appropriated over to being (1974: 31).

This foundational relationship of correspondence between 'human' and 'being' is a relationship between Beings's coming to presence and human's giving themselves to the presence, which is not necessarily a 'sacrifice', but a gesture of a giving of an 'it' that belongs to a prior Hegelian 'substance-subject' (Malabou 2005: 118) that contains a differentiation between itself and its positioning itself as the being of a subject. A 'substance-subject' as a double movement of towards being and conscious subjectivity necessarily divided itself as a remainder to presence. This takes one to a plasticity of subjectivity that establishes the Heideggerain correspondence between being and consciousness, which later manifests itself in the form of a 'future' thought or subjectivity. Such a future thought is constituted by a temporal disjunction between prior determination of Being as a giving-to and a consequent affirmation of presence that leads one to a question, how can the transition from the in–itself to the for–itself open a dialectic between being and consciousness? The answer can be formulated in two different and interrelated ways:

1. Essenceless Subjects, called being-for-consciousness of the in–itself, which is 'pure being', which merely ascends without descending into the depths of subjectivity to become a Subject (Hegel 1977: 419). Such a being is a neuter, neither this nor that, it is rather 'to be in the middle of all that' and 'to be in the center'.[1] Such a positioning of being has too many correspondences, so much so that there are as many idioms as there are things. The 'many' of things and entities correspond to 'many' idioms of Being, which is essenceless-by-play [*ein wesenloses beyherspielen*].

2. Essenceless subjects assume an architectonic a 'totality of relations' within an episteme (Foucault 1972: 191) that embodies the signifiers of correspondences between being and consciousness within a particular period or discursive science.

These two ways are interrelated as a binary relation between play and form, as Aristotle conceived it in terms of *aletheia* or disclosure. Such an idea is further nuanced to include an idea of a ployletic determination of Subject that lies at the crossroads of being and play. This determination remains polyletic on the ground that it not only involves the subjectivity of the singular self, but what accompanies the singular self is the disclosure of a plurality of beings that does not yield a place to a singular subjecthood. In the same vein, the singular that is yet to become cannot arrogate itself to the status of being or non-being, rather it remains in a state of undecidability that eludes 'real presence'. This disclosure of an undecidable moment of existence acts as the background against which the being is conceived in lived experiences. The crossroads of being and play is a crossroads primarily because the radically undecidable being plays out its non-presence within the performance of play in a non-reflexive manner such that every real embodiment of being can participate in the play. The totality of relations that such a play generates can be conceived as a 'manifold'. In Plotnisky's description of this play, one realizes,

in Hegel such multiplicities can often be best described in terms of one another. Each may serve as a descriptive 'mathematics' ('calculus', 'algebra', 'geometry', 'topology', 'analysis' and so forth) or translation of the other, even though all of them are, jointly, placed in the service of the inaccessible. History is a calculus or allegory (one among many) of philosophy, philosophy is (again, one among many) that of history, matter of mind, mind of matter; consciousness of the unconscious, the unconscious of consciousness; and so forth. (2002: 168)

The features of the crossroads between being and play is determined by Plotinsky here as 'spirals' as far as Hegel is concerned, but such spirals are multiple foldings and pathways that constitute a certain 'thought-style' and a certain 'lure of technique' that produces a contrast between the 'real presences' and 'relational-responsive' (Shtter 2006: 53–4) opening to the not-yet-formed subjectivity, the 'other' of Subject. Such an opening to the other, with its not-yet-formed subjectivity, acts as a source of crossing every single determination of otherness into a plurality of being that play themselves out in the open without falling into an idea of 'givenness'. The givenenss of the 'other' in a non-intentional mode is outside the givenness of relationality that spirals around responses in the manifold of play, which is a detour through 'real presences'. As B.K. Agarwala in a prolific moment of entwining Jiva in what he called the 'lil "a Jiva', says:

The purpose of the game is merely to be played. The task of the game is just to play, to play it for no end other than playing it and thus to play it without end …

To play something is also to present it … the game presents itself, plays itself out, but it also means that the players present themselves in it. So in lilā not only lilā comes into presentation but also Brahman comes to present itself in the form of or appearance of Jiva caught in … vikshepa sakti of māyās. (2004: 142–3)

In the instance of playing a game, the players present themselves as 'pure presence' that does not present the 'being' of players, rather 'game' abstracts a limited structure of relationships and strategies that attempts to enforce a being in the world that is a kind of projection in the world. Such a projection is a disconcealment of the relation.

This is explained by Heidegger as Dasein's projection upon its own possibilities, as 'the possible impossibility of its own existence' (1956: 11–12). This possible impossibility is manifest in Dasein's anxiety that only manifests 'nothing' that produces a gap between Dasein's pre-ontological understanding of itself and the way the world appears to Dasein. The very being of the Dasein does not find its significance in the world. Heidegger expresses the state of anxiety as a double consciousness: (1) the presence of the being of the entities in the world that makes it manifest as 'nothing of the world', which is an 'attunement' of being and (2) the being of 'nothing of the world' is disclosed only in anxiety and boredom, that is, an inner strife of 'being there' (Heideggor 2002: 78–9). Both (1) and (2) taken together give the existential reality of perpetual anxiety over the state of being, which is also the historical condition for Dasein's existence. This is stated by Heidegger as existence of Being-in-the-World in relation to Being-with-the-Other, which Heidegger called 'destiny' in a historical sense,

The [destiny] is how we designate the historizing of the community, of a people. Destiny is not something that puts itself together out of individual fates, any more than being-with-one-another can be conceived as the occurring together of several subjects. Our fates have already been guided in advance, in our being with one another in the same world and in our resoluteness for definite possibilities. (Hidegger 1962: 436)

The notion of 'destiny' arises in Being-with that marks a common and shareable state of existence for Dasein. The fate of Dasein is guided in advance insofar as it shares a common destiny with other beings-in-the-world, which is the temporal-historical source of Dasein's fate. Such a fate is common, although it is not necessary that Daseins have a common identity. In a sense, Dasein simultaneously faces its being in concrete disclosure of historical moments as well as it transcends this facticity of being by way of overcoming its own no-thingness in the concrete role as an actor, with the possibility of being a victim or a victor. What is guided in advance as a common destiny appears in the form of the possibility that it has inherited, which is disclosed as a 'choice' for the Dasein, which Heidegger terms as a 'situation' in which the Dasein is thrown into. Such a 'throwness', paradoxically, discloses one or other possibility for the Dasein as a projected fate that takes over its being there, which again at the same time, turns into 'attunement', which is a state of being 'anxious'. Anxiety is directed to the world without a specific object, while fear is directed to a specific object. In anxiety, the Dasein is indifferent towards entities, but the significance of entities is intact and it stands in purposive interrelations. Heidegger diagnoses that in anxiety the world is turned insignificant and the Dasein collapses into itself. In anxiety nothing matters, there is no significance, no wholeness of relevance, so in a sense the world is not there. Heidegger spoke of 'the nothing of the world'. However, being affected by the insignificance of entities as a whole is quite different from experiencing no entities at all. Insignificance is not absence. 'The nothing of the world . . . does not mean that in anxiety one experiences the absence of the innerworldly occurrent. It must be encountered, so that it can have no relevance at all and can show itself in an empty mercilessness.' In their insignificance entities are very much there, they show themselves in their strangeness. Just as the indifference of deep boredom refers to Dasein's possibilities, anxiety, in its own way, comes with a kind of referring. It refers to entities as they are in themselves. As their significance recedes, they light up as entities in themselves, i.e. as entities that are independent of Dasein's possibilities. In pursuing a post–Kantian Hegelianism, one can characterize these entities as 'topological' that are encountered by Dasein in the crossroads of play between being and consciousness. Such entities in themselves acquire historicity by losing their essence as they annul the possibility of response.

This lack of response makes a reference to entities as a whole and not to any specific entity within the world. It does not refer Dasein to any possibilities, i.e. it does not refer Dasein's basic understanding to a way to be. This distinction that Heidegger draws between Dasein's possibilities and anxiety is reflected in the distinction between 'mere facticity' and 'historicity'. The former is termed as 'ontic' and the latter as 'ontological'. The 'ontic' is the non-objectifiable ground of experience that discloses the significance of the world in which the factical Dasein is said to 'live'. The 'ontological' is what is disclosed as 'possibility' in Dasein's Being-with, the modality of which lies in the encounter with the 'nothing of the world'. The encounter assumes the form of anxiety and/or 'not being-at-home' through which the world is disclosed to the Dasein as destiny.

Ontico-Ontological Difference

The 'ontic' reality relates to 'facticity', while the 'ontological' relates to the meaning of being as presence or absence as such as part of a system of thought and inhabitants of language. The question of difference arises at two levels: at the level of predicates that 'present' being and at the level of 'conditions of possibility' of that very presence. The presence of being (which is not an object or entity) is different from mere facticity of an experience of being; it is rather a reflected notion of being that arises from the very intentional constitution of subjectivity that enters into every instance of 'facticity', which is an already interpreted notion of facts. This already interpreted notion of things/facts in the intentional-reflected notion of being in the subjectivity of the Subject overcomes the duality between Subject and Object, Self and Other by way of an ontico-ontological difference that differentiates 'facticity' and 'being'. Heidegger granted Dasein or being-in-the-world only the status of 'ontology', while he granted the 'ontic' status to humans as the only creature that has a being. But this Heideggerain notion of Dasein as both 'ontic' and 'ontological' produces the notion of a centred being that presents itself in the world qua self-consciousness that ultimately establishes a connection of necessity between how the ontologically present being understands, interprets and acts in the world. This connection of necessity makes both 'ontic' and 'ontological' as mutually co-constitutive such that the difference that Heidegger talked of, between Dasein and the entities towards which Dasein bears a relation of comportment, is circumvented by bringing the difference under a co-reductive holism.

Difference and co-constitutivity between Dasein's being and the entities in the world that gets neutralized in a kind of holism does not bring out what Derrida called 'differences of forces' against a metaphysical determination of presence and sameness (1982a: 260). Against such a metaphysical determination either as an inside or an outside, difference of forces are the most 'active' agent to subvert any holist understanding of the mutually reinforcing relationship between intentionality/subjectivity and causality/objectivity. This subversion by the force of opposition is not to re-inscribe a dialectical temptation of co-reduction within a system of difference, but it is an affirmation of an event in time that manifests as 'being' without an identity either with itself or with any other being. This non-identity in the manifest being does not deprive it of the status of an existential/transcendental sense, rather it acquires the status of one being always in difference to itself resisting any ontological determination of difference.

This role of a continuous difference as an ontologically indeterminate process within the system of thought acquires a lot of significance in understanding the happenings around that are a part of the world co-constituted by humans and other agents. Such a co-constituted sense of happening combines several possibilities of commonality and specificity. To make a sense of these phenomenal possibilities, one has to imagine the play between the human subjects in the domain of the symbolic which produces a differential reality of tracing what happens. The theoretical importance of an ontological indeterminacy of the position of subject in the phenomenon of co-constitutivity lies in the possibility of making sense of the matrix of relation that constitutes a context of establishing a relationship with the other.

The process of tracing an event is a process of undergoing the transformations that are a part of series of heterogeneous differences that can only throw up an existential background for what is present, to itself and to the other. The particularity of what is present and the singularity of what is presented to the process of tracing is the impossibility of assuming the fullness of being in any fact or disclosure, but this impossibility brings into the field of consciousness the limits of Being's potentiality. An existentialist description of this limit takes the form of a distinction between 'potentiality-to-be' and the 'potentiality-not-to' as presented by Agamben in his reading of Existentialism (2001: 40). Agamben's reinterpretation of Heidegger hinges on this notion of dialectic between 'potentiality-to-be' and 'potentiality-not-to' that coexist not as opposites, but as 'time-now' and 'time-that-remains'. The former brings facticity to a stop at a juncture of history with the disclosure of the potential, that is, potentiality-to-be as disclosed within the temporal horizons of a given structure of subjectivity.

It is in this manner potentiality-to-be is constitutive of history as time-now and as being-there. In contrast, time-that-remains is the time that remains after the constitution of subjectivity has reached a definite achievement in the sense of an end. In relation to this end, the historicized subject with its sense of the world arises beyond the 'horizon' of chronological (historical) time that has thrown the being into a determined state of existence. As this determined state of existence is the potentiality-to-be, it does not address the aporia or space of ambivalence between the constituted subjectivity and the historicized subjectivity that emerges beyond determination. For example, in the event of Partition of the Indian subcontinent in 1947, the aporia between the partitioned self/subjectivity as constituted by chronological occurrences of events and the experiential and the lived subjectivity of being a refugee beyond the determination of history is an extremely rich resource of representation. This historicized Subject emerges in the 'operational time' that comes after the 'potential' that is realized as the 'other side of Being' or 'otherwise than being' (pace Levinas). In case of partition, such a potential is realized in the post-displacement search for home in an alien, if not hostile, country. This historicized subject becomes the 'logos' in the existential sense of disclosure that claims to 'realize an enunciation without any real reference' as a spectral/temporal entity. In Agamben's words:

our representation of chronological time, as the time in which we are, separates us from ourselves and transforms us into impotent spectators of ourselves—spectators who look at the time that flies without any time left, continually missing themselves—messianic time, an operational time in which we take hold of and achieve our representations of time, is the time that we ourselves are, and for this very reason, is the only real time, the only time we have. (2006: 68)

This is much more than Dasein that only encounters 'nothing of the world'. It is more in the sense that it distinguishes between state of existence as 'spectators of ourselves' that separates the being from the self/identity/subjectivity and the being that one is as represented in the temporalization of yet-to-come possibilities. The partitioned Dasein probably meets its destiny in the yet-to-come, without inheriting it from the already lived world, but in a sense by way of surpassing the lived and the realized in its non-coincidence with what their 'selves' are. Further, such an emergent subjectivity is also a contingent figure of representation, whose 'experience' can only be narrated as 'spectatorial'. As the partitioned self neither lies in the present nor in the past, its potential 'meets' what is yet-to-come in a spectatorial mode. This Agambenian twist to Dasein's possibilities sets aside the limits posed on consciousness by the ontology of no-thingness, which for Heidegger is a counter-thesis of his notion of Dasein, as also it overcomes the gap between representation and reality by ascribing a different relationship with what one is. What is significant here is the space of the beyond that exists in the form of time that is yet-to-come, or the time-that-remains after the end is reached within a certain mode of being-in-the-world and/or being-for-itself. The space beyond is the messianic possibility of that which comes after the moment of historicization as an event that surpasses the potentiality-to-be by way of a surprise or an incalculable coming. How does the incalculable enter the realm of existence has been an untamable question within the notion of being qua being and being qua other. The question concerning Messianism has long occupied the place of a major thematic resource for developing an Existentialist perspective upon life, especially when it is damaged or it is in crisis. The experience of agony, holocaust, victimhood, trauma and other such states of being have been turned into a fundamental feature of the human condition, all of which either in their totality or in their partiality only disclose the limits of human existence. Such a picture only states that the subjects at the limit of their ability bear such dislocations simultaneously as victims as well as the 'imaging consciousness' of such victimhood. Victims of the life-situations have their being caught in a perpetual loss of a part of their own being, which they only pre-reflectively possess but do not know; while the experience of loss is already a part of being-in-the-world, i.e. already caught in a relation of intentionality. The experience of victimhood jibes with 'a pre-judicative comprehension of non-being' that acts as the ground of negative judgements and realities that inhabit the knowledge of one's own self and world. This nihilating relation of consciousness to the world is not just the victim's self-knowledge, but it is made possible only because consciousness is of its very nature a 'no-thingness' that lies at the heart of being. This nihilating relation is Agamben's potentiality-not-to, without which being-there cannot realize its own historicity, which interestingly, comes only after the realization of potentiality-to-be. Victimhood exhausts the potentiality-to-be to its nihilating end, where one is not what one is and, therefore, the revival and redemption follows from such an end to emerge into that, which is yet-to-come. This is the authentic experience of time from which the chronological time is derived in its identity with a given state of existence.

In its authentic mode, Consciousness appears to itself not as a thing, but as a non-being, as an 'other' with a non-self-identity. Existentialist like Sartre conceived such a non-being as being-for-other, whose being for-itself is only an act of presencing in relation to others. If being is being-for-other, then all its knowledge about itself and the world arise out of a relationship with the other. Therefore, the meaning of being lies in the nature of relationship with the other and knowing the being amounts to knowing the other. Existentialists contend that knowing oneself as an other genetically constitutes the otherness of one's own being. Being a victim of circumstances is being the other to one's own non-being, which the self or the subject can never own, as owning one's own being is an impossibility. This impossibility is simultaneously a relation to oneself and also it is a non-relation, as it is only a postponement or and undergoing of experiential time without 'any hold upon future'. Therefore, non-being or absence of being to itself does not allow one to even be a victim, rather the non-being appearing as a being-for-the-other provides a false essence to the state of victimhood. This false essence is experienced now as a relation to the other. In terms of Levinas, to be being is to be in a state of being persecuted by the other and for Heidegger, being-in-the-world never attains authenticity, as it can never attain its true essence. This ontological failure of being is taken to be the constituent of the very human condition that does not allow the being to attain its true nature, i.e. the desired freedom that eludes being. This elusiveness is concomitant with experience of impossibility of the event of redemption or justice. Existentialist gave freedom a messianic image, which is always a 'yet to come', a forever waiting to make it happen. As it never comes, the agent or the subject of such messianic consciousness attempts to make this happen through their expectation and wait, i.e. they try to create another world in which it happens, an apocalypse that is conceptualized in terms of freedom and plenitude. Subjects surrounded by such existential incompleteness seek an escape route in events that are apocalyptic by their very occurrence, as if such ever-awaited moments of happening would transform the very human condition.

Utopia and the Sociality of Messainism

The human condition that allows perplexities of an ontological failure to comprehend Subject's relationship with its own modality of existence, often contributes to the return of the desire of self-presence, a kind of proximity to oneself as well as to another. Ananta Kumar Giri's notion of 'ontological sociality' marks a return to the desire of self-presencing that itself is an effect of being a subject of a participatory universalist planetary discourse. But this is a return definitely to a location different from the current space of self-affirmation, but well within the domain of proximity and alterity. By way of representing the universal in the participatory agenda of global social movements of ethico-political multitudes, Giri is posing a new challenge to a realist-foundationalist notion of social science as a science of alterity. What remains inarticulate in Giri's anti-foundational critique of contextually specific social movements is a journey towards what he called 'homelessness', possibly a disclosure of plurality and alterity within the self-enclosed notion of self and its transcendental presuppositions of transformation. One needs to continue this therapeutic search for an alternative to the subversion of both the particular and the universal by way of a calling that annuls the call in order to respond to each other. This then comes to a utopic rehearsal of the scheme of problem-solving by means of ingenious means[2] in which the hegemonic multitudes face the anarchic particularity of group solidarity. Ephemeral solidarities and shifting inner alliances that result in ethnic jokes, racial envies and insults between communities and multitudes produced over a few ontic barriers create an ongoing discourse of difference that suffer the anxiety of having an external enemy, who is stronger, but who is invisible. This is a different sense of sociality that is a return to a 'immense federal network of overlapping monads' as an anticipation of a rediscovery of political figure in the new thoughts about sociality.

These anticipations get reflected in the substantive theories of the coming of Messiah, for whose coming everyone waits. The messiah might not be god-man, but it could be anyone who waits for the coming. In the Jewish messianic thought, what comes as a messianic event is the difference or gap between what happens and what is going to come. The evidence for the content of Messianism lies in new representations of time that can actualize evidences for the faith in Messiah. But such an actualization is like Edgar Auber's gift of a self-portrait to Proust, on which Auber wrote, 'Look at my face: my name is Might Have Been; I am also called No More, Too Late, Farewell' (quoted in Agamben 2007: 27).

The evidence for presence within the 'sublime breach between the sensible and the intelligible' cannot be a property of the photograph or self-portrait, rather it is given a 'content' that is without a grasp, although, such content exists within the general idea of features of a face. Agamben likens this pre-philosophical endowment to a wonderful example:

Even in nature there are profanations. The cat that plays with a ball of yarn as if it were a mouse—just as the child plays with ancient religious symbols or objects that once belonged to the economic sphere—knowingly uses the characteristic behaviours of predatory activity (or, in the case of the child, of the religious cult or the world of work) in vain. These behaviours are not effaced, but thanks to the substitution of the yarn for the mouse (or the toy for the sacred object), deactivated and thus opened up to a new, possible use. (2007: 85)

In trying to meet this challenge of profanating substitution, it is helpful to distinguish three levels at which the entitlement relation can be characterized. At the first level, it is characterized by its instances. At the second level, it is characterized by true generalizations about its instances. At the third level, it is characterized by an explanation of why the true generalizations at the second level hold. A full treatment of the entitlement relation in a problematic domain should supply characterizations at all three levels. It is of course the third level that is the deepest and most challenging.

In the case of perceptual entitlement to the presence of the Messiah, one is entitled to take at face value the perceptions, in the absence of reasons for doubt and without further background information. What makes these perceptions have the content they do is the fact that when the subject is properly connected to the world, the holding of these contents gives a metaphysical explanation to such perceptual experiences of their holding. These are, intuitively, perceptions whose contents are observational, but such observations are already constituted by the article of faith in the Messiah. I argue that the third-level explanation of why one is entitled to take these experiences at face value is that their correctness is part of the best explanation of the occurrence of such events with such complex relational properties as apocalyptic experiences.

There are two arguments for the Third Principle. One is the intuitive argument that if an article of faith is not fundamentally a priori, but it rests on empirical information, judging in accordance with that relation would not be rational unless the thinker possessed that information—in which case, the entitlement would be fundamentally a priori after all. The more theoretical argument is from the nature of the a priori. A plausible philosophical theory of what makes a proposition (or transition) a priori is that its truth (truth-conduciveness) can be explained philosophically from the nature of the contents and states involved in judgement of the content (or in making the transition). If this philosophical theory is correct, the Third Principle is a corollary of the First and Second Principles taken together. Agamben's distinction between chronological, operational and messianic time corresponds to these three Phronetic principles of Messianism. In Agamben's elucidation:

We may now propose our first definition of messianic time: messianic time is the time that time takes to come to an end, or, more precisely, the time we take to bring to an end, to achieve our representation of time. This is not the line of chronological time (which was representable but unthinkable), nor the instant of its end (which was just as unthinkable); nor it is the segment cut from chronological time; rather, it is operational time pressing within the chronological time, working and transforming it from within; it is the time we need to make time end: the time that is left us. (2006: 65–6)

The ending of time is signified by a preparation for the future, which cannot be appropriated within the normal, as future, in Jewish Messianic thought, comes with an absolute surprise. This is also a disruption of the present or the 'lived time' that is a synthesis of past, present and future. It is an 'other' time that is non-lived and extra-ordinary, a time not consistent with production and reproduction of 'real life'.

An Ontological Return to the Other

The adventure of the metaphysics of presence in the form of 'real life' leads to a distinction between signs that have no permanent signified and signs that permanently identify a specific signified. The signs that do have no signified are termed as 'merely indicative' of the present and the knowing subject experiences it as 'presence'. The signs that have fixed meaning act as the possibility of repetition. These signs are expressive signs. It is quite paradoxical that indicative signs are repeated and it assumes the possibility of bearing certain fixed meaning just as expressive signs. Expressive 'signs' are non-derivative, and it gives rise to a fixed meaning that cannot retain its non-derivational character without being repeated while every repetition assumes an indicative function. An imagination of messianic justice carries forwards this blurring of distinction between indication and expression in the process of repetition. Such a blurring produces an 'other context' that makes possible a projection of what is included/excluded, recognized/misrecognized not on the basis of real/ideal/imaginary kind of distinction, but on the basis of 'repetition'. Repetition is conceived as the 'threshold of indistinction' between an articulation of what is 'proper' to an identity or culture and what is 'other' to it. This indistinction creates a messianic structure around the event that is distinguished by Derrida from any determinate messianism of a biblical kind; one may always recognize there the arid soil in which grew, and passed away, the living figures of all the messiahs, whether they were announced, recognized, or still awaited (Derrida 1994: 168). This wait is a limit that, as Derrida puts it in 'Force of Law', 'defines either an infinite progress or a waiting and awaiting', because the political relationship to the 'absolute future' also requires that one act, that one makes political decisions. Derrida formulates this argument in relation to justice in 'Force of Law':

justice, however unpresentable it remains, does not wait. It is that which must not wait. To be direct, simple and brief, let us say this: a just decision is always required immediately, right away, as quickly as possible. It cannot provide itself with the infinite information and the unlimited knowledge of conditions, rules or hypothetical imperatives that could justify it. And even if it did have all that at its disposal, even if it did give itself the time, all the time and all the necessary knowledge about the matter, well then, the moment of decision as such, what must be just, must [il faut] always remain a finite moment of urgency and precipitation; it must [doit] not be the consequence or the effect of this theoretical or historical knowledge, of this reflection or this deliberation, since the decision always marks the interruption of the juridico-, ethico-, or politico-cognitive deliberation that precedes it, that must [doit] precede it. (Derrida and Anidjar 2002: 255)

Agamben echoes this messianic structure, which Beardsworth associates with the promise: 'Justice, like magic, is nameless. Happy, without a name, the creature knocks at the gates of the land of the magi, who speak in gestures alone' (Agamben 2007: 22).

Justice comes with a subversion of the particular experience of forms of power and representation. As such it turns out to be a critique of the structure of identity and political mobilization, which is an attempt to rejuvenate an aesthetic of self-representation in the public space. The critique is possible by way of calling of a shared political space with the Other, which ironically repeats the experiences of xenophobia, racism and numerous other forms of colonization. In this context, it is necessary to recognize that every 'we' necessarily comes from the 'other' by way of a radical undecidability about who the people are and this is the very possibility of sharing a common cultural space. This is also a profane sense of otherness, which is never identical to itself that ruptures the forms of misrecognition emanating from the immanent conditions of hegemonic difference. Derrida describes the situation in this manner,

A certain experience of emancipatory promise; it is perhaps even the formality of a structural messainism, a messainism without religion, even a messainic without messianism, an idea of justice—which we distinguish from law or right or even human rights—and an idea of democracy—which we distinguish from its current concept and from its determined predicates today. (1994: 59)

Interpretation as an act of deciding the meaning of an event encounters this multiple possibilities of meaning not as an intended consequence but as an inevitable directedness to a referential frame, which cannot be determined by the interpretation of an event. Undecidability of the referential frame acts as a source of multiple interventions on the occurrence of an event, which provides support to the interpretation as well as reorders it from a critical position of justice. This is how Derrida pronounces, 'I have only one language and it is not mine.' It indicates the possibility of search for the 'other' or/and 'other of language'. The other, which is beyond language and which summons language is not a 'referent', but a 'dissemination' that is irreducible to language. For example, every claim of uniqueness of cultural and linguistic identity has the 'responsibility of testifying for universality'. But this universality is to be free from the violence of representing the universal in the particular—a hegemonic strategy that subverts the particular. It is rather an idea of universality that Deleuze articulated in this way,

Neither particular nor general, neither finite nor infinite, it is the object of the Idea as a universal. This differential element is the play of difference as such, which can neither be mediated by representation nor subordinated to the identity of the concept.

This notion of universality beyond the hegemony of the dominant discourse is the play between being and its condition of possibility that lies in a differentially structured universal that poses problems within the concept of 'universal'. The problem is to 'invent' a concept of difference that is without a concept sans an irreducible problem of being that exists. The 'problem' can be understood in the way one tries to make universal accommodative of a differential relation between one and many, the current problematic between pluralism and singularity as 'intrinsically defined' multiplicity that requires a repetitive internal plurality into many shades (231). Methodologically one is somewhat liberated here from the constraints of holistic universality of cultural plurality as one needs to operate within a fractured multiplicity of action and signification that calls for the possibility of extensive 'forms of self-ascription and self-determination' not just from the point of view of a fixed insider, but from the possibility of a free-moving and wandering entry and exit into multiple domains of culture. Such entry and exit provide new routes to universality and one needs to invent in the *sal andhifts* of politicultural boundaries and boundaries of culture. This should not necessarily mean a strong identification with the given norms of belonging, but leave room for alternate belongings without necessarily subverting the closure of a particular culture. This can be articulated in a possible sense of learning from the other,

I can learn the whoness of the other(s) only through their narratives of self-identification. The norm of universal respect enjoins me to enter the conversation in so far as one is considered as a generalized other; but I can become aware of the Otherness of others, of those aspects of their identity that make them concrete other to me, only through their own narratives.

This implies that the responsibility and moral obligation of understanding the other through their narrative claims cannot be mediated and altered by the predicaments of cultural and political dominance that sets up asymmetric terms for discounting the political legitimacy of cultural claims. The hybridic processes of boundary crossing between dominant and non-dominant cultures should open up processes of intercultural justice between culturally different identities.

The representational device of hybridity is not just loaded with concepts of cultural self and the unity between the self and the world, but concepts such as presence of the self and the world as the origin of representation are re-mark(s) that fold on itself and on thought. The fold acts as a replica or re-application of quasi-transcendental or quasi-ontological conditions within which the empirical or the ontical aspects of an identity/ culture arises. This is putting the rigid cultural norms upside down: instead of knowledge or belief about a culture requiring the idea of objective practices and truths, the truth merely appears in practice and it presupposes the trace of language and a dissemination of language without return to cultural origin. This dissemination of culture is a device for an ontological reinterpretation of the 'Other' as the proper Subject of the social. Derrida conceived this as 'what is proper to a culture is not be identical to itself'. In his words:

there is no self-relation, no relation to oneself, no identification with oneself, without culture, but the culture of one's self as a culture of the other, a culture of the double genitive and of the difference to oneself…signals that a culture never has a single origin (Derrida 1992: 9f)

This brings one to a methodological acceptance of the 'other' as the source of one's own culture with the implication that portrays the possibility of multiple meanings as a Nietzschean impossibility of having a language, which means a simultaneous excription and effacement of meaning. None can be said to possess language, making it do one's bidding, allowing him/ her to subordinate it as a vehicle for the transportation of meaning. Each person is possessed by the field of forces and powers with which language/ culture/identity is always associated. The gesture of the torturer is ironic, who would, through violence, demand his victim speak in the name of truth. But which speech is this? Not the speech of violence—unspeaking, false through and through, logically the only one it can hope to obtain—but a true speech, free and pure of all violence. So, for an idea of universal sociality, affirmation is produced by negation, since negation maintains itself by positing being for an object. And it seems, in consequence, that affirmation, which is supposed to get past nihilism, ultimately fails to escape the contagion of the negation from which it came. This is to say that there is no outside of self-identity that did not authorize itself by inscribing itself within language. The meaning of such a conscious act of negation directs itself to the wholly other that involves a serial erasure of the trace of the self and the other, 'It should be anticipated as the unforeseeable, the unanticipatable, the non-masterable, non-identifiable, in short, as that of which one does not yet have a memory' (Derrida 1992: 18).

In other words, the search for the social should begin with a negation of an ontological determination of experience and memory, it should rather be an invitation to understand the other, the wholly other that demands a revision of sense-making, meaning-creating, justice-endorsing capacities of ours in relation to the wholly other.

Notes

1. John Cage, Pour les oiseaux, interview with Daniel Charles, Paris, 1976.
2. Fredric Jameson talked of 'lottery society', a society based on solving the problem of distributive justice on sheer chance selection of some people (2005: 8–9).

References

Agamben, Giorgio (2001), *State of Exception*, tr. Kevin Attel, Stanford: Stanford University Press.

———(2006), *The Time That Remains*, Stanford: Stanford University Press.

———(2007), *Profanations*, tr. Jeff Fort, New York: Zone Books.

Agarwala, Binod K. (2004), 'Society as Play: A Reconstruction of the Concept of Lokayan in Vedantic Social Philosophy', in *Philosophical Contribution of Professor S.L. Pandey*, ed. R.L. Singh, Ram Nath Kaul Library of Philosophy, University of Allahabad.

Badiou, Alain (2005), 'Being's Prohibition of the Event', in *Being and Event*, tr. Oliver Feltham, London: Continuum.

Benhabib, Seyla, *The Claims of Culture*, New Jersey: Princeton University Press.

Deleuze, Giles, *Difference and Repetition*, tr. Paul Patton, London: Continuum.

Derrida, Jacques (1982), 'The Ends of Man', in *Margins of Philosophy*, tr. Alan Bass, Chicago: University of Chicago Press.

———(1992), *The Other Heading: Reflections on Today's Europe*, tr. P.A. Brault and M.B. Nass, Bloomington: Indiana University Press.

———(1994), *Spectres of Marx*, tr. Peggy Kamuf, London: Routledge.

Derrida, Jacques and Gil Anidjar (2002), *Acts of Religion*, London: Routledge.

Foucault, Michel (1972), *The Archaeology of Knowledge and the Discourse on Language*, tr. A.M.S. Smith, New York: Pantheon Books.

Hegel, G.W.F. (1977), *Phenomenology of Spirit*, tr. A.V. Miller, Oxford: OUP.

Heidegger, Martin (1956), *What is Philosophy?* New York: New College & University Press.

———(1962), *Being and Time*, tr. John Macquarrie and Edward Robinson, New York: Harper and Row.

———(1974), *Identity and Difference*, tr. J. Stambaugh, New York: Harper and Row.

———(1975), 'The Way Back into the Ground of Metaphysics', in *Existentialism from Dostoevsky to Sartre*, ed. Walter Kauffman, New York: Meridian Books.

———(2002), *Identity and Difference*, Chicago: University of Chicago Press.

Jameson, Fredric (2005), *Archaeologies of Future*, tr. Mathew Robert, London: Verso.

Malabou, Catherine (2005), *The Future of Hegel: Plasticity, Temporality and Dialectic*, tr. Lisabeth, During: Routledge.

Plotnisky, Arkady (2002), 'Topo-philosophies: Plato's Diagonals, Hegel's Spirals and Irrigaray's Multifolds', in *After Poststructuralism: Writing the Intellectual History of Theory*, ed. Tilottama Rajan et al., Toronto: University of Toronto Press.

Shotter, John (2006), 'A Return to "Real Presences": Participatory Forms of Active, Responsive Understanding', in *Post-Structuralism and Cultural Theory*, ed. Franson Manjali, New Delhi: Allied Publishers.

24

Creating Dialogical Creativity

ALEC SCHAERER

Introduction

The current stage of human evolution can be characterized as a widespread seducibility by the illusion that dominance will solve problems—revealing itself as sway on all levels, from choosing systems of thought where one imposes favoured presuppositions (for example axioms or definitions) up to bullying and killing people. These practices seem to offer some success at first, as some intended effects are achievable, but finally they always backfire at the operator. It became normal to 'justify' rash action under the guise of a 'need to decide under conditions of limited information', which occurs also in theory formation. The approaches of today's mainstream, based on primal assumptions, can indeed offer only limited insight and knowledge. Some may wonder why dominative attempts at research are here even being characterized as illusory. They are indeed so, insofar as imposed basic assumptions inevitably produce unintended consequences that can range— depending on their level—from a limitation of possible insight to aggravations of material conflict, which is precisely the opposite of what was desired.

   This essay aims at showing, by systematic means that improving insight in research and hence knowledge has better possibilities than to invent ingenious basic assumptions, and that moreover it can embody extensive creativity; at its very best it develops a capacity of profound 'listening' to— and therefore 'dialogue' with—the subject matter. For becoming successful, this endeavour must reach beyond the dubious choice of either post-modernistic vagueness or the mental blinkers of tense formal logics, instead venturing systematically into the foundation of strictly integral views and procedures.

Outlining the Problem

In the context of research and knowledge, creativity rarely is a part of the discussion. When the term arises at all, it aims at exceptionally elegant basic assumptions, or expresses some hope for innovative results. Often creativity is given a connotation of something a bit frivolous in comparison to the dead serious mindset required for allegedly reliable research and knowledge; at best it is relegated to Art as a jester to society. It occurs, therefore, only rarely that unflinching seriousness and sensitive creativity are contemplated as two deeply related aspects of proceeding on the path towards an all-embracing understanding of something. The neglect takes effect at the expense of society, which has to make do with fractional insight.

The notion of creativity was originally reserved for the works of the gods, operating out of universal consciousness—in contrast to the human activity of merely 'making'—and even now that notion is usually associated more with innovative agency than with a quest for adequacy to its context. Yet this adequacy, calling for a relational or even dialogical orientation, determines its functional quality. In research and knowledge creation, due to the predominant (and insofar 'normal') habit of setting out from fundamental assumptions—known as axiom, definition, hypothesis, postulate, premise, etc.—today's normal research (in contrast to creative research) cannot achieve fully the required 'listening' mode. Basic assumptions are acceptable as long as they are clearly provisional (Meinong [1910] remains authoritative)—mere tentative elements at the foundation of the query process for developing the adequacy of a theoretical system. Unfortunately, since research is organized in a peculiar institutionalization (what Heidegger called 'Betrieb'), fundamental assumptions often are not examined and tested, but quite firmly believed. But then they mutate into fundamental assertions—and get in the way of insight, because they are a way of 'talking into' the subject matter before it has had a chance of presenting itself fully to awareness.

The result in the respective theory is a warped account of the phenomena. Of course one still gets 'answers', and often they appeal to buyers by allowing desired applications—think for example of the gadgets that physics allows one to manufacture. But there is no warranty that the ideas offer a thorough understanding of the subject matter, in this example of materiality; think for example of the idea in physics that matter consists of little pieces. The quantum approach ended up by showing that this idea must be erroneous, and that reality consists of movement as such—but heuristically speaking, even quantum theory itself still remains within the idea of 'particles', even though later on it had to accept that the 'wave' view is just as justifiable. As a result it still remains in 'either-or' declarations, sometimes even elevating this idea to the status of a law allegedly governing reality. This holds even in cases where the entities are idealized objects—as for example with the Kantian approach of Cuffaro (2010). Till now no approach to physics has been developed that gets rid on principle of basic entities of some sort or another; even non-linear dynamics or string theory remain dependent on such elements. In the light of this structure of assumptions, it is no surprise that physics' purely theoretical understanding of materiality as such remains in a peculiar kind of vagueness, oscillating between fuzzinesses, probabilities and paradoxes—making look silly the 'materialistic' stances and assertions of many contemporary celebrities. Precise measurements of details do not make up for general gaps in pure theory. A relatively good potential is in approaches based on relativity theory, when pursued towards pure and uncompromised conceptuality (see for instance Ziegler 1996 or Gschwind 2004). Here consider physics, which has held a generally paradigmatic role for a long time in spite of reducing its phenomena to mechanics, until biology took the lead, albeit still in a mechanicist and insofar physicalist vein, still far from the Aristotelian objective of a physics allowing complete autonomy of the entity and encompassing in one homogenous approach as much the inert as living beings.

The cost of believing in the illusion of arbitrary control and domination—from exploiting the mind in conceptually self-induced feedback loops, up to exploiting physical bodies by means of mechanical coercion—is immense, because it breeds huge amounts of unnecessary conflict. Carrying this cost will finally give birth to a new impulse to the evolution of mankind because disturbing other beings is—existentially speaking—a constitutional principle. On the other hand this primacy is precisely the reason why the content to be learnt is banished in many cultural contexts—especially in the coercive ones—to remote parts of the 'unconscious' (the realm of repressed ideas). This fact in turn pressures the life process into forms and loops that require more physical deaths and new births, more new incarnations than a straightforward approach would require. The idea of control and domination is adequate for directing the mind in seeking transparency, but it wreaks havoc when the mental activity is not oriented in a globally adequate direction, i.e. one that does not coerce other beings. Intelligent beings have the choice of either dying away mentally from illusion and error by uncompromised method, or dying away physically by dint of effects of what was neglected. Either way, all will certainly die—but the two procedures of dying are quite different.

Outlining the Path Towards a Solution

Some may wonder why the facts are put here so harshly, talking right away about life and death. The point is that truly uncompromised thinking cannot afford conceptual penumbra, it must address totality and it must do this clearly. The fact that normal research cannot achieve this, because it sets out on less selective distinctions, reveals no law of nature, but a weakness of the undesirable sort. Too many individual and social reactions stem deeply but simply from a fear of loss, of death. Ultimately life is fully understandable only in the background of death. Interestingly enough, no being fears the principle of death that is indeed woven into all cycles of arising and vanishing; what it does fear is the pain in processes of dying that are determined by inadequate handling—be it by its own agency on its own body, or by the influence of other beings. In fact, dying out of complete self-fulfilment is of utmost beauty, it is sheer bliss and known in all spiritual traditions—in contrast to dying by external influence. In cell biology this opposition is known as apoptosis vs. necrosis, but today's theory of biology cannot explain why two types of death must exist (Schaerer [2002] offers a thorough account). Mental death as a result of authentic interest, dedication and devotedness to a subject matter, arises in intense impulses (when addressing totality: as samadhi, satori, epiphany, etc.) only when the forces of the psyche seeking their free flow (in tantra: *kundalini*) must override a barrier of prejudicial deposits (fundamentally believed suppositions), which can be of sympathetic or of antipathetic character (desire or fear). This is why many spiritual traditions, in addressing totality, advocate techniques for 'purifying the mind'—often forgetting that the presupposition whereby just this is required, and the actual efforts, produce precisely such deposits; the mind then enacts a self-fulfilling prophecy. No wonder it then feels like being God, experientially getting a glimpse of the totality of its own acts. Since humans are structured in a self-referential way—just like the universe at large (remember 'actio = reactio', or quantum nonlocality)—the insights into reality can be considerable. Nevertheless they still need to be reappraised through systematic logical and empirical working. Even after the wildest psychic breakthrough, everyday life always has its comeback and needs to be mastered. Contemplating life through the immediacy of death can indeed be helpful for getting at the essentials. It can strengthen the overview and thereby the basis for creativity (see, e.g. http://www.mycoted.com/ Category: Creativity_Techniques).

Some might wonder whether fundamental creativity in research can be developed without massive threshold manifestations. The answer is so simple and so intimately close to one that it escapes habitual everyday awareness: instead of 'talking' into the issue at stake, a person can open him/herself up to it as completely as he/she can, using mental strength for becoming 'weak' in favour of the subject matter, thereby allowing its nature to permeate the person. Many have pointed out the fruitfulness of this move, especially in the phenomenological-hermeneutical line of thought and research. Yet this line remained essentially in a mode of description of objects, proceeding by ever more intimate and detailed observation—usually not noticing the 'blind spot' that is inevitably engendered by this type of procedure. Whether the seemingly objective gesture is one of analysing, describing, distinguishing, measuring, observing, predicating, influencing, or intervening, is irrelevant, since invariably it is one of splitting up the subject matter according to content introduced by comparing reality with something alien to it. Any separative gesture produces a blind spot that embodies the 'inverse' of the implied content vector. For example, observation can observe everything except its act of observing, and measuring can never be measured, if only because any type of measuring requires an element or act of comparison, as nature offers no strictly immutable basic elements or constants. Even Planck's action quantum, or the 'velocity of light', are no strict absolutes, but the result of measuring as a type of access to reality as a whole that inevitably induces paradoxes. Especially logicians such as Heinz von Foerster (1979), Gotthard Guenther (for example in Goldammer 1999) or Francisco Varela (for example in Scharmer et al. 2002), discovered that the blind spot cannot be discovered within a conceptual system that installs a separative gesture: through the system one cannot 'see' what it cannot make distinguishable. One is unable to discern that it cannot make distinguishable what it cannot make distinguishable, namely, the paradoxical pattern that the conceptual system, by explicitly splitting up the universe between itself and everything else, must on the one hand be distinct from this distinction, while on the other hand it must exist implicitly within the distinction as part of totality and hence as an object of investigation. In this paradoxical situation, observing other observers in their activity of observing can look like a helpful move, but the blind spot can on principle never be overcome, it can only be shifted around into ever new aspects. Luhmann addresses it eloquently in his version of systems theory (e.g. in Luhmann 1984, 1997). But by axiomatically postulating something signified that is preconstituted (namely the structure of being a system) while promoting the blind spot as just the type of form that allows differences and causalities to be formulated, he justifies the primal tangle, establishes a self-constraint, and can therefore develop no solution on principle.

Of course the world can be depicted in an endless way on the path of description. But this does not at all warrant completeness of grasp, while the dangers of believing that it can offer totality should not be underestimated—see for example the interesting investigation by Erroll Morris in The New York Times of 20 June 2010 'The Anosognosic's Dilemma: Something's Wrong but You'll Never Know What It Is'. The finally relevant question is what one really wants: sophisticated management techniques up to arbitrary domination and control (including of one's own mind), or rather a systematically consistent theory. Primal distinctions beyond the usual ones are decisive. For example, whether one considers material or mental elements is irrelevant because both are appearances (in the physical and mental realm) governed by their overall order, not this order as such. Understanding 'things' in terms of 'things'—as attempted in today's mainstream—is inevitably limited, since nothing in the realm of representables can offer the required strict generality. Even when addressing 'being as such', like Heidegger, and bordering mystical unity, as in his later works, complete clarity is not automatically warranted. Heidegger, presupposing that reality 'hides' its essential traits, seeks truth through the activity of unveiling (*aletheia*)—not noticing that his basic assumption makes him describe endlessly ever more details, driven by his blindness for the effects of positing hiddenness. Heidegger has a point insofar as the structure (or intrinsic law) of reality as a whole can indeed not show itself palpably, because appearances follow their structure. Traditional approaches, oriented towards 'things' in the hope of being able to formulate true predicates, cannot be helpful for addressing something as intrinsic as the pure order of something. They inevitably lead to problems such as Kant's with his 'thing-in-itself', or those of essentialism when wanting to reach the essence of things by means of predication. Any object-oriented approach must fail because the chosen perspective overrules the subject matter as such. It is helpful to notice that those concepts that allow complete intelligibility—in a process perspective: laws and forces—are not observable, but accessible only in pure thought. Unfortunately, Heidegger does not study generally the nature of intrinsic laws and how appearances are structured in terms that are ultimately relevant to intelligibility. As a result he is compelled to report descriptively more and more—like practically all adepts of phenomenology and hermeneutics—in ever more detailed narration, endlessly, while the immanent means even of transcendental phenomenology do not allow a full clarification of the categoriality required for solving the crux on principle. There is another prominent stream of object-oriented thought, analytic philosophy, whose ultimate objects are mental and that also operates in a blind spot, in its case by pandering to naturalism— unaware of the blind spot in that line of thought; for this reason it can unfortunately not even contribute to a strictly integral approach to what naturalism aims at, namely, understanding nature in its complete sense.

Outlining the Basis for a Solution

For determining types of knowledge that allow a fully secure overview, ideas for 'logical', 'metaphysical' and 'moral' certainty were proposed, or 'explicit' versus 'tacit' knowledge, but there is little consensus on the whole. Mittelstrass (1982) distinguishes 'knowledge for the sake of orientation' versus 'knowledge for the sake of action' ('*Orientierungswissen*'/'*Verfügungs-wissen*'). But he too does not base the more complete type of knowledge (seeking/offering orientation) systematically in a universal way; in spite of his holistic intention he remains in the predicative line of the linguistic turn and its intrinsic self-limitation.

For closing the gap, a totally uncompromised distinction is useful, namely, between the language of intelligibility and the language of manipulability. The first consists of laws (forms of order, pure structure), which may be grasped by means of concepts, ideas, or representations that can be communicated by using names and predicates; all forms of understanding are ways of grasping the ultimately relevant order. The language of manipulability consists of names and predicates ('handles' for catching 'things' in representations); the majority of philosophical and scientific interaction occurs in this language. At first glance, it seems to allow complete intelligibility; only upon thinking through the network of all names and predicates, one notices that it cannot cover strictly the whole, that something is missing somehow, cannot fully be understood, or produces surprises. Remaining in the language of manipulability impedes knowing just what is going wrong. An example is causation—think for example of the 'covering-law' type of explanation (Hempel-Oppenheim) that uses this type of language and cannot allow to know on its own whether the explanandum is causally effective, a necessary condition, or an inevitable concomitant element. This distinction of two 'languages of thinking' is similar to Mittelstrass's two types of knowledge, but more promising, since he offers no proposal for overcoming the language of manipulability. Remaining within it while believing it can serve as language of intelligibility logically, must lead to believing the encountered limit is absolute—while only the belief in the language of manipulability is absolute. Such knots are unnecessary. The failures they produce often are noticeable only much later. For wanting to learn, many first need to experience failure, but it is more efficient to think clearly beforehand, addressing the fundamental issues.

A sound systematic basis can be found by following closely the process of querying. Any approach can operate only through a perspective, out of a specific interest. On the other hand, actively sustaining a query content for its own sake, until achieving its general conceptual fulfilment—without wanting to apply immediately the discovered research pattern to a specific process—has a purifying effect. One might think for instance of Aristotle, thoroughly interested in change, processuality, movement (*kínesis, metabolé*). The constancy in pursuit—which can easily take decades of research—is fruitful because it gradually allows inappropriate sidelines to die away in the unflinching dialogue with the subject matter.

The deeper one reaches, the better one can grasp the complementing polar 'background' of what one had conceived at first. Studying the genesis and use of concepts shows that any conceptual aspect A can in the very end be thought only in the 'mental background' of non-A, the content that is strictly polar to A. This fact gave rise to many streams of thought under the heading of dialectics, because increasingly knowing A leads to an awareness of its intrinsic conceptual dependency on non-A; hence becoming aware of non-A leads to realizing what A really implies. Hegel draws unceasingly from this well, and any logic is based on negation. The point is that A and non-A together cover totally the universe, under one aspect: the queried one (in this example: A). Knowing this allows an essential conclusion: upon completely exhausting a query perspective conceptually, its perspectivity and universality become fully compatible.

The other side of this coin is that any query ultimately leads to a polarized conceptual space, as required for fully understanding the query's content. This is the law of content logic imposed by nature that regulates ultimately all mental processes. A difficulty is that everyday life usually prevents one from considering the ultimate consequences of primal assumptions and queries. It continuously pushes a person into mixing up query vectors and therefore perspectives. Today's 'normality' encourages evasion, changing the subject, limited views and responsibility—not cathartic engagement in experiencing one's own mental activity and responsibility. This condition made broadly respectable such problematic strategies as Tarski's approach to the concept of truth, seeking to avoid formal paradox by introducing meta-language as a regulator of the respective object language—while in a new perspective the meta-language is again an object language, and the meta-language of all meta-languages is everyday language. As any avoidance-based approach, Tarski's proposal too cannot offer the strict generality hoped for. In any case, the (often neglected) activity of querying determines the outcomes by necessarily splitting up the totality of interconnections—in Hegel's words a 'circle of circles' (1830/1989: 15) or 'diamantine net' (1830/1989: 246 addition)—compelling it to appear under the conceptual conditions imposed by the query. The (intensely debated) activity of judging is by far not as relevant, because it depends contingently on the implied structure of beliefs and is invariably limited by them, while judgement on an opaque foundation cannot clarify directly the necessary conditions for the activity of querying in an objectively systematic way.

The more intellectual efforts are examined, the more examples of the said law of nature abound, showing why sustained attentiveness to the subject matter is crucial. When fathomed uncompromisingly, the query content itself leads to the definition of the conceptually polarized concepts. For instance, Aristotle querying the nature of change finally found 'form' vs. 'matter'; Kant querying the necessary condition for cognizing eventually discovered 'perception' vs. 'thinking' as essential concepts; or Saussure, scrutinizing the nature of the sign, ultimately reached 'the signifying' vs. 'the signified' as the relevant basis, etc.

The best example is a branch of mathematics called 'synthetic projective geometry', which represents the 'mother' of all geometries, including the now famous non-Euclidian ones. In this geometry all structures and mental activities arise in a dual way—for instance triangularity can be thought of as three joined points, defining three lines, or as three intersecting lines, defining three points, while joining and intersecting also constitute a duality. The key point in this geometry is that it always contains totality, i.e. infinity is never allowed to become a special case—as in Euclidian geometry, which then has its problem of parallels. The principle of polarity appears also in the foundation of logic as negation, an absolute opposite in terms of meaning. For becoming operative as an actual logic, negation needs a combinatorial element. It is no coincidence that those logical connectives that allow all other logical connectives to be formulated, namely, logical NAND ('not and') and logical NOR ('not or'), display in themselves the said structure and together constitute a duality. There is an arbitrary choice as to which path is to be followed. It is thus no accident that in George Spencer-Brown's (1971) primary algebra the unmarked state can be read as 'True' or as 'False', calling for an arbitrary choice, and that the two resulting structures are dual. Similarly, the dual structure of defining is 'expressing the negation of a chosen content, while the consequences must be contained within the totality of interrelations'. The traditionally distinct—and conceptually polar—mathematical concepts of 'operator' and 'operand' are the two sides of the same coin, namely, of the single fundamental action of positing a distinction. But the implied abeyance shows that reality per se imposes no decision; the thinking mind, when wanting to operate by formal means in a systematic setup, must posit this decision, which is then categorially relevant. The act is obviously not absolute as an act; only the law is absolute whereby thinking must posit its own foundation. So the activity of thinking is itself not compelled to be formal, it need not posit first of all a decision for constituting a structure whose characteristics will limit all subsequent views, while for instance the decision to view logic only in formal terms inevitably leads to the impression that there must be a fundamental undecidability. It is useful to think of Kurt Gödel, whose theorems (1931) and their sequels agitate the scientific community to this day.

In spite of a universal applicability within their query perspective, polar concepts resulting from fulfilling a query content still cannot offer complete insight into all relevant facts, as they necessarily leave something open: while 'A' formally defines 'non-A', strictly covering totality, completely knowing the content of A and non-A requires some additional investigation. For example in the Aristotelian case, querying the nature of processuality, one still does not know how the change is actually achieved in the 'form' aspect of a thing in process, or what the concrete qualities are of its 'matter' aspect that allow changes. In the approach proposed here, this implicit remainder is approached systematically. This is why this new approach is called systematic attentiveness.

A brief comment as to terminology: it is useful not to confuse the meanings of polarity, duality, and complementarity. Polarity here means a semantically absolute opposite that can be achieved only purely conceptually (not just a semantic opposition such as 'full vs. empty'); in contrast, duality here is a materialized opposite (for example enantiomers in chemistry, or converse mental representations such as 'on' vs. 'off', or 'join points' vs. 'intersect lines'); and complementarity is a result of applying foundational ideas (for instance measurement) that entail the impossibility of an aspect arising in a medium, while its complement does arise (for example in the quantum approach: position vs. momentum, rest mass vs. impulse, etc.).

Developing an Integral Solution on the Exposed Foundation

Intelligibility requires knowing how to use concepts and systems of concepts. Since Freud, some believe that all are subject to 'the unconscious'. But all woes are fathomable under the appropriate conditions; only pathological cases move without knowing why. A systematization denotes logically connecting chosen concepts with all other concepts of reality. The borderline between naive ideas and theory is not fixed, because in theorizing too the point is with how little completeness one contents oneself. As even some prominent examples show, possessing a theory does not warrant per se a grasp of the relevant totality. One of the reasons is that not all theories serve the same purpose—for instance, desiring manipulative control in a given realm, and wanting to understand for the sake of the subject matter itself, leads to different theories on the same subject matter. Habitual criteria for judging theories cannot be absolute. Many believe, for instance, that testability is a requirement of scientific theory. But it arises only when there is no fundamental conceptual certainty; then empirical tests become a necessity for judging a theory. The problem is that the overall order then must remain unclear, since no empirical test can cover totality. Where scientific thinking has finally nothing but beliefs at its basis, its use of theories can only have the function of making interrelations between appearances credible, as Goethe famously observed ([1833]1976). Others believe, when they possess a theory that models a subject matter, that they know the subject matter sufficiently (a point that for instance those economists forget who colonize other fields, contributing to 'economic imperialism').

On the other hand, highly intuitive approaches in an integral aim can benefit from a sound systematic basis, especially when the scientific community remains in doubt about their degree of validity. As an example the works of Otto Scharmer might be considered, consolidated in his 'Theory U' (Scharmer 2007). The example is interesting insofar as he is one of those few researchers who actually and concretely embody some of the creativity aimed at in *Pathways of Creative Research*. He spells out a social grammar of creative constructive change that is intuitively very appealing and has many followers, but especially representatives of 'hard' science miss the secure conceptual foundation. It has been shown how very close scrutiny reveals that even today's 'hard' sciences cannot offer their own secure conceptual foundation and hence end up in paradoxical statements about total reality, but that is another story.

All systematic considerations occur by means of concepts; the point is in recognizing that action in the conceptual realm is of the same type as action in the gross material realm: what varies is merely the instrumental material (concepts versus physical matter). Concepts are the only 'things' to have the fascinating feature of being simultaneously the result of mental action—being formed through experience—and the means for steering mental action and choosing new experiences, any intention is guided by content and hence something (at least potentially) conceptual. There is a self-referential dynamism in the mental setup that most methods and ways of theorizing do not address adequately. Hegel opened a door, had his difficulties, and was often misunderstood. The key to overcoming the habitual limits is first in allowing one's mental activity to become something one experiences by becoming aware of the ideas to which one lends one's will in thinking, and later in allowing the principle of non-limit to become the lodestar towards totality. For example, in the eco-social process, even the simplest exchange of goods requires implicitly the basic ideas that are relevant to economics.

The strictly polar concepts championed in systematic attentiveness are transcendental (i.e. they constitute conditions of intelligibility, which empirical data never do) and metaphysical (operating in the non-empirical language of intelligibility, and constituting a sound categorial basis on which to proceed). They do not offer object predicates (such as 'the object is red') but are of securely heuristic character (i.e. useful for knowing what to look out for—in the given example, in a phenomenological approach: 'watch out for the colour'. Being developed out of one query content, they concern precisely this perspective and should be used conjointly and within it, because otherwise the results are not fully adequate to the subject matter.

When derived stringently from the content of one query perspective, such polar concepts are strictly universally applicable within their query perspective. Therefore, speaking in terms of pure content logic, within their framework they are also applicable to themselves. This step towards a fulfilment of the pursuit constitutes the dynamizing act that overcomes the static situation of strict polarity ('A' vs. 'non-A') of being only halfway through the query, having the names but not yet all the meaning. Note that—in contrast—no predicative approach to external objects can ever allow full self-reference. For understanding why this limit is not relevant in purely conceptual thinking, it is helpful to consider that clear thoughts—in contrast to empirical views of mundane objects—contain no backside, they are not subject to any perspective other than the primal assumptions implicit in the consideration; for the rest their content reveals all of themselves. Exercising the 'inner' empiricism ultimately means considering content for its own sake, as in pure mathematics. In philosophy this procedure is known as the 'speculative method' and was employed particularly in German Idealism.

Wishing to clarify the meaning of 'A and non-A'—in the Aristotelian example: the 'form' and 'matter' aspects, as general concepts—is the same type of query as seeking the intrinsic order ('meaning') of processuality itself; the point is to unfold the conceptual space out of the content of the query. The topic still is processuality, and at first the primary interest is in its causal side ('form' aspect); this is why the conceptual poles ('form'/'matter') are applied to the 'form' aspect ('self-reference'). This step must clarify the actual qualities of agency versus the actual qualities of what allows it. Expressed as a question: What is the 'form' aspect of the 'form' aspect, and what is the 'matter' aspect of the 'form' aspect? The next step then is to ask what is the 'form' aspect of the 'matter' aspect, and what is the 'matter' aspect of the 'matter' aspect? Accounts to varying degrees of detail can be found in Schaerer (2001, 2002, 2003, 2004, 2006, 2008, 2009). Here are the results for the processual query, in a nutshell: the 'form of form' is the intrinsic law of the respective process (the structure of it unravelling just as it does); the 'matter of form' is the force (in the mind: will) producing the change; the 'form of matter' is the disequilibriability of the respective force structure (the way in which it can be disturbed, up to being killed); and the 'matter of matter' is the fundamental equilibrium that characterizes the material medium allowing all force structures to be set up at all, according to their intrinsic law.

Such fully self-referential moves thwart any formal logical system—but here one proceeds in content logic, which is the basis that determines also the laws of formal logic. Therefore, this path does not face the limit of assumption-based systems, since the query content is unravelled completely according to its own nature, in pure thought. The chosen topic is taken as it is, applying no arbitrary distinction, not even allegedly fundamental ones such as 'subjectivity vs. objectivity', 'descriptive vs. normative view' ('fact vs. value'), 'theoretical vs. practical reason', 'epistemic vs. ontic view', etc. What is then done is to mirror content for its own sake, as in pure mathematics. The resulting categorial structure is on the level of the arché (Greek: 'origins') with their 'double face': for instance in the processual perspective (where complete intelligibility requires laws and forces as terms), an epistemic query, investigating appearances as dynamic 'entities' (at the physical or the mental level), eventually discloses the respective structure of law–plus–force (*ratio cognoscendi*), while an ontic query, analysing the structural interrelations between concepts, in this case thinking in terms of law–plus–force, finally leads to the respective existential complex, namely to the structure of the world (*ratio essendi*). In the result, conceptual coherence and differentiation can be equilibrated in a precise way. This is a systematic condition for methods and theories to be adequate to the wholeness of wholes.

Fostering Integral Creativity by Means of the Exposed Approach

The traditional procedure is to focus on predicating features of objects and later becoming aware of the activity of predicating, collecting predicated features of the world and calling the collection 'knowledge'. Beyond that or rather, for constituting the origin of a fruitful process towards what knowledge ultimately aspires to—one can be aware of the activity of collecting predicates and then become aware of the nature and effect of the attitudes 'behind' the activity, which guides that activity in ways one did not realize before. The point is that these attitudes set up part of the operative order and are thus laws co-regulating the process. For becoming aware of the essentials, an overview is required; only then the procedure can be a truly creative one by being fully in charge of it. Normal research focuses on the object and then develops the type of approach in a more or less subjective and hence contingent way. The lack of objectivity limits the quality of its creativity (for instance Mayorek [2002] offers a detailed account of this lack). In contrast, in systematic attentiveness the focus is first of all on the operative and conceptual means through which one approaches anything. Thereby the aspect of corpuscular wholeness is combined (the self being open in a unified way) with the aspect of relational content (the chosen basic query content defines the required conceptual conditions). Cultivating one's own integrity induces more intimacy with the object or rather the subject matter than a dominating attitude can afford. As a tendency, instead of succumbing for instance to a dependency on cellular phones and aeroplanes, one will seek to develop oneself more towards telepathy and astral travel—just to give a few examples. In systematic attentiveness the dialogical quality can on principle be secured at the outset, in a way that is completely adequate to the object. This approach does not foster quick predication, but an awareness of the conceptual needs imposed by approaching the facts out of a particular interest, a specific query perspective. The approach remains in a heuristic mode, merely—but very securely!—indicating appropriate observational dimensions. As a consequence, the struggle between—in the jargon of quantum physics—an 'either-or' in the vein of 'particle' vs. 'wave' aspects does not need to arise, and no 'blind spot' is being generated, since there is no subjective primal perspective; instead, one pursues objective considerations concerning the general relation between a query content and ensuing conceptual necessity. When one allows oneself to be rooted meditatively in the overall interconnections one can be aware of the fact that any gesture—doubt, query, outcry, aggression, etc.—elicits organically the corresponding response out of the overall interconnections. There is no chasm between logical connectivity and material cohesion (Schaerer 2002: section 4.3).

As mentioned in the preceding section, allegedly basic distinctions can be done away with, such as 'subject vs. object', 'fact vs. value' or 'epistemic vs. ontic view' that split up the features of the subject matter according to criteria alien to it. One does not therefore, advocate dissociations such as theoretical versus practical philosophy, or epistemology versus ontology, or descriptive versus normative modes of thinking, or empirical versus rational theories, or science versus humanities—in which the dependency of the one side on the other side is too often forgotten. Instead, there is a proposal for methodology and activity in which theory and practice can constitute a dynamic unity, the ontological view has a sound epistemological basis and the epistemology is ontologically relevant, the values that situate the facts are transparent and the effects of values can openly be considered, the empirical activity has a rational basis and the rationality has no empirical gaps, while the proposed form of science is humanly integral and does not, therefore, become destructive while its humanity is adequate for a complete natural science, etc. The concretely practised mental activity can operate in a meditative mood, in universally adequate categories, without finally being compelled to fuzzinesses, probabilities, undecidabilities and paradoxes that must seem inevitable to minds remaining in 'postmodern' beliefs as a result of not having overcome the descriptive mode.

For keeping everything together, the point is to distinguish adequately the conceptual facts in terms of what is fundamentally required for intelligibility. Then one is not compelled to an inadequate fragmentation of the subject matter. For getting the point one can think for example of the physicist who does not distinguish conceptually the alive from the inert and is therefore compelled—by his ideationally real, but conceptually unclear choices—to deploy experimental setups that separate the alive from the inert, in arrays that either kill the object or allow only mechanistic features of it to be recognizable; such a physicist cannot even realize that he is moving around in a self-fulfilling prophecy.

Due to its intrinsic completeness on principle, systematic attentiveness is suitable for all scientific disciplines, from physics and chemistry to biology all the way to anthropology, social science, and even theology. It has no problem with the self-referentiality that inheres as much the nature of materiality as the mental structure and process, as required for understanding the extreme existential feature of complete self-referentiality. Systematic attentiveness unifies for instance subjectivity and objectivity, but in a more complete way than other approaches aiming at this bridging act—as for instance is often being claimed in analytic philosophy or in systems theory—because systematic attentiveness liberates from onesidednesses and anthropocentric biases by allowing a thorough grasp of the ultimate principles for intelligibility—for example in a process view: 'law', 'force', 'disequiliability', 'basic equilibrium'—that remain unclear in traditional approaches due to their inherent and nevertheless usually unnoticed self-limitations.

The generality of the produced conceptual instrumentation is the reason why systematic attentiveness offers, besides an improved dialogue with the specific subject matter, also a potential for easier and more encompassing inter- and trans-disciplinary comprehension. As outlined very briefly, it is simultaneously an epistemology (of integral character), an ontology (of movement per se), a theory (explaining the relation between mental gestures and resulting conceptual structures), a practice (of integral understanding), etc. Once the shared general query content has been chosen (for example the Aristotelian line of thought: change, process), the strictly universal applicability of the respective conceptual tetrad makes any given field and discipline accessible to any other by means of the same categorial framework. As the history of philosophy shows, some conceptual polarities have already been developed and can readily be used, while on principle it would be possible to choose a new query content and distil the corresponding polar concepts out of it, but such an operation might well require a few decades of careful work. Yet the existing polarities cover a lot of fields already. Their availability opens up a very relaxed space of communication and agreement, and thereby of creative interaction—as much with the subject matter as with other investigators and involved institutions. After all, the general tenet of systematic attentiveness—proposing first to let go of all beliefs, instead 'listening' to the subject matter instead of prematurely 'talking into' it—can be understood, enacted and shared by any civilized person in any given culture. It embodies a philosophy of participation and of fulfilment. In this way, systematic attentiveness could be an invisible but very effective ambassador for creating dialogical creativity.

References

Cuffaro, Michael E. (2010), 'The Kantian Framework of Complementarity', arXiv:1008.2904v1 [physics.hist-ph], available online.

Foerster, Heinz von (1979), 'Cybernetics of Cybernetics', University of Illinois, Urbana, available as a PDF at http://faculty.stevenson.edu/jlombardi/pdf%27s/cybernetics/cybernetics_cybernetics_hvf.pdf

Gödel, Kurt (1931), 'Über formal unentscheidbare Sätze der Principia Mathematica und verwandter Systeme I', *Monatshefte für Mathematik und Physik*, vol. 37, pp. 173–98.

Goethe, Johann Wolfgang von (1976 [1907]), 'Maximen und Reflexionen', 1st edn., (published posthumously), *Schriften der Goethe-Gesellschaft*, ed. Max Hecker; vol. 21, latest reprint Frankfurt am Main: Insel-Verlag.

Goldammer, Eberhard von (1999), 'The Blind Spot of Artificial Intelligence', A footnote to Gotthard Günther´s articles: "Can Mechanical Brains Have Consciousness?" and "Die Entdeckung Amerikas und die Sache der Weltraumliteratur", available online at http://www.vordenker.de/gunther_web/footnote.htm

Gschwind, Peter (2004), *Projektive Mikrophysik, Erweiterung der Teilchenphysik durch Umkreisgrössen*, Dornach: Philosophisch-Anthroposophischer Verlag am Goetheanum.

Hegel, Georg Friedrich Wilhelm (1989 [1830]), *Enzyklopädie der Philosophischen Wissenschaften*, 2 vols. Frankfurt am Main: Suhrkamp (stw); (1991), *Encyclopaedia of Philosophical Sciences*, tr. T.F. Geraets, W.A. Suchting, H.S. Harris, Indianapolis: Hackett.

Luhmann, Niklas (1984), *Soziale Systeme. Grundriß einer allgemeinen Theorie*, Frankfurt am Main: Suhrkamp.

———(1997), *Die Gesellschaft der Gesellschaft*, Frankfurt am Main: Suhrkamp.

Mayorek, Marek B. (2002), *Objektivität: ein Erkenntnisideal auf dem Prüfstand*, Tübingen: A. Francke.

Meinong, Alexius (1910), *Über Annahmen*, Leipzig: Johann Ambrosius Barth.

Mittelstrass, Jürgen (1982), *Wissenschaft als Lebensform*, Frankfurt am Main: Suhrkamp (stw).

Morris, Erroll (2010), 'The Anosognosic's Dilemma: Something's Wrong but You'll Never Know What It Is', *The New York Times*, 20 June.

Schaerer, Alec A. (2001), 'Why Matter Matters Massively', *Frontier Perspectives*, vol. 10, no. 2, pp. 52–9.

————(2002), 'Conceptual Conditions for Conceiving Life—a Solution for Grasping its Principle, not Mere Appearances', in *Fundamentals of Life*, ed. G. Palyi, C. Zucchi and L. Caglioti, Paris: Elsevier, pp. 589–624.

————(2003), 'Begriffliche Bedingungen für den Umgang mit Ganzheit und Gewißheit', *Marburger Forum*, Beiträge zur geistigen Situation der Gegenwart, 4. Jg., Heft 3; available online at www.marburger-forum.de.

————(2004), 'Kultur, Bildung oder Geist? Alle drei gemeinsam. Ein Mehrdimensionen-Ansatz zur integralen Erneuerung der Humanwissenschaften', in *Kultur, Bildung oder Geist? Skizzen zur Zukunft der europäischen Humanwissenschaften im 21. Jahrhundert*, ed. Roland Benedikter, Innsbruck-Wien-München: Studienverlag, pp. 455–95.

————(2006), 'Toward a Unified Knowledge-Based Society for Sustainability, Developing a Synthesis on the Methodological Level', in *Proceedings of the Symposium 'Unifying Knowledge for Sustainability in the Western Hemisphere'*, Denver, Colorado, 20–25 September 2004; also available online at http://www. fs.fed.us/rm/pubs/rmrs_p042/rmrs_p042_960_990.pdf.

————(2008), 'A General Methodology for Reconciling Perspectivity and Universality: Applied to the Discrepancy between Theoretical Economics and Eco-Social Reality', *International Journal of Transdisciplinary Research*, vol. 3, no. 1, pp. 1–43.

————(2009), 'The Basic Concepts of Theoretical Economics, Developing Systematically the Content of the Law of Real Value', *International Journal of Transdisciplinary Research*, vol. 4, no. 1, pp. 35–95.

Scharmer, C. Otto, W. Brian Arthur, Jonathan Day, Joseph Jaworski, Michael Jung, Ikujiro Nonaka, Peter M. Senge (2002), *Illuminating the Blind Spot. Leadership in the Context of Emerging Worlds*, available online at http://www.ottoscharmer. com/sites/default/files/2002_Illuminating_the_Blind_Spot.pdf

Scharmer, Claus Otto (2007), *Theory U. Leading from the Future as it Emerges. The Social Technology of Presencing*, Cambridge, MA: Society for Organizational Learning (SoL).

Spencer-Brown, George (1971), *Laws of Form*, London: Allen and Unwin.

Ziegler, Renatus, ed. (1996), *Universalkräfte in der Mechanik. Perspektiven einer anthroposophisch erweiterten mathematischen Physik*, Dornach: Philosophisch-Anthroposophischer Verlag am Goetheanum.

25

Knowing and Sharing: A Dialogical Journey

RANJAN KUMAR PANDA

In this essay, I intend to delve into the ontological and the epistemological aspects of the notion of *knowing* and *sharing*. In the pursuit of knowledge—knowing and sharing are integrated to unfold performativity. The logic of performativity emphasizes the significance of the dialogical character of knowing and sharing. Knowledge is sustained within the intentional epistemic framework of dialogical method of knowing and sharing. In this regard, the epistemological aspect of the dialogue brings out the intentional engagement of the knower with the other or the world, whereas its ontology refers to the autonomy of the self as an initiator and liberator of the dialogue, i.e. knowing as well as restoring knowledge. Thus, knowing and sharing in a mode of dialogical journey not only unfolds human epistemic engagement with the *other*/world but also unfolds human aspiration to know the *self.*

Knowing and sharing are unified concepts in the discourse of social epistemology. Their integration is significant from two points of views: the epistemic and the ethical. Knowing is an epistemic activity largely interpreted as embodiment of logical or rational thinking. In rational methodological discourse of theorization of reality the presence of the ethical is either overlooked or considered insignificant. Sharing, on the other hand, gives primacy to the ethical for having a successful dissemination of knowledge. Knowledge sharing demands the presence of the ethical without which the *epistemic framework* in which knowledge is cultivated cannot be developed. In this regard, the attempt in this chapter is to reflect on an alternative methodology in which knowing and sharing are integrated and open up a new space of creative thinking and learning. This methodology is grounded in the notion of intentionality that connects the *self* with the *other* and the *other* with the *self.* This intentional relationship reveals a *dialogical* mode of knowing and sharing knowledge. The significance of this transformative intentionality is based on the *dialogical* nature of human *thinking,* which helps in transforming the self as well as transforming the other for the realization of value of life.

Knowing: An Appraisal of Performitivity

Knowing is a performative act. The performitivity unfolds the intentional mode in which the knower and the known are engaged. The intentional characterization of this engagement helps in explicating the very act of knowing. Since knowing represents the act from the *first person point of view*, so the authenticity of this engagement is often contested. The first person point of view of knowing unfolds the subjectivity of the knower. So far as the intentional representation of knowledge is concerned this subjectivity is an objective fact of knowing. Now the question arises that can anyone have knowledge without the presence of the subject of knowledge—the knower? If the response is negative then one may further ask does the intervention of subjectivity affect seriously the knowledge claim. The answer cannot be negative this time, because the assertion of this claim leads to *solipsism*. Then, how can subjectivity be entertained without affecting the values of the epistemic framework, and this has been a very engaging task for many philosophers who have tried to retain the notion of subjectivity. One of the problems regarding the peculiarity of this subjectivity is that it can *deceive* the other while being engaged in the process of acquisition of knowledge. For example, a learner who listens to someone knowledgeable can imitate easily, rather than being genuinely involved in the process of learning. Listening could be imitated by exhibiting some gestures or reproducing whatever is literally heard. Thus, the listener can impress the speaker showing that he is attentive and sincere in acquiring knowledge. A genuine listener, on the other hand, makes an effort to reflect, relate to experience, and articulate meaningfully. There has been a long tradition of learning in India, which emphasizes knowing through listening involving *sravana*, *manana* and *nididhyasana* (Hirst 1996). Pupils as listeners used to formally participate in this process of listening and learning. For instance, traditionally, the Vedas were orally taught and restored by following this method of learning. Hence, the Vedas are known as *srutis*. In the ashram, the rishi or the sage used to recite and in the process of recitation, the pupils used to listen to the Vedic hymns, reflect on them and internalize them. *Manana* or internalization of the content helps the learner to relate to experiences of life. And that gives an opportunity to the learner to put them in practice (*nididhyasana*) in everyday life. However, this process of learning through recitation and listening unfolds the notion of performitivity embedded in knowing.

By reciting the Vedic hymns the rishi or the guru intends to disseminate the *content* to the listener (the *sishya*), indeed shows the acceptable form of sharing does not go against the logic of the *speech-acts* (see Searle 1969). Speaking is an activity through which communication is initiated. During communication, the *meaning* of the utterance of a statement is induced by the speaker to the hearer. The intentionality of the communication shows that the speaker not only expresses something to the hearer but also intends to suggest something and in response indeed expects something from the hearer. Thus, speaking is associated not only with action but also with thought. On the other hand, one may also ask the question that whether listening is equally associated with thinking and action. In other words, can listening be characterized as a performative act? The performitivity of *speech-acts* shows a kind of transition from *thought* to *action*, i.e. *thinking* and *doing*. The latter is a public state of affairs whereas the former is a personal state of affairs. Referring to this *transition* in the case of the performative character of thinking, Hintikka writes, 'This transition from "public" speech acts to "private" thought acts, however, does not affect the essential features of their logic' (1962: 13). To listen is to be *conscious of* or attend to what is being said. In this regard, listening signifies an intentional involvement of the hearer. That implies listening is nothing but *thinking* along with the speaker, i.e. listener's intentional engagement with the process of sharing. And this reciprocity between the speaker and the listener accomplishes the *speech-acts*.

Moreover, the notion of performative unfolds the logical connection between thinking and acting. Thinking being a private state of affairs does not lose its logical feature of performitivity. As Hintikka clarifies, 'In trying to make others believe something I must normally do something which can be heard or seen or felt. But in trying to make *myself* believe something, there is no need to say anything aloud or to write anything on paper' (1962:13). For instance, when a listener obeys the order, he/she believes in what is being stated. So, making one believe in something entails from thinking, it does not require any overt action to be displayed. It only suggests that listening is an intentional and self-conscious act. Citing the case of the metaphor of listening to music, Hintikka further remarks that one is 'aware of the sound of music by pausing to listen to it but rather by making sure that music is to be heard by playing it oneself. Ceasing to play would not only stop one's hearing the music, in the way ceasing to listen could; it would put an end to the music itself' (1962: 22). Thus, listening demands intentional involvement from the listener.

Showing the essential relationship between thinking and listening, Hintikka further refers to Descartes's conception of the performative character of *thinking*, i.e. *cogito* that confirms the *sum*. The Cartesian cogito involves *self-knowledge* that signifies *knowing* about oneself and also confirms the existence. In other words, self-knowledge is a marker of what one *thinks* about oneself, i.e. comprehension of one's own ability to carry out thought into action. This ability is semantic, which may not merely characterize in terms of physical capability, power, etc. Rather, the semantic ability helps in comprehending the *content* of thought and action. And, that helps in transferring the content of thought into action. In other words, it is an ability to perform action meaningfully and realize what is being performed. Hence, *cogito* involves self-reflexive intentional attitude through which the content is introspected and related thought and action. Thus, Hintikka writes,

What makes us connect the *cogito* with introspection is 'spiritualization' which takes place when an 'external' speech act is replaced by a thought act and on which we commented above. In *cogito* it is presupposed that a man not only can converse with his fellow men but is also able to 'discourse with himself' without 'spoken sound' in a way closely reminiscent of Plato's famous definition of thinking 'as a discourse that the mind carries on with itself' (and also reminiscent of Peirce's pertinent remarks on the dialogical character of thought). (1962: 19)

This *spiritualization*[1] is often vulnerable to critics, under the banner of scientism or the positivistic attitude of explaining the nature of human life. No doubt scientific enterprise has been very productive in recent years making life comfortable and this enterprise in a sense is limited and does not include everything about life. For instance, questions still being pondered over: 'What is a good society? What is the aim and purpose of human life? What is the nature of language and meaning? What is the nature of truth? The scientific answer to these has yet not been found. And these all quite primitive questions are discussed in philosophy' (see Searle 1999: 2070). Keeping the philosophical significance of the study, let this *strong* point of the Cartesian characterization of the *cogito* be accepted—thinking as inner form of speech act. And being engaged in thinking is thus performative.

However, to listen, in a performative framework is to *believe* the *content* of the words of the speaker. The grammar of the performative is such that the listener receives the *content* with absolute care and commitment, whereas the latter disseminates the *content* with complete trust and clarity. Commitment, care, trust, clarity, etc., are normative conditions of knowing. These features significantly characterize knowing as performance and thus help in transcending the act of imitation. Knowledge of *sruti* is thus restored from one generation to another cultivating a systematic and normative method of listening. The implication of this is significant so far as restoration of knowledge is concerned, particularly when scripts are not developed. Referring to the significance of oral tradition Narayan writes:

Oral traditions are media of collective expression replete with traces of experiences and activities of the people. Usually, in the course of time, something new gets added to it and something gets deleted from it. This flows continually in the mental outlook of society and people, and also in their everyday forms of behaviour. This is the standing base to which new changes are added by people. Thus oral tradition possesses continuity and changes as truth. The oral tradition in its forms is unchangeable and changeable, records time and space in itself. (1999: 70)[2]

The continuity is retained through the dialogical order of the orality in which changes do not affect the content of the epistemic framework. Presently, one can contextualize this with regard to the cultural knowledge of some tribals. In the absence of scripts, some of these tribes have succeeded in restoring their art, literature, medicine, etc. (Devy 2006). Knowledge development, thus, involves orality as dialogical modality in which knowledge is articulated and disseminated.

The grammar of knowing is to do with orality, which is performative in nature. As Narayan explains:

In orality, through words, symbols, myths and folk songs, the collective memory recurs. In spoken form, a word is repeated and transformed each time. But this transformation does not break the continuity of the internal effect of the words; most of the time, this effect increases. This increased internal effect of oral words evolves the collective memory of the people. The process of memorialization in the oral culture is different from that in a literature context. While in a literature context memorialization means word for word duplication of previous speech event; in an oral context memorialization usually involves replication of tradition, not of specific words. (1999: 71)

Hence, in this tradition of dialogical form of orality, one must understand the significance of the internal effect of the words. That is, listening per se is not accomplished by mere hearing something, rather by assimilating and incorporating the content with the form of *manana* (self-reflection) and *nididhyasana* (practice) would disclose the dialogical nature of thinking.

Thinking: A Note on the Dialogical Aspect of *Cogito*

Thinking or *cogito* is central to the discourse of knowing. *Cogito* though carries metaphysical baggage being associated with consciousness or the mind, but still it is part of the everyday experience that involves intention, expectation, feeling, action, etc. (Clarke 1992: 272). Thinking is central to human life (Wittgenstein 1980). It represents genuine acts of consciousness, which Descartes 'sought to accomplish by extending the meaning of the verb *cogitare*. He tried to interpret all the other acts of consciousness as so many modes of thinking', remarks Hintikka (1962: 22). In this regard, thinking is considered as the most indubitable and simply accessible feature of knowledge. Thinking is easily comprehensible. Nevertheless, the Cartesian metaphysics is grounded in *cogito* that provides certainty to knowledge claims. In other words, knowledge about the *thinking I* or *the self is* conceived from the first person point of view (Descartes 1986: 17–18). That is, to know one's own being is nothing but being conscious about one's self and its existence in the world. Thus *cogito* lays down the foundation for any sort of knowledge claims, including the scientific explanation of the reality.

This notion of thinking is questioned and critiqued as Descartes found that it could not be located in space as the body can be located. This dissociation is significant as thinking constitutes the power of self-movement, judgement, rationality, etc., and situates the mind beyond the finites of mechanism. On the other hand, understanding of the body is possible within the mechanistic framework of physics and physiology. This is the basis of mind–body dualism. There is no interest in settling this philosophical problem here, rather concerned with highlighting the significance of *cogito* as the foundation of the epistemic discourses. John Searle, one of the eminent critics of Cartesian dualism, also highlights this point:

For three centuries after Descartes, from the middle of seventeenth to the late twentieth century, the single greatest preoccupation of philosophers was with the problems of knowledge and scepticism. Descartes made epistemology—the theory of knowledge—central to philosophy. For Descartes, the primary question was what sort of solid foundational grounding can we give to our claims to knowledge, in the sciences, in commonsense, in religion, in mathematics, etc. (1999: 2072).

Cogito provides the foundation to all kinds of knowledge, particularly the very act of knowing. And, knowing is inseparable from thinking.

For Descartes, 'thinking is inseparable from me—as the knower'. Because to know is to reflect on or think about what is being known. In this, as Hintikka rightly remarked, the knower is engaged in the *dialogue* with oneself. This dialogical mode of thinking not only provides the objectivity for claims of knowledge, but also shows how knowledge has a subjective belongingness. As Searle writes, 'Consciousness is, by definition, subjective, in the sense that for a conscious state to exist it has to be experienced by some conscious subject. Consciousness in this sense has first person ontology in that it only exists from the point of view of a human or animal subject, an "I", who has the conscious experience' (1999: 2074). Subjectivity is construed as the basic feature of conscious thinking. To talk about thinking is to talk about the self—thinking is the expression of the self. A thinking self is a dialogical self that experiences its own subjectivity as well as relates to the other/world from the *first person point of view*. This relationship is important because it structures thought and experience. The nature of thinking can be learned while living with the people.[3] Hence, knowledge about thinking can be theorized by delving into the forms of life of human beings.

Knowing as performative act shows how knowledge claim is being expressed. Knowledge is generally expressed in propositional form, i.e. 'I know that . . .'. It discloses two things: the intentionality of knowing, and second, knowledge is about something that does not belong to the subject. Nevertheless, this belongingness can be retained with the intentional dialogical attitude of knowing. That is to say, the knower as the subject of knowledge is different from the object of knowledge. Knowing is an intentional attitude of the knower through which he/she reaches out to the object of knowledge or the known. It is through this *intentionality*, Edmund Husserl, another notable critic of Descartes, unfolds the dialogical modes of *cogito*.

Intentionality is a technical term theorized from the phenomenological point of view by Husserl (1982) and from the naturalistic point of view by Searle (1983). Nevertheless, intentionality essentially refers to *directedness* or *aboutness* involved in consciousness. For Husserl, intentionality is the essential property, which reveals the structures of consciousness such that it unfolds various modes of the *cogito*, through the objectification of the intended object. Thus, the location of intentionality is within the realm of human consciousness or what he calls the *lived experience,* which includes thinking, knowing, imagining, etc. Though intentionality is placed within the realm of consciousness, still Husserl presupposes a transcendental epistemology of the *intersubjective* consciousness, and also the ontology of the essences. That is, the Husserlian notion of intentional thinking rejects the Cartesian privacy associated with the self. Hence, *cogito* as part of *intersubjective* world does not lead to solipsism of the individual consciousness, nor does it lead straightway to idealism. Husserl's programme therefore is not exclusively Cartesian, but Kantian. As Smith and MacIntyre put it, '. . . Husserl's transcendental resolution of Descartes' epistemological programme is not Cartesian but Kantian. Husserl calls it "transcendental theory of knowledge"' (1982: 94). Through Husserl critiques Cartesian epistemology, still his approach remains epistemological rather than metaphysical. The epistemological question mainly relates to the Cartesian methodological investigation as Husserl develops phenomenology in the Cartesian way to provide foundation to the structure of science in particular and epistemology in general. He introduces the phenomenological method for a logical analysis of the mental phenomena, and not to abolish the distinction between the mental and the physical. Rather the enquiry is into the correlation between the two. It is interesting to note that from this epistemological consideration the ontological problems crop up which further leads to the idea of 'reduction'. Hence, Husserl gives due importance to the idea of reduction (*epoche*) or *bracketing*. By reduction, he means the delimitation of the domain of phenomenology to the transcendental realm of experience. He classifies reduction generally into three types: psychological, transcendental and eidetic. All these three types of reduction are phenomenological and so are relevant to the study of the concept of intentionality.

Cogito as the thinking self has many referential points, such as man, individual, agent, subject, person, knower, etc., which are characterized by intentionality and freedom. Intentionality constitutes not only man's experiences but also defines the actions performed by the self. The self as the constituting feature of experiences flows along with these experiences. The flow of intentionality manifested through experiences has the peculiarity of transcending outer modes of relation as well as reflecting on its own *loneliness*. The outer relations show how one develops himself/herself in real time and history with relations to his/her beliefs, desires, hopes, etc. Over and above it defines one's belongingness to the socio-cultural space in which she/he lives. Understanding its own subjectivity (kind of loneliness) brings a reflection to the very mode of intentionality that defines the socio-cultural engagement from the 'subjective perspective of the world'. Thus, the subjective becomes the antonym of the objective. In this mode of relationship the self transcends the socio-cultural, socio-political and socio-historical engagements reflecting on the formal conditions of such engagements. Thus, intentionality totalizes the various kinds of relationships that the self shares with the other (or the world) and with itself (Mohanty 2000: 73).

Sharing: A Reflection on the Normativity of Intentionality

Knowledge is shareable with the other. And sharing is an obligation. Though intentionality of knowing is basically understood as a voluntary act, still normatively speaking knowing involves obligation. That is, the knower is obliged to share the known with the other. It is because knowledge cannot remain within the domain of the subject or the knower. Knowledge has to be shared for the sake its own development, so that if need arises it can be recalled at any point of time. For example, the written form of Vedic text is available today because of rigorous and systematic practice. In this case the normativity of practice is important to restore knowledge. In this connection, knowledge development has pragmatic concern and the user of knowledge must examine the practical as well as the theoretical utility. The practical utility of knowledge is realized only when knowledge is applied to resolve certain practical difficulties. For instance, knowledge of the Ayurveda is slowly being revived as an alternative mode of health care because of its practical utility. Globally people have started embracing yoga for better health care—in the form of an alternative technique to solve certain practical difficulties. On the other hand, the theoretical utility of knowledge refers to internal growth and novelty of knowledge. In other words, knowledge in its use must add to its content and enrich itself.

In this regard, it may be argued that the right to share knowledge demands a normative standard for its correct usage. A non-normative framework might not help to prevent mis-utilization of knowledge. Teaching and learning have been just a ritual practised without understanding the ethos of the culture of education. Some institutions do not cultivate this rationale at all. Values are interpreted largely from the point of view of religion and dogma. As a result they have failed largely to communicate the sense of social responsibility. This is partly because the basic mode of sharing is misconstrued as voluntary act. And second, the intentionality of dissemination of knowledge has tried to comply largely with economic and psychological desires. The economic and the psychological conditions do influence the mode of knowledge formation and process of dissemination. On the contrary, it may be emphasized that knowledge sharing is an obligatory act. It must be normatively construed to go beyond the psychological and economic conditions of knowledge sharing.

Knowledge should be meaningfully articulated taking into consideration systematic formation, examination and practice. Each of them represents different intentional modes through which knowledge is created. Knowledge sharing becomes important because it shows the outer intentional modalities in which knowledge is communicated to the other. In the process of communication one has the opportunity to convey the *content* to the other for justification, for practice, etc. Sharing takes place in a communicative mode developing an intentional relationship between the knowledgeable-teacher and the learner. This relationship demands a performative mode of representation in which teaching and learning are synchronic events. The intentional mode of participation is such that the teacher becomes the learner while communicating knowledge and the learner becomes the *knowledgeable* while listening to it. This intentional shift is due to the self-reflexivity of human consciousness. And in the process both relate to knowledge-content. This mode of relating is nothing but the intentionality of experiencing the *content* of knowledge.[4]

The content signifies the meaning. Every learner of knowledge must learn to find the novelty in acquiring knowledge. The novel aspect of knowledge is nothing but the aspectuality in which the learner or the researcher relates to the known and defines the content. In this process the new content is added to the existing 'knowledge-content'—which is nothing but articulating the new meaning. Meaning added is meaning invented or meaning discovered—novelty shown. Moreover, showing the significance of knowledge does require the art of communicating it. As an art it emphasizes the process of effective imparting of knowledge. Moreover, effective learning is possible if there is mutual reciprocity between the teacher and the learner. This mutual reciprocity is not just to fulfil certain psychological reason but also is grounded in certain normative reason, which shows that the act of sharing knowledge is a normative act that takes place in a social and institutional framework.

Normativity is nourished in socio-cultural background of human life and making human living meaningful. The norms have the power of influencing and modifying human behaviour. In a normative framework action is regulated by the norms for the realization of values. The cultural life is value laden. Searle writes, 'Humans are distinct from other animals in that they have a capacity to create not merely a social but an institutional reality. This institutional reality is, above all, a system of deontic powers. These deontic powers provide human agents with fundamental key for organized human society: the capacity to create and act on desired— independent reasons for action' (2007: 125). Animals exhibit natural behaviour, which may be guided by desires and instincts or natural characteristics. Only humans try to control their natural instincts and regulate their actions in the direction where actions are justified by reasons, emotions, and virtues. Human actions are not just intentional but also normative.

The deontic power refers to the normative ability of judging the content of thoughts and action. This is something significant of the human beings engaged in knowledge creation. This ability pertains to all kinds of knowledge such as scientific, cultural, religious, moral, etc. It is the power to evaluate the very content of knowledge per se. The ability to exercise the power of judging right and wrong, the will to perform certain duties, desire to show empathy, aspiration to know the truth, etc., unfold an important mode of the function of human intentionality.

Knowing and Sharing: Two Perspectives of the Intentional Relationship between the Self and the Other/World

Intentionality needs a special recall for two reasons; first, to clarify the phenomenological perspective of Husserl in juxtaposition to the naturalistic perspective of Searle, and secondly to highlight the basic intentional relationship that exists between the knower and the known. This intentional relationship constitutes the epistemic structure between the self and the world.[5] The first point is important from the methodological point of view, whereas delving on the second point would show the significance of the notion of intentionality *per se* to present study of the notion of knowing and sharing. The epistemic structure between the self and the world is grounded in the intentionality of consciousness which by nature is world oriented, i.e. all conscious experience is the experience of something. Hence, the *of-ness* or *directedness* that experience displays is the logical act of consciousness. Husserl introduces the concept of *noema* to explain this *logical act* that maintains the relation between the consciousness (self) and the object (the world). Nevertheless, the logical dimension needs transcendental reflection on *noema* (the intended object) and the *noesis* (the act of directedness) and their relationship present in the *cogito*. Hence, both are part of the intentional structure of experience.

In view of the fact that *noema* and *noesis* are logically related, it is important to draw a distinction between the *content* of an *act* and the *intended object*. Emphasizing their relationship, Smith and MacIntyre writes 'For Husserl the content of an act includes only what is in the act that makes the act intentional experience it is; and, as he says, "the object is properly speaking nothing at all 'in' the presentation"' (1982: 113). Generally the *act* means the *way of conceiving the content* that determines the *object* or referent. So a particular object may have different contents and therefore different acts of directedness. However, the content possesses the feature of directedness. That is, the act is determined by the inner capacity of how the object is presented and judged. For example, how one listens to hymns or listens to lectures in a classroom is different from listening to a running cricket commentary. The former requires immediate reflection or *manana* to grasp the content, whereas the latter does not. Grasping is a semantic ability grounded in the intentional attitude of *consciousness* in which content is internalized.[6] The content is intentionally articulated according to the presentation of the object. Thus, Husserl draws a further distinction between *intentional content* and *real content*. The intentional content can be possessed by more than one person since it is the logical object of the varying acts of consciousness. The real content, however, consists of two essential parts: 'the part of experience that makes the act of particular kind (the act's real quality) and the part that gives its directedness towards particular object and directedness which specifies the object in a specific way (the act's real matters)' (Smith and MacIntyre 1982: 116).

Moreover, *noema* and *noesis* are inseparable in the sense that one is inadequate to give the proper explanation of the structure of lived experience. Moreover, *noema* can be known not through the object perceived but by the act of experiencing the object in the perception. Here, the act of perception is different from the object of perception. Thus it is a special sort of *reflective act*, which presupposes the existence of *noema*. *Noesis* is the act intending the object and so the object is presented in the act. The way the object is represented is the *noema*: 'each *noema* includes an ideal correlate of the generic "way" in which the subject is conscious in an act' (Smith and Macintyre 1982: 131). The knower's relation to the object varies from context to context: the relationship is the way the agent becomes aware of the object. The fundamental component of *noema* is the logical essence of the object presented in the consciousness. Thus, the Husserlian idea of *noema* as the logical content of consciousness and the medium of reference has two significant roles. One, *noema* is the sense, which is expressed by general terms. Second, the *noema* of a particular object bears unique general features. In this way every representation has distinctive noematic content, because it shares some common features as a result of which it is understood. Even if the act of intending varies from person to person they all can entertain one *noema* for determining the reference.

Searle's naturalistic approach shows how intentionality is developed through an evolutionary process. Language and meaning is grounded in the logical feature of intentionality. They are the later additions to the intentional form of life of human beings. Moreover, there are two dimensions of this intentionality, which are: the function of intentionality as a non-reductive mental feature and intentionality as a crude biological feature with its naturalistic grounding. Searle is known for his argument against the reductive enterprise of naturalistic study of human life. This thesis is strengthened with reference to his notion of subjectivity. That is, intentional relationship between the self and the world unfolds the epistemic mode of subjectivity. Searle consistently maintains this right from his theorization of performative expressions. So far as the notion of sharing is concerned, performatives signify action (*doing*), which transcends the limitation of making a mere representation. Saying something is indeed making a representation. But mere *saying* does not necessarily involve the context in which it is appropriate to make that expression. Hence, while representation involves an informative content, still it can be made without communicative intention. Performatives carry *communicative intention*, that is, the agent not only makes a representation through the performance but also expects that the content effectively reaches the listener. That is the listener acts in accord with the epistemic structure of normativity of knowing. This intentional interaction between the speaker and the listener entails *intentional fitness*.

The notion of fitness is grounded in intentionality, which unfolds self-referentiality, i.e. the intentional fitness from *mind/self* to *the world* and from the *world* to *the mind/self*. As Searle explains, 'What is crucially important to see is that for every speech act that has a *direction of fit* the speech act will be satisfied if and only if the expressed psychological state is satisfied, and conditions of satisfaction and *psychological mode* are identical' (1983: 12). Every intentional or representational state has content. In other words, the intentionality of the content as an intrinsic feature of representation brings out the compatible relationship between {mind → [language] → intentional content} → [to the world] and vice-versa. This logical compatibility unfolds the two essential components of intentional states called *propositional content* and *psychological mode*. Whenever someone is representing something he also expects that there would be a change in the state of affairs according to the representation of belief. That shows the directedness of intentional content from mind/*self-to-the world/other*. And if changes occur favourably to their belief then directedness is *world/other-to-the mind/self*. Thus, intentional relationship is maintained between the mind and the world becomes more concrete through the intentional content.

Searlean internalism is agent centric. It locates the intentional content in the mind of the agent. The presence of intentional content signifies that content is experienced in the intentional act of the agent's representation (Searle 1983: 14). Representation is basically subjective in its nature. The subjectivity refers to the intentional mode of experience. The intentionality relates to the subject with the world as well as the subject with its own mental states. For Searle, 'The world itself has no point of view; my access to the world through my conscious states is always perspectival, always from my point of view' (1992: 95). The physical world will not have any intentionality. Since intentionality originates from the conscious act of the subject, therefore the first-person point of view lies in the *perspectival* feature of representation. Searle reiterates this while referring to his earlier claim that 'The logical properties of intentional states arise from their being representations, and the point is that they can, like linguistic entities, have logical properties in a way that stone and trees cannot have logical properties (though statements about stones and trees have logical properties) because intentional states, like linguistic entities and unlike stones and trees, are representations' (Searle 1992: 16). In this regard, the intentionality of the agent is the primary condition for the explanation of representational states. Representational states like belief, desire and intention are construed by intentionality. For example, my expression of a belief 'that mountain has smoke' is based on the direct perception of the mountain having smoke. The belief here is not having two-term relations between *a believer* and *a proposition*. Rather, proposition is the *content* of belief (Searle 1992: 18). The content is embedded in the *intentional act* of the agent.

J.N. Mohanty (1981) in his criticism of Searle's theorization of intentionality remarks that the intentional content cannot be causally explicable. According to Mohanty, Searle provides a causal theory of intentionality which is grounded in the hypothesis: 'consciousness is caused by the brain processes and realized in the brain processes' (Searle 1969). This hypothesis entails a physical ontology because the neurophysiological process of the brain causes the consciousness. Though the biological naturalism of Searle advocates a causal account of intentionality, still consciousness and its properties are irreducible to brain processes. In his agenda of naturalistic inquiry, Searle clarifies this point: 'The point I am making here is different. The epistemology of studying the mental no more determines its ontology' (1992: 23). The intentional explanation of the logical properties of representational states pertains to the realm of epistemology. The mind or conscious experience of thought provides the epistemic base for intentional act. Intentionality constitutes the epistemic base as the foundation of *internality* of thought and expression.

Intentionality of Self and Self-Knowledge: A Dialogical Enquiry

Intentionality being intrinsic to consciousness/thinking totalizes me—the self, thoughts and experiences. This totalization signifies not only a process of relationship that the self shares with the other, but also shows an inseparable relationship in which the self and the other are engaged. Such an understanding of this inseparable engagement brings out self-knowledge as well as the knowledge about the other (Mohanty 2000). The self-understanding is not generated by the other, rather it is out of the self's own cultivation—the cultivation of freedom (Verne 1979: 83). Intentionality and freedom are intrinsic features of human consciousness which constitute the self that constitutes culture of learning: 'it defines a way of life, a manner of thinking and acting shared by a group of people over time' (Dallmayr 1994:101). Here culture is not a still phenomenon, rather a dynamic field of *knowledge*, which has equal potentiality to interact with the self. This potentiality of dynamism is captured in reflective consciousness, so to say, a reflective mode of intentionality. As Fred Dallmayr puts it, 'captured in reflective judgement, culture provides an over all framework through which we understand the world; it offers a frame of reference which gives sense of meaning to individual terms and concepts (like the concept of development)' (1994: 101). The reflective intentionality of self constitutes not only the *epistemic framework* that formsmeaning in everyday life but also frames for the discourse of *meaning of life,* implying that there could be diversified flow of experiences in which multiple frameworks can take birth. The multiplicity of learning/cultural life is unified showing the normative traits of integration and aspiration for values. This aspiration works as internal force or operative idea in looking forward to revising and reconstituting the alternative *epistemic frameworks* of values, showing the result of free engagement in an operative idea of life as a whole that enters into the making and working of institutions. Hence, it may be said that freedom of the self creates values.

Freedom and experience are the breeding ground of creativity, while living in mode of knowing, reflecting and practising intellectual activities signifies culture of learning. The experiential mode of this relationship unfolds the field of interaction and communication in which the involvement of other is shown. The involvement develops the sense of belongingness in knowing, representing and contemplating on experience and they all form an intentional mode of engagement. As Mohanty points out, 'But a person, while being all these things, she acts, judges, demands, has rights, entertains values, is in connection with other individuals and their acts, judgements, evaluations, rights and values. This living space of a person is not field of objects, but an actual and valuational field of situations which constantly undertake her, and in which she is called upon to make new decisions, and from within which she projects new possibilities' (2000: 83). The culture of learning as experience looks at the living space as the field of intentional engagement and involvement that gives opportunity of putting forward new ideas and possibilities as well as opens up the scope for realizing them. This engagement becomes instrumental in developing *self-knowledge.*

The development of *self-knowledge* is the result of self-cultivation. The notion of cultivation is one of intrinsic potential quality of man. It initiates the *movement* of raising 'humanity through culture of learning'. The movement is an 'inner action' (Buber 1965). This action not only commences with the self but also forms the field of dialogue that turns to the other. In this regard, the movement has two important functions with regard to the notion of cultivation as defined by Dallmayr (1994); they are preservation and transformation. The idea of cultivation is meant to preserve the self and transform the process of educating it. The notion of educating the self for developing *self-knowledge* partly derives from one's involvement with various forms of cultural activities or with the community. Experiences encountered in the process of involvement are significant for 'self-formation'. The experiences are not 'isolated moments' of life. Rather, one's involvement builds up linkages—experience works as 'integrative processes' toward the development of the 'self- image' (Gadamer 2004: xiii).

The unfolding of *self-knowledge* opens up the space for one's existence, which is termed 'man's cultural existence'. As Werkmeister puts it, 'human existence is essentially a cultural existence. But since, culture itself is man's own creation, we are up against the fact that, in creating himself, man also creates his own culture; and in creating his culture; he creates himself. The two aspects of his existence and his becoming are inseparable' (1967: 33). The inseparable relationship represents the two aspects of his selfhood. One of the aspects of the self represents its identity through the socio-cultural system, e.g. as one would like to relate himself to his profession, to social status, etc., in which his association with the other becomes a public phenomenon. The self presents itself in this mode as *intersubjectivity.* Whereas another facet of the self represents 'the subjective dimension of the self'; as mentioned earlier, it is the aspect of the self-performing its intentional activities. In this mode, the self looks for new possibilities while interacting with the other. The latter, in fact, integrates the former.

Assimilation and integration proceed in the form of intentional experience, which is otherwise the subjectivity of the self. But it manifests another facet, i.e. its physical participation in the forum of a community that is regulated by a normative order. The assimilation itself represents an intersubjective forum. Nevertheless, bringing two facets of the self into one level of thought is indeed an intentional activity manifested in the act of *bundling*. Illustrating the desire for bundling, Buber writes:

Collectivity is not a binding but bundling together: individuals packed together, armed and equipped in common, with only as much life from man to man as will inflame the marching step. But community, growing community (which is all we have known so far) is the being no longer side by side but with one another of a multitude, though it also moves towards one goal, yet experiences everywhere a turning to, a dynamic facing of, the other, a flowing from *I* to *Thou*. (Buber 1965: 31)

Buber's emphasis on bundling relation not only lays down an intentional space for the integration of the self and the other, but also shows the similar rhythm in prevailing the form of community life in which values of life can be shared and cherished. Thus, the spirit of the intentional movement of the self-aspiring for relationship with the other opens up a kind of journey that the self undertakes in search of itself. In other words, it is a search for meaning (Pradhan 1996).

However, the idea of the search of meaning is embedded in the dialogical engagement between self and knowledge/culture of learning. There are two phases to this engagement, as mentioned earlier; one is viewing *learning as experience*, which shows one's existential engagement or participation with intellectual academic activities, whereas another phase refers to the process of distancing from the culture of academic conflicts and problems in which the self looks forward with vision and hope for values for future humanity. The process of distantiation requires a *creative dialogue* for sustainable engagement, which looks after the continuity of making choice for alternative *epistemic framework* of learning so far as one's existential engagement with the academic culture is concerned. It shows a creative mode of succession, which eventually overturns an existing perspective that can be perceived as narrow or erroneous. Thus, the form of creative dialogue not only develops the unity between the psychological, physical and the cultural but also helps in preserving and protecting the values of life.

The shift from the normativity of epistemic framework of learning to another form of learning and practice shows the *dialectic of value seeking*. The dialectic of value seeking motivates *self-criticism* and that helps the individual to foresee the value beyond the finitude of a given pattern of life. The self-criticism with regard to the dialectic of value seeking brings about '*self-transfiguration* through the interaction of vision and praxis' (Pande 1994: 54). Unless the underlying communication between the theoretical and the practical aspects of epistemic culture is conceived, the gap between the self and the other will not be bridged. The self may create a false distinction in every level of its experience.

In view of the intertwined relationship between culture of learning and academic practice, some may prefer to overemphasize the tension that persists in comprehending the link between the realm of theoretical meaning and practical meaning. Defining the tension Nandy writes: 'It is a creative tension with which some persons and cultures prefer to live. The gap between reality and hope which such a vision creates becomes a source of cultural criticism and a standing condemnation of the oppression of everyday life, to which we otherwise tend to be reconciled' (1999: 3). The creative tension results in cultural criticism. The self reflects on the asymmetry between the practice and the value aspired. Cultural criticism attempts to make reconciliation between theory and praxis by inviting interpretation from the other. Interpretation, as Mohanty suggests, is not a one-way process. It sustains rather in 'multiple processes'—simultaneously received from many ends and lays down 'multi-layered paths' to develop coherent understanding. Mohanty observes: 'such multi-layered process and the consequent synthesis of "overlapping" can lead us much of a better self-understanding as to a better understanding of the other' (2000: 122). Establishing the multilayered paths of learning, they share their viewpoints communicated in the process of dialogue. The communication reveals its profoundness, when, as Buber points out, 'Speech can renounce all the media of sense, and it is still speech' (1965: 3). Such speech facilitates a healthy conversation in silence.

To conclude, facilitating the *creative dialogue* in the realm of *self-criticism* as well as *cultural criticism* unfolds the complementary process of unification in which the development of the self and culture is realized. This living space of a person is not a field of objects, but an actual and valuational field of situations which constantly undertakes her, and in which she is called upon to make new decisions, and from within which she projects new possibilities (Giri 1997: 163). As cultural critique opens up the possibility of appropriating the dimension of the human self and its realization, the dialogical engagement continuously enriches the creative process of understanding the universal end of humanity. Humanity manifested in diversified form of cultural, religious, scientific, artistic, mystical, etc. activities of life needs a dialogical engagement for agreement and harmony. The notion of agreement signifies intersubjective solidarity, whereas harmony signifies the dimension of valuation. Thus, the dialogical engagement of value seeking would be an alarm to the notion of *spiritual awakening* in which peace would flourish showing the path towards infinity.[7]

Notes

1. The ashram is a place of learning. It was maintained by rishis/gurus who were involved in educating young children. It is also popularly known as *gurukula*.
2. Rishis are sages considered to be the most learned persons.
3. Charles Taylor finds this spiritual development of Descartes has an influence of Augustine and Plato; see the chapter 'In Interiore Homine' in Taylor (1989).
4. Oral tradition represents collective memory wherein things are continuously recollected by the communities themselves. Vedas and other scriptures were originally oral (see Narayan 1999: 70).
5. Posing this question Wittgenstein writes, 'How did I learn what "thinking" means?—It seems I can only have learned it by living with people. ...' (Wittgenstein 1980: 29).
6. I have discussed this referring to Grice, Marty and Searle, emphasizing that meaning has a psychological component. See the chapter 'Language, Representation and Meaning' in Panda (2008).
7. The phenomenological construction of the self and the world relationship is same as the relationship of the self and the other. This section of the paper was presented in ALWS, Vienna and published in pre-proceedings of the Symposium held in Kirchberg, 2006

References

Buber, Martin (1965), *Between Man and Man*, New York: Macmillan.

Clarke, Desmond M. (1992), *Cambridge Companion to Descartes*, Cambridge: CUP.

Dallmayr, Fred (1994), 'Culture and Global Development', *Journal of Contemporary Thought,* vol. 4, pp. 99–111.

Descartes, Rene (1986), *Meditation on First Philosophy*, tr. John Cottingham, Cambridge: CUP.

Devy, G.N. (2006), *A Nomad Called Thief*, Delhi: Orient Longman, pp. 95–122.

Gadamer, Hans-Georg (2004), *Truth and Method*, New York: Continuum.

Giri, Ananta Kumar (1997), 'Self, Other and the Challenge of Culture', *Journal of Contemporary Thought*, vol. 7, pp. 145-69.

Hintikka, Jaakko (1962), 'Cogito, Ergo Sum: Inference or Performance', *The Philosophical Review*, vol. LXXI, no. 1, pp. 3-32.

Husserl, Edmund (1982), *Ideas: Pertaining to a Pure Phenomenology and Phenomenological Philosophy, First Book, General Introduction to Pure Phenomenology*, tr. F. Kersten, The Hague: Martinus Nijhoff Publishers.

Mohanty, J.N. (1981), 'Intentionality and Noema', *The Journal of Philosophy*, vol. 78, no. 11, (Seventy-Eight Annual Meeting of the American Philosophical Association Eastern Division), pp. 706–17.

———(2000), *The Self and Its Other: Philosophical Essays*, New Delhi: OUP.

Nandy, Ashis (1999), *Tyranny, Tradition and Utopia*, New Delhi: OUP.

Narayan, Badri (1999), 'Dialogical and Not Exclusive', *Journal of Indian Council of Philosophical Research*, vol. XVII, no. 1, pp. 67–75

Panda, Ranjan K. (2006), 'A Perspective of Dialogical Engagement between Self and Culture', *Cultures: Conflict-Analysis-Dialogues*, ed. Georg Gasser, Christian Kanzian and Edmund Runggaldier, vol. XIV, Kirchberg am Wechsel: Wittgenstein Philosophical Society, pp. 243-5.

————— (2008), *Mind, Language and Intentionality*, Delhi: Bharatiya Kala Prakashan.

———(2012), 'Knowing as Semantic Ability', *Journal of Indian Council of Philosophical Research*, vol. XXIX, no. 2, pp. 167-92.

Pande, G.C. (1994), 'Culture and Cultures', *Journal of Indian Council of Philosophical Research*, vol. XI, no. 3, 41–61.

Pradhan, R.C. (1996), 'Life, Culture and Value: Reflections on Wittgenstein's *Culture and Value*', *Journal of Indian Council of Philosophical Research*, vol. 13, pp. 19–30.

Searle, John R. (1969), *Speech Acts: An Essay in Philosophy of Language*, Cambridge: CUP.

———(1983), *Intentionality: An Essay in Philosophy of Mind*, Cambridge: CUP.

———(1992), *The Rediscovery of the Mind*, Massachusetts: The MIT Press.

———(1999), 'The Future of Philosophy', *Philosophical Transactions: Biological Sciences*, (Millenium Issue), vol. 354, no. 1392, pp. 2069–80.

———(2007), *Freedom and Neurobiology: Reflection on Free Will, Language, and Political Power*, New York: Columbia University Press.

Smith, David W. and Ronald MacIntyre (1982), *Husserl and Intentionality*, Holland: D. Rediel Publishing Company.

Suthren Hirst, Jacqueline (1996), 'Strategies of Interpretation: Samkara's Commentary on Brhadaranyakopanisad', *Journal of the American Oriental Society*, vol. 116, no. 1, January-March, pp. 58–75.

Taylor, Charles (1989), *Sources of Self: The Marking of Modern Identity*, Cambridge, MA: Harvard University Press.

Verne, Donald P., ed. (1979), *Symbol, Myth and Culture: Essays and Lectures of Ernst Cassirer, 1935–45*, New Haven: Yale University Press.

Werkmeister, W.H. (1967), *Man and His Values*, Lincoln: University of Nebraska Press.

Wittgenstein, Ludwig (1980), *Remarks on Philosophical Psychology*, ed. G.H. von Wright and Heikki Nyman, vol. II, tr. C.G. Luckhardt and M.A.E. Aue, Oxford: Basil Blackwell.

Afterword

Towards a Rationality of Mystery: The Calling of Robust Ignorance

MARCUS BUSSEY and
MIRIAM SANNUM

There is little doubt that today one stands in the shadow of the great intellectual legacy of European rationalism/empiricism. It is clear that this tradition has broken many erstwhile limits to set human social, intellectual and technological energies free. Yet this tradition has also come at a cost—planetary environmental deterioration, new forms of predatory imperialism, a loss of diversity and meaning—and this cost calls to all of those who care for this world and its human and other-than-human inhabitants to do something bold on *behalf of, for* and also *with* this planet and its vibrant forms. One is required to be bold to chart new pathways into multiple futures. But how does one do that when the future cannot be read? Well, *plans* are needed and one needs *ideas* and one needs *scouts* to run ahead to explore possibilities. This book offers one such plan, a constellation of ideas and brings together a group of scouts charting news futures in creative research.

The plan needs to be loose and open—and such is Giri's idea of an ontological epistemology of participation. Such an epistemology is celebratory, a festival of encounters. This concept has both a personal and social dimension. At the personal level one can no longer escape from the necessity to engage in the *self-cultivation* needed to ground a reoriented epistemology of practice and co-creation. In this re-orientation the locus of knowing is seen to be shifting from the observer to the observer-observed, from the all-seeing eye to act of co-creating. Also found here is the double entendre of engagement with civilizational insights beyond the Western episteme. The Orient calls, thus a reorientation is emerging. Yet of course the Orient, as Edward Said (1995) reminded one, is not just the old east that dances in (haunts) the Western imagination—ultimately it is the Other. This other is the counterpoint and collaborator in what is yet to come. It lies beyond the horizon yet one should approach it filled with curiosity and hope.

This curiosity and hope fuel new pathways of creative research. This curiosity is a human attribute that has always leads one to look beyond, whilst the hope is a practical process of not accepting the limits given by any current hegemony (Bussey 2013). This is a calling for practical optimism in a time when hope seems somewhat diminished, even dangerous. And of course hope can be a problem. If one hopes clever people will find solutions to all problems, one is misguided. If one hopes that some new configuration of technology will change the rules of the current global problematique, they are misguided. If they hope that some divine intervention will save the earth they are misguided. All this must be done together and more: the limitations of passive hope have to be transcended.

Yet what remains if hope is abandoned? Or, more importantly, if one is abandoned by hope? This is not a time to cast hope aside. Instead hope requires something—effort, imagination and engagement. It demands practical, creative, resourceful and dangerous explorations into how the limits are approached, to knowing this world inherent in the current paradigm. It calls for a constructive optimism based on a practical hope that takes traditions and extends them in new ways. Such continuity draws on the enabling traditions so ably tapped in the chapters in this book, from Gandhi to Gadamer, Illich to Wilber and more. This creative and transformational traditionalism[1] is vital to any rethinking of research. It calls for new narratives based on the co-creative and spiritual possibilities inherent to the very limits faced. It invites in the energy and possibilities of joyful collaborations with the multitude that inhabit the ontological field. It calls to the self-cultivation of inter-knowing the world through a hopeful inquiry into its possibilities. Such a knowing is about acceptance and dancing together rather than about order and definition; such a knowing embraces the non-knowing that always accompanies the act of research and provides the substrata of inter-knowing at the heart of an ontological epistemology of participation.

So any *plan* must be open ended, inclusive and, we would argue, joyful. The *idea* central to this book of essays is the offering of a *soft ontology of intimacy*.[2] Intimacy is inherent to knowing as one cannot truly know without having merged with the known in a generative act (Bussey 2014). This is a kind of loving that trusts *the dynamics of knowing* to allow co-creation to emerge from the stepping into knowing. To step into knowing requires the cultivation of a robust ignorance[3]. People are not prisoners of ignorance but guests. Ignorance is not darkness to researchers cultivating the soft ontology of practical hope. This kind of ignorance eschews fear and the clinging to past modes of being that limit the heart and distort thought

(Sarkar 1982). What is pointed to here is an open, exciting ignorance that offers the basis for rethinking, reorienting and re-enchanting this world and people's relationship to it.

Traditionally ignorance has been used in research to explore what is known and what is not known. Consider Ph.D. and this is the kind of ignorance at work. Robust ignorance reaches beyond this known unknown to an engagement with the negative space implicit to all epistemological positions: the unknown unknowns. In this way it is acknowledged that there is a revealed way (known unknowns) and the silence (unknown unknowns) that surrounds that which is excluded from any dominant rationality. Robust ignorance brings in mystery as a way of understanding this negative space. It is like the Japanese word *ma,* which refers to *spaces or intervals between* visible, structural elements. There is a kind of Zen mind at work here. This quality invokes a *tolerance for uncertainty* (see Shah's Chapter 10), that develops into a robust engagement moving from the known elements of any context to the many mysterious 'unknown' things that bring magic to the inhabited worlds.

Magic refers to the mystery at the heart of things. This calls for skills in research that relate to the self-cultivation so dear to Giri's project. To go inward, to contemplate and reflect and then act and test are part of this process of cultivation. It is a form of meditative enquiry moving beyond the formal to the informal, beyond the external to the interior domains of reflection as action inquiry. This book offers many approaches to such self-cultivation and the research it engenders. In addition, tools such as visioning, deep listening, engagement with the creative arts, spiritual and meditative practices, experiential research, ensemble learning, social sculpturing, and play all have their own capacity to extend the robust ignorance at the heart of the rationality of mystery. Reason in this context becomes non-linear and intuitive. It functions by navigating and generating networks that work into the unknown, unknowns that punctuate reality.

The *scouts* in this programme of self-cultivation and co-creation are seekers and collaborators across-between-beyond fields of enquiry, often described as 'disciplines', who explore new modalities of research into humanity's relationship with this world. This volume offers some fascinating possibilities in this regard, enacting the ontological sociality Giri calls for. Such explorations are layered—both tentative and assertive, open and creative. They invite possibilities rather than mandating any specific alternative. They involve engagement, as Giri argues in Chapter 2, with theory as a process of closure, with the nature of any given reading of the social as the context for theory and also with the relationship of the theory-maker (a kind of psychotic/paranoid modernist God) with the act of theorizing. In this regard, theory as Theory is overthrown and a new theory of possibilities and openness turns towards *humility* and the limits to its own aspiration to define and disclose the bones of this world. Such analytic hubris must be relieved of the burden of Truth and instead invited to engage with the power of mystery as a creative calling. Thus the rationality of Modernity gives way to the rationality of Mystery.

To approach a Mystery, centred rationality calls for a robust ignorance. This kind of reason has a deeply counter-intuitive quality but it is also—or perhaps because of this—a *libratory reason*. It invites an anticipatory imagination to unveil new possibilities and draws on what Cornel West (1999) calls the prophetic pragmatism needed to question personal and civilizational 'conditionedness'. The contributors to this collection act as scouts. They offer deep insights into the human relationship with knowledge production working from many sites. Each in their own way is doing the necessary scouting to develop maps to future possibilities. They are seeking, not as imperialists sort to chart and define new possessions, but as co-creators of new territories of possibility: territories where power comes from *within and between* each one rather than being granted/conferred by virtue of birth, citizenship and class/caste.

New worlds need new ways of knowing that go hand in hand with the new ways of being that organically emerge from transformed environments. As each *scout* returns from their explorations of such worlds, they bring insights and visions of alternatives to the one-size-fits-all approach to knowing preached, practised and enforced by the academy. Free people can only be free when their thought is free. Thought can only be free when the values and processes that support it are open, inclusive and multiple. The violence of the current epistemic regime is, we believe, crumbling. There is too much that is unknown and it is becoming increasingly clear that this is not a problem but a gift. *Not to know* is an invitation to refresh one's approach to the world, to embrace a reasoning that works within the mystery of being as a critical spiritual resource for emancipation. This implies, as suggested, a robust ignorance that invites new pathways of creative research that promote the kind of critical inquiry celebrated in this volume.

Notes

1. For more on creative traditionalism see Bussey 2015.
2. Drawing on Giri's suggestion of a soft ontology implicit to his ideas of weak naturalism, weak identity and weak integration (Giri 2013).
3. This concept takes its lead from Nicholas of Cusa's (1990) description of 'learned ignorance' and also from Sebastien Castellio's (1981) 'art of doubting'.

References

Bussey, M. (2013), 'Re-Imagining Limits', *Sociological Bulletin,* vol. 62, no. 1, pp. 129–31.

———(2014), 'Intimate Futures: Bringing the Body into Futures Work', *European Journal of Futures Research,* vol. 2, no. 53, pp. 1–8.

———(2015), 'Heritage Futures: Thow Kwang Dragon Kiln and Creative Traditionalism in Singapore', in *Angel by the Water: Essays in honour of Dennis Reginal O'Hoy,* ed. M. Butcher, Kennington, Victoria: Holland House Publishing, pp. 128–39.

Castellio, S. (1981), *De Arte Dubitandi Et Confidendi Ignorandi Et Sciendi,* tr. W.F. Bense, Leiden: Brill.

Cusa, N. (1990), *Nicholas of Cusa on Learned Ignorance: A Translation and an Appraisal of De Docta Ignorantia,* tr. J. Hopkins, Minneapolis: The Arthur J. Banning Press.

Giri, Ananta Kumar (2013), 'Rethinking Integration', *Sociological Bulletin,* vol. 62, no. 1, pp. 100–9.

Said, E.W. (1995), *Orientalism,* London: Penguin.

Sarkar, P.R. (1982), *The Liberation of Intellect: Neohumanism,* Calcutta: Ananda Marga Publications.

West, C. (1999), *The Cornel West Reader,* New York: Basic *Civitas* Books.

Editor and Contributors

ANANTA KUMAR GIRI is a Professor at the Madras Institute of Development Studies, Chennai, India. He has taught and done research in many universities in India and abroad, including Aalborg University (Denmark), Maison des sciences de l'homme, Paris (France), the University of Kentucky (USA), University of Freiburg & Humboldt University (Germany), Jagiellonian University (Poland) and Jawaharlal Nehru University, New Delhi. He has an abiding interest in social movements and cultural change, criticism, creativity and contemporary dialectics of transformation, theories of self, culture and society, and creative streams in education, philosophy and literature. Dr Giri has written and edited around two dozen books in Odia and English, including *Global Transformations: Postmodernity and Beyond* (1998); *Sameekhya o Purodrusti* (Criticism and Vision of the Future, 1999); *Patha Prantara Nrutattwa* (Anthropology of the Street Corner, 2000); *Conversations and Transformations: Toward a New Ethics of Self and Society* (2002); *Self-Development and Social Transformations? The Vision and Practice of Self-Study Mobilization of Swadhyaya* (2008); *Mochi o Darshanika* (The Cobbler and the Philosopher, 2009); *Sociology and Beyond: Windows and Horizons* (2012), *Knowledge and Human Liberation: Towards Planetary Realizations* (2013); *Philosophy and Anthropology: Border-Crossing and Transformations* (co-edited with John Clammer, 2013); and *New Horizons of Human Development* (editor, 2015).

B.K. AGARWALA is currently working as a Professor of Philosophy at North-Eastern Hill University, Shillong, India, after teaching for more than two decades at Lucknow University, Lucknow. He began his academic career with a brief stint at Visva-Bharati, Shantiniketan. Agarwala is actively engaged in research in Critical Philosophy of Kant. Political Philosophy and Philosophical Hermeneutics are also major areas of his interest. He has published scholarly essays in political philosophy and Kant's Critical Philosophy in international Journals like *Journal of Indian Council of Philosophical Research*, *Sandhān*, and *Indian Philosophical Quarterly* and in books edited by eminent scholars.

PRASENJIT BISWAS teaches philosophy a North Eastern Hill University, Shillong. He is also a human rights activist. Some of his published books are *The Postmodern Condition: Understanding Richard Rorty, Jacques Derrida and Jurgen Habermas* (2005), *Ethnic Life-Worlds In North East India: An Analysis* (with Chandan Shuklabadya) and *Construction of Evil in North East India: Myth, Narrative and Discourse* (with C.J. Thomas, 2012).

MARCUS BUSSEY is currently Discipline Head of History and Program Leader in Futures Studies at his university. He is a futurist and researcher with the arts Research in the Creative Humanity's Centre, *University of the Sunshine Coast.* He is interested in cultural processes that energize social transformation. He uses futures thinking to challenge the dominant beliefs and assumptions that constrain human responses to rapid cultural, social and technological change. Marcus has a fascination with the poetics of anticipation and its expression through aesthetics, heritage, myth and literature. His workshops, research and writing all focus on the quest for individual and collective empowerment and creative and hopeful pathways to the future.

INGRID DASH is presently an independent scholar and researcher based in Lund, Sweden. She has written her doctoral theses in education from Lund University entitled Flexibility in *Knowing School Mathematics in the Context of Swedish and an Indian School Class* in 2009.

MARK EDWARDS is a lecturer at the Business School, University of Western Australia where he teaches in the areas of business ethics and organizational change. His current research focuses on a variety of fields including performative ethics, cultural change in disability services and global sustainability. His research has been published in several academic journals including *Mind, Culture and Activity, Australian Journal of Public Administration, Journal of Business Ethics* and *Systems Research and Behavioural Science.*

DES GASPER works at the International Institute of Social Studies in The Hague, a graduate school within Erasmus University Rotterdam, Netherlands, where he is currently Professor of Human Development, Development Ethics and Public Policy. He also lived and worked for many years in the UK and Africa. In recent years his research has been on theories of well-being and human security, and the implications of climate change and international migration. The work uses various methods for value-critical discourse analysis. His publications include *Arguing Development Policy* (co-editor R.J. Apthorpe, 1996); *The Ethics of Development* (2005); *Trans-National Migration and Human Security* (co-editor T-D. Truong, 2011); and *Gender, Migration and Social Justice* (2014).

PETER HERRMANN has taught and worked in many universities in Europe and around the world. He is also adjunct professor at the University of Eastern Finland (UEF), Department of Social Sciences (Kuopio, Finland), honorary associate professor at Corvinus University in Budapest, Faculty of Economics, Department of World Economy and visiting scholar at National University of Ireland Maynooth. He had been teaching at several Third Level Institutions across the EU and beyond; and is correspondent to the Max Planck Institute for Foreign and International Social Law/Max Planck Institute for Social Law and Social Policy (Munich, Germany).

LOIS HOLZMAN is co-founder (with Fred Newman) and director of the East Side Institute, an international training and research center for new approaches to therapeutics, education and community building; and a founder of the biennial *Performing the World* conference, which brings together those for whom theatrical performance and the creative arts are essential for personal and social transformation. Holzman is a passionate advocate for conceptual tools and practices that empower people to transform the alienation and passivity of our culture. As a developmental psychologist and activist scholar, she promotes postmodern, culture-change approaches to human development and learning. Her books include *Unscientific Psychology: A Cultural-Performatory Approach to Understanding Human Life* (with Newman), *Vygotsky at Work and Play*, and *The Overweight Brain: How Our Obsession with Knowing Keeps Us from Getting Smart Enough to Make a Better World*. She is a regular commentator on *Psychology Today* (A Conceptual Revolution) and the Psychology of Becoming blog.

AASE MOELLER-HANSEN works as an adviser for refugees and immigrants in Norway, organizing vocational training, and work and language training for adult refugees and immigrants. She is also an activist in social movements for peace, justice and sustainable development. As a member of Attac and Womens' International League for Peace and Freedom, she has been a co-organizer of workshops, lectures, exhibitions and Bergen Social Forum in Norway.

MARKUS MOLZ is Managing Director of the *Alliance for the Furture* (www. a4future.org) and Coordinator of the *University for the Future Initiative* (www.u4future.net). He also serves as a founding Board Member of the *Institute for Integral Studies* (www.integral-studies.org) and Associate Editor of *Integral Review* (http://integral-review.org). His background combines integral studies and transdisciplinary social research, educational innovation, consulting and creation for co-creative gatherings. His current focus is on institutionalising *transformative higher education* and *social transformation laboratories* catalysing the contemporary Great Transition.

WENDY OLSEN is a Reader at University of Manchester currently teaching at the Department of Social Statistics. She is the author of many books and articles on rural transformations in India, philosophies of social sciences and methodologies including *Data Collection: Key Debates and Methods in Social Research* (2012).

RANJAN K. PANDA is Professor of Philosophy, Department of Humanities and Social Sciences, Indian Institute of Technology Bombay. He specializes in the area of Philosophy of Mind. Philosophy of Education has been his most recent area of interest. His publications include 'Knowledge and Knowledge Structure' (*Indian Journal of Analytic Philosophy*, 2010); 'Ethics of Knowledge Sharing: A perspective of Social Ontology' (*Ethics in Progress Quarterly*, 2012); 'Knowledge as Semantic Ability' (*JICPR*, 2012); 'Learning from Stories' (*Lokaratna*, 2013) and 'Virtue of a Learner' (*Anekanta: The Journal of Polysemic Thought*, 2014).

JAMES PEACOCK is Kennan Professor of Anthropology at the University of North Carolina, Chapel Hill, USA. He served as president of the American Anthropological Association and is a fellow of the American Society for Arts and Sciences. His fieldwork is primarily in Indonesia and USA. Publications include *Rites of Modernization*, *Muslim Puritans* and *The Anthropological Lens*. His work includes *Gerakan Muhammadiyah* (*The Muhammadiyah Movement*, 2016), which is an Indonesian translation of his book about Muhammadiyah.

BOIKE REHBEIN is professor for the sociology of Asia and Africa at Humboldt University Berlin. He was acting chair of sociology at Freiburg from 2004 to 2006 and director of the Global Studies Programme from 2006 before moving to Berlin in 2009. His areas of specialization are social theory, globalization, social inequality and mainland Southeast Asia. His recent books in English include *Globalization, Culture and Society in Laos* (2007); *Globalization and Emerging Societies* (ed. with Jan Nederveen Pieterse, 2009); *Globalization and Inequality in Emerging Societies* (2011); *Critical Theory after the Rise of the Global South* (2015; translated from German).

KARL-JULIUS REUBKE worked as a chemist in the Research and Development section of Bayer AG from which he retired in 2003. He taught Chemistry and Bhagavad Gita in Panyotai Waldorf School, Sai Mai, Bangkok (2008–2011) and at Sloka Waldorf School, Hyderabad, India. He has been a Member of Anthroposophical Society since 1982 and lectures in different places on religious traditions of death and dying about which he published *Die fremden Gesichter des Todes* (2008). He has worked and walked closely with Ekta Parishad, India, since 2003 and is Founder/President of Freunde von Ekta Parishad e.V. (Friends of Ekta Parishad). He has published a book in Germany on Ekta Parishad titled *Indien im Aufbruch* (2006) and his book in English on Ekta Parishad, *Mission for Change* is coming out soon.

NEELA BHATTACHARYA SAXENA is Professor of English and Women's Studies at Nassau Community College, NY. She is the author of *In the Beginning is Desire: Tracing Kali's Footprints in Indian Literature* (2004) and *Absent Mother God of the West: A Kali Lover's Journey into Christianity and Judaism* (2015). Some of her other publications include, 'Mystery, Wonder and Knowledge in the Triadic Figure of Mahavidya Chinnamasta: A Shakta Woman's Reading' in *Woman and Goddess in Hinduism,* 'Shekhinah on the 'Plane of Immanence': An Intimation of the Indic Great Mother in the Hebraic Wholly Other' in the *Journal of Indo-Judaic Studies,* 'Gaia Mandala: An Eco-Theological Vision of the Indic Shakti Tradition' in *InterCulture,* 'The Fun House Mirror of Tantric Studies: A Rejoinder to David White's *Kiss of the Yogini*' in *Evam;* 'Color of God: Resplendent Clay of Hinduism as the Glow of the Ineffable' in *Living Our Religions;* 'Gynocentric Thealogy of Tantric Hinduism: A Meditation upon the Devi' in *Oxford Handbook of Feminist Theology;* 'Peopling an Unaccustomed Earth: Jhumpa Lahiri's Supreme Fictional Journeys into Human Conditions' in *Argument;* and 'Prodigy, Poet and Freedom Fighter: Sarojini Naidu, the Nightingale of India -1879 – 1949' in *Marginalized: Indian Poetry in English*. She writes a blog called 'Stand Under the Mother Principle' (http://neelabsaxena. blogspot.com/).

MIRIAM SANNUM is an ecologist and pedagogue, currently working with non-formal adult education at Studieförbundet Vuxenskolan (SV) in the south west part of Sweden. She started working as an ecologist with environmental matters and sustainable development within a municipal organisation in 1988. She has worked with thousands of people in rural areas and villages. She has also worked with hundreds of political leaders on national, regional and local levels. In 2005 she initiated the Academy for Sustainable Development – AkHUt – which invites people from different contexts to a 'space in-between' to deep listen, experiment, play and explore openings for innovative results to emerge. Miriam is also interested in the opportunities for deep learning for sustainable futures that encounters in and with nature can offer; how experiences of connection and revelation of paradoxes, fractals, symbols and metaphors can serve as guidance. Miriam is also affiliated with UNESCO's Regional Centre of Expertise Västra Götaland, Sweden.

L. ANTHONY SAVARI RAJ is Professor of Philosophy & Head, Department of Arts at Manipal University Jaipur, Rajasthan, India. He has served as a

Lecturer and Senior Lecturer at the Department of Philosophy, University of Madras, for more than a decade. His areas of interest and expertise include Intercultural Philosophy, Cross-cultural Philosophy of Religion, Modern Western Philosophy, Ecophilosophy, Interreligious Dialogue, and Raimon Panikkar's Thought. He has enjoyed several National and International Research Fellowships, such as the Charles Wallace Visiting Fellowship, University of Bristol, UK, and the Woodstock International Visiting Fellowship, Georgetown University, Washington, DC, USA. He has authored two books including *A New Hermeneutic of Reality: Raimon Panikkar's Cosmotheandric Vision* (Bern, et al, 1998), and has to his credit numerous research articles in several reputed national and international scholarly journals. He has been a Visiting Professor of Philosophy and Religion in several prestigious institutions of India, including Indian Institute of Technology (IIT, Chennai) and has enjoyed the 2012–2013 Fulbright-Nehru Visiting Lectureship at George Mason University (Department of Religious Studies), Fairfax, VA, USA.

ALEC SCHAERER was as an architect and town planner and he ran diverse international projects, of which several were in the Middle East. Seeking uncompromised ways of thinking he became interested in the potential for a systematic methodological approach and holistic perception of situations in their complete contexts, beyond blind spots. His publications include many articles in the realm of methodology, and most notably *Systematische Ganzheitlichkeit - Eine methodologische Vermittlung zwischen Perspektivität und Universalität, mit einem Grundriß der Anwendbarkeit dieses Ansatzes auf die Geowissenschaften* (2011).

SCOTT SCHAFFER is Associate Professor of Sociology at the University of Western Ontario in London, Canada, where he specializes in contemporary and global social theory, social ethics, social change, and development. He is the author of *Resisting Ethics* (2004), and has contributed to recent collections of works on cosmopolitanizing cosmopolitanism.

TRENT SCHROYER taught at Ramapo College, New Jersey, USA and has been interested in alternative economics and human futures. Originally a specialist in European Critical Theory, teaching at the Graduate Faculty of the New School in New York City, his book *The Critique of Domination* was nominated for a National Book Award in 1973. In 2000 he was invited by Siddhartha, from Fireflies Ashram, to bring Americans to India to tour grassroots groups and witness the cultural alternatives that work in India. The following three tours have resulted in a semester long study abroad program in 2004 that is now ongoing every year. Since 1988 he has participated in networks of International Scholars and Citizen's Organizations concerned with Sustainability, Alternative Economic Strategies and Cultural Alternatives to Development. He served as Program co-coordinator and President of the Other Economic Summit (TOES) for the counter G-8 summits in the United States in 1990, 1997 and 2004.

PAUL SCHWARTZENTRUBER is retired theologian and Director of a Retreat Centre from Canada. He has worked as a volunteer for the last 6 years in India for the Gandhian land rights organization Ekta Parishad and the International Institute for Nonviolence and Peace. He has written recent articles on Gandhi, Illich, George Grant, Simone Weil and Thomas Merton that were published in the journal *Ahimsa/Nonviolence.*

JENS SIEFFERT studied communication and media science, and political science at the University of Leipzig (Germany) and Charles University in Prague (Czech Republic). Jens Seiffert was a fellow of the Frederick Ebert Foundation between 2003 and 2007. Since 2009 he is a scholarship holder of the foundation for the promotion of PR-science of the University of Leipzig. He was visiting lecturer at several universities throughout Europe (Antwerp, Gent, Salzburg, Lund).

MIHIR SHAH is an economist who was Member, Planning Commission, Government of India from 2009 to 2014. He was chiefly responsible for drafting the paradigm shift in management of water resources in India's 12th Five Year Plan. He also initiated a makeover of MGNREGA, the largest employment programme in human history, with a renewed emphasis on rural livelihoods and people's empowerment. Before joining the Planning Commission, he spent 20 years living and working in India's most disadvantaged tribal areas, forging a new paradigm of inclusive and sustainable development, through Samaj Pragati Sahayog (SPS), an organization he co-founded in 1990. Dr Shah is also Visiting Faculty at Ashoka University, where he teaches a course on the *Political Economy of India's Development.*

ANDREW SMITH is Reader in Sociology at the University of Glasgow. His main area of research interest is the study of literature, sport and creative cultures more generally, in the colonial and postcolonial contexts. He is the author of *C.L.R. James and the Study of Culture*; and of essays on the representation of imperial defeat (*Race and Class*), ethnicity and everyday life (*Ethnic and Racial Studies*), the experience of shopworking (*New Left Review*) and Nigerian e-mail scams (*Cultural Studies*).

PIET STRYDOM originally an émigré from the apartheid regime, is since 2011 a retired member of the School of Sociology and Philosophy, University College Cork, Ireland. He is associate editor of the *European Journal of Social Theory*. Besides many articles, some well noted, in journals, anthologies and encyclopaedias, major publications include *Contemporary Critical Theory and Methodology* (2011), *New Horizons of Critical Theory: Collective Learning and Triple Contingency* (2009), *Risk, Environment and Society* (2002), and *Discourse and Knowledge* (Liverpool UP, 2000). He edited *Philosophies of Social Science* (2003, with Gerard Delanty) as well as special issues of the *European Journal of Social Theory* and the *Irish Journal of Sociology*.

BETSY TAYLOR is a cultural anthropologist whose primary fieldwork has been in Central Appalachia and North-East India. Her recent research is on emerging forms of civil society and social movements, community-based natural resource management, critical regional studies, globalization and sustainability. Her scholarly writings engage questions of environmental identities, the construction of identity (gender, class, place, ethnicity, religious), the constitution of public space, public involvement and civic engagement. In addition to numerous scholarly articles, she is co-author (with Herbert Reid) of *Recovering the Commons: Democracy, Place, and Global Justice* (2010). She has worked on many projects for community-driven, integrated, sustainable development in Appalachia and India—including health, agriculture, forestry, culture and environmental stewardship. Betsy Taylor is currently Research Scientist in the Dept. of Religion and Culture at Virginia Tech. At the University of Kentucky, she served as Co-Director of Environmental Studies, Research Director for the Appalachian Center and on the faculty of the Social Theory programme.

Index